SPORT PSYCHOLOGY

Concepts and Applications

SPORT PSYCHOLOGY

Concepts and Applications

FOURTH EDITION

RICHARD H. COX

University of Missouri-Columbia

WCB McGraw-Hill

Boston, Massachusetts   Burr Ridge, Illinois   Dubuque, Iowa
Madison, Wisconsin   New York, New York   San Francisco, California   St. Louis, Missouri

WCB/McGraw-Hill

A Division of The McGraw·Hill Companies

SPORT PSYCHOLOGY: CONCEPTS AND APPLICATIONS, FOURTH EDITION

This book is printed on acid-free paper.

1 2 3 4 5 6 7 8 9 0 QPF/QPF 9 0 9 8 7

ISBN 0–697–29507–9

Vice president and editorial director: *Kevin T. Kane*
Publisher: *Edward E. Bartell*
Executive editor: *Vicki Malinee*
Developmental editor: *Sarah Reed*
Marketing manager: *Pamela S. Cooper*
Project manager: *Sheila M. Frank*
Production supervisor: *Mary E. Haas*
Designer: *Kiera M. Cunningham*
Photo research coordinator: *Lori Hancock*
Compositor: *Shepherd, Inc.*
Typeface: *10/12 Times Roman*
Printer: *Quebecor Printing Book Group/Fairfield*

Cover photo: © *Tim Pannell/Sharpshooters*

Library of Congress Cataloging-in Publication Data

Cox, Richard H., 1941–
    Sport psychology : concepts and applications / Richard H. Cox. --
4th ed.
      p.   cm.
    Includes bibliographical references (p.) and index.
    ISBN 0-697-29507-9
    1.   Sports--Psychological aspects.   2. Coaching (Athletics)–
–Psychological aspects.   3. Athletes--Psychology.   I. Title.
GV706.4.C69   1998
796' .01—dc21   97-34896

www.mhhe.com

BRIEF CONTENTS

CHAPTER 1   INTRODUCTION TO SPORT PSYCHOLOGY   2

CHAPTER 2   PERSONALITY AND THE ATHLETE   16

CHAPTER 3   ATTENTION IN SPORT   52

CHAPTER 4   ANXIETY AND AROUSAL IN SPORT   84

CHAPTER 5   AROUSAL ADJUSTMENT STRATEGIES   134

CHAPTER 6   COGNITIVE-BEHAVIORAL INTERVENTION
IN SPORT   166

CHAPTER 7   CAUSAL ATTRIBUTION IN SPORT   206

CHAPTER 8   MOTIVATION AND SELF-CONFIDENCE
IN SPORT   236

CHAPTER 9   SOCIAL PSYCHOLOGY OF SPORT   274

CHAPTER 10   PSYCHOBIOLOGY OF SPORT
AND EXERCISE   334

CONTENTS

Preface   xiii
Acknowledgments   xvi

CHAPTER 1   INTRODUCTION TO SPORT PSYCHOLOGY   2
Sport Psychology Defined   4
History of Sport Psychology as a Discipline   5
Issue of Certification   7
What Does the Sport Psychologist Do?   10
Ethics in Sport Psychology   10
Summary   13
Review Questions   13
Glossary   14
Suggested Readings   15

CHAPTER 2   PERSONALITY AND THE ATHLETE   16
The Structure of Personality   19
Theories of Personality   21
   Psychodynamic Theories   21
   Social Learning Theory   22
   Humanistic Theory   23
   Trait Theories   23
The Measurement of Personality   24
   Rating Scales   25
   Unstructured Projective Procedures   25
   Structured Questionnaires   27
The Credulous vs. Skeptical Argument   29
Personality and Sports Performance   30
   Athletes vs. Nonathletes   30
   Developmental Effects of Athletic Participation
      upon Personality   31
   Personality Sport Type   32
   Player Position and Personality Profile   34
   Personality Profiles of Athletes Differing in Skill
      Level   35
   The Female Athlete   37
The Interactional Model   39
   Trait-State Approach   41
   Psychological Profile of the Elite Athlete   42
   Psychological Profile of the Elite Disabled
      Athlete   45
Summary   46

Review Questions 47
Glossary 48
Suggested Readings 50

CHAPTER 3   ATTENTION IN SPORT   52
Information Processing 54
 Memory Systems 56
 Measuring Information 58
Selective Attention 63
Limited Information Processing Capacity 65
Attentional Narrowing 67
Measuring Attentional Focus 70
Attentional Focus Training 72
 Types of Attentional Focus 72
 Thought Stopping and Centering 73
Associative vs. Dissociative Attentional Strategies 76
Summary 79
Review Questions 80
Glossary 80
Suggested Readings 82

CHAPTER 4   ANXIETY AND AROUSAL IN SPORT   84
Neurophysiology of Arousal 86
 Autonomic Nervous System 86
 Brain Mechanisms 87
 Preferred State of Arousal 90
Defining Anxiety and Stress 91
Measurement of Anxiety 95
Multidimensional Nature of Anxiety 97
 Time-to-Event Nature of Precompetitive
  Anxiety 98
 Differential Effect of Somatic and Cognitive
  Anxiety on Performance 98
 Intensity and Direction Issues 101
 Shortened Version of the CSAI-2 102
 The Sport Grid 103
Relationship between Arousal and Athletic
 Performance 104
 Inverted-U Theory 104
 Drive Theory 113
Alternatives to Inverted-U Theory 115
 Fazey and Hardy's Catastrophe Model 115
 Hanin's Zone of Optimal Functioning
  (ZOF) 118
 Flow: The Psychology of Optimal
  Experience 121
 Apter's Reversal Theory 123

Summary 128
Review Questions 129
Glossary 130
Suggested Readings 133

CHAPTER 5 AROUSAL ADJUSTMENT STRATEGIES 134
Relaxation Procedures 140
    Progressive Relaxation 141
    Autogenic Training 143
    Meditation 144
    Biofeedback 147
    Hypnosis 150
Arousal Energizing Strategies 157
    Goal Setting 158
    Pep Talks 159
    Bulletin Boards 159
    Publicity and News Coverage 160
    Fan Support 160
    Self-Activation 160
    Coach, Athlete, and Parent Interaction 160
    Precompetition Workout 160
Summary 162
Review Questions 163
Glossary 163
Suggested Readings 165

CHAPTER 6 COGNITIVE-BEHAVIORAL INTERVENTION IN SPORT 166
Coping Strategies in Sport 170
Imagery in Sport 172
    Mental Practice as a Form of Imagery 172
    Theories of How Imagery Works 174
    Internal and External Imagery 176
    Measurement of Imagery 177
    Effectiveness of Imagery in Enhancing Sports Performance 177
    Developing Imagery Skills 179
Cognitive-Behavioral Intervention Programs Using Imagery and Relaxation 181
    Visual-Motor Behavioral Rehearsal 181
    Stress Inoculation Training 183
    Stress Management Training 185
Goal Setting in Sport 186
    Goal Setting Defined 186
    Applying Locke's Goal-Setting Theory to Sport and Exercise 188
    Getting the Most Out of Goal Setting 189

Psychological Skills Training for Sport 191

Some Helpful Guidelines for Psychological Skills
Training 192

Measurement of Psychological Skill 194

Psychological Skills Education 195

Other Aspects of Psychological Skills
Training 198

Summary 199

Review Questions 200

Glossary 201

Suggested Readings 203

CHAPTER 7   CAUSAL ATTRIBUTION IN SPORT   206

The Attributional Model 209

Fritz Heider's Contribution 209

Bernard Weiner's Contribution 211

Dan Russel's and Ed McAuley's
Contribution 212

Other Considerations 216

Causal Attributions in Competitive Situations 217

Internal/External Attributions 217

Stability Considerations 222

Gender Differences in Sport 225

Egocentrism in Attribution 228

Attributional Training 230

Summary 232

Review Questions 233

Glossary 234

Suggested Readings 235

CHAPTER 8   MOTIVATION AND SELF-CONFIDENCE
IN SPORT   236

Achievement Motivation 238

The McClelland-Atkinson Model 240

Models of Self-Confidence 243

Bandura's Theory of Self-efficacy 244

Harter's Competence Motivation Theory 245

Vealey's Sport-Specific Model of Sport
Confidence 247

Nicholls' Developmentally Based Theory
of Perceived Ability 249

Gender and Self-Confidence 253

Perceived Gender Roles 255

Gender Role and Anxiety 257

Effects of External Rewards on Intrinsic
Motivation 258

Developing Self-Confidence and Intrinsic Motivation
in Youth Sport Participants 263
 The Individual Athlete 263
 The Coach or Teacher 265
 The Parent 266
Summary 267
Review Questions 268
Glossary 269
Suggested Readings 271

CHAPTER 9 **SOCIAL PSYCHOLOGY OF SPORT** **274**
Aggression in Sport 276
 Defining Aggression 278
 Theories of Aggression 280
 The Catharsis Effect 283
 Measurement of Aggression 284
 Fan Violence 284
 Effects of Aggression on Performance 285
 Situational Factors in a Sport Setting 285
 Reducing Aggression in Sport 287
Audience Effects in Sports 288
 Social Facilitation 289
 Effects of an Interactive Audience
  on Performance 290
 Audience Characteristics 292
Team Cohesion 295
 Measurement of Team Cohesion 296
 Determinants of Team Cohesion 299
 Consequences of Team Cohesion 301
 Developing Team Cohesion 304
Leadership in Sport 306
 Theories of Leadership 307
 Coach-Athlete Compatibility 322
 Geographical Location and Leadership
  Opportunity 324
Summary 327
Review Questions 328
Glossary 330
Suggested Readings 331

CHAPTER 10 **PSYCHOBIOLOGY OF SPORT
AND EXERCISE** **334**
Exercise Psychology 336
 Psychological Benefits of Exercise 337
 Evidence of the Benefits of Chronic
  Exercise 339
 Treating Anxiety and Depression 341

Theoretical Explanations for the Relationship
  between Exercise and Improved
  Mental Health 344

Exercise Adherence and Determinants 346

Theories of Exercise Behavior 349

Fitness as a Moderator of Life Stress 352

The Immune System, Cancer, HIV,
  and Exercise 354

Social Physique Anxiety, Exercise Addiction,
  and Eating Disorders 357

Staleness, Overtraining, and Burnout in Athletes 362

Process Leading to Burnout 363

Overtraining and Mood Disturbance 366

Models of Burnout 367

Symptoms of and Interventions for Burnout 370

Recommendations for Athletes, Coaches,
  and Parents 371

Psychology of Athletic Injuries 372

Psychological Predictors of Athletic Injury 372

Interventions 377

Psychological Adjustment to Injury 377

Psychological Factors Influencing
  Rehabilitation 378

Drug Abuse by Athletes 379

Psychophysiological Effects of Certain Banned
  Substances 381

Position Statement of NSCA 382

Combating Drug Abuse in Sport 383

Summary 385

Review Questions 387

Glossary 389

Suggested Readings 391

References 394

Author Index 441

Subject Index 449

PREFACE

I have written this book specifically for the undergraduate student interested in exercise and sport psychology as an academic discipline. By supplementing the text material with current articles from research journals, instructors can also readily adopt the text as a foundation text for graduate students. In recent years, there has been a tremendous interest in applied sport psychology for the purpose of enhancing athletic performance. With this surge of interest in applied sport psychology, it is of critical importance that a knowledge base be presented and understood by teachers, coaches, and researchers. In this text I develop concepts that are supported by the research literature and provide examples of how these concepts can be applied in exercise and sport settings.

NEW TO THIS EDITION

In writing the fourth edition, I thoroughly edited and updated every chapter in order to make the book as current as possible. In so doing I have continued to provide documentation of important topics. However, in order to avoid too much documentation I have carefully selected the most important and current references. I have also made a concerted effort to include research applications associated with women, youth sport athletes, and disabled athletes when ever possible and appropriate. Numerous new illustrations and photographs have been carefully selected and included. Many of the new photographs include pictures of women, children, and disabled athletes. Subtle changes and improvements occur throughout the fourth edition. In some chapters significant changes or additions are made. Some of these important improvements are as follows:

Chapter 1, "Introduction to Sport Psychology," now contains an important table that clarifies the relationship between sport psychology associations and professional journals. Other improvements in this chapter relate to the removal of less important material.

Chapter 2, "Personality and the Athlete," now contains a new section on the humanistic theory of personality development. The inclusion of this important theory provides a more rounded treatment of the explanation of how personality develops in an individual.

Chapter 3, "Attention in Sport," has been improved by eliminating peripheral information while at the same time focusing the discussion on new research related to physiological activation and attentional style.

Chapter 4, "Anxiety and Arousal in Sport," has been improved by clarifying a number of difficult to understand concepts, and by adding two new sections. One new section deals with intensity and direction issues associated with anxiety and performance, while a second addresses the psychology of optimal experience (Flow).

Chapter 5, "Arousal Adjustment Strategies," has been improved through updating and editing, but in addition the hypothesis that arousal adjustment strategies should closely match specific anxiety symptoms is addressed in greater detail. This is called the "matching hypothesis."

Chapter 6, "Cognitive-Behavioral Intervention in Sport," now contains a new section on coping strategies in sport, which will help readers to understand how coping strategies can manage stress, and how coping strategies can be developed, practiced, and refined.

Chapter 7, "Causal Attribution in Sport," now appears prior to the chapter on motivation and self-confidence in sport. This important change was made to make it possible to show application of the principles of causal attribution in the development of motivation and self-confidence.

Chapter 8, "Motivation and Self-Confidence in Sport," the focus of this important chapter continues to be on explaining how intrinsic motivation and self-confidence can be developed in children. Additions to the content include a discussion of the effects of external rewards on intrinsic motivation, and the importance of a child's goal orientation in developing intrinsic motivation.

Chapter 9, "Social Psychology of Sport," spectator and athlete aggression, audience effects, team cohesion, and leadership continues to be the focus of this important chapter. Careful editing and the inclusion of new research have added significantly to the quality of this chapter.

Chapter 10, "Psychobiology of Sport and Exercise," has been significantly bolstered in the fourth edition. Separate sections are now provided on the important topics of exercise psychology, overtraining and burnout, psychology of athletic injuries, and drug abuse by athletes. The section on exercise psychology has been upgraded by including new sections on theories of exercise behavior, social physique anxiety, exercise addiction, and eating disorders.

PEDAGOGY

A significant number of pedagogical aids have been included in the text for the benefit of students, teachers, and coaches. Most significantly, many sports-related examples are included throughout each chapter. "Concepts and applications" boxes are inserted after major themes and topics in each chapter. These boxes highlight and refocus the reader's attention to important concepts immediately after they are discussed. These concepts are derived from the pertinent scientific literature and are followed by suggested applications for the coach or teacher.

Other important pedagogical aids included in each chapter are key terms, chapter summaries, review questions, a glossary, and recommended readings.

The key terms, which appear at the beginning of each chapter, draw the student's attention to important terms and concepts. They appear in the glossary and in boldface type where they are introduced in the text.

SUPPLEMENTS

An Instructor's Manual and Test Bank is also available. This manual includes test questions for every chapter, along with answer keys.

ACKNOWLEDGMENTS

I am indebted to a host of people who have contributed to the completion of this work.

First of all, to my wife, Linda, and my four children, Candice, Clayton, Ryan, and David, for their patience and forbearance.

Second, to the reviewers of the fourth edition, who went the extra mile to ensure that the work would be a success:

Terry Brown
Faulkner University

David Furst
San Jose State University

Marion Johnson
Colorado State University

Paul Rhoads
Williams Baptist College

Jay Shaw
Eastern Montana College

Third, to my colleagues, who were always willing to share ideas and resources.

Finally, I am most grateful to the reserve librarians at the University of Missouri-Columbia, who were more than happy to help me locate foreign and other references not in the library.

Richard H. Cox

SPORT PSYCHOLOGY
Concepts and Applications

1 INTRODUCTION TO SPORT PSYCHOLOGY

KEY TERMS

- *AAASP*
- *academic sport psychology*
- *APA*
- *applied sport psychology*
- *clinical/counseling sport psychologist*
- *CSPLSP*
- *educational sport psychologist*
- *Griffith, Coleman Roberts*
- *Henry, Franklin M.*
- *ISSP*
- *Lawther, John*
- *NASPSPA*
- *Ogilvie, Bruce*
- *research sport psychologist*
- *Slater-Hammel, Arthur*
- *SPA*
- *Sport Psychology Registry*
- *Triplett, Norman*
- *USOC*

Sport is something that everyone can enjoy. Courtesy University of Missouri–Columbia Sports Information

Hardly a subject associated with sport is more intriguing than the subject of sport psychology. Perhaps this is because it is a comfortable subject for so many people associated with sport. The average spectator does not care to offer a biomechanical explanation for why an athlete achieves a near superhuman feat, yet the same spectator is often more than willing to give a psychological explanation. In many ways this is good, but it is also the reason many athletes and coaches don't feel the need for a professional sport psychologist on their team. As we look at some of the great basketball and football coaches of our time, it is easy to see why. John Wooden, former coach of U.C.L.A., would have to fall into this category. Coach Wooden's athletes were always prepared mentally for competition. They may not always have had the best talent, but they always seemed to be in control of the emotional and psychological aspects of the game. Can the sport psychologist learn something about performance enhancement from coach Wooden? Yes, I think so, but I also believe that great coaches such as John Wooden, Pat Head Summitt, and Bobby Knight could benefit a great deal from a qualified sport psychologist. Successful coaches and athletes are people who make it a point to study their sport and master the mental elements of the game. This process can be speeded up and refined through the correct application of the scientific principles of sport psychology. A Canadian research report revealed that elite athletes generally recognize the need for a professional sport psychologist. This perception was observed to increase as athletes came into actual contact with sport psychologists' services (Orlick & Partington, 1987).

This text offers the prospective coach and scholar the opportunity to learn correct principles and applications of sport psychology, even though sport psychology is not a perfect science. We have a great deal to learn about mental preparation for sport competition. We will always have a need for the scientist who is interested in discovering new knowledge. As you read this text I encourage you to keep an open mind and become interested in sport psychology as a science.

In the paragraphs that follow I will discuss a number of peripheral issues that provide background information for the study of sport psychology. Specifically, this chapter provides a definition of sport psychology, sketches a brief history of the discipline, discusses the issue of certification, reviews various roles of the sport psychologist, and finally, discusses ethics associated with sport psychology services.

SPORT PSYCHOLOGY DEFINED

Sport psychology is a science in which the principles of psychology are applied in a sport or exercise setting. These principles are often applied to enhance performance. However, the true sport psychologist is interested in much more than performance enhancement and sees sport as a vehicle for human enrichment (Hinkle, 1994; Russell, 1996). A win-at-all-costs attitude is inconsistent with the goals and aspirations of the best sport psychologist. As a sport psychologist, I am interested in helping every sport participant reach his or

her potential as an athlete. If helping a young athlete develop self-control and confidence results in superior athletic performance, so be it. However, it is also possible that a quality sport experience can enhance an athlete's intrinsic motivation without the athlete necessarily winning. Taken as a whole, sport psychology is an exciting subject dedicated to the enhancement of both athletic performance and the social-psychological aspects of human enrichment.

HISTORY OF SPORT PSYCHOLOGY AS A DISCIPLINE

Sport psychology as a field of study is extremely young and still evolving. In writing this brief sketch of the rise of sport psychology in North America, I have relied a great deal on excellent historical reviews by David Wiggins (1984), Robert Singer (1989), Jean Williams and Bill Straub (1986), and Bill Morgan (1994).

Perhaps the first clear example of historical research being conducted in the area of sport psychology was reported by **Norman Triplett** (1897). Drawing upon field observations and secondary data, Triplett analyzed the performance of cyclists under conditions of social facilitation. He concluded from this "milestone" research that the presence of other competitors was capable of facilitating better cycling performance. While Triplett provided an example of one of the earliest recorded sport psychology investigations, he was not the first person to systematically carry out sport psychology research over an extended period of time. This distinction is generally attributed to **Coleman Roberts Griffith,** often referred to as the father of sport psychology in America (Kroll & Lewis, 1970). Griffith is credited with establishing the first sport psychology laboratory at the University of Illinois in 1925. Over an extended period of time, Griffith studied the nature of psychomotor skills, motor learning, and the relationship between personality variables and motor performance.

It was not until the 1960s that sport psychology began to emerge as separate and distinct from other areas of motor behavior research. It was only after the Second World War that American universities began to offer courses in the parent discipline of motor learning. Such notables as **Franklin M. Henry** at the University of California, **John Lawther** at Pennsylvania State University, and **Arthur Slater-Hammel** at Indiana University pioneered these courses (Landers, 1995).

Another significant event in the 1960s was the publication of *Problem Athletes and How to Handle Them* by Bruce Ogilvie and Thomas Tutko (1966). This book and the authors' personality inventory for athletes—the Athletic Motivation Inventory—caught on with coaches and athletes. However, Ogilvie and Tutko's work was not well received by the sport psychology scientific community of the time; their contribution to sport psychology is much better received today than it was only a few short years ago. **Bruce Ogilvie** is referred to as the father of *applied* sport psychology (Williams & Straub, 1986).

A number of professional sport psychology organizations have evolved since the 1960s. In 1965 the **International Society of Sport Psychology (ISSP),** which sponsors worldwide meetings and publishes the *International Journal of Sport Psychology* and *The Sport Psychologist,* was organized in Rome. The purpose of the ISSP is to promote and disseminate information about the practice of sport psychology throughout the world.

In 1965, a small group of physical educators from Canada and the United States met in Dallas, Texas, to discuss the feasibility of forming a professional organization distinct from the American Association of Health, Physical Education, and Recreation (AAHPER). The efforts of this small group came to fruition in 1966 when it was recognized by the ISSP. The name of the new organization became the **North American Society for the Psychology of Sport and Physical Activity (NASPSPA).** The first annual meeting of NASPSPA was held prior to the 1967 AAHPER national convention in Las Vegas. Since that time, NASPSPA has evolved into an influential academic society focusing on sport psychology (Salmela, 1992).

NASPSPA's primary goal has been to advance the knowledge base of sport psychology through experimental research (Williams & Straub, 1986). This has been reflected in the kind of articles that have appeared in periodicals such as the *Journal of Sport and Exercise Psychology.*

Shortly after the emergence of NASPSPA in the United States, another significant professional organization came into existence in Canada in 1969. This organization was called the **Canadian Society for Psychomotor Learning and Sport Psychology (CSPLSP).** CSPLSP was originally organized under the auspices of the Canadian Association for Health, Physical Education, and Recreation, but became an independent society in 1977.

Somewhat concurrently with the emergence of the Canadian association (CSPLSP), the **Sport Psychology Academy (SPA)** emerged in the United States as one of six academies within the **National Association for Sport and Physical Education (NASPE).** NASPE is an association within the AAHPERD. The six academies were formed to represent the knowledge base or disciplines within physical education (Oglesby, 1980). The *Research Quarterly for Exercise and Sport* (RQES) is the official research journal of AAHPERD.

In recent years two sport psychologies have emerged (Martens, 1987). The first is referred to as **academic sport psychology** and the second as **applied sport psychology.** The former or traditional (academic) sport psychology continues to focus on the disciplinary or research-oriented aspects of the field. Conversely, applied sport psychology focuses on the professional or applied aspects of the field of sport psychology.

The division took place because many sport psychologists who were interested in application did not think NASPSPA was meeting their needs. Consequently, the **Association for the Advancement of Applied Sport Psychology (AAASP)** was formed in the fall of 1985. Four years later it began publishing the *Journal of Applied Sport Psychology* (Sylvia, 1989a). Even though it appears that two competing sport psychology organizations have emerged, I believe they will continue to work together to advance the discipline

Table 1.1

Summary of Major Professional Societies that are Dedicated or Partially Dedicated to the Discipline/ profession of Sport Psychology.

Genesis	Name of Association or Society	Journal Affiliation
1954	American College of Sports Medicine (ACSM)	MSSE
1965	International Society of Sport Psychology (ISSP)	IJSP, TSP*
1967	North American Society for the Psychology of Sport and Physical Activity	JS&EP
1977	Canadian Society for Psychomotor Learning and Sport Psychology (CSPLSP)	None
1977	Sport Psychology Academy (SPA) (Division within AAHPERD)	RQES
1985	Association for the Advancement of Applied Sport Psychology (AAASP)	JASP

*not an official affiliation

of sport psychology and facilitate its application in the real world of sport. Many of the prominent sport psychologists who are actively involved in research are also members of the AAASP and, conversely, many of the practicing sport psychologists are also active members of NASPSPA.

While not normally thought of as a sport psychology journal, *Medicine and Science in Sports and Exercise* (MSSE) is the official journal of the American College of Sports Medicine (ACSM) and regularly publishes articles relating to both exercise and sport. While not associated with any association or society, the *Journal of Sport Behavior* (JSB) and the *Journal of Interdisciplinary Research in Physical Education* (JIRPE) publish exercise and sport psychology research. A summary of professional societies and associated research journals is provided in table 1.1.

Interestingly, a recent split took place in the **American Psychological Association (APA),** resulting in the formation of the American Psychological Society (Raymond, 1990). In this case, however, dissatisfied academic research psychologists complained that the APA had become too application-oriented. They worried that clinical and applied psychology was being emphasized at the expense of science and research. In 1986, the APA formed yet another section within its structure called Division 47, which is dedicated to issues dealing with exercise and sport psychology. In years to come, the future of applied sport psychology will be greatly influenced by the success of and directions taken by this new organization.

ISSUE OF CERTIFICATION

Historically, sport psychology emerged as a discipline from physical education. In recent years, however, a significant interest in the discipline has developed among individuals prepared in psychology and counseling. This has raised the issue among practicing sport psychologists as to which people are qualified to call themselves "sport psychologists" and to provide services to athletes. This

Sports competition brings out the best in these athletes. Courtesy University of Missouri–Columbia Sports Information

issue has been discussed at length in recent years. Perhaps the most enlightening exchange on the topic was made between John Silva III (1989b), the first president of AAASP, and Frank Gardner (1991), a psychologist who took issue with Silva's assertions.

Some have gone so far as to argue that only licensed psychologists should be allowed to call themselves sport psychologists, and suggest that the appropriate title for a nonlicensed "sport psychologist" would be "mental training consultant" (Taylor, 1994). Most agree, however, that even licensed psychologists should have significant academic training in the exercise and sport sciences before practicing applied sport psychology (Taylor, 1994).

A partial solution to the issue of professionalization of sport psychology was presented by the **United States Olympic Committee (USOC)** (1983) and clarified by May (1986). The USOC developed the **Sport Psychology Registry** to identify three categories in which a person can demonstrate competence. These categories correspond to three types of sport psychologists: the **clinical/counseling sport psychologist,** the **educational sport psychologist,** and the **research sport psychologist.** The purpose of the Sport Psychology Registry was to identify individuals in the area of sport psychology who could work with specific national teams within the Olympic movement. The registry was not meant to be a licensing or authorizing committee.

The AAASP took the issue of who is qualified to deliver sport psychology services one step further. It adopted a certification document outlining the process an individual must take to be given the title "Certified Consultant, Association for the Advancement of Applied Sport Psychology." As part of the certification criteria, the applicant is required to hold an earned doctorate in an area related to sport psychology (e.g., psychology, sport science, or physical education). In addition, numerous specific courses and experiences are identified. While this certification process adopted by the AAASP may not be

Baseball is an excellent game in which to observe sport psychology in action. Courtesy Ball State University Sports Information

the final one, it is a good beginning since it recognizes that an individual needs specialized training in psychology and physical education (sport and exercise science) to be certified as a practicing sport psychologist.

It should be mentioned, however, that not all sport psychologists are in agreement about the merits of the AAASP certification process. Anshel (1993), for example, argued that the AAASP certification process is discriminatory and counterproductive. He argues that there is scant evidence that certified consultants make better consultants than noncertified consultants. Nevertheless, it appears that the AAASP certification initiative is a move in the right direction. It requires both licensed and unlicensed psychologists to meet minimum standards in order to be certified by the AAASP.

The issue of what sport psychology is and who is qualified to practice applied sport psychology was recently addressed by the European Federation of Sport Psychology (FEPSAC, 1996a). This body took the position that the term *sport psychology* was properly used in a broad sense, and included all qualified persons, independent of their specific academic field. It did, however, acknowledge that different countries may have restrictions on the use of the term *psychologist*.

WHAT DOES THE SPORT PSYCHOLOGIST DO?

In an effort to promote the virtues of sport psychology to coaches, athletes, and prospective students, many thoughtful professionals have suggested contributions that sport psychologists can make to sport (Singer, 1984; Taylor, 1991). In the paragraphs that follow, different roles and functions of the sport psychologist are outlined. Generally, these roles and functions describe the sport psychologist in the categories of clinician, educator, and researcher.

The Clinical/Counseling Sport Psychologist The clinical/counseling sport psychologist is a person trained in clinical or counseling psychology and is a licensed psychologist. Generally, the clinical sport psychologist also has a deep interest in and understanding of the athletic experience. Training may also include coursework and experience in sport psychology from programs in physical education. Clinical sport psychologists are individuals who are prepared to deal with emotional and personality disorder problems that affect some athletes. The athletic experience can be very stressful to some athletes, and can negatively affect their performance or their ability to function as healthy human beings. In these cases, sport psychologists trained in counseling psychology or clinical psychology are needed.

The Educational Sport Psychologist Most sport psychologists who received their academic training through departments of physical education (i.e., sport and exercise science) consider themselves to be educational sport psychologists. These individuals have mastered the knowledge base of sport psychology and serve as practitioners. They use the medium of education to teach correct principles of sport psychology to athletes and coaches. In general, their mission and role is to help athletes develop psychological skills for performance enhancement. They also help athletes, young and old, to enjoy sport and use it as a vehicle for improving their quality of life.

The Research Sport Psychologist For sport psychology to be a recognized and respected social science, the knowledge base must continue to grow. It is the scientist and scholar who serves this important role. For the practicing sport psychologist to enjoy professional credibility, there must exist a credible scientific body of knowledge.

ETHICS IN SPORT PSYCHOLOGY

While the ethical application of sport psychology principles is discussed throughout this text, it is important to emphasize the topic. In recent years it has become clear that theories and techniques derived from the study of sport psychology can provide the winning edge for athletes and athletic teams. In this text, you will learn many of the psychological theories and techniques that can make you a more effective teacher and/or coach. This does not mean, however, that you will be qualified to provide psychological services to coaches and athletes. It takes much more than one course in sport psychology to become a sport psychologist. This is true despite the fact that at the present time there are

Working with athletes can be both challenging and rewarding.
Courtesy University of Missouri–Columbia Sports Information

limited licensing procedures in sport psychology; anyone can claim to be a sport psychologist. However, without certain minimal qualifications this would be unethical. When one considers the dangers involved in the inappropriate application of psychological theory, personality assessment, and intervention strategies, it is no wonder that many professionals are concerned (Silva, 1989b).

The practice of sport psychology, whether by a coach or by a licensed psychologist, involves two diverse components. The first has to do with teaching, while the second is clinical in nature. For example, the sport psychologist uses teaching principles to help an athlete learn how to use imagery and/or relaxation techniques effectively. A well-trained and informed coach or teacher should be able to give such service (Smith, 1992). However, when the sport psychologist is called upon to provide clinical services such as crisis counseling, psychotherapy, or psychological testing, it is important that that person be specifically trained and licensed. To do otherwise would be unethical and irresponsible.

To help the sport psychologist deal effectively with the ethical issues of the profession, the NASPSPA issued a set of "Ethical Standards for Provision of Services by NASPSPA Members" (Staff, 1982). These standards are summarized by nine principles:

1. *Responsibility* Sport psychologists accept responsibility for the consequences of their acts and make every effort to ensure that services are used appropriately.

2. *Competence* Sport psychologists provide services and use techniques for which they are qualified by training and experience.

3. *Moral and Legal Standards* Sport psychologists refuse to participate in practices that are inconsistent with legal, moral, and ethical standards.

4. *Public Statements* Sport psychologists accurately and objectively state their professional qualifications and affiliations.

5. *Confidentiality* Sport psychologists respect the confidentiality of information obtained from clients or subjects in the course of their work.

6. *Welfare of the Client* Sport psychologists respect the integrity and protect the welfare of the people and groups with whom they work.

7. *Professional Relationships* Sport psychologists are sensitive to the needs and concerns of colleagues in other sport-related fields.

8. *Assessment Techniques* In the development, publication, and utilization of assessment techniques, sport psychologists promote the best interests of their clients.

9. *Research with Human Participants* In conducting psychological research, sport psychologists are first of all concerned with the welfare of the participants according to federal, state, and professional standards.

While the ethical standards published in 1982 by the NASPSPA have served a useful purpose, they are woefully inadequate for the current day. In 1982, there were very few practicing sport psychologists. This situation has changed drastically in the last fifteen years. The need for a detailed set of ethical principles and a code of conduct to govern the practices of sport psychology consultants seems obvious. To address this need, the Association for the Advancement of Applied Sport Psychology has generally adopted the published guidelines of the American Psychological Association (APA) to govern the behavior of AAASP certified consultants. The ethics code outlined in the APA guidelines "provides a common set of values upon which psychologists build their professional and scientific work" (APA, 1992, p. 1599). Petitpas, Brewer, Rivera, and Raalte (1994) surveyed AAASP members to obtain data on ethical beliefs and behaviors associated with the practice of applied sport psychology.

Their research indicated that most questionable ethical practices identified by respondents corresponded to violations of APA ethical standards. These results provide support for the position that adoption of the APA ethical standards is a viable and prudent practice.

SUMMARY

Sport psychology is a science in which the principles of psychology are applied in a sport setting. It is an exciting subject dedicated to the enhancement of both athletic performance and social-psychological aspects of human enrichment. Norman Triplett (1897) is cited as the first individual to conduct sport psychology research. Triplett analyzed performance of cyclists under conditions of social facilitation. Coleman Roberts Griffith established the first sport psychology laboratory at the University of Illinois in 1925. In recent years, numerous scholarly societies have emerged to represent the discipline and application of sport psychology. In the United States, the most prominent are the North American Society for the Psychology of Sport and Physical Activity (NASPSPA) and the Association for the Advancement of Applied Sport Psychology (AAASP).

The issue of who is qualified to provide sport psychology services has been addressed by numerous professional organizations. The United States Olympic Committee developed the Sport Psychology Registry to identify individuals qualified to work with Olympic athletes. The AAASP developed procedures whereby qualified individuals could earn the title "Certified Consultant, AAASP." The roles and functions of the sport psychologist fall into the categories of clinical/counseling services, education, and research.

Concern is emerging over ethics associated with providing applied sport psychology services. The NASPSPA has published standards of ethical behavior. More recently, most professionals in the field have seen the wisdom of adopting APA standards of ethical behavior.

REVIEW QUESTIONS

1. What is sport psychology?

2. Provide a brief history of the development of sport psychology as a discipline in North America.

3. Provide a chronological review of the emergence of sport psychology societies in North America. What is the role and function of each society? How do they relate to each other and to the International Society of Sport Psychology?

4. Provide a chronological review of the emergence of scholarly journals dedicated to the expansion of knowledge in sport psychology. How do the various journals relate to the societies identified in question #3?

5. Explain the difference between academic and applied sport psychology. What practical impact do these two divisions have upon the discipline of sport psychology?

6. Why is the question of who is qualified to provide psychological services to athletes an important one? How is the question being addressed?

7. Explain the differences between clinical/counseling, educational, and research sport psychology. What are the roles and functions played by sport psychologists in these three categories?

8. Address the issue of ethics in sport psychology. Is ethics associated with sport psychology services a concern? How can these concerns be addressed?

GLOSSARY

AAASP Association for the Advancement of Applied Sport Psychology.

academic sport psychology An unofficial division dedicated to the development of sport psychology as a scientific discipline.

APA American Psychological Association.

applied sport psychology An unofficial division dedicated to the advancement of sport psychology as an applied science. Proponents of applied sport psychology are keenly interested in providing services to athletes.

clinical/counseling sport psychologist Type of sport psychologist that is required to be licensed and have specialized training in clinical and/or counseling psychology.

clinical/counseling sport psychology Category of applied sport psychology that requires licensure and specialized training in clinical and/or counseling psychology.

CSPLSP Canadian Society for Psychomotor Learning and Sport Psychology.

educational sport psychologist Type of sport psychologist that uses education as a medium for teaching athletes and coaches correct principles associated with sport psychology.

educational sport psychology Category of sport psychology in which education is the medium used for teaching athletes and coaches correct principles about applied sport psychology.

Griffith, Coleman Roberts Father of sport psychology in North America. In 1925, and while at the University of Illinois, he established the first sport psychology laboratory in North America.

Henry, Franklin M. Sport psychology pioneer from the University of California, Berkeley.

ISSP International Society of Sport Psychology.

Lawther, John Sport psychology pioneer from Pennsylvania State University.

NASPE National Association for Sport and Physical Education. An association within AAHPERD.

NASPSPA North American Society for the Psychology of Sport and Physical Activity.

Ogilvie, Bruce Father of applied sport psychology in North America.

research sport psychologist Type of sport psychologist who is mainly interested in research and in expanding the knowledge base in sport psychology.

research sport psychology Category of sport psychology in which the main interest is in research and expanding the knowledge base.

Slater-Hammel, Arthur Sport psychology pioneer from Indiana University.

SPA Sport Psychology Academy, a division within NASPE.

Sport Psychology Registry List of individuals in the area of psychology of sport who are qualified to work with Olympic Athletes. The Registry was initiated by the USOC.

Triplett, Norman Person who conducted and published what appears to be the first clear example of sport psychology research in North America.

USOC United States Olympic Committee.

SUGGESTED READINGS

American Psychological Association. (1992). Ethical principles of psychologists and code of conduct. *American Psychologist, 47,* 1597–1611.

Dember, W. N. (1974). Motivation and the cognitive revolution. *American Psychologist, 29,* 161–168.

Gardner, F. L. (1991). Professionalization of sport psychology: A reply to Silva. *The Sport Psychologist, 5,* 55–60.

May, J. R. (1986, Summer). Sport psychology: Should psychologists become involved? *The Clinical Psychologist, 39,* 77–81.

Silva, J. M. III (1989). Toward the professionalization of sport psychology. *The Sport Psychologist, 3,* 265–273.

Singer, R. N. (1989). Applied sport psychology in the United States. *Journal of Applied Sport Psychology, 1,* 61–80.

Taylor, J. (1991). Career direction, development, and opportunities in applied sport psychology. *The Sport Psychologist, 5,* 266–280.

Wiggins, D. K. (1984). The history of sport psychology in North America. In J. M. Silva & R. S. Weinberg (Eds.), *Psychological foundations of sport* (pp. 9–22). Champaign, IL: Human Kinetics.

2 PERSONALITY AND THE ATHLETE

KEY TERMS

- able-bodied athlete
- AMI
- Cattell 16 PF
- credulous argument
- disabled athlete
- factor analysis
- first-order traits
- gravitational hypothesis
- iceberg profile
- interactional model
- mental health model
- meta-analysis
- MMPI
- multivariate approach
- personality
- personality trait
- physically challenged athlete
- POMS
- projective procedures
- psychological core
- psychological profile
- psychological state
- role-related behavior
- Rorschach test
- second-order traits
- skeptical argument
- source traits
- surface traits
- Thematic Apperception Test
- trait
- typical responses

An athlete expresses
her personality through
her performance.
Courtesy University of
Missouri–Columbia
Sports Information

Consider the following scenario. You are in a group of fifty athletes competing for one of fifteen places on your country's Olympic volleyball team. On the first day of the tryouts you are taken into a room and asked to take a three-hour battery of pencil-and-paper tests. The test administrator tells you to answer all the questions as honestly as you can and that the results will help the selection committee determine your personality profile. You are not too concerned about the psychological testing because you know that you are one of the top setters and defensive players in your country. After four days of grueling workouts in which you perform very well, you are taken aside by the coach and informed that you are not going to be selected for the Olympic team. In tears, you ask the coach how this could be, since you feel that you had an excellent tryout and that you performed as well as or better than many of the other athletes. The coach tells you with regret that your personality profile, as measured through the tests you took, indicates that you lack the mental toughness and aggressiveness necessary for world-class competition.

A scenario such as this actually happened (Ryan, 1976), and still happens on a regular basis in other sports and other equally critical situations (Davis, 1991). If athletic performance can actually be predicted from psychological testing, then the use of personality tests to make team selections makes some sense. However, if it cannot be done with at least 90 percent accuracy, the process could be considered highly unethical.

In many ways, the study of personality as it relates to sports participation is one of the most intriguing and exciting areas of sport psychology. Ruffer (1975, 1976a, 1976b), for example, cites 572 sources of original research in a compilation of references on the relationship between personality and athletic performance. However, in recent years the interest of researchers has waned. Fewer articles appear in journals such as the *Journal of Sport and Exercise Psychology,* the *International Journal of Sport Psychology,* the *Journal of Sport Behavior, The Sport Psychologist,* and the *Journal of Applied Sport Psychology.*

Based on the great interest in personality research, one might incorrectly conclude that the relationship between personality and athletic performance would by now be crystal clear. Unfortunately, this is not the case. In fact, a random sample of the references cited by Ruffer could easily reveal conflicting conclusions. However, during the last ten years, thanks to the critical eye of many sport psychologists, many of the problems plaguing scientific inquiry have been identified and rectified.

This chapter looks at many of these problems and examines what progress has been made. It begins with a basic study of personality, its structure, measurement, and development. This is followed by a candid review of the personality-performance relationship, and the introduction of an interactional approach to studying the effect of personality on human behavior and performance.

Figure 2.1

Hollander's notion of personality structure. From *Principles and Methods of Social Psychology,* 3rd Edition, by Edwin P. Hollander. Copyright © 1976 by Oxford University Press, Inc. Adapted by permission.

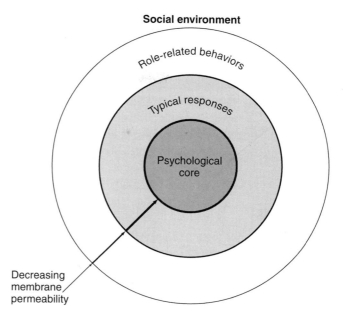

Social environment

Role-related behaviors

Typical responses

Psychological core

Decreasing membrane permeability

THE STRUCTURE OF PERSONALITY

The concept of personality is so broad that it is difficult to define precisely. Regardless of what definition is put forth, there will be those who argue that it is either too broad or too narrow. One definition that has stood the test of time was proposed by Allport (1937), who said **personality** "is the dynamic organization within the individual of those psychophysical systems that determine his unique adjustments to his environment" (p. 48). Hollander (1971) gave a similar yet simpler definition when he wrote that personality is "the sum total of an individual's characteristics which make him unique" (p. 394). No matter what definition is selected, both Allport and Hollander agree that the personality of each individual is unique.

Perhaps the best way to understand personality is to look at its structure. Such a structure has been outlined by Hollander (1971) and adapted to sport psychology by Martens (1975). A schematic view of personality structure is illustrated in figure 2.1. While the basic concepts for the structure of personality as shown in this figure are outlined by Hollander, the unique manner of presenting these concepts should be attributed to Martens.

As illustrated in figure 2.1, a personality can be divided into three separate but related levels. These are (1) the psychological core, (2) typical responses, and (3) role-related behaviors. The psychological core is further represented as being internal and consistent in nature, while typical responses and role-related behaviors are considered external and dynamic.

The relative effect of the social environment on the three levels of personality is reflected by the thickness or permeability of the lines that separate each level from the environment. *Permeability* means the degree to which a membrane or dividing structure can be penetrated. For example, a sieve used for straining vegetables is very permeable, while a concrete wall is relatively impermeable.

As can be observed in the figure, role-related behaviors are most susceptible to the influence of the environment, while the psychological core is somewhat insulated from the environment.

The **psychological core** of an individual holds that person's image of what she is really like. It includes the individual's self-concept. The psychological core represents the centerpiece of a person's personality; it includes basic attitudes, values, interests, and motives. In short, it's "the real you."

Typical responses represent the usual manner in which we respond to environmental situations. For example, a person may exhibit typical mannerisms in responding to such things as frustration, humor, and anxiety. Typical responses are learned modes of dealing with the environment. Unless a person is playacting or has an unstable personality, typical responses will be a valid indicator of a person's psychological core. For example, if a person consistently responds to all types of environmental situations with feelings of apprehension and tension, we may confidently conclude that this is an anxious person. However, if we were to conclude from a single observation that a person was aggressive because he displayed aggression on one occasion, we could be very wrong. The person may have exhibited aggressive behavior because of the situation (responding to a physical attack) or may have been playacting.

Role-related behavior represents the most superficial aspect of our personalities. We engage in role-related behavior to fit our perception of our environment. Consequently, as the environment or our perception of it changes, our behavior changes. These are not typical responses, and are certainly not valid indicators of the psychological core. Consider the example of the athlete who is being recruited to play football at a major university. The university representative asks the high school football coach about the athlete's personality. The coach responds that he is very quiet, hardworking, and untalkative. When this same question is asked of the athlete's girlfriend, she replies that he is actually very sociable, outgoing, and talkative. We would certainly be on dangerous ground if we tried to affix a particular personality trait to someone based upon role-related behavior.

A clear understanding of Hollander's personality structure should be of great value as we proceed with our discussion of personality. In measuring an athlete's personality, we want to get to the *real* person, or in Hollander's terms, the psychological core. Yet it should be clear from Hollander's personality structure that this can best be done at the level of typical responses. Psychologists have long attempted to measure personality directly, through the use of projective tests such as the Thematic Apperception Test. However, as we shall learn, projective tests may suffer from low reliability and validity. Consequently, the most common and objective manner of measuring personality is on the level of typical responses using some type of questionnaire. This should not be construed to indicate, however, that questionnaires are devoid of problems.

CONCEPT & APPLICATION 2.1

Concept The personality of an individual may be represented by three distinct levels. The most superficial level is role-related behavior, while the deepest and most meaningful is the psychological core. The psychological core is best reflected in the athlete's typical responses.

Application To understand athletes, the coach must not be deceived by role-playing behavior. The athlete may play the role of a "hotshot," but in truth be rather insecure. Take the time to study your athletes and find out what they are really like, deep down in their psychological core.

THEORIES OF PERSONALITY

In this section we will consider four major theoretical approaches to the study of personality: psychodynamic theory, social learning theory, humanistic theory, and trait theory. Each will be briefly discussed.

PSYCHODYNAMIC THEORIES

Perhaps the most influential proponent of psychodynamic theory was Sigmund Freud (1933). However, in the years since Freud, a number of psychoanalytic theorists have proposed modifications to Freud's original theory. Among the neo-Freudians are Carl Jung, Erich Fromm, and Eric Erickson (Mischel, 1986). Most of the neo-Freudian positions evolved from the theorists' personal experiences with patients during psychotherapy.

Freud's psychodynamic theory and his method of treating personality disturbances were based primarily upon self-analysis and extensive clinical observation of neurotics. Two distinguishing characteristics of the psychodynamic approach to personality have been its emphasis upon in-depth examination of the *whole* person, and its emphasis upon unconscious motives.

In Freud's view, the id, ego, and superego form the tripartite structure of personality. The id represents the unconscious instinctual core of personality; in a sense, the id is the pleasure-seeking mechanism. In contrast, the ego represents the conscious, logical, reality-oriented aspect of the personality. The superego represents the conscience of the individual; it is the internalized moral standards of society impressed upon the person by parental control and the process of socialization. Freud proposed that the ego aids in the resolution of conflicts between the id and the superego. Essentially, Freud advocated a conflict theory of personality. In this respect, the three parts of the psychic structure are always in conflict. The individual's personality is the sum total of the dynamic conflicts between the impulse to seek release and the inhibition against these impulses (Mischel, 1986).

The individual's unconscious sexual and aggressive instincts are major determinants of behavior, according to Freud. Athletic aggression represents a potential example of this approach. Instinct theory provides one explanation for the phenomenon of violence in sport, as we will later learn.

Certain personality types are attracted to rock climbing. Courtesy David Frazier Photo CD

SOCIAL LEARNING THEORY

From the viewpoint of social learning theory, behavior is not simply a function of unconscious motives (as in psychoanalytic theory) or underlying predispositions. Rather, human behavior is a function of social learning and the strength of the situation. An individual behaves according to how she has learned to behave, as this is consistent with environmental constraints. If the environmental situation is prominent, the effect of personality traits or unconscious motives upon behavior should be minimal.

The story is told of the boy who brought his report card to his father and wanted to know if his poor performance was inherited or due to his social environment. This was certainly a no-win situation for the father. However, from a social learning theory perspective, the answer would clearly be his social environment. According to social learning theory, a child's performance and behavior is a function of the child's experiences and environment.

The origin of social learning theory can be traced to Clark Hull's 1943 theory of learning, and B. F. Skinner's (1953) behaviorism. Hull's stimulus-response theory of learning was based on laboratory experimentation with animals. According to stimulus-response theory, an individual's behavior in any given situation is a function of his learned experiences. Other researchers, such as Miller and Dollard (Miller, 1941), Mischel (1986), and Bandura (1977), extended the Hullian notions of complex human behavior.

Two of the primary mechanisms through which individuals learn are modeling and social reinforcement. *Modeling,* or imitative behavior, refers to the phenomenon of learning through observation. Albert Bandura's social learning theory is based primarily upon this important concept. According to

Bandura, behavior is best explained as a function of observational learning. *Social reinforcement* is based upon the notion that rewarded behaviors are likely to be repeated. Martens (1975) has defined social reinforcement as verbal and nonverbal communication passing between two individuals that can increase the strength of a response.

A youth league football player observes on television that professional athletes are often able to intimidate quarterbacks and wide receivers through aggressive hard-hitting tackles. Using the professional athlete as his model, he tries the same tactics on his youth league team, and is reinforced by the coach with a pat on the back. This example illustrates how young athletes develop questionable behaviors through modeling and social reinforcement.

HUMANISTIC THEORY

The major proponents of the humanistic theory of personality are Carl Rogers and Abraham Maslow (Ewen, 1984; Smith & Vetter, 1991). Unlike the pessimistic Freud, Rogers and Maslow argue that human nature is inherently healthy and constructive. At the center of the humanistic theory of personality is the concept of *self-actualization.* The human organism possesses an innate drive or tendency to enhance itself, to realize capacities, and to act to become a better and more self-fulfilled person. In the developing personality, openness to experiences that then shape the individual is of critical importance. It is not necessarily the experience that shapes the individual, but the individual's perception of that experience. Self-actualization is an ongoing process of seeking congruence between one's experiences and one's self-concept. Rogers's influence on the development of the humanistic theory of personality is largely due to his method of psychotherapy, which is nondirective and client-centered. The therapist does not attempt to impose her values on the client, but rather helps the client to find her own solutions to problems. Further, the therapist is accepting, empathetic, and honest, and expresses unconditional positive regard for the client. Maslow's contribution to the humanistic theory is in the development of his hierarchical motive system based on the notion of hierarchical needs. For Maslow, the end goal of all human experience is self-actualization, but to get there the person must first have lesser needs fulfilled.

TRAIT THEORIES

The basic position of trait or factor theory is that personality can be described in terms of **traits** possessed by individuals. These traits are considered synonymous with predispositions to act in a certain way. Traits are considered to be stable, enduring, and consistent across a variety of differing situations. Those who exhibit the trait or need to achieve success, for example, can be expected to have a predisposition toward competitiveness and assertiveness in many situations. A predisposition toward a certain trait means not that the individual will *always* respond in this manner, but that a certain likelihood exists.

Among the most ardent advocates of trait psychology are psychologists such as Gordon Allport, Raymond Cattell, and Hans Eysenck. Cattell (Cattel, Eber &

Tatsuoka, 1980) claims to have successfully identified sixteen different and independent source traits that he believes describe a personality. Using a similar approach, British psychologists (Eysenck & Eysenck, 1968) have concentrated on the dimensional traits of neuroticism-stability and introversion-extroversion.

Since the notion of an enduring, somewhat genetically-founded, trait approach to personality offends the social learning theorist, it is important to point out that Cattell has never ignored the importance of the environment. Cattell (1965) believes that typical responses are a function of both the situation (environment) and the personality disposition. This is evident from his formula, $R = f(S \cdot P)$, in which R = response, S = situation, and P = personality. This revelation may be somewhat startling to social learning advocates who oppose trait theory on the grounds that it does not consider the environment.

The great strength of the trait theory of personality is that it allows for the easy and objective measurement of personality through the use of inventories. If it can be demonstrated that a collection of traits can accurately describe a person's psychological profile, then this certainly is superior to a psychoanalytic approach, in which personality is inferred through less objective techniques. Conversely, the weakness of the trait approach is that it may fail to consider the whole person, since personality according to this approach is represented by a collection of specific traits.

CONCEPT & APPLICATION 2.2

Concept Four basic approaches for explaining the phenomenon of personality are the psychodynamic, social learning, humanistic, and trait theories.

Application In attempting to explain behavior on the basis of personality, it is important to recognize the ramifications of adopting one theoretical approach over another. The teacher or coach's belief system will influence athlete-coach interactions.

THE MEASUREMENT OF PERSONALITY

This section will identify and briefly discuss various techniques used for assessing personality. It should be pointed out that the various methods of assessing personality correspond closely to the basic personality theories we have just discussed. For example, projective tests such as the Rorschach test are closely linked to the psychoanalytic theory of personality. Conversely, the various paper-and-pencil inventories are linked to the trait theory. In this brief overview of personality measurement techniques, the reader should be aware that many issues regarding personality assessment remain unresolved. The methods outlined here are not perfect; nor do psychologists agree on the meaning of the results of any particular test.

Cofer and Johnson (1960) identified three basic classes of measurement techniques. These are (1) rating scales, (2) unstructured projective tests, and (3) questionnaires. Each of these three categories will now be discussed, with particular emphasis upon the questionnaire method. The questionnaire method is highlighted because of its demonstrated objectivity, validity, and reliability (Whiting, Hardman, Hendry, & Jones, 1973). Additionally, it is the measurement technique most commonly used by sport psychologists today.

RATING SCALES

Characteristically, *rating scales* involve the use of a judge or judges who are asked to observe an individual in some situation. The judges employ the use of a checklist or scale that has been predesigned for maximum objectivity. Usually, if the checklist is used properly and the judges are well trained, the results can be fairly reliable and objective.

Typically, two types of situations are involved in personality assessment using rating scales. These are the *interview* and the *observation of performance.* In the interview, the judge asks the subject numerous open-ended and specific questions designed to ascertain personality traits and general impressions. Generally, several interviews are necessary to gain impressions about underlying motives (the core of personality). If the interview is conducted properly, carefully, and systematically, the results can be reliable and valid. However, much depends upon the skill and sensitivity of the person conducting the interview.

Observation of a subject during some type of performance situation is the second kind of rating system used for ascertaining personality. As with the interview, observations can be effective if the checklist being used is well designed and planned, and if the observer is highly trained. Typically, for personality assessment, the checklist would contain specific traits and behaviors that the observer would look for. These traits, as they were observed, would then be rated in terms of strength and clarity.

UNSTRUCTURED PROJECTIVE PROCEDURES

The foregoing rating methods are generally used for ascertaining data on traits of personality, although in many instances inferences may be made concerning underlying motives. **Projective procedures** may also be used to identify traits, but they are commonly used to determine information about underlying motives. Projective techniques allow subjects to reveal their inner feelings and motives through unstructured tasks. These unstructured techniques are used primarily in clinical psychology and are somewhat synonymous with the psychoanalytic approaches to explaining personality. The underlying assumption in the unstructured test situation is that if subjects perceive that there are no right or wrong responses, they will likely be open and honest in their responses.

Several kinds of unstructured tests have been developed. Among them are the Rorschach Test (Sarason, 1954), the Thematic Apperception Test (Tompkins, 1947), the Sentence Completion Test (Holsopple & Miale, 1954), and the

House-Tree-Person Test (Buck, 1948). For our purposes, only the Rorschach (also known as the "inkblot") and Thematic Apperception Tests (TAT) will be discussed. The inkblot and the TAT are by far the most commonly used projective tests.

The Rorschach Test

Herman Rorschach, a Swiss psychiatrist, was the first to apply the inkblot to the study of personality (Fredenburgh, 1971). The **Rorschach test** was introduced in 1921, and remains the most famous of all the projective testing devices. The test material consists of ten cards. Each card has an inkblot on it, which is symmetrical and intricate. Some of the cards are entirely in black and white, while others have a splash of color or are nearly all in color. The cards are presented to the subject one at a time and in a prescribed order. As the cards are presented, the subject is encouraged to tell what he or she sees. The tester keeps a verbatim record of the subject's responses to each, and notes any spontaneous remarks, emotional reactions, or other incidental behaviors. After all the cards have been viewed, the examiner questions the subject in a systematic manner regarding associations made with each card.

The Rorschach test has not been used extensively by sport psychologists to evaluate personality in athletes. Early research on its use suggested that it lacked objectivity, reliability, and validity (Ryan, 1981). Research over the last fifteen to twenty years, however, strongly refutes these early conclusions. Weiner (1994) reports that the test is psychometrically sound, with verifiable retest reliability and criterion and construct validity. However, the test requires highly trained clinicians in order to yield reliable and accurate results. The use of the Rorschach test in research involving athletes is desirable, but only when administered by highly trained psychologists.

The Thematic Apperception Test

The **Thematic Apperception Test,** developed by Henry Murray and his associates in 1943 at the Harvard University Psychological Clinic, has been used almost as extensively as the Rorschach test. The TAT is composed of nineteen cards containing pictures depicting vague situations and one blank card. The subject is encouraged to make up a story about each picture. In contrast to the vague blots in the Rorschach test, pictures in the TAT are rather clear and vivid. For example, the sex of the characters in the picture and their facial expressions are generally identifiable. It is believed that subjects reveal or project important aspects of their personalities as they weave the characters and objects in the pictures into either an oral or a written story.

Like the Rorschach test, the TAT has not been used extensively by sport psychologists to measure personality in athletes. This is not to say that it should not be used; however, its validity and reliability are highly dependent upon the skill and training of the individual administering and interpreting the results.

STRUCTURED QUESTIONNAIRES

The structured questionnaire is a paper-and-pencil test in which the subject answers specific true-false or Likert scale-type statements. A typical Likert scale-type statement is illustrated in the following example:

In athletic situations, I find myself getting very uptight and anxious as the contest progresses.

DEFINITELY FALSE								*DEFINITELY TRUE*	
1	2	3	4	5	6	7	8	9	10

There are many different kinds of questionnaire-type personality inventories. Some of them have been designed for use with abnormal patients, while others are for normal individuals. Generally speaking, certain specific personality characteristics or traits are believed to be identified through the administration of these questionnaires. The three questionnaires selected for our discussion have been used extensively in sport psychology literature. The reader is referred to Ostrow (1996) for a more complete description of available personality inventories. Indeed, the reader is referred to this work regarding psychological inventories generally.

Minnesota Multiphasic Personality Inventory (MMPI)
The **Minnesota Multiphasic Personality Inventory (MMPI)** appeared in the early 1940s as a new kind of psychometric tool for the assessment of personality. It was designed to provide objective assessment of some of the major personality characteristics that affect personal and social adjustment in persons of disabling psychological abnormality. Nine scales were originally developed for clinical use and were named for the abnormal conditions on which their construction was based. The twelve scales now in the test include the following: hypochondriasis (Hs), depression (D), hysteria (Hy), psychopathic deviation (Pd), masculinity-femininity (Mf), paranoia (Pa), psychasthenia (Pt), schizophrenia (Sc), hypomania (Ma), lying (L), validity (F), and correction (K). The test is designed for subjects sixteen years of age or older who have had at least six years of successful schooling. While the test was designed for abnormal individuals, it can be and has been used with normal individuals (Dahlstrom & Walsh, 1960; Hathaway & McKinley, 1967).

Cattell Sixteen Personality Factor Questionnaire
Perhaps the most sophisticated paper-and-pencil test of personality is the **Personality Factor Questionnaire (16 PF)** designed and tested by Cattell (1973). Cattell employed the methods of **factor analysis** in his study of personality and firmly believed that his test measured the sixteen **source traits** or **first-order traits** of personality. Factor analysis procedures allow the researcher to identify major factors associated with a particular test. Cattell and his associates conducted extensive research over forty years to find support and verification for these source traits (Cattell, Eber & Tatsuoka, 1980).

Additionally, Cattell believed that the sixteen source traits can be reduced to four **second-order traits,** or **surface traits.** The surface traits of introversion-extroversion, anxiety, tough-mindedness, and independence represent a cluster of several source traits and relate to learned behavior (Fredenburgh, 1971). Thus we may infer that second-order factors are learned, while primary factors (source traits) are fundamental structures of personality.

The Athletic Motivation Inventory

The **Athletic Motivation Inventory (AMI)** was developed by Thomas Tutko, Bruce Ogilvie, and Leland Lyon at the Institute for the Study of Athletic Motivation at San Jose State College (Tutko & Richards, 1971, 1972). According to its authors, the AMI measures a number of personality traits related to high athletic achievement: drive, aggression, determination, responsibility, leadership, self-confidence, emotional control, mental toughness, coachability, conscience development, and trust.

The reliability and validity of the instrument has been questioned by Rushall (1973), Corbin (1977), and Martens (1975). However, Tutko and Richards (1972) say that thousands of athletes have been tested and that the AMI was originally based upon the 16 PF and the Jackson Personality Research Form (Ogilvie, Johnsgard & Tutko, 1971).

Perhaps the real concern of sport psychologists is not that the test is more or less reliable than other personality inventories, but that the developers implied that it could predict athletic success. No other organization, researcher, or promoter has made similar claims about other more distinguished personality inventories.

A study by Davis (1991) supports this position. Davis studied the relationship between AMI sub-scales and psychological strength in 649 ice hockey players who were eligible for the National Hockey League (NHL) entry draft. The criterion measure of psychological strength was based on an evaluation of on-ice play by NHL scouts. The results showed that less than 4 percent of the variance in scout ratings was accounted for by AMI scores ($r = .20$). This outcome suggests that the AMI is a poor predictor of psychological strength of ice hockey players.

CONCEPT & APPLICATION 2.3

Concept Many structured personality inventories are available for measuring the personality traits of athletes. Each of these inventories or tests was designed for a specific purpose and with a particular subject in mind. Tests should be selected with care.

Application In terms of reliability and validity, there is little doubt that the Cattell 16 PF is the best test to be used for measuring the personality of athletes. When using this test, consult your team sport psychologist, your school psychologist, or other trained professionals regarding the correct administration of the test and interpretation of results.

Coaches also exhibit interesting personality styles. Courtesy Ball State University Sports Information

THE CREDULOUS VS. SKEPTICAL ARGUMENT

Several years ago, Morgan (1980a) published an article entitled "Sport Personology: The Credulous-Skeptical Argument in Perspective." In this article, Morgan explained that many sport psychologists are polarized on the issue of the credibility of personality research. On one side, a few researchers believe that positive and accurate predictions can be made about sport performance from personality profiles based on measured traits. Proponents of this position are considered **credulous** in nature and are generally willing to use results of personality testing in predicting athletic success. On the other side are sport psychologists who tend to be **skeptical,** minimizing the value of personality assessment in predicting athletic success.

While the credulous vs. skeptical argument in sport personality research raged in the literature for many years, it seems clear that this served no useful purpose. In fact, it accomplished little more than to further polarize the thinking of the two camps. Personality is not a *strong* predictor of athletic performance, but it is a predictor. Based upon what is known about personality, it is unreasonable to expect a high correlation between a personality disposition and a physical skill. A person's basic personality should be viewed as just one factor that can contribute to athletic success.

John McEnroe
dominated men's
professional tennis in
the 1980s through
superior skill and a
volatile personality.
Courtesy Kansas State
University Sports
Information

PERSONALITY AND SPORTS PERFORMANCE

Since 1960, several comprehensive literature reviews have attempted to clarify
the relationship between personality and sport performance (Cofer & Johnson,
1960; Cooper, 1969; Hardman, 1973; Ogilvie, 1968, 1976; Morgan, 1980b). Of
these, the review by Morgan (1980b) provided the most comprehensive
treatment of the subject. While not fully endorsing the credulous position,
Morgan argued that the literature shows a consistent relationship between
personality and sport performance when (a) response distortion is removed, and
(b) data are analyzed using a multivariate approach. A **multivariate approach**
is used when multiple measures of personality are analyzed simultaneously, as
opposed to separately. Since personality is multifaceted and complex, it is
appropriate that statistics used to analyze personality measures also be complex.
While it is good to remember that the relationship between sport performance
and personality is far from crystal clear, it seems equally true that certain general
conclusions can be drawn. In the paragraphs that follow, I will attempt to
synthesize some of the research and offer some general conclusions.

ATHLETES VS. NONATHLETES

Athletes differ from nonathletes on many personality traits (Geron, Furst &
Rotstein, 1986). It is often a matter of conjecture whether these differences favor
the athletes or the nonathletes. Schurr, Ashley, and Joy (1977) clearly showed
that athletes who participate in team and individual sports are more independent,
more objective, and less anxious than nonathletes. From Hardman's (1973)
review it is also clear that the athlete is often more intelligent than average.
Additionally, Cooper (1969) describes the athlete as being more self-confident,

competitive, and socially outgoing than the nonathlete. This is supportive of Morgan's (1980b) and Kane's (1976) conclusions that the athlete is basically an extrovert and low in anxiety.

In several recent investigations, a number of comparisons have been made between an athlete's score on various personality and psychological inventories and scores associated with norm groups. For example, compared to published normative data, the scores of professional cowboys indicate that they tend to be alert, enthusiastic, forthright, self-sufficient, reality based, and practical (McGill, Hall, Ratliff & Moss, 1986). Compared to norm groups, elite rock climbers exhibit low anxiety, emotional detachment, low superegos, and high levels of sensation seeking (Magni, Rupolo, Simini, DeLeo & Rampazzo, 1985; Robinson, 1985).

While the evidence favors the conclusion that the athlete differs from the nonathlete in many personality traits, the problem arises in the definition of what constitutes an athlete. In the Schurr et al. (1977) research, an athlete was defined as a person who participated in the university intercollegiate athletic program. This would seem to be a viable criterion. However, this classification system has not been universally adopted by researchers. Some studies, for example, have classified intramural and club sports participants as athletes. Other studies have required that participants earn awards, such as letters, in order to be considered athletes. Until some unifying system is adopted, it will always be difficult to compare results from one study with those from another.

CONCEPT & APPLICATION 2.4

Concept Generally speaking, athletes differ from nonathletes in many personality traits. For example, it can be demonstrated that athletes are more independent, objective, and extroverted than nonathletes, but less anxious.
Application As a coach, expect your athletes to be generally higher in such traits as independence, extroversion, and self-confidence, and lower in anxiety, than nonathletes. One cannot, however, rank athletes on the basis of these traits or make team roster decisions based on them. A statistical relationship (often low) does not suggest a cause-and-effect relationship.

DEVELOPMENTAL EFFECTS OF ATHLETIC PARTICIPATION UPON PERSONALITY

Given that athletes and nonathletes differ on the personality dimensions of extroversion and stability (anxiety), is this due to the athletic experience (learning), or to a natural selection process in which individuals possessing certain personality traits gravitate toward athletics? Perhaps the final answer to this question will never be known; however, the evidence typically supports the genetic or *gravitational hypothesis* (Morgan, 1974). Individuals who possess stable, extroverted personalities tend to gravitate toward the athletic experience.

As the competitive process weeds out all but the keenest of competitors, those who remain are those having the greatest levels of extroversion and stability. This could be described as sort of an athletic Darwinism (survival of the fittest). Some of the studies that support the gravitational model are those by Yanada and Hirata (1970), Kane (1970), and Rushall (1970a).

The viability of the gravitational model, however, does not preclude the possibility that sport participation can enhance personality development. In this respect, Tattersfield (1971) has provided longitudinal evidence that athletic participation before maturity has a developmental effect upon personality. Specifically, Tattersfield monitored the personality profiles of boys participating in an age-group swimming program across a five-year training period. Significant changes toward greater extroversion, stability, and dependence were observed in the boys during this period. From an educational perspective, all but the factor of dependence would be considered positive in nature.

CONCEPT & APPLICATION 2.5

Concept Athletes tend to be more extroverted, independent, and self-confident than nonathletes because of a process of "natural selection," and not due to learning. Individuals who exhibit certain personality traits tend to gravitate toward athletics. An important exception to this principle occurs in the formative years before the young athlete reaches maturity. During the early maturing years, the youth sport experience is critical in forming positive personality traits such as self-confidence and independence.

Application Coaches and teachers who work with young boys and girls must be very careful that the athletic experience is a positive one in the lives of young people. Athletic programs designed for youth should place a premium on the development of feelings of self-worth, confidence, and independence, and relegate winning to a position of secondary importance. Winning must not be more important than the needs of the boys and girls.

PERSONALITY SPORT TYPE

Can personality profiles of athletes in one sport be reliably differentiated from those of athletes in another sport? Perhaps the first real attempts to answer this question were made with bodybuilders. Research by Henry (1941), Thune (1949), and Harlow (1951), for example, suggested that bodybuilders suffer from feelings of masculine inadequacy, and are overly concerned with health, body build, and manliness. A study by Thirer and Greer (1981), however, would tend to cast doubt on these earlier stereotypes. In a well-conceived and controlled study, the authors concluded that intermediate and competitive bodybuilders were high in achievement motivation and resistance to change, but relatively normal in all other traits measured. They found no support for the previous generalities and negative stereotyping sometimes applied to bodybuilders.

Kroll and Crenshaw (1970) reported a study in which highly skilled football, wrestling, gymnastic, and karate athletes were compared on the basis of Cattell's 16 PF. The results showed that when the football players and wrestlers were contrasted with the gymnasts and karate participants, significantly different personality profiles emerged. The wrestlers and football players had similar profiles, while the gymnasts and karate athletes differed from each other, as well as from the wrestlers and football players.

Similarly, Singer (1969) observed that collegiate baseball players (a team sport) differed significantly from tennis players (an individual sport) in several personality variables. Specifically, tennis players scored higher than baseball players on the desire to do one's best, desire to lead, and the ability to analyze others, but were less willing to accept blame.

Schurr, Ashley, and Joy (1977), in their signal research, clearly demonstrated that personality profile differences exist between players of team and individual sports, and between players of direct and parallel sports. Team sport athletes were observed to be more anxious, dependent, extroverted, and alert-objective, but less sensitive-imaginative, than individual sport athletes. Direct sport athletes (basketball, football, soccer, etc.), were observed to be more independent and to have less ego strength than parallel sport athletes (volleyball, baseball, etc.).

Clingman and Hilliard (1987) examined the personality characteristics of super-adherers and found them to differ significantly from the population norm in the personality traits of achievement, aggression, autonomy, dominance, endurance, harm avoidance, and play. Super-adherers are runners, swimmers, cyclists, and triathletes who are dedicated to endurance activities. While data were not provided, the expectation is that the super-adherer would also differ from athletes in other sports in certain personality traits.

CONCEPT AND APPLICATION 2.6

Concept Generally speaking, it can be demonstrated that differences exist in the personalities of athletes who engage in different types of sports. Perhaps the clearest distinction occurs between athletes involved in team sports and those involved in individual sports. For example, team sport athletes are more extroverted, dependent, and anxious than individual sport athletes. Certainly, one might expect some differences to emerge between football players and tennis players in terms of personality traits.

Application Personality profiles may be used by trained sport psychologists to help athletes decide which sports to devote their energies to, but they should never be used to coerce the athletes into making such decisions. If a young athlete with a tennis player's personality wants to be a golfer, so be it. Occasionally, an athlete reaches a junction in her athletic career when she must decide between two sports in order to devote adequate time to academic work. Perhaps consideration of the athlete's personality profile would be useful at this point.

The literature shows that athletes in one sport often differ in personality type and profile from athletes in other sports (Franken, Hill & Kierstead, 1994). It seems reasonable, for example, to expect a football player to be more aggressive, anxious, and tolerant of pain than a golfer or a tennis player. However, the point still needs to be made that the state of the art (or science) is still not so refined that one could feel justified in arbitrarily categorizing young athletes based on their personality profiles.

PLAYER POSITION AND PERSONALITY PROFILE

In the previous section, the notion of personality types among athletes of differing sports was discussed. It was concluded that in many circumstances, clear differences exist between the personality profiles of athletes from different sports. The same concept can be applied to whether athletes of a certain sport exhibit different personality profiles based on player position.

In recent years we have experienced an age of superspecialization in team sports. In baseball, outfielders are inserted based on whether they hit left- or right-handed. In football, the offense and defense rarely come in contact with each other. In volleyball, hitters and setters have specialized roles that dictate the sorts of defensive and offensive assignments they fulfill. Similar kinds of specializations can be observed with most other team sports.

While this area of research would seem to be of interest to coaches and athletes, very little has been reported on it. Cox (1987a) asked the following question relative to the sport of volleyball. Do center blockers, strong-side hitters, and setters display different psychological profiles due to their different assignments? The subjects were 157 female volleyball players who participated in an invitational volleyball tournament. The results indicated that the three groups of athletes were very similar in terms of their psychological profiles, with the exception of certain attentional focus variables. Compared to middle blockers and strong-side hitters, setters were observed to have a broad internal focus and be able to think about several things at one time. The setter on a volleyball team is like a point guard on a basketball team or the quarterback on a football team. She must be cognizant at all times of what plays to call and of the strengths and weaknesses of front-line attackers, as well as the strengths and weaknesses of the opposing team's blockers and defensive alignment.

In a similar study reported by Schurr, Ruble, Nisbet, and Wallace (1984), a comparison was made between player position in football and personality traits. Using the Myers-Briggs type inventory (MBTI), the authors concluded that linesmen differ significantly from backfield players in terms of judging and perceiving traits. Linesmen tend to be more organized and practical, while defensive and offensive backs are more flexible and adaptable. Interestingly, no reliable differences were noted between offensive and defensive linesmen, while offensive backs tend to be more extroverted and defensive backs more introverted.

American football players were the subjects in another study, in which position players were differentiated as a function of psychological skills possessed by the athletes (Cox & Yoo, 1995). Backfield players tend to exhibit higher anxiety control, concentration, and confidence than do linesmen, regardless of whether they play offense or defense. In this investigation, defensive linebackers were categorized as backfield players.

CONCEPT & APPLICATION 2.7

Concept In many cases, athletes playing different positions on the same team can be differentiated as a function of personality and/or psychological characteristics. This is especially pronounced in sports in which athletes are required to do very different kinds of things. Point guards in basketball, setters in volleyball, quarterbacks in American football, and goalies in soccer and/or ice hockey can be expected to exhibit personality/psychological characteristics decidedly different from those of some other position players.

Application Personality characteristics of athletes can and should be considered in the selection of players for certain specialized positions. Results of personality tests and the like may be helpful in identifying a self-confident, energetic, and outgoing extrovert to run your multiple offense in volleyball or your motion offense in basketball. You may also ascertain that an individual has these same important characteristics by simply observing athletes in competitive situations. It may not take a pencil-and-paper test to tell you that Mary excels at taking charge of the team when she is on the court. One should not forget, however, that physical characteristics such as speed, power, and quickness are also critically important.

PERSONALITY PROFILES OF ATHLETES DIFFERING IN SKILL LEVEL

Sufficient evidence exists to suggest that elite, high-level performers can be distinguished from lower-level performers when psychological state *and* trait profiles of the athletes are considered. This point has been well documented by Morgan and his associates (Morgan & Costill, 1972; Morgan & Johnson, 1977, 1978; Morgan & Pollock, 1977; Nagle, Morgan, Hellickson, Serfass & Alexander, 1975) using elite distance runners, wrestlers, and oarsmen.

Nevertheless, the ability to distinguish between successful and unsuccessful athletes in any particular sport using personality traits *only* has never been particularly successful (Davis & Mogk, 1994; Morgan, 1980b). For example, Kroll (1967), using collegiate wrestlers, and Kroll and Carlson (1967), using karate participants, could not successfully distinguish between the successful and unsuccessful performers. Rushall (1972), using football players, and Singer (1969), using tennis and baseball players, likewise could not distinguish between the successful and unsuccessful players. In addition, Craighead, Privette, and Byrkit (1986) were unable to distinguish between starters and nonstarters in high school boys' basketball.

Added to this lack of relationship between personality traits and skill level are the results of the Schurr et al. (1977) research. Successful and unsuccessful sport participation in this study was determined based on whether or not the athlete earned a letter or award. The results of this comparison using the second-order factors of the 16 PF failed to show a significant relationship between performance and personality. It does not seem reasonable to expect that a group of first-string athletes could be separated from a group of second-string athletes based solely on personality traits. Both of these groups consist of highly skilled athletes in the first place, or they would not be on the team. Additionally, the task of differentiating between two groups of relatively successful performers on the basis of skill itself is a very tenuous and arbitrary task. Why, then should a coach expect to be able to do the same thing based on personality traits? A study by Williams and Parkin (1980) provides credence to this line of reasoning. Specifically, they compared the personality profiles (Cattell's 16 PF) of eighteen international-level male hockey players with those of thirty-four national-level and thirty-three club players. Their results showed that the international players had significantly different profiles from the club players, but that the national-level players could not be distinguished from players in either of the other two groups.

Research by Garland and Barry (1990) and Davis (1991) does little to alter this view. Garland and Barry (1990) categorized 272 American collegiate football athletes as a function of skill (e.g., regulars, substitutes, or survivors). Results showed that the personality traits of tough-mindedness, extroversion, group dependence, and emotional stability accounted for 29 percent of the variance in skill ($R = .54$). While this is not a high correlation, it is clearly much higher than those reported in earlier investigations. Davis (1991), however, reported that skill level in prospective professional ice hockey players could not be predicted as a function of personality traits.

One exception to the general rule that skill level cannot be differentiated as a function of personality may occur when elite athletes are compared with athletes of lesser ability. Notice that in the Williams and Parkin (1980) study cited above, international-level hockey players exhibited personality profiles that differed from those of club-level players, but not national-level players. Silva (1984) provided a plausible explanation for this phenomenon. As illustrated in figure 2.2, as aspiring elite athletes move up the athletic pyramid, they become more alike in their personality and psychological traits. At the base or entrance level of sport, athletes are very heterogeneous, or have different personalities. However, certain personality traits will enhance an athlete's likelihood of advancing to a higher level, while other traits will undermine it. Through a process of "natural selection," at each higher level of the athletic personality pyramid, the athletes become more alike, or more homogeneous, in their personality traits. When trying to differentiate between athletes of varying skill levels in the middle and lower parts of the pyramid, we meet with failure. Elite athletes, however, will exhibit similar profiles and will differ as a group from less skilled groups.

Figure 2.2

The personality-performance athletic pyramid. From Personality and sport performance: Controversy and challenge by John M. Silva, III. In *Psychological foundations of sport* by Silva, J. M. III and R. S. Weinberg (Eds.), 1984. Human Kinetics Publishers, Inc. Reproduced by permission of publisher.

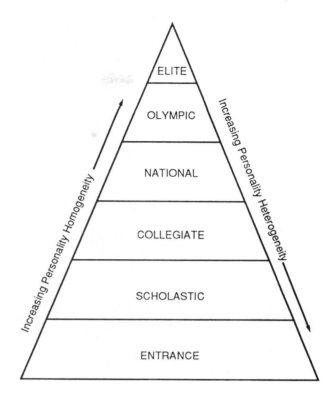

CONCEPT & APPLICATION 2.8

Concept Personality traits, as measured through various inventories, are not strong predictors of skill level in sport. It is unlikely that you can consistently and reliably discriminate among athletes of differing skill on the basis of personality testing.

Application Results of personality testing may be used by coaches and other professionals to gain insights into an athlete's behavior, but never should be used for the purpose of skill discrimination.

THE FEMALE ATHLETE

The conclusions and generalizations that have been drawn from the previous comparison areas have been done primarily through research conducted on male rather than female subjects. This is not to say that the conclusions would have been any different if female subjects had been used. Indeed, we should expect the results to be essentially the same. However, after a thorough review of the available literature, Morgan (1980a) drew this conclusion: "Comparisons of college athletes and nonathletes, or athletes from different sport groups, did not

Setting in volleyball requires outstanding physical and psychological skill. Courtesy Ball State University Sports Information

appear to be consistent in the literature dealing with females" (p. 60). Morgan blames methodological and design problems for the inconsistent results. He points out that this inconsistency seems to disappear when the successful or elite female athlete is compared with the "normative" female.

After reviewing much of the available literature on the female athlete and personality, Williams (1980) cautiously concluded that the "normative" female differs in personality profile from the successful female athlete. Specifically, the female athlete is found to exhibit personality traits much like those of both the normative male and the male athlete (i.e., assertive, achievement-oriented, dominant, self-sufficient, independent, aggressive, intelligent, and reserved). For example, in comparison with available norms, female bodybuilders were observed to be more extroverted, more vigorous, less anxious, less neurotic, less depressed, less angry, and less confused (Freedson, Mihevic, Loucks & Girandola, 1983). On the other hand, the normative female tends toward

passiveness, submissiveness, dependence, emotionality, sociability, low aggression, and low need achievement.

Additionally, Williams (1980) cites numerous studies that show low personality variation within sport groups such as fencing, ice hockey, track and lacrosse. This observation would suggest the existence of specific personality types or profiles for different sports.

Thus, it would appear that like her male counterpart, the female athlete differs from the nonathlete in terms of personality. As with male athletes, female athletes from one sport are likely to differ to some degree from female athletes in another sport in terms of their personality profiles. Differentiation between athletes of varying skill levels on the basis of personality factors is feasible only at the level of the elite performer.

CONCEPT AND APPLICATION 2.9

Concept While it is true that most personality research has involved male rather than female subjects, there is ample evidence that the principles apply equally to athletes of both sexes. *Application* In this respect the coach should not consider the female athlete to be in any way different from the male athlete. However, all athletes must be treated as individuals, and it must be recognized that gifted athletes of either sex can exhibit psychological profiles that differ from the norm.

THE INTERACTIONAL MODEL

To determine trends in sport personality research, Vealey (1989) conducted a systematic review of the literature from 1974 to 1987. Her review revealed that sport personality research has shifted from an interest in examining relationships between traits and sport performance to an interest in the influence on sport behavior of the interaction between the environment (situation) and the personality with sport performance. This approach has come to be referred to as the interactional or **interactional model** approach to studying the effects of personality on athletic performance. The interactional model is not a theory of personality, but a concept introduced first by Bowers (1973) and later by Carron (1975) to suggest a situation-specific approach to understanding the complex relationship between personality, the environment, and performance.

An athlete brings a basic personality into a sporting event. However, the most powerful and salient part of this whole scenario may not be the athlete's personality, but the situation in which the athlete is placed. For example, if you are asked to pinch-hit in the bottom of the ninth inning with the bases loaded, two outs, and the score tied, you can bet that you are going to be anxious. *This will be true, regardless of whether you are high in trait anxiety or not, or are characteristically an anxious person.* The degree to which someone's basic

Figure 2.3

Illustration showing the
contribution of personality
and situation to total
athlete behavior.

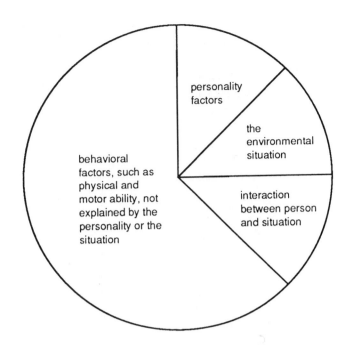

personality
factors

the
environmental
situation

behavioral
factors, such as
physical and
motor ability, not
explained by the
personality or the
situation

interaction
between person
and situation

personality can and will influence performance is dependent upon the interaction between the person (personality) and the situation (environment).

The relationship between the personality of the individual and the situation is illustrated in figure 2.3. In this figure, the total pie represents all the factors that can contribute to athletic behavior or performance. Only a small part of the total pie is due to factors associated with the athlete's personality. Another small portion is due to factors directly related to the situation and independent of or unrelated to the person. Next, a certain part of the pie is represented by the interaction between the personality and the situation. When factors associated with the athlete's personality, the environmental situation, and the interaction between these three are summed, approximately 30 to 50 percent of the athlete's behavior is accounted for. If we were to consider only the athlete's personality, then we could explain only about 10 to 15 percent of the athlete's performance or behavior.

A close examination of figure 2.3 should make it very clear that personality alone accounts for only a small part of the total pie. When the environmental situation is taken into consideration, much more of the total pie is accounted for. However, even then, the largest part of the pie is dominated by unexplained factors. This should not be interpreted to mean that the contribution of personality to performance is trivial. It simply means that athletic performance is made up of many other factors, such as physical abilities, motor abilities, and difficulty of the task (level of competition).

TRAIT-STATE APPROACH

Consistent with the notion of an interactional approach for studying personality and performance is the concept of an interaction between an athlete's personality and the athlete's psychological response to a specific situation. As we learned earlier, a **personality trait** is believed to be a relatively permanent disposition. Conversely, a **psychological state** is believed to be a situation-specific, somewhat transient, mood response to an environmental stimulus. For example, the predisposition to be anxious in a wide variety of situations is a personality trait, whereas the actual manifestation of anxiety is situation-specific and is called state anxiety.

One way sport psychologists measure psychological state is through the use of the **Profile of Mood States (POMS).** The POMS is not the only state measure of psychological mood, but over the last ten years it has been by far the most commonly used measure (Snow & LeUnes, 1994). The original POMS is a 65-item unipolar inventory that measures six affective states: tension, depression, anger, vigor, fatigue, and confusion (McNair, Lorr & Droppleman, 1971). A 72-item bipolar version of the original POMS was developed by Lorr and McNair (1988). The bipolar version also has six sub-scales, but they are presented in a bipolar form (composed-anxious, agreeable-hostile, and the like). For ease of administration, several shortened versions of the original unipolar POMS have been developed. They include a 37-item version by Schacham (1983), a 40-item version by Grove and Prapavessis (1992), and a 27-item version by Terry, Keohane, and Lane (1996). The 27-item version was conceptualized as a POMS for children.

The interactive relationship between personality traits and mood states is evident in the literature (Prapavessis & Grove, 1994a, 1994b). When athletes are categorized as high or low on some personality variable, it is observed that these diverse groups may also differ on selected mood states. For example, rifle shooters categorized as high on the personality characteristic of commitment also score high on the precompetitive measure of tension.

Earlier we observed that an observable but generally weak relationship exists between personality traits and athletic performance. Interestingly, this same sort of relationship holds for athletic performance and mood states measured prior to competition. Mood states measured immediately prior to an athletic event are not strong predictors of performance during the event, but mood states measured immediately following the event are highly predictive of performance during the event. This is about what one would expect relative to psychological mood. Immediately following an event, successful performers tend to be lower in the negative moods of tension, depression, and anger than unsuccessful performers (Hassmen & Blomstrand, 1995; Meyers, Sterling, Treadwell, Bourgeois & LeUnes, 1994; Renger, 1993). Rowley, Landers, Kyllo, and Etnier (1995) put this all in perspective when they demonstrated through **meta-analysis** procedures (statistical summary and comparison of independent samples) that a small but significant difference exists between successful and unsuccessful athletes relative to measured mood states (POMS). The Rowley et al. (1995) study was based on effect sizes gleaned from studies conducted between 1971 and 1992.

Mood states measured immediately prior to competition are not particularly effective in discriminating between successful and unsuccessful performers. However, several researchers have demonstrated that if the athletes are categorized by expected performance as opposed to actual performance, the predictive relationship between mood states and performance is much improved (Hall & Terry, 1995; Terry, 1993, 1995a, 1995b). This is accomplished by asking athletes prior to competition how they expect to perform in the competition. Following the event, the athletes are categorized into two groups, those who performed below their pre-event expectations and those who performed above their pre-event expectations. These two diverse groups can be identified on the basis of precompetitive mood state scores. This observation has far-reaching implications, since it suggests that precompetitive mood is predictive of athletic performance when performance is measured subjectively. In many ways, predicting whether or not an athlete will perform up to her own personal expectations is more useful than predicting whether she will perform up to some absolute standard (i.e., the median of the group).

PSYCHOLOGICAL PROFILE OF THE ELITE ATHLETE

Utilizing the interactional model, sport psychologists have been able to identify a **psychological profile** for the elite athlete. As can be observed in figure 2.4, the psychological profile of a mentally healthy elite athlete is readily distinguished from that of a less successful mentally unhealthy athlete (Morgan, 1979b). Three of the ten psychological factors illustrated in figure 2.4 are personality traits, while the remaining seven are mood states. Together, selected personality traits and mood states are effective predictors of athletic ability. Silva, Shultz, Haslam, and Murray (1981) reported being able to accurately classify 80 percent of a group of elite wrestlers using the interaction model. Similarly, Silva, Shultz, Haslam, Martin, and Murray (1985) demonstrated that 78 percent of a group of qualifiers for the United States Olympic Wrestling Team could be accurately classified using an interactional model. For both studies, the percentage of correct classification increased when physiological variables were also included.

Based upon the interactional model, Morgan and associates (Morgan, 1979a; Morgan & Johnson, 1977, 1978) have concluded that the successful elite athlete generally exhibits the psychological profile of a mentally healthy individual. The **mental health model** proposes that successful world-class athletes generally enjoy greater positive mental health than do unsuccessful performers. This is not to say, however, that *all* elite athletes are mentally healthy, or that *all* unsuccessful athletes are mentally unhealthy.

While the mental health model has generally been applied to the elite Olympic-level athlete, it follows that it should also apply to highly successful

Figure 2.4

Psychological profiles of unsuccessful (negative profile) and successful (positive profile) elite athletes. From Prediction of performance in athletics by W. P. Morgan. In *Coach, athlete, and the sport psychologist* by P. Klavora and J. V. Daniel (Eds.), 1979. School of Physical and Health Education, Publications Division, University of Toronto. Reproduced by permission of publisher.

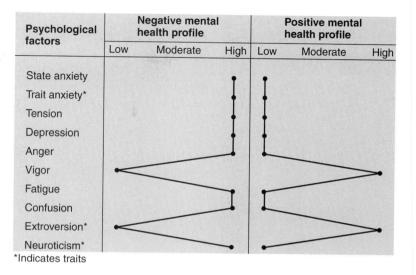

*Indicates traits

CONCEPT & APPLICATION 2.10

Concept The psychological profiles of elite world-class athletes can be accurately distinguished from those of less gifted athletes between 70 and 80 percent of the time. Personality profiles that do not include situational measures of psychological states are not nearly so accurate. Additionally, when one gets below the level of the elite performer, even psychological profiles that include trait and state measures are suspect in terms of predicting performance.

Application On the level of the elite performer, the coach is justified in using psychological profiles for the purpose of *assisting* in the selection of athletes, but never for the purpose of discriminating between them. Decisions of this type should never be made on the basis of personality traits alone. Situation-specific state measures should also be included. For example, one certainly would not decide to cut a player on the basis of scores on the AMI or any other personality inventory.

---

athletes at all levels. Indeed, Newcombe and Boyle (1995) reported that the mental health model applies to successful high school athlete as well.

A second important concept that has emerged from Morgan's research is that of an **iceberg profile** to illustrate the successful world-class athlete. In essence, the iceberg profile is simply one aspect of the mental health model. However, the very concept of an iceberg profile serves to illustrate some important relationships between psychological factors and successful athletic performance. On the Profile of Mood States (POMS), the successful world-class athlete is typically well below the population mean on all mood states except for vigor. In

Physically challenged
athletes exhibit
personality profiles
similar to those of able-
bodied athletes.
Courtesy David Frazier
Photo CD

Figure 2.5

The iceberg profile and
the elite athlete. From
Prediction of performance
in athletics by W. P.
Morgan. In *Coach, athlete,
and the sport psychologist*
by P. Klavora and J. V.
Daniel (Eds.), 1979.
School of Physical and
Health Education,
Publications Division,
University of Toronto.
Reproduced by
permission of publisher.

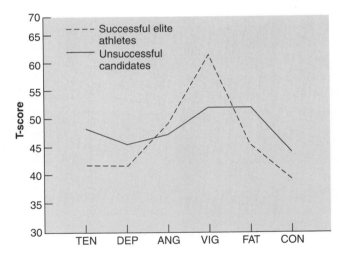

the case of vigor, the successful athlete clearly emerges well above the mean of
the population. As can be observed in figure 2.5, the profile of the successful
world-class athlete looks very much like an iceberg, while in contrast, the less
successful athlete has a rather flat profile.

Numerous investigations have demonstrated the reality of the iceberg profile
relative to the elite athlete. Some of the more recent investigations involved
female long-distance runners (Morgan, O'Connor, Sparling & Pate, 1987), male
long-distance runners (Morgan, O'Connor, Ellickson & Bradley, 1988), elite

triathlon athletes (Bell & Howe, 1988), and rodeo athletes (Meyers, Sterling & LeUnes, 1988).

In summary, the successful world-class athlete is low in the trait measures of anxiety and neuroticism, and high in extroversion. In terms of psychological mood states, the world-class athlete is low in anxiety, tension, depression, anger, fatigue and confusion, but high in vigor. In total, the psychological profile of the successful world-class athlete is consistent with positive mental health.

PSYCHOLOGICAL PROFILE OF THE ELITE DISABLED ATHLETE

The interaction approach in sport psychology has focused primarily on the elite **able-bodied athlete.** In recent years, however, more attention has been devoted to describing the psychological characteristics of the elite **disabled** or **physically challenged athlete.** This surge of interest in the disabled athlete is due partly to the encouragement of notable sport psychologists who have argued that this group of athletes has been ignored (Ogilvie, 1985).

Interestingly, the elite disabled athlete exhibits a psychological profile that is very similar to the profile of the elite able-bodied athlete (Asken, 1991; Shephard, 1990). Elite wheelchair athletes, for example, exhibit personality characteristics that are similar to those of able-bodied athletes, but dissimilar to those of disabled wheelchair nonathletes. Wheelchair athletes are higher in self-esteem and physical orientation than disabled nonathletes (Roeder & Aufsesser, 1986).

In addition, the iceberg profile of the elite able-bodied athlete (see figure 2.5) is readily observed in elite disabled wheelchair athletes (Greenwood, Dzewaltowski & French, 1990; Henschen, Horvat & French, 1984). As with the elite able-bodied athlete, the physically challenged elite athlete is generally a mentally healthy individual who displays low levels of tension, depression, anger, fatigue, and confusion. These findings are very striking, considering the extreme physical and psychological trauma that many of these remarkable athletes have had to overcome (Asken, 1991).

The iceberg profile of the elite athlete has also been observed in elite visually impaired male athletes (Gench, Mastro & French, 1987). Visually impaired female athletes, however, possess psychological characteristics typical of average nonathletic females. In a follow-up investigation, Mastro, Canabal, and French (1988) studied mood states of sighted and unsighted "beep baseball" players. Beep baseball is an interesting game in which the catcher, the pitcher, and two outfield spotters are sighted; the remaining defensive players are unsighted. Mastro et al. observed that the sighted and unsighted players exhibited similar mood state profiles. Although both groups reported mood state scores that were below the population norm (able-bodied), the unsighted players reported being more tense and depressed when compared to the sighted players.

While unrelated to mood state, an interesting investigation by Cox and Davis (1992) compared the psychological skills of elite wheelchair athletes to those of able-bodied collegiate-level athletes. Psychological skills measured included anxiety control, concentration, confidence, mental preparation, motivation, and team emphasis. The wheelchair athletes displayed psychological skills that were superior to those of a group of collegiate track and field athletes, as well as a group of collegiate athletes from four sports combined. It was hypothesized that the differences in psychological skill were due to relative skill level. The wheelchair athletes were competing for berths on the United States Seoul Paralympics team, while the collegiate athletes represented a skill level clearly below elite for the able-bodied athlete.

CONCEPT & APPLICATION 2.11

Concept The psychological profile of the elite physically challenged athlete is similar to that of the elite able-bodied athlete. Both groups of athletes exhibit the iceberg profile relative to mood states.

Application When working with elite disabled athletes, it is important to recognize that they do not suffer from psychological disabilities as well. They are mentally healthy individuals who have overcome tremendous adversity to become elite athletes.

SUMMARY   Personality is defined as the dynamic organization within the individual of those psychophysical systems that determine the person's unique adjustments to the environment. The structure of personality is described on three levels: the psychological core, typical responses, and role-related behavior. Four theories or approaches to studying personality were reviewed. These were (1) the psychodynamic approach, (2) social learning theory, (3) humanistic theory, and (4) the trait theory approach. A number of different approaches to measuring personality were also discussed. These included rating scales, projective procedures, and pencil-and-paper inventories. A number of different personality inventories were described, including the Cattell 16 PF, considered to be the best written personality traits test.

Several factors were considered concerning whether a relationship exists between athletic performance and an athlete's personality. The following conclusions were drawn: (1) athletes differ from nonathletes on many personality traits; (2) athletes who exhibit certain personality traits gravitate towards athletic involvement; (3) athletes in one sport often differ in personality, type, and profile from athletes in other sports; (4) an association exists between personality and player position in some sports; (5) it is difficult to discriminate between players of differing skill level based purely upon personality variables; (6) elite athletes can be discriminated from athletes of low ability based on personality variables; (7) female athletes are very similar to male athletes in the general conclusions that have been drawn; and (8) the psychological profile of the elite physically challenged athlete is similar to that of the elite able-bodied athlete.

The relationship between athletic performance and psychological variables is enhanced significantly when an interaction model is used. The interaction model considers both the personality of the athlete and the environmental situation in predicting behavior. Utilizing the interactional model and measurement of situation-specific mood states, it is possible to identify a psychological profile for the elite athlete.

REVIEW QUESTIONS

1. Define personality and describe its structure. How does an understanding of the various levels of personality help you generally understand the nature of the personality?

2. What are the key features of the four basic theories of personality? In your judgment, what is the best approach? Why?

3. Discuss the various ways in which sport psychologists can measure personality. What are the strengths and weaknesses of each? Compare the three personality inventories that are discussed in the text.

4. Summarize the basic research that has been conducted and synthesized relative to the relationship between personality and sports performance. Discuss the basic research within the context of the credulous vs. skeptical argument.

5. Do athletes and nonathletes differ in terms of personality? Qualify and explain your answer.

6. Does the athletic experience mold an individual's personality, or does the individual gravitate toward sport as a function of personality? Qualify and explain your answer.

7. Is there such a thing as a personality sport type? Do athletes in one category of sport differ in personality from those in another category? Qualify and explain your answer.

8. Is there a relationship between the position that an athlete plays on a sports team and selected personality variables? Qualify and explain your answer.

9. Is it possible to discriminate among athletes of varying skill levels utilizing personality testing? Qualify and explain your answer.

10. Do female athletes have psychological profiles different from those of male athletes? Qualify and explain your answer.

11. Explain and discuss the interactional model relative to personality and the environment.

12. What is the strength of the relationship between mood states measured prior to competition and athletic performance? How can this relationship be strengthened?

13. Discuss the interactional model relative to psychological traits/states, the mental health model, and the iceberg profile of the elite athlete.

14. Does the elite disabled athlete possess a psychological profile that is similar to that of the elite able-bodied athlete? Qualify and explain your answer.

GLOSSARY

able-bodied athlete An athlete who does not possess physically challenging disabilities.

AMI The Athletic Motivation Inventory, developed by Tutko, Ogilvie, and Lyon for measuring eleven personality traits.

Cattell 16 PF Cattell's Personality Factor Questionnaire, measuring the sixteen source traits of personality.

credulous argument The argument that athletic performance can be predicted from personality traits.

disabled athlete *See* physically challenged athlete.

factor analysis A complex statistical procedure wherein test items are grouped into factors or clusters.

first-order traits Synonymous with Cattell's innate source traits.

gravitational hypothesis The notion that athletes possessing stable, extroverted personalities gravitate toward athletics.

iceberg profile Profile of the elite athlete on the six mood states measured by the POMS. Vigor is the only state for which elite athletes score well above the population mean, causing the profile to resemble an iceberg when charted on a graph.

interactional model Approach to sport personality based on the notion that both personality traits and situational states should be used in any prediction equation.

mental health model Developed by Morgan, model proposing that the elite athlete is a mentally healthy individual.

meta-analysis Statistical summary and comparison of independent samples associated with a literature review.

MMPI Minnesota Multiphasic Personality Inventory; a 12-scale test designed for abnormal subjects.

multivariate approach The practice of measuring and analyzing correlated dependent variables simultaneously, as opposed to separately, as in the univariate approach.

personality The dynamic organization of psychological systems that determines an individual's uniqueness.

personality trait A relatively stable personality disposition to respond to the environment in predetermined ways.

physically challenged athlete An athlete possessing physically challenging disabilities.

POMS Profile of Mood States; a 65-item inventory designed to measure a person's affective states.

projective procedures Psychological tests commonly used to determine information about underlying motives. Responses are unstructured and open-ended.

psychological core A person's true self; the centerpiece of the individual's personality.

psychological profile Based upon a number of inventories, a distinct pattern of responses that a particular group of subjects, such as elite athletes, displays.

psychological state Situation-specific, somewhat transient mood response to an environmental stimulus.

role-related behavior The most superficial aspect of a personality; the behavior we engage in to fit our perception of the environment.

Rorschach test A projective test in which the subjects describe an inkblot.

second-order traits The four surface traits of introversion-extroversion, anxiety, tough-mindedness, and independence, reduced from Cattell's sixteen source traits.

skeptical argument The argument that athletic performance cannot be predicted from personality traits.

source traits Sixteen major personality traits discovered by Cattell in his personality studies.

surface traits Synonymous with Cattell's notion of four surface or learned traits.

Thematic Apperception Test Personality test in which the personality is projected through storytelling.

trait Relatively stable personality predisposition.

typical responses Manner in which a person typically responds to environmental situations.

SUGGESTED
READINGS

Asken, M. J. (1991). The challenge of the physically challenged: Delivering sport psychology services to physically disabled athletes. *The Sport Psychologist, 5,* 370–381.

Bowers, K. S. (1973). Situationalism in psychology: An analysis and a critique. *Psychological Review, 80,* 307–336.

Cattell, R. B. (1973, July). Personality pinned down. *Psychology Today, 7,* 40–46.

Fung, L., & Fu, F. H. (1995). Psychological determinants between wheelchair sport finalists and non-finalists. *International Journal of Sport Psychology, 226,* 568–579.

Morgan, W. P. (1980). The trait psychology controversy. *Research Quarterly for Exercise and Sport, 51,* 59–76.

Morgan, W. P., O'Connor, P. J., Ellickson, K. A., & Bradley, P. W. (1988). Personality structure, mood states, and performance in elite male distance runners. *International Journal of Sport Psychology, 19,* 247–263.

Newcombe, P. A., & Boyle, G. J. (1995). High school students' sport personalities: Variations across participation level, gender, type of sport, and success. *International Journal of Sport Psychology, 26,* 277–294.

Ostrow, A. C. (Ed.) (1997). *Directory of psychological tests in the sport and exercise sciences.* Morgantown, WV: Fitness Information Technology, Inc.

Rowley, A. J., Landers, D. M., Kyllo, L. B., & Etnier, J. L. (1995). Does the iceberg profile discriminate between successful and less successful athletes? A meta-analysis. *Journal of Sport & Exercise Psychology, 17,* 185–199.

Schurr, K. T., Ashley, M. A., & Joy, K. L. (1977). A multivariate analysis of male athlete characteristics: Sport type and success. *Multivariate Experimental Clinical Research, 3,* 53–68.

Silva, J. M., III, Shultz, B. B., Haslam, R. W., Martin, T. P., & Murray, D. F. (1985). Discriminating characteristics of contestants at the United States Olympic Wrestling Trials. *International Journal of Sport Psychology, 16,* 79–102.

Terry, P. C. (1995b). The efficacy of mood state profiling with elite performers. A review and synthesis. *The Sport Psychologist, 9,* 309–324.

3 ATTENTION IN SPORT

KEY TERMS

- *associaters*
- *attentional focus*
- *attentional narrowing*
- *attentional style*
- *bit*
- *capacity model*
- *centering*
- *chunking*
- *cue utilization theory*
- *dissociaters*
- *distractibility*
- *gate out*
- *information conveyed*
- *information processing model*
- *LTM*
- *memory storage*
- *processing capacity*
- *refocusing*
- *response delay*
- *retrieval*
- *RT probe*
- *selective attention*
- *sensory register*
- *STM*
- *TAIS*
- *thought stopping*

To succeed, the quarterback in American football must concentrate and effectively narrow his attentional focus. Courtesy Kansas State University Sports Information

Few topics in sport psychology are as important to athletic performance as attention, or concentration. Consider the following illustration. In the 1985 baseball World Series, a situation occurred that highlights the critical nature of concentration in athletic competition (Fimrite, 1985). It was the bottom half of the ninth inning in game 6 between the Kansas City Royals and the St. Louis Cardinals. The Cardinals held a 3 to 2 game lead in the series and had a 1 to 0 lead in the game. It looked like the Cardinals were going to win the game and the series. Through a series of miscues on the part of the Cardinal defense and a questionable call at first base, the Royals had the bases loaded and one out with a pinch hitter at the plate. Dane Iorg, a left-handed pinch hitter, was inserted into the lineup to face right-handed relief pitcher Todd Worrell. Iorg had been used by the Royals all year as a pinch hitter with only moderate success. As Dane stepped into the batter's box, the tension began to mount. What was going through this young athlete's mind? Here he was, in the World Series, bases loaded, ninth inning, and the game on the line. As the TV cameras zeroed in on the batter, you could just see the total concentration and attention that he was giving to the pitcher. Dane let the first pitch, a fastball, go by. Then he stroked the next pitch into right field for a game-winning single. He was a hero! As history has recorded, the Kansas City Royals went on to win the seventh game and the World Series. This story highlights the critical importance of selective attention to sport and to successful performance. If Dane Iorg had become too narrowly focused or had allowed the historical significance of the event to overwhelm him, he could have been just an easy out, and his name would not appear in this book.

According to William James (1890), attention is "the taking possession by the mind, in clear and vivid form, of one out of what seem several simultaneously possible objects or trains of thought. . . . It implies withdrawal from some things in order to deal effectively with others" (pp. 403–404). In sport, nothing can be more important than paying attention to the object at hand. On the surface, the idea of paying attention seems simple enough, but psychologists have long recognized that the attention process can be very complex. In discussing the complex nature of attention, this chapter is divided into several related sections. Each section builds upon the previous section and helps explain why attention is important in sport. Important concepts to be introduced include these: information processing, selective attention, limited information processing space, attentional narrowing, measurement of attention, attentional focus training, and attentional strategies used by endurance athletes.

INFORMATION PROCESSING

In the following pages, the meaning and importance of information processing to athletic performance will be discussed. However, to help you understand the nature of information processing, we will begin with an example of information processing *overload*.

Perhaps the most critical difference between the modern games of basketball, volleyball, and football and these same games twenty years ago is in the complexities of their offenses. Twenty years ago, volleyball was a relatively predictable game in which the spiker attacked from one of two positions on the court. These two positions were the left and right sides of the court near the sidelines. The ball was always set high and there was never any deviation from this pattern. This changed in the late 1960s and early 1970s, when the Japanese revolutionized the game with their version of the multiple offense. In this remarkable offense, attackers spiked the ball from numerous positions at the net. In so doing, the spikers often switched attack positions and called for sets of varying heights and speeds. The result was predictable. Defensive net players were jumping at the wrong time, responding to the wrong attackers, crashing into their own players, and generally falling all over themselves. From an information processing point of view, they were simply overwhelmed. Up to this point, the blockers had only been required to attend to one or two spikers at a time. But now they had to deal with three or four times as much information. Later on, when opposing teams were able to study the multiple offense, defensive players were taught to ignore irrelevant movement and fakes and to concentrate on the important elements of the attack.

In a very general way, there are two basic approaches to explaining behavior. The first and probably better understood is the behavioral, or stimulus-response, approach. In this way of looking at things, the world is explained through a series of stimulus-response (S-R) connections. In fact, psychologists such as B. F. Skinner (1938) would have us believe that all behavior can be reduced to a mathematical model in which specific stimuli go in and predicted responses come out. With animals, this approach has been extremely successful. However, for human beings this approach seems too simplistic. There seems to be more to human behavior than the simple act of strengthening the bond between a stimulus and a response. Certainly, a great deal goes on in the brain between the time that a stimulus is given and the time that a response is initiated. This notion is well accepted by cognitive psychologists, and is illustrated in figure 3.1. It is referred to as the **information processing model** of behavior. The information processing model contains a stimulus and a response, but a large number of mental operations occur between the two. The three general stages of information processing also appear in figure 3.1.

In its most elemental form, information processing involves the storage of information in memory, the retrieval of information from memory, and the execution of a movement in response to information (Keele, 1973). For a person to experience a stimulus and respond to it at a later time, there must be a **memory storage** capability. That is, the person must have a memory, or place to save important information. Once the information has been saved, the person must be able to reactivate or retrieve it. **Retrieval** enables us to use the information to make decisions about forthcoming responses. A football quarterback stores thousands of pieces of information about offenses and

Figure 3.1

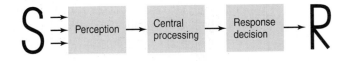

defenses. As he approaches the line of scrimmage after calling one play in the huddle, he may observe the defensive alignment and change the play prior to the snap (this is termed "calling an audible"). What has happened here? The answer is simple. Previously stored information about the opposing team was retrieved from memory and used to initiate a different but appropriate response. This is information processing in action, and it takes place constantly on the athletic field or court. The concept is based on the notion of a storage or memory system, which we will discuss next.

MEMORY SYSTEMS

One basic question we may ask about memory is whether there is one memory system or there are several. While many researchers have tried to show that the different types of memory are clearly distinct from one another, the current thinking is that the distinction among memory systems is for convenience and should not be interpreted to mean that they reside in different parts of the brain. With this in mind, the three basic memory systems will be described.

Sensory Information Store

The first stage in the human memory system is the sensory information store, sometimes called the **sensory register.** This storage system is capable of holding large amounts of sensory information for a very brief amount of time before most of it is lost (Sperling, 1960). Information is thought to remain in the sensory register for up to one-half second before it is either lost or transferred to a more permanent storage system. The images in the sensory store may be iconic (visual) or echoic (auditory), or they may come from any of the other senses, such as touch or taste. The limitations of the sensory register are illustrated in a volleyball-officiating situation. Events often occur so rapidly in a play at the net that it is hard for the referee to make an immediate decision. However, if the decision is not immediate, the referee will discover that the iconic image is no longer available. The same situation occurs in basketball officiating when the ball is knocked out of bounds by one of two opposing players. The information in the sensory register decays very rapidly, and may be effectively scanned for only about one-half second. That portion of the information that we can effectively attend to is passed on to a short-term memory system for further processing.

Short-Term Memory (STM)

The **short-term memory (STM)** is the center, or crossroads, of activity in the information processing system. Information comes into STM for rehearsal from both the sensory store and permanent memory. Information that comes into

Competitive cyclists
focus all of their
attention on a high-
speed race. Courtesy
David Frazier Photo CD

STM from the sensory store is often new or original information. If we do not rehearse and memorize it quickly, we will likely forget it. For example, when a telephone operator gives us a new telephone number for a friend, we repeat it several times while dialing. If we did not repeat it, we would forget the number before we could dial. This is an example of rehearsing new information in STM. Conversely, a quarterback uses STM to rehearse information already permanently stored in memory. For example, just before a game, the quarterback will retrieve from memory the plays that he has learned and will rehearse them to make sure he knows them well. This process tends not only to refresh his memory of the plays, but also to strengthen their representation in memory. Generally, if a person can rehearse information for twenty to thirty seconds in STM, it will be sufficiently learned to be passed on to long-term memory for permanent storage.

The absolute capacity of short-term memory is relatively limited. It would be very difficult, for example, for the average person to retain more than seven separate words or numbers in STM at one time. However, through the process of **chunking,** it is possible for an individual to retain far more than this. Chunking is the process of combining several separate pieces of information into larger ones. The larger chunks are combined in such a way that they can be rehearsed as a unit. Key words or phrases are then used to represent and recall the larger chunks. In the sport of football, for example, a single number or phrase is often used to represent a complex series of actions on the part of several players. In this way it is possible for the quarterback to rehearse in memory several complex plays without getting them confused. He rehearses the plays as chunks, or units. The details of each chunk (play) do not immediately need to be scrutinized. In this manner, the capacity of short-term memory can be greatly increased (Baron, 1989).

Concept The working capacity of short-term memory can be effectively enhanced through the process of "chunking."

Application Grouping separate words, thoughts, ideas, and motor movements into meaningful wholes is a skill that can be learned. The wholes, or "chunks," can be memorized, rehearsed, and practiced much more efficiently in this way. Athletes should be taught how to utilize this skill when trying to learn and manage large amounts of verbal or motor information.

Figure 3.2

The three stages of memory, showing rehearsal in STM and retrieval in LTM.

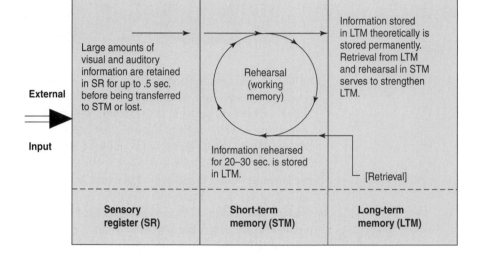

Long-Term Memory (LTM)

Whereas information in short-term memory is present for only a brief period of time, information in **long-term memory (LTM)** is relatively permanent. The purpose of the memory system is to store information in LTM. Once information is stored in LTM, it is theoretically permanent. This may seem difficult to understand, since we all have occasionally had trouble remembering things we thought were permanently learned. In conjunction with STM, information in long-term memory can be continually updated, reorganized, and strengthened. New information can also be added to LTM. The relationship between the three basic memory systems is illustrated in figure 3.2.

MEASURING INFORMATION

Our consideration of information processing as it relates to attention would not be complete without some discussion of the procedures sport psychologists use to measure information.

The difficulty of any athletic event can be calculated in terms of the amount of information conveyed, responded to, and transmitted. The more information an event conveys, the more difficult the perceptual-motor event is. For example, an athlete would react more quickly to a single light source than to one of several lights that might flash, because several lights convey more information (Keele, 1973). Placed in the context of a sport situation, a basketball center who always dribbles once before shooting is less difficult to guard (conveys less information) than a center who may do one of several things before shooting.

The amount of **information conveyed** by an event is equivalent to the number of questions that would have to be asked to accurately predict the event's occurrence. If one question needs to be asked, the event conveys one bit of information. The word **bit** is short for *binary digit;* the number of bits corresponds to the number of questions that must be asked to accurately predict an event's occurrence. Thus, a five-bit perceptual-motor problem would convey more information and would be considerably more difficult than a one-bit problem.

CONCEPT & APPLICATION 3.2

Concept The difficulty of an athlete's response to a specific environmental situation can be represented in terms of information conveyed. Information conveyed increases proportionally with situation difficulty.

Application The difficulty of specific athletic situations should be carefully evaluated by the coach in terms of the amount of information conveyed. Once the difficulty has been determined, the coach can work with the athlete to either reduce incoming information (give a specific assignment) or increase outgoing information (learn a new move).

Consider the situation in which a baseball pitcher has complete control of four basic pitches. If each pitch has an equal probability of being thrown, then the probability of any one pitch being thrown will be 25 percent. On the average, how many bits of information does this problem convey? There are two ways to solve this problem. The first is simply to determine how many questions are needed to select the appropriate pitch, and the second is to calculate information conveyed using a simple mathematical formula.

First, how many questions are needed to solve this problem? Consider the problem as displayed in figure 3.3. My first question would be, "Is she going to throw one of the pitches in the top row?" If the answer is no, my second question would be, "Is she going to throw a fastball?" If the answer is no, I don't need to ask a third question, since I know there is only one possibility left, a curve. Therefore, the average amount of information conveyed by this problem is two bits. If a pitcher only has two pitches that she throws with equal

Figure 3.3

Pitcher A has four pitches at his command. The probability of his throwing any one of the pitches is 25 percent. What is the average amount of information conveyed?

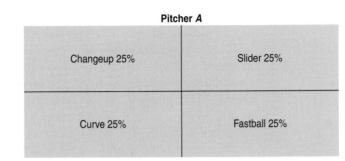

Pitcher *A*

Changeup 25%	Slider 25%
Curve 25%	Fastball 25%

likelihood, the information conveyed will be one bit. Suppose a pitcher only had one pitch? Say it's a fastball. How much information would this convey? Since you don't have to ask which pitch is coming, the event carries no information and should present a good batter with little difficulty.

It is also possible to calculate information conveyed using a mathematical formula. However, since the mathematical approach is rather tedious and complex, it is beyond the scope of this text. Students interested in pursuing the mathematical derivation of information conveyed may do so by consulting the writings of Fitts and Posner (1967) and Keele (1973).

Estimating information conveyed is relatively easy when events are equally likely to occur. For example, estimating the amount of information conveyed in figure 3.3 was relatively easy. However, if the probability that each of several events will occur is unequal, then the calculation of information conveyed is complex, requiring a mathematical approach. Consider the baseball example displayed in figure 3.4. In this case the pitcher (pitcher B) has four pitches at his command, but he does not throw them each with equal regularity; rather, he tends to throw his fastball 70 percent of the time. Would this situation convey more or less information than the equal-probability case displayed in figure 3.3? The answer is that it would convey less information (1.25 bits) than the equal-probability case (2.00 bits), and therefore present less of a challenge to the hitter. It is harder to outguess a pitcher who throws four pitches with equal probability than to outguess a pitcher who throws the same four pitches with unequal probability. Why is this so? Because you would be right 70 percent of the time if you "sat on" or looked for, the pitcher's fastball.

The practical implication of all this is enormous. Since bits of information represent difficulty or complexity, athletes should increase the amount of information that their movements convey to the opposition. At the same time, they must learn to reduce the amount of information that is being presented to them. How can they do this?

First of all, let's consider how information conveyed can be increased. For one thing, you can learn to make each of your responses equally likely. If you are a basketball center, don't always dribble the ball before shooting. Develop several alternatives, and use them with equal probability. If you are a spiker in volleyball, master all the different shots and use them with equal probability.

Figure 3.4

Pitcher B has four pitches at his command. However, the probabilities are not equal. What is the average amount of information conveyed?

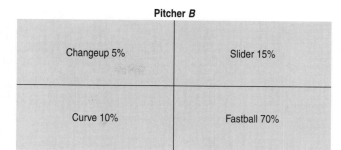

Pitcher *B*

| Changeup 5% | Slider 15% |
| Curve 10% | Fastball 70% |

You also need to disguise your responses so that you don't "telegraph" your intentions. What good does it do to have four pitches at your command if you tip the batter off by some idiosyncrasy? Finally, and perhaps most important, master as many offensive moves as you can. A tennis player capable of making eight different shots conveys more information than a player who can make only four. The difference between eight shots and four shots, if they are all equally likely, is one bit of information, which is a great deal to the opposing player.

CONCEPT & APPLICATION 3.3

Concept An athletic response can be made more difficult to interpret in terms of information conveyed.

Application Let's use the baseball pitching example. Your pitcher's difficulty in terms of information conveyed can be increased in three ways. First, the pitcher must master as many different pitches as possible. Second, the pitcher must throw each pitch with equal probability. Finally, the delivery should provide no cues to the batter as to which pitch is coming. A combination of these three factors maximizes the amount of information conveyed

Finally, let's consider how to reduce the information a person conveys. One way is to study the other person. Take the baseball pitching example. Say you are a major league player. Find out from your scouts how many different pitches the opposing pitcher has at his command. If he has several, find out which one he throws most often and with what regularity. Does he have a pitch he likes to throw in critical situations? If so, what pitch is it? How about mannerisms? Does he telegraph pitches? Even in the major leagues, some pitchers are quite predictable, although the best are not. Another approach to minimizing information is to use positioning and strategy. Basketball players, boxers, and volleyball players do this. If you are guarding a basketball player who loves to fake right and drive left, then overplay that person on the left so that she cannot drive left. This will leave the right side open, and since that player does not prefer this, the information is effectively reduced.

Digging a hard-driven spike is a complex information problem that requires the athlete's undivided attention. Courtesy Kansas State University Sports Information

CONCEPT & APPLICATION 3.4

Concept Through careful analysis and study, the amount of difficulty conveyed by an athletic situation can be reduced.

Application A case in point is the reduction in information conveyed by the "wishbone" offense in football. By teaching defensive players to key

in on specific offensive players, coaches have learned to defeat or at least contain this high-powered offense. In this case, the important thing is for athletes to focus their attention on their assignment and to ignore other distracting movements.

In most dynamic sporting events the critical and decisive difference between success or failure lies in delay in responding, or **response delay.** Response delay is literally a function of the amount of information conveyed. For example, in basketball, the offensive player with the ball can usually defeat a quicker defensive opponent if the offensive player can cause a delay in responding. If the offensive player is both an inside and an outside threat, a feint toward the basket will allow the offensive player the split second necessary to get an outside jump shot off. The feint increases the information conveyed and in turn increases the response time of the defensive player to try to stop the jump shot. A nearly identical situation develops in the game of badminton when the attacking player feints a smash or deep clear, but hits a drop shot instead.

Interestingly, there is some evidence that response delay can be reduced through practice, as well as through reduction in information conveyed. Castiello and Umilta (1992) demonstrated, for example, that volleyball players are faster than nonplayers at reorienting their attention after being distracted. It is believed that this is a skill learned by volleyball players who are required to respond (or not respond) to deceptive actions of opposing setters. In a related way, Loehr and Hahn (1992) have suggested several reasons tennis players lose their concentration, experience a loss of attentional focus, and perhaps suffer a response delay. These reasons include (a) too much off-court stress, (b) too much or too little arousal prior to or during play, (c) low blood sugar, and (d) poor fitness.

SELECTIVE ATTENTION

Humans' ability to **gate out,** or ignore, irrelevant sensory information, and to pay **selective attention** to relevant information, is of incalculable value. Perhaps the best way to dramatize this point is to consider the schizophrenic patient who may suffer an impaired capacity to sustain attention. At one extreme, the patient may attend to some internal thought to such an extent that he becomes catatonic. At the other extreme, the patient may be incapable of selectively attending to anything. Although young schizophrenic patients describe their difficulties in different ways, the following extract is considered typical (McGhie & Chapman, 1961):

> I can't concentrate. It's diversion of attention that troubles me . . . the sounds are coming through to me but I feel my mind cannot cope with everything. It is difficult to concentrate on any one sound . . . it's like trying to do two or three different things at one time. . . . Everything seems to grip my attention although I am not particularly interested in anything. I'm speaking to you just now but I can hear noises going on next door and in the corridor (p. 104).

Each of us has experienced the feeling of overstimulation that can result in an inability to concentrate, but can you imagine experiencing this problem every waking hour? If it were not for our ability to concentrate on one or two relevant items at a time, we simply could not function. While you are reading this page, you are selectively attending to one thing at the expense of several others.

The ability to selectively attend to the appropriate stimuli is critical in most athletic situations. In basketball, the athlete must concentrate on the basket while shooting a free throw rather than being distracted by the noise from the crowd. In volleyball, the athlete must selectively attend to the server instead of being distracted by thoughts of a previous play. In baseball, the base runner must attend to the pitcher, and not to the jabbering of the second baseman. In football, the quarterback must selectively attend to his receivers, while gating out the sights and sounds of the huge defensive linesmen who are lunging at him. Of course, some athletes are better than others at selectively attending to important cues. This is one difference between the good athlete and the outstanding athlete.

As we watch sport on television and in person, many times athletes can be observed engaging in various psychological ploys to gain an advantage. Usually these ploys are manifested in some sort of verbal dialogue, such as commenting on things unrelated to the contest. In baseball, base runners have been picked off first or second base while engaging in innocent chatting with infielders. When and if these ploys (intentional or otherwise) are successful, this is usually related to inappropriate selective attention. The athlete simply is not attending to the appropriate stimuli. This, as well as information overload, will cause a delay in responding.

CONCEPT & APPLICATION 3.5

Concept Selective attention is perhaps the single most important cognitive characteristic of the successful athlete.

Application All sporting events contain critical "keys," or cues, that must be selectively attended to. In volleyball, blocking may be the most decisive offensive weapon in scoring points, because a team is generally blocking when it is serving, and points can only be scored off the serve. To take advantage of this situation, the blockers must selectively attend to the assigned attacker and must not be distracted by actions of the setter, by fakes by other spikers, or even by the ball.

A number of complex models have been proposed to explain the phenomenon of selective attention. These models include the Broadbent Model (1957, 1958), Norman's Pertinence Model (1968), and Treisman's Attenuation Model (1965). Each of these models proposes mechanisms that allow us to selectively attend to one item at the expense of several others, while at the same time allowing for a shift in attention from one important item to an even more important item. A concrete sports-related example of this would be the defensive basketball player intent upon cutting off the passing lane to the person she is guarding, only to be beaten by the back-door play. In this example, the shift from selectively attending to cutting off the passing lane to anticipating the back-door play was too slow.

For highly trained and skilled athletes, the process of selective attention is very efficient. When skilled basketball players step up to the free throw line, they refuse to allow anyone or anything besides the task at hand to capture their attention. Coaches refer to this process as "concentration." However, some athletes never do learn how to cope with distraction. Every little event distracts them, or they concentrate on the wrong things (e.g., dribbling), and missed relevant cues.

CONCEPT & APPLICATION 3.6

Concept Selective attention is a skill that can be learned.

Application There is no doubt that some athletes are better at selective attention than others. However, there is no reason to believe that this skill cannot be learned. The secret is for the coach to identify the important cues and then to provide drills that require the athlete to selectively attend to them. A good example might be shooting free throws in basketball. The key, of course, is to concentrate on the basket. However, few athletes learn to do this during practice, since there are rarely any distractions to cause their attention to wander. A game-like situation with fans and opponents would help the athlete to learn selective attention.

LIMITED INFORMATION PROCESSING CAPACITY

An alternative approach to studying attention is to view it in terms of information **processing capacity,** or *space.* In the previous section we discussed attention in terms of our ability to selectively gate out irrelevant information. In this section, we are concerned with the capacity to attend to more than one thing at a time. In view of our discussion of selective attention, this may seem paradoxical. However, we can readily see that human beings seem to be able to attend to more than one thing at a time. For example, a skilled basketball player can dribble a basketball, hold up one hand and signal a play, and respond to a teammate who is cutting to the basket. A person driving a car can carry on a conversation with a passenger, steer the car, and shift gears all at the same time. How can this be? Didn't we just conclude that the human mind can attend to only one piece of information at a time? Not necessarily; we concluded only that the human mind is capable of selectively attending to one thing at the expense of others.

According to Kahneman (1973), a person's limited ability to do several things at the same time seems to indicate that the total amount of attention that can be deployed at one time is limited. Different tasks impose demands on this limited capacity. When the supply of attention does not meet the demands of the tasks, performance suffers. This way of conceptualizing attentional capacity is consistent with Keele's (1973) observation that limited information processing capacity is the same as limited processing space. If some motor task cannot be performed simultaneously with another verbal or motor task, then one or both tasks are said to take space. Conversely, if several tasks can be performed at the same time, then apparently some or all of them require no space. Thus, in this **capacity model** of attention, when two tasks cannot be performed simultaneously without a decrement in performance, we ask not where the bottleneck is, but rather how much information processing space each task demands.

In the capacity model of attention, more than one piece of input can be attended to at one time and more than one response can be made at one time, if the demands on available space are not too severe. If any particular task requires all available space, then only that task will be attended to, and all others will suffer a performance decrement.

The concepts of selective attention and limited information processing capacity are germane to the sport psychologist, coach, or teacher who is

CONCEPT & APPLICATION 3.7

Concept Each athlete's information processing capacity, or space, is limited.

Application If, as a coach, you require athletes to attend to more information than they have processing space to handle, you are inviting failure. Processing space is not the same as intelligence.

Figure 3.5

Relative amounts of available information processing space for a beginning basketball player and a skilled player.

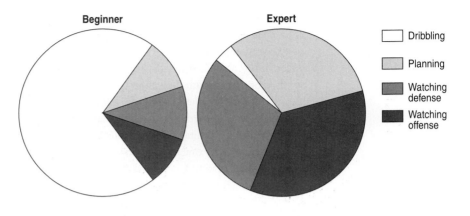

interested in improving athletic performance. Wrisberg and Shea (1978) demonstrated through the use of the **reaction time probe technique (RT probe)** that the attentional demands of a motor act decrease as learning increases. In other words, as a motor act becomes automatic or learned, the demands on the limited information processing capacity of the athlete decrease, and the athlete can attend to other cues. In the RT probe procedure, the subject must perform a simple reaction time task while at the same time performing a primary motor task. If reaction time is slower than normal, then the primary task is judged to require attention, and hence, information processing space. The significant difference between a beginning basketball player and a skilled one appears in the demands placed on information processing space. In a game, dribbling requires nearly all of the available processing space of the beginner. He or she cannot hear the coach, see the basket, see other players, or do anything except attend to the task of dribbling. On the other hand, the skilled player has reduced the attentional demands of dribbling to such a degree that he can see and hear all kinds of relevant cues while dribbling. The important concept of processing space is illustrated in figure 3.5.

CONCEPT & APPLICATION 3.8

Concept The information content of various skills and processes can be reduced so that available information processing space seems to increase.

Application For a beginning soccer player, the mere act of dribbling the ball will require so much information processing space that there is room for nothing else. The athlete will not be

able to pass to the open player, see plays develop, or even avoid an opponent. However, once the skill of dribbling is mastered, the player will be able to do all of this and more. It is not that information processing space has increased, but that the information content of dribbling has been reduced to nearly zero.

A close play at home requires appropriately focused attention from the catcher, baserunner, and umpire. Courtesy Kansas State University Sports Information

In critical game situations, a highly disciplined tennis player can benefit from this even if the opponent is equally skilled. For example, in a close game of professional tennis, one can expect close calls by line judges to significantly distract each player. The professional who is able to gate out the adverse decisions and attend to the game should have a decisive advantage. This is true because playing flawless tennis and fretting over a bad call both demand information processing space. To try to attend to both will result in a decrement in performance.

ATTENTIONAL NARROWING

An athlete's ability to attend to appropriate stimuli during competition has been termed **attentional focus.** The concept of attentional focus includes the ability of an athlete both to narrow and to broaden her attention when necessary. For example, in basketball, the guard who initiates a fast break must be able to broaden her attentional focus in order to see teammates on either side as they break toward the basket. This same player must be able to narrow attentional focus while shooting free throws in order to gate out distractions from the crowd.

The notion of **attentional narrowing** is best understood in terms of **cue utilization.** As explained by Easterbrook (1959), attentional narrowing is a function of available cues. Environmental cues provide the athlete with needed information for a skilled performance. In any sport task, many cues are available to the athlete. Some are relevant and necessary for quality performance; others are irrelevant and can damage performance. Under conditions of low arousal, the athlete picks up both relevant and irrelevant cues. The presence of irrelevant cues should result in a decrement in performance. As arousal increases, the athlete's attention begins to narrow (Landers, Qi & Courtet, 1985). At some optimal point, attentional narrowing gates out all of the irrelevant cues and allows the relevant cues to remain. At this point performance should be at its best. If arousal increases still further, attention continues to narrow and relevant cues will be gated out, causing a deterioration in performance.

High levels of arousal may also lead to the phenomenon of **distractibility.** In addition to gating out potentially relevant cues, high arousal may also decrease an athlete's ability to selectively attend to one stimulus at a time. Rather, the athlete's attention shifts randomly from stimulus to stimulus. Distractibility has the effect of decreasing the athlete's ability to discriminate between relevant and irrelevant cues, and to focus upon relevant cues. The athlete who is suffering from distractibility tends to experience sudden and significant decrements in performance (Schmidt, 1988). The phenomenon of attentional narrowing is illustrated in figure 3.6.

When a quarterback drops back for a pass, he needs a relatively wide band of attentional focus in order to pick up his receivers. However, if the band is too wide, he will pick up such irrelevant cues as the noisy crowd and the cheerleaders. This will cause a decrement in performance (arousal level is too

Figure 3.6

Cue utilization and the arousal-performance relationship. From Daniel M. Landers, The arousal-performance relationship revisited. *Research Quarterly for Exercise and Sport,* 1980, *51,* 77–90. Reproduced by permission of the publisher, the American Alliance for Health, Physical Education, Recreation and Dance, 1900 Association Dr., Reston, VA 22091.

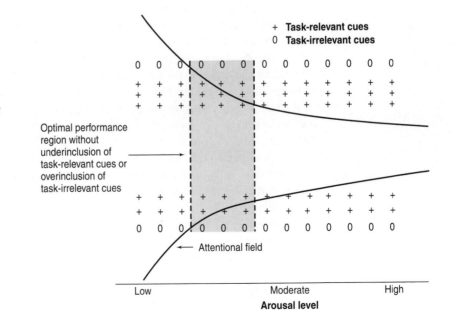

CONCEPT & APPLICATION 3.9

Concept Attentional narrowing has the effect of reducing cue utilization.

Application Broad attentional focus allows the athlete to attend to important cues, but the distraction of irrelevant cues can hurt performance. Narrow attentional focus allows the athlete to attend to only the most critical cues, but can also hurt performance, because many relevant cues can be eliminated. Successful athletes are often required to adjust their attentional focus so that it is appropriately narrow in one situation, yet broad in another. A point guard in basketball must have broad attentional focus to be able to pass to the open player on offense, but must have a narrow band of attention on the foul line.

low). As arousal level increases, attention narrows and irrelevant cues are eliminated. However, in a very intense game situation, arousal may be very high. Consequently, further narrowing of attention may cause the quarterback to gate out such relevant cues as the secondary receivers, the position of defensive backs, and the possible outlet pass.

As we have observed, changes in attentional focus are critically linked to changes in physiological activation. In recent years, scientists interested in studying human performance have used a variety of techniques to study the phenomenon of attention during the execution of skilled motor tasks. Utilizing the reaction time probe technique, Rose and Christina (1990) demonstrated the attentional demands of precision pistol shooting. The closer one gets temporally to the actual pulling of the trigger, the more narrowed the shooter's attention becomes. Populin, Rose, and Heath (1990) observed this same phenomenon in studying the attentional demands of catching a baseball. When attentional focus was disrupted, catching errors increased. Similarly, distractors in the form of turbulent flight conditions have been shown to decrease an airplane pilot's attentional focus, and hence, flying performance (Leirer, Yesavage & Morrow, 1989). Research involving the measurement of electrical activity in the brain in the seconds leading up to the execution of skilled motor performance (archery, rifle/pistol shooting, putting in golf) have further demonstrated the phenomenon of attentional narrowing. Attentional narrowing in the last second before the execution of a precision task is associated with specific shifts in electrical brain activity from one hemisphere to another (Crew & Landers, 1993; Konttinen & Lyytinen, 1992, 1993; Konttinen, Lyytinen & Konttinen, 1995; Landers, Han, Salazar, Petruzzello, Kubitz & Gannon, 1995).

Performing an athletic event requires an athlete to narrowly focus upon the task at hand in order to realize success. Quality attentional focus can gate out the debilitating effects of distractors and irrelevant cues. As the time to execute a skill gets closer, the requirement to narrowly focus attention increases. The ability to focus narrowly on relevant cues is a skill that can be learned, but also a skill that is influenced by arousal. Too much arousal undermines the athlete's ability to narrowly focus attention in a quality manner, while too little arousal may introduce unwanted competition between irrelevant and relevant cues (Singer, Cauraugh, Murphey, Chen & Lidor, 1991).

MEASURING ATTENTIONAL FOCUS

Landers (1988) has identified three primary ways in which attention may be measured by sport psychologists. In method one, a *behavioral* assessment of attention is made using the reaction time probe technique. In this procedure, attention demands of a primary task are estimated based on a subject's performance on a secondary reaction time task.

The second method used by sport psychologists for assessing attention is through *physiological indicators*. As illustrated in figure 3.6, physiological arousal and attentional focus are closely related. As the level of arousal increases, an individual's attentional focus tends to narrow.

The third method identified by Landers for assessing attention is through the use of the *self-report*. While behavioral and physiological indicators of attention tend to measure attentional abilities at a specific point in time, the self-report method has tended to be more of an indicator of attentional focus as a personality trait or disposition. The primary originator of the self-report method for assessing attentional focus is Robert Nideffer (1976a, 1976b, 1980a, 1980b). Nideffer called his self-report inventory the **Test of Attentional and Interpersonal Style (TAIS).** Basing his research on reviews by Silverman (1964) and Wachtel (1967), Nideffer reasoned that an athlete's attentional processes could be represented as a function of two independent dimensions. The first he called *width* and the second he called *direction*. As illustrated in figure 3.7, the width dimension of the athlete's attentional focus ranges from broad to narrow, while the direction dimension varies from internal to external. Figure 3.7 also gives examples of athletic situations that fall at certain points on the two-dimensional scale. Some situations require the athlete both to broaden and to narrow attentional focus at the same time. For example, the quarterback in American football needs to narrow his focus relative to charging linemen, but broaden it to relative the three or four receivers he has on the field.

The vertical axis in figure 3.7 identifies the attentional focus dimension of direction. Some athletes seem to be internally directed, while others seem externally directed. Bowlers must attend to certain external cues, such as the arrows on the lane and the spots on the floor. However, one might expect marathon runners to be inward-directed and to attend to internal cues that will help them, whereas a linebacker in football might be categorized as ideally having a broad-external attentional style. However, it is important to point out that the superior linebacker should also be able to narrow his focus while tackling, and to internalize while contemplating the next defensive play. Thus, the effective athlete should have an attentional focus that is appropriately

Figure 3.7

Attentional styles of various types of athletes. Dotted lines suggest flexible styles that can accommodate varying situations. From R. M. Nideffer, Test of attentional and interpersonal style. *Journal of Personality and Social Psychology*, 1976, *34*, 394–404. Copyright 1976 by the American Psychological Association. Adapted by permission of Robert M. Nideffer, Ph.D., Enhanced Performance Associates, San Diego, CA.

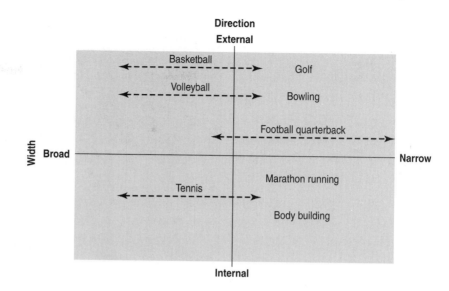

flexible. The manner in which an athlete directs her attention is referred to as **attentional style.**

The TAIS have been a popular inventory for assessing focus from a trait perspective. Researchers, however, have had difficulty confirming the two-dimensional structure of attentional focus that is assumed by the underlying variables measured by the TAIS (Bergandi, Shryock & Grasha, 1981). A more extensive treatment of this issue may be found in Cox (1994). In an effort to make the measurement of attentional focus more situation-specific, several sports-related versions of the TAIS have been developed and reported in the literature (Albrecht & Feltz, 1987; Bergandi, Shryock & Titus, 1990; Etzel, 1979; Van Schoyck & Grasha, 1981).

CONCEPT & APPLICATION 3.10

Concept The use of TAIS to measure an athlete's attentional focus can provide useful information for helping the sport psychologist assess an athlete's perception of himself relative to selected personality factors (Nideffer, 1990). *Application* Like the personality and mood state inventories discussed in the previous chapter on personality, it is a mistake to assume that the TAIS can, by itself, predict athletic performance with a high degree of accuracy. The attentional constructs of width and depth of focus are useful concepts to consider in helping athletes maximize their abilities. This is true, regardless of whether the TAIS provides a perfect assessment of these dimensions. As with personality inventories, the TAIS should not be used for purposes of discriminating among athletes.

Appropriately narrowed attentional focus is required of basketball players. Courtesy University of Missouri-Columbia Sports Information

ATTENTIONAL FOCUS TRAINING

In this section I will discuss ways in which athletes can use principles of attention for enhanced performance. A high level of performance in any human activity requires a certain amount of concentration and attention. If you are a pretty good athlete in any particular sport, then you have mastered some aspects of attention control already. The student who has learned to read a book while others in the room are watching television has developed a high degree of attentional focus. To maximize athletic performance, the athlete must develop a highly refined and developed ability to focus and refocus. As you studied the section of this chapter on cue utilization, you learned that the width of your attentional focus narrows as you become more alert and aroused. Thus, it should be apparent to you that attention is tied very closely to the degree of mental and physical activation. As one attends precisely to an event, there is an associated increase in certain internal arousal mechanisms (Fitts & Posner, 1967).

TYPES OF ATTENTIONAL FOCUS

As outlined by Nideffer (1978, 1986), four different types of attentional focus can be attained. These four types of attention have already been illustrated in figure 3.7 as a function of width and direction of attention. An athlete's attentional focus may be categorized as broad-internal, broad-external, narrow-internal, or narrow-external. Different types of attentional focus are required for different athletic situations and events (Nideffer, 1985).

Whether attention will be directed internally or externally is primarily a function of required cognition, or thought. For example, in order to mentally rehearse a skill or mentally plan a strategy, we must focus internally. Internal attentional focusing can be accomplished with the eyes open or closed. Conversely, external attention is required for the athlete to focus on people, events, or objects in the external environment.

Whether attention should be broad or narrow is primarily a function of arousal and the number of environmental elements that must be scanned. In order for an athlete to be able to take into account several different game situations and objects, he must employ a broad attentional focus. In order to have a broad external focus, the athlete must be able to reduce the level of arousal activation in his body. That is why a young quarterback who is in danger of being sacked may fail to see the open receiver. Due to increased arousal, the athlete narrows attention too much and fails to see the big picture. Experienced quarterbacks are often able to find the open receiver, even when a full-scale rush is on. Conversely, the baseball or softball player must focus on a single element when trying to hit a moving ball with a bat. This situation requires an acute or sudden burst of narrowed attention as the ball is released and approaches the plate. Prior to the vital pitch, the batter must display a fairly broad external focus in order to remain relaxed, see the coach's signs, and avoid becoming tense.

Because of the complex nature of attentional focus, it is easy to see why an athlete might adopt an inappropriate pattern of attention for a specific situation. Figure 3.8 illustrates the fluctuation in attentional style that might be necessary for a quarterback in football. Attentional control training requires the athlete to be aware of the various types of attentional focus and to learn to apply each at the appropriate time. Once the athlete understands which type of focus is necessary for specific athletic situations, attentional control can be self-taught and practiced. Harris and Harris (1984) identified a number of strategies that can be used to improve general concentration. However, for best results, the athlete must practice attentional focus skills in game-like situations.

THOUGHT STOPPING AND CENTERING

Along with learning various attentional styles, it is critically important that the athlete learn to use attention to stop negative thoughts and to focus on positive thoughts. This is a problem that confronts athletes regularly. To overcome feelings of self-doubt, it is necessary to apply the principles of selective attention as discussed in this chapter. In other words, the athlete must develop a high degree of attentional control. As defined by Nideffer (1981), attention control is a technique designed to keep the athlete from slipping into a cycle of anxiety and self-doubt.

It is important that the athlete approach every sport situation with a positive attitude and belief that she will succeed. When negative thoughts come into consciousness, they must be removed or displaced with positive thoughts. The

Figure 3.8

Attentional focus changes for a quarterback in football. From Concentration and attention control training by Robert M. Nideffer. In *Applied sport psychology,* Jean M. Williams, editor, by permission of Mayfield Publishing Company. Copyright © 1986 by Mayfield Publishing Company.

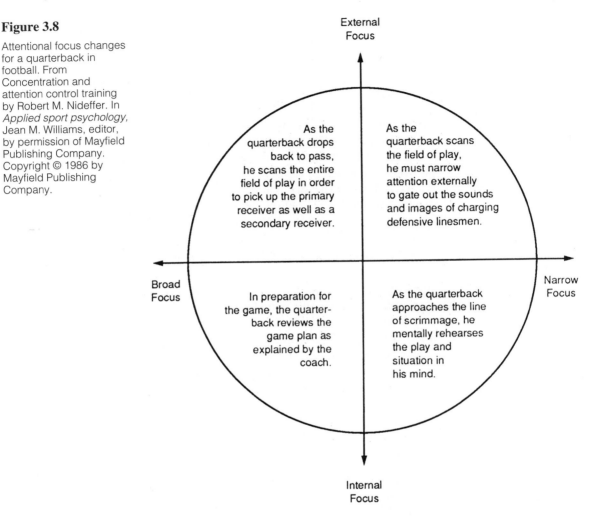

External
Focus

As the quarterback drops back to pass, he scans the entire field of play in order to pick up the primary receiver as well as a secondary receiver.

As the quarterback scans the field of play, he must narrow attention externally to gate out the sounds and images of charging defensive linesmen.

Broad
Focus

Narrow
Focus

In preparation for the game, the quarterback reviews the game plan as explained by the coach.

As the quarterback approaches the line of scrimmage, he mentally rehearses the play and situation in his mind.

Internal
Focus

process of stopping a negative thought and replacing it with a positive one is referred to as **thought stopping** (Ziegler, 1980). It is a basic principle of psychology that an athlete cannot give quality attention to more than one attention-demanding task at a time. In this case, it is the mental task of thinking a positive as opposed to a negative thought. Once the negative thought has been displaced, the athlete centers her attention internally. The process of **centering** involves directing thoughts internally. It is during the internal process of centering that the athlete makes conscious adjustments in attention and arousal. According to Nideffer (1985), the process of centering involves the conscious awareness of the body's center of gravity, while at the same time the internalization of thought processes. Immediately following the centering process, the athlete narrowly focuses her attention on a task-relevant external cue. It is at this point that skilled action is taken. Any delay between directing attention externally and skill execution will only invite distractions in the form of negative thoughts or unwanted environmental stimuli.

Let's take a specific example. Say you are standing at the foul line and are about to shoot a game-winning (or game-losing) foul shot. The thought goes through your mind, "I'm going to miss, I can feel it. The basket is too small, it's a mile away, and I'm scared!" You are losing control. To successfully use the thought-stopping and centering procedure, you must first use the principle of selective attention to drive out the negative thought with a positive thought. You might say to yourself, "No, I'm an excellent shooter; I'm the best person on the team to be shooting in this situation." At this point you center your attention internally as you make minor adjustments in your level of arousal. Many athletes accomplish this by taking a deep breath and exhaling slowly. Then you turn your attention to the basketball hoop and focus upon a task-oriented suggestion, such as "follow through, and put a little backspin on the ball." By using the thought-stopping and centering procedure correctly and practicing it in many different situations, you will have an instant weapon to use against the occasional loss of attentional control.

The following basic steps are used in the thought-stopping and centering procedure:

1. Displace any negative thought that comes into your mind with a positive thought.

2. Center your attention internally while making minor adjustments in arousal.

3. Narrowly focus your attention externally on a task-relevant cue associated with proper form.

4. Execute the sport skill as soon as you have achieved a feeling of attentional control.

Learning the thought-stopping and centering procedure takes practice. The critical point to understand is that negative thoughts can be displaced, and that through the process of centering, the thoughts that capture attention can be controlled. The conscious process of thought stopping and centering will divert the athlete's attention from threatening thoughts and anxiety-producing stimuli. Selective attention will effectively gate out the unwanted thoughts if the correct thoughts are pertinent and meaningful to the athlete.

CONCEPT & APPLICATION 3.11

Concept Thought-stopping and centering skills help an athlete avoid errors caused by negative thoughts and diverted attention.
Application Thought-stopping and centering skills practiced and developed prior to competition can be used when they are needed. Specific positive thoughts, relevant cues, and task-oriented suggestions should be practiced and readied for competition.

Closely related to the notion of centering and focusing is the important psychological skill of **refocusing.** In a sporting event, it is easy for an athlete to allow his attention and concentration to be distracted after initially being very centered and focused. Often this occurs as a result of an error or an official's call. The athlete, rather than refocusing attention on appropriate cues, centers attention inwardly on the distraction. The failure to develop refocusing skills has been the downfall of many athletes. For example, Landers, Boutcher, and Wang (1986) observed a significant relationship between archery performance and focusing on past mistakes. The athlete who focuses on errors and distractions instead of refocusing on the task will generally suffer a performance decrement.

From a human performance point of view, there is ample evidence to support the position that attention is an important ingredient for improving athletic performance (Magill, 1985; Schmidt, 1988). In the specific case of thought stopping and centering, Nideffer (1981) presented several case histories involving athletes who reportedly benefited from the procedure. In a study Weinberg, Gould, and Jackson (1980) conducted to determine the effects various cognitive strategies had on tennis serves of advanced and beginning tennis players, attentional focus (centering) was one of the strategies associated with improved performance.

ASSOCIATIVE VERSUS DISSOCIATIVE ATTENTIONAL STRATEGIES

As defined by Morgan (1978) and Morgan and Pollock (1977), **associaters** are marathon runners who internalize the direction dimension of attentional focus and attend to the body's feedback signals. **Dissociaters** are marathon runners who externalize the direction dimension of attentional focus and gate or block out feedback from the body. Morgan believed that elite marathon runners tend to be associaters, while less proficient runners tend toward being dissociaters. Morgan's basic theory has generated a great deal of interest on the part of sport psychologists and serious runners in recent years.

In a study by Morgan, O'Connor, Ellickson, and Bradley (1988), 72 percent of a group of elite distance runners reported using an associative strategy during competition, while 28 percent reported using both associative and dissociative strategies. None of the athletes in this investigation reported using an exclusively dissociative strategy during competition. Different results were obtained for training runs, however. Only 21 percent of the athletes reported using an exclusively associative strategy during training, while 43 percent indicated they used an exclusively dissociative strategy. The remaining 36 percent reported using both dissociative and associative strategies. Similar results were reported by Masters and Lambert (1989) and by Kirkby (1996). Elite runners utilize a predominantly associative strategy during competition and a predominantly dissociative strategy during training runs. The rest of the time, they shift back and forth between the two attentional strategies.

To assist researchers in ascertaining the attentional style utilized by long-distance runners, Silva and Appelbaum developed the Running Style Questionnaire (RSQ).

Figure 3.9

Mental strategies and perception of effort of marathon runners. From H. H. Schomer, Mental strategies and perception of effort of marathon runners. *International Journal of Sport Psychology,* 1986, *17,* 41–59. Adapted with permission of the publisher.

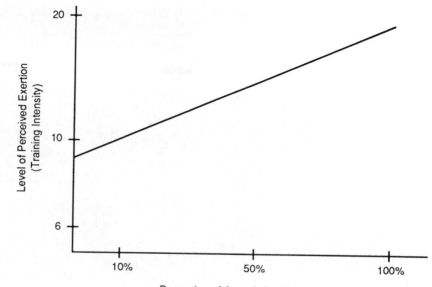

An adapted version of the RSQ was utilized and reported by Smith, Gill, and Crews (1995). The RSQ is composed of several open-ended and multiple-choice questions designed to ascertain cognitive/attentional style in distance runners.

A second approach to ascertaining attentional style, used by long-distance runners, has been extensively tested and reported by Schomer (1986, 1987a, 1987b, 1990). In this approach, a lightweight tape recorder is taped to the athlete's back and a tiny microphone clipped to the front of the runner's vest or shirt. At predetermined intervals, athletes record their thoughts, cognitive focus, and perceived exertion. The contents of the recordings are later analyzed by trained researchers to categorize thoughts and feelings consistent with attentional style. Perhaps the most interesting and well-documented outcome of Schomer's research is the relationship between perceived exertion and proportion of associative mental strategy utilized by athletes. Schomer determined that a linear relationship exists between associative thought processes and increased intensity of the workout. As the level of perceived exertion increases, marathon runners tend to internalize their attentional focus. This principle is illustrated in figure 3.9. Schomer also concluded that from the standpoint of safety, the long-distance runner is better off using an internal attentional focus. This strategy allows the athlete to be aware of danger signals that might warn her of potential injuries.

Building on his earlier research, Schomer (1990) also demonstrated that it is possible to train long-distance runners to utilize an associative strategy to their advantage. This was accomplished through the use of two-way radios, so that trainers could interact with athletes relative to their cognitive strategies. Schomer's finding that a positive linear relationship exists between training intensity (perceived exertion) and proportion of associative thought processes was

Figure skating requires
complete mental and
physical control.
Courtesy Corel Photo
CD/Winter Sports

independently confirmed by Tammen (1996). This observation that perceived
exertion and proportion of associative strategy are clearly related is indirect
evidence of the superiority of the associative attentional style over the dissociative
style in terms of running performance. It is likely necessary for the marathon
runner to occasionally lapse into a dissociative (external) mind-set in order to
"gate out" the stress connected with long-distance running. A quick return,
however, to the associative (internal) style is necessary to maintain the intensity
necessary to perform well. This line of thinking is supported by Harte and Eifert
(1995), who reported that running while listening to one's own heartbeat results in
emotional stress, due to its tedious nature. They reasoned that listening to one's
own heartbeat while running was associative, or internal, in nature.

While most of the literature related to attentional style has involved elite
distance runners and marathoners, an investigation by Wrisberg and Pein (1990)
reveals some interesting comparisons with recreational runners. The type of
attentional style adopted by recreational runners is related to experience. The
less experienced recreational runner tends to adopt an associative strategy, while
the more experienced recreational runner prefers a dissociative style. It is
hypothesized that the inexperienced runner uses an associative style because he
has not yet learned how to dissociate. The dissociative style is used by
experienced recreational runners because it is more pleasant to focus upon
external thoughts, sights, and sounds than to focus upon bodily stimuli.

CONCEPT & APPLICATION 3.12

Concept Proportion of associative (internal) attentional focus is directly related to perceived exertion in skilled marathoners and long-distance runners. Consequently, the proportion of internal focus increases during competition, but decreases during training runs.

Application In order to be an effective long-distance runner, it is important that the athlete be able to internally focus a large proportion of the time. Through careful coaching, the athlete can learn to use an associative attentional strategy. It would be a mistake, however, to insist that an athlete associate all of the time. Dissociating is more relaxing, and provides a needed psychological break for the marathoner.

SUMMARY

The information processing model of attention recognizes the presence of many variables and processes between a stimulus and a response. Memory plays an important role in information processing. The three types, or stages, of memory are the sensory register, short-term memory, and long-term memory. Information is measured in bits. The amount of information conveyed by a particular problem can be quantified in terms of questions asked, or in terms of a mathematical formula.

The ability to gate out irrelevant information and attend to important information is called selective attention. A number of structural models of selective attention have been proposed. Three models mentioned in this chapter were the Broadbent model, Norman's pertinence model, and the Triesman model.

The notion of limited information processing capacity helps explain the difference between skilled and unskilled athletes. If a particular task requires all of a person's information processing space, then none will be left over for attending to other tasks that also require attention.

Easterbrook's cue utilization theory deals with the phenomenon of attentional narrowing. As an athlete's arousal increases, the athlete's attentional focus narrows. The narrowing process tends to gate out irrelevant cues, and sometimes relevant ones as well.

An athlete's attentional style can be measured through the use of Nideffer's Test of Attentional and Interpersonal Style (TAIS). Situation-specific versions of the TAIS have been developed.

Thought stopping and centering is an attentional focusing strategy designed to counter negative thoughts and feelings of self-doubt. Negative thoughts are displaced with positive thoughts and task-oriented suggestions.

Marathon runners tend to both internalize (associate) and externalize (dissociate) in terms of attentional focus. Associative strategy is not necessarily the most effective strategy in terms of performance enhancement, but it is the safest and is highly correlated with intensity of the running pace. As intensity increases, so does the degree of attentional associating.

REVIEW
QUESTIONS

1. What is information processing?

2. How much information is conveyed by a pitcher who has mastered four pitches that he throws with equal probability?

3. How could the amount of information conveyed by a pitcher who throws four pitches with unequal probability be increased?

4. Define selective attention.

5. How can selective attention help the quarterback in American football? The server in tennis and volleyball? The shooter in basketball and the receiver in volleyball?

6. How does the concept of selective attention differ from that of processing capacity?

7. In terms of information processing space, explain the difference between the beginning and the advanced basketball players, both of whom are dribbling the ball.

8. What is the effect of arousal upon attentional focus?

9. Provide a detailed explanation of Easterbrook's cue utilization theory. What do you feel are the strengths and weaknesses of the theory? Explain.

10. Discuss various ways that attention and attentional focus can be assessed. Provide a brief discussion of Nideffer's Test of Attentional and Interpersonal Style (TAIS) relative to the measurement of attentional focus.

11. Discuss ways in which an athlete's attentional abilities can be enhanced.

12. What are thought stopping and centering? How are they related to attention, and how can their application improve athletic performance?

13. Discuss the different attentional styles displayed by distance runners and relate them to actual competitive situations.

14. What are the implications of the research finding that the proportion of associative (internalizing) strategy utilized during competition is directly related to perceived exertion?

GLOSSARY

associaters Long-distance runners who internalize or adopt an internal attentional focus.

attentional focus In sports, an athlete's ability to focus on relevant information during competition.

attentional narrowing The narrowing of an athlete's attentional focus due to an increase in arousal.

attentional style An athlete's particular style of attending to stimuli.

bit A term that stands for binary digit, a unit of information measurement. The number of bits corresponds to the number of questions needed to accurately predict the occurrence of an event.

capacity model A model of attention based on limited information processing space.

centering The process whereby an athlete's attention is brought to focus on an important task-oriented suggestion.

chunking Cognitive process of combining several separate pieces of information into larger ones.

cue utilization theory Theory proposed by Easterbrook that predicts attentional narrowing and gating out of environmental cues.

dissociaters Long-distance runners who externalize or adopt an external attentional focus.

distractibility Characterizes an athletes inability to selectively attend to relevant stimuli due to very high levels of arousal.

gate out To exclude or ignore irrelevant sensory information.

information conveyed The amount of information, in bits, contained in a particular problem. For example, a reaction-time problem containing four lights conveys two bits of information if all four lights are equally likely to flash.

information processing model A model based on the theory that humans process information rather than merely respond to stimuli. Many cognitive processes are involved. For example, information must be stored, retrieved and rehearsed.

LTM Long-term or permanent memory.

memory storage The notion that all information reaching memory for future recall must be stored.

processing capacity The notion that people have a limited amount of space available for the processing of information.

refocusing The process of returning attention to a relevant stimuli after being distracted.

response delay Delay in reacting or responding to an environmental stimulus.

retrieval The mental process of retrieving information to make decisions about forthcoming responses.

RT probe Used in attention research to determine if a certain primary task requires information processing space.

selective attention The notion that humans are capable of attending to one stimulus at the exclusion of others.

sensory register A short-term sensory store that effectively retains information for about one-half second before it is lost or transferred to a more permanent storage system.

STM Short-term memory, considered to be the center of activity in the information processing system. New information must remain in STM for a minimum of 20 to 30 seconds or it will be lost.

TAIS Nideffer's Test of Attentional and Interpersonal Style.

thought stopping In sport, the process of replacing a negative thought with a success-oriented, positive thought.

SUGGESTED READINGS

Fitts, P. M., & Posner, M. I. (1967). *Human performance.* Belmont, CA: Brooks/Cole.

Harte, J. L., & Eifert, G. H. (1995). The effects of running, environment, and attentional focus on athletes' catecholamine and cortisol levels and mood. *Psychophysiology, 32,* 49–54.

Keele, S. W. (1973). *Attention and human performance.* Pacific Palisades, CA: Goodyear.

Landers, D. M. (1982). Arousal, attention, and skilled performance: Further considerations. *Quest, 33,* 271–283.

Morgan, W. P., O'Connor, P. J., Ellickson, K. A., & Bradley, P. W. (1988). Personality structure, mood states, and performance in elite male distance runners. *International Journal of Sport Psychology, 19,* 247–263.

Nideffer, R. M. (1976). Test of attentional and interpersonal style. *Journal of Personality and Social Psychology, 34,* 394–404.

Nideffer, R. M. (1990). Use of the Test of Attentional and Interpersonal Style (TAIS) in sport. *The Sport Psychologist, 4,* 285–300.

Schomer, H. H. (1986). Mental strategies and the perception of effort of marathon runners. *International Journal of Sport Psychology, 18,* 133–151.

Sperling, G. (1960). The information available in brief visual presentations. *Psychological Monographs, 74*(11), 1–29.

Tammen, V. V. (1996). Elite middle and long distance runners associative/dissociative coping. *Journal of Applied Sport Psychology, 8,* 1–8.

4 ANXIETY AND AROUSAL IN SPORT

KEY TERMS

- anxiety
- arousal
- arousal reaction
- autonomic nervous system
- autotelic experience
- catastrophe theory
- central nervous system
- cerebral cortex
- cognitive state anxiety
- direction of anxiety
- distractibility
- distress
- drive
- drive theory
- electroencephalogram
- eustress
- Flow
- hyperstress
- hypostress
- hypothalamus
- intensity of anxiety
- inverted-U theory
- metamotivational modes

- noise
- objective demand
- optimal arousal
- parasympathetic nervous system
- paratelic orientation
- precompetitive anxiety
- prestart state anxiety
- reticular formation
- reversal theory
- signal detection theory
- signal plus noise
- somatic state anxiety
- Sport Grid
- state anxiety
- stress
- stress process
- sympathetic nervous system
- telic orientation
- trait anxiety
- Yerkes-Dodson law
- zone of optimal functioning

High levels of physiological arousal seem to facilitate performance in some athletes. Courtesy University of Missouri-Columbia Sports Information

The story is told of an African hunter who, after losing his weapon, was pursued by a lion. He was running along as fast as he could go with the lion in hot pursuit, when he spotted a tree limb about 12 feet off the ground. Without breaking stride, he leaped with all his might, hoping to jump higher than he had ever imagined possible. As luck would have it, he missed the limb going up, but he caught it coming down! This tale illustrates an interesting fact about the phenomenon of arousal. When extremely aroused, we are often capable of astonishing feats. However, note that the man in the story *missed* the tree limb going up. Luckily for him he caught it on the way down—but what does this say about his accuracy?

In this chapter, the important concepts of arousal and anxiety will be discussed. These two terms are often used interchangeably, but in some instances can mean very different things. According to Posner and Boies (1971), arousal is one of three important components of attention; the other two are selective attention and limited information processing capacity. As an athlete becomes more keenly aroused, he becomes more attentive and narrowly focused. Arousal is synonymous with the condition of alertness; the aroused individual is in a physiological state of readiness. This state of readiness can be represented on a continuum that goes from deep sleep to extreme excitement. The quality of an athlete's performance often depends upon how aroused the athlete is (Duffy, 1962; Malmo, 1959).

The state of being anxious as a result of an environmental stimulus is associated with an elevation in arousal. For this reason, many people have assumed that the two states are the same. When confronted with physical violence, for example, an individual will typically feel a rush of fear and anxiety that is associated with an increase in such things as heart rate and breathing. An increase in arousal, however, can also be associated with the emotions of joy, happiness, and exhilaration, which often accompany the thrill of sports victory. Arousal is a neutral physiological phenomenon that can be associated with both negative (anxiety) and positive (exhilaration) affect, yet is not synonymous with either.

NEUROPHYSIOLOGY OF AROUSAL

To understand arousal is to understand what basic changes take place in the body when the athlete is activated. **Arousal** is the degree of activation of the organs and mechanisms that are under the control of the body's autonomic nervous system. In a subsequent chapter of this book, various strategies for adjusting the level of arousal in the athlete will be discussed. For this reason, it is critical that the sport psychologist understand the neurophysiology of arousal.

AUTONOMIC NERVOUS SYSTEM

The nervous system in humans contains two major divisions: the peripheral nervous system, or the nerves in the skeletal muscles of the body, and the autonomic system, or the nerves in the smooth muscles and glands of the body.

That part of the nervous system directly related to activation and arousal is the **autonomic nervous system** (ANS). It is autonomic in the sense that we do not normally have voluntary control over the organs and glands innervated by it. This is not entirely true, of course, but normally we do not control such bodily functions as heart rate, blood pressure, skin conductivity, and respiration.

The autonomic nervous system is itself divided into two divisions, the **sympathetic** and the **parasympathetic nervous systems.** The sympathetic division is primarily responsible for changes in bodily functions associated with arousal. For example, it is the sympathetic division that brings about sweating of the hands, increased heart rate, pupil dilation, increased respiration, release of glucose from the liver, and decreased kidney output. The sympathetic division releases catecholamines (adrenalin and noradrenalin) at the postganglionic innervation site of the gland or smooth muscle (with the exception of palmar sweat glands).

The sympathetic division tends to result in arousal of the organism, while the parasympathetic division selectively reduces the effects of the sympathetic division. Stimulation of the parasympathetic division results peripherally in pupil constriction, decrease in heart rate, decrease in respiration, and in general, a return to a homeostatic balance of bodily functions.

The sympathetic nervous system responds very quickly to environmental or cognitive stimuli, while the parasympathetic nervous system is comparatively slow. When confronted with a sudden physical threat, the body's physiological response to it is nearly instantaneous. Conversely, it might take hours for body and mind to return to a relaxed resting state following a highly emotional and demanding athletic event.

BRAIN MECHANISMS

Fundamental to the concept of arousal is the notion that levels of activation come under control of progressively higher levels of the nervous system. Structures of the **central nervous system** (CNS) that are closely related to the phenomenon of arousal include the cortex of the brain, the hypothalamus, and the reticular formation, or ascending reticular activating system (see figure 4.1).

The **cerebral cortex** is the area of the brain responsible for higher brain functions and conscious thought processes. The functional part of the cerebral cortex is comprised of a thin layer of neurons. The total cerebral cortex contains approximately ten billion neurons. The electrical activity of the cortex is measured with the electroencephalograph (EEG). The EEG can monitor frequency and amplitude of electrical potential changes in the brain. High states of arousal are associated with EEG waves that are desynchronized, fast, and of low amplitude. Low states of arousal are associated with a synchronous pattern of EEG waves (Guyton, 1976).

The **hypothalamus,** a part of the mid-brain, has been shown to be an important part of the arousal system. Lesions of the posterior section of the hypothalamus cause sleep and drowsiness (Ranson, 1939), while electrical stimulation of these same areas has been reported to cause alertness and

Figure 4.1

Three important brain
structures associated with
arousal. From Phillip W.
Groves and Kurt
Schlesinger, *Introduction
to biological psychology,*
2nd ed. © 1979, Wm. C.
Brown Publishers,
Dubuque, Iowa. All rights
reserved. Reprinted by
permission.

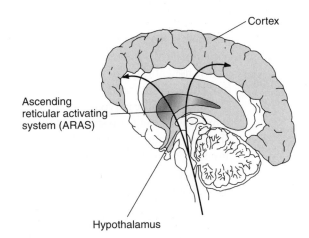

excitement (Hess, 1957). Stimulation of the posterior hypothalamus also causes
the secretion and release of catecholamines (neurotransmitting substances) by
the adrenal medulla (Sage, 1984a).

The **reticular formation** is a complex set of neurons and nuclei that extends
throughout the brain stem from the medulla to the posterior hypothalamus. This
network of neurons sends diffuse fibers throughout the nervous system and
cortex. It appears that the reticular formation organizes sensorimotor behavior
through its interconnections with the cortex, hypothalamus, and nervous
system. Along with the cortex and hypothalamus, the activity of the *ascending
reticular activating system (ARAS)* is closely associated with the onset of
arousal. The ascending axons of the ARAS facilitate the higher brain center
neurons. Stimulation of the ARAS of sleeping animals results in EEG waves
resembling those they would have if awake (Milner, 1970). Lesions of the
ARAS in cats result in somnolence (Lindsley, Schreiner, Knowles & Magoun,
1950). When an individual perceives a situation to be threatening or arousing,
the reticular formation is activated, and this in turn governs the arousal
sequence (Lykken, 1968).

An overview of the process by which the **arousal reaction** is initiated is
illustrated in figure 4.2. Any type of sensory stimulus from the environment or
from the cerebral cortex can initiate the arousal reaction at the level of the
reticular formation (Guyton, 1976). The reticular activating system responds
very quickly to bring about a general activation of other brain structures. Almost
simultaneously, the sympathetic nervous system is activated by centers in the
cortex, spinal cord, brain stem, and hypothalamus. Stimulation of sympathetic
nerves to the adrenal medulla and other body organs causes large quantities of
adrenalin and noradrenalin to be released into the circulating bloodstream. Until
these drugs are reabsorbed into body tissues, the organism will remain in an
aroused state.

Figure 4.2

Simplified illustration of the anatomical and physiological basis of the arousal reaction.

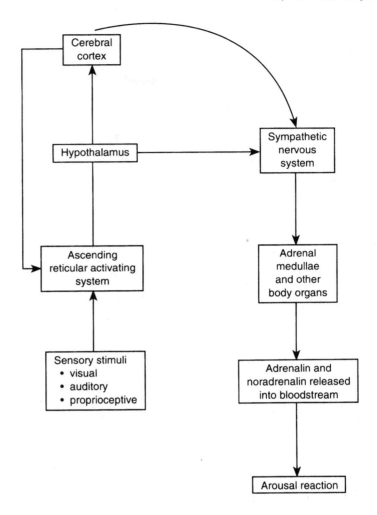

CONCEPT & APPLICATION 4.1

Concept Stimuli from the environment that are interpreted by the brain as threatening to the individual will automatically initiate the arousal reaction.

Application It is extremely important for the athlete and the coach to understand the rudiments of the physiology of arousal. Intervention and stress-management strategies are based in a large degree on learning to reverse the arousal reaction. One must first understand what the arousal reaction is and what causes it.

PREFERRED STATE OF AROUSAL

Arousal varies along a continuum from deep sleep to extreme excitement. Yet researchers have consistently observed that organisms seek to attain a level of arousal that is ideal for the task at hand, that is, a level of **optimal arousal.** Schultz (1965) called this internal drive for seeking a state of optimal arousal *sensoristasis*. Duffy (1957) observed that the optimal degree of activation appears to be moderate—not too much arousal and not too little. The hypothesized curve representing the relationship between arousal and the quality of performance is quadratic, taking the form of an inverted U. Further discussion on this curve appears later in this chapter.

Electrophysiological Indicators of Arousal

Many electrophysiological methods exist for measuring arousal level. Some of the more common methods will be outlined here. We should remember that no single measure of arousal can be considered completely accurate; correlations among the various measures of arousal are very low (Lacey & Lacey, 1958; Tenenbaum, 1984). This means, for example, that someone exhibiting a fast heart rate might not exhibit a decrease in palmar skin resistance.

Electrocortical Activity As discussed earlier, the electrical activity of the brain can be measured by an electroencephalograph (EEG), which measures the amount of electrical activity put out between two scalp electrodes. An **electroencephalogram** (EEG) is the tracing of the brain waves made by an electroencephalograph. Three types of brain waves are associated with the arousal states of sleep (theta waves), awakeness (alpha waves), and excitement (beta waves). Depression of EEG alpha-wave activity is considered to be a strong indicator of heightened arousal (Landers, 1980).

Biochemical Indicators The arousal, or activation, response in the brain triggers the release of catecholamines into the bloodstream by the adrenal medulla. Thus, one way to determine arousal levels is to directly measure the amount of adrenalin and noradrenalin in the bloodstream (Lykken, 1968). The accurate assessment of catecholamines requires immediate blood samples, since they readily diffuse into body tissues.

Heart Rate The heart rate of an aroused person is easily obtained with an electrocardiograph (ECG), a device for measuring the electrical activity of the heart. The heart rate can also be indirectly measured with a pulse monitor or by finger palpation. The heart rate is not considered to be a good single indicator of arousal. Its correlation with other more viable indicators is quite low (Lykken, 1968).

Muscle Tension The electrical potential of muscles can be measured with an electromyograph (EMG), a device that measures electrical activity in a muscle. Woodworth and Schlosberg (1954) have shown that muscle tension levels are roughly equivalent to levels of arousal. Weinberg (1978) and Weinberg and Hunt (1976) have successfully used EMG recordings to indicate arousal levels in motor performance research.

Respiration Rate Rate of respiration is not entirely under the control of the autonomic nervous system, but it is still a fairly reliable indicator of heightened arousal. With a spirometer, a person's respiratory rate, tidal volume, inspiratory reserve volume, expiratory reserve volume, inspiratory capacity, and vital capacity can be measured.

Blood Pressure Arterial blood pressure can be measured with a sphygmomanometer. Blood pressure is an indication of the relative dilation or constriction of the blood vessels associated with the autonomic nervous system. Since blood pressure is generally monitored through repeated application of the pressure cuff and stethoscope, only intermittent recordings can be obtained. For this reason, blood pressure is not considered to be a very good measure of arousal (Martens, 1974).

Palmar Sweating In a threatening situation, the increased levels of activation are associated with an increase of sweat from sweat glands on the hands. According to Harrison and MacKinnon (1966), sweat glands of the human palm do not function in response to environmental changes, but are activated by alerting stimuli. Techniques for counting palmar sweat glands are detailed by Sutarman and Thompson (1952), Johnson and Dabbs (1967), and Dabbs, Johnson, and Leventhal (1968).

Galvanic Skin Response Associated with increased palmar sweating during periods of heightened arousal is a corresponding change in the resistance of the skin to the passage of an electrical current (ohms of resistance). Increased palmar sweating causes a decrease in skin resistance, or galvanic skin response (GSR). A decrease in skin resistance to the passage of electricity from one electrode to another is equal to an increase in skin conductivity. The galvanic skin response is mediated through the sympathetic cholinergic nerve supply to the skin and is attributed to changes in the number of active sweat glands (Montagu & Coles, 1966). Therefore, increased skin conductivity is directly related to an increase in the number of active palmar sweat glands.

DEFINING ANXIETY AND STRESS

The following story about a young athlete illustrates the potentially debilitating effects of anxiety on athletic performance. Ryan is a physically gifted sixteen-year-old athlete. He participates in several sports for his high school during the academic year and plays summer baseball as well. Some of the team sports he excels in are football, basketball, and baseball. However, his favorite sport is track and field, which is primarily an individual sport.

Ryan is a highly anxious young man with a tendency toward perfectionism. In Ryan's particular case, these traits had very little negative effect on his performance in the team sports he played. He would often get uptight about a big game, but he could always rely upon his teammates to help him out. The fact that team games involved other players seemed to help control the negative impact his anxiety could have had on his performance. Ryan occasionally

The debilitating consequences of anxiety affect athletes regardless of gender. Courtesy Ball State University Sports Information

"clutched" during baseball games, but the outcome of the game was rarely affected. Usually, only Ryan and Ryan's parents were aware of the anxiety and tension that was boiling within.

However, track and field was a different matter. Ryan was a sprinter and hurdler. His physical power and mesomorphic build made him especially well equipped for running and jumping events that required speed and leg power. Unfortunately, his basic anxiety and worry about failing had a serious effect on his performance during competition. During practice, Ryan always did well. In fact, during three years of high school Ryan had never lost a race to a teammate during practice. In actual competition, things were different. Ryan began preparing mentally for his races days in advance of the actual competition. During the days and hours preceding competition, his anxiety would rise to fearful levels. By the time actual competition came, Ryan could hardly walk, let alone run or jump. Several times he had to vomit before important races. His coach talked to him a great deal about learning to relax and not worry about the race, but didn't give him specific suggestions on how to accomplish this. Finally, the coach decided to remove Ryan from his favorite events because he was actually a detriment to the team. This was more than Ryan could take. He approached the coach one day and announced that he was going to give up

Figure 4.3

The four basic variations of stress. As adapted from H. Selye (1983), The stress concept: Past, present, and future. In C. L. Cooper (Ed.), *Stress Research* (pp. 1–20). New York: John Wiley & Sons Limited. Adapted with permission.

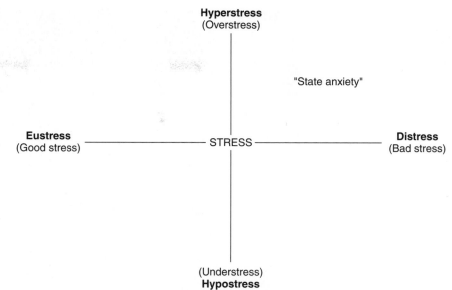

athletics altogether and concentrate on his studies. This story has a successful conclusion, but it will be shared later, at the beginning of the chapter on arousal adjustment strategies.

We can think of **anxiety** as being situation-specific or general in nature. A situation-specific anxiety response to a threatening stimulus is referred to as *state anxiety*. **State anxiety** is an immediate emotional state that is characterized by apprehension, fear, tension, and an increase in physiological arousal. **Trait anxiety,** on the other hand, is a personality predisposition. It is a predisposition to perceive certain environmental situations as threatening, and to respond to these situations with increased state anxiety (Spielberger, 1971). According to Endler (1978), any combination of five factors may be responsible for an increase in state anxiety. These five factors include (a) threat to a person's ego, (b) threat of personal harm, (c) ambiguity, (d) disruption of routine, and (e) threat of a negative social evaluation.

Anxiety has often been linked with the term *stress,* yet stress is a much broader and more comprehensive term. In the classic sense, **stress** is the "nonspecific response of the body to any demand made upon it" (Selye, 1983, p. 2). Stress, like arousal, is a neutral physiological response to some sort of stressor. The stressor could be in the form of physical exercise, joyful excitement, or threat to the body. All instances of stress, regardless of their origins, result in identical reactions in the body. As explained by Hans Selye (pronounced "sale-ye"), there are four basic variations of stress. As illustrated in figure 4.3, these four are dichotomized as eustress and distress, and as hyperstress and hypostress. **Hyperstress** (overstress) occurs when the amount and degree of stress exceeds our ability to adapt to the stress. Conversely, **hypostress** (understress) occurs

The thrill of victory often results in positive stress, or eustress. Courtesy Ball State University Sports Information

when we suffer from a lack of sensory stimulation (physical immobility and boredom). **Eustress** is conceptualized as "good stress," and is manifested in the form of joy, exhilaration, and happiness. Conversely, **distress,** or "bad stress," is manifested in the form of tension, anxiety, and worry. In order to neutralize the negative effects of stress in our lives, we must strike a balance between too much and too little stress, find as much eustress as possible, and do all in our power to minimize or eliminate the debilitating effects of distress. Based on their respective definitions, state anxiety (as defined by Spielberger) and distress (as defined by Selye) are virtually identical.

Another interesting and useful way to conceptualize stress is in the form of a process. The **stress process,** as described by Martens (1982) and by McGrath (1970), refers to the process associated with the manifestation of state anxiety (distress). This process is explained in terms of an objective demand, a perceived threat, and a state anxiety reaction. The **objective demand** represents the situation that the athlete is placed in; it is considered a stimulus. Whether or not the athlete sees the objective situation as threatening depends on her subjective evaluation of the situation and the interactive effect of trait anxiety. The relationship between the objective situation and the response can also be explained in terms of an imbalance. Distress will occur if the perceived demand is not balanced by the athlete's perception of her ability to respond effectively to the threat. The stress process is illustrated in figure 4.4.

An anecdote attributed to Tuckman (1972) and related by Fisher (1976) serves to clarify the relationships illustrated in figure 4.4. Two researchers were studying the effects of fear of drowning on the physiological responses of a subject. The subject was strapped to the side of a swimming tank with the water

Figure 4.4

The stress process. From *Competitive anxiety in sport* (p. 9) by R. Martens, R. S. Vealey, & D. Burton, 1990, Champaign, IL: Human Kinetics. Copyright 1990 by Human Kinetics Publishers, Inc. Reprinted by permission.

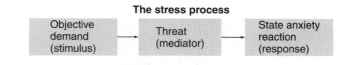

The stress process

Objective demand (stimulus) → Threat (mediator) → State anxiety reaction (response)

steadily rising. For some reason the researchers left the test area and forgot about their subject. When they remembered, they were aghast and numb with fear. Dropping everything, they raced to the test area to find the water level dangerously high. Quickly, they unstrapped the subject and pulled him from the water. Safely on the pool deck, they asked the subject if he was frightened. The subject responded that he wasn't at all worried, because it was just an experiment and he knew that the researchers wouldn't let any harm come to him! The subject perceived the test situation (objective demand) to be nonthreatening, and therefore the state anxiety reaction was not evoked.

CONCEPT & APPLICATION 4.2

Concept Whether or not an athlete responds to a threatening situation with high levels of state anxiety will depend entirely on the athlete's perception of the situation.

Application Each athlete is unique and should be treated as an individual. Do not attempt to predict an athlete's anxiety response to a competitive situation based on your own perception of the same situation. The athlete's own perception of the situation will determine the level of anxiety response, if any.

MEASUREMENT OF ANXIETY

In recent years, the preferred method of measuring trait and state anxiety has been through the use of pencil-and-paper inventories. For your perusal I have listed in table 4.1 a number of the most common anxiety inventories as used or developed by sport psychologists. For a more comprehensive description and listing of anxiety inventories, see Ostrow (1996).

While pencil-and-paper inventories are the most common measures of anxiety, behavioral and physiological assessment can be very effective. One category of behavioral measurement is direct observation, where the experimenter looks for objective signs of arousal in the subject and records them. Such things as nervous fidgeting, licking the lips, rubbing palms on pants or shirt, and change in respiration could all be interpreted as behavioral signs of activation. Such a system was developed and used by Lowe (1973) for ascertaining arousal through "on-deck activity" of batters in Little League baseball.

Along these lines, Harris and Harris (1984) prepared a list of overt behavioral responses that can be used by the athlete to identify indicators of distress, or state anxiety. The list is arranged in alphabetical order in table 4.2 and may be

Table 4.1

Common Anxiety Inventories Utilized or Developed by Sport Psychologists.

Trait/State	Inventory	Reference
Trait	Spielberger's Trait Anxiety Inventory (TAI)	Spielberger (1983)
	Cognitive Somatic Anxiety Questionnaire (CSAQ)	Schwartz, Davidson, and Goleman (1978)
	Sport Competition Anxiety Test (SCAT)	Martens et al. (1990)
	Sport Anxiety Scale (SAS)	Smith, Smoll, and Schutz (1990)
State	Spielberger's State Anxiety Inventory (SAI)	Spielberger (1983)
	Activation-Deactivation Checklist (AD-ACL)	Thayer (1967)
	Competitive State Anxiety Inventory (CSAI)	Martens (1977, 1982)
	Competitive State Anxiety Inventory-2 (CSAI-2)	Martens et al. (1990)

Table 4.2

Checklist for Monitoring Distress-Related Behavioral Responses of the Athlete.

From *The Athlete's Guide to Sports Psychology: Mental Skills for Physical People* (p. 36) by D. V. Harris and B. L. Harris, 1984, Champaign, IL: Human Kinetics. Copyright 1984 by Leisure Press.

Reprinted by permission.

Butterflies in stomach	_____	Increased heart rate	_____
Clammy hands	_____	Increased respiratory rate	_____
Cotton mouth	_____	Irritability	_____
Desire to urinate	_____	Muscle tension	_____
Diarrhea	_____	Nausea	_____
Feeling of fatigue	_____	Resorting to old habits	_____
Flushed skin	_____	Sense of confusion	_____
Forgetting details	_____	Trembling muscles	_____
Heart palpitations	_____	Visual distortion	_____
Hyperventilation	_____	Voice distortion	_____
Inability to concentrate	_____	Vomiting	_____
Inability to make decisions	_____	Yawning	_____

CONCEPT & APPLICATION 4.3

Concept The state anxiety response to stressful situations can be observed and recorded through the use of a behavioral checklist.

Application The athlete should systematically chronicle anxiety-related behavioral responses. Once these are recorded, the coach will be able to help an athlete identify and control competitive stress.

used by the athlete as a checklist to monitor state anxiety response during practice, immediately before competition, and during competition.

From the perspective of applied (nonlaboratory) field research, pencil-and-paper inventories and behavioral assessment techniques seem most feasible. This will remain true as long as electrophysiological indicators require cumbersome and expensive instruments. Advances in the field of applied psychophysiology, however, may change this perspective. Improvements in the use of telemetry may soon make it possible to monitor an athlete's heart rate, blood pressure, and muscular tension while she is competing in such dynamic activities as swimming, batting in baseball, and sprinting in track. Landers (1980b) has long argued that both physiological and psychological assessments of anxiety should be taken to measure anxiety and arousal. In this regard, however, it is important to point out that the relationship between physiological and psychological measures of state anxiety are quite low (Karteroliotis & Gill, 1987). Consequently, if both physiological and psychological measures of state anxiety are recorded simultaneously, it is possible that conflicting results may be obtained (Tenebaum, 1984).

CONCEPT & APPLICATION 4.4

Concept Pencil-and-paper inventories, behavioral checklists, and electrophysiological measures all provide somewhat independent measures of state anxiety.
Application Notwithstanding the lack of correlation among the various measures, it is useful to measure state anxiety from at least two perspectives. A pencil-and-paper inventory provides an easily administered assessment of state anxiety *prior* to the event, while the other two techniques theoretically assess state anxiety *during* the event.

MULTIDIMENSIONAL NATURE OF ANXIETY

As indicated earlier in this chapter, Endler (1978) identified five different dimensions, or facets, of anxiety. Studies by Fisher and Zwart (1982) and Gould, Horn, and Spreeman (1983) have provided support for Endler's multidimensional theory of anxiety in the sport domain. Any psychological test or theory that focuses on only one dimension of anxiety at the expense of others is considered to be unidimensional in nature. As indicated by Endler (1978), Spielberger's trait and state inventories are somewhat univariate in nature, because they do not address potentially important causes of anxiety.

Multidimensional anxiety theory has resulted in a number of inventories that approach anxiety from a multidimensional as opposed to unidimensional perspective. A case in point is the well-known and often-utilized Competitive State Anxiety Inventory–2 (CSAI-2) developed by Martens, Vealey, and Burton (1990). Relative to competition, the CSAI-2 assesses sport-specific cognitive and somatic state anxiety. **Cognitive state anxiety** is the mental component of state anxiety caused by such things as fear of negative social evaluation, fear of failure, and loss of self-esteem. **Somatic state anxiety** is the physical component of anxiety and reflects the *perception* of such physiological responses as increased heart rate, respiration, and muscular tension.

TIME-TO-EVENT NATURE OF PRECOMPETITIVE ANXIETY

Our ability to obtain independent measures of cognitive and somatic state anxiety has greatly enhanced our knowledge about the athletic situation. One of the factors that is believed to significantly influence the quality of the athletic experience is the level of state anxiety during the time leading up to competition. This is referred to as **precompetitive anxiety.** We now know quite a bit about the temporal changes in anxiety during the period of time leading up to and immediately following the beginning of the event. Precompetitive cognitive anxiety starts relative high and remains high and stable as the time-to-event approaches. Conversely, somatic anxiety remains relatively low until approximately 24 hours before the event, and then increases rapidly as the event approaches. Once performance begins, somatic anxiety dissipates rapidly, whereas cognitive state anxiety fluctuates throughout the contest as the probability of success/failure changes (Fenz, 1975; Hardy & Parfitt, 1991; Jones & Cale, 1989; Jones, Swain & Cale, 1991; Martens et al., 1990; Schedlowski & Tewes, 1992; Parfitt, Hardy & Pates, 1995; Swain & Jones, 1992). The relationship between competitive state anxiety and time-to-event is graphically illustrated in figure 4.5.

CONCEPT & APPLICATION 4.5

Concept Cognitive and somatic state anxiety are differentially manifested as the time to competitive event approaches.

Application Bodily perceptions of increased sympathetic nervous system activity (somatic anxiety) are normal and healthy indicators of an approaching athletic contest. If allowed to dissipate, they should be viewed as indicators of physiological readiness. Conversely, cognitive state anxiety has the potential of causing a decrement in athletic performance if it is not controlled (Bird & Horn, 1990).

DIFFERENTIAL EFFECT OF SOMATIC AND COGNITIVE ANXIETY ON PERFORMANCE

The capability to ascertain the independent measures of cognitive and somatic state anxiety has increased our knowledge of the relationship between precompetitive anxiety and athletic performance. The nature of the relationship between competitive state anxiety and performance depends in part upon the dimension of state anxiety measured. For example, the relationship between somatic anxiety and performance tends to be quadratic in nature and takes the

Precompetitive cognitive anxiety starts relatively high and remains high and stable as the time-to-event approaches. Courtesy Ball State University Sports Information

Figure 4.5

Changes in competitive state anxiety prior to competition (decline in cognitive anxiety fluctuates with probability of success/failure).

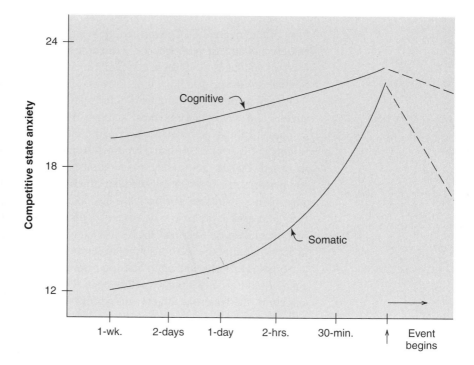

Figure 4.6

Multidimensional
relationship between
athletic performance and
state anxiety.

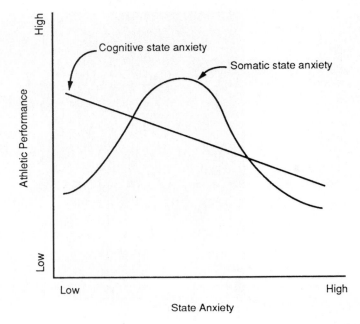

form of the inverted U. Conversely, the relationship between cognitive state anxiety and athletic performance is linear in nature (although negative, or inverse) and takes the form of a straight line (Burton, 1988; Gould, Petlichkoff, Simons & Vevera, 1987).

As can be observed in figure 4.6, the relationship between cognitive state anxiety and performance is linear and negative. As cognitive state anxiety increases, athletic performance decreases. This is consistent with the volleyball findings of Cox (1986) when a unidimensional measurement of state anxiety was used (CSAI). Conversely, the relationship between somatic state anxiety and performance is quadratic and takes the form of the inverted U. As somatic state anxiety increases, performance also increases up to an optimal level, and then decreases as somatic state anxiety continues to increase.

It would appear that the CSAI-2 has led to a major breakthrough in our understanding of the relationship between state anxiety and athletic performance. Worry and apprehension associated with cognitive state anxiety is a major hindrance to athletic performance. The lower the level of cognitive state anxiety is, the better the athlete will perform. The notion that a "little" anxiety is good for the athlete is not true, if the anxiety is cognitive.

Conversely, increases in the somatic indicators of state anxiety (increased heart rate, muscle tension, jitteriness, etc.) are associated with increased athletic performance up to an uncertain optimal level, and then thereafter result in a decrement in performance. This is the classic inverted-U relationship between anxiety/arousal and performance.

CONCEPT & APPLICATION 4.6

Concept The relationship between somatic state anxiety and athletic performance takes the form of the inverted U, while the relationship between cognitive state anxiety and performance is linear and negative.

Application The real threats to quality athletic performance are worry, self-doubt, and

apprehension. Knowing this, the coach must help the athlete cope with these debilitating threats. At the same time, an optimal level of somatic state anxiety should be encouraged and maintained. Too much somatic state anxiety is detrimental, as is too little.

INTENSITY AND DIRECTION ISSUES

The basic relationships illustrated in figure 4.6 provide a foundation for an understanding of the relationship between state anxiety and performance. In subsequent sections of this important chapter, I will introduce other factors that enter into this relationship. Among them is the notion of individual differences. The relationships illustrated in figure 4.6 are based on groups of people. Any single individual or athlete might exhibit a pattern very different from that of the group. The CSAI-2 measures **intensity** of state anxiety and says nothing about the individual's perception of whether his response, be it high or low, would hinder or facilitate performance. The athlete's perception of whether his "felt" response, relative to a specific item on the CSAI-2, was good or bad for future performance has been labeled **direction** of state anxiety. Direction of state anxiety is the athlete's interpretation of whether his felt level of intensity was debilitative or facilitative relative to performance (Edwards & Hardy, 1996; Jones, 1991, 1995; Jones & Hanton, 1996; Jones, Hanton & Swain, 1994; Jones & Swain, 1992, 1995).

To take into account the directional component of competitive state anxiety (CSA), the CSAI-2 was revised (Jones & Swain, 1992). The basic CSAI-2 is composed of 27 items, each set to a 4-point Likert Scale running from "not at all" to "very much so." The revised CSAI-2 requires a second response from the subject relative to each item. The second response requests that the individual indicate on a 7-point scale whether he thought the level of intensity he marked would be debilitative or facilitative. The actual scale runs from a –3 to a +3, with a minus indicating debilitative and a plus indicating facilitative (–3, –2, –1, 0, +1, +2, +3).

Jones et al. (1994) and Jones and Swain (1995) administered the revised CSAI-2 to athletes and then categorized them as either being elite or nonelite. Based on the intensity measure of state anxiety, they were unable to differentiate between the two groups, but based upon the direction component, they could differentiate. The elite athletes viewed their intensity responses to be much more facilitative than the nonelite athletes thought their responses were. In a related investigation,

Jones and Hanton (1996) divided athletes up into two groups, with high and low expectations about goal attainment. The athletes who had a high expectation that they would achieve their goals were categorized in the high-expectancy group. Conversely, the athletes who had a low expectation that they would achieve their goals were categorized in the low-expectancy group. Based upon the results of the revised CSAI-2 administration, researchers were not able to differentiate between the two groups based on anxiety intensity scores; however, they were able to differentiate based on directional scores. Individuals in the high-expectancy group viewed their intensity responses to be much more facilitative than those in the low-expectancy group considered theirs to be. Jones and Hanton (1996) interpreted these results to mean that athletes who expect to attain their goals feel "in control," and view anxiety symptoms as facilitative as opposed to debilitative. Based upon this new research, it seems clear that an athlete's perception of whether or not anxiety symptoms are facilitative or debilitative is more important than whether the absolute intensity of anxiety is high or low.

CONCEPT & APPLICATION 4.7

Concept Intensity of competitive state anxiety is an indicator of the absolute level of state anxiety associated with a competitive situation, whereas direction of competitive state anxiety is the athlete's perception of whether the indicated intensity is debilitative or facilitative relative to performance.

Application From the perspective of individual differences, it is more important for the coach or teacher to know whether an athlete perceives a certain level of anxiety to be positive or negative than for her to know the absolute level. Two athletes may exhibit high levels of somatic and cognitive anxiety immediately prior to competition, but one of them may view these high levels as having a positive, or facilitative, influence on the competition. This knowledge should provide the coach with valuable information as to how to best prepare the athlete for competition.

SHORTENED VERSIONS OF THE CSAI-2

In recent years, the most common inventory used for measuring precompetitive competitive state anxiety has been the CSAI-2. The inventory is 27 items in length, takes about 5 minutes for an individual to complete, and is administered as close in time to the start of competition as possible. This generally ranges from 60 minutes before competition, for high-profile events, to 15 minutes before intramural events. Admittedly, a great deal of variation in precompetitive state anxiety could occur during this time frame. In addition, athletes are often reluctant to allow any sort of distraction during the time they are preparing mentally for competition. With these reasons in mind, Murphy, Greenspan, Jowdy, and Tammen (1989) developed a 3-item version of the CSAI-2 called the Mental Readiness Form (MRF). Improved versions of the MRF were

Figure 4.7

The Sport Grid. Reprinted by permission of the publisher. From T. D. Raedeke and G. L. Stein (1994). Felt arousal, thoughts/feelings, and ski performance. *The Sport Psychologist, 8*, 360–375.

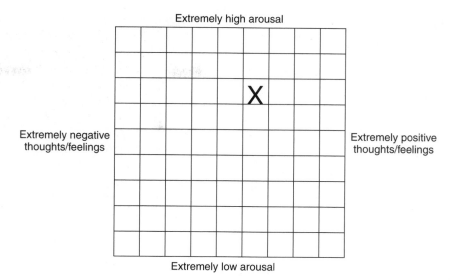

developed by Krane (1994). The two improved versions of the MRF were set to 11-item Likert scales and titled the MRF-Likert and MRF-3. In addition to the MRF, Cox, Russell, and Robb (1998) developed the Anxiety Rating Scale (ARS), which is also a 3-item version of the CSAI-2 set to a 7-item Likert Scale. Both of these scales provide the researcher and practitioner with a nonintrusive way to measure competitive state anxiety prior to, or even during, competition. Neither Krane nor Cox et al. recommend the use of the shortened versions of the CSAI-2 over the 27-item parent test if time is not an important consideration.

In addition to the MRF and ARS described above, Stadulis, Eidson, and MacCracken (1994) reported the development of a 15-item version of the CSAI-2 called the Competitive State Anxiety Inventory–2 for children (CSAI-2C). The CSAI-2C is a shortened version of the parent test modified to include language appropriate for children ages ten to twelve.

THE SPORT GRID

Russell, Weiss, and Mendelsohn (1989) proposed the use of the Affect Grid as a single-item scale for assessing affect along the dimensions of high/low arousal and positive/negative affect. The basic concepts developed by Russell et al. (1989) were modified by Raedeke and Stein (1994) into the Sport Grid. The **Sport Grid** provides a simple and direct way for an athlete to indicate with a single mark on a grid whether he feels physiologically aroused (using a high/low continuum) and whether he is experiencing positive or negative thoughts and feelings at a specific point in time (using a positive/negative continuum). Like the MRF and the ARS, described in the previous section, the Sport Grid offers a quick and nonintrusive way for an athlete to indicate how he is feeling immediately before an important competitive event. The Sport Grid is illustrated in figure 4.7. Notice the striking similarity between this figure and figure 4.3.

Figure 4.8

Relationship between
drive and inverted-U
theories.

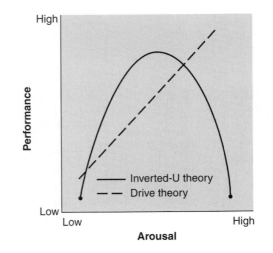

RELATIONSHIP BETWEEN AROUSAL
AND ATHLETIC PERFORMANCE

Throughout this chapter, an effort has been made to avoid confusing the terms
anxiety and *arousal*. In this section, however, it will be necessary to use the term
arousal as somewhat synonymous with *state anxiety*. This is the case because
researchers have routinely employed a test of state anxiety as the primary means
for determining a subject's arousal level. Consequently, most of the reported
research will relate negative anxiety (state anxiety) to sport and motor
performance.

The primary focus of this section will be upon two main theories that purport
to explain the relationship between arousal and athletic performance: inverted-U
theory and drive theory. **Inverted-U theory** includes many subtheories that
explain why the relationship between arousal and performance is curvilinear as
opposed to linear in nature. Conversely, **drive theory** proposes a linear
relationship between arousal and performance. In the most elementary case, the
distinguishing characteristics of inverted-U and drive theory are illustrated in
figure 4.8.

INVERTED-U THEORY

The inverted-U theory has been around for as long as the arousal/performance
relationship has been studied. It simply states that the relationship between
performance and arousal is curvilinear as opposed to linear, and takes the form
of an inverted U (figure 4.8). While it is described as a theory or hypothesis,
researchers such as Duffy (1957) and Malmo (1959) consider it to be an
observed fact.

One of the difficulties encountered in testing the inverted-U theory with
humans is our inability to precisely measure arousal. For example, if in a
particular study researchers fail to demonstrate that heightened arousal causes a

Under the influence of high arousal, athletes are capable of jumping great heights. Courtesy Kansas State University Sports Information

decrement in performance, it is not particularly damaging to the theory. The reason for this is that it can always be argued that for that particular task, arousal was not high enough. If it had been higher, we may argue, performance would have declined. The problem is that from a human rights standpoint, the amount of arousal researchers can induce is limited. For example, if arousal is induced through electrical shock, how much can the researcher elevate the voltage without violating the subject's rights? Not very much.

The foundation for inverted-U theory is the classic work of Yerkes and Dodson (1908). Using dancing mice as subjects, Yerkes and Dodson set out to discover the relationship between arousal and task difficulty in their effect on performance. Performance was measured as the number of trials needed for the mice to select the brighter of two compartments. Arousal consisted of high, medium, and low intensities of electrical shock. Task difficulty was manipulated in terms of the differences in brightness between two compartments (high, medium, and low difficulty). Results showed that the amount of practice needed to learn the discrimination task increased as the difference in brightness between the two compartments diminished. These findings led to the **Yerkes-Dodson law,** which states, "an easily acquired habit, that is, one which does not demand difficult sense discrimination or complex associations, may readily be formed under strong stimulation, whereas a difficult habit may be acquired readily only under relatively weak stimulation" (pp. 481–482).

The results of the Yerkes-Dodson research are illustrated in figure 4.9. As can be observed in this figure, the optimal level of electrical shock (arousal) for a difficult task was much lower than that needed for an easy task. Additionally, an optimal level of arousal (electrical shock) is indicated for each task. Before and after the optimal point, performance drops off. This is the inverted U.

In terms of practical sport application, the Yerkes-Dodson law is illustrated in figure 4.10. This figure shows that as the complexity of a skill increases, the amount of arousal needed for optimal performance decreases.

As can be observed in figure 4.10, a high level of arousal is necessary for the best performance in gross motor activities such as weight lifting. Conversely, a lower level of arousal is best for a fine motor task such as putting in golf. Each sport skill has its theoretical optimal level of arousal for best performance. Regardless of which type of skill is being performed, they all conform to the inverted-U principle. Specifically, performance is lowest when arousal is very high or very low, and highest when arousal is moderate, or optimum.

CONCEPT & APPLICATION 4.8

Concept The relationship between athletic performance and arousal takes the form of the inverted U.

Application Preparing athletes for competition involves more than psyching them up. It involves finding the optimal level of arousal for each athlete.

Another important consideration relating to the Yerkes-Dodson law is skill level. Just as putting in golf is a complex activity compared to weight lifting, learning to dribble a basketball is more difficult for a beginner than performing the same task as an expert. The optimal level of arousal for a beginner should be considerably lower than the optimal level for an expert performing the same task. As illustrated in figure 4.11, this concept explains why highly skilled athletes often perform better in competitive situations than do novices (Oxendine, 1970).

Evidence of an inverted-U relationship between athletic performance and arousal is documented in the literature. Klavora (1978) and Sonstroem and Bernardo (1982) were able to demonstrate that basketball performance is related to level of arousal, with best performance occurring at moderate levels of arousal and poorest performance at high or low levels. Similarly, Gould, Petlichkoff,

Figure 4.9

Results of the Yerkes-
Dodson (1908) research
showing the effect of
arousal and task difficulty
on performance. From
R. M. Yerkes and J. D.
Dodson, The relationship
of strength of stimulus to
rapidity of habit formation,
*Journal of comparative
neurology and
psychology,* 1908, *18,*
459–482. Adapted with
permission of Alan R. Liss,
Inc., Publisher and
Copyright holder.

Figure 4.10

Application of the Yerkes-
Dodson law in athletic
events.

Figure 4.11

Application of the Yerkes-
Dodson law to tennis
players at various skill
levels.

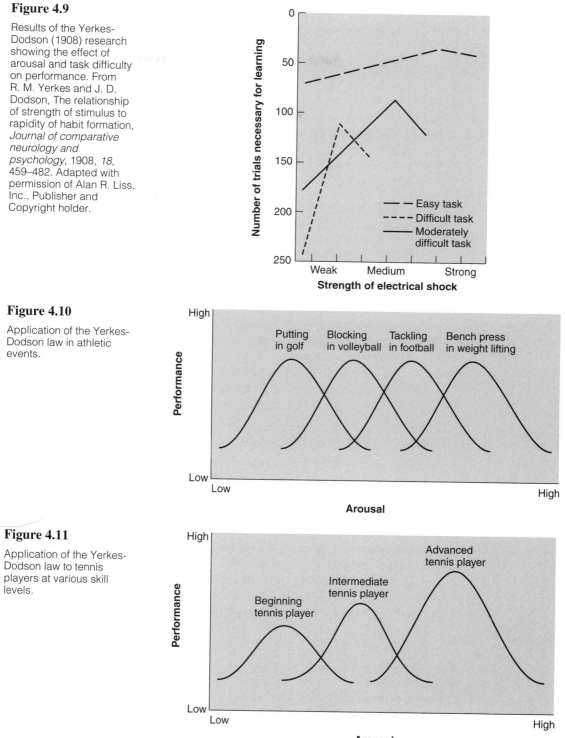

CONCEPT & APPLICATION 4.9

Concept The optimal level of arousal varies as a function of the complexity of the task and the skill level of the athlete.

Application Highly skilled athletes and athletes performing simple tasks need a moderately high level of arousal for maximum performance. Less skilled athletes and athletes performing complex tasks require a relatively low level of arousal for maximum performance.

Simons, and Vevera (1987) and Burton (1988) reported that best performance in pistol shooting and swimming, respectively, were related to somatic anxiety in a way consistent with inverted-U predictions. In a related study, Beuter and Duda (1985) observed that heightened arousal has a detrimental effect on the motor performance of children. Under conditions of optimal arousal, children perform smooth and automatic movement patterns. However, under conditions of high arousal, movement patterns come under volitional control and are observed to be less smooth and efficient. The inverted-U relationship between performance and arousal has also been documented with nonathletic tasks such as reaction time (Lansing, Schwartz & Lindsley, 1956), auditory tracking (Stennet, 1957), and hand steadiness (Martens & Landers, 1970).

While it seems relatively clear that the nature of the relationship between athletic performance and arousal takes the form of the inverted U, it is not clear why this occurs. In the following subsections, three theories that predict the inverted-U relationship will be briefly reviewed.

Easterbrook's Cue Utilization Theory

Easterbrook's (1959) notion of cue utilization theory was introduced in chapter 3 and illustrated in figure 3.6. The basic premise of cue utilization or attentional narrowing theory is that *as arousal increases, attention narrows.* The narrowing of attention results in some cues being gated out, first irrelevant cues and later relevant cues. From figure 3.6 it should be clear that attentional narrowing predicts an inverted-U relationship between arousal and performance. When arousal is low, the attentional band is wide and both irrelevant and relevant cues are available. The presence of the irrelevant cues is distracting and causes a decrement in performance. At a moderate, or optimal, level of arousal, only the irrelevant cues are eliminated, and therefore performance is high. Finally, when arousal is high, attentional focus is narrow and both relevant and irrelevant cues are gated out. This results in a decrement in performance, as predicted by the inverted-U theory.

Cue utilization theory also addresses the problem of task complexity and learning. With a complex or unlearned motor skill, there is a greater number of task-relevant cues to manage. Consequently, with increased arousal, the

Coaches can get psyched up too! Courtesy Ball State University Sports Information

probability of errors increases at a faster rate than it would for a simple motor skill (Landers, 1980b).

The phenomenon of attentional narrowing is easily applied to a sport setting. When a football quarterback drops back for a pass, an optimal level of attention will cause a gating out of irrelevant cues. However, if arousal becomes too high, the quarterback may either suffer from **distractibility** or gate out relevant cues as a result of his narrow band of attention. Research supporting the concept of attentional narrowing is strong, but has taken place primarily in a laboratory setting (Bacon, 1974; Bahrick, Fitts & Rankin, 1952; Bursill, 1958; Weltman & Egstrom, 1966; Weltman, Smith & Egstrom, 1971). An exception to this general rule is a sports-related study reported by Landers, Qi, and Courtet (1985).

Taken as a whole, this brief review of attentional narrowing research provides support for Easterbrook's cue utilization theory. Increased arousal causes attention to become narrower and more restricted. This can enhance performance up to a certain point, but thereafter it causes a performance decrement. Thus, attentional narrowing theory supports an inverted-U relationship between arousal and performance.

CONCEPT & APPLICATION 4.10

Concept Increased arousal has the effect of narrowing an athlete's attention.
Application Athletes who participate in a sport that requires broad attentional awareness need lower levels of arousal for best performance. The setter in volleyball must be particularly aware of all aspects of the game. Narrow vision would seem to be particularly damaging to the setter's play selection.

CONCEPT & APPLICATION 4.11

Concept Decreased arousal has the effect of broadening an athlete's attentional focus.
Application Athletes who participate in a sport that requires narrow attentional focus need appropriately increased levels of arousal for optimal performance. An athlete attempting a single feat of power and force will need a narrowed focus of attention.

Signal Detection Theory

Another theory that predicts a quadratic relationship between arousal and performance is **signal detection theory** (SDT). Signal detection theory has not been field tested for the inverted-U concept; however, from a theoretical point of view it should be of interest to the reader.

In its simplest form, signal detection theory holds that the intensity of **noise** (*N*) in the nervous system falls along a continuum ranging from low to high. The addition of a signal to the noise naturally increases the neural activity. It is the subject's task to discriminate between noise (*N*) alone and **signal plus noise** (*SN*). The signal is typically a sound.

Repeated random presentations of test intervals in which a signal may or may not be presented is theoretically represented by two bell-shaped curves. One curve represents the noise distribution, and the other represents the signal plus noise distribution (see figure 4.12). These two curves are believed to be normally distributed, with the greatest frequency of observations occurring at about the mean of each distribution.

The task of participants in an SDT experiment is to respond by saying "yes" if they detect a signal and "no" if they do not. Obviously, the constant presence of neural noise makes the task potentially difficult. If the neural activity seems high, the participant will be likely to respond "yes." If the neural activity associated with a test interval seems low, she will be likely to respond "no." A participant's ability to discriminate between the noise and the signal plus noise distributions is called the participant's "sensitivity." In figure 4.12, sensitivity is indicated by d'. It represents the distance between the means of the *N* and *SN* distributions.

Figure 4.12

Relationship between level of arousal and signal detectability. From "Stress and performance" by A. T. Welford 1973, *Ergonomics, 16*(5), 567–580. Copyright © 1973 by Taylor & Francis, Ltd. Adapted with permission of the publisher.

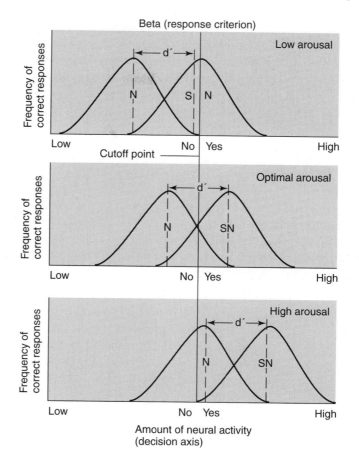

One important factor that determines whether a participant will give a yes or no response to a particular stimulus is the participant's response bias, or *response criterion* (beta). Some people exhibit a very stringent criterion and refuse to respond "yes" unless they are positive they have heard a signal. Others have a lenient criterion and will respond "yes" even if the signal appears weak. Participants with a stringent criterion miss detecting many signals, while those with a lenient criterion often identify signals that do not actually occur.

Welford (1973) has hypothesized that a high or a low level of arousal has the effect of altering the position of a participant's response criterion, as shown in figure 4.12. Increased arousal causes brain cells to become activated and more ready to fire. Increased activation of brain cells would increase the neural activity of any particular point along the decision axis in figure 4.12. As this occurred, both distributions would tend to shift to the right due to increased neural activity. Since the response criterion is relatively stationary, shifting the distributions to the right would cause the response criterion to shift to the left in relation to the two distributions. This process would be reversed during sleep or low arousal.

In the low-arousal situation, the errors tend to be a failure to detect a signal (error of omission). In the high-arousal situation, the errors tend to be false identification of signals (error of commission). In the optimal-arousal situation, the errors are ideally balanced between false alarms and misses. This model is very appealing, because one would expect errors to increase with high and low levels of arousal.

CONCEPT & APPLICATION 4.12

Concept Athletes in sports that require instant decisions require a moderate level of arousal to avoid errors of commission or omission. *Application* An overly aroused batter in baseball will tend to swing at bad pitches (error of commission), while an underaroused hitter will allow called strikes (error of omission). A moderate level of arousal will tend to balance out the two kinds of decision errors.

From this explanation, it should be clear that with extreme shifts in the response criterion from the left to the right, we have the inverted-U relationship between signal detectability and arousal. For example, consider what would happen in the high-arousal situation if beta shifted clearly to the left of both distributions. This would result in a totally lenient response criterion, by which subjects would respond "yes" every time they were asked if they detected a signal. Assuming a signal was presented 50 percent of the time, this would yield a 50 percent error rate. Conversely, if in the low-arousal situation, the criterion shifted completely to the right of both distributions, the subject would respond "no" to every test observation. Again, a 50 percent error rate would result. Thus, high and low levels of arousal yield a decrement in performance, while an optimum level of arousal yields the best performance.

In sport, the SDT model can be applied to officials who must routinely make split-second decisions. Was the pitch a ball or a strike? Was the runner safe or out? The SDT model is easily applied to these situations by simply assigning the two curves to each of two possible decisions (Cox, 1987b; Hutchinson, 1981). The theory can be used to determine an official's bias and sensitivity. As with athletes, when the official is underaroused or overaroused, he will make more errors than when he is optimally aroused.

Information Processing Theory
The basic predictions of information processing theory for the arousal/performance relationship are identical to those of signal detection theory. Both theories predict the inverted-U relationship between performance and arousal, and both support the Yerkes-Dodson law. Welford (1962, 1965) gives a basic outline of the theory's predictions. However, the theory is presented without the support of research evidence in the motor domain.

According to Welford (1962), brain cells become active with increased levels of arousal, and they begin to fire. As this happens, the information processing system becomes noisy, and its channel capacity is reduced. At low levels of arousal, the system is relatively inert and performance is low. At high levels of arousal, a performance decrement occurs because of the reduced information processing capacity of the channels. At some optimal level of arousal, the information processing capacity of the system is at its maximum, and performance is at its best.

DRIVE THEORY

Perhaps the great contribution of drive theory is that it helps to explain the relationships between learning and arousal, and between performance and arousal. Many young athletes are just beginning the process of becoming skilled performers. The effect of arousal upon a beginner may be different from its effect upon a skilled performer. The basic relationship between arousal and an athlete's performance at any skill level is given in the following formula:

$$Performance = Arousal \times Skill\ Level$$

As developed by Hull (1943, 1951) and Spence (1956), drive theory is a complex stimulus-response theory of motivation and learning. It is a theory of competing responses, in which increased **drive** (arousal) facilitates the elicitation of the dominant response. The basic tenets of drive theory are as follows:

1. Increased arousal (drive) will elicit the dominant response.

2. The response associated with the strongest potential to respond is the dominant response.

3. Early in learning or for complex tasks, the dominant response is the incorrect response.

4. Late in learning or for simple tasks, the dominant response is the correct response.

We can make several practical applications of these drive theory tenets. First, heightened levels of arousal should benefit the skilled performer, but hamper the beginner. The coach with a relatively young team should strive to create an atmosphere relatively low in anxiety and arousal. Low levels of arousal should increase the beginner's chances of a successful performance. In turn, the experience of success should strengthen self-confidence. Skilled athletes, on the other hand, will benefit from an increase in arousal. Similar applications can be made to the performance of simple and complex tasks. For example, a complex task, such as throwing a knuckleball in baseball, will always require a low level of arousal. Conversely, a very simple task, such as doing high push-ups, would seem to benefit from arousal. A case in point is a reported study by Davis and Harvey (1992). Utilizing drive theory predictions, the researchers hypothesized that increased arousal caused by major league baseball pressure situations would cause a decrement in batting (a complex task). Four late-game pressure situations were compared with nonpressure situations relative to batting

This athlete celebrates a successful block in volleyball. Courtesy University of Missouri-Columbia Sports Information

CONCEPT & APPLICATION 4.13

Concept The effect of increased arousal on an athlete performing a complex task or learning a novel task will be to elicit an incorrect response, which is the dominant response.

Application With beginners it is important that the environment be one of low arousal and stress. Young athletes tend to make more mistakes if they become excited and overly activated.

CONCEPT & APPLICATION 4.14

Concept The effect of increased arousal on an athlete performing a simple or well-learned task will be to elicit a correct response, which is the dominant response.

Application Highly skilled athletes will often benefit from increased arousal. Psyching up a basketball star like Michael Jordan could have grave consequences for the opposing team.

performance. Results showed a decrement in batting performance associated with increased arousal, as predicted by drive theory.

Drive theory received tremendous amounts of attention from researchers between 1943 and 1970. However, since then, interest in the theory has diminished significantly. The theory was extremely difficult to test, and the tests that were conducted often yielded conflicting results. For an in-depth review of research associated with drive theory, the reader is referred to Cox (1990).

ALTERNATIVES TO INVERTED-U THEORY

From 1970 to the present, inverted-U theory has been the favored theory of sport psychologists to explain the relationship between arousal and performance. During this time, drive theory was largely abandoned by researchers. Just as drive theory was supplanted by the inverted-U theory in the 1970s and 1980s, inverted-U theory is in danger of being supplanted by a number of theories that are gaining support. Some appear to be complex variations of the inverted-U theory, while others appear to represent a clear departure from the notion of the inverted U. Critics of inverted-U theory point out that it is far too simplistic to account for the complex relationship between arousal and performance (Jones & Hardy, 1989; Raglin, 1992; Weinberg, 1990). In this section, four theories that purport to more adequately explain the relationship between arousal and performance will be introduced and explained.

FAZEY AND HARDY'S CATASTROPHE MODEL

As illustrated in figure 4.8, inverted-U theory predicts a smooth bell-shaped (inverted-U) curve relationship between physiological arousal and athletic performance. The basic assumptions of the theory are that (a) small incremental increases in arousal result in small incremental increases or decreases in performance, and that (b) moderate arousal results in optimal performance. **Catastrophe theory** questions both of these basic assumptions, but more specifically, the notion that small incremental increases in arousal result in small changes in performance. At critical points in the performance curve, quite the opposite may be observed. When faced with debilitating stress and arousal, athletes do not experience small incremental decreases in performance; they suffer large and dramatic decrements that may be described as catastrophic in nature. In addition, once the athlete suffers a catastrophic decrement in performance, small incremental reductions rarely bring performance back to the pre-catastrophic level (Fazey & Hardy, 1988). Inverted-U theory cannot account for these sudden and extreme reductions in performance. A case in point is the real-life experience (nightmare) of professional golfer Greg Norman (Reilly, 1996). After the third round of the 1996 Masters golf tournament, Greg Norman held a six-shot lead over his nearest competitor, with one round (eighteen holes) to go. On Sunday, during the fourth round, came the most "catastrophic" four holes in Greg's professional golf career. On the ninth through the twelfth holes, he surrendered his six-stroke lead to Nick Faldo. He then went on to lose the Masters by five strokes.

Fazey and Hardy's catastrophe model is illustrated in figure 4.13. In this model, physiological arousal is represented on the back horizontal edge of the

Figure 4.13

Fazey and Hardy's (1988) catastrophe model of the relationship between anxiety and performance. From J. Fazey and L. Hardy, 1988. The inverted-U hypothesis: A catastrophe for sport psychology? *Bass Monograph No. 1.* Leeds, U.K.: British Association of Sports Sciences and National Coaching Foundation. Reprinted with permission.

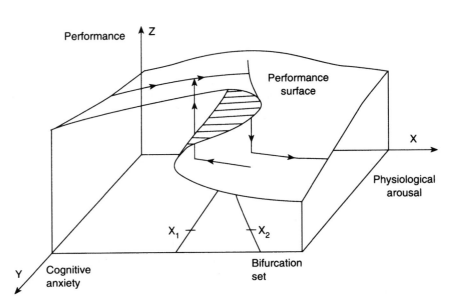

floor of the three-dimensional model (X). Cognitive anxiety is represented as being at a right angle to arousal and on the left edge of the floor of the model (Y). Performance is represented as being the height of the performance surface (Z). For every (X,Y) coordinate on the floor of the model, a point exists on the performance surface directly above it. In the model, arousal is referred to by Fazey and Hardy as the *normal factor,* and cognitive anxiety, as the *splitting factor* (Hardy, 1996; Krane, 1992).

If cognitive anxiety is very low, the relationship between arousal and performance is predicted to take the form of the traditional inverted U, as represented by the back edge of the performance surface. Cognitive anxiety is represented in the model as the decisive factor for determining whether performance changes will be smooth and small, abrupt and large, or somewhere in between. With increasing physiological arousal, a catastrophe is predicted to occur at point (X_2), when cognitive anxiety is high. At this point, performance drops over the edge of the upper fold's performance surface down to a very low point on the same surface. Thus, with a very small increase in physiological arousal, a very large and abrupt decrease in performance occurs. Notice that the severity of the catastrophic decrease in performance depends on the level of cognitive anxiety. A small decrease in physiological arousal will not result in performance returning to its former lofty height, even though a small incremental increase in physiological arousal resulted in the performance catastrophe in the first place.

If cognitive anxiety remains high (unchanged), a significant decrease in physiological arousal will be necessary to return performance back to a position on top of the upper fold of the performance surface. The point where this occurs is represented as (X_1) on the floor of the three-dimensional model. Notice that the distance between point one (X_1) and point two (X_2) on the floor of the model is a function of cognitive state anxiety. The distance between this "bifurcation set" increases as cognitive anxiety increases. When physiological arousal recedes to point one (X_1), with no change in cognitive anxiety, performance jumps abruptly back to its pre-catastrophic level. The requirement that discontinuity (represented by sudden large jumps) occurs at different points along the normal factor (physiological arousal) is known as *hysteresis*.

Another subtle prediction of the model is that when physiological arousal is very low, an increase in cognitive anxiety will result in an increase in performance (the height of Z is greater at the front of the model than at the back). Conversely, when physiological arousal is very high, a decrease in cognitive anxiety will result in increased performance (the height of Z is greater at the back than at the front). This aspect of the model was supported by research involving netball players (Edwards & Hardy, 1996).

The basic tenets of Fazey and Hardy's catastrophe model were tested by Hardy and Parfitt (1991) and Hardy, Parfitt, and Pates (1994). In both of these studies, cognitive anxiety and physiological arousal were manipulated. Setting cognitive anxiety at a high level and systematically increasing physiological arousal resulted in catastrophic decrements in basketball and bowling performance. Minimal changes in performance were observed when cognitive anxiety was low and physiological arousal was systematically increased. Both of these studies provided strong support for the basic tenets of catastrophe theory.

Several investigators have replaced physiological arousal with somatic anxiety and tested the revised catastrophe model in competitive situations. In these investigations, cognitive and somatic state anxiety were measured immediately before batting in softball (Krane, Joyce, Rafeld, 1994), or before diving off a 3-meter board (Durr, 1996). In the Krane et al. (1994) investigation, very minimal support was found for the revised model, in that somatic anxiety was related to batting performance in certain critical game situations (situations in which cognitive anxiety would be expected to be high). As somatic anxiety increased, performance increased to a point, but then began to decline

CONCEPT & APPLICATION 4.15

Concept If cognitive state anxiety is high, an increase in physiological arousal can result in a sudden and large decrement in athletic performance.

Application Large and sudden decrements in performance will not occur if cognitive state anxiety can be minimized or eliminated. Failing this, it will be necessary to closely monitor physiological arousal to avoid triggering a catastrophe in performance. If a catastrophe in performance does occur, it is best to give the athlete a rest to allow physiological arousal to return to a low level.

(a curvilinear relationship). In the diving research (Durr, 1996), little interaction was observed between somatic and cognitive anxiety. Rather, regardless of the level of cognitive anxiety, performance decreased as somatic anxiety increased (negative linear relationship). At the present time, it appears that catastrophe theory is best supported when the model is conceptualized as originally presented by Fazey and Hardy (1988).

HANIN'S ZONE OF OPTIMAL FUNCTIONING (ZOF)

Hanin's theory also questions the two basic assumptions of inverted-U theory, but more specifically the notion that a moderate level of state anxiety results in best performance. **Zone of optimal functioning** (ZOF) theory postulates that the level of optimal state anxiety best for one athlete may be very different from that optimal for the next athlete. Hanin (1986), for example, reported that a group of 46 elite female rowers had a mean optimal **prestart state anxiety** (precompetitive) of 43.80, with individual levels ranging from 26 to 67. Thus, for some athletes, the optimal level of state anxiety was very low, while for others it was very high. State anxiety was measured using a Russian version of Spielberger's State Anxiety Inventory (SAI). Hanin's concept of a zone of optimal functioning has been discussed in detail by Hanin (1980, 1986, 1989) and by Raglin (1992).

According to Hanin, if an athlete's optimal prestart state anxiety level can be determined, it should be possible to help an athlete achieve that ideal level through arousal control techniques. An athlete's optimal prestart anxiety level can be determined either directly or *retrospectively*. Direct measurement of optimal prestart anxiety level is accomplished by actually measuring state anxiety immediately before a number of competitions and determining the level of anxiety that corresponds to the best performance. Since this method of determining optimal prestart anxiety is often time-consuming and impractical, the retrospective method offers an attractive alternative. In the retrospective method, athletes are merely asked to reflect upon past performances and to complete the SAI according to how they remember feeling immediately before their best-ever performance. Hanin (1986) reported data showing that actual and retrospective measures of state anxiety are identical in some situations. In other situations, retrospective measures of state anxiety tend to be inflated relative to actual measures.

The notion that an individual's optimal precompetitive anxiety level obtained retrospectively is essentially the same as that obtained through actual observation (i.e., identifying precompetitive anxiety level associated with best performance) has been confirmed by Harger and Raglin (1994) and by Inlay, Carda, Stanbrough, Dreiling, and O'Connor (1995). Harger and Raglin concluded that an athlete can accurately recall her precompetitive anxiety two days following competition. Inlay et al. (1995) reported a correlation of .85 between actual best precompetitive anxiety scores and recalled scores after a three-month delay. They observed, however, that the correlation dropped significantly after a seven-month delay.

Once optimal prestart state anxiety is determined, a zone of confidence (confidence interval) is placed around it. The upper and lower boundaries of the ZOF are established by adding and subtracting four points to the optimal prestart state anxiety score. This procedure allows for error in selecting the optimal level of anxiety. Hanin reported that four anxiety points correspond to a .5 standard deviation of observed precontest optimal state anxiety scores. Therefore, a ZOF is defined as an individual's optimal prestart level of state anxiety, plus or minus a population estimate of a .5 standard deviation. It is not known whether the standard deviation would change as a function of nationality, gender, sport, or skill level. If an athlete exhibited an optimal prestart state anxiety level of 60, her ZOF would be 56 to 64. Based on Hanin's theory, it would be expected that best performance would be achieved when state anxiety was within this zone, as opposed to some "moderate" level of state anxiety. By monitoring an athlete's prestart state anxiety, it should be possible to utilize some form of intervention to increase or decrease state anxiety to move it into the ZOF.

CONCEPT & APPLICATION 4.16

Concept In the absence of an actual ideal precompetitive state anxiety score, an estimate may be obtained by asking the athlete to complete a state anxiety inventory relative to how she retrospectively recalls feeling before her best performance.

Application Once the ideal precompetitive anxiety score is identified, a zone of optimal functioning can be easily formed by adding and subtracting .5 standard deviations. In the case of Spielberger's SAI, the zone would range from 4 points below to four points above the ideal score (Hanin, 1980).

Hanin also presented data to suggest that prestart state anxiety can be accurately predicted by the athlete as much as one week in advance. In this case, the athlete is asked to complete the state anxiety inventory (SAI) according to how he thinks he will feel before the start of an important forthcoming competition. Again, if the predicted level of prestart anxiety is outside of the ZOF, then the coach can utilize some form of intervention to assist the athlete in adjusting anxiety as the time-to-competition approaches. If the athlete reports that he expects prestart anxiety to be low, the coach can work on ways to increase state anxiety before the competition begins.

Strong support for the concept of a zone of optimal functioning (ZOF) has been reported by Prapavessis and Grove (1991), Raglin and Turner (1993), and Turner and Raglin (1996). In all three of these investigations, predictions based upon ZOF theory were compared to predictions based upon Morgan's mental health model approach (discussed in chapter 2) or upon inverted-U theory. In each case, the results favored ZOF theory. In the case of the two Raglin and

Turner articles, track and field performance scores associated with state anxiety that fell within a predetermined ZOF were significantly larger than those for which anxiety levels fell outside of the zone. Conversely, performance scores associated with state anxiety that fell within normatively based moderate zone of functioning were not significantly larger than those falling outside of that zone. Other support for the theory comes from Morgan, O'Connor, Spartling, and Pate (1987); Raglin and Morgan (1988); Raglin, Morgan, and Wise (1990); Gould, Tuffy, Hardy, and Lochbaum (1993); and Russell (1996b).

CONCEPT & APPLICATION 4.17

Concept An athlete will perform best if his state anxiety is within a certain zone of optimal functioning.
Application Once an athlete's zone of optimal functioning has been determined (directly or through retrospection), arousal control techniques can be utilized to assist the athlete in achieving the optimal-level prestart state anxiety. Some athletes monitor prestart pulse rate as a means of determining if they are within their ZOF.

Most reported research on zone of optimal functioning theory has been supportive, but not all has. A study reported by Raglin and Morris (1994) showed that collegiate volleyball players tended to perform within their predetermined ZOF when they were playing difficult matches against highly skilled opponents. When they were playing easy matches against less skilled opponents, however, their precompetitive anxiety levels tended not to be in their predetermined ZOF. It is not generally necessary that athletes be in their zones of optimal functioning against lesser competition. They will likely prevail anyway. This explains, however, why it is possible for a weaker team to defeat a stronger team on occasion. If a strong team overlooked a supposedly weak team or failed to take it seriously, it is possible that its players could suffer an unexpected loss before they could appropriately adjust their arousal levels. We will discuss more on this important topic in the next two chapters.

In Hanin's original research on the topic of the zone of optimal functioning, his focus was upon state anxiety and upon forming a ZOF around an optimal level of state anxiety. In recent years, however, he has turned the focus of his research toward *positive* as well as negative (anxiety) affect (Hanin & Syrja, 1995). Rather than using Spielberger's SAI or Marten's CSAI-2, he began using inventories like the Positive and Negative Affect Schedule (PANAS). This change in emphasis was important in the development of the concept of an optimal zone of functioning. An athlete's zone of optimal functioning is not based only on negative affect. It is logically based as well on positive moods, such as self-confidence, vigor, and happiness. Hanin's recent shift to the concept of a positive and negative zone of optimal functioning provides an excellent

Wheelchair athletes strive for peak performance through physical and mental preparation. Courtesy © David Young-Wolf/Photo Edit

introduction to the concept of Flow, or the psychology of optimal experience, as discussed in the following section.

FLOW: THE PSYCHOLOGY OF OPTIMAL EXPERIENCE

Mihaly Csikszentmihalyi (1975, 1990) is credited with being the originator of the Flow construct. The individual most responsible for applying the principles of Flow to sport and exercise is Susan Jackson (1992, 1995, 1996). As defined by Jackson (1995), "**Flow** is a state of optimal experiencing involving total absorption in a task, and creating a state of consciousness where optimal levels of functioning often occur" (p. 138). In his original conceptualization of the Flow construct, Csikszentmihalyi (1990) described Flow as an end in itself, something that is to be enjoyed and appreciated. The key term in the Flow construct is that of the **autotelic experience.** An autotelic experience "refers to a self-contained activity, one that is done not with the expectation of some future benefit, but simply because the doing itself is the reward" (p. 67). When applied to sport and exercise, Flow is not an acronym, but a way of expressing a sense of seemingly effortless movement. The nine defining characteristics of the Flow experience are these (Csikszentmihalyi, 1990):

1. Requirement of a challenge/skill balance.

2. Merging of action and awareness (sense of automaticity and spontaneity).

3. Goals that are clearly defined.

4. Clear, unambiguous feedback.

5. Total concentration on the skill being performed.

6. Sense of being in control without trying to be in control (paradox of control).

7. Loss of self-awareness (becoming one with the activity).

8. Loss of time awareness.

9. Autotelic experience (end result of all of the above).

   The nine defining characteristics of the Flow experience form the basis of an instrument developed by Jackson and Marsh (1996) for measuring Flow. The Flow State Scale (FSS) is composed of 36 items that measure the nine dimensions identified by Csikszentmihalyi. Each item is set to a 5-point Likert scale (1 = strongly disagree to 5 = strongly agree). A sample item on the FSS might be as follows:

My concentration was focused entirely on the task at hand

STRONGLY DISAGREE				*STRONGLY AGREE*
1	2	3	4	5

   It has been tempting for some authors to use the terms "peak experience" or "peak performance" as identical to the Flow experience. Flow is a combination of emotional ecstasy and personal best performance (Kimiecik & Stein, 1992; McInman & Grove, 1991). An athlete may perform a personal best in a track and field event, yet not really consider the total experience as a peak moment. Conversely, one may experience an autotelic experience in sport and not realize a personal best score in terms of performance. In studying the Flow experience, Jackson (1992, 1995) identified factors believed to facilitate Flow, as well as other factors believed to prevent the occurrence of the Flow state. These factors are listed in table 4.3.

   One interesting way to view the Flow experience is as a positive interaction between skill and challenge (Kimiecik & Stein, 1992; Stein, Kimiecik, Daniels & Jackson, 1995). This concept is illustrated in figure 4.14. The Flow experience is most likely to occur when the athlete is highly skilled, yet feels personally challenged by the competition that she faces. If the athlete feels personally

CONCEPT & APPLICATION 4.18

Concept When the conditions are just right, the athlete may enjoy a psychological experience that yields both high performance and personal ecstasy. Flow is an end in itself, something that is to be enjoyed and appreciated. It is sometimes, but not necessarily, associated with peak performance.

Application Conditions necessary for Flow to occur are listed in table 4.3. They include a positive mental attitude, positive affect, attentional focus, perception of being well prepared physically, and a oneness with teammates and/or coach. These are all attributes that an athlete should strive for at all times. If at some time they yield the ecstasy of the Flow experience, this is all the better.

Table 4.3

Factors Believed to Facilitate or to Prevent the Occurrence of the Flow State (Jackson, 1992).

Effect on Flow State	Factor
Facilitate	1. Development of a positive mental attitude. 2. Positive precompetitive affect. 3. Positive competitive affect (during contest). 4. Maintaining appropriate attentional focus. 5. Physical readiness (perception of being prepared). 6. Unity with teammate(s) and/or coach.
Prevent	1. Experiencing physical ptroblems and mistakes. 2. Inability to maintain appropriate attentional focus. 3. Negative mental attitude. 4. Lack of audience response.

Figure 4.14

The relationship between the psychological construct of Flow and the presence of skill and challenge. Adapted from Kimiecik, J. C., and Stein, G. L. (1992). Examining Flow experiences in sport contexts: Conceptual issues and methodological concerns. *Journal of Applied Sport Psychology, 4,* 144–160. Adapted with permission of the publisher.

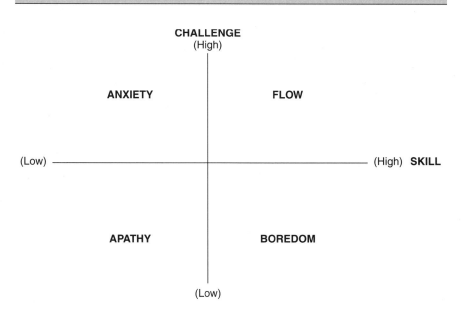

challenged by the competition, yet feels that her skills are not up to the challenge, anxiety is likely to occur (compare with figure 4.4). Apathy is the likely outcome when an individual with a low skill level is confronted with a nonchallenging situation. Finally, boredom will likely ensue when a highly skilled athlete is confronted with a nonchallenging competitive situation.

APTER'S REVERSAL THEORY

Reversal theory, as proposed by Apter (1982), is as much a theory of personality as it is a theory of arousal. Individuals are described as being either **telic** or **paratelic** dominant. Telic-dominant individuals have a goal-directed orientation towards life, while paratelic individuals are fun-loving and have a "here-and-now" orientation. At the same time, however, Apter notes that the telic and paratelic orientations are not enduring traits or personality dispositions. While an individual tends to be dominant in either the telic or the paratelic orientation, each person has the capability to switch back and forth between the two. **Reversal theory** receives its name from this proclivity towards switching back and forth between the two orientations. Apter's concept of reversal theory is described in detail by Apter (1982, 1984), and by Kerr (1985, 1987, 1989).

Reversal theory is described as having characteristics associated with both drive theory and inverted-U theory. In drive theory, the organism seeks to reduce drive (anxiety) by satisfying the craving for such needs as food, water, or sex. Drive reduction has the effect of moving an organism from a state of being anxious to a state of relaxation. In optimum arousal (inverted-U) theory, the organism seeks to overcome boredom by increasing arousal. In this case, an increase in arousal brings on the desirable psychological state of excitement. Combining these two conditions into a single theory (reversal theory) produces a hedonic goal (pleasure seeking) to bring about a situation of relaxation or excitement as opposed to anxiety or boredom. Reversal theory as explained in these terms is illustrated in figure 4.15. As can be observed in this figure, the objective is to increase hedonic tone, not to increase or decrease arousal.

The two curves in figure 4.15 are representative of the two frame-of-mind orientations in reversal theory. The orientation leading from anxiety (unpleasant) to relaxation is labeled the telic mode, while the orientation leading from boredom (unpleasant) to excitement is labeled the paratelic mode. The telic mode is goal-oriented and serious. While in this frame of mind, the individual views increased arousal to be unpleasant and stressful. Conversely, the paratelic mode is activity-oriented and excited with the here-and-now. Increased arousal could be viewed as threatening and stressful in the telic mode and as exciting and exhilarating in the paratelic mode.

Because reversal theory hypothesizes the involuntary switching back and forth between the telic and paratelic orientations, it is referred to as being **metamotivational** as opposed to motivational in nature. Metamotivational modes go in pairs of opposites, with only one pair operating at a time (Kerr, 1985). Three factors interact with each other to bring about a psychological reversal (Apter, 1984). These three factors are (a) contingent events, (b) frustration, and (c) satiation.

An example of a *contingent event* might be as follows. An athlete enters a game situation where the atmosphere is extremely tense and competitive. This is a situation conducive to a telic orientation. Midway through the game, however, her team starts to gain momentum as they score one important point after another. The athlete's mood, along with the moods of her teammates, begins to shift noticeably towards the paratelic mode and away from the telic mode. High levels of arousal and excitement are still present, but the mood has changed, and the emotional environment has shifted from one of high anxiety and tension to one of fun and excitement.

Figure 4.15

The hypothesized relationship between arousal and hedonic tone (pleasure seeking) for the anxiety-avoidance (telic) and the excitement-seeking (paratelic) systems. Adapted from Apter, M. J. (1982), *The experience of motivation: The theory of psychological reversals,* New York: Academic Press.

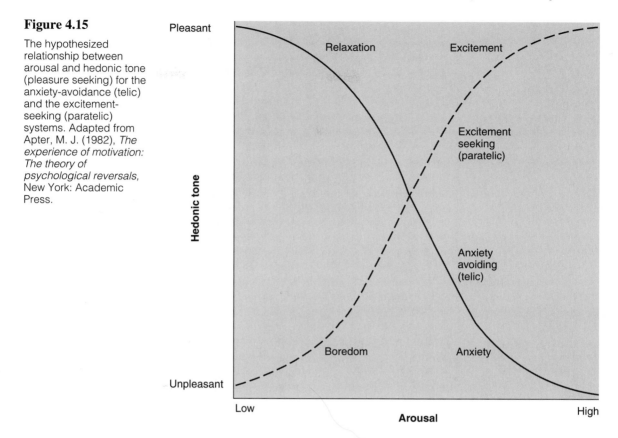

The following describes a famous Olympic incident that could be an example of *frustration* causing a reversal. In the 1972 Munich Olympic Games, members of the U.S.A. men's basketball team leaped and hugged one another with joy (paratelic mode) when they believed they had won the gold medal against the former Soviet Union. This psychological frame of mind quickly changed to the telic mode when they were informed that the game was not over and that 3.0 seconds were being put back on the clock (Smith, 1992).

The third factor that can bring about a change in metamotivational mode is *satiation,* or an innate dynamic force for change. As the period of time an individual spends in one metamotivational mode increases, the probability of a reversal also increases (Kerr, 1993). This situation might occur with a tennis player who has just spent two hours working on refining his backhand drive down the line (telic mode). Taking a water break, he meets some friends who invite him to join in a friendly game of mixed doubles. Partly from satiation and partly from a desire for a change, the tennis player experiences a metamotivational reversal from the telic to the paratelic mode. Suddenly, the tension and singlemindedness of his practice session shifts to a carefree feeling of enjoyment, enthusiasm, and excitement about the game of tennis.

Peak performance in sport often occurs while an athlete experiences a psychological phenomenon called Flow. Courtesy Corel Photo CD/Winter Sports

While psychological reversals are inevitable, a certain dominance or disposition exists to prefer one metamotivational orientation over the other. Preference for one orientation over another is calculated with the Telic Dominance Scale (TDS), a 42-item inventory designed to measure a person's seriousness, inclination to set goals, and tending to avoid arousal (Murgatroyd, Rushton, Apter & Ray, 1978).

The attractiveness of reversal theory is closely associated with its flexibility and dynamic nature. The theory underscores the importance of taking a situation-specific and individualistic approach to studying the relationship between arousal and performance. If an athlete is in the telic mode, increased arousal could result in a state anxiety level that could cause a decrement in performance. Conversely, if an athlete is in the paratelic mode, decreasing arousal through some sort of intervention could actually bring about boredom. Neither of these scenarios is likely to have a facilitative effect upon athletic performance. A great deal of care must be used to determine the appropriate approach to use with an athlete that is suffering from a decrement in athletic performance. From a reversal theory perspective, figure 4.16 illustrates the various options that are available to the athlete who is experiencing either debilitating state anxiety or boredom.

An athlete suffering from debilitating anxiety while in the telic mode has two possible options open to her. The first option is to decrease the level of arousal through a stress management strategy (progressive relaxation). The second option

Figure 4.16

Possible options available to the athlete experiencing high anxiety while in telic mode, or boredom while in paratelic mode. Adapted from Kerr, J. H. (1989). Anxiety, arousal, and sport performance: An application of reversal theory. In D. Hackfort & C. D. Spielberger (Eds.), *Anxiety in Sports: An international perspective* (p. 148), New York: Hemisphere Publishing Corporation.

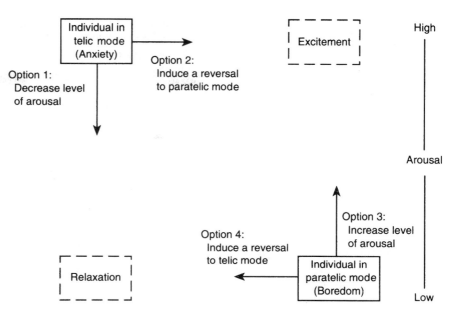

is to induce a reversal to the paratelic mode. If this can be accomplished, the athlete will view the anxiety-provoking situation as exciting and challenging (pleasurable), as opposed to threatening and unpleasant. The psychological reversal can be triggered through a reinterpretation of the unpleasant high arousal (Kerr, 1989). For example, the athlete might engage in some sort of pleasant fantasy that is associated with high arousal (e.g., dunking the basketball).

Similarly, an athlete who is suffering from boredom while in the paratelic state has two options available to her. The first option is to increase the level of arousal to induce a sense of excitement (psyching-up strategy). The second option is to induce a reversal to the telic state. If this can be accomplished, the athlete will view the unpleasant situation as relaxing and tranquil as opposed to boring. For example, the athlete might reflect upon the peacefulness of the moment and imagine she is relaxing in a hot tub.

CONCEPT & APPLICATION 4.19

Concept In addition to arousal control (to be discussed in chapter 5), reversal theory offers a second strategy for dealing with boredom and/or anxiety in sport.

Application Athletes should be instructed in the thought processes necessary to reinterpret the ways in which they respond to high and low arousal. If interpreted differently, the boredom of waiting for the next round of competition could be viewed as relaxing. Additionally, the anxiety associated with worrying about an important competition could be reinterpreted as excitement about a stimulating opportunity.

As shown in figure 4.15, reversal theory posits that athletes seek an increase in hedonic tone as they strive for excellence. The bored athlete strives for more excitement and enthusiasm, and the distressed athlete strives for calm and relaxation. Increased hedonic tone should result in improved athletic performance (Rainey, Amunategui, Agocs & Larick, 1992). Individuals with a strong paratelic orientation should seek involvement in sports that involve excitement and some physical risk (e.g., skiing, surfing, diving); those with a strong telic orientation should pursue safe, low-risk sports associated with relaxation and low arousal (e.g., archery, golf, walking) (Kerr and Svebac 1989). Best performance from an athlete should occur in conditions associated with pleasant moods and in situations in which an athlete's preferred level of arousal is matched by his actual felt level of arousal (Males & Kerr, 1996).

SUMMARY

Anxiety is associated with, but is not the same as, arousal. Arousal is a neutral physiological phenomenon that is associated with both negative (anxiety) and positive (exhilaration) affect, yet not synonymous with either. The neurophysiology of arousal was discussed relative to the autonomic nervous system, specific brain mechanisms, and electrophysiological indicators of arousal and activation. The two divisions of the autonomic nervous system are the sympathetic and parasympathetic. The sympathetic division is responsible for heightened arousal, while the parasympathetic division helps maintain homeostasis. Three brain structures and mechanisms that are of significant importance in arousal are the ascending reticular activating system, the hypothalamus, and the cerebral cortex. Some of the electrophysiological indicators of arousal are electrocortical activity (measured by EEG), heart rate, muscle tension (measured by EMG) and galvanic skin response (GSR).

The relationship between anxiety, arousal, and stress were discussed and explained. Trait anxiety was defined as a personality disposition, and state anxiety as a situation-specific response to a stressor. The five factors triggering state anxiety include ego threat, physical danger, ambiguity, disruption of routine, and social evaluation. Stress can be experienced in four ways: eustress, distress, hyperstress, and hypostress. State anxiety and distress are the same thing. Methods for measuring anxiety were briefly discussed. The multidimensional nature of anxiety was introduced and explained relative to precompetitive cognitive and somatic anxiety. The concept of direction of anxiety was introduced as a corollary to intensity.

The relationship between arousal and athletic performance is represented best by the inverted-U curve. The foundation of inverted-U theory is the classic work of Yerkes and Dodson (1908). Three theories that predict a curvilinear relationship between performance and arousal are cue utilization theory, signal detection theory, and information processing theory. Cue utilization is based on the principle of relevant and irrelevant cues and attentional narrowing. Signal detection theory is based upon the notion of errors of commission and omission and of a subject's response criterion. Information processing theory emphasizes channel capacity and neural activity. Each of the inverted-U theories hypothesizes that an optimal level of arousal is necessary for best performance. Drive theory was discussed in terms of the effects of arousal on learning and performance. In its simplest form, drive theory posits a linear relationship between athletic performance and arousal, or drive.

Four alternatives to inverted-U theory were introduced, explained, and illustrated. Fazey and Hardy's catastrophe model was introduced as a theory of performance and arousal that rejects the inverted-U concept of a smooth quadratic curve. Small increases in somatic anxiety can result in large decrements in performance if cognitive anxiety is sufficiently high. Hanin's zone of optimal functioning theory rejects the inverted-U theory concept that a moderate level of arousal leads to optimum performance. Many athletes perform at their very best at very high or very low levels of state anxiety. Optimal precompetitive state anxiety can be estimated retrospectively.

Flow is a term used to describe the psychology of optimal experience, or the state of mind that an athlete is in when she becomes totally absorbed with the task at hand. Nine identifying characteristics of the Flow experience have been defined, as well as factors that facilitate the occurrence of the Flow state. The Flow experience is measured using the Flow State Scale (FSS).

Apter's reversal theory has characteristics associated with both drive and inverted-U theory. While in a telic frame of mind, the athlete seeks to reduce the level of arousal in order to bring about a state of relaxation. While in a paratelic frame of mind, the athlete seeks to increase arousal in order to increase excitement. The individual's ability to switch back and forth between telic and paratelic modes is referred to as a psychological reversal.

REVIEW QUESTIONS

1. Explain the role that the autonomic nervous system has in arousal and activation. What are the divisions of the autonomic nervous system? What are the different functions of the two divisions of the autonomic nervous system?

2. Identify specific brain structures and mechanisms associated with the onset and control of arousal. How do these structures interact with each other and the environment to bring about general arousal?

3. What are some of the electrophysiological techniques for assessing arousal? Discuss advantages and disadvantages of each.

4. Differentiate between the terms *arousal* and *anxiety*.

5. What is the difference between state and trait anxiety?

6. According to Endler, what are the five factors associated with anxiety? Give examples of each.

7. Define distress and eustress. How do these terms relate to stress and anxiety?

8. Diagram the stress process. Show its interrelationships with trait anxiety, state anxiety, and the perception of imbalance between the objective demand situation and the athlete's response to it.

9. Briefly discuss the measurement of trait and state anxiety.

10. Discuss the multidimensional nature of anxiety relative to the period of time leading up to and preceding the start of a competitive event.

11. Differentiate between direction and intensity when measuring state anxiety. How are the two different dimensions measured? How do they relate to athletic performance?

12. Discuss the research conducted by Yerkes and Dodson (1908) and explain how their findings relate to inverted-U theory.

13. As hypothesized by inverted-U theory, what is the nature of the relationship between arousal and athletic performance?

14. Discuss the concepts of distractibility and optimal arousal relative to inverted-U theory and athletic performance.

15. Explain how cue utilization theory proposes an inverted-U relationship between arousal and performance. How can the theory take into consideration such factors as skill level and complexity of the task?

16. Explain how signal detection theory proposes an inverted-U relationship between arousal and performance. What is a subject's response criterion? How is sensitivity of a subject determined?

17. Discuss the arousal/performance relationship in terms of drive theory.

18. Provide a brief description of Fazey and Hardy's catastrophe model. Show how cognitive anxiety and arousal interact to bring about changes in performance. Compare the model with the inverted-U theory.

19. Provide a brief description of Hanin's zone of optimal functioning (ZOF) theory. In what ways is ZOF similar and dissimilar to inverted-U theory? Is ZOF an alternative or variation of the inverted-U theory?

20. Provide a brief description of Flow, the psychology of optimal experience. In what way is Flow related to Hanin's concept of zone of optimal functioning? In what way is it different? How does Flow relate to the concept of the inverted U?

21. Provide a brief description of Apter's reversal theory. Provide some examples of ways this theory could be useful in explaining human behavior.

GLOSSARY

anxiety A subjective feeling of apprehension and heightened physiological arousal.

arousal Activation of the various organs of the body that are under the control of the autonomic nervous system.

arousal reaction Arousal of the individual through sudden activation of the reticular activating system.

autonomic nervous system Division of the peripheral nervous system responsible for glandular and emotional responses.

autotelic experience A self-contained activity, one that is done as an end in itself. Associated with Flow, the psychology of optimal experience.

catastrophe theory Theory of arousal that predicts that small incremental changes in arousal can result in catastrophic changes in performance.

central nervous system The brain and spinal cord.

cerebral cortex A layer of approximately ten billion neurons on the surface of the brain.

cognitive state anxiety The mental component of state anxiety, causing worry and apprehension.

direction of anxiety The athlete's interpretation of whether the felt level of anxiety (intensity) was debilitative or facilitative relative to performance.

distractibility A condition that occurs with high arousal, in which an athlete's attentional focus moves randomly from cue to cue, resulting in poor performance.

distress Negative stress, or state anxiety.

drive A condition similar to anxiety and arousal, originally conceived in terms of need reduction.

drive theory A complex theory of learning that predicts a linear relationship between drive (arousal) and learning.

electroencephalogram Tracing depicting measurement of the electrical activity of the brain.

eustress The positive or pleasant aspect of stress.

Flow State of optimal experiencing involving total absorption in a task, and creating a state of consciousness where optimal levels of functioning often occur (Jackson, 1995).

hyperstress Situation in which stress exceeds an individual's ability to adapt.

hypostress Denotes a situation which sensory stimulation is too low.

hypothalamus A portion of the brain stem that is involved in the regulation of sleep, wakefulness, and bodily activation.

intensity of anxiety The athlete's perception of the level of felt anxiety he is experiencing.

inverted-U theory Model describing the hypothesized relationship between arousal and performance. The term originates from the shape of the curve that results when this relationship is plotted on a graph.

metamotivational modes In reversal theory, frame-of-mind orientations represented in pairs of opposites, with only one pair operating at a time.

noise In signal detection theory, random firing of the nervous system.

objective demand Environmental situation or stimulus the athlete is in. Whether or not the athlete sees the objective situation as threatening depends upon her subjective evaluation of the situation and the role of trait anxiety in her personality.

optimal arousal The notion that for every skill there exists an optimal level of arousal for maximum performance.

parasympathetic nervous system A branch of the autonomic nervous system that operates to maintain bodily homeostasis (pupil constriction, decrease in heart rate, decrease in respiration).

paratelic orientation Personality orientation towards the "here-and-now" (i.e., fun-loving orientation).

precompetitive anxiety The anxiety of an athlete during the weeks, hours, and minutes leading up to the start of an event.

prestart state anxiety *See* precompetitive anxiety.

reticular formation A diffuse area of the core of the brain responsible for general alerting and activation of the brain.

reversal theory A theory of personality and arousal proposing that an individual's psychological orientation switches back and forth between the telic and the paratelic modes.

signal detection theory Psychophysical method using noise and signal plus noise to determine a person's response bias and sensitivity.

signal plus noise Signal presented against a noise background.

somatic state anxiety Somatic or physiological dimension of state anxiety, causing increased heart rate, increased respiration, clammy hands, stomach butterflies, etc.

Sport Grid Simple method for allowing an athlete to assess his perceived level of arousal along the dimensions of positive/negative affect and intensity (high/low).

state anxiety An emotional state characterized by apprehension, fear, and tension accompanied by physiological arousal.

stress "The nonspecific response of the body to any demand made upon it" (Selye, 1975).

stress process The process by which an objective demand situation results in a state anxiety reaction, if the situation is perceived to be threatening.

sympathetic nervous system A branch of the autonomic nervous system that is responsible for changes in bodily functions associated with arousal (sweating of the hands, increased heart rate, pupil dilation, etc.).

telic orientation A goal-directed personality orientation that is associated with anxiety under conditions of high arousal.

trait anxiety A relatively permanent personality disposition to perceive a wide variety of situations as threatening, and to respond to those situations with increased state anxiety.

Yerkes-Dodson law A principle based on the classic work by Yerkes and Dodson (1908) that predicts an inverted-U relationship between arousal and performance.

zone of optimal functioning In Hanin's theory, the specific prestart level of state anxiety, unique to each athlete, that produces the athlete's best performance.

SUGGESTED READINGS

Apter, M. J. (1984). Reversal theory and personality: A review. *Journal of Research in Personality, 18,* 265–288.

Csikszentmihalyi, M. (1990). *Flow: The psychology of optimal experience.* New York: Harper and Row.

Easterbrook, J. A. (1959). The effect of emotion on cue utilization and the organization of behavior. *Psychological Review, 66,* 183–201.

Endler, N. S. (1978). The interaction model of anxiety: Some possible implications. In D. M. Landers & R. W. Christina (Eds.), *Psychology of motor behavior and sport–1977* (pp. 332–351). Champaign, IL: Human Kinetics.

Fazey, J., & Hardy, L. (1988). *The inverted-U hypothesis: A catastrophe for sport psychology?* British Association of Sports Sciences Monograph No. 1. Leeds: The National Coaching Foundation.

Hanin, Y. L. (1986). State-trait anxiety research on sports in the USSR. In C. D. Spielberger & R. Dias-Gurerrero (Eds.), *Cross-cultural anxiety* (pp. 45–64). Washington, DC: Hemisphere.

Jackson, S. A. (1996). Toward a conceptual understanding of the flow experience in elite athletes. *Research Quarterly for Exercise and Sport, 67,* 76–90.

Jones, G., & Hanton, S. (1996). Interpretation of competitive anxiety symptoms and goal attainment expectancies. *Journal of Sport & Exercise Psychology, 18,* 144–157.

Lacey, J., & Lacey, B. (1958). Verification and extension of the principle of autonomic response-stereotype. *American Journal of Psychology, 71,* 50–73.

Martens, R., Vealey, R. S., & Burton, D. (1990). *Competitive anxiety in sport.* Champaign, IL: Human Kinetics.

Raedeke, T. D., & Stein, G. L. (1994). Felt arousal, thoughts/feelings, and ski performance. *The Sport Psychologist, 8,* 360–375.

Selye, H. (1983). The stress concept: Past, present, and future. In C. L. Cooper (Ed.), *Stress research* (pp. 1–20). New York: John Wiley & Sons.

Sonstroem, R. J., & Bernardo, P. (1982). Intraindividual pregame state anxiety and basketball performance: A re-examination of the inverted-U curve. *Journal of Sport Psychology, 4,* 235–245.

Spielberger, C. D. (1971). Trait-state anxiety and motor behavior. *Journal of Motor Behavior, 3,* 265–279.

Tenenbaum, G. (1984). A note on the measurement and relationships of physiological and psychological components of anxiety. *International Journal of Sport Psychology, 15,* 88–97.

Turner, P. E., & Raglin, J. S. (1996). Variability in precompetition anxiety and performance in college track and field athletes. *Medicine and Science in Sports and Exercise, 28,* 378–385.

Yerkes, R. M., & Dodson, J. D. (1908). The relationship of strength of stimulus to rapidity of habit formation. *Journal of Comparative Neurology and Psychology, 18,* 459–482.

5 AROUSAL ADJUSTMENT STRATEGIES

KEY TERMS

- *anxiety-prone athlete*
- *anxiety/stress spiral*
- *arousal adjustment*
- *arousal energizing strategies*
- *autogenic training*
- *autohypnosis*
- *biofeedback*
- *heterohypnosis*
- *hypnosis*
- *hypnotic induction*
- *hypnotic trance*
- *intervention*

- *mantra*
- *matching hypothesis*
- *meditation*
- *mental device*
- *neutral hypnosis*
- *posthypnotic suggestion*
- *progressive relaxation*
- *psyching up*
- *relaxation response*
- *stress management*
- *transcendental meditation*
- *waking hypnosis*

Controlled arousal and determination often result in optimal performance. Courtesy University of Missouri-Columbia Sports Information

135

In the previous chapter on anxiety and arousal in sport, the case study of a young high school athlete named Ryan was introduced. Recall that Ryan was an extremely gifted multiple-sport athlete who experienced difficulty in dealing with anxiety while competing in track events. Specifically, he would become so anxious prior to sprinting and hurdling events that he literally could not run efficiently. During practices, Ryan experienced little or no tension and anxiety. During three years of high school track, he had never lost a race during practice with teammates.

It was clear that Ryan was going to be a track "drop-out" if some sort of intervention was not provided. Ryan's father talked to a professor of sport psychology at the local college to find out if there was something that could be done to help Ryan. After three weeks of studying Ryan's anxiety response to competition, the sport psychologist concluded that an individualized intervention program could be developed to help him. The program that was recommended was one very similar to autogenic training, described later in this chapter. In this program, Ryan learned what caused his anxiety and how to cope with it when it occurred. Ryan's success at reversing the damaging effects of anxiety did not happen overnight. However, during his senior year he made up for many of his earlier failures by setting a state record in the 200-meter sprint.

In chapter 4, I discussed the concepts of arousal and anxiety in great depth. You are now familiar with both of these terms and aware of several theories that purport to explain the relationship between arousal/anxiety and performance. Too much or too little arousal may result in poor athletic performance. Consequently, the goal for the athlete and the coach is to identify the optimal level of arousal for any particular event.

The purpose of this chapter is to identify strategies to help athletes intervene to alter their existing levels of arousal or anxiety. Perhaps one of the most famous examples of this occurred before the first heavyweight boxing match between Muhammad Ali and Ken Norton in 1973. Norton hired a professional hypnotist to help him with his self-confidence and anxiety. He won the match in a stunning upset, effectively calling attention to hypnosis as an intervention strategy.

Other famous athletes who have effectively used arousal control strategies include Jimmy Connors and Chris Evert in tennis, Jack Nicklaus in golf, Nolan Ryan in baseball, and Karl Malone in basketball. A number of collegiate and professional sports teams have utilized the services of trained sport psychologists to help athletes control arousal and prepare mentally for competition. A few examples include Dan Smith with the Chicago White Sox (baseball), Robert Rotella with the University of Virginia (basketball), Chris Carr with Ball State and Washington State Universities (general), Linda Bunker with women's professional golf, and Dan Gould with Olympic wrestlers.

In this chapter, the terms **arousal adjustment** and **intervention** will be used to refer to various strategies for altering existing levels of anxiety and arousal. Other authors have chosen to use the term **stress management** to refer to the same thing (Zaichkowsky & Sime, 1982). The important point to remember is

Figure 5.1

The effects of a pep talk on the activation levels of four different athletes.

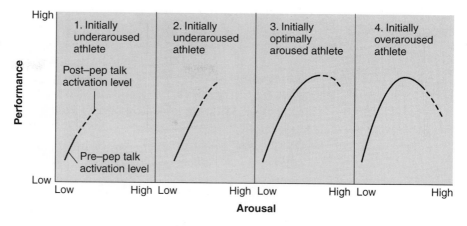

that certain strategies are available to the athlete to change the existing level of arousal in the body. A reduction in physiological arousal often results in a parallel reduction in anxiety and tension. Muscular tension is one of the factors that often accompanies cognitive and somatic anxiety. Tension is not synonymous with anxiety, but it is a component part of it. Tension specifically refers to the tightness that we feel in certain muscle groups as a result of excessive worry and anxiety.

Coaches have been looking to the sport psychologist to learn how to maintain optimal levels of arousal in athletes. This is a most promising development, since many coaches have improperly prepared their athletes for competition. The typical approach has been to "psych up" the athlete through various kinds of pep talks and activation techniques. There is, of course, a proper time to get athletes excited and aroused, but often these techniques are applied at the wrong time. It is commonplace, for example, to see high school volleyball coaches leading their players in cheering and psyching-up sessions immediately before a match. Generally, these athletes have only an intermediate level of skill, and the extra arousal serves only to induce unforced errors. This problem is illustrated in figure 5.1. Each athlete in this figure begins with a different initial level of arousal. Increasing arousal affects each athlete differently. In most cases, intervention procedures are best applied on an individual basis; each athlete should be treated differently. Some will need a pep talk, but others may need an entirely different form of intervention.

As can be observed in figure 5.1, using a pep talk to increase the arousal level of four different athletes has interesting ramifications. Only in situations 1 and 2 did the pep talk have the desired effect. In situation 3, the athlete was already at an optimal level of activation, and it was destroyed by the coach's pep talk. In situation 4, the athlete was overactivated to begin with; the intervention was totally inappropriate. How many coaches overactivate their athletes by their pregame locker room pep talks? It is also important to recall the important lesson learned from our earlier discussion on catastrophe theory (chapter 4).

A basketball team demonstrates the exhilaration and thrill of victory. Courtesy Ball State University Sports Information

When an athlete has a high level of cognitive state anxiety, it is possible that even a small increase in physiological arousal could result in a large catastrophic decrement in performance.

It was reported a few years ago (McCallum, 1994) that the Milwaukee Brewers professional baseball team brought in a California motivational group called Radical Reality to "motivate" its players. During one of the presentations, one of the Radicals ripped a phone book in two with his bare hands. The next day, one of the team's pitchers tried to duplicate the phone book stunt and dislocated his left shoulder. The rookie right-hander was scratched from his next scheduled pitching appearance and reassigned to a minor league team. This example of misdirected "psyching up" underscores the danger of undifferentiated attempts to raise or lower the arousal level of athletes.

Indiscriminate use of intervention strategies to control anxiety and arousal has prompted sport psychologists to propose a closer match between a debilitating symptom and its cure. This is the **matching hypothesis,** which holds that interventions matched to anxiety symptoms will be more effective in reducing debilitating anxiety (Maynard & Cotton, 1993; Maynard, Hemmings & Warwick-Evans, 1995; Maynard, Smith & Warwick-Evans, 1995). Athletes who perceive high levels of cognitive anxiety to be counterproductive to high performance should be instructed on ways to control their thoughts. Conversely, athletes who perceive high levels of somatic anxiety to be counterproductive to high performance should be instructed in techniques to relax and reduce their physiological arousal. Studies have shown, for example, that appropriate and planned reductions in negative mood can result in increased running economy in runners (Crews, 1992).

CONCEPT & APPLICATION 5.1

Concept Group activation strategies such as pep talks may help some athletes reach an optimal level of arousal, but may cause others to become overaroused.

Application Indiscriminate use of activation procedures to psych up athletic teams should be avoided. Instead, help each athlete to find her own optimal arousal level.

This chapter contains two major sections. Both relate directly to arousal control. The first deals with relaxation procedures (including hypnosis) that are designed to lower and control physiological arousal, anxiety, and muscular tension. Hypnosis is discussed in this chapter because of its similarity to relaxation procedures such as autogenic training and meditation. Section two deals with intervention strategies used to increase physiological arousal in the athlete.

Topics such as imagery, visual-motor behavior rehearsal, goal setting, and psychological skills training are not treated in this chapter, but are addressed in the next chapter, on cognitive-behavioral intervention strategies. In most cases, arousal control is viewed as a precursor to imagery, visual-motor behavior rehearsal, and other cognitive intervention programs.

RELAXATION PROCEDURES

I think a lot of it has to do with me pressing. It's in my head. I'm trying harder, and the harder I try, the worse it goes. I've just got to try and relax. But the more I miss, the harder it is to relax, so it's just a vicious circle.

Jeff Jaeger
Place kicker, Cleveland Browns, 1987

While some athletes may suffer from low levels of arousal, the more difficult problems occur with athletes who experience excessively high levels of anxiety and tension. For these athletes, any strategy calculated to heighten arousal can only cause greater anxiety and tension. Typically, what happens is that an initial increase in anxiety leads to a decrease in performance. This decrease in performance itself results in even greater anxiety, resulting in the **anxiety/stress spiral.** There is only one way out of this spiral, and that is to reverse the process by reducing the anxiety and tension. *Relaxation procedures* can effectively reduce tension and anxiety associated with sport. In this section, we will discuss some of them.

Four popular relaxation procedures can be adequately categorized under the broad heading of relaxation. These are (1) progressive relaxation, (2) autogenic training, (3) meditation, and (4) biofeedback. Each procedure is unique but they all yield essentially the same physiological result. That is, they all result in the **relaxation response.** The relaxation response consists of physiological changes that are opposite to the "fight or flight" response of the sympathetic nervous system. Specifically, procedures such as progressive relaxation, autogenic training, and meditation result in decreases in oxygen consumption, heart rate, respiration, and skeletal muscle activity, while they increase skin resistance and alpha brain waves (Benson, Beary & Carol, 1974).

Benson et al. (1974) explained that four different factors are necessary for eliciting the relaxation response. Each of these factors is present to some degree in the specific relaxation techniques that we will discuss. These four elements or factors are (1) a **mental device,** (2) a passive attitude, (3) decreased muscle tone, and (4) a quiet environment. The mental device is generally some sort of word, phrase, object, or process used to shift attention inward.

CONCEPT & APPLICATION 5.2

Concept An important part of any relaxation procedure is to focus attention on a mental device.

Application Two mental devices are highly recommended for the athlete. The first is to take a deep breath and exhale slowly, and the second is the use of a *mantra,* or key word or phrase. Athletes can focus on the key phrase and slow air release as they relax.

Before discussing specific relaxation procedures, it is essential that the issue of *need* be addressed. Except in a general way, athletes who are *not* overly aroused may not benefit from relaxation intervention. In fact, the danger exists that an athlete who is "misdiagnosed" by his coach as tense and anxious may become drowsy and broadly focused as a result of arousal reduction. This problem is identified because coaches are inaccurate estimators of an athlete's competitive state and trait anxiety (Hanson & Gould, 1988). Using two well-known sport-specific anxiety inventories, coaches were asked to complete the inventories as they thought an athlete would. The results showed that a large discrepancy exists between a coach's perception and an athlete's perception of the athlete's anxiety level. A coach should make sure that an athlete is actually suffering from anxiety and tension before applying an arousal adjustment intervention.

CONCEPT & APPLICATION 5.3

Concept It is difficult for a coach to accurately estimate an athlete's level of competitive state anxiety.

Application If a coach believes that an athlete is suffering a decrement in performance due to elevated competitive state anxiety, she should consider recommending an arousal control intervention. However, before actually referring the athlete for treatment, the coach should make sure that she has not misdiagnosed the athlete. This can be accomplished through the administration of a state anxiety inventory, discussed in the previous chapter.

PROGRESSIVE RELAXATION

Modern progressive relaxation techniques are all variations of those outlined by Edmond Jacobson (1929, 1938). Jacobson began his work with progressive relaxation in the early part of the twentieth century. It was Jacobson's basic thesis that it is impossible to be nervous or tense in any part of the body where the muscles are completely relaxed. In addition, Jacobson believed that nervousness and tenseness of involuntary muscles and organs could be reduced if the associated skeletal muscles were relaxed. According to Jacobson, an anxious mind cannot exist in a relaxed body.

Jacobson's **progressive relaxation** procedure requires that subjects lie on their backs with their arms to the side. Occasionally a sitting posture in a comfortable chair is recommended. In either case, the room should be fairly quiet and arms and legs should not be crossed, to avoid unnecessary stimulation. While the goal of any progressive relaxation program is to relax the entire body in a matter of minutes, it is essential that in the beginning the subject practice the technique for at least one hour every day. Once the relaxation procedure is well learned, the relaxation response can be achieved in a few minutes.

Jacobson's method calls for the subject to tense a muscle before relaxing it. The tensing helps the subject recognize the difference between tension and relaxation. Once the subject can do this, he should be able to relax a limb completely without tensing it first. Jacobson warns that only the first few minutes of any relaxation session should be devoted to muscle tensing. The remaining time should be devoted to gaining complete relaxation. For a muscle to be considered relaxed, it must be completely absent of any contractions and must be limp and motionless.

Jacobson's full progressive relaxation procedure involves systematically tensing and relaxing specific muscle groups in a predetermined order. Relaxation begins with the muscles of the left arm and proceeds to those of the right arm, left and right legs, abdomen, back, and chest and shoulders, concluding with the neck and face muscles. The full training procedure lasts many months. In the beginning stages, an entire session should be devoted to the total relaxation of a single muscle group. While it is unrealistic to expect an athlete to devote this much time to learning to relax, Jacobson's point is well taken. A well-developed relaxation training program requires a great deal of practice in the beginning. It is unrealistic to expect an athlete to elicit the relaxation response at will after only one or two 15-minute practice sessions. However, after several months of practice and training, it should be possible to evoke the relaxation response in a matter of seconds (Nideffer, 1981).

Abbreviated versions of Jacobson's full forty-session procedure have been proposed (Bernstein & Borkovec, 1973; Greenberg, 1990). A review by Carlson and Hoyle (1993) provided evidence that abbreviated progressive relaxation training procedures are effective in reducing anxiety, tension, and stress. Numerous variations of Jacobson's original progressive relaxation procedure have proven to be effective (Greenberg, 1990). For example, it is not necessary that the procedure always start with the left arm. Greenberg suggests that in some cases a muscle contraction could be best accomplished by applying resistance to an immovable object.

The ultimate goal of any relaxation training program is to evoke the relaxation response to counter stress in a specific situation. For example, a professional golfer does not have 30 minutes to relax prior to a $15,000 putt. The golfer must be able to accomplish this while waiting to putt, a skill that takes many hours of practice to master.

Research has clearly shown that progressive relaxation procedures are effective in eliciting the relaxation response. Additionally, numerous investigations have shown that when used in conjunction with other cognitive or arousal control interventions, it is associated with increased sports performance (Greenspan & Feltz, 1989; Onestak, 1991; Neiss, 1988). Greenspan and Feltz (1989) critically reviewed nine investigations in which forms of relaxation intervention were involved. The majority of the studies showed that increased performance was associated with arousal control in combination with some other cognitive technique. Few studies, however, have shown that progressive relaxation procedures alone effectively enhance performance. For example, Wrisberg and Anshel (1989) showed that relaxation used in conjunction with imagery was effective in enhancing the basketball shooting performance of young boys. Neither imagery nor relaxation training alone was effective in enhancing shooting performance. In conjunction with adequate warning, muscle relaxation training is effective in enhancing an athlete's tolerance to pain (Broucek, Bartholomew, Landers & Linder, 1993).

CONCEPT & APPLICATION 5.4

Concept Learning how to relax the muscles of the body is a foundation skill for all stress management and intervention strategies.

Application As a first step in learning how to control anxiety and stress, the athlete must become proficient at relaxing the mind and the body.

AUTOGENIC TRAINING

Autogenic training and progressive relaxation both elicit the relaxation response. Whereas progressive relaxation relies upon dynamic contracting and relaxing of muscles, **autogenic training** relies upon feelings associated with the limbs and muscles of the body. Autogenic training is very similar to autohypnosis, and is based upon early research with hypnosis. The procedure was first developed by the German psychiatrist Johannes Schultz (Schultz & Luthe, 1959). In working with hypnotized patients, Schultz noted that they invariably reported two bodily sensations associated with the relaxation response. These two sensations were heaviness in the limbs and a feeling of general warmth in the body, arms, and legs. In its simplest form, autogenic training consists of a series of mental exercises designed to bring about these two bodily states. Limbs feel heavy because of a total lack of muscle tension, and the body feels warm due to dilation of blood vessels (a parasympathetic nervous system response) (Greenberg, 1990).

Various authors have suggested different exercises and self-statements to bring about the relaxation response using autogenic training (Davis, Eshelman & McKay, 1988; Greenberg, 1990; Vanek & Cratty, 1970). Essentially, autogenic training is composed of three component parts that are often intermingled. The first and most important part is the six initial steps designed to suggest to the mind a feeling of warmth in the body and heaviness in the limbs. These six self-statement steps are as follows:

1. Heaviness in the arms and legs (beginning with the dominant arm or leg).

2. Warmth in the arms and the legs (again, beginning with the dominant arm or leg).

3. Warmth in the chest and a perception of reduced heart rate.

4. Calm and relaxed breathing.

5. Warmth in the solar plexus area.

6. Sensation of coolness on the forehead.

The second component part of autogenic training involves the use of imagery. In this step, the subject is encouraged to visualize images of relaxing scenes while at the same time focusing upon feelings of warmth and heaviness in the arms and legs. The third component of autogenic training involves the use of *specific themes* (Davis et al., 1988) to assist in bringing about the relaxation response. One particularly effective specific theme is the use of self-statements to suggest to the mind that the body is indeed relaxed.

As with progressive relaxation, research has clearly shown that when used properly, autogenic training is effective in bringing about the relaxation response (Benson et al., 1974). Autogenic training requires several months and a great deal of practice to master. Once mastered, it can be utilized to bring about the relaxation response in a matter of minutes. Whereas the relaxation benefits of this technique are well documented, very little evidence exists to suggest that autogenic training by itself enhances athletic performance. Vanek and Cratty (1970) and Spigolon and Annalisa (1985) provide anecdotal evidence to suggest that autogenic training is related to improved athletic performance.

Various authors have outlined autogenic training and relaxation programs that can be adopted by the athlete (Harris & Harris, 1984; Nideffer, 1985; Orlick, 1986). In addition, numerous relaxation and autogenic training tapes can be commercially purchased or developed (Rotella, Malone & Ojala, 1985). Table 5.1 includes a series of instructions and statements that can be used for teaching athletes to relax using autogenic training. Using this list and others, the athlete could develop and record her own autogenic training tape.

MEDITATION

Meditation, as a form of relaxation, is tied directly to the concepts of selective attention discussed in chapter 3. In practicing **meditation,** the individual attempts to uncritically focus his attention on a single thought, sound, or object. Meditation will result in the relaxation response if practiced in a quiet environment that is associated with a passive attitude and decreased muscle tone (Benson et al., 1974).

The practice of meditation as a form of relaxation and thought control has its origin in Eastern cultures more than four thousand years ago. The individual most responsible for exporting meditation to the Western cultures was Maharishi Mahesh Yogi of India. Referred to as **transcendental meditation,** Maharishi Mahesh Yogi's brand of meditation has been widely accepted in the United States and throughout the world. Other forms of Eastern culture meditation practices include Chakra yoga, Rinzai Zen, Mudra yoga, Sufism, Zen meditation, and Soto Zen (Greenberg, 1990). The most common *mental device* used in transcendental meditation is the silent repetition of a **mantra.** The mantra is a simple sound selected by the instructor as a mental concentration

Table 5.1

Suggested Instructions and Statements That May Be Included in an Autogenic Training Presentation.

1. Locate a quiet room or environment where you will not be disturbed.
2. Find a comfortable area where you can sit or lie down on your back.
3. Close your eyes and put away thoughts of the outside world.
4. Begin by practicing some deep breathing to help you to relax.
5. Slowly inhale, exhale, inhale, exhale, inhale, exhale.
6. Each time you exhale, *feel* the tension being expelled from your body.
7. Now that you are feeling relaxed and your breathing has stabilized, begin suggesting to yourself that your limbs are beginning to feel heavy.
8. "My right arm feels heavy," "my left arm feels heavy," "both of my arms feel heavy," "my right leg feels heavy," "my left leg feels heavy," "both of my legs feel heavy," "my arms and legs feel heavy."
9. "My right arm feels warm," "my left arm feels warm," "both of my arms feel warm," "my right leg feels warm," "my left leg feels warm," "both of my legs feel warm," "my arms and legs feel warm."
10. "My chest area feels warm and my heartbeat feels slow and regular."
11. Focus for a few minutes upon your heart rate, while at the same time repeating to yourself that your heartbeat feels slow and regular.
12. Focus for a few minutes upon your breathing, while at the same time repeating to yourself that your respiration feels calm and relaxed.
13. Repeat several times: "My stomach area feels warm."
14. Repeat several times: "My forehead feels cool."
15. While experiencing feelings of warmth and heaviness in your limbs, warmth in your solar plexus and coolness in your forehead, imagine to yourself that you are on a warm sandy beach enjoying a cool lemonade while watching the waves flow in and out.
16. While enjoying this relaxing visual image (or some other one), repeat relaxing statements to yourself.
17. "I feel quiet."
18. "I feel warm and relaxed."
19. "My mind is at ease."

device. One such sound, "om" or "ahhom," has been popular (Nideffer, 1976a). Other mental devices that have been used in meditation include the *mandala* (a geometrical figure), *nadam* (imagined sounds), and *pranayama* (breathing).

In practice, the subject sits in a comfortable position with eyes closed. The subject concentrates on deep breathing while at the same time repeating the mantra silently. Reportedly, the sound of the mantra soon disappears as the mind experiences more subtle thought levels and finally arrives at the source of the thought. While most Oriental approaches teach a sitting meditation position, both Zen and transcendental meditation emphasize that standing or sitting are acceptable (Layman, 1980). Davis et al. (1988) and Greenberg (1990) offer excellent ideas for enhancing and facilitating the meditation experience. Similar to transcendental meditation, Tai Chi is a moving form of meditation which originated in China. The stress reduction effects of Tai Chi are comparable to those received from moderate physical exercise (Jin, 1992).

Football offensive linemen benefit from arousal adjustment skills. Courtesy University of Missouri-Columbia Sports Information

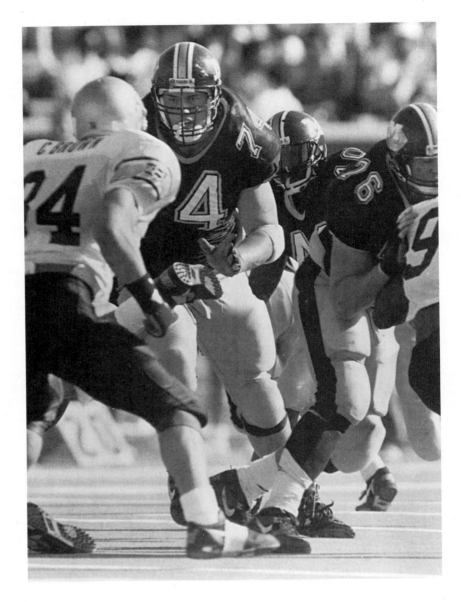

CONCEPT & APPLICATION 5.5

Concept Meditation, if properly used, can result in the relaxation response and offers an excellent vehicle for practicing and refining selective attention skills.

Application Meditation offers the individual sport athlete one of the best tools for relaxing and learning to control attention in preparation for athletic competition. Sporting events such as diving, gymnastics, and field events (track and field) could effectively utilize meditation as means to prepare for the next dive, routine, or toss.

While it is clear that the various forms of meditation can reduce anxiety and tension by evoking the relaxation response, it is not clear whether its practice has a facilitative effect on athletic performance. Like the effects of other forms of relaxation, the effects of meditation upon athletic performance are likely to be indirect. Meditation has a direct effect on reducing anxiety, tension, and stress, which in turn should have a facilitative effect on the performance of the anxiety-prone athlete. Attempts to link meditation training directly with improved athletic performance have met with mixed success. Meditation seems to be beneficial for performing gross motor skills such as the 50-meter dash, agility tasks, standing broad jump, and coordination tasks (Reddy, Bai, and Rao, 1976). But it seems to be of little facilitative value for performing fine motor tasks such as the rotary pursuit, mirror tracing, or pistol shooting (Hall & Hardy, 1991; Williams, 1978; Williams & Herbert, 1976; Williams, Lodge & Reddish, 1977; Williams & Vickerman, 1976).

BIOFEEDBACK

It has been demonstrated that humans can voluntarily control functions of the autonomic nervous system. Research on animals by DiCara (1970) and on humans by Benson et al. (1974) has verified this. **Biofeedback** is a relatively modern technique that is based upon this principle (Davis et al., 1988; Greenberg, 1990).

Biofeedback training uses instruments to help people control responses of the autonomic nervous system. For example, a subject monitors an auditory signal of her own heart rate and experiments with different thoughts, feelings, and sensations to slow the heart rate. Once the subject learns to recognize the feelings associated with the reduction of heart rate, the instrument is removed and the subject tries to control the heart rate without it. This is the goal of the biofeedback therapist. People suffering from chronic anxiety or illnesses caused by anxiety can often benefit from biofeedback training, because when they learn to reduce functions of the sympathetic nervous system, they are indirectly learning to reduce anxiety and tension (Brown, 1977; Danskin & Crow, 1981). Biofeedback is essentially the same as progressive relaxation, autogenic training, and meditation. Using the latter three techniques, the subject relaxes; this lowers arousal and decreases the activity of the sympathetic nervous system. With biofeedback, the subject begins by lowering certain physiological measures with the help of an instrument. This decreases arousal and increases relaxation.

Instrumentation

Theoretically, biofeedback can be very useful to athletes who suffer from excessive anxiety and arousal. If athletes could be trained to control their physiological responses in the laboratory, they should be able to transfer this ability onto the athletic field. The main drawback to biofeedback in athletics is expense. The cost of purchasing a machine for measuring heart rate, EEG, EMG, or GSR changes is out of reach for the average school's athletic budget. However,

Figure 5.2

Skin temperature can be monitored with a cardboard-backed thermometer. From *Biofeedback: An introduction and guide* by David Danskin and Mark Crow. Reprinted by permission of Mayfield Publishing Company. Copyright © 1981 by Mayfield Publishing Company.

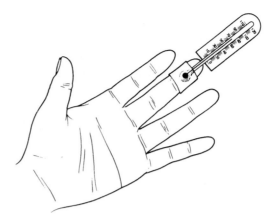

not all biofeedback measurement techniques are expensive, and many are still in the experimental stages. Some of the basic measurement techniques used in biofeedback training are as follows (Danskin & Crow, 1981; Schwartz, 1987).

Skin Temperature The most commonly used and least expensive form of biofeedback is skin temperature. When an athlete becomes highly aroused, additional blood is pumped to the vital organs. Part of this additional blood supply comes from the peripheral blood vessels, leaving the hands feeling cold and clammy. Thus, the effect of stress is to decrease the skin temperature of the extremities. Subjects can monitor skin temperature to discover what kinds of responses, thoughts, and autogenic phrases are most effective in increasing it. Typically, subjects are trained to use progressive relaxation techniques and autogenic phrases to assist them in the biofeedback process. Although sophisticated instruments are available, a simple and inexpensive cardboard-backed thermometer can be used to monitor skin temperature. The cardboard is cut off just above the bulb and the thermometer is taped to the finger, as illustrated in figure 5.2.

Electromyography Another very popular biofeedback technique employs the use of an electromyographic feedback instrument (EMG). Electrodes are attached to a particular group of muscles in the arm or forehead, and the subject tries to reduce muscular tension by using auditory or visual cues of muscle electrical activity. Auditory cues typically come through earphones in the form of clicks. Visual cues come through an oscilloscope that the subject watches.

Electroencephalogram A third major instrument used for biofeedback is the electroencephalogram (EEG). Use of the EEG is commonly called brainwave training. Tiny electrical impulses from billions of brain cells can be detected by electrodes placed on the scalp and connected to an EEG. Four basic types of brain waves are associated with EEG recordings. Beta waves predominate during periods of excitement and high arousal. Alpha waves predominate when the subject relaxes and puts his mind "in neutral." It is the alpha waves that the subject tries to produce. The other two types are theta waves, which predominate during drowsiness, and delta waves, which are associated with deep sleep (Fisher, 1976).

Other Methods While skin temperature, EMG, and EEG are the most common methods used in biofeedback training, several others are used to a lesser degree. These are the galvanic skin response (GSR), heart rate, and blood pressure. Other methods of biofeedback training techniques are still in the experimental stages. One is the use of a stethoscope to monitor heart rate. Still others involve monitoring of respiration rate, vapor pressure from the skin, stomach acidity, sphincter constriction, and blood chemistry.

Biofeedback and Performance

In a laboratory setting, the athlete learns to control the autonomic nervous system. The feelings and experiences associated with learning how to reduce sympathetic nervous system responses in the laboratory are then transferred to the athletic environment. In some cases, biofeedback may be practiced in the athletic environment. For example, Costa, Bonaccorsi, and Scrimali (1984) reported the use of biofeedback training with team handball athletes to reduce precompetitive anxiety.

As observed by Wenz and Strong (1980), the difference between success and failure of two equally matched athletes often depends on an individual's ability to cope with the perceived stress of competition. Biofeedback provides a way for athletes to determine their levels of physiological arousal and to learn how to make conscious changes calculated to reduce anxiety and improve performance. A number of scientific investigations have been conducted to determine the effect of biofeedback on athletic performance. Zaichkowsky and Fuchs (1988) reviewed 42 studies that examined the effect of biofeedback training on sports and athletic performance. Of these 42 studies, 83 percent found biofeedback training to be successful in facilitating sport and athletic performance, as well as beneficial to the athlete's well-being. More recently, Petruzzello, Landers, and Zalazar (1991), Boutcher and Zinsser (1990), and Blumenstein, Bar-Eli, and Tenenbaum (1995) have reported that biofeedback training is highly effective in eliciting the relaxation response and moderately effective in facilitating improved performance in athletes.

CONCEPT & APPLICATION 5.6

Concept Biofeedback is an effective and powerful tool for reducing the debilitating effects of anxiety and stress.

Application If an athlete cannot control anxiety and stress using progressive relaxation, autogenic training, or meditation, then biofeedback training should be attempted. To begin feedback training, it may be necessary to identify a professional therapist. Equipment necessary for biofeedback training may not be readily available to the athlete or coach.

CONCEPT & APPLICATION 5.7

Concept As evidenced by a review by Zaichkowsky and Fuchs (1988), biofeedback training is effective in facilitating athletic performance.

Application The use of biofeedback equipment for learning how to monitor and manipulate physiological arousal as a means of controlling and eliminating debilitating negative affect has proven to be very effective. If an athlete's performance is negatively influenced by inappropriate high (or low) levels of arousal, then biofeedback training can help. The availability of biofeedback equipment and trained clinicians should be investigated.

HYPNOSIS

Of all the arousal adjustment strategies, hypnosis is the least understood. Yet a close analysis reveals that in many important ways hypnosis (especially self-hypnosis) is identical to autogenic training and meditation. This is especially true during the induction phase of hypnosis. The process of inducing the hypnotic trance results in the relaxation response, with accompanying reductions in oxygen consumption, respiration rate, and heart rate (Benson et al., 1974). These are the very same physiological changes that take place with the application of progressive relaxation, autogenic training, and meditation. Once an individual is hypnotized, however, and asked to perform some act (waking hypnosis), then certain physiological differences may emerge. For example, if while hypnotized the subject were asked to imagine that a raging tiger was approaching, the person's heart rate and respiration rate would expectantly go up, not down.

A case study in which hypnosis was used to help an amateur boxer was documented by Heyman (1987). In this chronology, a single-case experimental design was presented in which hypnosis was systematically used as an intervention strategy. The athlete was described as suffering a performance decrement due to anxiety caused by crowd noise. As a result of the controlled and professionally applied use of hypnosis, the athlete was able to show some improvement. While there may be some potential risks associated with the indiscriminate use of hypnosis by an untrained therapist (Morgan & Brown, 1983), most concerns about hypnosis are unfounded. It is probably fair to say that hypnosis is more clouded by myths and misconceptions than any other form of psychological intervention (Clarke & Jackson, 1983).

The following discussion should demystify hypnosis to some degree and explain its relationship to sport performance. Our discussion is divided into four subsections: (1) a definition of hypnosis, (2) obtaining the hypnotic trance, (3) self-hypnosis, and (4) the effect of hypnosis on athletic performance.

Hypnosis Defined

Ulett and Peterson (1965) define **hypnosis** as the uncritical acceptance of a suggestion. This is a definition that almost all psychologists can agree upon,

The batter will have to be mentally and physically focused to hit this pitch. Courtesy University of Missouri-Columbia Sports Information

since it does little to explain what causes hypnosis or how it differs from the waking state. Four events occur when a subject is hypnotized. First, the subject elicits the relaxation response and becomes drowsy and lethargic. Second, the subject manifests responsiveness to suggestions. Third, the subject reports changes in body awareness and feeling. Finally, the subject knows that he or she is hypnotized (Barber, Spanos & Chaves, 1974).

There are at least two theoretical explanations for the phenomenon of hypnotism. (Barber et al., 1974). The first represents the hypnotic trance viewpoint, while the second represents the cognitive-behavioral viewpoint. The traditional or hypnotic trance viewpoint is that the hypnotized subject is in an altered state, or hypnotic trance. The cognitive-behavioral viewpoint rejects the notion of a trance and simply bases the hypnotic phenomenon on the personality of the subject. That is, subjects carry out hypnotic behaviors because they have positive attitudes, motivations, and expectations that lead to a willingness to think and imagine using the themes suggested by the hypnotist. Since only about 16 percent of subjects who go through the hypnotic induction procedure can reach a deep trance (Edmonston, 1981), the cognitive-behavioral viewpoint is certainly plausible. The student is referred to Kihlstrom (1985) and Onestak (1991) for additional discussion on theoretical explanations for hypnosis.

The acceptance of Barber's cognitive-behavioral viewpoint certainly would tend to demystify hypnosis. However, by itself it may be too simplistic an explanation. Regardless of which position one takes, the conclusion is the same: A subject is extremely responsive to suggestions, more responsive than he was during the waking state.

Achieving the Hypnotic Trance

Five phases are associated with inducing the **hypnotic trance** in a subject. They are preparation of the subject, the induction process, the hypnotic phase, waking up, and the posthypnotic phase.

When subjects are prepared for hypnotism, they must be relieved of any fears and apprehensions they have about hypnotism. Some myths may need to be exposed. For example, subjects may be under the impression that they will lose control, that they will be unaware of their surroundings, or that they will lose consciousness. They must have complete trust in the hypnotist and must want to be hypnotized. They also must be told that they will remain in control at all times and will be able to come out of the hypnotic trance if they want to.

It is during the **hypnotic induction** phase that the hypnotist actually hypnotizes the subject. There are many induction techniques. The best ones are associated with relaxation, attentional focus, and imagery. In fact, the steps involved in eliciting the relaxation response using these techniques are essentially identical to those in hypnosis. The only difference is that the word *hypnosis* is never used in eliciting the relaxation response. It should also be pointed out that in terms of physiological responses, hypnotic induction is identical to the relaxation responses associated with progressive relaxation, transcendental meditation, and autogenic training. Coleman (1976) verified this in a study in which he compared the physiological responses associated with hypnotic induction and relaxation procedures.

Generally, induction procedures are fairly standard. They are typically composed of a series of suggestions aimed at eliciting the subject's cooperation and directing his attention to thoughts and feelings about being relaxed and peaceful. The selection of an induction technique is generally based on the hypnotist's comfort with it, or her belief that the subject's attentional style or personality is compatible with it. Some of the more common techniques involve fixation on an object, monotonous suggestions ("you feel sleepy"), and imagery. Regardless of which technique is used, the effect is the same. The subject becomes very lethargic, experiences the relaxation response, and becomes very susceptible to suggestions. The hypnotist can use a number of techniques to make the subject become more responsive to hypnotism. Most of these are associated with relaxing the subject and gaining his confidence. Others include using the word *hypnotism* to define the situation and the manner in which suggestions are given. For example, a good time to suggest to the subject that he is becoming tired is when the hypnotist observes that the subject's eyelids are drooping. The hypnotist must also avoid making suggestions that the subject may fail.

Individuals who are highly hypnotizable exhibit a number of common characteristics (Masters, 1992; Taylor, Horevitz & Balague, 1993). As a group, they exhibit highly developed dissociative abilities. Masters (1992) hypothesized that marathoners are more susceptible to hypnosis than a normative sample. Indeed, 50 percent of his sample of 48 marathon runners scored in the high range of susceptibility. High hypnotizable individuals also enjoy vividness of imagination, and are capable of becoming deeply involved in an experience.

Once the hypnotic state has been induced, the subject is in **neutral hypnosis.** In this state, physiological responses are identical to those of the relaxation response. The hypnotized subject is generally asked to respond, either in imagination or physically, to suggestions of the hypnotist. Typically, these suggestions are alerting and arousing, and bring about the "alert" trance, or **waking hypnosis** (Edmonston, 1981). If subjects are asked to carry out suggestions while in a trance, they are doing so in the state of waking hypnosis. Subjects may, of course, be given suggestions of deep relaxation while in the hypnotic state. Generally, subjects will be given suggestions to carry out after they are awake. These are referred to as **posthypnotic suggestions.** Ken Norton was given posthypnotic suggestions for his fight with Muhammad Ali.

The fourth phase of hypnosis is coming out of the trance. Actually, a hypnotized subject can come out of the trance anytime. The only reason subjects do not come out on their own is that they don't want to. The relationship between the hypnotist and the subject can be a very pleasant one. When the hypnotist wishes to bring a subject out of a trance, he or she does so simply by suggesting that the subject wake up on a given signal. For example, the hypnotist might say, "Okay, when I count to three you will wake up." Occasionally a subject will resist coming out of the trance. If this happens, the subject is taken back into a deep trance and asked why he or she doesn't want to come out. After a few minutes of discussion and another suggestion to wake up, the subject will generally do so.

Suggestions given to subjects during hypnosis are often designed to influence them during the posthypnotic phase, or after they have come out of the hypnotic trance. Posthypnotic suggestions given to athletes should focus on the way they should feel in certain competitive situations. For example, a baseball player may be told that "when you get into the batter's box, you will find that you feel relaxed and confident." Specific suggestions such as "you'll be able to get a hit almost every time," should be avoided, since failure will tend to undermine the effectiveness of the suggestions (Nideffer, 1976a).

Autohypnosis

There are two kinds of hypnosis. The first kind is **heterohypnosis,** and the second is called **autohypnosis,** or self-hypnosis. Our discussion up to this point has dealt primarily with heterohypnosis, that which is induced by another person, usually a trained hypnotist or psychologist. Heterohypnosis should be practiced only by trained professionals. Even though an attempt has been made in this text to demystify hypnosis, this does not mean that potential dangers do not exist. Heterohypnosis is based upon a rather delicate rapport between the hypnotist and the subject. Consequently, if heterohypnosis is to be practiced on athletes, it should be done so by a competent psychologist (Morgan & Brown, 1983).

CONCEPT & APPLICATION 5.8

Concept A trained psychologist should be present and in charge if heterohypnosis is used as a cognitive strategy.

Application The hypnotized person is very susceptible to suggestions. For this reason, failure to employ a professional may do more harm than good.

Autohypnosis is not based on a relationship with another individual. Yet all the effects that can be achieved through heterohypnosis can be achieved through autohypnosis. It should also be emphasized that in one sense, all hypnosis is self-hypnosis, since people cannot be hypnotized unless they want to be. Furthermore, hypnosis is a natural state of consciousness that we slip into and out of dozens of times a day (Pulos, 1979).

As explained by Ulett and Peterson (1965), there are two kinds of autohypnosis. The first is self-induced, and the second is induced as a posthypnotic suggestion following heterohypnosis. The latter method is easier to achieve. In this method, subjects are told during hypnosis that they will be able to hypnotize themselves anytime they wish simply by following some relaxation and attentional focus induction procedures. Because they have already been hypnotized, they know how it feels and they enjoy the feeling. Therefore, it is much easier for them to hypnotize themselves. With each repetition of self-hypnosis, it becomes easier and easier to achieve. What initially begins as relaxation will later become effective hypnosis, as subjects learn to narrow their field of attention.

The phases involved in autohypnosis are identical to those outlined for hypnosis generally. If a coach or teacher wishes to employ autohypnosis as an intervention strategy for reducing anxiety and improving concentration and imagery, he should go over these steps with the athlete. First, the athlete must be completely comfortable regarding the use of hypnosis. The athlete should begin with the reminder (suggestion) that he is in complete control and can disengage from the hypnotic trance at any time. The induction procedures are the same as those for heterohypnosis. Some common strategies for induction are to sit in an easy chair and stare at a spot on the wall, imagine a blank screen, or look into a mirror.

Posthypnotic suggestions given during autohypnosis should always be couched in positive terms, stressing what is to be accomplished rather than dwelling on negative things to be eliminated. For example, the athlete may wish

These athletes enjoy an exciting moment in sport. Courtesy University of Missouri-Columbia Sports Information

to concentrate on being more positive when she prepares to receive a tennis serve from a tough opponent. A suggestion such as "I will feel relaxed and agile," would be better than "I'm going to hit a winner." The second suggestion contains the seeds of defeat, since you can't always hit a winner. Suggestions such as "I won't feel nervous" are negative, because they only call attention to the problem. The athlete should have specific suggestions already in mind before the hypnotic phase begins. In some cases, the athlete could have the suggestions written on a card that he could read during the hypnotic trance.

CONCEPT & APPLICATION 5.9

Concept Self-hypnosis, or autohypnosis, can be just as effective as heterohypnosis, and does not place the athlete in a situation of dependence.

Application If hypnosis skills are taught, autohypnosis is preferable to heterohypnosis. Autohypnosis is very similar to autogenic training and is safe.

Improving the Effectiveness of Hypnosis

Taylor et al. (1993) identify five factors that can influence the effectiveness of hypnosis. The first factor is the competence of the professional therapist, or the skill of the athlete, if autohypnosis is being employed. The therapist attempting to induce a hypnotic trance or teaching self-hypnosis skills must be well trained in all aspects of hypnosis. Second, the quality of the relationship between therapist and individual being hypnotized is important. The individual must have complete confidence and trust in the therapist. Third, the therapist must do her homework and get to know the person being hypnotized. A failure to have a deep understanding of the athlete's goals and aspirations could be counterproductive. Fourth, effective outcomes require practice of the procedures and instructions given during hypnosis. There is really nothing magical about hypnosis. Considerable effort on the part of the athlete receiving hypnosis is required for best results. Finally, it works best if therapist and athlete both recognize the limitations of hypnosis. Hypnosis will be of little help in overcoming major physical limitations. An athletic injury, for example, needs time to mend.

Hypnosis and Athletic Performance

Is hypnosis effective in facilitating athletic performance? Research on this topic yields a number of basic principles that can be summarized. These important principles are based on extensive reviews and recent published articles (Baer, 1980; Ito, 1979; Johnson, 1961; Morgan 1972a; Morgan & Brown, 1983; Ulrich, 1973; Weitzenhoffer, 1963). A list of basic principles gleaned from the literature is provided below, along with some commentary.

1. The more open and susceptible an athlete is to suggestions, the more likely it is that he will benefit from suggestions given to him under hypnosis. This is also the type of individual who is more likely to be hypnotized.

2. Once an individual is hypnotized, the deeper the trance he is able to achieve, the more likely it is that suggestions given under hypnosis will be effective.

3. Positive suggestions are effective in facilitating performance, regardless of whether or not the athlete is hypnotized. This principle underscores the importance of uncritical acceptance of suggestions from the teacher or coach. If an athlete will accept positive suggestions uncritically, it makes little difference whether she is hypnotized at the time or not.

4. General arousal techniques are more useful than hypnotic suggestions in enhancing muscular strength and endurance. Hypnosis tends to relax an athlete. Muscular strength and endurance activities require increased levels of arousal and activation, not relaxation.

5. Negative suggestions almost always cause a decrement in performance. This is perhaps the most important principle of all. Negative suggestions given to an athlete under hypnosis are particularly powerful. Negative suggestions given to an athlete at any time can be counterproductive. Often, negative suggestions are given inadvertently.

6. Hypnosis may be able to help a successful athlete, but it cannot make a good performer out of a poor one. A lot of practice, goal setting, and physical ability are required to accomplish this.

CONCEPT & APPLICATION 5.10

Concept Giving negative suggestions to hypnotized individuals must be guarded against. Positive suggestions may result in a benefit to performance, but negative suggestions almost always are detrimental to performance. *Application* It may seem obvious that one should not give negative suggestions to athletes, whether they are under hypnosis or not. The inexperienced coach or sport psychologist may, however, give negative suggestions without realizing it. For example, telling a hurdler to watch out for soft ground on the first turn of a race may be the equivalent of a negative suggestion, if it is too late for a practice run.

AROUSAL ENERGIZING STRATEGIES

Generally speaking, **arousal energizing** or **psyching-up strategies** are techniques designed to increase an athlete's arousal and activation level. While overanxiety and overarousal may be a major stumbling block for the **anxiety-prone athlete,** too little activation can also be a problem. This is especially so for highly skilled athletes who must defeat a relatively weak team in order to play a better team in a tournament. Under arousal causes the downfall of talented teams every year in the National Collegiate Athletic Association basketball tournament. Invariably, one or two highly seeded teams will be beaten by weaker teams simply because they were not ready for them.

It is interesting that when athletes are asked to "get psyched," they report using all kinds of different strategies not normally associated with activation. For example, in a study by Caudill, Weinberg, and Jackson (1983) using track athletes, 25 percent reported using relaxation/distraction procedures to psych up. These are cognitive strategies normally reserved for reducing activation. Other psych-up strategies reported by these subjects were preparatory arousal (7 percent), imagery (16 percent), self-efficacy statements (25 percent), and attentional focus procedures (16 percent).

It is important that athletes learn to prepare for competition using the strategy best for them. This may involve using one strategy to control anxiety and another to get psyched up. However, for a team rather than an individual, a different strategy may be needed. For example, if a coach determines that her team is not taking an opponent seriously, she must do something to get the players prepared. The coach runs the risk of overactivating a few anxiety-prone members of the squad, but this is usually better than running the risk of an uninspired effort from the whole team. If the coach identifies the players with very high trait-anxiety profiles, she can work with them individually.

Numerous research articles have reported the facilitative effect of arousal energizing strategies on strength and endurance tasks (Gould, Weinberg & Jackson, 1980; Shelton & Mahoney, 1978; Weinberg & Jackson, 1985; Wilkes & Summers, 1984). The results of research and these conclusions are consistent

Competitive weight lifters psych themselves up for difficult lifts. Courtesy Kansas State University Sports Information

with Oxendine's (1970) basic theory that an above-average level of arousal is essential for optimal performance in gross motor activities involving strength, endurance and speed. It also follows that heightened arousal would help an athlete whose precompetitive arousal level was below optimal. If the athlete is either overaroused or optimally aroused for a particular activity, then arousal energizing strategies are inappropriate. However, if the athlete is underaroused, then psych-up procedures are appropriate.

Coaches can use a number of specific strategies to psych up their athletes (Taylor, 1992; Voelz, 1982). If these strategies are properly planned and not overused, they can help get a team fired up for competition.

GOAL SETTING

Goal setting is an extremely effective tool for psyching up an athlete or a team. Athletes rarely need to be psyched up for high-visibility games such as city or state rivalries. However, how does an athlete get excited about playing a team that his team has defeated ten times in a row? How does a professional baseball player get psyched up to play the last twenty games of a season when the team is fifteen games behind in the standings? These and situations like these present a tremendous challenge to athletes, coaches, and managers. The solution lies in effective goal setting.

In preparing a highly seeded basketball team with 25 wins and 2 losses to play an unranked team in the NCAA playoffs, the coach must do something to keep the team from overlooking a potential "giant killer." One useful strategy is to help each member of the team to set personal performance goals for the game. The star rebounder might be challenged to accept the personal goal of getting thirteen "bounds" in the game. Similarly, the guards might be challenged to keep their turnovers below three between them. With each member of the team working to achieve realistic but difficult goals, it is likely that the team as a whole will perform well. Goal setting will be discussed in greater detail in the next chapter, on cognitive-behavioral strategies.

Figure 5.3

Poster showing performance goals for a volleyball team. From C. Voelz, 1982, *Motivation in coaching a team sport.* Reprinted by permission of American Alliance for Health, Physical Education, Recreation and Dance, 1900 Association Drive, Reston, Virginia 22091.

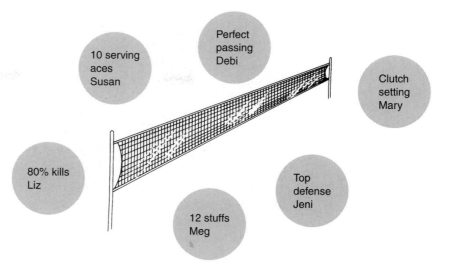

PEP TALKS

A pep talk by the coach or a respected member of the team is the most common method now used to increase the activation level of athletes. But like any verbal communication, it can be either effective or ineffective. Perhaps the most important element of the pep talk is an emphasis on the ingredient that is lacking in the team. If the team is obviously taking an opponent lightly, it must be impressed upon them that on a given night, any team can be a "giant killer." Some of the elements of an effective pep talk may include personal challenges, stories, poems, silence, reasoning, and voice inflections.

BULLETIN BOARDS

In many ways the messages on a bulletin board are identical to those in a pep talk, but they are visually rather than verbally conveyed. Poster-board displays should be placed where team members cannot miss them. Such places as locker room dressing areas and confined training areas are ideal. The bulletin board should always convey positive, motivating thoughts and ideas. Catchy phrases such as "when the going gets tough, the tough get going" can be effective. Athletes remember these simple phrases and will repeat them later, when they need reinforcement. Other messages on the display board might include personal challenges to members of the team. One such display for a volleyball team might look like the one in figure 5.3. This poster could either reflect great performances for the season or challenge performances for the next match.

Challenging or inflammatory statements by opposing teammates or coaches should also appear on the bulletin board. If an opponent is quoted as saying that she will dominate a certain player, this should be posted for all to see. It will give the team something to get excited about.

PUBLICITY AND NEWS COVERAGE

The school newspaper and other advertisements can be very helpful in generating a team spirit. If the members of the team sense that the student body is behind them, they will work harder to get prepared. Ads can be placed in the newspaper by the coach to call attention to an important game or contest. These same ads can be used to recruit new players for the team. For many teams, publicity comes easy, but for others it does not. It may be necessary to cultivate a close relationship with the media and school sports reporters. Invite them to games and send them positive information about players and upcoming contests.

FAN SUPPORT

Those who enjoy sport for its recreational value do not need people watching in order to enjoy the game. However, if you practice 10 to 15 hours a week and have a 20-game schedule, it doesn't hurt to have fan support. Fans tell the athletes that what they are doing is important to people other than themselves. A full season of daily basketball, football, or tennis can burn out many players. Those responsible for promoting the team must do all they can to get people to support the team by coming to watch them.

SELF-ACTIVATION

Often, lethargic activity on the part of an athlete can be reversed through the application of mental strategies to increase activation. Over the years I have observed Jimmy Connors psyching up in a tennis match by slapping himself on the thigh and using positive self-statements. Research has clearly shown that specific attempts to "get psyched" using various internal cognitive strategies is effective in enhancing strength and muscular-endurance activities (Weinberg & Jackson, 1985).

COACH, ATHLETE, AND PARENT INTERACTION

The interactions between an athlete's parents, the athlete, and the coach are an often-overlooked source of motivation for an athlete (Hellstedt, 1987). Coaches are often wary about the overinvolved and demanding parent. However, often just the opposite situation occurs, and parents are excluded from active involvement in motivating a young athlete. Parents provide tremendous support for an athlete's involvement that sometimes goes completely unnoticed. Parents provide transportation for games and practices, and sacrifice vacations and leisure time to watch their son or daughter perform. When called on, they are observed serving as scorekeepers, "water boys," bus drivers, and sometimes assistant coaches. What a tremendous source of support and motivation a parent can be when properly nurtured!

PRECOMPETITION WORKOUT

In the mid-sixties when the Japanese were dominating the international volleyball scene, I observed an interesting phenomenon. Prior to an international men's match between the United States and Japan, the Japanese team came out two hours early and went through a full workout. This was no warm-up as

Kayaking in white water is not for the faint of heart. Courtesy Digital Stock Photo CD/Active Lifestyles

typically observed prior to competition, but a full-blown practice session to exhaustion. The Japanese team went on to defeat the U.S.A. in three relatively easy games. I have often wondered if this was a viable strategy that would have proven effective against the powerful U.S.A. men's team of the 1984 and 1988 Olympics.

Husak and Hemenway (1986) were apparently thinking along similar lines when they tested the effects of competition-day practice on the activation and performance of collegiate swimmers. In this investigation, members of a collegiate swimming team engaged in brisk workouts four to six hours prior to competition. The results did not yield a significant performance effect, but they did show a reduction in feelings of tension and anxiety on the part of the precompetition workout group. Because tension and anxiety can easily hamper performance in swimming competition, precompetition workouts could be an effective tool for preparing an athlete for competition. Precompetition workouts that enhance and increase activation are apparently effective in reducing precompetitive anxiety.

CONCEPT & APPLICATION 5.11

Concept Athletes are sometimes underaroused, and psych-up strategies are necessary in these situations.

Application Goal setting, pep talks, bulletin boards, news coverage, fan support, parental involvement, and self-activation measures are all effective for getting athletes psyched up for competition. However, these techniques should not be overused or indiscriminately applied.

SUMMARY   Arousal adjustment strategies assist the athlete in either decreasing or increasing physiological arousal. When used to reduce arousal and anxiety, use of such strategies is called *stress management*. Any strategy that is calculated to change the existing physiological or mood state of the athlete is referred to as an *intervention*. Interventions designed to adjust arousal or control anxiety should be matched with the particular symptoms of the athlete. The chapter is divided into two main sections that relate to arousal adjustment and control: (a) relaxation procedures, and (b) arousal energizing strategies.

Relaxation procedures discussed include progressive relaxation, autogenic training, meditation, biofeedback, and hypnosis. All of these techniques result in the relaxation response when properly applied. Progressive relaxation involves the systematic tensing and relaxing of all the muscles in the body. The basic idea of progressive relaxation is that it is impossible to be nervous or tense in any part of the body where the muscles are completely relaxed. Whereas progressive relaxation relies upon dynamic contracting and relaxing of muscles, autogenic training relies upon feelings of warmth and heaviness associated with the limbs and muscles of the body. Meditation, as a form of relaxation, is tied directly to the concepts of selective attention discussed in chapter 3. In practicing meditation, the individual attempts to uncritically focus his attention on a single thought, sound, or object. Biofeedback training uses instruments to help people control responses of the autonomic nervous system.

Of all the arousal adjustment strategies, hypnosis is the least understood. Yet a close analysis reveals that in many important ways hypnosis is identical to autogenic training and meditation. The process of inducing the hypnotic trance results in the relaxation response, with accompanying reductions in oxygen consumption, respiration rate, and heart rate. Hypnosis is defined as the uncritical acceptance of a suggestion. The following principles apply relative to hypnosis and athletic performance: (a) the more open and susceptible an athlete is to suggestions, the more likely it is that she will benefit from suggestions given to her under hypnosis; (b) once an individual is hypnotized, the deeper the trance is that she is able to achieve, the more likely it is that suggestions given under hypnosis will be effective; (c) positive suggestions are effective in facilitating performance, regardless of whether or not the athlete is hypnotized; (d) general arousal techniques are more useful than hypnotic suggestions in enhancing muscular strength and endurance activities; (e) negative suggestions almost always cause a decrement in performance; and (f) hypnosis may be able to help a successful athlete, but it cannot make a good performer out of a poor one.

Techniques proven to be effective in psyching up the athlete were discussed. Goal setting, pep talks, use of bulletin boards, news coverage, fan support, self-activation, parent involvement, and precompetition workouts were identified as effective strategies for increasing the activation level of athletes.

REVIEW
QUESTIONS

1. Explain why it is dangerous to assume that small increases or decreases in physiological arousal will result in incremental changes in performance.

2. What is the matching hypothesis? Explain the principle and show its application.

3. What is the relaxation response?

4. Name the four elements involved in evoking the relaxation response. Describe each element in detail.

5. Discuss and describe Jacobson's progressive relaxation program.

6. Discuss and describe Schultz's autogenic training program.

7. Discuss and describe meditation as an arousal adjustment method. What is the relationship between meditation and transcendental meditation?

8. In what specific ways are progressive relaxation, autogenic training, and meditation similar and dissimilar? What is the "mental device" in each method?

9. Compare biofeedback with the other relaxation procedures and discuss the instrumentation involved.

10. Discuss the relationship between the four arousal reduction techniques (relaxation procedures) and athletic performance.

11. Define hypnosis and discuss the two basic theoretical explanations for the phenomenon.

12. Explain the steps and procedures involved in achieving the hypnotic trance.

13. Contrast heterohypnosis and autohypnosis. Which method is preferred in sport and why?

14. How can the effectiveness of hypnosis be improved? Give illustrations and examples for application.

15. What does research say about hypnosis and athletic performance? Give an application for each principle.

16. When are psych-up strategies effective? Name some psych-up strategies and explain how they can be appropriately applied.

GLOSSARY

anxiety-prone athlete An athlete who has a predisposition toward responding to competitive situations with elevated state anxiety.

anxiety/stress spiral The circular effect of anxiety causing poor performance, which results in even more anxiety.

arousal adjustment Intervention technique or process in which physiological arousal is effectively decreased or increased.

arousal energizing strategies Techniques designed to increase an athlete's arousal and activation level (*see* psyching up).

autogenic training A relaxation training program in which the athlete attends to body feedback.

autohypnosis Hypnotizing oneself, as opposed to being hypnotized by another.

biofeedback A program in which the athlete learns to elicit the relaxation response with the aid of physiological measurement equipment.

heterohypnosis Hypnosis requiring the assistance of a hypnotist or psychologist.

hypnosis The uncritical acceptance of a suggestion.

hypnotic induction The process of bringing a subject into the hypnotic trance.

hypnotic trance The state of being hypnotized, or willing to uncritically accept suggestions.

intervention As used in this chapter, a process of intervening or interrupting existing levels of anxiety and arousal to adjust physiological arousal, thereby benefiting performance.

mantra A key phrase or mental device used in transcendental meditation to help the athlete focus attention internally.

matching hypothesis The notion that interventions matched to anxiety symptoms will be more effective in reducing debilitating anxiety.

meditation A form of relaxation that applies directly to the concepts of selective attention.

mental device A word, phrase, object, or process used to help elicit the relaxation response.

neutral hypnosis A hypnotic state in which the athlete's physiological responses are identical to the relaxation response.

posthypnotic suggestion A suggestion given during the alert hypnotic trance that is to be carried out when awake.

progressive relaxation A muscle relaxation procedure in which skeletal muscles are systematically tensed and relaxed.

psyching up Use of cognitive strategies to increase an athlete's arousal and activation level.

relaxation response Physiological changes that reverse the effect of the sympathetic nervous system.

stress management Programs and procedures designed to manage or reduce stress (*see* intervention).

transcendental meditation A relaxation procedure that originated in India and features the repetition of a mantra to elicit the relaxation response.

waking hypnosis The stage of hypnosis during which the athlete is asked to carry out suggestions that are alerting and arousing.

SUGGESTED READINGS

Benson, H., Beary, J. F., & Carol, M. P. (1974). The relaxation response. *Psychiatry, 37,* 37–46.

Carlson, C. R., & Hoyle, R. H. (1993). Efficacy of abbreviated progressive muscle relaxation training: A quantitative review of behavioral medicine research. *Journal of Consulting and Clinical Psychology, 61,* 1059–1067.

Davis, M., Eshelman, E. R., & McKay, M. (1988). *The relaxation & stress reduction workbook* (3rd ed.). Oakland, CA: New Harbinger.

DiCara, L. V. (1970). Learning in the autonomic nervous system. *Scientific American, 222,* 30–39.

Edmonston, W. E., Jr. (1981). *Hypnosis and relaxation: Modern verification of an old equation.* New York: John Wiley and Sons.

Greenberg, J. S. (1990). *Comprehensive stress management* (3rd ed.). Dubuque, IA: Wm. C. Brown.

Jacobson, E. (1929). *Progressive relaxation.* Chicago: University of Chicago Press.

Kihlstrom, J. F. (1985). Hypnosis. *Annual Review of Psychology, 36,* 385–418.

Maynard, I. W., Hemmings, B., & Warwick-Evans, L. (1995). The effects of a somatic intervention strategy on competitive state anxiety and performance in semiprofessional soccer players. *The Sport Psychologist, 9,* 51–64.

Morgan, W. P., & Brown, D. R. (1983). Hypnosis. In M. H. Williams (Ed.), *Ergogenic aids in sport.* Champaign, IL: Human Kinetics.

Neiss, R. (1988). Reconceptualizing relaxation treatments: Psychobiological states in sports. *Clinical Psychology Review, 8,* 139–159.

Petruzzello, S. J., Landers, D. M., & Salazar, W. (1991). Biofeedback and sport/exercise performance: Applications and limitations. *Behavior Therapy, 22,* 379–392.

Schultz, J. H., & Luthe, W. (1959). *Autogenic training: A psychophysiological approach in psychotherapy.* New York: Grune and Stratton.

Taylor, J., Horevitz, R., & Balague, G. (1993). The use of hypnosis in applied sport psychology. *The Sport Psychologist, 7,* 58–78.

Wallace, R. K., & Benson, H. (1972). The physiology of meditation. *Scientific American, 226,* 85–90.

Zaichkowsky, L. D., & Fuchs, C. (1988). Biofeedback applications in exercise and athletic performance. *Exercise and Sport Science Reviews, 16,* 381–421.

Zaichkowsky, L. D., & Sime, W. E. (1982). *Stress management for sport.* Reston, VA: AAHPERD Publications.

6

COGNITIVE-BEHAVIORAL INTERVENTION IN SPORT

KEY TERMS

- *ACSI-28*
- *attention and arousal set theory*
- *attentional cueing*
- *between-play routines*
- *cognitive-behavioral intervention*
- *cognitive restructuring*
- *coping strategies*
- *external imagery*
- *goal setting*
- *imagery*
- *internal imagery*
- *mental practice*
- *outcome goal orientation*
- *outcome goals*
- *performance goal orientation*

- *performance goals*
- *performance routines*
- *postshot routines*
- *preshot routines*
- *PSEP*
- *PSIS-5*
- *psychological method*
- *psychological momentum*
- *psychological skill*
- *psychological skills training*
- *psychoneuromuscular theory*
- *self-talk*
- *SIT*
- *SMT*
- *symbolic learning theory*
- *TOPS*
- *VMBR*

Imagery is an example of a cognitive strategy commonly employed in golf. Courtesy Kansas State University Sports Information

In the previous chapter on arousal control, our focus was upon interventions or strategies designed to reduce or increase arousal. In the present chapter, our focus is upon **cognitive-behavioral interventions** designed to enhance or positively influence the performance and learning of sport skills. In our discussion of controlling arousal, our primary focus was upon relaxation-based interventions designed to lower or in some way control physiological arousal. In this chapter we show how physical relaxation techniques are combined with cognitive restructuring techniques to bring about changes in behavior and improvements in athletic performance. We may think of these techniques as cognitive-behavioral interventions, because they bring together both physical relaxation and cognitive restructuring (Gold & Dry, 1994).

Early work by Ellis (1967) is helpful in understanding the utility of **cognitive restructuring** to change behavior. In a sense, cognitive restructuring is little more than using our cognitive (mental) skills to restructure, or change, the way we view certain situations. Ellis's theory was based on what he called the ABC theory of personality, which states that ". . . when human beings are affected by mental or emotional (rather than by physical) conditions, it is never stimulus, A, which causes them to react emotionally at point C; rather it is their own interpretation of, or what they tell themselves about A, at point B" (p. 83). In essence, A is the stimulus, C is the person's response to the stimulus, and B is the person's belief system that determined how she would respond to the stimulus. This scenario is repeated over and over again each day of our lives. We respond not to the actual danger or threat of an objective situation, but to our perception or belief about that situation. Some people are terrified of flying. Is this because of some inherent danger associated with flying? Or is this due to the person's belief system and perceptions associated with flying? Airplane accidents do occur, of course, but given the vast numbers of safe flights completed, accidents are rare indeed. Since commercial airplane travel is statistically safe, where does the fear come from? It comes from the belief system of the fearful individual. This principle has great application to the athlete. Because negative responses are often due to our belief system, wouldn't it make sense to change or modify our belief system? This is exactly what cognitive restructuring is all about. How we think and feel about something determines how we will respond to it. If an athlete responds to a situation with an irrational thought, it may result in an emotional disturbance, causing a decrement in performance. All of the concepts that we will introduce and discuss in this chapter have the potential of modifying the way we view, interpret, and respond to objective situations or stimuli.

A very simple example of cognitive restructuring is the technique of **self-talk** that athletes often use to maintain quality attentional focus and arousal during competition. In a sense, this is autogenic training in action, designed not only to control the level of arousal, but also to control thoughts (Van Raalte, Brewer, Lewis, Linder, Wildman & Kozimor, 1995; Van Raalte, Brewer, Rivera & Petitpas, 1994). Negative self-talk is associated with losing and poor performance, while

Figure 6.1

Intrapersonal and interpersonal model of the psychological makeup of the athlete. Adapted with permission from Iso-Ahola, S. (1995). Intrapersonal and interpersonal factors in athletic performance. *Scandinavian Journal of Medicine and Science in Sports, 5,* 191–199.

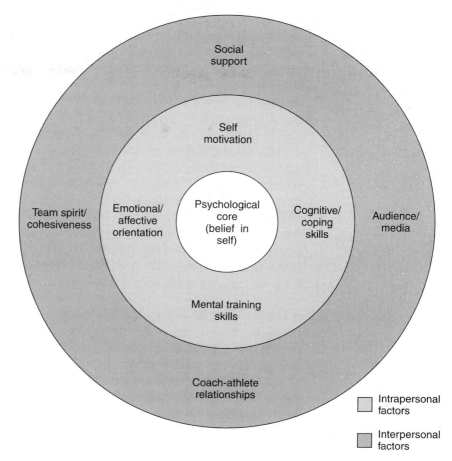

positive self-talk is associated with winning and improved performance. Recall that negative suggestions given during hypnosis are also detrimental to performance. Other cognitive factors that have an impact upon how an athlete responds to specific situations include coping, imagery, and goal-setting skills. Each of these topics will be discussed in detail in the sections that follow. In addition, I have included a section on psychological skills training, which brings together cognitive skills introduced in this chapter with relaxation skills from chapter 5.

Before beginning our discussion of these important concepts, I would like to introduce a unifying model. This is an interactive model proposed by Iso-Ahola (1995) that illustrates how important concepts in this book come together to explain the dynamic psychological makeup of the athlete. The model, illustrated in figure 6.1, shows schematically how key intra- and interpersonal factors interact to explain the psychology of the athlete. At the center of the model is the psychological core of the athlete (compare with figure 2.1), or belief in himself. The core affects and is affected by intrapersonal and interpersonal factors surrounding the athlete. Intrapersonal factors form the second layer of the model, or the layer immediately surrounding the psychological core. As illustrated in the model, the most important intrapersonal factors are self-motivation and intrinsic motivation (to be discussed in chapter 8), cognitive and coping skills (discussed in this chapter), emotional/affective orientation (discussed in chapters 3, 4, and 5), and mental training skills (discussed in this chapter). Finally, interpersonal factors form the outer layer of the model. Factors that make up this layer include social support, coach/athlete relationships, audience effects, and finally, team spirit and cohesiveness.

Gold, Eklund, and Jackson (1992a, 1992b) conducted an extensive in-depth study of the psychological makeup of twenty U.S.A. Olympic wrestlers from the 1988 Olympics in Seoul, Korea. Cognitive-behavioral interventions and strategies of these athletes were studied and compared with performance. Their results showed that the most successful athletes are confident athletes possessing well-developed cognitive-behavioral skills to prepare them for the grueling pressure of Olympic competition. Skills developed by the athletes to deal with pressures of competition may be categorized as cognitive-behavioral coping skills, the topic of the first section in this chapter.

COPING STRATEGIES IN SPORT

Coping has been defined by Lazarus and Folkman (1984) as "constantly changing cognitive and behavioral efforts to manage specific external and/or internal demands that are appraised as taking or exceeding the resources of the person" (p. 141). **Coping strategies,** then, are dynamic, conscious efforts on the part of the individual to eliminate or manage distress. Distress occurs when an individual perceives an imbalance between demands and resources (compare with figure 4.4). Coping strategies can be categorized into two main types: (a) problem focused, and (b) emotion focused. Problem-focused coping strategies are cognitive-behavioral efforts to change for the better the problem causing distress. Emotion-focused coping strategies seek to regulate distressing emotions through arousal control techniques. Coping can be assessed using the 66-item Ways of Coping Checklist (WCC) developed by Folkman and Lazarus (1985), and modified for sport by Crocker (1992). Research with athletes has shown that individuals cope in very complex and diverse ways.

Athletes who possess well-developed and practiced coping skills will be more effective in managing the stress and demands of training and competition. Gould and colleagues (Gould, Eklund & Jackson, 1993; Gould, Finch & Jackson, 1993) studied coping strategies reported by Olympic wrestlers and National Champion figure skaters. Thirty-nine different coping themes were reported by the wrestlers. The 39 themes reduced down to four broad dimensions: (a) thought control strategies (e.g., self-talk, positive thinking, thought control), (b) attentional focus strategies (e.g., concentration control, tunnel vision), (c) emotional control strategies (e.g., arousal control, relaxation, visualization), and (d) behavioral strategies (e.g., set routines, rest, control of the environment). With the exception of the seeking of social support, coping strategies reported by figure skaters tended to be similar to those reported by wrestlers. Seeking of social support was not one of the themes reported by wrestlers, but was a consistent theme reported by figure skaters. The notion that females utilize social support as a coping strategy to a greater degree than males was reported by Crocker and Graham (1995).

Some evidence is available to suggest that the appropriateness of a coping strategy may be related to perception of control (Johnston & McCabe, 1993; Lazarus & Folkman, 1984). If an athlete perceives that the solution to a stressful situation is within her control, then an approach coping strategy is called for. In an approach coping strategy, the individual must confront the stressful situation straight on. For example, if an athlete is worried about an upcoming competition, she should be proactive, determine the source of the worry, and implement a strategy to address it. Conversely, if an athlete perceives that the solution to a stressful situation is out of her control, then an avoidance coping strategy is called for. In an avoidance coping strategy, the individual focuses on a strategy that does not confront the stressor directly. If an athlete is worried about an upcoming competition, she might focus attention on some other activity in order to gate out negative thoughts about competition.

As with all of the cognitive-behavioral interventions discussed in this chapter, for best results, coping strategies must be developed, practiced, and refined. Danish, Petitpas, and Hale (1992) suggest the use of life development intervention (LDI) specialists to assist individuals in developing strategies for coping with distress. The LDI specialist must possess (a) counseling skills, (b) the ability to assist in setting and attaining goals, and (c) proficiency in helping individuals identify existing coping skills and transfer them from one domain to another. A sport psychologist with LDI training should be available to youth and adult athletes.

CONCEPT & APPLICATION 6.1

Concept As with all of the cognitive-behavioral interventions discussed in this chapter, coping strategies must be developed, practiced, and refined. Effective and appropriate coping strategies do not happen by accident.

Application As research has indicated, strategies used by athletes are often very individualistic, complex, and creative. Relaxation training, visualization, and goal setting are all excellent intervention strategies that can be built into an athlete's arsenal of coping skills. These strategies should be utilized by the athlete in creative and individualistic ways to address situations of excessive demand and distress. In the sections ahead, we will learn more about these important cognitive strategies.

IMAGERY IN SPORT

Game 6 of the 1987 baseball World Series provided an excellent example of the use of imagery by a professional athlete. During game 6, Don Baylor, the Minnesota Twins' designated hitter, faced pitcher John Tudor of the St. Louis Cardinals. It was the bottom of the fifth inning; St. Louis was leading 5 to 3, there were no outs, and there was one man on second base. Baylor had last faced Tudor in 1983, when he was with the Yankees and Tudor was with the Red Sox. Preparing to face Tudor in this classic match-up of game 6, Baylor recalls, "I reminisced about the last time he pitched me then. Let's just say I was somewhat more ready for him than he was for me." (Wulf, 1987). History records that Baylor took Tudor's first pitch deep into the left-field stands for a two-run homer.

Block (1981) identified human **imagery,** the use of visualization to imagine situations, as one of the most important topics in cognitive science. Two general theories have evolved. The first states that when we imagine a scene in our mind's eye, we are scanning an actual image that has somehow formed in our brain. This is not to say that a brain surgeon could find actual physical pictures lodged in our brain, but that the images are as real to us as an image taken from the retina of the eye. This position is held by the so-called pictorialists. The second position is that of the descriptionist. The descriptionist argues that there is no such thing as a mental image. That is, when we imagine a physical scene in our mind's eye, we are not really seeing an internal image, but the graphic and detailed nature of our language makes it seem so. Our thoughts, as it were, actually manufacture an image so clear that we think we are seeing one.

Consistent with Block's (1981) notion of the nature of imagery, Fisher (1986) clarifies that imagery is the language of the brain. In a real sense, the brain cannot tell the difference between an actual physical event and the vivid visualization of the same event. For this reason, imagery can be used by the brain to provide repetition, elaboration, intensification, and preservation of important athletic sequences and skills.

MENTAL PRACTICE AS A FORM OF IMAGERY

While the literature has tended to use the terms *mental practice* and *imagery* interchangeably, this may not be entirely correct. **Mental practice** implies that an individual is practicing a physical task in some covert way, although actual images of the task may or may not be present. Conversely, it is possible for an athlete to visualize or imagine a particular scene without really practicing anything. Murphy and Jowdy (1992) attempted to clarify the difference between these two terms by referring to imagery as a mental process and to mental practice as a particular technique. Other terms that have been used as essentially equivalent to imagery include *symbolic rehearsal, visualization, covert practice, cognitive rehearsal,* and *mental rehearsal.* Because mental practice often involves some form of imagery, the literature associated with mental practice provides us with important clues about the effectiveness of imagery for enhancing athletic performance.

Excellent literature reviews conclude that mental practice as a cognitive strategy is more effective than no practice, but less effective than physical practice (Feltz & Landers, 1983; Grouios, 1992; Hinshaw, 1991). Mental practice used in a complementary fashion with physical practice often yields the best results. Recent research reveals that mental practice is effective in enhancing figure skating performance (Palmer, 1992) and trampoline performance (Isaac, 1992). An important study by Hird, Landers, Thomas, and Horan (1991) confirms that mental practice is more effective with tasks having a large cognitive component, and that the ratio of physical practice to mental practice is important. For example, a ratio of 75 percent physical practice and 25 percent mental practice is more effective in facilitating pegboard performance than a ratio of 25 percent physical practice and 75 percent mental practice.

An important study by Kohl, Ellis, and Roenker (1992) demonstrates that learning (retention) as well as performance is influenced by mental practice. In this investigation, mental practice was shown to be as effective as physical practice in learning a novel pursuit rotor task. A combination of mental practice and actual practice results in the greatest level of learning and retention.

Evidence also suggests that mentally practicing a motor task, such as basketball, prior to physically practicing the task is more beneficial than mentally practicing the task following physical practice. The amount of time actually spent mentally practicing a task is important. Mentally practicing for 1 to 3 minutes is more beneficial than mentally practicing for 5 to 7 minutes at a time (Etnier & Landers, 1996).

CONCEPT & APPLICATION 6.2

Concept When used in conjunction with actual practice, mental practice effectively enhances motor performance. Mental practice by itself is more effective than no practice, and in certain circumstances is as effective as actual practice. *Application* In order to realize maximum performance, athletes should be taught to mentally practice sports skills in conjunction with actual practice. In addition, mental practice should be used by itself in situations where actual practice is not practical (e.g., waiting in the locker room).

Another important finding associated with mental practice is that advanced performers benefit from mental practice to a much greater extent than beginners. Clark (1960) compared the effect of mental practice with that of physical practice in the learning of the Pacific Coast one-hand basketball foul shot. He placed 144 high school boys into physical and mental practice groups on the basis of varsity, junior varsity, or novice experience. All subjects were given a 25-shot pretest before and a 25-shot posttest after fourteen days of practice (30 shots per day).

Results showed that mental practice was almost as effective as physical practice for the junior varsity and varsity groups, but physical practice was far superior to mental practice for the beginners. Corbin (1967a, 1967b) observed similar results using a wand-juggling task. From the results of these studies, it seems clear that for mental practice to facilitate performance, a certain amount of skill is necessary. In other words, a coach or teacher should not expect mental practice to be effective with athletes who are unskilled in their sports. The more skillful they are, the more useful mental practice will be for them.

CONCEPT & APPLICATION 6.3

Concept The more skillful and experienced an athlete is, the more he will be able to benefit from the use of mental practice.
Application To avoid discouraging young athletes from the use of mental practice, make sure that he is familiar enough with the activity to know the difference between a good and a bad performance. An athlete must know what a skill looks like and how it feels in order to effectively mentally practice it.

Finally, mental practice is most effective for activities that require some thought—those that have a large cognitive component (Ryan & Simons, 1981). For example, a balancing task would have a small cognitive component, while a finger maze would have a large cognitive component. In terms of sport, one should expect better results using mental practice for tennis than using it for a rope-pulling contest.

THEORIES OF HOW IMAGERY WORKS

While a great deal of research has been published to the effectiveness of imagery and mental practice in sport, sport psychologists know very little about the reasons they are effective or how they work. Why should mentally practicing or imaging a physical task result in improved learning and performance? A number of possible explanations to this basic question have been proposed (Grouios, 1992; Hecker & Kaczor, 1988; Janssen & Sheikh, 1994; Murphy & Jowdy, 1992). For the sake of brevity and simplicity, only three theoretical explanations will be discussed.

Psychoneuromuscular Theory

Psychoneuromuscular theory posits that imagery results in subliminal neuromuscular patterns that are identical to the patterns used during actual movement. Even though the imagined event does not result in an overt movement of the musculature, subliminal efferent commands are sent from the brain to the muscles. In a sense, the neuromuscular system is given the opportunity to "practice" a movement pattern without really moving a muscle. A study reported by Jowdy and Harris (1990) confirms that increased electrical

Mental preparation involves the individual, the team, and the coach. Courtesy University of Missouri-Columbia Sports Information

activity in the muscles is associated with mental practice and imagery, regardless of the type of imagery used (kinesthetic or visual). Imagery assists the brain in developing a motor schema for executing a particular motor pattern. Psychoneuromuscular theory is the most plausible explanation for why imagery facilitates physical performance and learning.

Symbolic Learning Theory

Symbolic learning theory differs from psychoneuromuscular theory in that subliminal electrical activity in the musculature is not required. Mental practice and imagery work because the individual literally plans her actions in advance. Motor sequences, task goals, and alternative solutions are considered cognitively before a physical response is required. The short-stop in baseball provides an excellent example of this theory in action. Prior to each pitch to the hitter, the short-stop cognitively reviews in her mind the various possible events and the appropriate response for each event. If there is one out in the eighth inning, the bases are loaded, and the score is tied, the short-stop's play will depend upon the type of ball that is hit to her. By mentally rehearsing the various stimuli and possible responses before each pitch, the short-stop can improve her chances of making the correct play.

Attention and Arousal Set Theory

Attention and arousal set theory combines the cognitive aspects of symbolic learning theory with the physiological aspects of psychoneuromuscular theory. Imagery serves to improve performance in two ways. From a physiological perspective, imagery may help the athlete to adjust his arousal level for optimal performance. From a cognitive perspective, imagery may help the athlete to selectively attend to the task at hand. If the athlete is attending to a task-relevant image, he is less likely to be distracted by irrelevant stimuli.

In the final analysis, the best theory might be eclectic in nature and include elements of all three theories. From a logical perspective, it would seem impractical to exclude any one of these theories in favor of another.

INTERNAL AND EXTERNAL IMAGERY

The two types of imagery are *internal* and *external*. **Internal imagery** is considered to be primarily *kinesthetic* in nature, as opposed to visual. It is kinesthetic in the sense that the individual actually imagines herself carrying out a motor task from within her own body. Shut your eyes and imagine for a moment that you have a basketball in your hand and you are preparing to shoot a free throw. If your perspective at this moment is from within your body looking toward the basket, this is an example of internal imagery. You imagine yourself bouncing the ball a few times, you position yourself for the shot, and you shoot. What do you see? You see your hand releasing the ball and traveling toward the basket. However, you do not see the rest of your body. Even though you are imagining the shot and not actually carrying it out, your brain is sending out "subliminal" electrical impulses to your muscles and limbs regarding the execution of the shot. For these reasons, internal imagery is referred to as kinesthetic in nature.

External imagery, however, is considered to be primarily *visual* in nature. In what way does it differ from internal imagery? Let's take the basketball free throw example again. Shut your eyes and imagine that you are going to shoot a free throw, only this time, imagine that you are outside your body, watching yourself from a distance. You see yourself bounce the ball a few times, position yourself for the shot, and then shoot it. You see all of these things, but you don't "feel" them. You can see, for example, that your right foot is about 6 inches in front of your left foot, and you notice that your elbow is pointing towards the basket immediately prior to the release of the ball.

Internal imagery is generally believed to be superior to external imagery, for two reasons. First, elite athletes report using internal imagery to a greater degree than novice or less elite athletes (Barr & Hall, 1992; Mahoney & Avener, 1977). The second reason is that internal imagery results in measurable subliminal electrical muscle activity (EMG) in the muscles associated with the imagined actions (Barr & Hall, 1992; Hale, 1982; Harris & Robinson, 1986; Jacobson, 1931).

CONCEPT & APPLICATION 6.4

Concept Two kinds of imagery are available to the athlete.

Application Internal imagery allows athletes to kinesthetically experience the correct execution of a skill, while external imagery allows them to see themselves performing the skill. Athletes should develop skill in both internal and external imagery.

While research generally suggests that internal imagery is superior to external imagery, this conclusion is not completely supported by the literature (Epstein, 1980; Rotella, Gansneder, Ojala & Billings, 1980). It would seem reasonable to assume that some type of guided combination of both would be beneficial. The athlete can benefit both from "feeling" himself perform a motor skill and from "seeing" himself performing the skill.

MEASUREMENT OF IMAGERY

Research involving imagery is often difficult to control. If, for example, you wish to study the effectiveness of imagery in facilitating the performance of a motor task, you might form two groups: a control group that does not use imagery, and an experimental group instructed to use imagery. Now, how do you manage the quality of imagery used by the experimental group, or even whether they are really using it? How do you keep the control group from using imagery, even though you did not ask them to use it? If you do not randomly assign participants to treatment conditions, or you did, but you have a small sample size, how do you know that the participants in one group do not possess more advanced imagery skills at the outset than those in the other group? These are all important issues that researchers must deal with in order to design and conduct research involving the use of imagery in sport.

The use of imagery to facilitate or enhance the performance of sports skills has increased in recent years. Paralleling this increase in interest in imagery has been the development of inventories designed to measure an athlete's ability to control and manipulate the vividness of images (Moran, 1993). In addition, O'Halloran and Gauvin (1994) have suggested that individual preferences regarding the use of imagery is an important variable to measure. For easy reference, I have provided the reader with a list of many of the current inventories available for assessing various aspects of imagery use (see table 6.1). Based on Moran (1993), this list contains reference to most, but not all, available inventories. Also, while an attempt is made in table 6.1 to identify the major aspect of imagery measured by the inventory, it is important to understand that these inventories tend to be multidimensional, measuring more than one aspect of imagery.

EFFECTIVENESS OF IMAGERY IN ENHANCING SPORTS PERFORMANCE

In a previous section, we documented that mental practice is effective in enhancing the learning of a motor task. It follows, therefore, that the use of imagery and visualization should also facilitate performance of a well-learned motor task. Athletes who utilize imagery to prepare for competition should realize a facilitatory effect (Sheikh & Korn, 1994).

When considering the effectiveness of imagery in sports performance, it is important to take into consideration the skill of the athlete. The more skilled the athlete is, the more benefit she can derive from the use of imagery. Novices do not benefit very much from imagery and mental practice because they do not

Table 6.1

Most Common Tests of Mental Imagery.

From Moran, A. (1993). Conceptual and methodological issues in the measurement of mental imagery skills. *Journal of Sport Behavior, 16,* 157–170. Adapted with permission of the publisher.

Title	*Aspect*	*Source*
1. Questionnaire on Mental Imagery (QMI)	Vividness	Betts (1908)
2. Shortened form of Questionnaire on Mental Imagery (SQMI)	Vividness	Sheehan (1967)
3. Gordon's Test of Imagery Control (GTIC)	Control	Richardson (1969)
4. Individual Differences Questionnaire (IDQ)	Preferred Style	Paivio (1971)
5. Vividness of Visual Imagery Questionnaire (VVIQ)	Vividness	Marks (1973)
6. Group Test of Mental Rotations (GMRT)	Control	Vandenberg & Kruse (1978)
7. Preferred Imagic Cognitive Style (PICS)	Preferred Style	Isaacs (1982)
8. Movement Imagery Questionnaire (MIQ)	Vividness	Hall & Pongrac (1983)
9. Vividness of Movement Imagery Questionnaire (VMIQ)	Vividness	Isaac, Mark & Russell (1986)
10. Imagery Use Questionnaire (IUQ)	Multidimensional	Hall, Rodgers & Barr (1990)
11. Imagery Use Questionnaire for Soccer (IUQ-SP)	Multidimensional	Salmon, Hall & Haslam, (1994)
12. Sport Imagery Questionnaire (SIQ)	Multidimensional	Hall, Mack & Paivio (1996)
13. Revised Movement Imagery Questionnaire	Multidimensional	Hall & Martin (in press)

have a well-developed image of what a skilled performance should look like. This is not to say that beginners should not be given the opportunity to benefit from using imagery, but that one should not expect imagery to play a significant role in performance enhancement at this stage (Pie, Tenebaum, Bar-Eli, Levy-Kolker, Sade & Landers, 1996).

While it is generally understood that imagery plays a cognitive-behavioral role in enhancing the performance of sports skills, it is also true that imagery plays a motivational role. The motivational function of imagery is to energize the individual to achieve success, while its cognitive function is to increase skill through covert practice (Martin & Hall, 1995). The value and importance of emotion and motivation in enhancing athletic performance should not be underestimated. While overarousal is often a problem to be addressed, underarousal and undermotivation is also a serious concern to the athlete. You cannot remove "passion" and emotion from an athlete and expect superior performance. Imagery has an energizing and motivational function, and should be utilized for this purpose to a greater extent (Botterill, 1996).

Research showing the efficacy of using imagery in sport has focused primarily on the adult sports performer, but recent evidence also supports its use with children and with physical activities outside of traditional sport. For example, imagery enhances the performance of children in table tennis, and of adult dancers required to execute complex dance movements (Hanrahan, Tetreau & Sarrazin, 1995; Ahang, Qi-Wei, Orlick & Zitzelsberger, 1992).

Given the effectiveness of imagery in enhancing performance, it is of value to realize that an individual's ability to utilize imagery can be improved through training. The athlete does not have to rely on some sort of inherited trait for imaging (Rodgers, Hall & Buckolz, 1991). However, there does seem to be some sort of innate preference of individuals for either imagic or verbal thinking. Research suggests that individuals who have a preference for imagic thinking benefit most from the application of imagery to sport (O'Halloran & Gauvin, 1994).

CONCEPT & APPLICATION 6.5

Concept Just as mental practice is effective in enhancing the learning of a motor skill, use of imagery by skilled athletes is effective in enhancing athletic performance.

Application The athlete should wonder not whether he should use imagery to enhance performance, but what he needs to do to learn how to use it effectively. Like physical skills, imagery skills must be practiced and learned. Principles that can be utilized by the athlete to learn how to use imagery properly are summarized in table 6.2.

DEVELOPING IMAGERY SKILLS

As with relaxation training, imagery abilities can be improved with practice. Hickman (1979, pp. 120–121) listed thirteen steps to effective training in mental imagery and rehearsal. These are summarized in the following six steps:

1. Find a quiet place where you will not be disturbed, assume a comfortable position, and relax completely.

2. Practice imagery by visualizing a circle that fills the visual field. Make the circle turn a deep blue. Repeat the process several times, imagining a different color each time. Allow the images to disappear. Relax and observe the spontaneous imagery that arises.

3. Create the image of a simple three-dimensional glass. Fill it with a colorful liquid, add ice cubes and a straw. Write a descriptive caption underneath.

4. Select a variety of scenes and develop them with rich detail. Include sport-related images such as a swimming pool, a tennis court, and a beautiful golf course. Practice visualizing people, including strangers, in each of these scenes.

Table 6.2

Principles Associated with the Application of Imagery to Sport.

1. Imagery ability and application skills can be developed and learned.
2. Imagery is most effective when used by skilled athletes.
3. Imagery must be approached with a positive attitude.
4. Knowing how to relax is an important precursor to the effective use of imagery.
5. Both internal (kinesthetic) and external (visual) imagery are of value to the performer.
6. Imagery is an effective cognitive strategy for enhancing performance.
7. Imagery is an effective energizer that can be used to motivate the athlete.
8. Athletes categorized as high imagers and who prefer imagic thinking benefit more from the use of imagery than those low in these abilities.
9. Negative-outcome imagery is more powerful in causing a decrement in performance than positive-outcome imagery is in facilitating athletic performance.
10. Imagery is widely used by athletes of many different sports.
11. Highly skilled athletes use imagery to a greater extent than less skilled athletes do.
12. Imagery can be effectively used by children to enhance performance.

5. Imagine yourself in a sport setting of keen interest to you. Visualize and feel yourself successfully participating in the scene. Relax and enjoy your success.

6. End the session by breathing deeply, opening your eyes, and adjusting to the external environment.

The potential of imagery as an effective cognitive strategy is enormous. An athlete can physically practice shooting basketball free throws for years, and yet never feel comfortable or confident doing the same thing in a game situation. Generally, practice conditions do not match the anxiety and fear associated with the real-life situation. In an effective mental imagery session, athletes can imagine themselves successfully making basket after basket in pressure-packed game situations.

CONCEPT & APPLICATION 6.6

Concept Imagery allows the anxiety-prone athlete to practice relaxation skills in a stressful situation.

Application Since actual practice situations are rarely as stressful as competition, the athlete should use imagery to create numerous anxiety-provoking situations.

COGNITIVE-BEHAVIORAL INTERVENTION PROGRAMS USING IMAGERY AND RELAXATION

In this section I will discuss three different cognitive-behavioral intervention programs that link imagery and relaxation together into one comprehensive program. Research has demonstrated that individualized packaged intervention programs are more effective than nonindividualized programs in which participants select their own strategies. Athletes benefit most from intervention strategies that are designed to fit their needs and are presented in a systematic and organized fashion. Merely informing an athlete about various cognitive strategies is not particularly effective (Seabourne, Weinberg, Jackson & Suinn, 1985).

Cognitive intervention programs designed for performance enhancement and arousal control have one thing in common: they all include a linkage between relaxation training and imagery. The basic notion is that imagery use is enhanced through relaxation training. While Murphy (1994) cited evidence to the contrary, the vast majority of the published research supports this position (Kendall, Hrycaiko, Martin & Kendall, 1990; Suedfeld & Bruno, 1990; Wrisberg & Anshel, 1989).

The three cognitive-behavioral intervention programs to be introduced in this section include **Visual Motor Behavior Rehearsal (VMBR), Stress Inoculation Training (SIT), and Stress Management Training (SMT).** A summary of the essential components of all three is provided in table 6.3. While our focus will be upon these three intervention programs, this is not to imply that these are the only programs that are available, or that others are less effective.

VISUAL MOTOR BEHAVIOR REHEARSAL (VMBR)

Visual Motor Behavior Rehearsal (VMBR) was developed by Suinn (1972, 1994) as an adaptation of Wolpe's (1958) desensitization procedures for humans. The process of desensitization was used to help patients to overcome phobias. For example, a patient fearing heights would be desensitized to this phobia through a series of systematic approximations to the fearful stimuli. Although Suinn used VMBR to treat people with depressions, he was especially interested in applying the techniques to athletes. His particular method of training consisted of (1) relaxing the athlete's body by means of a brief version of Jacobson's progressive relaxation techniques, (2) practicing imagery related to the demands of the athlete's sport, and (3) using imagery to practice a specific skill in a lifelike stressful environment.

Basically, VMBR combines relaxation and imagery into one procedure. It also requires the athlete to mentally practice a specific skill under simulated game conditions. Theoretically, this would be better than actual practice, since the practice environment rarely resembles a game situation. Coaches and teachers typically go to great lengths to minimize distractions to their athletes during practice sessions. VMBR teaches the athlete to use relaxation and imagery techniques to create lifelike situations. Going through these stressful

Table 6.3

Summary of Three Cognitive-Behavioral Intervention Programs That Utilize Imagery and Relaxation.

Intervention Program	Characteristic Steps
Visual Motor Behavioral Rehearsal (VMBR)	1. Relaxation training for mastery 2. Practice of imagery in sports-related environment 3. Sport-specific application of imagery and relaxation
Stress Inoculation Training (SIT)	1. Conceptualization phase 2. Skills acquisition phase (relaxation, imagery, problem solving, cognitive restructuring) 3. Inoculation against stress through small manageable steps
Stress Management Training (SMT)	1. Conceptualization of stress 2. Skills acquisition phase (relaxation, imagery, problem solving, cognitive restructuring) 3. Practice managing strong emotional stress responses

experiences mentally should make it easier to deal with the stress of actual competition. Suinn generally recommends the use of internal kinesthetic imagery for VMBR training, but suggests that in addition the athlete should use external imagery to identify performance errors.

Numerous investigations have been reported that demonstrate that VMBR is effective in enhancing athletic performance, as well as in reducing the debilitating effects of overarousal and state anxiety. These include studies involving basketball (Gray & Fernadez, 1990; Kolonay, 1977), karate (Seabourne, Weinberg & Jackson, 1984), tennis serving (Noel, 1980), pistol shooting (Hall & Hardy, 1991), and archery (Zervas & Kakkos, 1995). In summary, it appears that VMBR training is effective in reducing an athlete's negative affect relative to the sports tasks mentioned above. Furthermore, the potential for VMBR training to improve athletic performance is very good, but its effectiveness depends on the type of task, the skill level of the performer, and the athlete's ability to relax and use imagery.

CONCEPT & APPLICATION 6.7

Concept VMBR is an effective intervention program that incorporates principles derived from relaxation training and imagery to reduce anxiety, focus attention, and enhance performance.

Application An athlete who suffers from the debilitating effects of anxiety, as well as a nonaffected athlete, can benefit from Visual Motor Behavior Rehearsal.

Excellent imagery and relaxation skills are necessary for optimal gymnastic performance. Courtesy University of Missouri-Columbia Sports Information

STRESS INOCULATION TRAINING (SIT)

Stress inoculation training (SIT) is a cognitive-behavioral program developed by Meichenbaum (1977, 1985) that incorporates relaxation training, imagery, and other cognitive processes into a single plan. The key element of SIT is the progressive exposure of the athlete to situations of greater and greater stress as a way to inoculate the athlete against the debilitating effects of stress. SIT is composed of three phases. In the *conceptualization phase,* the focus of the sport psychologist is upon establishing a collaborative relationship with the athlete and helping him to better understand the nature of stress and its effect upon emotions and performance. This phase may include interviews, administration of questionnaires, and other strategies to assess the athlete's expectations and goals. During the *skills acquisition phase,* the major objective of the sport psychologist is to help the athlete develop coping skills such as progressive relaxation, cognitive restructuring, imaging, problem solving, and self-instructional training. In the final *application and follow-through phase,* the

Many different psychological approaches are used by coaches to mentally prepare athletes for competition. Courtesy Kansas State University Sports Information

athlete is encouraged to implement his learned coping skills and responses in day-to-day situations. Small manageable units of stress (whatever distresses the athlete) are introduced to the subject. The athlete is first asked to imagine (in vitro) himself coping with progressively more threatening scenes while in a relaxed state. In this way, the athlete anticipates stressful interactions and practices ways to behave or cope with them. Next, the athlete is introduced to real-life situations (in vivo) in which the level of stress is gradually increased, allowing the athlete to practice his learned coping strategies. In this graded way, the athlete is inoculated against stress.

Threatening situations are presented through imagery, films, role playing, and real-life situations. For example, if the fear of competition is stressful, the athlete is allowed to experience both imagined and real competitive situations. As soon as the athlete is able to cope with a low level of stress, the situation is changed, and a more stressful situation is presented. In this way, the athlete becomes inoculated against progressively increasing levels of stress. Eventually, the athlete's fear of competition is minimized to such a degree that he can cope with it.

Research with SIT in athletic situations has demonstrated its effectiveness in reducing stress and increasing athletic performance in basketball (Hamilton & Fremouw, 1985; Meyers, Schleser & Okwumabua, 1982), gymnastics (Carroll, 1989; Kerr & Leith, 1993; Mace, Eastman & Carrol, 1986), rappelling (Mace & Carroll, 1985), squash (Mace & Carrol, 1986), and cross-country running (Ziegler, Klinzing & Williamson, 1982), as well as in increasing athlete's pain tolerance (Whitmarsh & Alderman, 1993).

CONCEPT & APPLICATION 6.8

Concept Similar to VMBR, SIT effectively reduces stress and has been shown to enhance performance of subjects.

Application The principle of gradually exposing a fearful athlete to situations of progressively

greater threat is one that can be readily applied by the practitioner. As the athlete masters the skills of relaxation and imagery, he will be better prepared to cope with situations of increased difficulty.

STRESS MANAGEMENT TRAINING (SMT)

Stress Management Training (SMT) is a cognitive-behavioral intervention program developed by Smith (1980) that incorporates relaxation training, imagery, and other cognitive processes. Like Stress Inoculation Training (SIT), SMT is composed of three stages. The significant difference between the two stress management programs is in stage three. SIT emphasizes the ability to manage small incremental changes in stress, while SMT practices managing stress associated with imagined high-stress situations.

In phase one, the *conceptualization phase,* the athlete is taught to understand the nature of stress generally, and to understand the source of her stress specifically. She learns what causes stress and how to cope with it. During this phase she also learns that she already possesses a number of useful coping strategies for dealing with stress. In phase two, the *skill acquisition phase,* the athlete learns and practices integrated coping responses. The coping responses are based on relaxation, imagery, deep breathing, and other cognitive-behavioral skills. She learns to "trigger" these coping skills through cognitive self-statements. In phase three, the *skill rehearsal phase,* induced affect is used to generate high levels of emotional arousal, which are reduced by the subject through the application of coping responses learned during skill acquisition. In SMT, the athlete is asked to imagine as vividly as possible a relevant stressful situation. Research supports the use of SMT for reducing stress and for enhancing athletic performance (Crocker, 1989; Crocker, Alderman & Smith, 1988; Ziegler et al., 1982).

CONCEPT & APPLICATION 6.9

Concept Similar to VMBR and SIT, Smith's Cognitive-Affective SMT program effectively reduces stress and has been shown to enhance performance of subjects.

Application The principle of helping an athlete to experience competition-like stress through

imagery is an effective way to help the athlete overcome real-life competitive stress. The athlete who can visualize herself successfully performing a skill with associated competitive stress is more likely to transfer this ability to a real-life situation.

GOAL SETTING IN SPORT

As explained by Locke and Latham (1990), **goal setting** is a cognitive theory of motivation that effectively energizes individuals to become more productive. Locke and Latham's basic theory is that (a) a linear relationship exists between degree of goal difficulty and performance, and (b) goals that are specific and difficult lead to a higher level of performance than "do your best" goals.

GOAL SETTING DEFINED

There are many worthwhile goals in sport. Goals can be defined in terms of such things as goal difficulty, specificity, measurability, proximity, and personal orientation. A goal is generally defined as the aim or object of something we are trying to obtain (Locke & Latham, 1985).

As an illustration, let us select a goal and define it in terms of various distinguishing characteristics. Let us say that I wish to become a better tennis player, so I set a goal to "become a better tennis player." On the surface, this seems to be a worthwhile goal. However, a number of characteristics about it make it difficult to achieve. The goal is very general, impossible to measure, and nebulous relative to how and when the goal is to be obtained. How could this goal be improved? Because becoming a better tennis player involves improving several physical and mental skills, it is necessary to set several specific goals, each defined in measurable terms. A skill analysis might reveal that the weakest part of my game is the serve. Therefore, this might be a good place to begin. My new and improved goal could be "to get 75 percent of my first serves, and 90 percent of my second serves, into the opposing player's court." This is a better goal than the first one, because it is specific, measurable, and obtainable. The only detail remaining is to define some short-term goals that will help me to achieve the final goal. For example, I might set a goal to get 60 percent of my first and 80 percent of my second serves in. I would use this as a short-term goal to be achieved by the end of the next tournament.

Perhaps the most important ingredient of goal setting is whether or not the goals are accepted by the athlete (Locke, 1991). Athletes often set goals that are imposed upon them by parents, coaches, or other athletes. If the athlete does not accept a goal as his own, it is quite meaningless. The coach's goal to win 75 percent of a season's softball games is meaningless if the athletes do not also accept this as their goal.

CONCEPT & APPLICATION 6.10

Concept For an athlete to benefit from goal setting, he must accept the goal as his own. Goals that are set by the coach may or may not be accepted by the athlete.

Application The athlete must be intimately involved in the process of goal selection. Nothing is wrong with the coach's suggesting specific goals, but it is the athlete who must accept the goal or goals as his own.

Goal orientation is another important factor to consider in goal setting. Individuals who prefer to set goals that are directly tied to the outcome of a competition are said to have an **outcome goal orientation.** These individuals think in terms of winning and not necessarily in terms of the quality of play. Conversely, the individual who has a **performance,** or process **goal orientation** tends to think in terms of quality of performance, and not necessarily in terms of the outcome of the competition. It is perhaps simplistic, however, to imply that an outcome orientation is always bad and a process goal (emphasizing the means over the end) always good. If an athlete does not have the goal of winning, there is a good chance that she won't. The very act of wanting to win is energizing and leads to greater effort. It is true, however, that an overemphasis upon winning can lead to disappointment (failure) or to an unfulfilling victory ("winning ugly"). In the long run, it is desirable that athletes focus upon a performance orientation without abandoning their goals of achieving success.

CONCEPT & APPLICATION 6.11

Concept Focusing upon performance or process goals will not assure success, but such goals will help the athlete to improve in those areas that are likely to lead to success.

Application Athletes generally do not know the difference between outcome and performance goals. This is an area in which the coach or sport psychologist can make an important impact.

Help athletes distinguish between the two types of goals and to set performance goals that will help them realize success. For example, focusing upon a strong and accurate first serve in tennis will be more likely to help an athlete achieve success than will an unfocused desire to win. This way, even if she doesn't win a particular tournament, she will end up being a better server.

As explained by Locke, Shaw, Saari, and Latham (1981), there are four basic ways in which goal setting can influence performance. The first is in the form of directed attention. Goal setting causes the athlete to focus his attention upon the task and upon achieving the goal relative to the task. Second, goal setting mobilizes effort. An athlete who sets a goal to achieve a certain level of volleyball spiking proficiency must work hard to achieve that goal. Third, goal setting increases the long-term persistence of the athlete to achieve a goal. It is not enough to work hard during a single practice or week of practice; goal setting mobilizes the need to persist and work hard for an entire season. Finally, goal setting promotes the development of new learning strategies. In setting tennis volleying goals, it is possible that the athlete might learn new and interesting strategies for rushing the net following a strong ground stroke.

APPLYING LOCKE'S GOAL-SETTING THEORY IN SPORT AND EXERCISE

When sport psychology researchers began applying Locke's goal-setting theories to sport, they naturally assumed that results would be consistent with Locke and Latham's (1990) report that 354 out of 393 industrial, organizational, and academically based studies supported their theory. However, only about 50 percent of the published exercise and sport science studies suggested that individuals given difficult but specific goals would outperform individuals merely asked to "do their best." This means that the other 50 percent failed to demonstrate support for the theory when it was applied to sport and exercise. This situation created an environment in which a series of articles were published by Locke (1991, 1994), who suggested that negative results were largely a function of poorly designed studies, and by Weinberg and Weigand (1993, 1996) who argued that negative results were due to a number of uncontrollable factors, including the nature of the task. One of the main arguments put forth by Weinberg and Weigand was that you can't stop control subjects in the "do your best" group from setting their own goals, thus biasing the results.

While the exchange between Locke and Weinberg was interesting, the consumer of the goal-setting research was left wondering about the usefulness of goal setting in motivating athletes to superior performance. In my own mind, there is no doubt that goal setting is a powerful and effective cognitive strategy for enhancing performance of athletes. In support of this position, I offer results of two very important studies. The first is a study reported by Lerner and Locke (1995), in which the researchers carefully considered all of the research design issues they believed had plagued earlier studies. They used sit-ups as the performance task and developed a strategy to make sure the "do your best" control group subjects would not set covert personal goals. The results of this pivotal investigation provided strong support for Locke and Latham's theory of goal setting in sport and exercise. The second study was a meta-analysis reported by Kyllo and Landers (1995). They scrutinized 36 studies that yielded 136 effects (measures of statistical strength). The overall results of the meta-analysis yielded the following relevant conclusions: (a) setting goals in sport and exercise results in an improvement over baseline measures, (b) moderate goals are superior to difficult goals, and (c) making goals public is effective.

While self-efficacy is not a specific topic of this chapter, it is interesting to note that both of these important studies noted the strong impact that an athlete's self-efficacy had upon goal setting. Athletes who believe that goal setting will result in improved performance almost always realize a positive benefit. Self-efficacy, as a psychological construct, will be discussed in the chapter on motivation.

When used correctly, goal setting is an effective and powerful energizer and motivator. Individuals who set goals, work towards them, and monitor them regularly will benefit from this cognitive-behavioral strategy. Two excellent reviews of goal-setting theory and of research related to the topic are provided by Weinberg (1994) and by Weinberg, Stitcher, and Richardson (1994).

Table 6.4

Summary of Selected Goal Setting Principles for Sport.

1. Specific goals are better than general goals.
2. Goals should be written or described in behavioral terms so they can be measured.
3. Difficult goals are better than easy goals or "do your best" goals.
4. Short-term goals are helpful in achieving long-term goals.
5. Performance goals are preferred to outcome goals.
6. Good goal setting mechanics require that goals be written down and closely monitored to maintain their motivational value.
7. Goals must be accepted by the athlete in order to be effective.

GETTING THE MOST OUT OF GOAL SETTING

The following principles, and associated explanations, have been gleaned from research conducted in industrial, organizational, academic, sport, and exercise settings. Goal setting principles are also summarized in table 6.4.

1. *Specific goals are better than general goals.* It is difficult for an athlete to recognize whether or not progress towards a goal has been accomplished unless the goal is relatively specific. Specific goals result in improvement greater than that produced by general goals. Getting 90 percent of one's volleyball serves in the court is a better goal than simply becoming a more accurate server.

2. *Goals should be measurable.* Along with goals being specific, they also must be measurable. How can it be determined if a goal has been achieved if it cannot be measured? A softball player's goal to increase her batting average by 50 percentage points is a goal that can be measured and achieved, but a goal to make better contact with the ball cannot. Goals should always be written or described in behavioral or observable terms.

3. *Difficult to moderately difficult goals are better than easy goals.* A vast body of industrial, organizational, academic, and sport research points to the utility of challenging workers and athletes to strive to achieve goals that appear to be difficult to achieve. Locke and Latham recommended goals that can be reached by only 10 percent of the individuals striving to achieve the goals. Reason dictates, however, that it would be counterproductive to set goals that are unreachable, especially if the individual recognizes that they are unreachable. While Locke recommended goals that only 10 percent can reach, I have modified this statement to include moderately difficult goals. This is based on the meta-analysis of Kyllo and Landers (1995), which showed that moderate goals were superior to difficult goals in sport and exercise. The utility of the recommendation to set very difficult goals, however, does have some historical precedent. Breaking the four-minute mile, for example, must have seemed to be an unrealistic goal to thousands of athletes before Roger Bannister did it in May 1954.

4. *Use short-term goals to achieve long-term goals.* Short-term goals should be used as a means to realize long-term goals (Bar-Eli, Hartman & Levy-Kolker, 1994). The relationship between long and short goals is illustrated in figure 6.2.

Figure 6.2

A goal-setting staircase showing the relationship between short- and long-term goals. From Gould, Dan. Developing psychological skills in young athletes, in *Coaching science update.* Copyright © 1983 Coaching Association of Canada, Ottawa, Canada. Reprinted by permission.

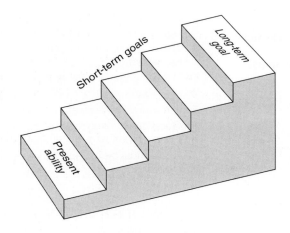

In order to obtain a long-term goal such as becoming a varsity basketball player, an athlete must meet several short-term goals along the way. A professional baseball pitcher's goal to win twenty games in a single season might very well start with the goal to win ten games before the annual All Star Game break.

5. *Set performance goals instead of outcome goals.* Research has consistently supported the setting of processes or **performance goals,** as opposed to **outcome goals** (Zimmerman & Kitsantus, 1996). Performance goals refer to methods and strategies designed to help achieve skill mastery. These are goals that can be achieved, even if the goal to win is not achieved. For example, a basketball player who sets a personal performance goal to bring down ten rebounds in a single game can achieve this goal even if the team fails to win. If your only goal is to win (an outcome goal), you will be quite disappointed if you lose. There is, however, some consolation in losing a contest if you successfully achieve a personal goal. Young athletes do not understand the difference between outcome and performance goals. It would be wise for the coach or parent to sit down with a young athlete and discuss personal performance goals that could lead to individual and team success.

6. *Mechanics of goal achievement.* An important characteristic of effective goal setting is to outline a specific strategy or plan for meeting the goal. Many goals are not reached simply because no systematic plan for achieving them has been outlined. For example, exactly how does one achieve the goal of becoming an 85 percent free throw shooter? If left to chance, it will most likely never happen. The coach and athlete together must devise a plan for achieving this goal. The athlete may have to stay after practice every day and shoot an extra 100 baskets. Other strategies, such as increasing wrist and arm strength, may also be considered. Finally, a good goal-setting program requires constant monitoring and evaluation by player and coach. A day should not go by without the athlete considering goals and evaluating progress. It may be that a particular goal cannot be achieved. In this case, the athlete should redefine the goal in a more realistic manner. However, in most cases the regular evaluation of

progress will help athletes see improvements that will provide them additional motivation to achieve their goals.

7. *Goals must be accepted by the athlete.* In order for a goal to be effective, the athlete must believe that it is her goal. The athlete may not feel "ownership" for goals that are set by the athlete's coach or parents. The coach or parent may assist in identifying and verbalizing goals, but in the final analysis the goal(s) must belong to the athlete. It is the athlete that must be motivated, therefore it is the athlete that must set and strive to achieve the goal.

CONCEPT & APPLICATION 6.12

Concept The most effective goals are specific, are reasonably challenging for the athlete, and combine short-term subgoals with a long-term final goal.

Application Effective goal-setting skills do not come naturally to the athlete; they must be taught. Coaches must work with athletes to help them set goals that are motivational and have the potential for performance enhancement.

PSYCHOLOGICAL SKILLS TRAINING FOR SPORT

Psychological skills training for sport is a concept that brings together many of the attentional, arousal control, and cognitive-behavioral strategies that have been discussed in this text. It is a concept that implies that psychological skills, like motor skills, can be learned by the athlete and used to enhance performance as well as quality of life. Psychological skills include but are not the same as coping skills. By definition, coping skills are used by the athlete to eliminate or manage stress. This is one of the psychological skills that an athlete must learn, but there are others as well. Psychological skills training involves the learning of procedures and practices that are proactive in nature, as opposed to mere responses to negative stress. At the conclusion of this section, I will introduce and

---

CONCEPT & APPLICATION 6.13

Concept Organized sports psychological skills training programs are effective in enhancing both performance and self-confidence.

Application With the assistance of a sports psychologist, the coach should incorporate psychological skills training into the daily practice schedules of athletes. The program should be designed to maximize the mental preparation benefits without detracting from individual and team skill development. Free throw shooting practice, for example, would be an ideal time to discuss and practice imagery skills.

Psychological skills
training for sport
enhances
performance. Courtesy
University of Missouri-
Columbia Sports
Information

explain the details of a well-established psychological skills program for athletes.
At this juncture, it is useful to point out that situation-specific psychological skills
programs have been utilized to improve performance in tennis (Draw & Burton,
1994), golf (Thomas & Over, 1994), alpine ski racing (Taylor, 1995, youth
basketball and football (Hughes, 1990; Jeffries & Esparza, 1992), and activities
engaged in by disabled wheelchair athletes (Hanrahan, 1995).

SOME HELPFUL GUIDELINES FOR PSYCHOLOGICAL SKILLS TRAINING

Vealey published an article in 1988 that provides some important guidelines for
the continued development of psychological skills programs for athletes. Her

critical points are important to the continued development of sport psychology, now and for the future. In this important paper, Vealey identified six critical needs associated with the continued development of psychological skills training for athletes. I will discuss each of these needs briefly.

1. Populations other than elite athletes must be targeted for psychological skills training. The trend has been to focus upon elite athletes at the expense of athletes and sports participants in general. This trend has led to the conclusion that only certified sport psychologists are qualified to work with athletes. Who is going to provide psychological skills training for youth and for disabled athletes? Is it realistic to assume that every youth sport team has the financial resources to hire a certified or licensed sport psychologist to teach its players psychological skills? A better approach is to equip teachers and coaches at all levels with the skills necessary to train their own athletes in psychological skills (Smith, 1992). In many European countries, coaches receive training in skills and techniques associated with psychological preparation of athletes. This is a model that should be better developed in North America.

2. The second need is to move beyond education to implementation. Coaches and practitioners must be given opportunities to receive "hands-on" training in psychological skills training techniques. Training opportunities may come in the form of workshops, university extension services, and professional conferences.

3. In developing a psychological skills training program, it is important to differentiate between psychological skills and the methods for developing these skills. A case in point is imagery. Imagery is a **psychological method** that is used to develop **psychological skill** in visualizing correct performance. It is also used in achieving optimal arousal and optimal attentional control. Similarly, goal setting, relaxation training, and thought control are methods used to develop psychological skills that lead to enhanced performance and self-confidence. Approaching an achievement situation with confidence and with the knowledge that the body and mind are prepared for optimal performance is a psychological skill.

4. It is important that psychological skills training programs take a holistic approach as opposed to a narrow, unidimensional, performance enhancement approach. A holistic approach takes into consideration all aspects of the environment in attempting to solve a problem. The sport psychologist must approach the problem of optimal performance from a multidimensional perspective. Lack of psychological skill is not the only reason that an athlete fails to make contact with a softball, or to make a free throw in basketball. The sport psychologist must not view his role as fundamentally tied to enhancing the athletic performance of elite athletes. Consistent with this theme is the implementation by many university athletic departments of "total person programs" as a way to help athletes develop themselves holistically. This is an approach that should be embraced in the grade schools and high schools as well.

Downhill skiing requires a great deal of mental preparation, physical skill, and courage. Courtesy Digital Stock Photo CD/Active Lifestyles

5. In chapter 1 of this text, three kinds of sport psychologists were identified: educational, research, and clinical/counseling sport psychologists. The fifth need is for educational sport psychologists to adopt a human development model as opposed to a clinical/counseling model for working with athletes at all levels. Athletes suffering from clinical depression or some other serious malady should be referred to the clinical/counseling licensed psychologist who is also trained in sport psychology. As recommended by Anshel (1992), educational and research sport psychologists should (a) continue to validate (research) cognitive-behavioral techniques, (b) recognize the role of licensed clinical/counseling psychologists, and (c) educate the public about the human development skills of the sport psychologist.

6. Finally, there is a need for sport psychologists to nurture the symbiotic relationship between theory, research, and practice. The viability of psychological skills training programs depends upon an interactive and cooperative relationship between the researcher and the practitioner who applies the research in the field. Applied sport psychology is only as strong as the knowledge base that supports the cognitive and behavioral techniques used by the sport psychologist. Conversely, the theorist must view research as something that can be applied at a later time, as opposed to viewing it as an end in itself.

MEASUREMENT OF PSYCHOLOGICAL SKILL

Several inventories have been developed that are designed to measure psychological skills used by athletes. Each of the inventories I will mention has demonstrated the ability to distinguish among groups of athletes performing at different levels of skill. Before adopting a specific inventory, the practitioner should become familiar with the reliability, validity, and statistical properties of the selected inventory.

Psychological Skills Inventory for Sports. The **Psychological Skills Inventory for Sports (PSIS-5)** was developed by Mahoney, Gabriel, and Perkins (1987). The PSIS-5 (5th version) is a 45-item inventory that measures the psychological skills of anxiety control, concentration, confidence, mental preparation, motivation, and team orientation. While the PSIS-5 has exhibited the ability to discriminate among levels of skilled performers, recent research has questioned the underlying structure of the six factors it measures (Chartrand, Jowdy & Danish, 1992).

Athletic Coping Skills Inventory. The **Athletic Coping Skills Inventory (ACSI-28)** was developed by Smith, Schutz, Smoll, and Ptacek (1995). The ACSI-28 is a 28-item inventory that measures the psychological skills of coping with adversity, peaking under pressure, goal setting/mental preparation, concentration, freedom from worry, confidence and achievement motivation, and coachability. The ACSI-28 is a modest predictor of hitting and pitching performance among professional baseball players (Smith & Christensen, 1995).

Test of Performance Strategies. The **Test of Performance Strategies (TOPS)** was developed by Thomas, Hardy, and Murphy (1996). The TOPS is a 64-item inventory that measures psychological behaviors of athletes during competition as well as practice. Eight factors are measured relative to practice behaviors, and eight relative to competition. Seven of the eight factors are common to both practice and competition. The eight factors that measure psychological behavior during practice include activation, relaxation, imagery, goal setting, self-talk, automaticity, emotional control, and attentional control. The eight factors that measure psychological behavior during competition include all of the above except attentional control. Attentional control is replaced with negative thinking when the test is used to measure psychological behaviors during competition.

PSYCHOLOGICAL SKILLS EDUCATION

A number of organized programs for teaching psychological skills to athletes have been proposed. One such program, developed by Boutcher and Rotella (1987), has provided the field of sport psychology with a basic model for teaching these skills. It is instructive to review this program in some detail. The **Psychological Skills Education Program (PSEP)** was developed for athletes who perform closed skills. One such closed skill is weight lifting (clean-and-jerk); another is free throw shooting in basketball, a sport that is primarily open-skill in nature. Open-skill sports such as basketball and football are classified as such because they are open to the environment. An opponent cannot interfere with an athlete's attempt at a clean-and-jerk in weight lifting, but an opponent can alter or interfere with a pass, dribble, or jump shot in basketball, because these skills are open to the environment. PSEP was conceived as a four-phase program in which various intervention strategies are applied in the final phase. These four phases are illustrated in figure 6.3.

In phase one, the *sport analysis* phase, the sport psychologist does a thorough analysis of the characteristics of the closed skill that is involved. If the athlete is

Figure 6.3

Schematic of Boutcher
and Rotella's (1987)
Psychological Skills
Education Program.

Phase 1	Phase 2	Phase 3	Phase 4
Analysis of closed skills	Psychological assessment of athletes	Conceptualization/ motivation	Development of mental skills
* Biomechanical	* SCAT	* Commitment	1. In controlled environment, learn arousal control and intervention strategies.
* Physiological	* POMS	* Desire to Excel	
* Motor sequence	* Cattell 16 PF	* Long-term Motivation	
	* TOPS		2. Apply intervention techniques in real-life situations.
	* Etc.		
			3. Development of performance routines. * Preshot * During-play * Postshot

trying to improve her golf swing, the sport psychologist must become familiar with the important biomechanical elements of the golf swing, as well as the physiological and psychological requirements. The important point is that the sport psychologist should not prematurely attribute all problems to a psychological cause.

In phase two, the *individual assessment* phase, the psychological strengths and weaknesses of the athlete must be determined from a psychological perspective. It is at this point that various psychological inventories should be administered and interpreted. Appropriate inventories might include the Sport Competition Anxiety Test (SCAT), the Profile of Mood States (POMS), Cattell's 16 Personality Factor Questionnaire, and the Test of Performance Strategies (TOPS). If, after interpreting the selected inventories, the sport psychologist concludes that the athlete demonstrates abnormal clinical symptoms, she should be referred to the appropriate professional sources.

In phase three, the *conceptualization/motivation* phase, the sport psychologist discusses with the athlete the kind of commitment that is needed in order to change inappropriate behaviors. It is during this phase that the athlete must come to grips with her own desire to excel. Whether or not an athlete has the desire to develop effective psychological skills must be determined prior to entering into phase four.

In phase four, the *development of mental skills phase,* the athlete learns specific intervention techniques that can influence psychological mood and performance. These mental techniques may include arousal adjustment, mental imagery, self-talk, and thought stopping. In learning the various intervention techniques, the athlete is taken through three training stages. In the *first stage,* the athlete learns the intervention technique in a quiet, non-threatening environment. Relaxation and mental imagery, for example, might first be learned in the quiet of the person's own home, or perhaps in a secluded out-of-doors setting. In *stage two,* the athlete applies the intervention technique in real-life settings. For instance, the techniques of relaxation might be applied in practice and pre-game situations where there might be a tendency to become anxious and tense.

After the athlete has succeeded in the development of cognitive intervention techniques that can be transferred to game situations, *stage three* focuses on the development of performance routines. **Performance routines** can be categorized as preshot, between-play, or postshot in nature. **Preshot routines** take place immediately preceding the initiation of a shot or play. **Between-play routines** take place during breaks in the action of games such as tennis, basketball, volleyball, and baseball. **Postshot routines** take place during the period of time immediately following the execution of a motor skill.

Performance routines, whether used before, during, or after the execution of a closed motor skill, are designed to help the athletes focus attention appropriately. While little has been written about the between-play and postshot routines, they are potentially as important as the preshot routine. Many sporting activities take several hours to complete and provide many before- and after-shot opportunities for the athlete to engage in some useful mental activity. For example, what should baseball outfielders be thinking about during the period of time the catcher is warming up a relief pitcher? One possibility would be to engage in relaxing conversation with teammates or fellow competitors. Another would be to imagine restful scenes on a secluded beach or a walk along a mountain stream.

The kinds of planned postshot routines that athletes engage in are also of importance. There is a natural tendency, in noncontinuous sports, to dwell on the negative aspects of an unsuccessful performance. A planned postshot routine would include a strategy to clear the mind for the next shot and to save critical skill analysis for the practice field.

Research has validated the use of performance routines in sport (Cohn, Rotella & Lloyd, 1990; Hill & Borden, 1995; Predelbon & Docker, 1992; Wrisberg & Pein, 1992). Examples of preshot, between-play, and postshot routines are provided in table 6.5. To be effective, performance routines must be practiced and must exhibit temporal consistency. This means that the temporal length of the routine must be consistent, and execution of the routine must occur at a consistent time prior to execution of the skill. For example, a preshot routine for shooting a basketball free throw, should always take about the same amount of time to execute, and be initiated at approximately the same point in time relative to releasing the basketball (Wrisberg & Pein, 1992).

Table 6.5

Examples of Performance Routines Used in Sport.

Routine	Sport	Situation	Steps
Preshot	Golf	Putting	1. Stand behind the ball and "read" the line of the putt.
			2. Approach the ball and take two practice swings.
			3. Align the putter to the target, set the feet, and take two glances at the hole.
Between-Play	Tennis	Changing Courts	1. Take care of your body and your equipment (water and towel off).
			2. Give your mind some relief (focus on positive thoughts).
			3. Focus on strategy for next game.
Postshot	Volleyball	Passing	1. Clear mind of results of previous pass by yourself or teammate.
			2. Focus on making a perfect pass to the setter.
			3. Use self-talk to remind yourself that you are an excellent passer.

CONCEPT & APPLICATION 6.14

Concept Preshot routines are effective strategies for channeling an athlete's attention on the execution of a motor skill.

Application A young athlete needs assistance in crafting a preshot routine that fits his personality. All preshot routines need not be identical.

However, they should cause the athlete to focus attention upon appropriate stimuli and should be of uniform length. The sequencing of activities within the routine should also remain unchanged from one shot to the next.

OTHER ASPECTS OF PSYCHOLOGICAL SKILLS TRAINING

Positive self-talk is a concept that is well established in the applied sport psychology literature. When used in conjunction with arousal control and attentional focus, self-talk is tantamount to positive suggestions given during self-hypnosis or autogenic training. Self-talk phrases form the basis of another learned behavior called *attentional cueing*. **Attentional cueing** utilizes self-talk statements to trigger images and attentional focus points designed to guide the athlete during competition (Hill & Borden, 1995). Three different types of self-talk include task-relevant statements, mood words containing emotional meaning, and positive self-affirmation statements (Rushall, Hall & Rushall, 1989). In the sport of cross-country skiing, task-relevant statements might include the phrases "up hill, quick and grip, weight back." Mood words containing emotional meaning might include "go, blast, drive, burst." Self-affirmation statements might include the phrases "feel great, feel strong, feel fast."

Psychological momentum is a phenomenon that has been documented in the literature relative to tennis (Silva, Hardy & Grace, 1988), basketball free throw shooting (Shaw, Dzewaltowski & McElroy, 1992), volleyball (Burke & Houseworth, 1995), ice hockey (Gayton, Very & Hearns, 1993), and pocket billiards (Adams. 1995). As defined by Taylor and Demick (1994), psychological momentum is "a positive or negative change in cognition, affect, physiology, and behavior caused by an event or series of events that will result in a commensurate shift in performance and competitive outcome" (p. 54). The key element in this definition is the *precipitating event* that leads to the "momentum chain." An important meditating variable is the experience of the athletes involved (both teams, or both opponents). Experienced athletes are better able to recognize and act upon precipitating events, more likely to possess the skills necessary to take advantage of precipitating events, and better able to mobilize defenses against negative momentum. *Negative momentum* may be characterized as conditions necessary to precipitate positive momentum on the part of the opposition. Examples of precipitating events in tennis might include a dramatic shot, breaking an opponent's serve, winning game after long deuce, a critical unforced error, and not converting 15-40, 0-40 break serve opportunities. Examples of precipitating events in basketball might include a slam-dunk, a critical 3-point play or shot, a steal and conversion, and making the first free throw in a one-and-one situation.

SUMMARY

The focus of this chapter was upon cognitive-behavioral intervention strategies designed to change or influence existing thought and behavioral patterns. Topics discussed included coping strategies, imagery and mental practice, goal setting, and psychological skills training for sport.

Coping strategies were defined as dynamic, conscious efforts on the part of the individual to eliminate or manage distress. Distress occurs when an individual perceives an imbalance between demands and resources. Coping strategies can be categorized into those that are problem focused, and those that are emotion focused.

Differences and similarities between mental practice and imagery were discussed. Principles and practices relating imagery and mental practice to performance enhancement were reviewed. Psychoneuromuscular theory, symbolic learning theory, and attention/arousal set theory were discussed as possible explanations for the efficacy of imagery in sport. The two kinds of imagery are internal and external. Several inventories designed to measure imagery ability were identified. Based upon the literature, principles of the application of imagery to sport were identified and discussed. Six steps for improving imagery skills were identified.

Visual motor behavior rehearsal (VMBR), stress inoculation training (SIT), and cognitive-affective stress management training (SMT) were identified as cognitive intervention programs that include relaxation and imagery. Each of the programs was discussed relative to procedures and research support.

Goal setting was defined as a cognitive theory of motivation that effectively energizes individuals to become more productive. Locke and Latham's (1985, 1990) basic theory that specific and difficult goals are better than "do your best" goals was discussed, and sport psychology literature was reviewed relative to the theory. Several important principles associated with effective goal setting were reviewed and discussed, including these: (a) specific goals are better than general goals, (b) goals should be measurable, (c) difficult to moderately difficult goals are better than easy goals, (d) short-term goals assist in achieving long-term goals, (e) performance goals are better than outcome goals, (f) good goal achievement mechanics are required, and (g) goals must be accepted by the athlete.

Psychological skills training (PST) was discussed in terms of (a) guidelines for the future of PST, (b) measurement, and (c) an educational program for developing psychological skills. Relative to guidelines for the future, six needs were discussed. Measurement of psychological skills was discussed in terms of the Psychological Skills Inventory for Sports (PSIS-5), the Athletic Coping Skills Inventory (ACSI-28), and the Test of Performance Strategies (TOPS). Finally, Boutcher and Rotella's (1987) Psychological Skills Education Program (PSEP) was reviewed in detail. The PSEP is conducted in four basic phases: sport analysis, individual assessment, conceptualization and motivation, and development of mental skills. The development of mental skills phase is divided into three stages that include the learning and application of specific intervention techniques.

REVIEW QUESTIONS

1. Explain and give examples of cognitive restructuring relative to Ellis's ABC theory of personality.

2. Discuss and explain Iso-Ahola's model of the psychological makeup of the athlete.

3. Provide a definition of coping, and discuss coping strategies used by athletes. How do problem-focused and emotion-focused coping strategies differ? Provide examples.

4. Distinguish between the terms *mental practice* and *mental imagery.*

5. Is imagery of greater use to the novice or to the accomplished athlete? Provide logic and research documentation with your answer.

6. Why should mentally practicing or imaging a physical task result in improved learning and performance? Identify and review three theories that purport to explain this facilitative relationship.

7. Distinguish between the two types of imagery. Is one method superior to the other? Explain.

8. Review and discuss the principles associated with the application of imagery to sport.

9. How can imagery skills be improved? Explain and elaborate.

10. Name and describe three cognitive-behavioral intervention programs that utilize both imagery and relaxation.

11. Explain how the three intervention programs identified in question #10 are similar and dissimilar.

12. Describe goal-setting theory as proposed by Locke and Latham. Review the industrial, organizational, academic, and sport-related support for the theory.

13. Differentiate between the terms *outcome orientation* and *performance orientation* relative to goal setting. Which orientation is preferred? Give illustrations of each.

14. Identify, review and explain the seven principles of good goal setting. Give examples of good and bad goals for each principle.

15. As identified by Vealey (1988), what are the six needs associated with the future of psychological skills training? Provide an explanation for each.

16. Identify and briefly discuss three inventories used to measure psychological skill in sport.

17. Provide a detailed explanation of Boutcher and Rotella's (1987) Psychological Skills Education Program (PSEP).

18. Discuss the nature of performance routines in sport. Provide a detailed discussion of the nature and utility of the preshot routine in sport.

19. Discuss psychological momentum as a verifiable psychological phenomenon in sport.

GLOSSARY

ACSI-28 The Athletic Coping Skills Inventory (ACSI-28), developed by Smith, Schutz, Smoll, and Ptacek (1995), which assesses psychological skills of athletes.

attention and arousal set theory Theory combining the cognitive aspects of symbolic learning theory with the physiological aspects of psychoneuromuscular theory to explain the phenomenon of performance enhancement through imagery.

attentional cueing The use of self-talk statements to trigger images and attentional focus points designed to guide the athlete during competition.

between-play routines Sequenced performance routines that take place during breaks in the action in an athletic contest.

cognitive-behavioral intervention A mental as opposed to physical intervention designed to bring about a change in behavior.

cognitive restructuring The use of cognitive or mental skills to restructure or change the way one views certain situations.

coping strategies Dynamic, conscious efforts on the part of the individual to eliminate or manage stress.

external imagery Visual imagery in which athletes "watch" themselves perform.

goal setting The process of setting goals in order to increase motivation and achieve an end result.

imagery Use of visualization to imagine situations.

internal imagery Kinesthetic imagery in which the subject feels himself "within" his own body while performing.

mental practice Practicing a physical skill mentally or cognitively, without overt movement of the limbs or body.

outcome goal orientation A psychological orientation to focus upon the outcome of an athletic contest (i.e., wins and losses) rather than the quality of play.

outcome goals Goals that focus upon the outcome of a contest (i.e., wins and losses) as opposed to the quality of the play.

performance goal orientation A psychological orientation to focus upon the quality of an athlete's performance, as opposed to the outcome of a contest.

performance goals Goals that focus upon the quality of an athlete's performance, as opposed to the outcome of a contest.

performance routines Planned sequences of mental or physical steps designed to assist the athlete in focusing attention upon relevant stimuli.

postshot routines Performance routines that take place immediately following the execution of a skilled movement.

preshot routines Performance routines that take place immediately before the execution of a skilled movement.

PSEP Psychological Skills Education Program, designed by Boutcher and Rotella (1987) to teach athletes how to prepare mentally for sports participation.

PSIS-5 Psychological Skills Inventory for Sports, developed by Mahoney, Gabriel and Perkins (1987) to assess psychological skills relevant to athletic performance.

psychological method A technique, such as imagery or relaxation, that is designed to improve the psychological skill of an athlete.

psychological momentum The perception, based upon a series of successful experiences, that an athlete or a team has the impetus to achieve victory.

psychological skill The ability to approach an achievement situation with the confidence and knowledge that the body and mind are prepared for optimal performance.

psychological skills training Preparation of an athlete to approach an achievement situation with confidence and the knowledge that the body and mind are prepared for optimal performance.

psychoneuromuscular theory A theory that purports to explain the phenomenon of performance enhancement through imagery based upon subliminal neuromuscular patterns.

self-talk A form of verbal self-affirmation.

SIT A four-phase stress management program called Stress Inoculation Training, whose goal is to "inoculate" an athlete against stress by guiding the athlete through progressively more stressful situations.

SMT A stress management program called Cognitive-Affective Stress Management Training, in which the athlete practices stress-coping skills in stressful situations.

symbolic learning theory A theory that purports to explain the phenomenon of performance enhancement through imagery as based upon advanced planning.

TOPS Test of Performance Strategies, designed by Thomas, Hardy, and Murphy (1996) to assess psychological behaviors relevant to athletic performance.

VMBR A stress management program called Visual Motor Behavior Rehearsal, which uses imagery and relaxation techniques to help athletes deal with stress.

SUGGESTED READINGS

Boutcher, S. H., & Rotella, R. J. (1987). A psychological skills education program for closed-skill performance enhancement. *The Sport Psychologist, 1,* 127–137.

Folkman, S., & Lazarus, R. S. (1985). If it changes it must be a process: Study of emotion and coping during three stages of a college examination. *Journal of Personality and Social Psychology, 48,* 150–170.

Gould, D., & Udry, E. (1994). Psychological skills for enhancing performance: Arousal regulation strategies. *Medicine and Science in Sports and Exercise, 26,* 478–485.

Greenspan, M. J., & Feltz, D. L. (1989). Psychological interventions with athletes in competitive situations: A review. *The Sport Psychologist, 3,* 219–236.

Grouios, G. (1992). Mental practice: A review. *Journal of Sport Behavior, 15,* 42–59.

Iso-Ahola, S. (1995). Intrapersonal and interpersonal factors in athletic performance. *Scandinavian Journal of Medicine and Science in Sports, 5,* 191–199.

Kyllo, L. B., & Landers, D. M. (1995). Goal setting in sport and exercise: A research synthesis to resolve the controversy. *Journal of Sport & Exercise Psychology, 17,* 117–137.

Lerner, B. S., & Locke, E. A. (1995). The effects of goal setting, self-efficacy, competition, and personal traits on the performance of an endurance task. *Journal of Sport & Exercise Psychology, 17,* 138–152.

Locke, E. A., & Latham, G. P. (1990). *A theory of goal setting & task performance.* Englewood Cliffs, NJ: Prentice-Hall.

Meichenbaum, D. (1985). *Stress inoculation training.* New York: Pergamon Press.

Moran, A. (1993). Conceptual and methodological issues in the measurement of mental imagery skills in athletes. *Journal of Sport Behavior, 16,* 157–170.

Murphy, S. M. (1994). Imagery interventions in sport. *Medicine and Science in Sports and Exercise, 26,* 486–494.

Smith, R. E., Schutz, R. W., Smoll, F. L., & Ptacek, J. T. (1995). Development and validation of a multidimensional measure of sport specific psychological skills: The athletic coping skills inventory-28. *Journal of Sport & Exercise Psychology, 17,* 379–398.

Taylor, J., & Demick, A. (1994). A multidimensional model of momentum in sports. *Journal of Applied Sport Psychology, 6,* 51–70.

Vealey, R. S. (1988). Future directions in psychological skills training. *The Sport Psychologist, 2,* 318–336.

Weinberg, R. S. (1994). Goal setting and performance in sport and exercise settings: A synthesis and critique. *Medicine and Science in Sport and Exercise, 26,* 469–477.

Zhang, L., Qi-Wei, M., Orlick, T., & Zitzelsberger, L. (1992). The effect of mental imagery training on performance enhancement with 7–10-year-old children. *The Sport Psychologist, 6,* 230–241.

7 CAUSAL ATTRIBUTION IN SPORT

KEY TERMS

- *attributional training*
- *attribution theory*
- *Causal Dimension Scale*
- *Causal Dimension Scale II*
- *competitive situation*
- *controllability*
- *covariation principle*
- *ego-enhancing strategy*
- *ego-protecting strategy*
- *external control*
- *illogical model*

- *internal control*
- *learned helplessness*
- *locus of control*
- *logical attribution*
- *logical model*
- *open-ended attribution*
- *origin-pawn relationship*
- *self-serving hypothesis*
- *stability*
- *structural rating scale*

Athlete's affect
associated with
outcome is indicative of
perceived cause.
Courtesy Kansas State
University Sports
Information

The key element in *attribution theory* is perception. When athletes are asked, "To what do you attribute your great success?" they are being asked for their perceptions. The fact that their perceptions of why they are successful may be completely erroneous is beside the point. The manner in which athletes answer questions like these reveals their perceptual biases.

Consider the following scenario. Two experienced volleyball players were matched against a pair of less experienced players in intramural doubles competition. The outcome was predictable: the experienced team won the match 15–1, 15–3. After the match the losers explained to the victors that they lost because one of them had injured his shoulder and they had had a bad day. In point of fact, they lost because they played a team with far more ability. However, this was not apparent to the losers, who attributed their loss to bad luck and an injured shoulder. In so doing, they were subconsciously protecting their egos. While this may not have made them better volleyball players, it served to protect their feelings of self-esteem.

Consider a second example, a variation that occurs regularly in youth sports competition. A group of youngsters was returning home after suffering a humiliating 17–0 soccer defeat at the hands of a superior team. As the children began to give causes for the defeat, it became apparent to the father of two of the youngsters that each child had a little different perception of the cause of the loss. One child explained that they lost because of poor officiating. A second and a third exclaimed that they thought they lost the match because of the poor condition of the playing field. A fourth child reported, with tears in her eyes, that they lost because they weren't any good. Each response revealed important information about the way children attempt to make sense out of their experiences.

Attribution theory is a cognitive approach to motivation. It assumes that people strive to explain, understand, and predict events based upon their cognitive perception. According to attribution theory, the intent of every human being is to explain his own actions in terms of their perceived causes. Fritz Heider (1944, 1958), the originator of attribution theory, described his theory as one of common sense, or "naive psychology."

However, as viewed by Weiner (1985) and Roberts (1982), attribution theory is far more than a layperson's theory of perceived motivation. It is a complex theory in which perceived attributions are viewed as greatly influencing a person's actions, feelings, confidence, and motivation. How an athlete feels about herself is directly related to the athlete's perception of cause and effect.

Most of the research that uses attribution theory deals with understanding when and why people select certain categories of attribution. For example, if an athlete systematically attributes failure to bad luck, we might suspect an unwillingness to accept responsibility. The attributions that athletes select reveal their motivational structures. Furthermore, helping athletes to change their perceptions can have a significant effect on their motivation to achieve. For this reason, motivation and attribution theory are very closely related. For example, some young people feel they fail because they lack innate ability. Since innate ability is relatively permanent, it is hard for those children to see that things will ever change for the better. However, if young athletes can be encouraged to consider bad luck or lack of effort as a cause for their failure, they need not feel that things cannot change. After all, luck can improve, and one can always try harder.

CONCEPT & APPLICATION 7.1

Concept Attributions that athletes select to explain their outcomes reveal much about their motivational structures.

Application Coaches should not disregard the kinds of attributions athletes use to explain their outcomes. Instead, coaches should analyze them to understand the athletes' basic attribution structures. Athletes who give inappropriate attributions may need help in explaining their outcomes.

This chapter deals with attribution theory under three broad categories: model development, causal attributions in competitive situations, and egocentrism in attribution.

THE ATTRIBUTIONAL MODEL

The basic attribution model was proposed by Heider (1944, 1958). However, several significant contributions by Weiner (1972, 1979) have made it much more useful. Most recently, contributions by Russell (1982) and by McAuley, Duncan, and Russell (1992) have improved our ability to measure attribution.

FRITZ HEIDER'S CONTRIBUTION

Fritz Heider is the acknowledged founder of attribution theory. The basis for Heider's model was the notion that people strive for prediction and understanding of daily events in order to give their lives stability and predictability. A simplified version of Heider's basic model is illustrated in figure 7.1.

Outcomes are attributed internally to the person (personal force) or externally to the environment (environmental force). Effective personal force is composed of the attributional factors *ability* and *effort,* while effective environmental force is composed of the attributional factors *task difficulty* and *luck.*

According to Heider, an interaction occurs between the personal force of ability and the environmental force of task difficulty that yields a separate dimension referred to as *can* (or *cannot*). This is a sensible suggestion. If a task is difficult and yet is accomplished, it must be due to great ability. However, depending on the difficulty of the task and the ability of the subject, several other attributions can give rise to the *can* or (*cannot*) dimension.

Figure 7.1

Simplified schematic of
Heider's (1958) model of
causal attributions.

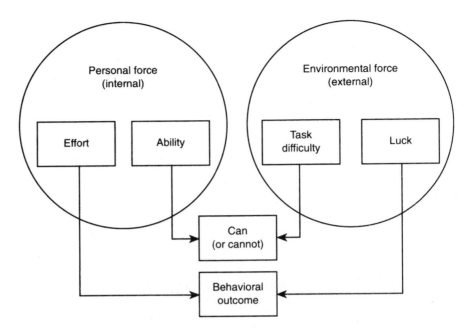

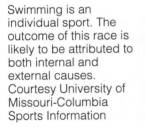

Swimming is an
individual sport. The
outcome of this race is
likely to be attributed to
both internal and
external causes.
Courtesy University of
Missouri-Columbia
Sports Information

The highly unstable factor of luck also enters into many attribution situations.
Luck is an environmental factor that can favorably or unfavorably change an
outcome in an unsystematic way. However, keep in mind that what one person
calls luck another person may call ability. For example, a tennis player who
consistently places the first serve into the deep back-hand corner of the opponent's
serving area should be considered skilled. However, the opponent may continue to
attribute the event to luck. All these factors (trying, ability, task difficulty, and
luck) combine to result in a behavioral outcome, to which an individual attributes
a cause. Heider reasoned that the personal and the environmental components of
causation are additive. Thus, the following formula represents his reasoning:

Behavioral outcome = Personal force + Impersonal force

Figure 7.2

Weiner's classification scheme for causal attributions. From Bernard Weiner, *Theories of motivation: From mechanism to cognition.* Copyright © 1972 by Houghton Mifflin Company. Used with permission.

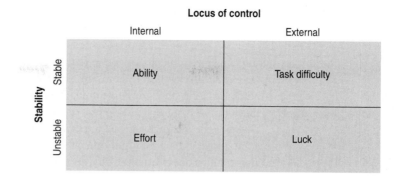

BERNARD WEINER'S CONTRIBUTIONS

Using Heider's basic formulation, Weiner (1972) made several significant contributions to the attribution model that made it easier to understand and apply in achievement situations. Weiner took Heider's four main factors and restructured them into two main causal dimensions. These two dimensions he labeled *stability* and *locus of control*. As can be observed in figure 7.2, **stability** is composed of stable and unstable attributes, while **locus of control** includes internal and external loci of control. Locus of control is a psychological construct that refers to people's belief about whether they are personally in control of what happens to them. Athletes who exhibit **internal control** tend to believe their behaviors influence outcomes. Those who exhibit **external control** tend to attribute their outcomes to outside forces such as fate, chance, and other people.

Weiner then incorporated Heider's four main factors (trying, ability, task difficulty, and luck) into his classification scheme for causal attribution. Ability was classified as a stable internal factor, while trying, or effort, was classified as an unstable internal factor. Both ability and effort are internal or personal in nature. However, ability is relatively unchanging or stable, while effort is constantly changing or unstable. A soccer player's ability may not change much from game to game, but the effort expended might fluctuate a great deal.

Conversely, task difficulty and luck are external in terms of locus of control. Task difficulty (ability of an opponent, for example) is relatively stable and unchanging, while luck is unstable and variable.

Within this four-choice framework, Weiner envisioned that people would generally attribute their successes and failures to one of the four factors depicted in figure 7.2. If a female sprinter loses a race to a faster opponent and then reasons that the loss is due to bad luck, what she is really saying is that the cause is external and unstable, and given another chance she would win. But if she loses and attributes the loss to a lack of ability, she is saying the cause is internal and is not going to change; if she ran the race a second time, she would still lose.

Weiner's original conceptualizations included the four specific classes of attribution shown in figure 7.2. Frieze (1976) provided evidence to support this four-category system. She found that 85 percent of the open-ended attributions reported in her research could be easily categorized in terms of stability and locus of control. However, Roberts and Pascuzzi (1979) reported that only 45 percent of the open-ended attributions that children use in a sport setting can be easily categorized in terms of effort, ability, difficulty, and luck. **Open-ended attribution** systems allow athletes to identify their own causes without any suggestions or constraints from the individual recording the attribution.

Weiner (1972), however, never meant to imply that there could not be more than two dimensions for classifying attributions. In fact, he later identified another dimension, **controllability** (Weiner, 1979). Under this dimension, attributions are classified as being either controllable or uncontrollable. A controllable attribution is one in which the athlete's perception is that the outcome is under her personal control; an uncontrollable attribution is one in which she thinks it is not. One drawback to the controllability dimension is that it is difficult to conceive of an attribution that is both external and controllable. Thus, two of the eight potential three-dimensional cells would have to be empty.

Due to the similarity of the terms *locus of control* and *controllability,* the introduction of the controllability dimension is confusing. For this reason Weiner (1985) suggested that the locus of control dimension be called *locus of causality.* As explained by Weiner (1985), the distinction between locus of causality and controllability is a subtle one. An athlete may perceive that failure is due to ability and therefore internal, yet feel little control over ability. For example, I might lose a 100-meter race to a faster opponent, attribute the loss internally to low ability (speed), yet feel that I don't have control over how fast I can run. The issue of controllability is discussed further in the next section.

DAN RUSSELL'S AND ED MCAULEY'S CONTRIBUTIONS

Traditionally, there have been three ways of measuring causal attribution. The first is the **structural rating scale** method, in which the athlete is asked to rate several attributions in terms of how they apply to an event. The list of attributions usually includes ability, effort, difficulty, and luck. The second method is the structural percentage rating scale method. With this the attributions are again supplied, but the subject must rate them in terms of percentage of contribution. The third method is referred to as an open-ended system. The athletes make their own attributions or select them from a long list of potential attributions. The researcher then assigns the open-ended statements to specific categories of the attribution model shown in figure 7.2.

The weakness of the two structural methods of assessing attributions is that they are too constrained. Subjects are forced to select attributions from a list that may not contain a statement that matches their perception of what caused an event. The weakness of the open-ended system is that it leaves the experimenter with the task of assigning attributions to the appropriate dimensions. The researcher and the athlete may not agree on the meaning of a causal attribution, and too often the open-ended attributions are ambiguous.

To deal with attribution distortion and misclassification, Russell (1982) developed the **Causal Dimension Scale** (CDS). In using the CDS, athletes are asked to indicate their perceived cause for an outcome, and then to rate the cause relative to nine questions. The scale is composed of three questions for each of the dimensions of locus, stability, and controllability. The score range for each dimension is between 3 and 27. The higher the score is, the more internal, stable, and controllable the athlete perceives the attribution to be. Thus, if an athlete attributed her outcome to "I had a good day" and then received a locus score of 25, a stability score of 21, and a controllability score of 10, you could label her attribution as internal, stable, and uncontrollable. Using the three-dimensional model shown in figure 7.3, you could also classify the attributional response in the *ability* category.

Russell avoided the problem of empty cells for the external/controllable interactions by slightly modifying the dimension of controllability. He redefined a controllable cause as one that could be controlled, changed, or affected by either the athlete or some other person. Others affecting an outcome could be teammates, opponents, coaches, or fans. This modification resulted in eight possible categories of attributions based on the three dimensions of locus of control, stability, and controllability.

According to Russell's classification system, the attributions of ability, task difficulty, and luck are uncontrollable. In addition, mood has replaced effort as one of the original four attributions listed by Weiner. Effort, formerly considered to be an internal/unstable attribution, is the only attribution that Russell classifies as controllable. However, within the controllable category it may be further categorized in terms of stability and locus of control. This conceptualization places a great deal more emphasis on effort as a viable attribution. This is reasonable, since it would include the efforts of other people such as referees, coaches, and judges. Athletes often attribute their successes and failures to other people, such as referees and umpires.

CONCEPT & APPLICATION 7.2

Concept Formal attempts to measure an athlete's attribution structure should employ an open-ended system in conjunction with the Causal Dimension Scale.

Application Open-ended attributions allow freedom of choice. In conjunction with the Causal Dimension Scale, these freely selected attributions can be correctly categorized. Although it is usually reserved for researchers, the practice of gathering data on perceived causality can be a valuable source of information for the coach.

Figure 7.3

Two views of a three-dimensional model that Russell (1982) used to illustrate causal perceptions in terms of locus of control, stability, and controllability.

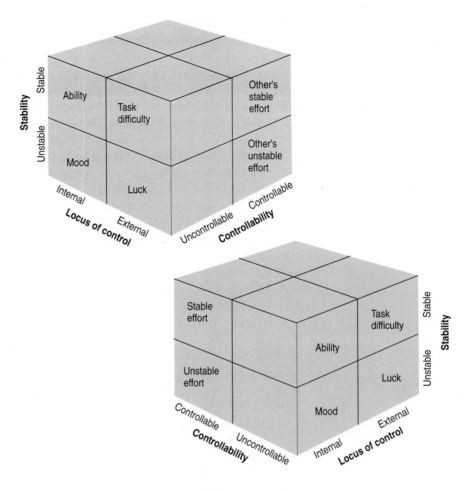

The development of the Causal Dimension Scale essentially solved the problem of misclassification or misinterpretation of attributions given by athletes for competitive outcomes. In addition, as illustrated in figure 7.3, Russell's addition of controllability to the attribution model made it possible to conceptualize all three dimensions of attribution into three-dimensional space. Prior to Russell's 1982 article on the development of the Causal Dimension Scale, it was very difficult to envision how controllability and locus of control could coexist in three-dimensional space.

The adoption of the Causal Dimension Scale in attribution research marked a fundamental departure from the traditional approach to interpreting attribution data. Rather than categorizing attributions in two-dimensional space, as illustrated in figure 7.2, or in three-dimensional space, as illustrated in figure 7.3, researchers tend to report results as a function of relative stability, locus of control, and controllability. For example, McAuley (1991) reported that exercise frequency is associated with somewhat stable, somewhat internal, and personally controllable attributions.

Figure 7.4

Illustration showing four dimensions used to measure causality in the revised Causal Dimension Scale (CDS II) (McAuley, Duncan, & Russell, 1992).

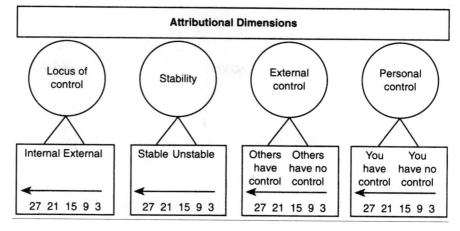

Since its development in 1982, the Causal Dimension Scale has been used extensively by researchers. As a result, it has become apparent that the controllability dimension of the scale is defective. Psychometric investigations revealed that the controllability dimension of the scale exhibited low internal consistency and a propensity to correlate highly with the locus of control dimension (Russell, McAuley & Tarico, 1987). These results suggest that the controllability dimension lacks consistency and is highly related to the locus of control scale, making it an inconsistent, redundant measure of locus of control.

An article by McAuley, Duncan, and Russell (1992) documents the development of the **Causal Dimension Scale II** (CDSII), a revision of the original version of the scale. The revised version differs from the original in that it comprises four rather than three causal dimension scales. The four dimensions of the CDSII are locus of control, stability, personal control, and external control. The original CDS scale failed to distinguish adequately between causes that were controlled by the individual and those controlled by other people. Attributions were simply controllable or uncontrollable, with no clear indication of who was controlling the cause. As indicated in figure 7.4, the CDSII measures four specific dimensions of causality.

The actual inventory is composed of 12 items, with 3 items representing each of the dimensions of locus of control, stability, external control, and personal control. Values for each dimension can range from 3 to 27, with higher values representing attributions that are more internal, stable, controllable by others, and personally controllable. A sample item from the personal control dimension is as follows:

Is the cause something:

YOU CAN REGULATE								*YOU CANNOT REGULATE*
9	8	7	6	5	4	3	2	1

A successful drive to the basket will likely yield an internal attribution suggesting competence. Courtesy Kansas State University Sports Information

OTHER CONSIDERATIONS

The process of identifying and categorizing causal attributions has come a long way since Heider first defined it. However, a number of conceptual problems persist. For instance, researchers and practitioners may fail to recognize that the kinds of attributions people make are based on a socialization process that may vary across cultures. Socialization plays an important part in the emphasis that we place on attributions. Attributions depend on what we learn to value. For example, ability is very important for Iranian children, and evolves as an important attribution regardless of whether a child fails or succeeds. American children, on the other hand, tend to value effort and intent regardless of innate ability (Salili, Maehr & Gillmore, 1976). These socialization differences will undoubtedly affect the kinds of attributions made.

In addition to social-cultural differences, we also have evidence of differences due to race and ethnicity. Morgan, Griffin, and Heyward (1996), for example, observed that young track and field athletes' attributions do not differ as a function of gender, but do differ as a function of race/ethnicity. Young Anglo athletes perceive success as internal and stable to a greater degree then African or Native American athletes do. This certainly is an advantage for the young Anglo athletes. They perceive success as something that they caused and that will likely occur again.

A second problem that has often plagued attribution research is that the experimenter can bias a subject's perception of outcome. In many sports-related attribution studies, subjects do not perceive themselves to be succeeding or failing until the researcher biases their perceptions by asking, "To what do you attribute your success (or failure)?" Sometimes success and failure are perceived differently by researcher and athlete. For example, let's say I play tennis with one of the world's best players. I don't expect to win, but if I can win one or two games, I will consider myself a success.

Spink and Roberts (1980) studied this problem in a sport setting and demonstrated that a person's causal attributions are affected by the ambiguity of the outcome. They determined that clearly perceived wins or losses were attributed to internal factors such as ability or effort, while ambiguous results were attributed to external factors such as task difficulty and luck. An ambiguous outcome was defined as one in which the athlete's subjective perception of success differed from the objective outcome.

CAUSAL ATTRIBUTIONS IN COMPETITIVE SITUATIONS

A **competitive situation** is defined as one in which participants expect that their performance will be evaluated by others in some way. It is an opportunity to compete with others for some internal or external reward. The competitive situation provides rich opportunities in which to study attribution theory. There are usually a perceived winner and loser, and an opportunity for participants to explain reasons or causes for outcomes. In this section we look specifically at internal/external locus of control and at stability considerations in competitive situations.

INTERNAL/EXTERNAL ATTRIBUTIONS

Regarding the internal and external dimensions of attribution, several lines of research have evolved. Three are of particular interest to us in this section. One has dealt with the notion of locus of control at the exclusion of the stability dimension. Another has investigated the relationship between affect and attribution. The third has concentrated on the notion of covariation.

Locus of Control

Locus of control, or the extent to which people believe they are responsible for their behavioral outcomes, has often been cited as an important factor in achievement-oriented behavior. As discussed earlier, people with an internal locus of control tend to believe their behaviors influence outcomes, while those with an external locus of control tend to attribute outcomes to outside forces such as fate, chance, and other people. This dichotomy closely resembles DeCharms and Carpenter's (1968) **origin-pawn relationship.** People who are *origins* like to be in control and originate their own behavioral outcomes. Those who are *pawns* feel powerless and acted on by external sources.

Perhaps the person most responsible for developing the conceptual framework for the locus of control dimension in attribution was Julian B. Rotter

(1966, 1971). Rotter (1966) developed the 29-item Internal-External Locus of Control Scale to measure the extent to which people believe they possess some control over their lives. The Rotter scale has been used by many researchers to classify subjects on the basis of the locus of control dimension. After using the scale for many years, Rotter (1971) stated the following generalities about locus of control: (1) children coming from a lower socioeconomic environment tend to be external, (2) children tend to become more internal with age, and (3) highly external people feel they are at the mercy of their environment and are continually being manipulated by outside forces.

As an alternative to the Rotter scale for measuring locus of control, Levenson (1981) developed the Levenson IPC scale. It measures the internal (I) dimension in much the same way the Rotter Scale does, but breaks the external dimension down into two important subdivisions. These two subdivisions are powerful others (P) and chance (C). Levenson reasoned that individuals with an external locus of control view their lack of control as being orderly and predictable (controlled by powerful others), or unordered, unpredictable, and out of control (chance).

While it is not appropriate for human beings to always give internal attributions to outcomes, research makes it abundantly clear that in the sports environment it is better to have an internal as opposed to an external locus of control. It is better that young athletes and people in general view themselves as in control of their own destiny, as opposed to seeing themselves as at the mercy of external events. Accepting credit for a success is psychologically preferred to attributing the success to some external force, such as luck or the actions of others. While painful, it is also desirable that we accept responsibility for our actions when we fail. If we do not accept responsibility for our errors and failures, how can we possibly improve and become stronger? The key is to accept responsibility for our failures when appropriate, but to do so in such a way that the attribution does not suggest that failure is inevitable for the future. This approach can be instilled in children by teaching them to use internal but unstable (changeable) attributions for failure. We will discuss the stability dimension in greater detail in the next section.

Research suggests that an internal orientation is more mature than an external orientation. Consequently, we should expect that children's attributions should shift towards a more internal orientation as they mature (Jambor & Rudisill, 1992). Furthermore, we have evidence that sports and exercise can have the effect of shifting a child's locus of causality from the external to the internal. Duke, Johnson, and Nowicki (1977) monitored the locus of control of 109 children ages 6 to 14 during an eight-week sport fitness camp, and observed a significant shift towards internal control as a result of the experience.

In keeping with the theme that an internal locus of control is more mature than an external locus of control, two studies are of interest. Scheer and Ansorge (1979) noted that gymnastic coaches typically rank-order their gymnasts from poorest to best for gymnastic meets, on the theory that judges expect scores to improve as the meet progresses. Interestingly, the results showed that judges who themselves had an internal locus of control were uninfluenced by order. Conversely, judges who had an external locus of control were influenced by order. This suggests that the judges who had an internal orientation were able to overcome the order bias and judge solely on the basis of performance. Another study showed that captains (leaders) of female adult volleyball teams exhibit a greater tendency towards internal locus of control than their teammates have (Aguglia & Sapienza, 1984).

Even though an internal locus of causality appears to be preferable to an external locus of control, this should not be construed to mean that all external attributions are immature. Sometimes external attributions are appropriate and expected. For example, it would be completely normal for athletes to complain that they lost because of poor officiating if their team had been called for twice as many fouls as the other team.

CONCEPT & APPLICATION 7.3

Concept An internal locus of control is typically a more mature orientation.

Application Externals can be identified by using Rotter's Internal-External Locus of Control Scale or by observing that the athletes attribute most outcomes to external causes. These athletes can be encouraged to adopt a more internal orientation through the development of self-confidence and of the habit of attributing outcomes internally when appropriate.

Attribution and Affect

The kinds of attributions we make in response to outcomes are closely associated with affect, or emotion. An internal attribution generally results in greater affect than an external attribution. For example, imagine you have just scored a 68 on a new eighteen-hole golf course. You feel elated! You have never done so well; your true ability has finally shown itself. But when you check some other people's scores, you discover that everyone has scored in the 60s, even your friend who never gets below an 80! You can no longer attribute your success internally, because the low score is obviously due to a lack of difficulty, an external attribution.

Weiner (1981) and McAuley, Russell, and Gross (1983) suggested some specific cause-and-effect relationships among attribution, outcome, and affect. In terms of locus of control, the expected pattern of emotional responses, given success or failure, is illustrated in figure 7.5. When people attribute success to internal causes, they typically respond with pride, confidence, and satisfaction. Conversely, if they attribute success externally, they will likely experience gratitude and thankfulness.

Figure 7.5

The influence of outcome and locus of control upon affect.

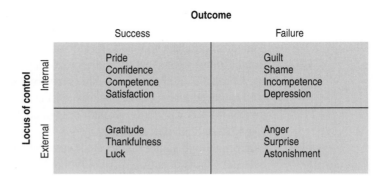

While the affect for success, regardless of attribution, tends to be positive and enthusiastic, the affect for failure is typically negative and sometimes subdued. For example, an athlete who fails at a task and attributes the failure internally is likely to feel guilty, especially if other teammates are involved. On the other hand, failure that is explained externally might result in an outburst of anger or surprise. Consider the tennis player who loses an important point due to a line call. If the athlete feels that the line judge was in error, the response may predictably be anger.

Weiner, Russell, and Lerman (1979) extend the attribution-affect connection one step further and suggest that attributions may be surmised from observing affect. In other words, one ought to be able to determine the cause to which a child attributes failure or success by simply observing the child's emotional response. If a child strikes out in a baseball game and responds with a look of surprise, one can conclude that the child attributed failure to an outside source (the umpire, perhaps).

The kinds of attributions that young athletes make in response to success and failure are closely linked to their feelings of self-esteem and self-confidence. Internalizing a failure results in feelings of guilt, shame, and depression. Individuals suffering from low-esteem are more likely than individuals high in self-esteem to internalize a failure and respond with negative affect. Losers are much more likely to search for reasons they failed than winners are to search for reasons they succeeded. This is especially true if a negative outcome was unexpected. If you lose a contest that you expected to win, you want to know why (Biddle & Hill, 1992).

CONCEPT & APPLICATION 7.4

Concept The kinds of attribution that athletes make for success and failure are closely associated with their emotions.

Application Coaches should learn to recognize athletes' unspoken attributions from the athletes'

emotional responses. If an athlete hides emotions, the coach should be able to predict how that person is feeling based upon the attributions the athlete makes.

Figure 7.6

Illustration of the covariation of performance principle in attribution.

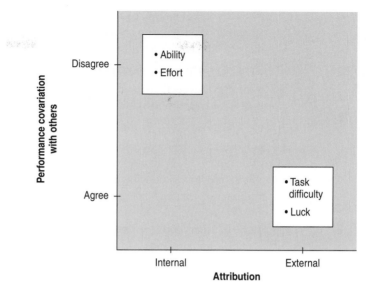

Covariation Principle

A person's attributions for success or failure can be predicted on the basis of the performance of others on the same task. This phenomenon has been named the **covariation principle.** According to this principle, when the performance of others agrees (covaries) with the performance of the participant, attributions will be external. If the performance of others disagrees (lacks covariation) with the performance of the participant, attributions will be internal. For example, if I beat someone in tennis whom everyone else has lost to, I will certainly attribute my victory to an internal cause such as superior ability. Conversely, if I defeat someone in tennis whom everyone else has also defeated, I will likely attribute my success to an external cause such as my opponent's low ability. Because there is logic in these predicted attributions, they are referred to as **logical attributions.** The covariation principle is illustrated in figure 7.6. When your performance agrees with the performance of others, your attributions are likely

---

CONCEPT & APPLICATION 7.5

Concept According to the covariation principle, outcomes that agree with the performance of others usually result in external attributions, while outcomes that disagree usually result in internal attributions.

Application This principle can help the coach tell when the athlete is making inappropriate attributions for success and failure. For example, if an athlete hits a home run off a pitcher who strikes most batters out, this outcome should be attributed internally.

to be external in nature, e.g., task difficulty or luck. Conversely, when your performance disagrees with the performance of others, your attributions are likely to be internal in nature, e.g., ability or effort.

STABILITY CONSIDERATIONS

In the previous section our concern was with locus of control and affect. In this section we will turn to a discussion of the stability dimension of causal attribution.

Attribution and Expectancy

Suppose an athlete with a history of success is unexpectedly defeated. To what is this athlete likely to attribute the failure? Or suppose an athlete who consistently loses suddenly experiences success. To what is this athlete likely to attribute the success? One might expect both athletes to attribute their unexpected outcomes to some type of unstable factor such as luck, officiating, or effort. In other words, we might expect an ascription to an unstable attribution whenever an outcome is different from what should be expected based on previous experience. We should expect a stable attribution to be selected in response to an expected outcome (success or failure). For example, if an athlete with a history of success defeats another who has a history of failures, we should expect both of them to attribute their outcomes to some type of stable attribution, such as ability or task difficulty.

Thus, past experience significantly affects the kinds of causal attributions given for success and failure (Frieze & Weiner, 1971; Iso-Ahola, 1977; Roberts, 1977; Spink, 1978). If the outcome is inconsistent with past experience, attributions tend to be unstable. If the outcome is consistent with past experience, attributions tend to be stable. These relationships are graphically illustrated in the left and right portions of figure 7.7. If, based on past history, an athlete rarely succeeds, and in fact does fail, the probability is very low that he will give an unstable attribution (left), but very high that he will give a stable attribution (right). If, based on past history, an athlete almost always succeeds, but in fact fails, the probability is very high that he will give an unstable attribution (left), but very low that he will give a stable attribution. Using figure 7.7, attribution predictions can also be made when the athlete experiences a successful outcome. This information can be useful to the coach or sport psychologist who is trying to help an athlete cope with failure or success.

Given these generalizations, it follows that we can predict athletes' future expectations about performance based on the kinds of attributions they give for their present performance. If an athlete attributes a loss to bad luck, she is saying that things may be different next time. But if the loss is attributed to a lack of ability, the athlete is saying that the result will be the same next time. This observation points to the utility of ascribing failures to unstable causes, since it does not imply repeated failure. It would be wise to encourage a young athlete to attribute a failure to lack of effort. This will suggest that more effort can change the outcome from failure to success. Experimental support for these conclusions has been provided by Duquin (1978), Roberts (1980), and Ryan (1981).

Figure 7.7

Relationship between attribution, outcome, and expectancy (based on past performance).

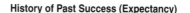

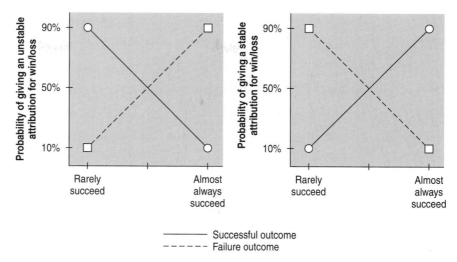

Concept Athletes tend to give stable attributions in response to expected outcomes and unstable attributions in response to unexpected outcomes. *Application* Attributions along the stability dimension should suggest to the coach the kind of performance expectations the athlete has for the future. An unstable attribution suggests that the athlete expects future outcomes to change, while a stable attribution suggests that she expects future outcomes to remain the same.

Learned Helplessness

In competitive situations, some people act as if events are out of their control, and failure is inevitable. The person who displays these characteristics is suffering from **learned helplessness** (Seligman, 1975). This is a psychological state in which people feel events are out of their control.

"Learned helpless" children who show a deterioration of performance under the threat of failure tend to attribute their failure to stable factors such as lack of ability. Conversely, "learned helpless" children who show enhanced performance under the threat of failure tend to choose unstable factors such as luck or lack of effort (Dweck, 1980). Attributing success to stable factors suggests to the child that success is a realistic expectation for the future; attributing failure to stable factors suggests to the child that failure is a realistic expectation for the future. These and other attributional predictions about stability are illustrated in figure 7.8.

A coach or teacher should promote feelings of self-efficacy and self-confidence by encouraging children to make appropriate attributions for success and failure. Children who succeed should be encouraged to view the success as

Figure 7.8

Flow chart showing the results of both stable and unstable attributions for success and failure.

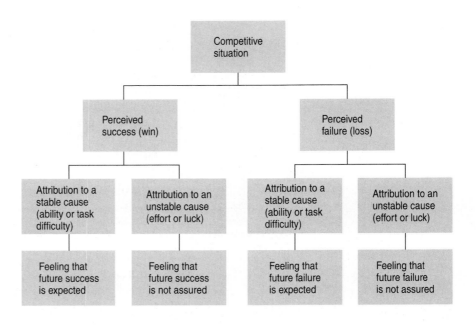

both stable and internal—internal, because the child needs to feel pride in this accomplishment; stable, because the child needs to feel that success is likely to occur again. Attributing success to ability should be beneficial, since it is both internal and stable. Children who experience repeated failure should be encouraged to select an unstable and perhaps internal attribution (Grove & Pargman, 1986). Such an attribution will assure the child that failure is not inevitable, because the cause is not stable. But an internal attribution will help the child accept responsibility for the results. It would not be wise to continually encourage an external/unstable attribution, because the child may come to feel that bad luck or poor officiating are the cause of all disappointments. However, a good mix of internal and external unstable attributions would be beneficial.

Dweck (1975) proposed and tested such a therapeutic strategy. A sample of "learned helpless" children were categorized into a failure deprivation condition and an attribution retraining condition. In the deprivation condition, the children's confidence was bolstered through programmed success. The children in the attribution retraining condition were told after experiencing a failure to attribute the failure to an unstable cause such as effort. The results showed that by the end of the training period, the attribution retraining children fared far better than the success-only children in the face of a contrived failure. Therefore, helping children to change their attributions may be more beneficial than merely manipulating success. This does not mean that experiencing success is not important. It is. But performance and self-efficacy can also be enhanced by helping children make confidence-building or confidence-protecting attributions.

CONCEPT & APPLICATION 7.7

Concept Attributing failure to an internal/stable cause is potentially damaging to a young athlete's self-esteem.

Application Young athletes should be encouraged to attribute failure to unstable causes that can be expected to change. For example, effort would be an ideal attribution for failure.

CONCEPT & APPLICATION 7.8

Concept Attributing success to an internal/stable cause such as ability is good for a young athlete's self-confidence.

Application The development of self-confidence is the most important goal of any youth sport program. Coaches should encourage athletes to take credit for their successes.

GENDER DIFFERENCES IN SPORT

Males typically attribute successful performance to high ability and strong effort, and unsuccessful performance to bad luck. This is a self-enhancing attributional pattern fashioned to build and protect the athlete's ego. Ability is both an internal and a stable attribution, while effort is an internal and controllable attribution. Attributing success to ability and/or effort says that the athlete feels responsible for the success and believes it is likely to occur in the future. Conversely, attributing failure to bad luck says that the athlete believes that failure was not his fault and that it is not likely to happen again (unless more bad luck happens).

Females typically attribute successful performance to good luck and social support, and unsuccessful performance to lack of ability. This is a self-defeating pattern of attribution that is unlikely to build self-confidence. Luck and social support are external attributions that are controlled by external forces. Attributing success to good luck implies that the athlete expects to succeed only as long as her luck holds up. Attributing success to social support is nice, but what happens when the social support is withdrawn? This is an external force that is controlled by others. Finally, attributing lack of success to low ability is very damaging, because it suggests that the athlete believes that the failure was her fault, and the pattern is not likely to change.

The above generalizations are typical of men and women, but they are not the rule. Many males exhibit logical as opposed to ego-enhancing attributional patterns, and many women exhibit confidence-building attributional patterns. Are we to assume that the self-defeating pattern of attributions exhibited by many

In team sports, outcome may be attributed to personal effort as well as to the effort of others. Courtesy University of Missouri-Columbia Sports Information

females is somehow innate—or is it learned? Hendy and Boyer (1993) addressed this issue in an important study involving triathlon athletes. The results of the study showed that the attributional patterns of the male athletes were very similar to the pattern described above, but the attributional patterns of the female triathlon athletes were very different. Females attributed more importance than males on such controllable factors as psychological state, diet, and body weight as reasons for success and failure. After a success, the females downplayed the importance of external factors like climate, luck, social support, and equipment. They did not give away credit for their success or blame low ability for their failure. These results are very optimistic and lead us to believe that self-defeating attributional patterns are learned, and therefore can be unlearned.

A classic story related to former Olympic volleyball great Mary Jo Peppler is of interest. In her book *Inside Volleyball for Women* (Peppler, 1977), she commented on the male characteristic of believing that failure was highly unlikely. As an Olympic volleyball player, and all-American, she promoted volleyball by giving demonstrations and clinics at high schools. As part of her exhibition, she and another female athlete would challenge any group of six young men to a game. She marveled that no matter how badly the boys were beaten, they were always ready to try again with complete confidence that they would win the next time. She suggested that young female athletes should develop this characteristic.

CONCEPT & APPLICATION 7.9

Concept Young women and girls who lack self-confidence tend to ascribe internal and stable causes to their failures, while young men and boys tend to attribute failure to unstable causes or to no cause at all.

Application As with the learned helpless child, girls and women who suffer from perceptions of low self-esteem should be encouraged and coached to consider unstable causes such as effort or luck for their failures in sport.

Attributing success to internal causes leads to high future expectations. Courtesy University of Missouri-Columbia Sports Information

EGOCENTRISM IN ATTRIBUTION

People are assumed to follow logic when they make attributions to behavioral outcomes. For example, in regard to the covariation principle, it was observed that people tend to make attributions consistent with a certain logic. That is, if a person "aces" a test, but then realizes that everyone else has aced it too, that person will ascribe the cause externally (e.g., an easy test). This is considered to be a **logical model** for making attributions to outcomes.

However, evidence suggests that people are not always entirely logical in making causal attributions for their behavior. Instead of making logical attributions, they often make self-serving ones. In this regard, a person might attribute successes to internal causes and failures to external causes. Attributing all successes to internal causes is called **ego-enhancing strategy,** while attributing all failures to external causes is called **ego-protecting strategy.** Both strategies are self-serving and are considered **illogical models** of attribution. Mann (1974) observed this strategy among football fans. Mann found that fans of winning football teams tended to attribute game outcomes to internal causes, such as ability, while fans of losing teams tended to attribute game outcomes to external causes, such as luck and biased officiating.

Perhaps the first serious review of the available literature on the **self-serving hypothesis** I just described was conducted by Miller and Ross (1975). In their review, they pointed out that for the illogical model to be true, it must be shown that people indulge in both ego-protective attributions under conditions of failure and ego-enhancing attributions under conditions of success. Their basic conclusion was that the self-serving bias proposition was largely unsupported, since the literature provided strong evidence that people use ego-enhancing strategies under conditions of success, but only minimal evidence that they use ego-protective strategies under conditions of failure.

A review of the sport psychology literature since Miller and Ross's (1975) signal work reveals a significant interest in the self-serving hypothesis, but does little to clarify the issue. Of the articles reviewed, only one demonstrated unambiguous support for the illogical hypothesis for both the ego-enhancing and the ego-protecting notions (Zientek & Breakwell, 1991). As with the Miller and Ross (1975) conclusions, studies generally showed that people experiencing success typically attributed their success to internal factors such as effort and ability. But when it came to the ego-protecting bias, the results tended to be qualified in terms of some situational factor. Consistent with these findings, Mark, Mutrie, Brooks, and Harris (1984) proposed a reformulation of the basic self-serving hypothesis. Supported by Grove, Hanrahan, and McInman (1991), the reformulated theory holds that athletes make primarily internal attributions for both success and failure. Athletes make internal attributions for success because they are ego-enhancing. However, they make internal attributions for failure so that they are not perceived as making excuses for their lack of success. Results of the Grove et al. investigation further suggests that attributions associated with success are altered along the lines of perceived stability and controllability, as opposed to locus of control. Winners attribute their success to stable and controllable causes more frequently than losers do.

Regarding the notion that attributions for losing tend to be qualified in terms of situational factors, Kimiecik and Duda (1985) observed that the self-serving hypothesis was supported for children involved in one-on-one basketball competition when a forced-choice attribution model was used (ability, effort, difficulty, or luck). However, when an open-ended attribution model was used, winners selected internal and external causes equally, and losers selected primarily internal attributions. Additionally, Brawley (1984) provided evidence to support his contention that self-serving attributions may not be necessarily self-serving after all. An athlete's ability to assign accurate causes to outcomes may be limited by memory. Athletes recall events about their own behavior to a much greater extent than they recall events about their opponents' or teammates' behavior, both of which may be responsible for outcome.

Even though the literature does not clearly support the self-serving bias hypothesis, several interesting factors are worth noting. Iso-Ahola (1977a), Spink (1978a), and Spink and Roberts (1980) studied the relationship between the self-serving hypothesis and decisiveness of outcome. All three studies hypothesized that subjects would attribute clear success and failure to internal causes, but ambiguous outcomes to external causes. The Spink and Roberts research supported this hypothesis, although success and failure were determined subjectively as a function of subjects' perceptions of "desirable qualities in themselves." Thus, for some people a loss at racquetball, for instance, could be perceived as a success. The results of the other two studies were identical to each other. Clear wins and ambiguous wins were attributed to internal causes (a familiar result), while clear losses and ambiguous losses were attributed to low effort and task difficulty. Thus, losers selected both internal and external causes. However, Iso-Ahola (1977a) noted that subjects tended to view lack of effort as an external attribution rather than an internal one. That is, the subjects reasoned that they did not try very hard because of some external factor (e.g., poor officiating). With this interpretation of the effort attribution, the results support the self-serving hypothesis.

In another investigation, Iso-Ahola (1978) identified still another situational factor that could affect the interpretation of attributional results. In this study, subjects were asked to imagine that they either agreed or disagreed with an objective assessment of their performance on a motor maze task. The results indicated that subjects tended to use a self-serving strategy for selecting attributions under the objective success-failure conditions. However, when the subject's own perceptions of success and failure were considered, the attributions were generally logical and non-self-serving.

In an interesting study by Gill (1980), the question of self-serving bias was investigated in regard to team outcomes rather than individual outcomes. Subjects were members of women's basketball teams. After winning or losing, players were asked to assign primary responsibility for success or failure either to their own team or to their opponents. Results showed that players attributed success to their own team and failure to the other team. Thus, in terms of group attributions, the self-serving hypothesis seemed to be supported. In another part of the study, players were asked to assign primary responsibility for success or failure to themselves (an internal attribution) or to their teammates (an external attribution). The results failed to support the self-serving hypothesis. Members of winning teams assigned primary responsibility to their teammates and members of losing teams assigned primary responsibility to themselves. Thus in this case, a reverse egocentric pattern emerged.

Bradley (1978) summarized the situation somewhat by suggesting that the attributional process is probably neither purely logical nor purely illogical (self-serving). Rather, the disposition to use a self-serving strategy is within each individual to some degree. Some people will rarely use it, preferring to accept responsibility for their own actions in most cases. However, others may find it comforting to reject personal responsibility for outcomes in order to protect delicate egos.

It is good to remember at this point in our discussion that Dweck (1980) suggested that "learned helpless" children can be helped by being taught to attribute their failures to unstable internal factors such as low effort. It is also important to keep in mind that an ego-enhancing/ego-protecting approach to attribution may be better from the standpoint of improving self-efficacy. Athletes should learn to accept responsibility for their own performances, but not at the expense of their self-confidence. I personally would rather hear young athletes state that they struck out in baseball because of a bad call or because of a great curve ball than that they struck out because of a lack of ability (even if they do lack ability). It is healthy for athletes to ascribe failure to ability *if* they perceive ability to be something they can improve on. In this case, ability would be an unstable attribution, since it could be changed. Unfortunately, young athletes often fail to see skill as dynamic and changing.

CONCEPT & APPLICATION 7.10

Concept Athletes are not always completely logical in their attributions. They will often engage in illogical or ego-enhancing strategies to explain events.

Application Athletes who make self-serving attributions for every event are in danger of losing contact with reality. After all, losing is not always something or someone else's fault. However, to a certain extent, self-enhancing and self-protecting strategies are good for the athlete's self-confidence.

ATTRIBUTIONAL TRAINING

Research with children suggests that **attributional training** can positively influence a child's future expectations and performance (Rudisill, 1988). Attributional training can also be effective with adults, although not so effective as it is with children. Adults respond well to attributional training as long as their perceived competence is not too low. Athletes who suffer from maladaptive achievement patterns (learned helplessness) exhibit attributional styles that differ from nonmaladaptive athletes. Athletes with maladaptive achievement patterns give failure attributions that are more internal, stable, uncontrollable, and global than those of the nonmaladaptive athletes (Prapavessis & Carron, 1988). This means that the athlete who suffers from maladaptive achievement patterns attributes failure to causes that are personal (internal), are unchanging (stable), are out of his control (uncontrollable), and apply generally to his life (global). For an example, an athlete with low self-esteem with a history of failure might explain a recent failure thus: "I am just no good at this." This explanation, correctly interpreted, may tell the coach that this young person believes that he is responsible for the failure, there is no likelihood for change in the future, he has no control over the situation, and he is likely to experience failure in most athletic mastery attempts.

If the athlete suffering from maladaptive achievement patterns wins a contest, he is likely to attribute the success to causes that are impersonal (external), changing (unstable), out of his control (uncontrollable), and specific to the event. In this case, the individual suffering from learned helplessness might explain a recent unexpected success this way: "Everyone gets lucky sometime." Correctly interpreted, this explanation may tell the coach that this young person believes that he was not responsible for the success, it is not likely to happen again, he has no control over it, and the success is not likely to have a positive effect on his life generally.

In attribution training, it is a good idea to objectively determine the nature of attributions given by individuals for outcomes. Earlier we introduced the Causal Dimension Scale (CDS) and the CDSII as means for determining the true nature of attributions given. One of these instruments, or an appropriate adaptation, can be used to assist in correctly interpreting the true meaning of attributions given by young athletes for outcomes (Grove & Prapavessis, 1995).

Once it has been determined that attributions given by a maladaptive athlete are indeed counterproductive and potentially damaging to the individual, steps should be taken to restructure how the person perceives attributions. Consider the following hypothetical script:

Coach	"Sally, it appears that you feel that your failure to return serve in your last match was due to lack of skill."
Sally	"Not just skill. I really don't have what it takes to be a good tennis player. I'm just not coordinated and never will be."
Coach	"Actually, I've known lots of good tennis players who felt that way when they first started. I'm sure you are no different."
Sally	"Do you really think so?"
Coach	"Yes, I do. You have a whole week before your next match. I'll work with you on your footwork. I'm sure you will do better next time. Practice really helps, but it does take time."

In the prior script, the coach has subtly suggested to the athlete that the cause of her failure may be something that can change (skill), and that she can do something about it (practice). The coach did not encourage Sally to reject responsibility for her outcomes (bad luck), but suggested that the outcome can change (unstable attribution) and that Sally is in control. The coach must be very patient and positive when engaging in attribution training. One should not expect an athlete to immediately alter a long-standing maladaptive attribution pattern. It takes patience and time. To help students and athletes choose suitable attributions, the following steps are recommended:

1. Record and classify attributions that students and athletes make to successful and unsuccessful outcomes.

2. For each outcome, discuss with the athlete causes or attributions that might lead to a greater expectancy for success and increased effort.

3. Provide an attributional training program for athletes who consistently give attributions that lead to negative implications for future outcomes.

4. For best results, combine planned goal setting with attributional manipulation.

CONCEPT & APPLICATION 7.11

Concept Attributional training is effective in helping young athletes overcome feelings of learned helplessness. Attributional training involves teaching individuals to adopt more appropriate and positive explanations for their successes and failures.

Application The first step in attributional training is to pay attention to the reasons young athletes give for outcomes. Attributions provide valuable information about the way young people see themselves. If properly used, attributional information can be used to understand an athlete and to help her appropriately restructure the way she views reasons for success and failure.

SUMMARY   Attribution theory is based on the kinds of perceptions people have for why they succeed or fail. Attributions are causal explanations for outcomes. Fritz Heider is the acknowledged founder of attribution theory, but Bernard Weiner is credited with making significant contributions to it in terms of interpretation and application. People are believed to make attributions along three dimensions: locus of control, stability, and controllability. Dan Russell and Ed McAuley are credited with making significant contributions relative to the accurate assessment and measurement of attributions.

Attribution theory is very useful in understanding behavior exhibited in competitive situations. Locus of control is a basic dimension used by athletes in explaining causality. A person who believes he is in control of his own destiny exhibits an internal locus of control, while one who feels at the mercy of outside forces exhibits an external locus of control. The kinds of attributions that people give for outcomes are related to previous experience. Future expectations can also be predicted from attributions. Emotions are closely associated with attribution. Internal attributions for success result in feelings of self-confidence, while the same attributions for failure result in feelings of shame and guilt. Making stable attributions about failure promotes a loss of confidence; making unstable attributions about the same outcome gives one the feeling that failure can be reversed.

A general observation is that males typically attribute success to high ability and strong effort, and unsuccessful performance to bad luck. Conversely, females typically attribute successful performance to good luck and social support, and unsuccessful performance to lack of ability. Evidence suggests that the self-defeating pattern of attributions exhibited by females is learned and can be corrected.

Egocentrism in attribution occurs when athletes routinely assign failure to external causes and success to internal causes. This is a self-serving strategy and is considered to be an illogical model of attribution. The self-serving strategy of assigning attributions is not universal among athletes, but it is used occasionally by most people.

Research with children suggests that attributional training can positively influence a child's future expectations and performance. Attributional training can be effective with adults, but not so effective as it is with children. Practical suggestions for providing attribution training for young athletes are introduced and discussed.

REVIEW QUESTIONS

1. Who are the people responsible for the development and refinement of attribution theory? What are their specific contributions?

2. Name the three dimensions used to describe causal attribution. What are the categories of each? Name the basic attributions identified by Weiner.

3. What is the Causal Dimension Scale (CDS) and why is it important? Who was responsible for its development?

4. Discuss the development of the Causal Dimension Scale II (CDSII). Why was it necessary to revise the original scale? How do the scales differ?

5. What is the origin-pawn relationship? What does it have to do with locus of control in attribution theory?

6. In what way are affect and attribution related? Provide some examples and explain how knowledge of the relationship can be important to the coach.

7. What is the covariation principle? Provide examples and explain the utility of the principle.

8. What types of attributions do people typically give for situations in which outcome is consistent with previous performance? Inconsistent? Why do you think this is so?

9. What is learned helplessness, and how can attribution training help to alleviate this situation?

10. Discuss gender differences associated with attributions given by males and females for various competitive outcomes. Are differences innate or learned?

11. Discuss the phenomenon of egocentrism in attribution. Is it desirable or undesirable? Explain.

12. Discuss the process of attribution training. Give steps involved and provide examples of its application.

GLOSSARY

attributional training Process by which attributions given for failure are manipulated in order to overcome feelings of learned helplessness.

attribution theory A cognitive approach to motivation in which perceived causation plays an important role in explaining behavior.

Causal Dimension Scale A scale developed by Russell for assigning attributions to one of three dimensions: locus of control, stability, and controllability.

Causal Dimension Scale II Revised version of the Causal Dimension Scale that divides the controllability dimension into external control and personal control.

competitive situation Situation in which participants expect their performance to be evaluated in some way.

controllability Attributional dimension in which causes for events are perceived to be either within or beyond a person's control.

covariation principle Principle that when the performance of others agrees (covaries) with the performance of the athlete, attributions about that performance will be external.

ego-enhancing strategy A strategy by which one attributes all success to internal causes.

ego-protecting strategy A strategy by which one attributes all failures to external causes.

external control The perception that external factors determine outcomes.

illogical model Use of an ego-enhancing or ego-protecting strategy for selecting attributions.

internal control The perception that factors within a person determine that person's outcome.

learned helplessness A condition in which people feel that they have no control over their failures, and that failure is inevitable.

locus of control A psychological construct that refers to people's beliefs about whether they can personally control what happens to them.

logical attribution An attribution one would expect an individual to give if not biased by a desire to enhance or protect the ego.

logical model The notion that people make logical attributions about outcomes.

open-ended attribution An attribution freely made by the athlete without any categorical constraints.

origin-pawn relationship A term coined by DeCharms and Carpenter (1968), who observed that some people (origins) like to control their outcomes, while others (pawns) feel powerless to control their outcomes.

self-serving hypothesis The observation that people will sometimes make illogical attributions to enhance or protect their egos.

stability An attributional dimension that suggests that an outcome will either change or remain stable.

structural rating scale A method of selecting attributions in which options are structured and limited.

SUGGESTED READINGS

Biddle, S. J. H., & Hill, A. B. (1992). Relationships between attributions and emotions in a laboratory-based sporting contest. *Journal of Sports Sciences, 10,* 65–75.

Dweck, C. S. (1980). Learned helplessness in sport. In C. H. Nadeau, W. R. Halliwell, K. M. Newell, & G. C. Roberts (Eds.), *Psychology of motor behavior and sport, 1979.* Champaign, IL: Human Kinetics.

Hendy, H. M., & Bower, B. J. (1993). Gender differences in attribution for triathlon performance. *Sex Roles, 29,* 527–542.

McAuley, E., Duncan, T. E., & Russell, D. W. (1992). Measuring causal attributions: The revised causal dimension scale (CDSII). *Personality and Social Psychology Bulletin, 18,* 566–573.

Rejeski, W. J., & Brawley, L. R. (1983). Attribution theory in sport: Current status and new perspectives. *Journal of Sport Psychology, 5,* 77–99.

Roberts, G. C. (1982). Achievement motivation in sport. In R. Terjung (Ed.), *Exercise and sport science reviews* (Vol. 10). Philadelphia: Franklin Institute Press.

Rotter, J. B. (1971). External control and internal control. *Psychology Today, 5*(1), 37–42, 58–59.

Rudisill, M. E. (1989). Putting attribution theory to work—improving persistence and performance. *Journal of Physical Education, Recreation, and Dance, 60,* 43–46.

Russell, D. (1982). The causal dimension scale: A measure of how individuals perceive causes. *Journal of Personality and Social Psychology, 42,* 1137–1145.

Wankel, L. M., & Kreisel, S. J. P. (1985). Factors underlying enjoyment of youth sports: Sport and age group comparisons. *Journal of Sport Psychology, 7,* 51–64.

Weiner, B. (1985). An attributional theory of achievement motivation and emotion. *Psychological Review, 92,* 548–573.

8 MOTIVATION AND SELF-CONFIDENCE IN SPORT

KEY TERMS

- *achievement motivation*
- *achievement situation*
- *additive principle*
- *androgyny*
- *approach-avoidance conflict*
- *cognitive evaluation theory*
- *competence motivation*
- *competition*
- *cross-gender-typed*
- *ego oriented*
- *extrinsic motivation*
- *fear of failure*
- *fear of success*
- *feminine attribute*
- *gender role*
- *gender-typed*

- *goal orientation*
- *intrinsic motivation*
- *masculine attribute*
- *mastery environment*
- *McClelland-Atkinson model*
- *motive to achieve success*
- *multiplicative principle*
- *participation motivation*
- *participatory modeling*
- *perceived ability*
- *psychological construct*
- *self-confidence*
- *self-efficacy*
- *social comparison*
- *sport confidence*
- *task oriented*

Successful sport experiences develop self-confidence and the motivation to achieve success. Courtesy Kansas State University Sports Information

Two young boys were asked to participate in a sandlot baseball game. One of them happily joined in and became active in team selection, competition, skill development, and socialization. The other youngster's immediate reaction was to follow his friend. However, after a few seconds of deliberation he declined, citing schoolwork and chores. He feared that if he participated, he would be shamed by being the last player chosen, and would be ridiculed for making errors.

As this story suggests, not everyone approaches an achievement situation with the same enthusiasm. An **achievement situation** is one in which someone expects that his performance is going to be evaluated. This occurs regularly in sport, and is referred to by Martens (1982) as **competition.** Competition is nothing more than a sport-specific achievement situation.

ACHIEVEMENT MOTIVATION

Achievement motivation can be defined as the athlete's predisposition to approach or avoid a competitive situation. However, in a broader sense, achievement motivation includes the concept of desire, or desire to excel. The athletic literature and folk history are full of examples of athletes who have excelled because of an internal desire, as opposed to physical attributes such as size and strength. Former Boston Celtic player Larry Bird may be a case in point. Bird has never been accused of possessing great quickness, speed, or vertical jumping ability, yet he remains one of the greatest players of all time. Much of his greatness is attributed to an intense internal desire to work hard and to achieve success. In introducing the topic of achievement motivation, a psychological construct is addressed that is much more than getting psychologically aroused or motivated for a single competitive event. I am talking about the fundamental internal drive that motivates athletes to literally commit a large portion of their lives to achieve a particular goal.

From the mid-1950s through the mid-1970s, the theory of achievement motivation that received the most attention in the psychological literature was the McClelland-Atkinson theory. During that time, two other basic theories competed with the McClelland-Atkinson model for general research appeal. Roberts (1982) identified these two as the test-anxiety approach and the Crandall approach (1963). Simply stated, the test-anxiety approach hypothesized that fear of test taking or fear of failure (test anxiety) was the critical factor in determining whether or not an individual would approach or avoid an achievement situation. Children who suffer from high levels of anxiety might be expected to avoid achievement situations. By contrast, the Crandall approach placed the emphasis upon an individual's expectation for reinforcement and on an individually determined standard of excellence. In practice, the child compares social expectations with minimal standards for success. If expectations are too high or reinforcements too few, the child drops out of the achievement situation.

A fundamental goal of this chapter is to understand the meaning of the term *motivation,* and explore why some individuals possess it in abundance, while others do not. An admirer once remarked to a highly accomplished concert pianist, "I would give half my life to play as you do." The pianist responded, "That's exactly what I did." What is it that motivates an individual to give much of her life to accomplish a goal? For some reason (or reasons), the individual comes to believe that the goal is worth spending a lifetime and large amounts of money to achieve. This, however, does not explain why the person comes to believe this, and why it becomes such an all-consuming goal.

Insight into this behavior comes from the work of behaviorists such as Hull (1943, 1951) and Spence (1956), who demonstrated that animals will go to extraordinary lengths to reduce an internal drive such as hunger, thirst, or the desire for sexual gratification. Drive theory, as proposed by Hull, Spence and other behaviorists, is a theory of motivation based upon drive reduction. Drive theory states that motivation is related to a desire to reduce or satisfy an internal drive. In the case of sport, the drive may be to become an All-American track star or to make a high school basketball or football team. Motivation to achieve success in sport is closely related to the kinds of experiences each child has as he is growing up. Many of these experiences lead to a strong desire to excel in sport, while others lead to sport avoidance. The following is an example of an experience that destroyed one child's desire to achieve success in sport (K. Dimick, Personal Communication, September 1990):

> This is the story of a child named Johnny who had not yet succeeded in hitting a baseball off of a Tee (T-ball). One day, after several attempts, the boy, for the first time in his young life, succeeded in hitting the ball. Overcome with happiness and joy, the boy jumped up and down with glee as his parents and other fans cheered his success. In his excitement, however, he forgot that he was supposed to run to first base. In anger, his volunteer coach grabbed him and said "Johnny, you dummy, you can't even run to first. You will never get another chance to bat on my team." Needless to say, Johnny became a sports drop out. Johnny's experience could have been one of the greatest in his life, but an untrained, insensitive volunteer coach turned it into one of his worst.

This story emphasizes my belief that the motive to achieve success in sport is not an innate drive, such as the drive to satisfy hunger or thirst, but one that is developed or learned. The root word for *motivation* is the word *motive,* which is literally the desire to fulfill a need. According to Maslow (1970), human beings have five basic needs. These needs are conceptualized by Maslow as being on a continuum from lower- to higher-level needs. To satisfy the higher needs, the lower-level needs must first be satisfied. This is referred to as a hierarchy of needs. The lower-level needs include physiological cravings (hunger, thirst) and the need for bodily safety. Once these fundamental needs are satisfied, the human being seeks to satisfy higher-level cravings associated with the needs to be loved, feel worthy, feel competent, and to realize self-fulfillment.

As explained earlier, one important theory that attempted to explain motivation was McClelland and Atkinson's theory of achievement motivation. While thoroughly studied between 1950 and 1970, the theory has been largely abandoned by most psychologists and sport psychologists in favor of more situation-specific cognitive theories. One reason the theory was abandoned was its complexity and reliance upon difficult-to-measure **psychological constructs,** or concepts. The one redeeming characteristic of the theory, however, was that these specific psychological constructs were systematically identified and studied in an attempt to explain the phenomenon of human motivation. For this reason, various components of the McClelland-Atkinson model, as well as several elaborations, will be discussed. In addition to the McClelland-Atkinson model, other topics to be discussed include various models of self-confidence, goal orientation as one of these models presents it, gender roles, threats to intrinsic motivation, and the development of motivation and self-confidence in young athletes. While this is not a chapter on youth sports (a broad topic), it is helpful to point out that much of the research that forms the knowledge base for this chapter comes from research involving youth sport participants.

THE McCLELLAND-ATKINSON MODEL

In its simplest form, the **McClelland-Atkinson model** of achievement motivation is based upon two psychological constructs. These two constructs are (a) the motive to achieve success, and (b) fear of failure. The **motive to achieve success** is believed to represent an athlete's **intrinsic motivation** to engage in an interesting and exciting activity.

Fear of failure is a psychological construct associated with cognitive state anxiety. According to the McClelland-Atkinson model, an individual's desire to enter into an interesting and exciting activity is a function of the relative strengths of these two constructs: motive to achieve success and fear of failure. If an individual's self-confidence associated with performing a certain task is stronger than her fear of failing at the task, she will approach and perform the task. In its simplest form, the model is represented by the following equation:

achievement motivation = intrinsic motivation − cognitive state anxiety

Consider this example: David is a fourteen-year-old boy who recently moved from a farming community in eastern Kansas to Chicago, Illinois. While in Kansas he learned to play basketball and was a member of his ninth-grade team. Upon moving to Chicago, he was encouraged to go out for the basketball team in his new high school. As he surveyed the situation, he quickly determined that many of the boys were bigger and stronger than he. This made him fearful that he might not make the team. Conversely, he believed that his basketball skills were quite good and that he would do well against the bigger boys. Furthermore, he loved the game of basketball and did not want to give it up just because he had moved to a new city. After considering his dilemma for several weeks, he decided to go out for the basketball team.

As observed in this example, the McClelland-Atkinson model presents a classic **approach-avoidance conflict** for the athlete. As illustrated in the achievement motivation equation, the decision to enter into an achievement situation is a function of the strength of the athlete's intrinsic motivation (approach) and his fear of failure (avoidance). While the model has intuitive appeal, research support in the motor domain has been mixed. Individuals who score high on the achievement motivation construct do not always perform better on motor tasks than subjects who score low on the construct. While there is some evidence that athletes high in achievement motivation will perform better than those low in achievement motivation, the relationship is complex and often uncertain. For example, using the McClelland-Atkinson model, Fodero (1980) demonstrated that a reliable relationship does not exist between achievement motivation and performance of elite gymnasts. It seems unlikely that athletic performance can be predicted solely on the basis of achievement motivation. The real value of measuring achievement motivation is in predicting long-term patterns of motivation, not in predicting success in a specific event.

CONCEPT & APPLICATION 8.1

Concept The real value of measuring achievement motivation is in predicting long-term patterns of motivation, not in predicting success in a specific event.

Application Personality tests of achievement motivation are valuable indicators of long-term motivation, but should not be used to make predictions of success in a specific athletic event. For example, the coach should not cut a player from the team because of a low score on achievement motivation.

Due to the McClelland-Atkinson model's inability to satisfactorily predict behavior, a number of elaborations or additions to the model have been proposed. Each of the elaborations was designed to improve the predictive ability of the model. The first elaboration to be proposed was the addition of **extrinsic motivation.** Extrinsic motivation comes in many forms, usually those of praise, money, awards, or trophies. By adding extrinsic motivation to the achievement motivation model, Atkinson acknowledged that factors external to the individual may influence an individual's overall motivation.

CONCEPT & APPLICATION 8.2

Concept Contrary to predictions of the McClelland-Atkinson model, individuals whose motive to succeed is low and fear of failure is high may still enter into a competitive situation if some sort of extrinsic motivation is promised.

Application Participation ribbons and awards for effort may be effectively used to encourage children who are fearful and high in the motive to avoid failure to participate in sport anyway.

Many concerned individuals contribute to the development of achievement motivation and self-confidence. Courtesy Kansas State University Sports Information

In addition to its difficult-to-measure psychological constructs, a second shortcoming of the McClelland-Atkinson model is its failure to accurately and consistently account for achievement motivation in women. Sarason and Smith (1971) observed that in studies with female subjects, results were both inconsistent and dissimilar to those for males. This deficiency in the model prompted Horner (1968) to propose the psychological construct of **fear of success** (FOS). This elaboration of the basic model was conceived to account for an apparent lack of motivation to succeed in women competing with men. Conceptually, the fear of success construct was subtracted from the basic achievement motivation equation. Including FOS in the model explains why a woman who enjoys a strong sense of intrinsic motivation and low anxiety would still refuse to enter into an achievement situation involving men. According to Horner (1972), otherwise very achievement-oriented women may suffer a self-inflicted decrement in performance and motivation when competing against men for traditional masculine goals. The female fears that if she succeeds in a male-dominated environment she will suffer a perceived loss of femininity and social rejection by members of both sexes.

An important study by McElroy and Willis (1979), however, tested the FOS construct in a sport setting and found no evidence to justify its inclusion in a sport-specific achievement environment. The authors composed a series of yes-no statements reflecting sport-specific situations and administered them to 262 female athletes from five different sports. Factor analytic procedures were used to isolate and identify two significant dimensions, intrinsic motivation and fear of failure. The analysis failed to support the presence of a fear of success (FOS) dimension for female athletes. McElroy and Willis suggested that the sport setting may be one area where women's achievement is accepted, and fear of success is not a salient factor.

The McElroy and Willis (1979) study is important because it suggests that female athletes do not view success as a masculine accomplishment. According to the original FOS construct proposed by Horner, women should fear success when competing against men for a traditional masculine goal. If athletic achievement was viewed by the subjects in this research to be associated with masculinity, a fear of success response pattern should have emerged. The fact that it did not is good news, since athletic participation is a positive experience that should not be stereotyped.

While women do not seem to have a personality disposition to avoid success to a greater degree than men, they do appear to fear activities inappropriate to their gender role (Peplau, 1976). Young women may avoid such activities as boxing, football, and wrestling, but feel perfectly comfortable playing tennis or volleyball.

CONCEPT & APPLICATION 8.3

Concept It is unlikely that women suffer from fear of success (FOS) to a greater degree than men.

Application A female athlete's reluctance to excel in certain achievement situations is probably due more to the masculine nature of the task than to fear of success. Fear of success is not an independent personality disposition. In choosing competitive activities for women, organizers should carefully consider whether the task is gender appropriate.

MODELS OF SELF-CONFIDENCE

Since the late 1970s a number of cognitive theories have been proposed and researched based upon the broad notion of **self-confidence.** As observed by Arkes and Garske (1982), researchers have recognized that the discriminating factor between individuals high and low in achievement motivation is self-confidence. Athletes who are self-confident and expecting to succeed are generally the same athletes who do succeed.

Increased interest in self-confidence research parallels a declining interest in the achievement motivation theory of McClelland and Atkinson. Clearly, the construct of self-confidence is similar to the achievement motivation notion of intrinsic motivation, or motive to achieve success. The confident athlete has a high motive to succeed and high expectations for success.

In this section, a number of cognitive models will be introduced that use terms essentially equivalent to the concept of self-confidence. These include Bandura's *self-efficacy,* Harter's *competence motivation,* Vealey's *sport confidence,* and Nicholls' *perceived ability.* Each reflects the notion of situation-specific self-confidence, as opposed to a global personality trait. For example, Bandura's self-efficacy refers to an individual's confidence that he can succeed at a specific task, as opposed to feeling generally confident about life.

BANDURA'S THEORY OF SELF-EFFICACY

Self-efficacy is synonymous with an individual's belief that he is competent and can succeed at a particular task. An individual who enjoys a high level of self-efficacy enters into a competitive situation with enthusiasm and self-confidence. The degree of self-efficacy possessed by an individual will determine whether that person will approach or avoid an achievement situation. While the concepts of self-confidence and self-efficacy may not be absolutely identical, it is clear that they are very similar. Bandura's theory of self-efficacy (1986) proposes that self-efficacy is fundamental to competent performance. In competitive situations, the higher the level of self-efficacy is, the higher the performance accomplishments are and the lower is the emotional arousal (Bandura, 1982).

Bandura's model of self-efficacy states that self-efficacy is enhanced by successful performance, vicarious experience, verbal persuasion, and emotional arousal. The most important of these four factors is successful performance. According to Bandura, successful performance raises expectations for future success; failure lowers these expectations. Once strong feelings of self-efficacy develop through repeated success, occasional failures will be of small consequence. Feelings of self-efficacy lead to improved performance, while a lack of those feelings results in slackening performance.

The most critical aspect of Bandura's theory is repeated success through **participatory modeling.** In participatory modeling, the subject first observes a model perform a task. Then the model assists the subject in successfully performing the task. The subject is not allowed to fail. As a result of repeated success, strong feelings of self-efficacy develop. Considerable support for Bandura's model exists in sport-related research (Feltz & Mugno, 1983; Gould & Weiss, 1981; Kavanagh & Hausfeld, 1986; Lan & Gill, 1984; Weinberg, 1985).

CONCEPT & APPLICATION 8.4

Concept The development of self-efficacy in young athletes is closely associated with the level of success that they are able to experience.

Application Participatory modeling should be used by teachers and coaches to assure that young athletes "feel" and experience repeated success. This will result in the athlete's feeling personally competent in an achievement situation.

Clearly, an athlete's belief that she is competent and can succeed in a task is related to her performance in that task (Schunk, 1995). This should not lead one to believe, however, that this relationship is particularly strong. Previous performance, for example, is a stronger predictor of future performance than is self-efficacy (George, 1994; Watkins, Garcia & Turek, 1994). The predictive power of self-efficacy can in many cases be enhanced when performance is process oriented as opposed to outcome oriented (Treasure, Monson & Lox, 1996). When the abilities of individual sport athletes are equalized, self-efficacy is a very strong predictor of performance. For example, self-efficacy is the best available predictor of wrestling performance in overtime matches. In these critical match situations, self-efficacy is particularly powerful (Krane, Marks, Zaccaro & Blair, 1996). As a general rule, compared with persons who doubt their capabilities, those exhibiting high self-efficacy work harder, persist in the task longer, and achieve at a higher level. This observation is true not only for individuals; groups that collectively exhibit high self-efficacy also tend to perform at a higher level than groups exhibiting low collective self-efficacy (George & Feltz, 1995).

CONCEPT & APPLICATION 8.5

Concept Self-efficacy can be enhanced in young athletes by using skilled models and emphasizing that innate ability alone does not determine performance outcome.

Application Coaches and teachers can facilitate the development of self-efficacy in young athletes by focusing on strengths as opposed to weaknesses, providing excellent role models, and emphasizing that hard work and sweat is as important as innate ability.

HARTER'S COMPETENCE MOTIVATION THEORY

Patterned after White's (1959) theory of effectance motivation, Harter (1978) proposed a theory of achievement motivation that is based on an athlete's feeling of personal competence. According to Harter, individuals are innately motivated to be competent in all areas of human achievement. To satisfy the urge to be competent in an achievement area such as sport, the person attempts mastery. An individual's self-perception of success at these mastery attempts develops feelings of positive or negative affect. As illustrated in figure 8.1, successful attempts at mastery promote self-efficacy and feelings of personal competence, which in turn foster high **competence motivation.** As competence motivation increases, the athlete is encouraged to make further mastery attempts.

Conversely, if a young athlete's attempts at mastery result in perceived rejection and failure, then low competence motivation and negative affect will be the end product. It is hypothesized that low competence motivation will result in a youth sport drop-out.

Sport-related studies have provided support for Harter's competence motivation theory. In each of these investigations the tool for measuring competence was Harter's (1982) Perceived Competence Scale for Children (PCSC). In this instrument, emphasis is placed on the assessment of a child's competence in three domains: cognitive (school competence), social (peer-related competence), and physical (skill at sports). A general measure of self-worth is also obtained from the 27-item scale of perceived competence.

Figure 8.1

Harter's competence motivation theory. From S. Harter, Effectance motivation reconsidered. *Human Development,* 1978, *21,* 34–64. Adapted by permission of S. Karger AG, Basel.

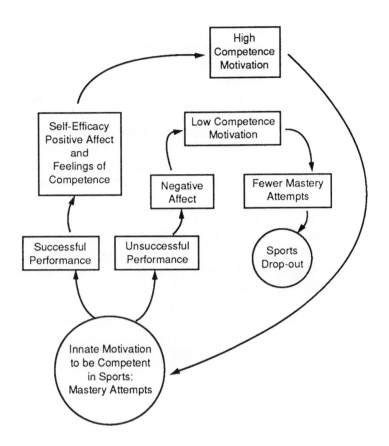

CONCEPT & APPLICATION 8.6

Concept Competence motivation may be enhanced in children through repeated successful mastery attempts.

Application Redefining success to include positive outcomes other than winning will allow more children to succeed. Success may come in the form of skill improvement, trying, or having fun.

The importance of developing competence motivation in sport has been verified by Weiss and Horn (1990). This investigation underscored the importance of accurately assessing personal competence. Boys and girls who underestimate their own competence tend to be candidates for sport drop-outs. Girls who underestimate their own competence tend to drop out of sport involvement, suffer from high trait anxiety, prefer unchallenging activities, and are controlled by external forces. The effect of underestimation on boys seems to be less damaging. Generally, children who accurately assess their own ability feel more in control and seek involvement in challenging activities.

An investigation by Black and Weiss (1992) reaffirmed the importance of significant others in developing competence motivation in young athletes. Young athletes who perceive their coaches as individuals who give positive feedback and encouragement are the same athletes who perceive themselves as highly motivated. The importance of a supportive coach or teacher cannot be overestimated. Coaches, teachers, and leaders must recognize that helping young people develop confidence in themselves is time well spent.

VEALEY'S SPORT-SPECIFIC MODEL OF SPORT CONFIDENCE

Vealey's (1986, 1988b) model of sport confidence is a unique approach to conceptualizing achievement motivation and self-confidence in sport. Perhaps the real strength of Vealey's proposed model is that it is situation-specific and represents a legitimate attempt at theory development within the discipline of sport psychology. All other theories discussed in this chapter have been borrowed from the parent discipline of psychology and then applied to sport.

In the model illustrated in figure 8.2, Vealey defines **sport confidence** as "the belief or degree of certainty individuals possess about their ability to be successful in sport" (p. 222). The athlete brings to the objective competitive situation a personality trait of sport confidence (SC-trait) and a particular competitive orientation. These two factors are then predictive of the level of situational state-specific sport confidence (SC-state) the athlete exhibits during competition. Situation-specific sport confidence (SC-state) is then predictive of performance, or overt behavioral responses. Behavioral responses give rise to subjective perceptions of outcome. Examples of subjective outcomes include such things as satisfaction, perception of success (independent of a win or a loss), and causes given for outcomes. Subjective outcomes in turn influence and are influenced by the athlete's competitive orientation and personality trait of sport confidence.

Vealey (1986) tested the basic tenets of her proposed model and found them to be viable. In doing so, she also developed instruments for measuring SC-trait (Trait Sport-Confidence Inventory), SC-state (State Sport-Confidence Inventory) and competitive orientation (Competitive Orientation Inventory).

Vealey's sport confidence model is very useful for explaining the relationship between general sport confidence and situation-specific sport confidence. An athlete who is very successful at one sport transfers much of the confidence derived from his success to other sport situations.

Figure 8.2

Vealey's model of sport confidence. From R. S. Vealey, Conceptualization of sport-confidence and competitive orientation: Preliminary investigation and instrument development. *Journal of Sport Psychology,* 1986, *8,* 221–246. Adapted by permission of Human Kinetics Publishers, Inc., Champaign, IL.

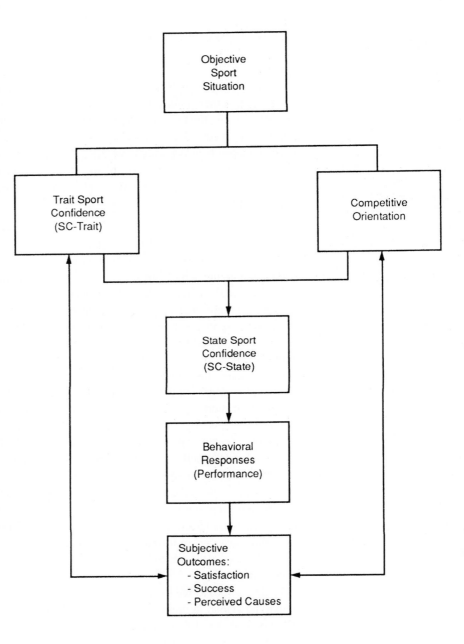

CONCEPT & APPLICATION 8.7

Concept An athlete who enjoys a general feeling of sport confidence will be able to transfer that predisposition to new and different situation-specific events.

Application It is important that each youth sport participant find success and a feeling of competence in at least one sport or activity. A situation-specific success experience will have the effect of enhancing the athlete's general perception of sport confidence. As the personality trait of sport confidence is developed, the athlete will experience greater levels of situation-specific sport confidence as new events are attempted.

NICHOLLS' DEVELOPMENTALLY BASED THEORY OF PERCEIVED ABILITY

Nicholls' developmentally based theory of achievement motivation is a logical extension of both Bandura's theory of self-efficacy and Harter's theory of competence motivation. According to Nicholls (1984) and Duda (1987), the defining feature of achievement motivation is the way children come to view their own **perceived ability.** Perceived ability, however, is viewed differently from one developmental level to another. At a young age, ability is judged by the child based on past performance. At a later age, ability is judged based on the performance of others (social comparison).

A child two to six years old views perceived ability in terms of how well she performed the task the last time. If the child notices an improvement in performance from time one to time two, she naturally assumes that ability has increased and that she is competent at performing the task. High amounts of effort in mastering the task are perceived by the child as evidence of high ability and competence. Competence is perceived by the child as a function of hard work and absolute capacity. At this early age, the child is said to be **task-oriented,** as opposed to ego-oriented.

At the age of six or seven, the child begins to view perceived ability in terms of how other children perform. The child becomes **ego-oriented,** as opposed to task-oriented. No longer is it enough to perform the task better than she performed it the last time; the child must now perform the task better than other children do. Perceived ability is now a function of one's own capacity as it is relative to that of others, as opposed to being a function of absolute ability. High ability and competence is only perceived as such if it is better than the performance of others.

After age 11 or 12, the child may exhibit either a task- or an ego-involved disposition, depending upon the situation at hand. Environmental factors causing a person to focus upon social comparisons will result in an ego-oriented disposition, while situations causing a person to focus upon personal mastery and improved performance will foster a task-oriented disposition. The evidence

Optimal athletic performance is associated with high levels of self-confidence. Courtesy University of Missouri-Columbia Sports Information

suggests that a task-oriented disposition is ultimately the most beneficial for the development of a positive self-image. A case in point is a study by Duda, Olson, and Templin (1991) that relates to mature attitudes towards the use of aggression in sport. Athletes who exhibit a task orientation towards sports performance tend to view acts of athletic violence as being less legitimate than athletes who exhibit an ego-involved orientation towards sports participation think they are.

CONCEPT & APPLICATION 8.8

Concept Developmental considerations must be taken into consideration when attempting to help children develop feelings of self-confidence, competence, and perceived ability.

Application At the age of six or seven, a child starts to evaluate his perceived ability relative to the performance of his peers. While this is a

developmental characteristic of this age group, efforts must be made to help the child view competence as a function of effort and absolute performance, as opposed to outcome only. If the adult leader emphasizes the importance of effort and personal improvement, winning and losing will become less important.

The goal-orientation climate that these children play in will affect their intrinsic motivation. Courtesy © Skjold Photos

As explained before, **goal orientation** plays an important role in Nicholls' theory of motivation. In recent years goal orientation, as it relates to motivation theory, has become one of the most researched topics in sport psychology. The notion of goal orientation was first introduced in chapter 6, when I discussed goal setting as a cognitive-behavioral intervention strategy. At that time, I noted that some athletes have an orientation towards outcome goal setting and others have an orientation towards process, or performance, goal setting. The concept of being task-oriented is similar to that of being process-oriented, and the concept of being ego-oriented is similar to that of being outcome-oriented.

Task-oriented athletes endorse mastery strategies and focus upon self-referenced criteria for determining success. They believe in working hard in practice and in skill development. They consciously avoid normative comparisons with their peers, and base their perception of success upon personal improvement. Faced with difficulty or failure, these athletes are more likely to persist and demonstrate desirable motivational behaviors. Conversely, *ego-oriented* athletes focus upon external criteria for determining success. They believe that chance and social comparisons are important success criteria. Success is measured normatively or in relation to how others perform. To the ego-oriented athlete, perceived ability is more important than hard work and effort. In the face of difficulty or failure, these athletes are less likely to persist and more likely to demonstrate undesirable motivational behaviors. Ego-oriented athletes are more likely to use an unfair or illegal advantage to achieve success (Duda & White, 1992; Kavussanu & Roberts, 1996; Lochbaum & Roberts, 1993).

In order to determine whether individuals exhibit task and/or ego goal orientations, a number of inventories have been developed. These are the Task and Ego Orientation in Sport Questionnaire (TEOSQ), the Perceptions of Success Questionnaire (POSQ), and the Sports Orientation Questionnaire (SOQ). The TEOSQ (Duda, 1989; White & Duda, 1994) is composed of 15 items that measure task and ego orientation. The POSQ (Roberts, 1993; Roberts & Treasure, 1995) is composed of 12 items that measure competitiveness (ego orientation) and mastery (task orientation). The SOQ (Gill, 1993; Gill & Deeter, 1988) is composed of 25 items and purports to measure competitiveness, win orientation, and goal orientation. It is unclear, however, exactly how each of these factors compares with basic task and ego orientations (Marsh, 1994).

Research on goal orientation has revealed that individuals who are high in task orientation can also be high in ego orientation; other combinations of the two orientations are also possible. In other words, the two orientations are somewhat independent of each other. The best combination is for a young athlete to be high in both orientations. Individuals with high task and ego orientations exhibit the highest levels of motivation and perceived competence. The worst combination in terms of motivation and perceived competence is to be low in both task and ego orientations. Individuals in this category tend to be primarily young women. Children dominated by a task orientation tend to be more motivated than children dominated by an ego orientation (Fox, Goudas, Biddle, Duda & Armstrong, 1994).

Perhaps of greater import than whether an individual is task- or ego-oriented is the climate that the individual is placed in. Just as individuals can be task- or ego-oriented, learning environments can also be task- or ego-oriented. An ego-oriented environment, with its emphasis upon social comparison, can be particularly harmful to low-ability youth. Conversely, high-ability children seem to thrive in either environment. The effects of a mastery, or task-oriented, learning environment can reverse the negative effects of an ego orientation. A **mastery environment** can also have a positive effect on a low-ability child who is fearful of any sort of competitive situation (Goudas, Biddle, Fox & Underwood, 1995; Papaioannow, 1995; Theeboom, DeKnop & Weiss, 1995). So strong is the research on this principle that the European Federation of Sport Psychology (1996b) released a position statement which states, "A mastery motivational climate should be created. Under such favourable conditions, sport can enhance the child's initiative and independence, as well as self esteem and identity" (p. 224). In order to measure children's perception as to whether an environment is task- or ego-oriented, the Perceived Motivational Climate on Sport Questionnaire (PMCSQ) was developed by Seifriz, Duda, and Chi (1992).

CONCEPT & APPLICATION 8.9

Concept As a general rule, a task-involved goal orientation is preferred to an ego-involved goal orientation. Children who are high in both goal orientations are not negatively affected by the presence of the desire for social comparison. More important than the child's goal orientation, however, is the orientation of the learning environment that the child is placed in.

Application As recommended by the European Federation of Sport Psychology, a mastery- or task-oriented motivational climate should be created. A mastery-oriented climate creates conditions favorable for the development of a child's initiative, independence, and self-esteem. These same environmental conditions are effective in enhancing self-confidence and motivation in children with physical disabilities (White & Duda, 1993).

GENDER AND SELF-CONFIDENCE

The fear of success (FOS) construct as introduced earlier in this chapter suggested that in certain circumstances men and women may respond differently to a competitive situation. One such situation may be related to the nature of the activity. Women and men perceive certain activities to be gender-role-inappropriate, or appropriate for only one gender. For example, American football is considered to be a male-appropriate activity, ballet a female-appropriate activity, and swimming a neutral activity. Women suffer a decrement in self-efficacy when asked to perform motor tasks that they perceive to be female-inappropriate. They do not suffer a decrement when asked to perform neutral or female-appropriate activities. Both males and females rate themselves higher in ability in gender-appropriate tasks (Clifton & Gill, 1994). The work of Lenney (1977) supports these conclusions and suggests two other insights about women and self-confidence.

Lenney (1977) observed that previous reviewers had suggested that women display lower self-confidence than men across almost all achievement situations. Lenney analyzed the empirical validity of this suggestion and concluded that while this was often the case, it was not true in all achievement situations. Women are often low in self-confidence, a frequent and potentially debilitating problem. However, Lenney points out that whether a woman will respond with lower levels of self-confidence depends on certain situational variables. She then identified the three important variables that influence gender differences in self-confidence.

The first of these is the nature of the task. While it is not clear exactly what types of tasks yield this effect, it is clear that women respond to some tasks with a great deal of confidence, but to others with little confidence. For example, a woman might be expected to respond with a low level of confidence to a task that was inappropriate to her gender role. Bodybuilding once was considered such a task, although this is changing rapidly.

Second, the nature of gender differences in self-confidence depends on the availability of clear and unambiguous information. Females provided with clear feedback regarding their performance will exhibit as much self-confidence as men. However, if the feedback is unclear and ambiguous, women tend to have lower opinions of their abilities and to respond with lower levels of self-confidence than men. For example, women might be more likely to show a lack of confidence if they were asked to execute a sideward roll in volleyball without being told what was good or bad or for what purpose they were doing it.

Finally, the third factor that influences a gender difference in self-confidence is that of **social comparison** cues. When women work alone or in a situation not involving social comparison, they are likely to respond with self-confidence levels equal to those of men. However, when placed in a situation where their performance is compared with others in a social context, they typically respond with lower levels of self-confidence (Corbin, 1981).

Lenney's hypotheses regarding women and self-confidence were derived primarily from research in which cognitive (non-motor) tasks were studied. Lirgg (1991) conducted a meta-analysis to determine if research involving physical activity would also support Lenney's assertions. Being tested were Lenney's assertions that females would be less confident than males when the task was male-appropriate or when the situation was competitive in nature. The results of the meta-analysis supported Lenney's hypothesis that females will show lower self-confidence than males when performing male-appropriate tasks. As long as the task was not female-inappropriate, however, the analysis did not support Lenney's contention that females will be less confident than males in competitive (social comparison) situations. While research shows that females do not lack self-confidence in all situations, strategies to increase self-confidence in women may be beneficial. Suggested strategies include these: (a) ensure success, (b) avoid gender-inappropriate activities, (c) avoid ambiguity through effective communication, (d) use effective modeling of correct performance, and (e) decrease competitive situations during learning (Lirgg & Feltz, 1989).

A recent investigation reported by Lirgg, George, Chase, and Ferguson (1996) provides additional insight into the issue of gender-inappropriate tasks and self-confidence (self-efficacy). Self-efficacy of men and of women was assessed relative to performing a decidedly feminine task (baton twirling) or a decidedly masculine task (kung fu) under conditions of differing beliefs about ability. Results showed that men were unswayed by either the gender-inappropriate nature of the task or their conception about ability. Conversely, women were affected by both the nature of the task and their conception about ability. The combination of a perceived masculine task and a belief that ability is unchangeable (innate) leads to lower self-efficacy in women. Women, however, respond with significantly higher levels of self-efficacy if they believe ability or skill on the masculine task can be learned.

CONCEPT & APPLICATION 8.10

Concept Self-confidence is affected to a greater degree in women than in men in situations of ambiguity, social comparison, and gender-inappropriate tasks. There are, however, a number of mediating variables that influence the degree to which a woman's self-confidence can be affected. One such mediating variable is the woman's conception relative to ability.

Application Performing a decidedly masculine task can result in feelings of low self-confidence in women. However, these feelings can be modified by a woman's conception about ability.

If she believes that ability on the masculine task is innate and unchanging, she will have feelings of low self-confidence relative to performing the task. Conversely, if she believes that ability on the task is something that can be learned and acquired, her feelings of self-efficacy and confidence will increase significantly. It is important that all sports participants, especially females, be taught that motor tasks can be learned and mastered even if they appear difficult or gender-inappropriate to begin with.

PERCEIVED GENDER ROLES

As I have mentioned, one of the factors that interacts with a person's gender to influence perceived competence and motivation is the person's perceived **gender role.** Men and women both exhibit masculine and feminine attributes. A **masculine attribute** is defined as a characteristic considered to be desirable to both sexes, but found in greater abundance in males. A **feminine attribute** is defined as a characteristic considered to be desirable to both sexes, but found in greater abundance in females. A woman, for example, might exhibit an abundance of masculine attributes that would define her gender role as somewhat masculine, so she would be described as a masculine female. Similarly, a man who exhibited an abundance of feminine attributes might be described, in terms of gender role, as a feminine male. An example of a masculine attribute desirable to both sexes might be the attribute of assertiveness, or being forthright and confident. An example of a feminine attribute desirable to both sexes might be the attribute of nurturing, or wanting to care for someone.

Utilizing either the Personal Attributes Questionnaire (PAQ), developed by Helmreich and Spence (1977), or the Bem Sex-Role Inventory (BSRI), developed by Bem (1974), an individual's gender role can be determined and categorized as shown in figure 8.3. Female subjects classified as high in femininity and low in masculinity would be categorized as feminine. Women low in femininity but high in masculinity would be categorized as masculine. High scores in both masculinity and femininity indicate **androgyny.** Since the items in both the feminine and the masculine scales are considered socially desirable for both genders, the androgynous classification should be very desirable for both men and women. Finally, subjects scoring low on both the feminine and the masculine scales are classified as undifferentiated, since they are not high in either dimension.

Figure 8.3

Classification system used by Helmreich and Spence (1977) when they analyzed scores from the Personal Attribute Questionnaire. From R. Helmreich and J. T. Spence, Sex roles and achievement. In *Psychology of motor behavior-1976 (Vol.2)*, R. W. Christina & D. M. Landers (Editors). Copyright © 1977 by Human Kinetics Publishers, Inc. Adapted by permission of the publishers.

	Masculinity Scale	
	Below median	**Above median**
Below median	**Undifferentiated** Subjects categorized below median on both feminine and masculine scales.	**Masculine** Subjects categorized above median on masculine scale, but below on feminine scale.
Above median	**Feminine** Subjects categorized above median on feminine scale, but below on masculine scale.	**Androgynous** Subjects categorized above median on both masculine and feminine scales.

(Femininity Scale, left axis)

Successful female athletes enjoy high levels of self-confidence. Courtesy Kansas State University Sports Information

In terms of gender role, women characterized as masculine or androgynous exhibit higher levels of self-confidence and motivation than women characterized as feminine or undifferentiated (Harris, 1980b). From an achievement motivation perspective, this suggests that it would be prudent to teach women desirable masculine attributes and encourage them to adopt these characteristics in competitive situations.

CONCEPT & APPLICATION 8.11

Concept The androgynous female athlete is likely to be higher in intrinsic motivation than the feminine female athlete.

Application Many feminine qualities, such as compassion and empathy, are desirable human

qualities. And many masculine qualities, such as assertiveness and independence, are desirable human qualities. Athletes must be taught that to be womanly does not mean that desirable masculine qualities are to be shunned.

GENDER ROLE AND ANXIETY

In a study designed to investigate the relationship between gender role and competitive trait anxiety (SCAT), Andersen and Williams (1987) classified male and female subjects as being feminine-female, feminine-male, androgynous-female, androgynous-male, masculine-female, and masculine-male. Undifferentiated males and females were excluded. Individuals with the same gender-role orientation and gender are referred to as **gender-typed** (feminine-female and masculine-male), while individuals having different gender-role orientation and gender are referred to as **cross-gender-typed** (feminine-male and masculine-female). Androgynous persons are those individuals who assume both gender roles (androgynous-female and androgynous-male).

As illustrated in figure 8.4, the Andersen and Williams (1987) results show a linear relationship between competitive trait anxiety (SCAT) and a person's gender and gender-role classification. The greatest degree of competitive trait anxiety is exhibited by female subjects who embrace a feminine gender role. Conversely, the lowest level of competitive trait anxiety is exhibited by male subjects who embrace a masculine gender role.

These results suggest that gender role may be a powerful predictor of sport nonparticipation. If feminine-females participate in sport, they are more likely than other gender-role groups to experience high levels of anxiety. As predicted by the McClelland-Atkinson model of achievement motivation, individuals with high levels of fear of failure (anxiety) may be reluctant to enter into a competitive situation.

CONCEPT & APPLICATION 8.12

Concept Girls and women who endorse a feminine gender role are more likely to experience feelings of anxiety and fear of failure than other gender-role groups when thrust into a sport environment.

Application Coaches and teachers of sport-related activities should anticipate the nature of the relationship between gender orientation and anxiety. With this in mind, special assistance should be given to vulnerable individuals in order to minimize their anxiety and nonparticipation.

Figure 8.4

Mean sport competitive
anxiety scores by gender-
role classification and sex.
From M. B. Andersen and
J. M. Williams, Gender role
and sport competition
anxiety: A re-examination.
*Research Quarterly for
Exercise and Sport,* 1987,
58, 52–56. Reproduced by
permission of the
American Alliance of
Health, Physical
Education, Recreation and
Dance.

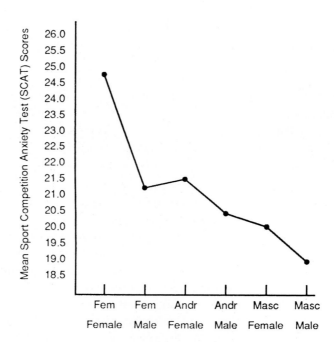

Knowing that females, and especially feminine-females, are susceptible to high levels of anxiety associated with competition, it may be beneficial to consider arousal control techniques as a way to control anxiety. It is important, however, that intervention strategies not be applied indiscriminately. Ample evidence exists to suggest that men and women respond differently to arousal control intervention. A case in point is a study by Friedman and Berger (1991). In this investigation, gender and gender role was studied relative to three different stress reduction techniques. Results of the investigation suggested that gender and gender role are important predictors of the effectiveness of stress reduction and arousal control techniques. Masculine-males and masculine-females respond better to stress management techniques than feminine-males and feminine-females.

EFFECTS OF EXTERNAL REWARDS ON INTRINSIC MOTIVATION

Intrinsic motivation is defined as motivation that comes from within and is not determined by external rewards. As illustrated in figure 8.5, intrinsic motivation is enhanced by feelings of self-confidence and perceived competence. Self-confidence is in turn strengthened by positive feedback associated with successful mastery attempts (Woodcock & Corbin, 1992). Intrinsic motivation was first introduced at the beginning of this chapter in our discussion of the McClelland-Atkinson model of achievement motivation. In this model, intrinsic motivation is the same as the motive to achieve success. As an elaboration on the basic McClelland-Atkinson model, it was proposed that extrinsic motivation would have an *added effect* on intrinsic motivation.

Figure 8.5

Illustration showing the relationship between positive feedback, self-confidence, and intrinsic motivation.

When someone engages in an activity for its own sake and not for any other reason, we may conclude that she engages in the activity with an intrinsic motivation. On the other hand, if someone has an external reason for engaging in the activity, we would agree that she has an external reason to engage in it. If the external motivation is a reward, then it can be assumed that the reward may be part of the reason the person is participating.

It is appealing to assume that extrinsic rewards can enhance motivation. But what happens to an athlete's motivation if the rewards are withdrawn? Can external rewards actually damage rather than enhance motivation? Research on attribution theory indicates that external rewards can damage a young athlete's intrinsic desire to compete. The kinds of attributions that people give for receiving external rewards may have a negative impact on their intrinsic motivation.

According to the **additive principle,** a young athlete who is low in intrinsic motivation will participate in an achievement situation if there is sufficient reward or extrinsic motivation for doing so. Yet a great deal of research evidence seems to cast doubt on the additive principle. Specifically, it has been argued that the relationship between intrinsic and extrinsic motivation is multiplicative, not additive. That is, extrinsic rewards can either add to or detract from intrinsic motivation. This principle is illustrated in the story of an elderly man who wanted to chase away some noisy children who liked to play near his home (Siedentop & Ramey, 1977). The man tried several strategies to get the boys to play elsewhere, but to no avail. Finally, he came up with a new and interesting strategy. He decided to pay the boys to play near his house! He offered them 25 cents apiece to return the next day. Naturally, the boys returned the next day to receive their pay, at which time the man offered them 20 cents to come the following day. When they returned again he offered them only 15 cents to come the next day, and he added that for the next few days he would only give them a nickel for their efforts. The boys became very agitated, since they felt their efforts were worth more than a nickel, and they told the man that they would not return!

The boys in this story came to believe that the reason they were playing near the man's house was for pay and not for fun. Therefore their perceived locus of control shifted from an internal to an external source. When this happens, an activity can lose its intrinsic value. Is it possible that this is happening today in

Can trophies such as this one contribute to a decrease in intrinsic motivation? Courtesy Kansas State University Sports Information

professional baseball? There are no doubt many highly paid athletes who have shifted their locus of control from an internal source—love of the game—to an external source. If the high salaries were withdrawn, how many would continue playing the game?

A similar thing could be happening to our young athletes as they receive trophies, money, pins, and awards for athletic participation. Is the relationship between intrinsic and extrinsic rewards additive, or is it multiplicative? The **multiplicative principle** suggests that the interaction between intrinsic and extrinsic rewards could either add to or detract from intrinsic motivation.

Embedded in attribution theory are the concepts of discounting and overjustification (Lepper & Greene, 1975, 1976). These concepts suggest that adding external rewards as an incentive to participate in an otherwise interesting activity may represent an *overjustification* for participating, leading to a *discounting,* or reduction, in intrinsic motivation. For example, if a child begins playing baseball for fun but then is induced to do so for a trophy, this trophy may represent an overjustification for playing baseball. The child may come to perceive that she is playing for the purpose of receiving a trophy rather than for intrinsic reasons. Whenever an individual comes to believe that she is participating in an otherwise interesting activity for external rewards, intrinsic motivation is minimized.

The overjustification principle plays a role in the weakening of intrinsic motivation within adults as well as children. Consider the destructive effect that big salaries associated with free agency have had upon major league baseball players. In a moment of unusual candor, Candy Davis, wife of big-league relief pitcher Mark Davis, said of his new $13 million contract with the Kansas City Royals: "You'd think he discovered the cure for cancer or something." As history records, Mark Davis did not live up to his multimillion-dollar contract (Neff, 1990).

CONCEPT & APPLICATION 8.13

Concept An extrinsic reward that encourages athletes to attribute their participation to external causes can reduce intrinsic motivation.

Application Coaches should discourage any form of extrinsic reward that athletes may perceive to be more important than athletic participation itself.

Perhaps the single most important contribution to our understanding of the relationship between intrinsic motivation and extrinsic rewards comes from **Cognitive Evaluation Theory.** Cognitive Evaluation Theory (Deci & Ryan, 1985) is deeply seated in attribution theory, and in the locus of control origin-pawn relationship introduced earlier in the previous chapter, on attribution theory.

Deci theorized that extrinsic rewards can affect intrinsic motivation in two ways. The first is to produce a decrement in intrinsic motivation; this occurs as people perceive a change in locus of control from an internal to an external one. That is, when people come to perceive that their behavior is controlled by external forces, they respond with decreased levels of intrinsic motivation. This is referred to as the controlling aspect of extrinsic motivation, and serves to place an athlete in the position of a pawn who is acted upon. The second effect of extrinsic rewards is informational in nature, and results in an increase in intrinsic motivation. If an external award provides feedback to the person and enhances that person's sense of competence and self-determination, increased intrinsic motivation will be the end result. This is referred to as the informational aspect of extrinsic motivation, and it places an athlete in the position of an originator who does the acting.

Consider the following situation: A ten-year-old boy agrees to run in a five-mile road race with his father. As further incentive to train and finish the race, the father promises the boy ten dollars. Later on, the boy passes up a second opportunity to run in a race with his father because, as he puts it, "Why, what's in it for me?" This may seem like an extreme example, yet situations like this occur every day. Why did this boy lose interest in this intrinsically interesting activity? Because he came to perceive that the primary reason for his running in the race was money. The money, not the intrinsic fun of running, became the source of his motivation. Once the shift in locus of control was made from the internal cause to the external cause, the boy came to feel controlled by the external reward. He was running for the money and not for the intrinsic value of the experience; consequently, when the salient external motivation was withdrawn, intrinsic motivation was insufficient.

Let us consider a second example. A twelve-year-old girl competed in a singles tennis tournament and won an award for accomplishment. The inscription on the award said, "In recognition of your placing in the top ten of the City Tournament." This positive feedback about her performance gave the girl a feeling of competence and self-determination. She was proud of the award and went on to participate in several more tennis tournaments that year. Because she perceived that the award provided her positive information about her ability as a tennis player, it became intrinsically motivating.

CONCEPT & APPLICATION 8.14

Concept Extrinsic rewards (such as praise, awards, ribbons, and trophies) that athletes view as rewards for competent performance and encouragement for further participation will enhance intrinsic motivation.
Application Coaches and teachers should carefully consider the perceptions that young

athletes have about extrinsic rewards. If the rewards are perceived to represent excellence, they can be valuable. However, if they become more important than the sport itself, they can be damaging.

Research has also linked intrinsic motivation to goal orientation. Individuals displaying a task (mastery) orientation enjoy enhanced intrinsic motivation because of the self-referenced and self-determined nature of their involvement. Conversely, individuals displaying an ego orientation suffer a loss of intrinsic motivation because of the controlling nature of their involvement. Ego orientation is controlling because the goal to demonstrate competence in a task through social comparison becomes more important than the task or event itself (Frederick & Ryan, 1995; Walling, Duda & Chi, 1993). Competition may lead to a reduction in intrinsic motivation because of its controlling nature. When athletes compete only for the purpose of winning and demonstrating superiority over others (social comparison), the main reason for their participation is an external reward (winning), and not the joy of participation. Fortier, Vallerand,

CONCEPT & APPLICATION 8.15

Concept The development of an athlete's intrinsic motivation and self-confidence is the ultimate goal of youth sport programs.

Application Coaches and administrators should define program goals in terms of the intrinsic values the participants will gain.

Briere, and Provenchers (1995) reported that French Canadian recreational athletes enjoy higher levels of intrinsic motivation for their sport involvement than do competitive collegiate athletes. Similarly, Ryan (1980) reported that scholarship athletes exhibit lower intrinsic motivation than nonscholarship athletes. When we participate in sport for some reason other than the enjoyment of participation, we are in danger of suffering a decrement in intrinsic motivation.

Interestingly, research by Wankel and Kreisel (1985) identifies intrinsic factors as more important to youth sport participants than extrinsic factors. Eight hundred and twenty-two children were asked to indicate their reasons for participating in sport. The following intrinsic factors were listed as being most enjoyable and important:

> Excitement of sport
> Personal accomplishment
> Improving skill
> Testing skills against others
> Just doing the skills
> Pleasing others
> Being with friends

Extrinsic factors such as "winning the game" and "getting rewards" were identified as least enjoyable or important.

DEVELOPING SELF-CONFIDENCE AND INTRINSIC MOTIVATION IN YOUTH SPORT PARTICIPANTS

Three separate groups of people have primary responsibility for the development of self-confidence and intrinsic motivation in youth sport participants. These three groups include the participants themselves; the teacher, coach, or youth sport leader; and the participant's parents.

THE INDIVIDUAL ATHLETE

A line of research referred to as **participation motivation** documents the reasons that children give for participating in youth sport activities, and to a lesser extent the reasons they give for nonparticipation. The basic measurement tool used in these investigations is the Participation Motivation Inventory (PMI) or some modification of it (Gill, Gross & Huddleston, 1983). Based upon numerous investigations, the following motives for participation have been identified repeatedly by youth sport participants:

1. The motive to learn new skills and to improve on existing sport skills.

2. The motive to have fun and to enjoy participating in sport.

3. The motive to become physically fit and to enjoy good health.

4. The motive to enjoy the challenge and excitement of sports participation and competition.

5. The motive to enjoy a team atmosphere and to be with friends.

This athlete seems to be truly pleased with her performance and her trophy. Courtesy © Skjold Photos

While the prior list of motives for participation does not represent a complete list of reasons for participation in sport, it does represent the motives that children feel strongly about. All of these motives are consistent with what we have come to recognize as a task or mastery goal orientation. A task orientation is associated with increased intrinsic motivation.

CONCEPT & APPLICATION 8.16

Concept The motives that young athletes have for participating in youth sport programs are the same motives that lead to the development of intrinsic motivation and self-confidence.
Application Youth sport promises an exciting and challenging environment in which participants can realize enhanced self-esteem and motivation. Youth sport programs that are based on participation motives of organizers and parents may not be consistent with the motives of the participants themselves. In order to assist participants in the development of intrinsic love for sport and increased self-confidence relative to sport participation, the participant's motives for participation must be of primary concern.

THE COACH OR TEACHER

The coach or teacher and the organizers of youth sport programs (in and out of public schools) are primarily responsible for establishing the climate and environment for youth sport participation. As we learned earlier, an environment that fosters a task, or mastery, goal orientation is associated with increased intrinsic motivation, while one that fosters an ego, or performance, goal orientation is associated with decreased intrinsic motivation.

Epstein (1989) and Treasure and Roberts (1995) have proposed that a task-mastery-oriented climate can be created by the coach or teacher that will be instrumental in developing and fostering self-confidence and intrinsic motivation in youth sport participants. As originally coined by Epstein, the acronym TARGET has come to represent the manipulation of environmental conditions that will lead to a mastery climate conducive to the development of intrinsic motivation. It is proposed that coaches address each of these conditions in order to create a mastery environment. The conditions are as follows:

1. *Tasks*—Tasks involving variety and diversity facilitate an interest in learning and task involvement.

2. *Authority*—Students should be given opportunities to participate actively in the learning process by being involved in decision making and monitoring their own personal progress.

3. *Reward*—Rewards for participation should focus upon individual gains and improvement, and away from social comparisons.

4. *Grouping*—Students should be placed in groups so that they can work on individual skills in a cooperative learning climate.

5. *Evaluation*—Evaluation should involve numerous self-tests that focus upon effort and personal improvement.

6. *Timing*—Timing is critical to the interaction of all of these conditions.

CONCEPT & APPLICATION 8.17

Concept The climate and environment created by the coach or teacher can be a powerful determinant as to whether a young athlete will increase in intrinsic motivation and self-confidence.

Application TARGET structures provide specific suggestions as to how the coach can create an atmosphere conducive to the development of self-confidence and the motive to achieve success. Factors such as making practices interesting, involving athletes in decision making, basing rewards on individual gains, and creating an atmosphere of cooperation are all important TARGET structures. Other strategies used by coaches to enhance self-confidence include (a) instruction/drilling, (b) encouraging positive self-talk, (c) acting self-confident, (d) liberal use of praise, and (e) physical conditioning sessions.

In addition to the TARGET principle, successful coaches have identified a number of coaching practices that they feel enhance self-confidence and intrinsic motivation in youth sport participants (Gould, Hodge, Peterson & Giannini, 1989; Weinberg & Jackson, 1990). These practices include (a) the use of instruction/drilling, (b) encouraging the use of positive self-talk, (c) acting confident yourself, (d) liberal use of praise, and (e) physical conditioning.

THE PARENT

Just as the coach or teacher plays an important role in developing intrinsic motivation and self-confidence in young athletes, so do the athlete's parents. We have learned that young athletes tend to exhibit either a task (mastery) or an ego (performance) goal orientation. We have also learned that a task orientation is related to an increase in intrinsic motivation, while an ego orientation is associated with a decrease in intrinsic motivation. Where does a child's orientation towards task or ego goals come from? Is this an inherited personality disposition, or a learned behavior? The observation that the best predictor of whether or not a child will be task- or ego-oriented is the goal orientation of the parent suggests that goal orientation is a learned behavior (Ebbeck & Becker, 1994). If the parents are decidedly ego- or performance-oriented, there is a good chance that the child will favor this goal orientation as well. Similarly, young athletes who are task-oriented tend to have parents who favor this particular orientation.

Classic research by Winterbottom (1953) and by Rosen and D'Andrade (1959) point to the important role of parents in the development of achievement motivation. The following principles summarize much of their research:

1. Parents should encourage independence and reinforce a child's efforts at becoming independent.

2. Parents (especially mothers) should be warm and encouraging to their children.

3. Parents should comfort and support their children when setbacks, fear, and discouragement occur.

4. Parents should expect their children to be able, competent, and responsible.

5. Parents can demonstrate confidence in their children's ability by resisting the urge to "take charge" when they experience difficulty in mastering a task.

6. Parents should allow and expect many trials for a child to master a task. Do not keep track of trials. Appreciate small steps.

7. Keep track of a child's successes and applaud them. Do not dwell on failures.

8. Parents should pay attention to their child's efforts. Listen to their problems and pay attention to their feelings.

There can be no doubt about the importance of developing self-confidence in children. Parents, coaches, and teachers must be willing to go to extreme lengths to make sure that every youth sport participant has a positive experience. One cannot guarantee success, but specific steps can be taken to make sure that failure is not the dominant outcome.

CONCEPT & APPLICATION 8.18

Concept Parents play a pivotal role in developing intrinsic motivation in children. Their influence is manifested in the child's self-confidence, the child's goal orientation, and the child's basic motive to achieve success. It might not be an overstatement to say that next to the gift of life, the greatest gift a parent can give a child is the gift of self-confidence and self-assurance.

Application There is not much that youth sport programs can do to educate parents about promoting intrinsic motivation and confidence in their children prior to the age of sports involvement. The tender years from birth to the first school experience are known to be critical in the life of the developing child. However, once a child is involved, there exists a tremendous opportunity to draw the parent into the youth sports experience. Enlightened and well-trained coaches and teachers can enlist parental support and involvement in developing in their child the motive and desire to achieve success.

SUMMARY   Achievement motivation and McClelland and Atkinson's classic model of need achievement were defined and described. Components of the McClelland-Atkinson model that were discussed included the motive to achieve success (intrinsic motivation) and fear of failure. Extrinsic motivation and fear of success were introduced and discussed as elaborations of the basic model. While thoroughly studied between 1950 and 1970, the theory has been largely abandoned in favor of more situation-specific cognitive theories. The theory has continuing value because of the systematic way in which psychological constructs associated with motivation are explained. The fundamental prediction of the model is that individuals high in motive to achieve success will enter into achievement situations, while those high in fear of failure will not.

Categorized under the heading of self-confidence, four additional theories of motivation were introduced and discussed. These include Bandura's theory of self-efficacy, Harter's theory of competence motivation, Vealey's sport-specific model of sport confidence, and Nicholls' developmentally based theory of perceived ability. In each of these theories it is predicted that the young athlete will increase in self-confidence as he is given the opportunity to experience success in a supportive environment. Nicholls' goal orientation theory was discussed in detail relative to the concepts of task (mastery) and ego (performance) goal orientations.

Women do not necessarily have less self-confidence than men, but ambiguous tasks, gender-inappropriate tasks, and social comparison can dampen their self-confidence. Men and women both exhibit masculine and feminine attributes. Women high in desirable masculine attributes and androgynous women (high in both masculine and feminine attributes) exhibit higher levels of self-confidence than women high in feminine attributes. Women who adopt a feminine gender role exhibit higher levels of competitive trait anxiety than people in other gender and gender-role groups.

If an athlete comes to believe that an extrinsic reward for participation is more important than the activity itself, then intrinsic motivation will be diminished. Deci and Ryan's cognitive evaluation theory explains that rewards are perceived as being either informational or controlling. If they are controlling, then intrinsic motivation is diminished. If they are informational, intrinsic motivation is enhanced. An ego goal orientation is controlling in nature and may result in a reduction in intrinsic motivation.

Three separate groups have primary responsibility for the development of self-confidence and intrinsic motivation in youth sport participants. These three groups include the participants themselves, the teacher or coach or the youth sport leader, and the participant's parents. Teachers and coaches have control over the learning environment of young athletes, and are therefore responsible for creating a climate conducive to the development of self-confidence and intrinsic motivation. Parents have the greatest opportunity to facilitate the development of motivation in children and should be enlisted by coaches and teachers towards this end.

REVIEW QUESTIONS

1. What is an achievement situation, and how does it relate to competition?

2. Describe McClelland and Atkinson's basic model of achievement motivation, including elaborations. According to the model, when will an athlete approach or avoid a competitive situation?

3. Explain the relationship between self-confidence and achievement motivation.

4. Explain the relationship between the term *self-confidence* and such other terms as *self-efficacy, self-esteem, competence motivation, perceived ability,* and *sport confidence.*

5. What is the difference between situation-specific self-confidence and the global trait of self-confidence?

6. What is fear of success? How does it relate to achievement in women?

7. Describe Bandura's theory of self-efficacy. How is self-efficacy developed, according to this theory?

8. Describe Harter's theory of competence motivation. How is competence motivation developed, according to this theory?

9. Describe Vealey's sport-specific model of sport confidence. How do trait sport confidence, state sport confidence, and competitive orientation interact to bring about satisfaction and success?

10. Describe Nicholls' developmentally based theory of perceived ability. How is perceived ability developed, according to this theory?

11. Differentiate between task and goal orientation. How do these concepts relate to mastery and performance orientations? How are the constructs measured?

12. Explain how task and goal orientation interact with the environment to create a climate conducive to the development of intrinsic motivation and self-confidence.

13. According to Lenney (1977) what factors can contribute to low levels of self-confidence in women? Explain.

14. What is androgyny, and how does it relate to achievement motivation in women?

15. What is the difference between the terms *gender* and *gender role?*

16. What is the relationship between gender role and competitive trait anxiety? Explain.

17. Explain the relationship between perceived causality and extrinsic motivation.

18. Explain Deci and Ryan's Cognitive Evaluation Theory.

19. Using Deci and Ryan's theory, explain how and when extrinsic rewards can be damaging to intrinsic motivation.

20. Discuss the development of self-confidence and intrinsic motivation from the perspective of the participant.

21. Discuss the development of self-confidence and intrinsic motivation from the perspective of the coach or teacher.

22. Discuss the development of self-confidence and intrinsic motivation from the perspective of the participant's parent.

GLOSSARY

achievement motivation An athlete's predisposition to approach or avoid a competitive situation.

achievement situation A condition or expectation that one's performance will be subject to evaluation.

additive principle The notion that an athlete low in intrinsic motivation will participate in a competitive situation if there is an extrinsic reward or motivation.

androgyny A condition in which an individual has both masculine and feminine psychological characteristics.

approach-avoidance conflict Psychological conflict on which McClelland-Atkinson's theory of achievement motivation is based. The conflict is between the desire to enter into a competitive situation and the fear of failing in that situation.

cognitive evaluation theory A theory that proposes that external rewards may have either a controlling or informational effect upon the person receiving a reward.

competence motivation Similar to self-efficacy, it is a person's belief that he is competent while encourages attempts to master various tasks.

competition A sport-specific achievement situation in which performance is evaluated.

cross-gender-typed Characterized as having different gender-role and gender orientations (e.g., masculine-female).

ego orientation According to Nicholls' theory, the tendency to view success in terms of the performance of others.

extrinsic motivation External rewards such as praise, money, or trophies.

fear of failure In the McClelland-Atkinson model, the equivalent of cognitive anxiety.

fear of success In an elaboration of the McClelland-Atkinson model, women's fear of success in a masculine environment.

feminine attribute Characteristic considered to be desirable to both sexes, but found in greater abundance in females.

gender role A role associated with gender (male or female).

gender-typed Characterized as having the same gender-role and gender orientation (e.g., feminine-female).

goal orientation The tendency of an athlete to be either task or ego goal oriented.

intrinsic motivation An internal desire to achieve success.

masculine attribute Characteristic considered to be desirable to both sexes, but found in greater abundance in males.

mastery environment A motivational climate conducive to the development of independence, self-confidence, and self-esteem. The terms *mastery environment* and *task environment* are identical, as are the terms *mastery orientation* and *task orientation*.

McClelland-Atkinson model An approach-avoidance model of achievement motivation.

motive to achieve success In the McClelland-Atkinson model, an athlete's intrinsic motivation and self-confidence to engage in an interesting and exciting activity.

multiplicative principle The notion that extrinsic rewards or motivation may interact with intrinsic motivation to either add or detract from it.

participation motivation Reasons young athletes give for participating in sport.

participatory modeling Process in which the participant observes a model perform a task, after which the model helps the subject successfully perform the task.

perceived ability In the Nicholls model, the athlete's perception of how well she can perform a motor task.

psychological construct A psychological concept or theory devised to integrate diverse data on a phenomenon.

self-confidence Feeling or belief in one's own abilities.

self-efficacy A person's belief that he is competent and can succeed in a particular task.

social comparison Comparing one's own performance with another person's performance.

sport confidence The perception of confidence in a sport-related achievement situation.

task orientation According to Nicholls' theory, the tendency to perceive ability based on personal improvement, as opposed to a comparison with how others perform.

SUGGESTED READINGS

Bandura, A. (1977). Self-efficacy: Toward a unifying theory of behavioral change. *Psychological Review, 84,* 191–215.

Brodkin, P., & Weiss, M. R. (1990). Developmental differences in motivation for participating in competitive swimming. *Journal of Sport & Exercise Psychology, 12,* 248–263.

Ebbeck, V., & Becker, S. L. (1994). Psychosocial predictors of goal orientation in youth soccer. *Research Quarterly for Exercise and Sport, 65,* 355–371.

Fox, K. R., Goudas, M., Biddle, S., Duda, J., & Armstrong, N. (1994). Children's task and ego goal profiles in sport. *British Journal of Educational Psychology, 64,* 253–261.

Frederick, C. M., & Ryan, R. M. (1995). Self-determination in sport: A review using cognitive evaluation theory. *International Journal of Sport Psychology, 26,* 5–23.

Gill, D. L., & Deeter, T. E. (1988). Development of the SOQ. *Research Quarterly for Exercise and Sport, 59,* 191–202.

Gould, D., Hodge, K., Peterson, K., & Giannini, J. (1989). An exploratory examination of strategies used by elite coaches to enhance self-efficacy in athletes. *Journal of Sport & Exercise Psychology, 11,* 128–140.

Harter, S. (1978). Effectance motivation reconsidered: Towards a developmental model. *Human Development, 21,* 34–64.

Horner, M. S. (1972). Towards an understanding of achievement-related conflicts in women. *Journal of Social Issues, 28* (2), 157–175.

Lenney, E. (1977). Women's self-confidence in achievement situations. *Psychological Bulletin, 84,* 1–13.

Lirgg, C. D. (1991). Gender differences in self-confidence in physical activity: A meta-analysis of recent studies. *Journal*

of Sport & Exercise Psychology,
13, 294–310.

McClelland, D. C., Atkinson, J. W., Clark, R. W., & Lowell, E. L. (1953). *The achievement motive.* New York: Appleton-Century-Crofts.

Nicholls, J. (1984). Achievement motivation: Concepts of ability, subjective experience, task choice and performance. *Psychological Review, 91,* 329–346.

Schunk, D. H. (1995). Self-efficacy, motivation, and performance. *Journal of Applied Sport Psychology, 7,* 112–137.

Spence, J. T., & Helmreich, R. L. (1978). *Masculinity and femininity.* Austin: University of Texas Press.

Treasure, D. C., & Roberts, G. C. (1995). Application of achievement goal theory to physical education: Implications for enhancing motivation. *Quest, 47,* 475–489.

Vealey, R. S. (1986). Conceptualization of sport-confidence and competitive orientation: Preliminary investigation and instrument development. *Journal of Sport Psychology, 8,* 221–246.

9

SOCIAL PSYCHOLOGY OF SPORT

KEY TERMS

- *aggression*
- *assertiveness*
- *assertiveness training*
- *bracketed morality*
- *catharsis*
- *centrality*
- *consequences of team cohesion*
- *consideration*
- *determinants of team cohesion*
- *dysfunctional assertive behavior*
- *false consensus effect*
- *Fiedler's contingency theory*
- *frustration-aggression theory*
- *functional assertive behavior*
- *Group Environment Questionnaire*

- *home advantage*
- *hostile aggression*
- *initiating structure*
- *instinct theory*
- *instrumental aggression*
- *life cycle theory*
- *moral reasoning*
- *path-goal theory*
- *self-handicapping*
- *social cohesion*
- *social facilitation*
- *task cohesion*
- *team building*
- *universal behaviors*
- *universal traits*
- *Zajonc's Model*

Sport teams are composed of individual members. Courtesy Kansas State University Sports Information

As clearly illustrated in the previous eight chapters, sport psychology is a discipline that focuses upon the individual. Topics such as personality, attention, arousal, anxiety, anxiety control, cognitive intervention, attribution, and motivation all apply specifically to the individual. Conversely, the sociology of sport is a discipline that focuses upon social relations, group interactions, and sport-related social phenomena. Because groups are composed of individuals, it is often difficult to determine where psychology ends and sociology begins; hence the need for an area of study called the social psychology of sport. While it is beyond the scope of a textbook on sport psychology to provide a comprehensive review of the social psychology of sport, it is appropriate that selected topics be addressed. Chapter 10 is titled "Psychobiology of Sport and Exercise," and deals with psychological issues related to exercise and training. In a similar way, chapter 9 is titled "Social Psychology of Sport," and deals with psychological issues related to groups. The social psychology topics to be discussed include sport aggression, audience influence, team cohesion, and leadership issues in sport.

AGGRESSION IN SPORT

At New York's Shea Stadium during a 1978 Jets-Steelers football game, spectators overpowered a security guard and dropped him over a railing to a concrete walkway 15 feet below. In Toronto, four members of the Philadelphia Flyers hockey team faced maximum penalties of up to three years in prison on assault charges stemming from a wild brawl during the Stanley Cup play-offs of 1975. In the same year, Henry Boucha suffered a severe beating from Dave Forbes during a Boston-Minnesota hockey game, causing Boucha to lose 70 percent of his sight in one eye. In professional basketball, on December 9, 1977, Los Angeles Laker Kermit Washington literally shattered the face of forward Rudy Tomjanovich of the Houston Rockets with a devastating punch. On August 13, 1978, football fans were shocked by the crushing blow Jack Tatum gave receiver Darryl Stingley in an exhibition match between the Oakland Raiders and the New England Patriots. The blow left Stingley a quadriplegic. A 1987 *Sports Illustrated* article chronicled a rivalry between two NHL professional hockey teams. The Calgary Flames took a brawling home-and-home series from archrival Edmonton Oilers. The Flames won the first game 5 to 4 and the second 6 to 3. While the first game was a reasonable facsimile of fair play, the second was nothing but a brawl. It was described as a three-hour slugfest composed of 60 penalties and 250 total minutes of penalty time. In 1991, Rob Dibble, pitcher for the Cincinnati Reds major league baseball team, aimed his fastball at base runner Doug Dascenzo as he ran out a successful bunt. During a 1995 Houston Rockets professional basketball game against the Portland Trailblazers, the Rockets' Vernon Maxwell went into the stands in Portland and slugged an abusive fan. Maxwell was suspended for ten days and fined $20,000.

Two athletes strain to maintain their emotional composure. Courtesy University of Missouri-Columbia Sports Information

Fighting and violence among athletes is not limited to men. After Missouri's 72–70 home court basketball victory over rival Oklahoma on January 17, 1987, a brawl erupted. The center of attention was Oklahoma's volatile coach. With players slugging and kicking, the coach was observed on her back kicking an opposing player.

Most of the examples of aggression and violence described involved participating athletes. However, numerous examples of violence can be cited that involve spectators. One of the most repugnant examples of fan violence occurred in 1985 in Europe, where a soccer riot in Brussels left 38 dead and 437 injured after English hooligans attacked panic-stricken Italian fans. The riot occurred prior to the European Cup soccer final in Heysel Stadium in Brussels between Liverpool and Juventus, the soccer team of Turin, Italy. Well-liquored Liverpool hooligans attacked Juventus fans with broken bottles, tin cans, flag sticks, and metal bars. Within minutes hundreds of Italian fans found themselves pressed against a chain-link fence and a restraining wall. As more bodies pressed against the barriers, they collapsed, pitching hundreds of terrified fans into a hideous pileup in which 31 Italians, 4 Belgians, 2 Frenchmen, and 1 Briton were killed, most by suffocation. The event has since been referred to as

Black Wednesday by shamed residents of Liverpool. Similarly, more than 40 people were killed and 50 injured at an exhibition soccer match in Johannesburg, South Africa in 1991. Most of the deaths occurred when panicked spectators were crushed against a fence around the field and trampled by fleeing people. Two children were among the dead. Most recently, following a 1996 heavyweight boxing match in New York between Riddick Bowe and Andre Golota, a confirmed riot ensued. The fight ended after the seventh round as Golota was disqualified for throwing his fourth low blow to Bowe's groin. Thirty-five minutes after the bout, the crowd was ordered to evacuate Madison Square Gardens as riot police rushed in.

A number of critical questions come to mind as one contemplates the issue of sport aggression. Does participating in or observing violent sporting events serve as a *catharsis,* or release from aggressive tendencies, or do these events merely teach and encourage further aggression on and off the playing field? If these two questions can be answered, then is it possible to eliminate aggression and violence from sports? If so, how?

In this section, these questions and other critically important issues will be discussed. Topics to be addressed include defining aggression, theories of aggression, the catharsis hypothesis, measurement issues, fan violence, performance issues, situational factors contributing to aggression, and reducing aggression in sport.

DEFINING AGGRESSION

Two factors must be present in order for a behavior to be labeled **aggression** (Berkowitz, 1993). First, the behavior must be aimed at another human being with the goal of inflicting physical harm. Second, there must be a reasonable expectation that the attempt to inflict bodily harm will be successful. Consequently, the following behaviors, often mislabeled aggression, are not really examples of aggression:

1. Doing destructive violence to an inanimate object such as a door or a water cooler.

2. Unintentionally injuring another person during athletic competition.

3. Aggressive behavior in which there is no chance for the intended victim to be injured (e.g., aggressor and victim are separated by bars or teammates).

Over the years, two basic kinds of aggression have been identified. The first is **hostile aggression.** For individuals engaged in hostile aggression, the primary goal is the injury of another human being. The intent is to make the victim suffer, and the reinforcement is the pain and suffering that is caused. This sort of aggression is always accompanied by anger on the part of the aggressor. A good example of hostile aggression occurs when a baseball pitcher throws a high inside fastball at a batter who has angered him. The clear attempt to injure is present, and the goal is to cause suffering. The outcome of the contest is not a factor to be considered. The goal is to harm, not to win.

The second major kind of aggression is **instrumental aggression.** For individuals engaged in instrumental aggression, the intent to harm another individual is present, but the goal is to realize some external goal such as money, victory, or prestige. The aggressor views the aggressive act as *instrumental* in obtaining the primary goal. A parallel baseball example for instrumental aggression would be one in which the pitcher has been "ordered" by his manager to hit a batter in retaliation for some earlier infraction. The pitcher is not necessarily angry at the batter, but sees hitting the batter as instrumental in achieving the team goal of winning the game.

It must be emphasized that neither type of aggression is acceptable. The aggressor is guilty of purposely inflicting harm with the intent to injure another person. This must be discouraged at all levels of competition, especially the professional level, because young athletes everywhere emulate the pros.

CONCEPT & APPLICATION 9.1

Concept The difference between hostile and instrumental aggression lies in the perceived goal of the aggressor and not in intent.

Application Because the intent to harm is present in both forms of aggression, both must be discouraged from an ethical and moral reasoning standpoint.

A third category of behavior that is often confused with aggression is **assertiveness,** or assertive behavior. Generally, when coaches encourage their athletes to be more aggressive, what they really want is that they be more assertive. Coaches want their athletes to assert themselves and make their presence felt. Assertiveness involves the use of legitimate physical or verbal force to achieve one's purpose. However, there is no intent to harm the opponent. Even if an opponent is harmed as a result of a tackle in soccer, it is not necessarily aggression. It is merely assertive play, as long as it is within the spirit of the agreed-on rules and the intent to harm is not present. Assertiveness requires the expenditure of unusual effort and energy, but if there is no *intent* to harm, then any resultant harm is incidental to the game. Let's go back to our baseball example. If the pitcher throws a high inside fastball, with no intent to hit the batter, this is considered assertive play. The pitcher *must* establish control of the strike zone, or the batter will intimidate the pitcher into throwing either strikes or outside balls.

As can be observed in figure 9.1, an area of ambiguity lies between instrumental aggression, hostile aggression, and assertive behavior. This is to be expected, since at times only the athlete knows whether an "aggressive" act was intended. From a practical standpoint, it is the job of the official to penalize any behavior that is in violation of the rules, regardless of the intent of the violator.

Figure 9.1

Schematic showing the possible difficulties in discriminating among hostile aggression, instrumental aggression, and assertive behavior. From J. M. Silva, III, Assertive and aggressive behavior in sport: A definitional clarification. In *Psychology of motor behavior and sport*—1979 by C. H. Nadeau (Ed.). Copyright © 1980 Human Kinetics Publishers, Inc., Champaign, IL. Adapted by permission.

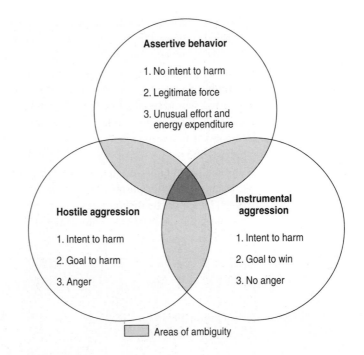

However, most sports make provisions for extraordinary penalties if the behavior is deemed to be intentional and/or dangerous. For clarity, let's return to the baseball pitching example. If in the judgment of the umpire a pitcher purposely throws a pitch at a batter with intent to harm, he must be penalized, regardless of why he did it. However, if a batter has his body over the strike zone, he is inviting an assertive pitcher to throw a fastball over the inside part of the plate. If the batter is hit, it is not the fault of the pitcher and it is not an example of sport aggression.

THEORIES OF AGGRESSION

A number of theories have been proposed to explain the phenomenon of aggression. These theories fall into four main categories: instinct theory, social learning theory, Bredemeier's theory of moral reasoning, and Berkowitz's reformulation of the frustration-aggression hypothesis.

Instinct Theory

Instinct theory is based upon the writings of Sigmund Freud and ethologists such as Konrad Lorenz. Freud (1950) viewed aggression as an inborn drive similar to hunger, thirst, and sexual desire. According to Freud, aggression is unavoidable since it is innate, but as with any drive it can be regulated through discharge, or fulfillment. Since humankind is innately aggressive, it benefits society to promote athletic sports and games that provide a socially acceptable outlet for aggression. An important corollary of the biological instinct theory is the notion that aggression results in a purging, or releasing, of the aggression

If looks could kill! Is this an example of aggression or assertive behavior? Courtesy Kansas State University Sports Information

drive. This purging of pent-up aggression is known as **catharsis.** According to instinct theory, striking an opposing player serves as a catharsis or release of pent-up aggression.

Social Learning Theory

Social learning theory posits that aggression is a function of learning, and that biological drive and frustration are inadequate explanations of the phenomenon. While the notion of a catharsis is an important component of both biological instinct theory and frustration-aggression theory, it has no place in social learning theory. Acts of aggression serve only to lay the foundation for more aggression and do not result in a reduction or purging of the drive to be aggressive. Perhaps the leading advocate of social learning theory, relative to aggression, is Bandura (1973). Bandura has argued that aggression has a *circular effect.* That is, one act of aggression leads to further aggression. This pattern will continue until the circle is broken by some type of positive or negative reinforcement. Smith (1980), for instance, argues that violence in ice hockey is due to modeling. Youngsters learn aggression by watching their role models, the professionals, on television or in person. As long as aggression in professional sports is tolerated, children will continue to have adult models of aggressive behavior.

Bredemeier's Theory of Moral Reasoning and Aggression

Based upon Jean Piaget's theory of cognitive development, Bredemeier's theory of **moral reasoning** proposes than an individual's willingness to engage in aggression is related to her stage of moral reasoning (Bredemeier, 1994). Since human aggression is viewed as unethical, Bredemeier reasoned that a relationship should exist between level of moral reasoning and overt acts of athletic aggression. Contact sport, because it legitimizes acts of aggression, may actually retard a person's moral development. The level of morality necessary for everyday life is often suspended during athletic competition. Bredemeier refers to this suspension of ethical morality as **bracketed morality.** Furthermore, athletic teams create a "moral atmosphere" that may be conducive to the willingness to aggress (Stephen & Bredemeier, 1996).

CONCEPT & APPLICATION 9.2

Concept A relationship exists between an athlete's level of moral and ethical reasoning and her willingness to engage in acts of aggression. *Application* Coaches and teachers can best control athletes' aggression by appealing to their sense of right and wrong. Athletes must be taught that aggression during an athletic contest is just as wrong as it is in normal everyday life.

Reformulated Frustration-Aggression Theory

As originally presented by Dollard, Miller, Doob, Mourer, and Sears (1939), **frustration-aggression theory** proposes that aggression is a natural response to frustration and that the aggressive act provides a catharsis, or purging, of the anger associated with the frustration. Berkowitz's (1958, 1993) reformulation of frustration-aggression theory takes into consideration the observation that frustration does not necessarily result in aggression and proposed that frustration creates a *readiness* for aggression. For aggression to actually occur, certain stimuli associated with aggression must be present. These stimuli are cues that the frustrated person associates with aggression. An example of this phenomenon in animals would be the "red flag" for the enraged and frustrated bull. In the presence of frustration, certain stimuli can serve as "triggers" to release a disposition towards aggression in a frustrated individual (Anderson, Deuser & DeNeve, 1995). Negative affect, associated with frustration, is the fundamental spur to the inclination for aggression. Anger is the root of hostile aggression, but depression is another example of negative affect that can trigger an aggressive act. The development of aggressive tendencies is complex, but certainly learning from parents, peers, and other aggressors is a paramount

Figure 9.2

Illustration showing factors
that can influence the
strength of an impulse to
commit an act of
aggression. Reproduced
with permission from
L. Berkowitz (1993).
*Aggression: It's causes,
consequences, and
control.* Philadelphia:
Temple University Press
(figure 3.6, p. 71).

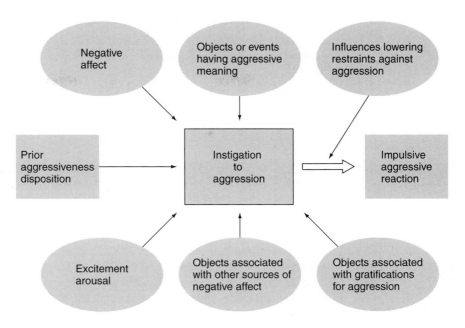

factor. Rewards in the form of incentives and self-gratification play an important
role in learning. Illustrated in figure 9.2 are factors that can influence the
strength of the impulse to be an aggressor.

CONCEPT & APPLICATION 9.3

Concept According to Berkowitz's
reformulation of frustration-aggression theory, a
frustrating event creates a readiness for
aggression.

Application Coaches must look for game
situations that could result in aggression. When
an athlete becomes frustrated and angry, the
coach should take that athlete out of the game to
give him time to calm down.

THE CATHARSIS EFFECT

Introduced earlier, the catharsis effect represents a release of pent-up frustration
that makes one feel better. It is a purging of the anger and frustration associated
with not being able to accomplish a goal. Venting your frustration upon a
punching bag or some other suitable object may provide an excellent release of
anger and pent-up emotion. Venting your frustration upon another human being
may also represent a catharsis or venting of pent-up negative affect. In this case,
however, the behavior is considered to be inappropriate and counter to the codes
of proper social conduct. If an act of aggression is associated with personal

gratification, there is a good chance that it will occur again. This is one way in which aggression can become a learned behavior. Evidence from social learning theory suggests that engaging in or observing acts of aggression results in learned aggressive behavior.

CONCEPT & APPLICATION 9.4

Concept Research shows that the athletic experience does not provide a viable outlet for pent-up aggression.
Application Aggressive behavior on the athletic field leads to further aggression. It is a behavior that is learned and often tolerated. Coaches must teach their athletes that acts of aggression will not make them feel better or help the team.

MEASUREMENT OF AGGRESSION

A number of inventories have been developed to measure aggressiveness as a personality disposition or trait. The two most current inventories include the Aggression Questionnaire (Buss & Perry, 1992) and the Aggression Inventory (Gladue, 1991). Sport-specific inventories include the Athletic Aggression Inventory (Bredemeier, 1978) and the Continuum of Injurious Acts (Bredemeier, 1985). The actual measurement of aggression, however, is much more difficult. Because aggression is defined as the intent to harm another human being, the measurement device must be able to capture this intent. This approach generally requires the use of trained observers using a standardized checklist of some kind (Harrell, 1980).

FAN VIOLENCE

Most of our discussion in this section has focused upon acts of aggression on the part of sport participants. Unfortunately, however, some of the worst examples of sports aggression and violence occur among the fans watching an athletic contest. I prefaced this section with some examples of both athlete aggression and fan violence. Intense rivalries, nationalism, and alcohol abuse are major factors contributing to fan violence. Every sports event is attended by individuals who may instigate fan violence. These are individuals who score high in the personality dispositions of anger and physical aggression. These individuals are attracted to violence and fighting among fans, and exhibit a false belief about the willingness of other fans to join in acts of violence. The **false consensus effect** emboldens individuals with a disposition for violence to believe that other fans share their infatuation for fighting and would willingly join them in precipitating an altercation (Russell, 1995; Russell & Arms, 1995).

EFFECTS OF AGGRESSION ON PERFORMANCE

Conventional wisdom argues that acts of aggression on the part of an athlete will constitute a distraction and result in a decrement in performance. Not only are aggressive acts on the part of an individual distracting to the individual, but they are likely to be distracting to the team as a whole. Research shows, for example, that the lower a team is in the standings, the more likely it will be to engage in aggression. An exception to this general observation may be in the sport of ice hockey, where it is often difficult to separate legitimate force (assertiveness) from illegitimate force (aggression). Because hostile aggression is associated with anger and hence with an increase in physiological arousal, it is possible that for some individuals an increase in anger may produce a level of physiological arousal conducive to best performance. Conversely, it may produce a level of arousal that is above an athlete's zone of optimal functioning.

CONCEPT & APPLICATION 9.5

Concept Aggression is most likely to hinder, not help, a team's chances for victory.
Application Coaches who want to be successful will not encourage aggression. An unpenalized act of aggression may help a team or individual win an athletic contest once or twice, but over the long run it will be a serious handicap and distraction.

SITUATIONAL FACTORS IN A SPORT SETTING

Much of the research in sport-related aggression has dealt with situation-specific factors. Factors associated with the occurrence of aggression in sport-specific situations are as follows:

1. *Environmental temperature.* Using archival data from major league baseball games played during the 1986, 1987, and 1988 seasons, Reifman, Larrick, and Fein (1991) observed a linear relationship between hit batters and environmental temperature. The data suggest that higher temperatures lead major league pitchers to become more aggressive in pitching to batters.

2. *Perception of victim's intent.* If athletes perceive that an opponent's intent is to inflict harm, they are more likely to respond with aggression against the opponent. This means that perception of an opponent's aggressive intentions may be more salient than such things as defeat and competition. Basketball players who perceive that their opponents' rough play is intentional and designed to inflict harm are more likely to respond with aggression than if they perceive that the roughness is incidental. A study by Harrell (1980) using male high school basketball players demonstrated this point. The most significant factor in predicting player aggression was the amount of aggression directed

Sport aggression occurs at all levels of competition. Courtesy Kansas State University Sports Information

against the subject. The athlete who perceives that an opponent is trying to inflict harm will respond in the same way.

3. *Fear of retaliation.* To some degree, the fear of retaliation on the part of the individual who is the target of aggression can inhibit another player from initiating that aggression. A basketball player is a little less likely to elbow her opponent in the ribs if she fears similar treatment from the opponent. This sort of respect for an opponent's ability to "give as good as she gets," however, can quickly escalate into open aggression and counteraggression (Knott & Drost, 1972).

4. *Structure of the game.* Two of the earliest studies of game variables and aggression were conducted by Volkamer (1972) with soccer and Wankel (1972) with ice hockey. These studies were quickly followed by investigations by Lefebvre and Passer (1974) with soccer, Cullen and Cullen (1975) with ice hockey, Martin (1976) with basketball and wrestling, Russell and Drewery (1976) with soccer, and Engelhardt (1995) with ice hockey. Following is a summary of the findings with respect to game variables:

a. *Point differential.* More aggressive penalties occur as the game score differential increases. When teams are tied or the scores are close, aggression is at a minimum. The penalty for aggression in a critical game situation is so high that players, coaches, and managers go out of their way to avoid it.

b. *Playing at home or away.* Whether home or visiting teams display more aggressive behavior may depend on the nature of the aggression and the type of game involved. Soccer teams tend to be more aggressive when playing away from home, whereas aggression is almost equal for home and visiting ice hockey teams.

c. *Outcome of participation.* Consistent with the frustration-aggression hypothesis, members of losing teams are observed to be more aggressive than members of winning teams.

d. *League standings.* The lower a team is in the standings, the more its members engage in aggression. The lowest incidence of aggression occurs with teams in first place.

e. *Periods of play.* As a general rule, acts of aggression increase as the game proceeds. Clearly, the lowest number of acts of aggression occurs during the first period of play.

CONCEPT & APPLICATION 9.6

Concept Acts of aggression occur more frequently among losing teams, during games with high point differentials, and after the first quarter of play.

Application Athletes who have a history of aggression should be closely monitored during these situations.

REDUCING AGGRESSION IN SPORT

Aggression in sport can be curtailed, or at least minimized, if all concerned are interested in doing so. The sad part is that some of the most influential people actually promote rather than discourage violence because they believe it sells tickets. As this attitude is allowed to continue, there is little hope of solving the problem. If it is allowed to continue on the professional level, it will continue to be promoted at the lower skill levels. Athletes in the youth leagues emulate their heroes on the collegiate and professional levels. They watch their sport heroes receive awards, applause, money, and adulation for behavior that borders on open aggression, and they want to become like them. In this section we will discuss ways to reduce aggression on the part of participants and spectators.

1. *Curtailing aggression by athletes.* In this section, strategies that can be implemented to curtail athlete aggression will be identified. Based on the literature, the following recommendations can be made:

a. Young athletes must be provided with models of nonaggressive behavior.

b. An athlete who engages in an aggressive act must be severely penalized.

c. Coaches who encourage or even allow their athletes to engage in aggressive acts should be fined, censored, and/or suspended from their coaching duties.

d. External stimuli or cues capable of evoking hostile aggression on the field of play should be removed.

e. Coaches and referees should be encouraged to attend in-service workshops for dealing with aggression and violence on the part of players.

f. Along with punishment for acts of aggression, athletes must also receive positive reinforcement for controlling their tempers in highly volatile situations.

g. Strategies and coping skills designed to curtail acts of aggression should be practiced.

2. *Curtailing aggression by spectators.* The following practices would help alleviate spectator aggression at sporting events:

a. The sale, distribution, and use of alcoholic beverages at sporting events should be limited.

b. Athletic events should be promoted as family affairs.

c. Responsible media can discourage aggression in sport by not glamorizing it.

d. The media should not promote or encourage the perception of friction or hatred between two teams prior to competition.

e. Interaction between members of opposing teams should be encouraged by coaches and managers during the days leading up to a contest.

f. As with the athletes and coaches, spectator aggression must be swiftly and severely punished.

AUDIENCE EFFECTS IN SPORTS

Perhaps no social-psychological effect is more important to athletic performance and outcome than the audience, or spectator, effect. The evidence is clear, for example, that there is significant advantage to playing at home in baseball, football, basketball, and ice hockey. The perception of a home court advantage is especially evident in men's collegiate basketball and professional soccer. Many basketball conferences have adopted the policy of sending the winners of their postseason tournaments to the NCAA tournament. Thus, the conference championship has in many cases been reduced to a scramble for a home court advantage in the first round of the conference postseason tournament.

In professional sports, two well-publicized examples of the home court advantage may be cited. Sports writers have coined the phrase "Celtic Mystique," when referring to the win-loss record of the Boston Celtics basketball franchise when playing at Boston Gardens. Prior to losing game number 4 to the Los Angeles Lakers in the 1987 NBA Championship series, the Celtics had won 94 of their previous 97 games in "friendly" Boston Gardens. The 1987 World Champion Minnesota Twins baseball team won 70 percent of its regular season home games. The Twins won all their home games when they defeated the heavily favored Detroit Tigers for the American League Pennant and the St. Louis Cardinals in the World Series.

Figure 9.3

The effects of an audience on athletes at various levels of skill. Figure from *Myths and Truths in Sports Psychology* by Robert N. Singer. Copyright © 1975 by Robert N. Singer. Reprinted by permission of HarperCollins Publishers.

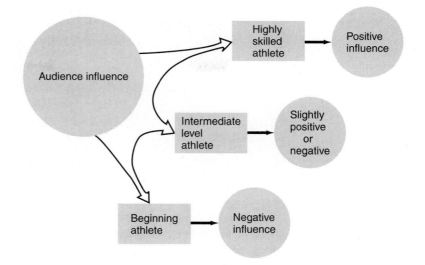

While many variables may help create the home court or home field advantage, none seem to be as important as the presence of a supportive audience. Determining how and why an audience presence affects athletic performance is the focus of this section. Topics to be discussed include social facilitation, home court advantage, home court disadvantage and audience characteristics (size, intimacy, sophistication, gender, and hostility).

SOCIAL FACILITATION

Social facilitation research is based on the notion that the presence of an audience of one or more spectators can facilitate performance. This is an appealing concept, since almost everyone has experienced the desire to perform better when friends, family, or members of the opposite gender are watching.

Research in the area of social facilitation was significantly influenced by the work of Robert Zajonc (pronounced "Zion"). Zajonc's classic paper on the topic remains the single most critical factor in the development of social facilitation as a field of inquiry (Zajonc, 1965). Based upon drive theory (see chapter 4), **Zajonc's Model** proposed that the presence of an audience has the effect of increasing arousal (drive) in performing subjects. Since increased arousal facilitates the elicitation of the dominant response, the presence of an audience will enhance the performance of a skilled individual while causing a decrement in the performance of an unskilled individual. This concept is illustrated in figure 9.3 for athletic competition.

While Zajonc's Model generated hundreds of research investigations, it suffered a fatal flaw from the perspective of sport psychology research. Social facilitation was defined as "consequences upon behavior which derive from the sheer presence of other individuals" (Zajonc, 1965, p. 269). To test the model, researchers were obligated to focus on the "sheer presence" of an audience with

Audience participation is a powerful influence on athletic performance. Courtesy Kansas State University Sports Information

no interaction between the performer and the audience. Since this situation *rarely* occurs in competitive athletics, the research generated from testing the model is not easily applied to sport. Therefore, the balance of this section will be devoted to research in which an interactive relationship between participants and spectators is assumed. For a review of social facilitation research, the reader is referred to Cox (1990).

EFFECTS OF AN INTERACTIVE AUDIENCE ON PERFORMANCE

Perhaps the most interesting topic associated with the interactive audience is that of the **home advantage.** The fact that the home advantage exists in such team sports as basketball, baseball, football, ice hockey, and soccer is well documented. In addition to the concept of a home court advantage in traditional team sports, we also have evidence of a home country advantage relative to the Olympics (Leonard, 1989) and to individual sports (Bray & Carron, 1993). Some authors have argued that the home advantage could be due to factors other than the audience, such as jet lag, travel fatigue, sleeping conditions, changed eating habits, unfamiliarity with local playing conditions, and referee bias. While it would be difficult to rule all of these factors out, researchers have shown that the negative effects of travel (Courneya & Carron, 1991) and lack of facility familiarity (Moore & Brylinski, 1995) are insufficient explanations for poor performance on the part of visiting teams. In the pages that follow, we will focus upon the most viable explanation for the home court advantage, the presence of a supportive and interactive audience.

Why Is There a Home Court Advantage?

The most plausible explanation for the home advantage in sport is the presence of a supportive and interactive audience. But how does this work? Does the audience energize the home team, or does it inhibit the performance of the visiting team? The best available answers for these questions come from two separate investigations.

The first investigation of interest, reported by Varca (1980), involved collegiate men's basketball games played during the 1977–78 season in the Southeastern Conference. Varca tested the hypothesis that the home court advantage was attributable to more functional assertive play on the part of the home team and more dysfunctional assertive play on the part of the visiting team. Increased arousal caused by the supportive crowd was believed to facilitate assertive play. In Varca's terminology, **functional assertive behavior** in basketball included superior performance in the skills of rebounding, steals, and blocked shots; while **dysfunctional assertive behavior** was limited to personal fouls, a behavior believed to inhibit performance. As predicted by Varca's hypothesis, significant differences were noted between home and away teams on the functionally assertive skills of stealing, blocking shots, and rebounding. The home teams enjoyed a superiority in these three important skills. Additionally, the visiting teams had significantly more fouls than the home team. Varca's research is very helpful in explaining why the presence of a roaring crowd could facilitate the home team's performance, but inhibit that of the visiting team. The skills involved in rebounding, stealing, and blocking shots are closely associated with strength and speed. These are the kinds of skills that would be facilitated by very high arousal. While trying to negate the functional assertive behavior of the home team, the visiting team gets whistled for personal fouls. This causes increased frustration, and more dysfunctional behavior results.

CONCEPT & APPLICATION 9.7

Concept The presence of a supportive and emotionally arousing crowd translates into a home court advantage in many situations. *Application* Since the home court advantage is a function of fan support, it is important to capitalize on this advantage by filling the stadium or fieldhouse. Additionally, the band, the cheering squad, and publicity should be used to generate excitement and enthusiasm.

The second study of interest was reported by Silva and Andrew (1987). Based on previous research, the investigators knew that the home team won more games than did the visiting team in collegiate basketball. They hypothesized, however, that the advantage favoring the home team was due not to increased performance caused by a supportive audience, but to inferior performance on the part of the visiting team—sort of an *away court disadvantage,* as opposed to a home court advantage. Archival data from 418 men's collegiate basketball games played in the Atlantic Coast Conference from 1971 to 1981 were utilized in the investigation. The unique aspect of this investigation was that performance of players during actual competition was compared with a pre-game standard of good performance provided by coaches.

While home teams did exhibit superior game statistics when compared to visiting teams, this occurred not because the home teams exhibited better game statistics than expected, but because the visiting teams exhibited game statistics worse than expected.

CONCEPT & APPLICATION 9.8

Concept Winning on the road can be enhanced by understanding the nature of the home court advantage.

Application When playing away from home, it is important that the coach develop a careful game plan and stay with it. The game plan should emphasize patience on offense, tactics to keep the crowd calm, and careful avoidance of penalties and fouls.

When Is the Home Court/Field a Disadvantage?

Is playing at home always an advantage, or can it sometimes be a disadvantage? For a number of reasons, playing at home can be a disadvantage. One reason might be that the fans expect you to win at home; this can result in additional pressure to play well. A second reason might be that playing before a very vocal and supportive audience can raise arousal to a level that results in a decrement of performance.

> Sometimes, playing at home in the postseason isn't an advantage. You get so charged up that you lose focus of what you have to do.
>
> Joe Torre, New York Yankees Manager, 1996

A case in point is the above observation by Joe Torre, manager of the New York Yankees baseball team, following the loss of the first two games of the 1996 World Series while playing at home. The Yankees went on to win the series in six games. In this series the Atlanta Braves lost three straight games at home as well. According to Baumeister and Steinhiller (1994), this is the heightened *self-attention,* or self-awareness, effect that plagues home teams during important home games. The presence of a supportive audience may have the effect of increasing the cost of not winning when you are expected to. The athlete or athletes begin to "press," which interferes with the execution of skillful play (Wright, Voyer, Wright & Roney, 1995).

AUDIENCE CHARACTERISTICS

Having determined that a home advantage usually exists in sport and that this advantage is related to the presence of a supportive and interactive audience, it is time to examine characteristics of the audience. Do certain audience characteristics lead to a greater home advantage? This question will be discussed in the following paragraphs.

Crowd Size, Intimacy, and Density

There is evidence in professional baseball that crowd size makes a difference. Schwartz and Barsky (1977), for example, demonstrated that audience size is related to performance in baseball. The winning percentage of home teams increased as the size of the crowd increased. This effect is most pronounced when first-division home teams play visiting teams from the second division (those with fewer wins). Also based upon the Schwartz and Barsky data is the observation that sports such as basketball and ice hockey enjoy a greater home advantage than baseball and football. Since baseball and football normally accommodate a far greater number of fans than basketball and/or ice hockey, factors such as audience density and audience intimacy may be more important than size for creating the home court advantage (Agnew & Carron, 1994). Audience density and audience intimacy are related to how tightly packed together the fans are and how close they are to the field of play. Successful teams that opt to move out of smaller, more intimate facilities into larger ones often do so at the expense of crowd density and intimacy.

Crowd Hostility

It is generally understood that a supportive and friendly crowd will help the home team. What is the effect, however, of a seemingly hostile and protesting crowd on player performance? Research by Greer (1983) demonstrated that sustained hostile spectator protests have a clearly negative impact on the visiting team. Home basketball games of two Division I basketball teams were monitored and studied. Observations of sustained spectator protest were identified and studied relative to subsequent skill performance. Following episodes of sustained fan protest (usually directed at officials), the performance of athletes was monitored for five minutes of running game time. The results of the research showed a slight improvement in the performance of the home team, paralleled by a more significant and pronounced decline in performance of the visiting team following spectator protest.

Arie Selinger, former head coach of the women's national volleyball team, can attest to the devastating effect of a hostile audience (Steers, 1982). Arie took his heavily favored women's team to Peru in 1982 to compete in the World Championships. Everything went according to plan until the U.S. team played Peru. That was when the crowd took over. For two hours, it was impossible to communicate verbally with players, coach, or officials. The highly unsportsmanlike fans were armed with whistles and noisemakers. Each time a U.S. player went back to serve, the noise was deafening. "The sound came down like thunder. You could feel the vibrations. You're totally disoriented. It's a terrible experience," said Coach Selinger. A father of one of the athletes summed it up this way: "The team prepared for nine months to win the World Championships and they were beaten by a wireless microphone and fifteen thousand plastic whistles."

A supportive crowd
energizes players and
fans alike. Courtesy
Kansas State University
Sports Information

Sometimes it is not necessarily the entire crowd that is hostile, but a small and highly vocal section of the crowd. A case in point is the "Antlers," a rowdy, raucous, almost-anything-goes men's basketball student jeering section composed of University of Missouri-Columbia undergraduates wearing black T-shirts, goofy hats, and painted faces. The antics of the "Antlers" are at times so offensive that they have to be censured by university administrators (Fallstrom, 1993).

CONCEPT & APPLICATION 9.9

Concept A supportive audience is important for the home team. However, the home team should make sure that the mood of an audience does not turn ugly and hostile.

Application It is unethical and unsportsmanlike to promote fan hostility in support of the home team. Coaches, managers, and team officials are morally obligated to avoid such a situation.

The "Antlers" provide raucous and sometimes rowdy support for the home team. Courtesy University of Missouri-Columbia Sports Information

TEAM COHESION

Albert Carron, a prominent sport social psychologist, defined group cohesion as "a dynamic process which is reflected in the tendency for a group to stick together and remain united in the pursuit of goals and objectives" (Carron, 1982, p. 124). Because an athletic team is a group, Carron's definition of group cohesion applies equally well as a definition for team cohesion. Intuitively, team cohesion is the elusive ingredient that changes a disorganized collection of individuals into a team.

Fundamental to the study of team cohesion is the understanding of group dynamics. Members of a team or group begin to interact with each other the moment the group is first formed. Once a group is formed, it ceases to interact with outside forces in the same manner that a collection of individuals would. The team becomes an entity in and of itself. From a Gestalt perspective, the whole (group or team) is greater than the sum of its parts.

In sport, it is a well-established principle that a group of individuals working together is far more effective than the same individuals working independently of one another. On a basketball team, there may be several individuals capable of scoring 20 or more points a game. However, in the interest of team success, the coach may require that one or more of these athletes assume nonscoring roles. For example, a point guard has the primary responsibility of setting up plays and getting the offense started, while the power forward must "crash" the boards and get offensive and defensive rebounds. Athletes who play these specialized roles rarely score as many points as shooting guards or forwards. Yet, out of the desire to be "team players," these athletes accept less glamorous roles for the common good of the team. Thus, as a group or team evolves, a certain structure develops. This structure varies from group to group and situation to situation, but it is critical for team success.

Not only do members of successful teams have the ability to work together (teamwork); they also enjoy a certain attraction to one another. In this respect, it seems logical that teams composed of members who like each other and enjoy playing together will somehow be more successful than teams lacking this quality. In 1979, the Pittsburgh Pirates won the World Series. Their theme was "We Are Family," suggesting that they owed their success to this ability to get along and work together for a common goal. Ironically, the Oakland Athletics of the early 1970s and the New York Yankees in 1978 also enjoyed World Series success, but with well-publicized disharmony within their ranks.

The team attraction, or "chemistry," necessary to bring the best out of a group of athletes appeared to be lacking in the 1988 Cincinnati Reds major league baseball team. After being picked to win the National League West, the Reds, led by Pete Rose, suffered a lackluster season. In attempting to explain how the talent-laden team could perform so poorly, relief pitcher [Rob Murphy] reportedly made the following observation (Kay, 1988):

> We've got a funny chemistry here. It's a strange mixture of guys. They're all good guys: I don't have any personal problems with any of them. They are guys who have great talent and good dispositions, but the mix—something's not there. I can't really explain it other than it's a strange chemistry (p. 15).

As a social psychological topic, team cohesion ranks as a very important factor for enhancing team performance and feelings of satisfaction among members. It has evolved as a fairly complex concept that requires study and additional research before it can be thoroughly understood. In the following paragraphs, team cohesion will be discussed as a function of measurement, determinants, consequences, and development.

MEASUREMENT OF TEAM COHESION

Early attempts to measure team cohesion led to confusion about the nature of team cohesion, as well as its relationship with other variables. The confusion was due primarily to two factors. The first had to do with the failure to

A tremendous amount of task cohesion and coordinated play are required to execute the "quick attack" in volleyball. Courtesy Ball State University Sports Information

discriminate between task and social cohesion, and the second, with the failure to discriminate between attraction to individual members of the group and the perception of closeness within the group as a whole.

Social and task team cohesion differ from each other in terms of orientation. Groups high in **task cohesion** identify closely with formal group goals and experience success in obtaining these goals. Groups that are high in **social**

cohesion tend to consider social interaction and member attraction to be more important than group goals. A measurement inventory that fails to discriminate between these two dimensions of team cohesion cannot accurately represent its multidimensional nature. The results of an investigation in which task and social cohesion were measured independently could differ markedly from an investigation in which the two aspects of cohesion were confounded.

It is quite easy to see how these two types of team cohesion could operate independently. Consider the world champion New York Yankees of 1978. This team was the best in the world in task cohesion. They could turn double plays, hit cut-off men, advance runners, and work together better than any other baseball team in the world. Yet their social cohesion was very low. Team members fought with each other, cliques were formed, and angry words were exchanged.

CONCEPT & APPLICATION 9.10

Concept Team cohesion is a multidimensional construct, not a unidimensional one.
Application A coach must recognize that a team can be low in one dimension of cohesion and be high in another. A team can be high in task cohesion and low in social cohesion and still be successful in terms of performance.

A measurement inventory that fails to differentiate between individual attraction to the group and group integration could be hopelessly confounded. Studies using indirect measures of team cohesion have resulted in conclusions different from those of studies that have measured team cohesion directly. Team cohesion is measured indirectly when members are asked about their attraction to members of the group. Team cohesion is measured directly when members are asked their assessment of the group as a whole.

The measurement problems associated with team cohesion have been addressed by the development of a conceptual framework from which a multidimensional team cohesion inventory could be fashioned (Widmeyer, Brawley, & Carron, 1985). As illustrated in figure 9.4, the conceptual model of team cohesion is composed of the athlete's perception of the team (group integration and individual attraction), and the athlete's group orientation (social and task cohesion). The conceptual framework, illustrated in figure 9.4, resulted in the development of the 18-item **Group Environment Questionnaire** (GEQ). The GEQ measures four dimensions of team cohesion: Group Integration—Task (GI-T); Group Integration—Social (GI-S); Individual Attractions to the Group— Task (ATG-T); and, Individual Attractions to the Group—Social (ATG-S). The following is a sample Group Integration—Task (GI-T) question from the questionnaire:

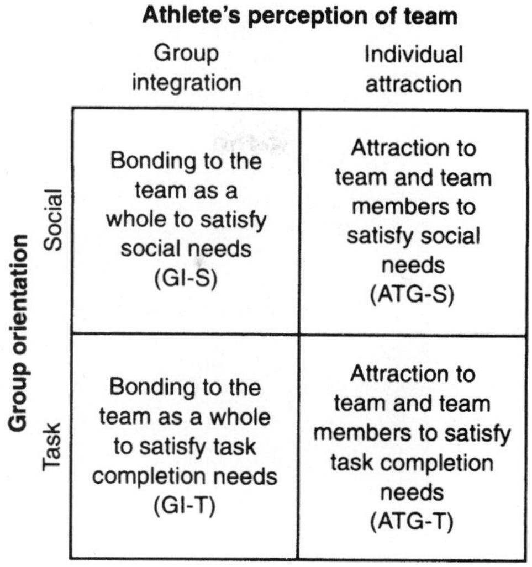

Figure 9.4

Widmeyer, Brawley, and Carron's conceptual model of team cohesion. From W. N. Widmeyer, L. R. Brawley, and A. V. Carron, *The measurement of cohesion in sport teams: The group environment questionnaire.* Copyright © 1985, Spodym Publishers. Used with permission of the publisher.

| | Athlete's perception of team | |
	Group integration	Individual attraction
Social	Bonding to the team as a whole to satisfy social needs (GI-S)	Attraction to team and team members to satisfy social needs (ATG-S)
Task	Bonding to the team as a whole to satisfy task completion needs (GI-T)	Attraction to team and team members to satisfy task completion needs (ATG-T)

(Group orientation)

Our team is united in trying to reach its goal for performance.

STRONGLY DISAGREE   *STRONGLY AGREE*

| 1 | 2 | 3 | 4 | 5 | 6 | 7 | 8 | 9 |

Since the development of the GEQ in 1985, it has become the primary measurement instrument of choice by sport social psychologists. Recent research has confirmed the factor structure and favorable psychometric properties of the GEQ (Carron & Spink, 1992; Li & Harmer, 1996).

Of interest relative to the measurement of team cohesion is the recent development of an instrument designed to measure team chemistry (Partington & Shangi, 1992). The 53-item Team Psychology Questionnaire (TPQ) measures seven dimensions of team chemistry. The seven dimensions of the TPQ are player talent and attitude, coach-technical, coach-interpersonal, task integration, social cohesion, team identity, and style of play. The TPQ follows a group cohesion model proposed by Russian psychologist Petrovsky (1983). As proposed by Petrovsky, members of a sports team are bound together at three levels: informally as friends (social cohesion), formally through team roles and coordination of effort (task cohesion), and through a link to a greater purpose (e.g., nationalism).

DETERMINANTS OF TEAM COHESION

Building upon Cartwright's basic model, Carron (1982) proposed a sport-specific framework for studying team cohesion determinants and consequences. As illustrated in figure 9.5, the basic conceptual framework is composed of four classes of determinants and two classes of consequences. The basic notion is that there are certain factors that lead to or determine team cohesion, and certain consequences associated with having or not having team cohesion. In this

Figure 9.5

Illustration showing determinants and consequences of team cohesion. From "Cohesiveness in sport groups: Interpretations and considerations" by A. V. Carron, 1982, *Journal of Sport Psychology* (Vol. 4, No. 2), p. 131. Copyright 1982 by Human Kinetics Publishers. Adapted by permission.

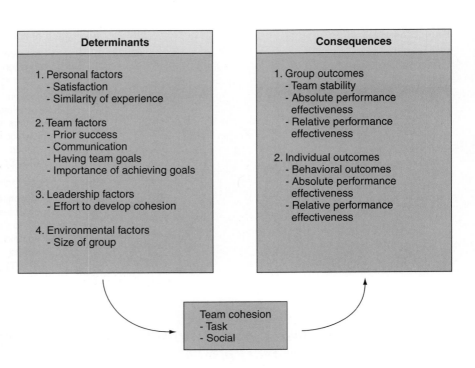

section I will focus attention upon the **determinants of team cohesion**; in the following section, upon the consequences of team cohesion.

In an important study reported by Widmeyer & Williams (1991), factors that determine team cohesion among female collegiate NCAA Division I golfers were investigated and reported. In this investigation, team cohesion was measured using the multidimensional GEQ. The results of this investigation revealed that each specific determinant shown in figure 9.5 was predictive of some aspect of team cohesion. The strongest predictor of team cohesion, however, was personal satisfaction. For intercollegiate golfers, the best way to develop team cohesion is by cultivating a personal feeling of satisfaction towards the team and team members.

CONCEPT & APPLICATION 9.11

Concept The feeling of personal satisfaction with the team as a whole and members generally is the strongest predictor of team cohesion in intercollegiate golf.

Application Other determinants of team cohesion, such as team success, group size, and interpersonal communication, are of small consequence in developing team cohesion compared to personal satisfaction. Golf coaches who value team cohesion should focus on developing a feeling of satisfaction among team members.

Widmeyer & Williams' research is a benchmark study because it systematically studied the relationship between Carron's (1982) taxonomy of team cohesion determinants and team cohesion among intercollegiate golfers. Whether the specific findings of Widmeyer & Williams can be generalized to team sports such as volleyball, basketball, and football remains to be seen. Is personal satisfaction with the team as a whole and members generally as strong a predictor of team cohesion in basketball as it is in golf? This is an important research question, since team cohesion is generally believed to be of greater consequence in team sports than in individual sports.

Although the Widmeyer & Williams study was the most comprehensive investigation to date dealing with determinants of team cohesion, other studies have focused upon specific antecedents. For example, team stability as an antecedent of team cohesion has been studied by Donnelly, Carron, & Chelladurai (1978), with the general finding that team stability fosters cohesion. Similarly, research by Widmeyer, Brawley, & Carron (1990) suggests that team cohesion decreases as team or group size increases.

CONCEPT & APPLICATION 9.12

Concept Team cohesion is related to size and stability of a team or group.
Application It is difficult to maintain team cohesion in teams or groups that are constantly changing and increasing in size. Coaches and leaders who wish to increase cohesion among members must avoid constant turnover and keep groups or sub-groups relatively small.

CONSEQUENCES OF TEAM COHESION

Most research on **consequences of team cohesion** has focused upon performance. The primary question that has been asked is to what degree team cohesion leads to improved team or individual performance. This basic question is also reflected in figure 9.5, where performance is described in terms of individual and group outcomes. Absolute and relative performance effectiveness refers to the difference between winning or losing a contest, as opposed to performing better than the last time. Having a team's performance reduced to a slash in the win or loss column is an absolute measure of performance effectiveness, whereas comparing a team's performance to how well it performed in the last outing is a relative measure of performance effectiveness. A similar dichotomy can be developed for the performance of individual sport athletes. From an absolute performance perspective, a golfer may not "win" a golf tournament, but from a relative perspective, she may have improved her score significantly.

In addition to the direct effects of team cohesion on performance, there are numerous other consequences of team cohesion that are indirectly related to performance. These include group self-esteem, future participation, lowered negative affect, team homogeneity, and self-handicapping. Each of these factors will also be briefly discussed in this section on consequences of team cohesion.

Direction of Causality

As was briefly mentioned above, numerous investigations have verified that a significant and positive relationship exists between direct measures of team cohesion and performance in both individual and team sports. The issue of direction of causality, however, has been a difficult issue to resolve. Does team cohesion lead to or cause successful performance, or does successful performance lead to or cause high team cohesion? As you might guess, this is not a good "either/or" question. It is likely that high team cohesion leads to high performance, but it is also likely that successful performance leads to perceptions of team cohesion. The critical issue is which direction is the most dominant. We would like to think that the direction from team cohesion to successful performance is most dominant. Almost all athletes, however, have experienced the "halo effect" of success. When teams are winning, it is a lot easier to feel at one with your team and with your teammates.

Early research on the causality issue generally supported the position that going from successful performance to perceptions of team cohesion yielded a stronger predictive relationship than going from perceptions of team cohesion to improved performance (Cox, 1990). The limitation of these early studies, however, was that they were all conducted using measurement instruments that tended to be unidimensional and focused to some degree upon indirect measures of cohesion. Since the development of the multidimensional Group Environment Questionnaire (GEQ) in 1985, few studies have addressed the causality issue. An exception to this general observation is an important study by Slater and Sewell (1994).

Slater and Sewell utilized a *cross-lagged correlational design* (CLCD) to study the causality relationship between team cohesion and performance. This particular correlational design was also used in several of the early studies on causality. The reader is referred to Cox (1990) and to Bakeman and Helmreich (1975) for detailed explanations of this design. As the title of this technique indicates, CLCD is based on measuring team cohesion and team performance once near the beginning of the competitive season, and once near the end of the competitive season. This configuration allows the researcher to compare correlation coefficients leading from early team cohesion to late performance to those that lead from early performance to late cohesion.

Utilizing male and female collegiate hockey teams, Slater and Sewell demonstrated that team cohesion measured early in the season predicted late-in-season hockey performance much more strongly than performance measured early in the season predicted late-in-season team cohesion. The unmistakable conclusion from this research is that the primary direction of causality is from team cohesion to performance, and not from performance to team cohesion.

CONCEPT & APPLICATION 9.13

Concept While successful performance can lead to perceptions of high team cohesion among team members, the primary direction of causality leads from perceptions of team cohesion to team performance.

Application Coaches must recognize the importance of developing both social and task cohesion in their teams and among their athletes. Team cohesion can be easily determined using the Group Environment Questionnaire (GEQ). Once measured, efforts should be made to increase team cohesion using methods and procedures discussed in the next section.

Improving Group Self-Efficacy

The importance of individual self-efficacy in developing self-confidence and in skilled performance was introduced in chapter 8. Research by Kim and Sugiyama (1992) likewise points to the importance of group or team self-efficacy in helping teams believe that they will be successful. Teams that have developed high levels of team cohesion tend to exhibit high levels of group efficacy as well.

Predicting Future Participation

For young athletes especially, it is important that the sport experience lead to the expectation of continued participation. Sport participants who exhibit high levels of social cohesion also exhibit high scores in the expectation that they will participate in sport during the following season. Thus social cohesion is a predictor of the intention to continue sport involvement (Spink, 1995). This prediction is undoubtedly related to the further observation that high levels of team cohesion are related to lowered state anxiety (Sprapavessis & Carron, 1996). Consistent with the McClelland-Atkinson model of motivation, individuals low in state anxiety are more likely to continue sports participation.

Homogeneity of Team Cohesion

It is not enough that starters alone exhibit high levels of team cohesion. Research indicates that homogeneity of team cohesion among both starters and nonstarters is an important predictor of successful team performance. Spink (1992) showed that successful volleyball teams are characterized by high levels of team cohesion on the part of both starters and nonstarters. Conversely, less successful teams are characterized by a lack of homogeneity (agreement) in team cohesion between starters and nonstarters. This observation suggests that the coach must develop high team cohesion among all the members of a team, and not just the starters.

Moderator of the Disruptive Effects of Self-Handicapping

Self-handicapping represents the strategies athletes use to proactively protect their self-esteem by creating excuses for their performance in forthcoming events by adopting or advocating impediments for success. Typical excuses might include missing practice due to injury or illness, partying and loss of sleep, school commitments or distractions, and family commitments or distractions. If success follows, the athlete or athletes can always internalize (take credit for) the victory, but if failure follows, they will have numerous external explanations as to why they have failed. This behavior causes disruption in the athlete's preparation for competition, and is therefore referred to as *self-handicapping.* Research (Carron, Prapavessis & Grove, 1994; Hausenblas & Carron, 1996) indicates that team cohesion has a moderating effect on the trait of self-handicapping. Athletes high on the trait of self-handicapping rate the severity of disruption associated with it as low when team cohesion was low, but high when team cohesion was high. There is something about being a member of a cohesive group that makes athletes sensitive to disruptions associated with self-handicapping.

DEVELOPING TEAM COHESION

A sport team can be viewed as having both *social,* or interpersonal, group activities and group *task*-related activities. As teams develop social and task cohesion, they proceed through four basic stages (Tuckman, 1965). These stages are referred to by Tuckman as *forming, storming, norming,* and *performing.* Thus, it is only in the final stage of team cohesion development that it would be possible to discriminate between two groups in terms of task performance. If teams have not worked together long enough to develop team cohesion, it is unlikely that cohesion would be a factor in helping a team accomplish its goals. During the forming and storming stages, team members are getting acquainted with one another. Measurements taken of team cohesion during these two stages would tend to be unreliable and unstable. During the norming and performing stages, team members begin to establish relationships and develop an awareness of one another's strengths and weaknesses. It is during these two latter stages that the measurement of team cohesion will be most meaningful.

Therefore, the practice of measuring team cohesion early in the season or before the season starts might not result in a reliable measure of cohesion. It would be better to wait until midseason, after team members have passed through the forming and storming stages of developing team cohesion. However, if the stability of the team remains basically unchanged from season to season, this may not be a serious problem. Professional sports teams tend to remain relatively stable across one or two seasons, whereas high school teams might change significantly from one year to the next.

High levels of team cohesion are associated with a host of positive individual and group consequences. For this reason, it is desirable that steps be taken to develop cohesion in sport teams. This can be accomplished through **team building.** Team building is a process by which the coach or leader develops and carries out strategies designed to increase social and team cohesion among members (Carron, Spink & Prapavessis, 1997). The following general principles are suggested for developing team cohesion in sport teams.

Successfully defending the goal in field hockey requires athlete cooperation. Courtesy Ball State University Sports Information

1. *Acquaint each player with the responsibilities of other players.* This can be accomplished by allowing players to play other positions during practices. This will give them an appreciation for the importance of other team players. For example, a spiker in volleyball who complains of poor setting should be given the chance to set once in a while.

2. *As a coach or teacher, take the time to learn something personal about each athlete on the team.* People will come to appreciate and cooperate with those who know little things about them, such as a girlfriend's name, a birthday, or a special hobby.

3. *Develop pride within the sub-units of large teams.* For example, in football the various special teams need to feel important to the team and take pride in their accomplishments. For smaller units such as basketball teams, this may not be as critical. However, the team as a whole should develop pride in its accomplishments.

4. *Develop a feeling of "ownership" among the players.* Individual players need to feel that the team is *their* team and not the coach's team. This is accomplished by helping players become involved in decisions that affect the team and them personally. Individual players need to feel that their voices will be heard.

5. *Set team goals and take pride in their accomplishments.* Individuals and teams as a whole must have a sense of direction. Challenging but obtainable goals should be set throughout the season. When these goals are reached, players

should collectively be encouraged to take pride in their accomplishments and then set more goals.

6. *Each player on the team must learn his role and come to believe it is important.* In basketball, only five players can be on the floor at one time. The process of keeping the other seven players happy and believing that they too are important is one of the great challenges of teaching and coaching. Each player on the team has a unique role. If players do not feel this, they will not feel they are part of the team, which will detract from team unity.

7. *Do not demand or even expect complete social tranquility.* While it is not conducive to team cohesion to allow interpersonal conflicts to disrupt team unity, it is equally unrealistic to expect interpersonal conflicts to be completely absent. Any time individuals are brought together in a group, there is potential for conflict. The complete elimination of any friction may actually suggest a complete lack of interest in group goals.

8. *Since cliques characteristically work in opposition to the task goals of a team, their formation must be avoided.* Cliques often form as a result of (1) constant losing, (2) players' needs not being met, (3) players not getting adequate opportunities to play, and (4) coaches who promote the development of cliques through the use of "scapegoats" or personal prejudice.

9. *Develop team drills and lead-up games that encourage member cooperation.* Many drills are designed solely for the purpose of skill development. Many other drills must be developed that teach athletes the importance of reliance upon teammates. For example, in basketball, drills that emphasize the importance of teammate assists could be emphasized.

10. *Highlight areas of team success, even when the team loses a game or match.* Since we know from the literature that performance affects feelings of satisfaction and cohesion, the coach must capitalize on this. If a volleyball team played good team defense in a losing effort, point this out to them.

LEADERSHIP IN SPORT

It is much easier to point to examples of great leadership than it is to explain what great leadership is. For example, in sport, it would be hard to find greater examples of leadership than such coaches as Knute Rockne, Vince Lombardi, John Wooden, and Pat Head Summitt.

Each of these men and women had (or has) an unquenchable desire to succeed, to excel, and to win. As Lombardi put it, "Winning is not everything, it is the only thing!" (Kramer, 1970). Roger Staubach was such a great field general that his teammates never gave up as long as he was in charge. As Billy Joe DuPree said of Staubach, "He never knew when it was over. At the end of a game, even if we're down by 20 points, he'll be standing there by himself trying to figure a way we can win it" (Luksa, 1980). John Wooden, the most successful coach in college basketball history, won ten NCAA national championships.

A coach diplomatically "discusses" a referee's disputed call. Courtesy Kansas State University Sports Information

Seven of those wins were in a row, beginning in 1967 and ending in 1973. Similarly, Pat Head Summitt, women's basketball coach at the University of Tennessee, has enjoyed unprecedented success as a leader and coach. Coach Summitt is one of the most successful coaches in America and ranks with any male coach in terms of success (Wrisberg, 1990). What made Wooden and Summitt such great coaches and leaders? We may never know the precise answer to a question like this, but we can study it and try to understand the many possibilities.

In some ways, the complexity of the concept of leadership is overwhelming. It is like a puzzle that makes little sense until each piece is put in its place. In an attempt to master this puzzle, this section has been organized into three subsections. The first addresses the major theories of leadership that have evolved. The second subsection deals with the nature of the coach-athlete interaction. The third discusses geographical location and leadership opportunity.

THEORIES OF LEADERSHIP

Early interest in leadership centered on the traits or abilities of great leaders. It was believed that great leaders were born and not made. Since these early beginnings, leadership research has evolved from an interest in the behavior of leaders to the notion of situation-specific leadership. The notion of an evolution in leadership thought is useful, but it suggests that the early researchers were somehow naive and behind the times. But a careful analysis of the early writings of some of the great researchers reveals that they were as aware of our "modern"

Figure 9.6

A classification scheme
for four types of
leadership theories. From
O. Behling and
C. Schriesheim,
*Organizational behavior:
Theory, research, and
application.* Copyright
© 1976 Allyn and Bacon,
Inc. Used with permission.

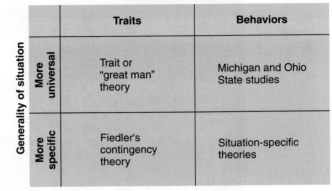

Characteristics of leaders

		Traits	Behaviors
Generality of situation	**More universal**	Trait or "great man" theory	Michigan and Ohio State studies
	More specific	Fiedler's contingency theory	Situation-specific theories

concerns for situation-specific leadership as we are today. For example, Metcalf and Urwick (1963, p. 277) quoted Mary Parker Follett as saying, "Different situations require different kinds of knowledge, and the man possessing the knowledge demanded by a certain situation tends in the best managed business . . . to become the leader of the moment." Stogdill (1948) expressed similar sentiment when he suggested that a successful leader in one situation may not necessarily be successful in other situations.

Perhaps the most significant contribution to understanding the various approaches to categorizing leadership theory has come from Behling and Schriesheim (1976). They developed a typology of leadership theory that is illustrated in figure 9.6. Their typology categorizes the four major approaches to studying leadership, according to whether the theory deals with leadership traits or leadership behaviors, and whether the traits or behaviors are universal or situational in nature.

Leadership traits are relatively stable personality dispositions such as intelligence, aggressiveness, and independence. Leadership behaviors have to do with the observed behavior of leaders and have little to do with their personalities. Traits found in *all* successful leaders are referred to as **universal traits,** as opposed to situational traits. Situational traits and situational behaviors are those traits and behaviors that may help make a leader successful in one situation, but are of little value in another. Research reported by Cratty and Sage (1964) underscores the importance of this concept. They conducted a study in which a fraternity pledge class (led by the pledge class president) competed against a loosely organized group of students who did not know one another. The task consisted of going through a maze while blindfolded. The a priori hypothesis was that the pledge class would do better because of their well-established lines of communication and leadership. In fact, the group having no previous association with each other outperformed the pledge class. The reason for this finding was due to the quality of the leadership. The pledge group tended to rely on the pledge president, who had no specific experience with such things as navigating a maze blindfolded. However, from among the independent group, a leader quickly emerged who had obvious skills at navigating the maze. The members of this group turned to him for instructions and tips that allowed them to outperform their competitors. They were not hampered by a leader who had no useful skills for this task.

Trait Theories of Leadership

Trait theory has as its origin in the "great man" theory of leadership, which suggests that certain great leaders have personality traits and personality characteristics that make them ideally suited for leadership. The heyday of trait leadership theory began with the development of objective personality tests in the 1920s and lasted until the end of World War II. Proponents of trait theory believe that successful leaders have certain personality characteristics or leadership traits that make it possible for them to be successful leaders in *any* situation. Since these personality traits are relatively stable, it should be possible to identify potential leaders simply by administering a personality inventory. This approach had a great deal of support from social scientists prior to and during World War II, but after the war, support waned rapidly.

The beginning of the decline in trait leadership theory occurred shortly after Stogdill (1948) published his review of 124 trait-related studies. His review and general conclusions led social scientists to discredit the universal trait theory of leadership. It was simply not possible to demonstrate that successful leaders possessed a universal set of leadership traits. A comparable review of sport-related literature led Sage (1975) to make the same conclusion relative to leadership in sport.

Since the early 1970s there was been a sharp decline in the number of sport studies investigating trait leadership theory. In some ways this is appropriate, since there does not seem to be a *universal* set of personality traits that would set the successful leader or coach apart from less successful colleagues. However, in some respects this is also unfortunate. While there may not be a universal set of traits associated with successful leadership, this is not to say that certain combinations of traits might not be beneficial in specific situations. Such an approach is evident in Fiedler's contingency model and in some of the situational theories that will be discussed later. In these theories, personality traits and/or characteristic behaviors are studied in light of the situation. Personality traits and behaviors that lead to successful leadership in one situation are observed to be of little value in another.

CONCEPT & APPLICATION 9.14

Concept There is no such thing as a universal set of personality traits common to all successful leaders.

Application Prospective coaches should not be discouraged if they do not share common personality traits with the famous leaders and coaches in sport.

Universal Behavior Theories of Leadership

Shortly after World War II the focus in leadership research turned from universal traits to **universal behaviors** of successful leaders. It was believed that successful leaders had certain universal behaviors. Once these universal behaviors were identified, they could be taught to potential leaders everywhere. This approach to leadership was very optimistic, since anyone could learn to be a successful leader simply by learning certain predetermined behavioral characteristics. If these universal behaviors could be mastered, then anyone could be a successful leader. Unlike trait theory, the belief was that *leaders are made, not born.* The driving force behind this approach to leadership came from two different sources at approximately the same time: Ohio State University and the University of Michigan.

CONCEPT & APPLICATION 9.15

Concept Leadership behaviors can be learned, while personality traits cannot.

Application The distinct advantage of the behavioral approach to effective leadership as opposed to the personality trait approach is that leader behaviors can be learned. Coaches who lack the necessary skills to be effective leaders can learn these skills by studying how effective coaches behave in specific situations.

Two important products or concepts emerged from the universal behavior research conducted at Ohio State University and the University of Michigan during the 1950s and early 1960s. First was the development and refinement of the Leader Behavior Description Questionnaire (LBDQ), from which most of the universal behavior research was derived (Halpin, 1966). Second was the identification of consideration and initiating structure as the two most important factors characterizing the behaviors of leaders. **Consideration** refers to leader behavior that is indicative of friendship, mutual trust, respect, and warmth between the leader and subordinates. Conversely, **initiating structure** refers to the leader's behavior in clearly defining the relationship between the leader and subordinates, and in endeavoring to establish well-defined patterns of organization, channels of communication, and methods of procedure.

These two kinds of behavior are considered to be relatively independent but not necessarily incompatible. That is, a leader could be high in both consideration and initiating structure. It is not necessary, according to the construct, to be high in one and low in the other. Interestingly, the Michigan studies resulted in two nearly identical universal behaviors associated with leadership (Kahn & Katz, 1960).

CONCEPT & APPLICATION 9.16

Concept Consideration and initiating structure are the two most important factors characterizing the behavior of leaders.

Application Coaches and leaders of sport teams should strive to establish well-defined patterns of organization and communication, while at the same time displaying the behaviors of friendship, trust, respect, and warmth.

Table 9.1

Leadership Styles Equivalent to Consideration and Initiating Structure.

Consideration	*Initiating Structure*
Relationship motivated	Task motivated
Democratic	Autocratic
Egalitarian	Authoritarian
Employee oriented	Production oriented

The two general dimensions of leadership behavior identified in the Ohio State and Michigan studies have provided a basic framework for many leadership studies. Often the terms *initiating structure* and *consideration* have not been used, but compatible terms have been. Yet the general nature of these two categories has resulted in confusion about the terms used to describe them. Table 9.1 presents some of these terms in relation to the labels that Halpin used. Such leadership styles as authoritarianism, production orientation, and autocratic leadership are roughly equivalent to the notion of initiating structure. Leadership styles with such labels as democratic, egalitarian and employee oriented reflect the notion of consideration. Leadership styles that are basically autocratic in nature tend toward behavior that can best be explained in terms of initiating structure or production emphasis. Leadership styles that are basically democratic in nature tend toward behavior that can best be explained in terms of consideration and employee orientation.

Fiedler's Contingency Theory

Fiedler's contingency theory provides an excellent example of a leadership theory that is situation-specific, but retains the notion of personality traits (see figure 9.7). Fiedler's theory is one of many that uses the contingency approach. The contingency approach to leadership suggests that leader effectiveness is somehow situation-specific, and that leader behaviors that are effective in one situation may not be in another. In a sense, effective leadership depends on specific environmental situations. However, Fiedler's theory differs from most situational theories, since the emphasis is on relatively stable personality traits, as opposed to behaviors. Thus, a particular personality disposition that seems to be effective in one leadership situation may not be effective in another.

Figure 9.7

Fiedler's contingency model for leadership. From F. E. Fiedler, The contingency model—new directions for leadership utilization. *Journal of Contemporary Business,* *4,* 65–79, 1974. Adapted with permission.

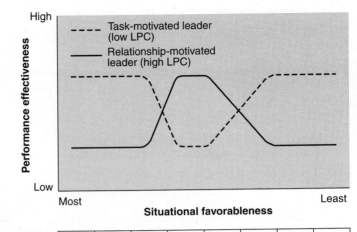

Leader-member relations	Good	Good	Good	Good	Poor	Poor	Poor	Poor
Task structure	High	High	Low	Low	High	High	Low	Low
Leader position power	Strong	Weak	Strong	Weak	Strong	Weak	Strong	Weak

According to Fiedler (1967), the contingency model of effective leadership posits that the effectiveness of a group is *contingent* on the relationship between leadership style (personality traits) and the degree to which the situation enables the leader to exert influence. The theory holds that the effectiveness of a group depends on two factors: the personality of the leader, and the degree to which the situation gives the leader power, control, and influence over the situation.

In terms of the personality, Fiedler believes that leaders are either relationship motivated or task motivated. Relationship motivation refers to concern with the interpersonal relationships between leader and followers. Successful performance of the task is of secondary importance to this type of leader. Task motivation, on the other hand, refers to the leader's concern with accomplishing the task at hand. The satisfactory completion of the task is important to this type of leader, while establishing and maintaining positive interpersonal relationships is secondary.

To measure these two personality types, Fiedler developed the Least Preferred Co-Worker (LPC) scale, which measures the leader's empathy for her least preferred team member. A high score on the LPC would indicate that the leader is able to have positive feelings toward a weak or nonproductive member of the group, and thus is relationship motivated. A low score on the LPC would indicate that the leader is unable to rate the least preferred co-worker very high, and thus is task motivated.

The second major factor in Fiedler's contingency model is situational favorableness. This construct indicates the degree to which the situation gives the leader control and influence over the environment. According to Fiedler, situational favorableness depends upon three subfactors: leader-member relations, task structure, and leader position power.

The interaction between the leader's personality style and the favorableness of the situation is graphically illustrated in figure 9.7. The horizontal axis indicates the eight cells of the situational favorableness dimension, with the left side of the graph representing the most favorable situation and the right side the least favorable situation. The vertical axis represents performance effectiveness for the relationship-oriented person (high-LPC leader) and the task-oriented person (low-LPC leader). The two curves in figure 9.7 represent Fiedler's basic predictions. Specifically, relationship-oriented leaders perform best in situations of moderate favorableness, while task-oriented leaders perform best in either favorable or unfavorable situations.

Fiedler's contingency theory has intuitive appeal and some research support (Fiedler, Chemers & Mahar, 1977). Perhaps the most controversial aspect of the theory is the basic proposition that leadership training programs are of little value. Leadership training programs only help the leader learn how to enhance power and influence. However, increased power and influence would not benefit the relationship-oriented person, who does best in a moderately favorable situation. Therefore, Fiedler proposes that there are only two ways to improve leadership effectiveness. The first involves changing a leader's personality. This is unlikely to happen, since core personality dispositions cannot be easily changed. The second approach involves modifying the degree to which the situation is favorable to a certain type of leader. Fiedler suggests that this could be done by adjusting some aspect of organizational structure, or looking for leaders who possess personality characteristics consistent with existing structure and situational favorableness.

Intuitively, there are many examples in which Fiedler's theory could apply in sport. Doug Collins, a former coach of the World Champion Chicago Bulls basketball team, provides a good example. Because of the nature of his emotional volatility, he was able to take a young team to near stardom during his early years with the Bulls. His volatile personality was useful in motivating a young and unpredictable team. However, this same personality characteristic became a liability as the Bulls matured as a team and began to tune him out (McCallum, 1991). History records that Collins was fired after the 1988–89 season and replaced by Phil Jackson.

A second example would be Johnny Keane. Following the failure of the New York Yankees to win the World Series in 1964, the Yankees fired Yogi Berra, a manager with a light touch, and hired the rules-conscious Johnny Keane.

> It would be the wrong team for him. He was a manager who was better with younger players than older ones, and this was a team of aging stars whose best years were behind them (Halberstam, 1994, p. 352).

The Yankees finished the 1965 season with a losing record of 77–85, and Johnny Keane was fired the following year.

CONCEPT & APPLICATION 9.17

Concept Leaders tend to be endowed with a disposition toward task orientation or relationship orientation.
Application Coaches should learn to recognize their own personality dispositions and work to compensate for their weaknesses through personal adjustments or through the help of assistant coaches. If the head coach is a task-oriented person, a relationship-oriented assistant coach might be hired to provide the personal touch.

Situation-Specific Theories of Leadership
Many contingency theories of leadership, or theories that hypothesize an interaction between the leader and the situation, have been studied. The basic difference between Fiedler's contingency theory and those that are to be discussed in this section is that Fiedler insisted on looking at relatively stable personality traits, as opposed to behaviors. The theories in this section view leadership as a function of the interaction between leader behavior in a specific situation and the situation itself (Glenn & Horn, 1993).

Some of the situation-specific theories are: path-goal theory (House, 1971); life cycle theory (Hersey & Blanchard, 1969); functional theory (Behling & Schriesheim, 1976); adaptive-reactive theory (Osborn & Hunt, 1975); the role-making model (Graen & Cashman, 1975); and the normative model of decision making (Vroom & Yetton, 1973). Unfortunately, space does not allow a thorough review of each of these theories; the first two will be considered because of their potential application to athletics. In addition, Chelladurai's (1978) multidimensional model of leadership, and Smoll and Smith's (1989) Model of Leadership Behaviors in Sport will be introduced as examples of leadership theory that has evolved from the sport sciences.

Path-Goal Theory In Fiedler's theory, the emphasis was on the personality of the leader and the favorableness of the situation. In **path-goal theory,** the emphasis is on the needs and goals of the subordinate or the athlete. In other words, the leader is viewed as a *facilitator.* The coach or leader helps athletes realize their goals. The leader's success is viewed in terms of whether or not the subordinates achieve their goals. Thus, the basic proposition of path-goal theory is that the function of the leader is to provide a "well-lighted path" to assist the follower in achieving goals (House & Mitchell, 1974). This is done by rewarding subordinates for goal attainment, pointing out roadblocks and pitfalls on the path to success, and increasing the opportunities for personal satisfaction. For example, if an athlete's goal is to break a school record in the mile run, it is the coach's job to provide a training program that is rewarding and enables the athlete to accomplish this goal.

Path-goal theory has not been investigated much either in or out of sport environments, perhaps due to its lack of clarity. However, Chelladurai and Saleh (1978) looked at the theory from a sport context and reported partial support for path-goal theory. Individuals who demonstrated a preference for team sports also indicated a preference for leader behavior that was calculated to improve performance through training procedures. Thus, leader behavior correlated with the athlete's preference for an interdependent type of sport. As predicted by the theory, a particular athlete personality consistently preferred a particular leader behavior.

CONCEPT & APPLICATION 9.18

Concept The basic proposition of path-goal theory is that the function of the leader is to assist the follower in achieving his goals.

Application To be an effective leader, the coach must assist the athlete in selecting worthwhile goals and by pointing out the "path" to follow to successfully reach goals.

Life Cycle Theory Like path-goal theory, **life cycle theory** places the emphasis in leadership behavior on the subordinates and not on the leader. The appropriate leadership style for any specific situation depends on the maturity of the subordinate (Hersey & Blanchard, 1969, 1977). Two types of leadership behavior, conceptualized in terms of relationship behavior (consideration) and task behavior (initiating structure), are possible. The appropriate combination of task and relationship behavior depends on the maturity of the follower. Maturity is defined in terms of the capacity to set and obtain goals, willingness and ability to assume responsibility, and education and/or experience. According to this model, the need for task structure behavior decreases with increased maturity. However, the need for relationship behavior forms an inverted U relative to maturity. At low and high levels of maturity, relationship behavior should be low, but at the moderate levels of maturity it should be high.

Case (1987) reported an investigation in which the basic tenets of Hersey and Blanchard's life cycle theory were tested in an applied setting. Leadership behaviors of successful head basketball coaches were ascertained using the LBDQ. A total of 399 basketball players completed the LBDQ regarding their respective coaches. Athletes were categorized according to the maturity dimensions of junior high, high school, college, and A.A.U. participation. Initiating structure (task behavior) and consideration (relationship behavior) leadership scores were calculated for 40 coaches and then categorized according to maturity (competitive) level. The results revealed a quadratic relationship between maturity and relationship behavior and between maturity and task behavior. Task behavior of successful coaches was low at the junior high and

Successful coaches
exhibit superior
leadership skills.
Courtesy Ball State
University Sports
Information

A.A.U. levels of maturity and high for the high school and collegiate levels.
Conversely, relationship behavior of successful coaches was high at the junior
high and A.A.U. levels of maturity and low for the high school and collegiate
levels. These results led Case to propose the life cycle model, illustrated in
figure 9.8.

Figure 9.8

Case's modified model of life cycle theory. From B. Case, Leadership behavior in sport: A field test of the situational leadership theory. *International Journal of Sport Psychology, 18,* 256–268, 1987. Adapted with permission.

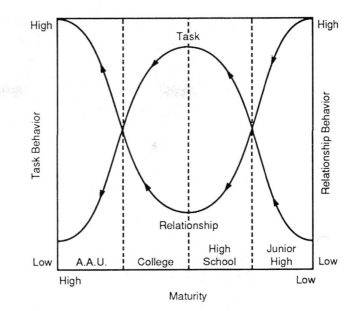

The Case model requires additional testing before it can be used for prediction purposes. Intuitively, the model is appealing because it is somewhat consistent with expectations. Young athletes who lack maturity and highly skilled and mature athletes would not be expected to respond well to a great deal of task structure. Yet, these same athletes might be expected to respond well to an environment in which concern for the athlete was openly expressed. Moderately mature athletes (high school and collegiate level) would require a fair amount of task structure in order to perform well. In this case, relationship behavior might appear to be less pronounced and less important.

CONCEPT & APPLICATION 9.19

Concept The type of leadership behavior appropriate for any given situation may be mediated by the maturity level of the athlete.

Application While it is difficult to predict which leadership behavior is best for specific maturity levels, coaches and leaders must be sensitive to the maturity level of the athlete.

Chelladurai's Multidimensional Model of Leadership Chelladurai's (1978) multidimensional model of leadership, illustrated in figure 9.9, provides an interactional approach to conceptualizing the leadership process. In this model, athlete satisfaction and performance are viewed as the products of the interaction of three components of leadership: prescribed leader behavior, preferred leader

Figure 9.9

Chelladurai's multidimensional model of leadership. From P. Chelladurai and A. V. Carron, *Leadership.* Copyright © 1978 by the Canadian Association for Health, Physical Education and Recreation. Used with permission of the publisher.

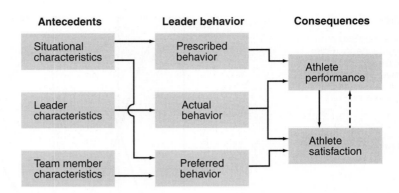

behavior, and actual leader behavior. *Prescribed leader behaviors* are those that conform to the established norms of the organization. In the military, for example, officers are expected to behave in a certain manner in the presence of their subordinates. *Preferred leader behaviors* are those behaviors that are preferred by the athletes. For example, members of a rugby team might prefer that the coach socialize with the team after a game. Finally, *actual leader behaviors* are those behaviors that the leader exhibits, irrespective of the norms or preferences of the team.

Based on the model illustrated in figure 9.9, Chelladurai hypothesized certain consequences of the *congruence* among the three types of leader behavior. As can be observed in table 9.2, congruence between all three types of leader behavior should promote ideal performance and satisfaction. A laissez-faire outcome is predicted when all three leader behaviors are incongruent with each other. If actual behavior is incongruent with both prescribed and preferred leader behavior, it is expected that the leader will be removed. If the prescribed and actual behaviors are congruent, but both are incongruent with preferred behavior, performance may be high, but athletes may be dissatisfied. Finally, if actual and preferred behavior is congruent, but prescribed behavior is incongruent, athletes may be satisfied, but performance may suffer.

General support for Chelladurai's model has been forthcoming. Athletes associated with specific sports and cultures tend to prefer a certain type of leadership style. When the coaches of these sport teams exhibit leadership styles that are incongruent with an athlete's preferred leadership style, athlete performance and/or satisfaction may decline (Chelladurai, 1984; Riemer & Chelladurai, 1995). The type of leadership style preferred by athletes varies as a function of gender, type of sport, and culture. In addition, teams that are high in team cohesion perceive their coach as possessing a number of desirable coaching characteristics (Gardner, Shields, Bredemeier & Bostrom, 1996).

Table 9.2

Leader Behavior Congruence and Outcomes.

+ Congruence with other types of behavior

– Lack of congruence with other types of behavior

Leader Behavior			*Outcome*
Prescribed	*Actual*	*Preferred*	
+	+	+	Ideal
–	–	–	Laissez-faire
+	–	+	Removal of leader
+	+	–	Performance
–	+	+	Satisfaction

CONCEPT & APPLICATION 9.20

Concept Discrepancies between an athlete's preferred coaching behavior and actual or prescribed coaching behavior has a measurable effect on the athlete's performance and/or satisfaction.

Application Athletes enter into the athletic environment with certain predetermined expectations about coaching behavior. Coaches should take this into account as they attempt to motivate athletes to superior performance.

Leadership Behavior Model As proposed by Smoll and Smith (1989), the Leadership Behavior Model is based upon situation-specific behaviors of the leader. As illustrated in figure 9.10, the model's central process is defined with solid lines leading from *coach behaviors* to *player perception* of coach behaviors to *player responses.* The dotted lines in the model represent the effect of various mediating variables upon the central process. In the model, coach individual difference variables include such factors as goals, intentions, perceptions of self/athletes, and gender. Player individual difference variables include such things as age, gender, perceptions about coach, motivation, anxiety, and self-confidence. Situational factors include things like nature of the sport, competitive level, success/failure, and team cohesion. The dotted line leading from player individual difference variables to coach behaviors was added to the model to reflect recent research by Kenow and Williams (1992). Coach behavior is influenced by the coach's perception of the individual athlete. A coach may treat an athlete who exhibits high anxiety or low self-confidence differently

Figure 9.10

Leadership behavior model. Adapted with permission of publisher from Smoll, F. L., & Smith, R. E. (1989). Leadership behaviors in sport: A theoretical model and research paradigm. *Journal of Applied Social Psychology, 19* (18), 1522–1551. © V. H. Winston & Sons, Inc., 360 South Ocean Boulevard, Palm Beach, FL 33480. All rights reserved.

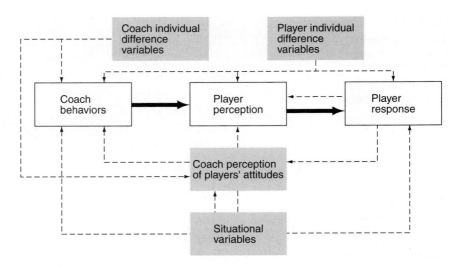

from other athletes. The model provides a framework for leadership behavior research in sport.

The science of observing and recording coaching behaviors has been refined through the development of various standardized scoring systems. The most thoroughly studied system is the Coaching Behavior Assessment System (CBAS), developed by Smith, Smoll, and Hunt (1977). The observed behaviors are reactive and spontaneous in nature. As can be observed in figure 9.11, eight types of reactive and four types of spontaneous behaviors are categorized by the CBAS. Reactive behaviors are coach reactions to player or team behaviors. For example, a player makes a mistake and the coach responds by verbally chastising the player. Spontaneous behaviors are initiated by the coach and do not occur in response to a player behavior.

Research with the CBAS has revealed a number of interesting relationships. When they are working with youth sport athletes, the dominant behaviors of coaches are positive reinforcement, general technical instructions, and general encouragement. The behaviors of keeping control (maintaining order) and administering punishment (punitive behavior) are perceived by players to occur much more often than they actually do. Another interesting finding is that coaches of youth sport teams spend a greater amount of their time providing technical instruction and feedback to low-expectation youth than to high-expectation youth. In other words, the coach does not favor the athletes she expects to be the better performers (Horn, 1984; Smoll, Smith, Curtis & Hunt, 1978).

The CBAS has also been utilized as a measurement tool to determine if behavioral training programs are effective in teaching youth sport coaches to be better and more effective leaders of youth. Research has demonstrated that well-conceived, well-planned efforts to train coaches are effective. Desirable

Figure 9.11

Coaching behavior assessment system. From Ronald E. Smith, Frank L. Smoll, and Earl Hunt, 1977. A system for the behavioral assessment of athletic coaches. *Research Quarterly, 48,* 401–407. Reprinted by permission of the publisher, the American Alliance for Health, Physical Education, Recreation and Dance.

Class I. Reactive behaviors

A. Player performs well
   1. Positive reinforcement (R)
   2. Nonreinforcement (NR)
B. Player makes mistake
   3. Mistake-contingent encouragement (EM)
   4. Mistake-contingent technical instruction (TIM)
   5. Punishment (P)
   6. Punitive TIM (TIM + P)
   7. Ignoring mistakes (IM)
C. Player misbehaves
   8. Keeping control (KC)

Class II. Spontaneous behaviors

A. Game-related
   9. General technical instruction (TIG)
   10. General encouragement (EG)
   11. Organization (O)
B. Game-irrelevant
   12. General communication (GC)

coaching behaviors can be identified and conveyed to new coaches. Furthermore, improved coaching behaviors of coaches result in benefit to the young athletes in the form of greater satisfaction and reduced anxiety (Barnett, Smoll & Smith, 1992; Smith, Smoll & Barnett, 1995; Smith, Smoll & Curtis, 1979).

CONCEPT & APPLICATION 9.21

Concept Well-planned leadership training programs are effective in teaching coaches how to be good leaders.

Application Effective coaching behaviors can be learned. Therefore, coaches should be encouraged to attend training sessions designed to teach effective leadership skills.

While the CBAS has been the most widely studied system for observing and documenting coaching behaviors in youth sports, it is not the only one. A case in point is the Arizona State University Observation Instrument (ASUOI) developed by Lacy and Darst (1984). The ASUOI is composed of 17 behavioral categories, 7 of which are directly related to instruction. It has been utilized in

Leaders must exhibit good communication skills. Courtesy Kansas State University Sports Information

studying coaching behaviors in American football, tennis, gymnastics, basketball, and soccer. Research with the ASUOI has tended to focus upon behaviors of coaches of adult athletes as opposed to those of youth sport athletes.

COACH-ATHLETE COMPATIBILITY

An important factor linked with leader effectiveness is coach-athlete compatibility, or the quality of the relationship between the coach and the athlete. Compatibility between coach and athlete has been shown to be an important determinant of team success and satisfaction. In studying coach-athlete compatibility, researchers compare behaviors of effective coach-athlete dyads with those of less effective dyads. Dyads (pairs) may be formed and compared utilizing an instrument called the Fundamental Interpersonal Relations Orientation-Behavior Questionnaire (FIRO-BQ). The FIRO-BQ was developed by Schutz (1966) to measure the level of affection, control, and inclusion that exists between members of a dyad. *Affection* refers to close personal emotional feelings between two people, while *control* refers to the perception of power, authority, and dominance. *Inclusion* refers to positive association among people and is related to communication, openness, and two-way interaction.

As illustrated in figure 9.12, compatible coach-athlete dyads are characterized by good communication and the presence of rewarding behavior flowing from coach to athlete. Conversely, incompatible coach-athlete dyads are characterized by a lack of communication and rewarding behavior. In compatible dyads, coach and athlete freely interact with each other. There is a feeling of mutual respect, an appreciation of each other's roles, and a desire to communicate honest feelings. These feelings are not present in the incompatible dyads. Rather, there is a feeling of detachment and isolation from each other. Effective and open

Figure 9.12

Some characteristics of
compatible and
incompatible dyads.

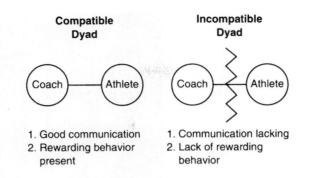

communication cannot take place in an environment of exclusion. Compatible
dyads are also characterized by coaches who consistently reward athletes for
effort and performance. Rewards come in the form of praise, acknowledgment
of effort, and recognition for outstanding performance. An enthusiastic "pat on
the back" is characteristic of compatible coach-athlete dyads (Horne & Carron,
1985; Weiss & Fredrichs, 1986).

Several investigations have shown that significant disparity exists between
coach and athlete perceptions of coaching behaviors and the environment.
Coaches tend to view the environment as ideal, while athletes often see a great
disparity between what is happening and what they think should be happening
(Bird, 1977; Fisher, Mancini, Hirsch, Proulx & Staurowsky, 1982).

The research on coach-athlete interaction suggests that the relationship
between the athlete and the coach has plenty of room for improvement. In light
of the lack of quality interaction between coach and athlete, Miller (1982)
suggested assertiveness training for coaches to help them relate to athletes.
Assertiveness involves appropriate expression of thoughts and feelings on the
part of the coach so that the self-esteem of the athlete is not damaged. Overly
assertive coaches may damage interpersonal relationships. Unassertive coaches,
on the other hand, allow players to take advantage of them. Miller's
assertiveness training module for coaches involves eight essential components
and eight associated therapeutic objectives. Using a volleyball example, actual
execution of the model involves the following three steps:

1. Describe the situation to the athlete. "Your assignment was to cover the
   power angle on that spike."

2. Tell how it affects the team. "When you follow through with your
   assignment, it provides the coverage necessary for an effective defense."

3. Tell what you think should be done. "I'd appreciate it if you would master
   your assignment and follow the strategy now and in the future."

The three steps in Miller's training program allow the coach to maintain a
quality relationship. The athlete receives specific information and is told exactly
how to perform. More important, the athlete is not shamed or embarrassed by
attacks on his self-esteem.

Coach-athlete
compatibility yields
good communication
and rewarding behavior
on the part of the
coach. Courtesy
University of Missouri-
Columbia Sports
Information

CONCEPT & APPLICATION 9.22

Concept The quality of coach-athlete interaction is a critical factor in team success and satisfaction.

Application Perhaps the most important factor in improving coach-athlete interaction is

communication. Coaches must encourage two-way communication between themselves and their athletes. If the athletes feel that the coach values their input, they will feel comfortable in a two-way interaction.

GEOGRAPHICAL LOCATION AND LEADERSHIP OPPORTUNITY

Of interest to sport psychologists are situations that seem to promote leadership opportunity. For example, Grusky (1963) designed a study that hypothesized that player position in baseball was related to leadership opportunity. Specifically, Grusky proposed that the *geographical location* of a baseball player was predictive of whether or not the player would later become a major league manager.

Grusky argued that the critical factor in player location was the opportunity for player interaction. He further proposed that the opportunity for high interaction was associated with centrality, communication, and the nature of the task. The term **centrality** refers to the spatial location of the athletes (central versus peripheral), while communication relates to the degree of verbal and visual interaction between players. The nature of the task is closely associated with interaction, since some tasks in baseball require a high degree of communication, while others do not. For example, the outfielder's task of catching a line drive is a highly independent task, while the infielder's task of turning a double play is highly interdependent.

In Grusky's design, the infielders and catchers were categorized as being high interactors, while the outfielders and pitchers were considered to be low interactors. Looking at all major league managers from 1921 to 1941 and 1951 to 1958, Grusky determined that 97 percent of them had played major league ball. Additionally, 77 percent of the managers were from the high interaction group, while only 23 percent were from the low interaction group. Thus playing position appeared to be highly related to leadership opportunity. Furthermore, former catchers made up 26 percent of the total sample of major league managers, but they made up only 11 percent of the original player sample during the years studied. Apparently, the position of catcher is highly related to player interaction and leadership opportunity.

Interestingly, of the six major league managers hired following the strike-shortened 1994 season, four were catchers in their playing days. Bob Boone, a manager of the Kansas City Royals, said of his playing days as a catcher, "I managed every game I played in. I just didn't have the control." Dan Duquette, Boston Red Sox general manager, was quoted as saying, "The catcher is involved with every pitch, every pitcher, and he's the only player on the field who has the whole field in front of him" (Chass, 1994, pp. 1, 4).

An important follow-up to the Grusky research was a study by Loy and Sage (1970) in which the relationship between player position in baseball and leadership qualities was again investigated. Using a sample of high school athletes, Loy and Sage hypothesized that player interaction, in terms of position, would be related to the selection of team captains and interpersonal attraction. As predicted, the results indicated that high interactors (catchers and infielders) were selected as the team captains much more often than low interactors (pitchers and outfielders). High interactors were also perceived to be better liked and more valuable to the team than low interactors.

Chelladurai and Carron (1977) proposed a geographical location model based on the dimensions of *propinquity* and *task dependence*. In so doing, they argued against the notion of centrality, since in many sports, being located in the geographical center of the team cannot be deemed crucial to task dependency or interaction. For example, the catcher in baseball and the point guard in basketball are not at the geographical center of the team, yet they are the individuals highest in interaction potential.

Chelladurai and Carron's dimension of propinquity is associated with the observability and visibility of an athlete by teammates. The catcher in baseball, though not always central to the action, is definitely the most observable and visible. The second dimension of task dependence is associated with the level of interaction required to successfully complete a task. For example, a double play in baseball is a highly dependent task requiring coordination between the shortstop and the second baseman.

Using the two-dimensional model, Chelladurai and Carron reconsidered the Grusky (1963) and Loy and Sage (1970) baseball data. The results of their analysis are illustrated in figure 9.13. As can be observed in this figure, the baseball position highest in propinquity and task dependence is the catcher. Lowest in these two dimensions were the outfielders. Clearly, certain positions on an athletic team enjoy greater propinquity and dependence. These positions are associated with greater leadership potential and opportunity.

More recently, Fabianic (1984) reconsidered the playing position hypothesis and related it to the paucity of minority managers in major league baseball. A highly visible characteristic of professional baseball is the relative absence of minorities serving in managerial positions. Traditionally it has been argued that blacks are seldom selected as managers because they did not occupy highly interactive positions as players (Loy & McElvogue, 1970).

Data from 1951 to 1980 and from 1980 alone show that the majority of baseball managers continue to be selected from the interactive positions (infield), even though infielders made up fewer players than noninteractive players combined (outfielders, pitchers, and designated hitters). Thus, according to Fabianic's analyses, managers continue to be selected from highly interactive positions. However, in 1980 minority (black and Hispanic) players made up 29 percent of all players and were distributed in the high and low interactive position groups in the same proportion. Based on expected representation, 9 of the total 32 managers should have been from minority groups—6 from the high interactive group and 3 from the low interactive group. Yet in 1980 there were only two managers representing minority groups (Maury Wills and Preston Gomez). Clearly, racial bias is involved in the selection of managers in professional baseball. While geographical location continues to be a salient factor in the selection of white managers, this generalization does not include minorities.

Most of the geographical location research dealing with leadership has focused on baseball. However, there is no reason why the Chelladurai and Carron two-dimensional model could not be applied to football (Bivens & Leonard, 1994), basketball, and volleyball. Based on the research by Grusky (1963), Loy and Sage (1970), and Fabianic (1984), we can predict that leadership opportunities in football, basketball, and volleyball would fall primarily to quarterbacks, point guards, and setters, respectively.

Figure 9.13

Categorization of baseball positions on the basis of propinquity and task dependence. From P. Chelladurai and A. V. Carron, A reanalysis of formal structure in sport. *Canadian Journal of Applied Sport Sciences, 2,* 9–14, 1977. Reproduced by permission of the publisher.

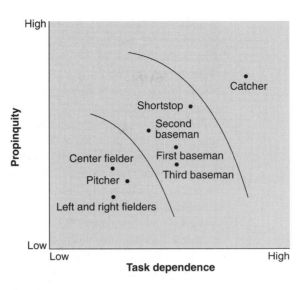

CONCEPT & APPLICATION 9.23

Concept The coach can develop leadership skills in young athletes by placing them in team positions requiring observability, visibility, and task dependence.

Application It is usually the athlete who already possesses leadership ability that becomes the quarterback in football or the catcher in baseball. Coaches should use this knowledge to help their players develop leadership skills. Young athletes who lack leadership ability could benefit from playing point guard on the basketball team or quarterback on the football team.

SUMMARY Four social psychology of sport topics were introduced and discussed in this chapter. They were aggression, audience effects, team cohesion, and leadership in sport.

Human aggression is a problem in society as well as in sport. Aggression is any form of behavior directed to the goal of harming or injuring another being. Differences between hostile and instrumental aggression were discussed relative to assertiveness. Instinct theory, social learning theory, moral reasoning and aggression theory, and the reformulated frustration-aggression theory were discussed to explain aggression. Catharsis, or energy release, was discussed as a potential by-product of aggression. Situational factors believed to be related to aggression were discussed. Procedures designed to reduce violence in sport were discussed in reference to both participants and spectators.

Social facilitation and Zajonc's Model were briefly discussed relative to the noninteractive audience paradigm. The majority of the discussion, however, focused upon the effects of the interactive audience upon the athlete. The home court advantage in sport is primarily a function of fan support. Teams that play at home tend to be more assertive in terms of functional aggressive behavior. Visiting teams may suffer a decrement in performance because of the increase in dysfunctional behavior, which results in more penalties called against them. Other factors that may affect the home court advantage or visiting team disadvantage include audience size and intimacy, crowd hostility, and home court disadvantage.

Team cohesion is a dynamic process reflected in the team's tendency to stick together and remain united in the pursuit of its goals and objectives. The conceptual model of team cohesion led to the development of the Group Environmental Questionnaire. The conceptual model is multidimensional in nature and considers task and social cohesion to be independent components of group cohesion. Determinants and consequences of team cohesion were discussed and considered. The difficulty of assigning causality to the cohesion-performance relationship was discussed. Various strategies for developing cohesiveness among athletes were examined.

Behling and Schriesheim (1976) proposed a typology of leadership theory that provides a logical approach to the study of leadership. This typology categorizes various theories in terms of traits and behaviors and of whether a theory emphasizes universal or situation-specific leader characteristics. According to this system, there are four basic types of leadership theories. The four basic theories discussed included trait theory, universal behavior theory, Fiedler's contingency theory, and Chelladurai's multidimensional model of leadership. Leadership was further discussed as a function of coach-athlete compatibility and geographical playing position.

REVIEW QUESTIONS

1. Describe the critical difference between aggression and assertiveness in sport.

2. How does hostile aggression differ from instrumental aggression?

3. Which theory of aggression do you think provides the best explanation of aggressive behavior in sport? Explain.

4. Discuss Berkowitz's reformulation of the basic frustration-aggression hypothesis.

5. Discuss catharsis relative to the various theories of aggression.

6. Discuss techniques available for measuring aggression and the personality trait of aggressiveness.

7. What is the false consensus effect, and what role does it play in fan violence and aggression?

8. What effect does aggression have upon athletic performance?

9. Identify various situational factors that help explain the elicitation of aggression among athletes.

10. Discuss procedures to reduce violence on the part of athletes and spectators.

11. Briefly explain Zajonc's Model of social facilitation.

12. What is the shortcoming of Zajonc's Model and associated research relative to understanding the influence of interactive audiences?

13. Provide an explanation, based on theory, as to why a home court advantage exists in sport.

14. What can the visiting team do to minimize the effect of the away court disadvantage?

15. Sometimes there is a disadvantage associated with playing at home. Discuss this phenomenon and provide some theoretical explanation for it.

16. What effect do audience characteristics such as crowd size, intimacy, and density have upon performance?

17. What effect does a hostile crowd have on the outcome of a sporting event?

18. Define team cohesion. Discuss this definition relative to its important points.

19. Provide a detailed discussion on the critical issue of the measurement of team cohesion. Include a discussion of theory associated with the development of the Group Environment Questionnaire.

20. Discuss determinants of team cohesion.

21. Discuss the relationship between team cohesion and team performance in terms of direction of causality.

22. Provide a detailed discussion of the consequences of team cohesion in general.

23. How is team cohesion developed?

24. Discuss Behling and Schriesheim's typology for categorizing leadership theories.

25. Compare the relative merits of trait theory, universal behavior theory, and Fiedler's contingency theory.

26. How many different kinds of situation-specific behavior theories of leadership are there? Discuss the relative merits of those discussed in the text.

27. How are coaching behaviors assessed in the sports setting? Provide some detail about this process and research results.

28. Discuss coach-athlete compatibility issues.

29. What do playing position, centrality, and race have to do with leadership opportunity? Explain.

GLOSSARY

aggression A sequence of behavior in which the goal is to injure another person.

assertiveness In sport, the expenditure of unusual effort and energy to achieve an external goal.

assertiveness training Training designed to assist either coaches or athletes to be appropriately assertive in their respective roles.

bracketed morality Suspension of ethics, or morality, during athletic competition.

catharsis The purging, or discharging, of pent-up emotions, anger, and frustrations by expressing one's feelings through aggression.

centrality In this context, the central spatial location of the athlete on a team.

consequences of team cohesion Consequences or outcomes derived from cohesion.

consideration Term indicating friendship, mutual trust, respect, and warmth between the coach and the athlete.

determinants of team cohesion Factors that lead to the development of team cohesion.

dysfunctional assertive behavior Aggressive or assertive behavior, such as fouling, that interferes with successful performance.

false consensus effect The belief on the part of some violence-prone fans that others share their infatuation for fighting and would willingly join them in precipitating an altercation.

Fiedler's contingency theory A situation-specific leadership theory that retains an emphasis on specific personality traits.

frustration-aggression theory As originally conceived by Dollard et al. (1939), the theory that frustration always results in aggression.

functional assertive behavior Aggressive or assertive behavior, such as rebounding, stealing, and shot blocking in basketball, that facilitates successful performance.

Group Environment Questionnaire Multidimensional cohesiveness questionnaire developed by Carron, Widmeyer, and Brawley (1985).

home advantage The notion that playing at home is an advantage because of fan support.

hostile aggression Aggression against another human being with the intent to harm; the reinforcement or goal is to inflict pain and suffering on the victim. It is always accompanied by anger.

initiating structure A leadership style in which patterns of organization, channels of communication, and procedures are well established.

instinct theory The theory that human aggression is an innate biological drive that cannot be eliminated, but must be controlled for the good of humankind through catharsis.

instrumental aggression Aggression against another human being with the intent to harm; the reinforcement is to obtain some external goal such as victory or prestige.

life cycle theory A situational theory that proposes that preferred leadership style depends upon the maturity of the athlete.

moral reasoning As related to aggression, the notion that an individual's willingness to engage in aggression is related to her stage of moral reasoning.

path-goal theory Theory of leadership in which the emphasis is on the needs and goals of the athlete.

self-handicapping Term describing strategies athletes use to proactively protect their self-esteem by creating excuses for their performance in forthcoming events by adopting or advocating impediments for success.

social cohesion The degree to which the members of a team like one another and enjoy one another's company.

social facilitation The benefits or detriments associated with the presence of a noninteractive audience.

task cohesion The degree to which members of a group work together to achieve a specific and identifiable goal.

team building The process by which the coach or leader develops and carries out strategies designed to increase social and team cohesion among members.

universal behaviors A certain set of leadership behaviors believed to be possessed by all successful leaders.

universal traits A certain set of personality traits believed to be possessed by all successful leaders.

Zajonc's Model A model of social facilitation based upon drive theory.

SUGGESTED READINGS

Anderson, C. A., Deuser, W. E., & DeNeve, K. M. (1995). Hot temperatures, hostile affect, hostile cognition, and arousal: Tests of a general model of affective aggression. *Personality and Social Psychological Bulletin, 21,* 434–448.

Baumeister, R. F., & Steinhilber, A. (1984). Paradoxical effects of supportive audiences on performance under pressure: The home field advantage in sports championships. *Journal of Personality and Psychology, 47,* 85–93.

Behling, O., & Schriesheim, C. (1976). *Organizational behavior: Theory, research and application.* Boston: Allyn and Bacon.

Berkowitz, L. (1993). *Aggression: Its causes, consequences, and control.* Philadelphia: Temple University Press.

Bredemeier, B. J. (1994). Children's moral reasoning and their assertive, aggressive, and submissive tendencies in sport and daily life. *Journal of Sport & Exercise Psychology, 16,* 1–14.

Carron, A. V. (1982). Cohesiveness in sport groups: Interpretations and considerations. *Journal of Sport Psychology, 4,* 123–138.

Carron, A. V., & Spink, K. S. (1993). Team building in an exercise setting. *The Sport Psychologist, 7,* 8–18.

Carron, A. V., Widmeyer, W. N., & Brawley, L. R. (1985). The development of an instrument to assess cohesion in sport teams: The group environment questionnaire. *Journal of Sport Psychology, 7,* 244–266.

Courneya, K. S., & Carron, A. V. (1991). Effects of travel and length of home stand/road trip on the home advantage. *Journal of Sport & Exercise Psychology, 13,* 42–49.

Courneya, K. S., & Carron, A. V. (1992). The home advantage in sport competitions: A literature review. *Journal of Sport & Exercise Psychology, 14,* 13–27.

Fiedler, F. E. (1974). The contingency model—new directions for leadership utilization. *Contemporary Business, 4,* 65–79.

Frank, M. G., & Gilovich, T. (1988). The dark side of self and social perception: Black uniforms and aggression in professional sports. *Journal of Personality and Social Psychology, 54,* 74–85.

Leith, L. M. (1991). Do coaches encourage aggressive behavior in sport? *Canadian Journal of Sport Sciences, 16,* 85–86.

Pollard, R. (1986). Home advantage in soccer: A retrospective analysis. *Journal of Sports Sciences, 4,* 237–248.

Reifman, A. A., Larrick, R. P., & Fein, S. (1991). Temper and temperature on the diamond: The heat aggression relationship in major league baseball. *Personality and Social Psychology Bulletin, 17,* 580–585.

Russell, G. W., & Arms, R. L. (1995). False consensus effect, physical aggression, anger, and a willingness to escalate a disturbance. *Aggressive Behavior, 21,* 381–386.

Silva, J. M., III. (1980). Understanding aggressive behavior and its effects upon athletic performance. In W. F. Straub (Ed.), *Sport psychology: An analysis of athlete behavior* (2d ed.). Ithaca, NY: Mouvement Publications.

Slater, M. R., & Sewell, D. F. (1994). An examination of the cohesion-performance relationship in university hockey teams. *Journal of Sports Sciences, 12,* 423–431.

Smith, R. E., Smoll, F. L., & Barnett, N. P. (1995). Reduction of children's sport performance anxiety through social support and stress-reduction training for coaches. *Journal of Applied Developmental Psychology, 16,* 125–142.

Smith, R. E., Smoll, F. L., & Curtis, B. (1979). Coach effectiveness training: A cognitive-behavioral approach to enhancing relationship skills in youth sport coaches. *Journal of Sport Psychology, 1,* 59–75.

Smoll, F. L., & Smith, R. E. (1989). Leadership behaviors in sport: A theoretical model and research paradigm. *Journal of Applied Social Psychology, 19,* 1522–1551.

Varca, P. E. (1980). An analysis of home and away game performance of male college basketball teams. *Journal of Sport Psychology, 2,* 245–257.

Widmeyer, W. N., Brawley, L. R., & Carron, A. V. (1985). *The measurement of cohesion in sport teams: The group environment questionnaire.* London, Ontario: Sports Dynamics.

Widmeyer, W. N., & Williams, J. M. (1991). Predicting cohesion in a coaching sport. *Small Group Research, 22,* 548–570.

Zajonc, R. B. (1965). Social facilitation. *Science, 149,* 269–274.

10

PSYCHOBIOLOGY OF SPORT AND EXERCISE

KEY TERMS

- *acquired immune deficiency syndrome (AIDS)*
- *acute exercise*
- *aerobic exercise*
- *amine hypothesis*
- *anabolic steroids*
- *anaerobic exercise*
- *anorexia analogue hypothesis*
- *anorexia nervosa*
- *bulimia nervosa*
- *burnout*
- *cardiovascular fitness hypothesis*
- *chronic exercise*
- *cognitive appraisal*
- *cognitive behavioral hypothesis*
- *coping behavior*
- *delayed anxiolytic response*
- *distraction hypothesis*
- *eating disorder*
- *endorphin hypothesis*

- *exercise addiction*
- *exercise adherence*
- *exercise self-efficacy*
- *human immunodeficiency virus (HIV)*
- *investment model*
- *life stress*
- *meta-analysis*
- *obligatory runner*
- *overtraining*
- *processes of change*
- *social interaction hypothesis*
- *social physique anxiety*
- *staleness*
- *stress inoculation*
- *stress response*
- *super-adherer*
- *training gain*
- *training stress*
- *training stress syndrome*
- *transtheoretical model*

Vigorous exercise benefits you physically and psychologically. Courtesy University of Missouri-Columbia Sports Information

The previous chapter, on the social psychology of sport, dealt with several issues that combined elements of psychology with elements of sociology. In a similar fashion, the present chapter, on psychobiology, deals with issues that combine elements of psychology with the study of biological functions of the body. Just as the social psychology of sport is viewed in this text as a subset of sport psychology, so also is the psychobiology of sport and exercise viewed as a subset of sport psychology. Each of these subset areas could easily evolve into separate disciplines. For the purpose of this textbook, however, they are considered to be subject areas within the broader field of sport psychology. I have taken this approach because of my basic belief that a textbook on sport psychology would be incomplete if it did not address social psychological and psychobiological issues related to sport and exercise. The psychobiological issues to be discussed in this chapter include exercise psychology; staleness, overtraining, and burnout in athletes; the psychology of athletic injuries; and drug abuse by athletes.

EXERCISE PSYCHOLOGY

Documentation of the physiological benefits of regular exercise has led to the inclusion of "lack of exercise" by the American Heart Association as a fourth risk factor for heart disease that can be modified or controlled by the individual. The other three risk factors are smoking, high blood pressure, and elevated cholesterol. Among other things, regular physical exercise helps lower cholesterol, decreases the percentage of body fat, mediates the effects of diabetes, reduces weight, and lowers blood pressure (Paffenbarger, 1994; Pate et al., 1995).

As stated by the President's Council on Physical Fitness & Sports (Staff, 1992), "if exercise could be packed into a pill, it would be the single most widely prescribed and beneficial medicine in the nation" (p. 5). But notwithstanding the documented physiological benefits of regular physical exercise, Dishman (1991) reports that (a) only 8 to 20 percent of the U.S. population regularly participate in vigorous physical activity; (b) 30 to 59 percent of the U.S. population have relatively sedentary lifestyles; and (c) 50 percent of the individuals who start regular physical activity programs drop out within six months.

Just as research has documented the physiological benefits of regular physical activity, research has also documented the psychological benefits of exercise. Based upon this research, a National Institute of Mental Health consensus panel listed eight statements supporting the positive benefits of physical exercise as a treatment for stress, depression, anxiety, and other manifestations of psychological dysfunction. Each statement listed by the panel underscores the therapeutic value of exercise for treating mental illness. This is an important development, because many health care professionals now prescribe exercise as a treatment for emotional disorders. Exercise is in many cases as effective as other forms of treatment, including psychotherapy and antidepressant drugs (Nicoloff & Schwenk, 1995).

Regular exercise has also been linked with many psychological benefits for individuals who do not suffer from mental illness (Paffenbarger, 1994; Pate et al., 1995). The strength of the relationship between regular exercise and positive mental health has led to the adoption of a position statement by the International Society of Sport Psychology (ISSP, 1992). The position statement reviews the literature on the relationship between exercise and psychological benefits and culminates in six specific statements. The six statements are listed below (reproduced with permission):

1. Exercise can be associated with reduced state anxiety.

2. Exercise can be associated with a decreased level of mild to moderate depression.

3. Long-term exercise is usually associated with reductions in neuroticism and anxiety.

4. Exercise may be an adjunct to the professional treatment of severe depression.

5. Exercise can result in the reduction of various stress indices.

6. Exercise can have beneficial emotional effects across all ages and both genders.

With this introduction, the broad topic of exercise psychology will now be addressed. Subtopics to be discussed include (a) benefits of exercise; (b) evidence of benefits of chronic exercise; (c) treating anxiety and depression; (d) theoretical explanations; (e) exercise adherence and determinants; (f) theories of exercise behavior; (g) fitness as a moderator of life stress; (h) the immune system, HIV, cancer, and exercise; and (i) social physique anxiety, exercise addiction, and eating disorders.

PSYCHOLOGICAL BENEFITS OF EXERCISE
The majority of the reported research on this topic has focused upon the relationship between chronic (as opposed to acute) bouts of exercise with changes in psychological states or personality traits. A **chronic exercise** program is one that involves daily or regular exercise across a long period of time. A study involving a chronic exercise regime is typically 10 to 12 months in length. Conversely, **acute exercise** bouts are usually of short duration, lasting approximately 30 minutes. The majority of the concepts that are discussed in this section are based upon research involving chronic as opposed to acute exercise. This is not to say, however, that bouts of acute exercise are ineffective in changing psychological states.

Numerous investigations have demonstrated that an acute bout of exercise can result in a reduction in negative affect or an increase in positive affect (Berger, Owen & Frantisek, 1993; Tuson, Sinyor & Pelletier, 1995). The beneficial effects of an acute bout of exercise are not necessarily dose sensitive. Consequently, a 20-minute bout of moderate exercise should be as beneficial

The psychological benefits of regular exercise have been scientifically documented. Courtesy University of Missouri-Columbia Sports Information

psychologically as a 40-minute bout (Hobson & Rejeski, 1993). Competition and performance outcome, however, may be a mediator of whether exercise results in improved affect. Research shows, for example, that successful adult runners realize a reduction in negative affect following competition, whereas unsuccessful runners do not (Clingman & Hilliard, 1994). Sometimes the beneficial effects of exercise are not evident until sometime following an acute bout of exercise. In the case of anxiety reduction, this observation is referred to as the **delayed anxiolytic response** (O'Connor, Bryant, Veltri & Gebhardt, 1993; Raglin, Turner & Eksten, 1993). Acute bouts of exercise, however, do not result in long-tern reductions in negative psychological mood. Regular chronic exercise is needed to maintain the short-and long-term benefits of exercise (Berger, Friedmann & Eaton, 1988). Two recent inventories have been developed to more effectively measure changes in affect associated with acute bouts of exercise. They are the Exercise-Induced Feeling Inventory (EFI) developed by Gauvin and Rejeski (1993), and the Subjective Exercise Experience Scale (SEES) developed by McAuley and Courneya (1994).

CONCEPT & APPLICATION 10.1

Concept While an acute bout of exercise can result in a measurable reduction in negative mood state, chronic exercise habits are required to maintain these psychological benefits.

Application In a sense, a single bout of exercise is like a single dose of medication. If the medication, or in this case exercise, is to be of long-term benefit, it must be maintained over a sufficiently long period of time.

EVIDENCE OF THE BENEFITS OF CHRONIC EXERCISE

Numerous investigations and reviews have shown a positive association between vigorous physical exercise and improved psychological mood (Biddle, 1995; LaFontaine, DiLorenzo, Frensch, Stucky-Ropp, Bargman & McDonald, 1992; Leith & Taylor, 1990; Long & Van Starvel, 1995; North, McCullagh & Tran, 1990; Petruzzelo, Landers, Hatfield, Kubitz & Salazar, 1991).

CONCEPT & APPLICATION 10.2

Concept A relatively large body of literature supports the position that regular exercise (generally, aerobic exercise) is associated with improved psychological affect.

Application The importance of this scientific finding should not be underestimated. Not only

can regular exercise improve cardiovascular fitness, but it is also believed to have a beneficial effect upon the psychological mood state of mentally healthy individuals.

Stress Inoculation

The ability of individuals to insulate, protect, or inoculate themselves against the stresses of life through regular exercise is called **stress inoculation.** Research shows that the psychological benefits associated with regular exercise do not normally require an increase in physical fitness (Rejeski, Brawley & Schumaker, 1996). Aerobic fitness, however, does appear to be a necessary precursor to the stress inoculation effect. Aerobically fit individuals appear to be inoculated against stress, illness, and the general hassles of life to a greater extent than less aerobically fit individuals. **Aerobic exercise** is continuous and rhythmic exercise in which a sufficient supply of oxygen is available to the exerciser. Children and adults who engage in healthy behavior that leads to physical fitness can insulate themselves from various physical and psychological health problems throughout their lives (Crews & Landers, 1987; Hinkle, 1992; Kubitz & Landers, 1993). While the exact mechanisms involved in stress inoculation are not known, it is believed that it may involve a complex pattern of central and autonomic nervous system adaptations.

Special Populations

It has already been mentioned that the positive benefits of regular exercise are particularly effective with clinical patients suffering form some psychological disorder. This makes sense, because these individuals have greater room for improvement. Research has also shown the beneficial effects of exercise on children and older adults. Children's exercise behaviors are greatly influenced by their parents' attitudes and behaviors regarding exercise. Factors that can influence a child's decision to be physically active include parents' beliefs, the children's perception of their own competence, and to some extent their goal orientation. A task, or mastery, orientation is a fairly strong predictor of exercise behavior in children (Brustad, 1996; Kimiecik, Horn & Shurin, 1996). Regarding exercise and the elderly, research shows that participation in aerobic exercise selectively preserves some cognitive functioning that normally declines with age. So for the elderly, there is not only the benefit of improved fitness and improved psychological affect associated with exercise, but also the prospect of slowing the decline of some cognitive functions. Exercise in the elderly is associated with the preservation of certain aspects of memory and spatial relationships (Shay & Roth, 1992). Finally, it is important to mention that the beneficial psychological effects of regular exercise extend to physically challenged individuals as well. Wheelchair-bound sport participants enjoy greater psychological benefits than non-sport participants (Campbell & Jones, 1994). This is consistent with previous research with wheelchair athletes. Throughout this text, whenever research involving wheelchair athletes has been cited, it has been shown that their responses to sport and exercise are the same as those of athletes who are not physically challenged.

CONCEPT & APPLICATION 10.3

Concept The psychological benefits of exercise extend to all individuals, regardless of age or degree of physical challenge.

Application We must not lose sight of the need to extend opportunities to be physically active to all populations of people. Children are in particular need, because it is at a young age that exercise behaviors for a lifetime are established.

Older adults are also in particular need because of the challenges of growing older. Physical activity can lessen or buffer the debilitating effects of aging, both physiological and psychological. Physically challenged individuals are in need as well, because it is often incorrectly assumed that they are incapable of meaningful physical activity.

Mediating Variables

Based upon the foregoing discussion, it can be concluded that a psychological benefit may be derived from regular moderate physical activity. In addition, research suggests that there may be intervening or mediating variables that can facilitate this relationship.

Time of Day Research suggests that time of day is not an important factor relative to benefits derived from exercise. Psychological benefits associated with exercise behavior are not dependent upon time of day. You get just as much affective benefit from running in the morning as from doing so at midday or in the evening (O'Connor & Davis, 1995).

Music Research suggests that listening to music during exercise can increase positive affect in the exerciser. Not only does listening to music during exercise enhance the beneficial effects of exercise, but it also reduces perceived exertion. At this time we can only speculate as to the effect that different kinds of music may have upon this observation (Boutcher & Trenske, 1990).

Attentional Focus Relative to attentional style, there is some evidence that an external, or dissociative, attentional style may result in greater psychological benefit. Runners who are asked to listen to their own heart rates during exercise (have an internal focus) exhibit greater emotional stress than runners who dissociate during exercise (Harte & Eifert, 1995).

TREATING ANXIETY AND DEPRESSION

While the previous section dealt with the general positive psychological benefits of exercise, this section will focus specifically upon anxiety and depression. Anxiety and depression are two of the most common mood disturbances in both normal and psychiatric individuals.

Since 1990, three important reviews dealing with anxiety, depression, and exercise have been published. North, McCullagh, and Tran (1990) reported the results of a **meta-analysis** (statistical summary and comparison of independent samples) involving 80 studies conducted from 1969 to 1989 on the effects of exercise on depression. The results of the meta-analysis are summarized as follows:

1. Acute and chronic exercise effectively reduce depression.

2. The greatest decrease in depression occurs with subjects requiring psychological care.

3. Exercise is associated with a reduction of both trait and state depression.

4. Exercise effectively reduces depression in mentally healthy subjects, as well as those undergoing psychiatric treatment.

5. All modes of exercise (anaerobic and aerobic) are effective in reducing depression.

6. Length of exercise program (in weeks) and number of sessions (per week) are related to amount of decrease in depression.

7. Exercise is more effective than relaxation and enjoyable activities in reducing depression.

8. Exercise combined with psychotherapy is more effective than exercise alone in reducing depression.

Petruzzello, Landers, Hatfield, Kubitz, and Salazar (1991) reported the results of a meta-analysis involving 104 studies conducted from 1960 to 1989 on the effects of exercise on anxiety. The effects of exercise on anxiety was further categorized as a function of type of measurement (self-reported state, self-reported trait, and psychophysiological). Some of the findings associated with the meta-analysis are as follows:

1. Exercise bouts must be longer than 20 minutes to effectively reduce anxiety.

2. Progressive relaxation is as effective in reducing state anxiety as exercise.

3. Exercise was more effective in reducing trait anxiety than progressive relaxation.

4. Anaerobic exercise does not result in reduction in anxiety.

5. Chronic and acute aerobic exercise bouts effectively reduce state anxiety.

6. Exercise programs must exceed 10 weeks before they can effectively reduce trait anxiety.

While the effects of exercise on anxiety generally parallel their effects on depression, one clear difference may be noted. **Anaerobic exercise** (high intensity/short duration) is effective in reducing depression but not effective in reducing anxiety. This conclusion suggests that if total mood improvement is desired, aerobic exercise is preferred over anaerobic exercise.

Gymnastic floor exercise requires mental and physical preparation. Courtesy University of Missouri-Columbia Sports Information

Noting that 10 to 25 percent of the American population suffer from mild to moderate depression and anxiety, LaFontaine, DiLorenzo, Frensch, Stucky-Ropp, Bargman, and McDonald (1992) reported a review of well-controlled studies from 1985 to 1990 on the relationship between aerobic exercise and anxiety/depression. The results of this review provide a summary of findings similar to those reported by North et al. (1990) and Petruzzello et al. (1991). As illustrated in table 10.1, the LaFontaine et al. (1992) conclusions provide strong support for the supposition that a strong and consistent relationship exists between exercise and reduction of negative affect. The psychological benefits of a consistent and well-designed exercise program are as impressive as the physiological benefits. The following statement in the "President's Council on Physical Fitness & Sports Newsletter" (Staff, 1992) applies equally to physiological and psychological health: "If exercise could be packed into a pill, it would be the single most widely prescribed and beneficial medicine in the nation" (p. 5).

Considering the strength of the relationship between exercise and improved mood state, it may seem strange that researchers refuse to affix a cause-and-

Table 10.1

Research Findings Supporting the Relationship between Aerobic Exercise and Reduced Anxiety and Depression.

LaFontaine et al., 1992

1. A consistent relationship exists between aerobic exercise and reduced levels of anxiety and depression.
2. Aerobic exercise is effective in the treatment of mild to moderate forms of chronic depression and anxiety.
3. Benefits are greatest in exercisers who are initially more depressed and anxious.
4. Reduced anxiety and depression associated with exercise may occur in the absence of an increase in measured cardiovascular fitness.
5. The hypothesis that exercise leads to or causes a reduction in anxiety and depression cannot be proven or refuted at this time.

effect relationship between the two (see item 5 in table 10.1). Given the weight of the evidence reviewed in this section, why can't it be stated that *exercise leads to reduced anxiety and depression?* There are a number of answers to this question, but perhaps the most compelling has to do with researchers' inability to rule out other causes. As we will discover in the next section, a number of theoretical explanations exist for the observed relationship between exercise and improved mood. Some of these theoretical explanations suggest that the cause may not be exercise at all, but some other factor that is associated with exercise. The finding that relaxation training and hatha yoga, for example, are also effective in reducing negative mood suggests that something other than exercise may be mediating the change (Brown, Wang, Ward, Ebbeling, Fortlage, Puleo, Benson & Rippe, 1995).

THEORETICAL EXPLANATIONS FOR THE RELATIONSHIP BETWEEN EXERCISE AND IMPROVED MENTAL HEALTH

Many hypotheses have been proposed to explain why exercise is associated with improved mental health. A number of these hypotheses will be reviewed and discussed in the following paragraphs. The first three explanations are considered to be psychological in nature, while the remaining three are physiological in nature (North et al., 1990). While it is tempting to subscribe to one hypothesis at the expense of the others, it is likely that the ultimate explanation is eclectic and multidimensional in nature.

Cognitive Behavioral Hypothesis

The basic premise of the **cognitive behavioral hypothesis** is that exercise encourages and generates positive thoughts and feelings that serve to counteract negative mood states such as depression, anxiety, and confusion (North et al., 1990; Simons, Epstein, McGowan, Kupfer & Robertson, 1985). This theoretical explanation parallels Bandura's theory of self-efficacy, discussed in chapter 8. According to Bandura (1977), when individuals master a task they perceive to be difficult, they experience an increase in self-efficacy. Exercise is perceived by nonexercisers as a difficult task. When the nonexerciser succeeds in becoming a regular exerciser, she experiences a feeling of accomplishment and self-efficacy. An increase in self-efficacy is helpful in breaking the downward spiral of negative affect associated with depression, anxiety, and other negative mood states.

Social Interaction Hypothesis

The basic premise of the **social interaction hypothesis** is that the social interaction associated with exercising with friends and colleagues is pleasurable and has the net effect of improving mental health (North et al., 1990). While the social interaction hypothesis provides a partial explanation for the psychological benefits of exercise, it does not provide an acceptable complete explanation. Evidence of the psychological benefits of regular exercise abounds, whether the exercising be in groups or alone. The North et al. (1990) meta-analysis, for example, confirmed that exercising alone and at home results in greater reductions in depression than exercising at other locations (usually with others).

Distraction Hypothesis

The basic premise of the **distraction hypothesis** is that exercise affords an opportunity for individuals to be distracted from their worries and frustrations. Support for this hypothesis comes from Sachs (1982a) and from Bahrke and Morgan (1978). Bahrke and Morgan (1978) observed that acute doses of meditation and quiet rest were as effective as exercise in reducing anxiety. The North et al. (1990) meta-analysis, however, concluded that chronic exercise is a more powerful and effective treatment for reducing negative mood than relaxation or other distracting but enjoyable activities. It may be that distraction provides a viable explanation for short-term reduction in depression and anxiety, but not for long-term reduction.

Cardiovascular Fitness Hypothesis

The basic premise of the **cardiovascular fitness hypothesis** is that improved mood state is associated with improved cardiovascular fitness (Morgan, 1969). The cardiovascular fitness hypothesis, however, is not generally supported by the literature (Emery & Blumenthal, 1988; North et al., 1990). The results of the North et al. (1990) meta-analysis suggest that the initial psychological benefits of chronic exercise occur during the first few weeks, before subjects experience substantial changes in cardiovascular fitness.

Amine Hypothesis

The basic premise of the **amine hypothesis** is that increased secretion of chemicals that serve as neurotransmitters is related to improved mental health. Neurotransmitters serve to transmit signals from nerve to nerve and from nerve to muscle. Studies have shown that depressed individuals often suffer a decrement in the secretion of various amines, such as norepinephrine, serotonin, and dopamine (Fawcett, Mass & Dekirmenjiar, 1972; Morgan, 1985; North et al., 1990), and that exercised rats experience an increase in brain norepinephrine (Brown & Van Huss, 1973). Theoretically, exercise stimulates the production of neurotransmitters that in turn have a positive effect upon psychological mood.

Endorphin Hypothesis

The **endorphin hypothesis** postulates that exercise is associated with brain production of chemicals that have a "morphine-like" effect on the exerciser (pain reduction and general euphoria). The general euphoria produced by the endorphins serves to reduce the levels of depression, anxiety, confusion, and other negative mood states. While this is an appealing concept, the evidence in support of the theory is meager. Human studies by Farrell, Gustafson, Garthwaite, Kalkhoff, Cowley, and Morgan (1986) and by Kraemer, Dzewaltowski, Blair, Rinehardt, and Castracane (1990) have failed to support a role for endorphins in the exercise and mood state relationship. Kraemer et al. (1990), for example, observed a decrease in blood plasma endorphins with an increase in positive mood.

CONCEPT & APPLICATION 10.4

Concept At least six plausible explanations exist for the relationship between improved mood and exercise. By itself, not one of the hypotheses provides a complete and satisfying explanation as to why exercise improves mental health.
Application The absence of a definitive explanation for the positive relationship between exercise and improved mood should not lessen the importance of the association. Exercise should be encouraged as a valid treatment for depression, anxiety, anger, and other psychological maladies. Nonexercisers, however, should consult their physician before beginning a strenuous exercise program.

EXERCISE ADHERENCE AND DETERMINANTS

The basic premise of this chapter is that exercise is associated with positive psychological and physiological benefits. The previous sections have reinforced the reality of this strong relationship. In contrast with these positive research findings is the grim reminder that 58 percent of the American population is sedentary, 10 to 25 percent of Americans suffer from mild to moderate depression and anxiety, and 50 percent of the people who start a structured exercise program drop out within the first six months (LaFontaine et al., 1992). With these facts in mind, it becomes clear that another important aspect of exercise psychology is to determine what motivates individuals to start exercising, what motivates them to adhere to an exercise program and what motivates them to try again after failing the first (or second) time.

A structural model proposed by Sallis and Hovell (1990) provides a framework for studying what these authors call the *natural history of exercise.* The natural history of exercise model, as illustrated in figure 10.1, proposes a framework for studying the *determinants* of exercise behavior.

As depicted in figure 10.1, the determinants of exercise behavior focuses upon the three *transitions* between the sedentary phase, the adoption phase, the

Figure 10.1

Four major phases of the natural history of exercise. Transitions denoted by T_1, T_2, and T_3. Adapted with permission from Determinants of exercise behavior by J. F. Sallis and M. F. Hovell, 1990. In K. B. Pandolf & J. O. Holloszy (Eds.), *Exercise and Sport Sciences Reviews, 18,* pp. 307–330. Copyright 1990 by Williams & Wilkins, Baltimore.

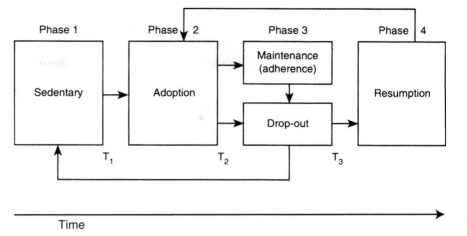

maintenance or drop-out phase, and the resumption phase. Research that has been or should be conducted on exercise determinants examines the three transitions between the four phases of the natural history of exercise.

Transition from Sedentary State to Exercise Adoption Determinants that motivate individuals to make the transition from a sedentary lifestyle to regular exercise are largely unknown. An exception to this general observation is a study reported by Sallis, Haskell, Fortmann, Vranizan, Taylor, and Solomon (1986). In this investigation, 1,400 adults were initially assessed with a battery of potential determinants. One year later these potential determinants were compared with exercise behaviors. As a result of these comparisons, several predictors of vigorous physical exercise were identified. Based on this investigation, individuals likely to adopt a vigorous exercise lifestyle exhibit the following characteristics:

1. Confidence they can succeed at a vigorous exercise program (exercise self-efficacy).

2. Knowledge about what constitutes a healthy lifestyle.

3. Knowledge about the importance and value of regular exercise.

4. The perception that they enjoy a high level of self-control.

5. Good attitudes about the value and importance of regular exercise.

6. Initial condition of not being overweight or obese.

The importance of self-efficacy as a determinant of exercise behavior has been documented (Rudolph & McAuley, 1996). Highly efficacious individuals experience lower perceptions of effort expenditure during exercise, and report positive affect associated with vigorous exercise.

Table 10.2

Primary Determinants of Adherence and Nonadherence to Vigorous Exercise Programs.

A. *Determinants of Adherence*
  1. Self-motivation
  2. Self-efficacy
  3. Behavioral coping skills
  4. Social influence (family members, group cohesion, co-exercisers, etc.)
  5. Available time
  6. Easy access to facilities
  7. Personal perception of good health
  8. High risk of heart disease

B. *Determinants of Nonadherence (Dropping Out)*
  1. Being a blue-collar worker
  2. Being overweight or obese
  3. Experience of discomfort during exercise
  4. Smoking
  5. Mood state disturbance

Transition from Adoption to Maintenance or Drop-Out Status

The statistic that 50 percent of individuals who start a vigorous exercise program drop out within six months is alarming, since the psychological and physiological benefits of vigorous exercise cannot be maintained unless exercise is maintained (Sallis & Hovell, 1990). Most of the research conducted on exercise determinants has focused on the transition from adoption to maintenance. The focus of this large body of literature has been upon predictors of **exercise adherence** and nonadherence (Carron, Hausenblas & Mack, 1996; Dishman, 1987; Sallis & Hovell, 1990). As summarized in table 10.2, determinants of exercise adherence include self-motivation, self-efficacy, coping skills, social influence, time, access to facilities, perception of health, and risk of heart disease. Conversely, determinants of nonadherence include being a blue-collar worker, obesity, discomfort during exercise, smoking, and increase in negative mood. Because a large percentage of people who start an exercise program either drop out or suffer a relapse, an important intervention is to teach new exercisers coping skills to deal with factors that are associated with nonadherence (Simkin & Gross, 1994).

Transition from Drop-Out Status to Exercise Resumption

As stated by Sallis and Hovell (1990), the transition from being an exercise drop-out to resuming a vigorous exercise program has been completely ignored

CONCEPT & APPLICATION 10.5

Concept An incomplete list of determinants of both exercise adherence and nonadherence has been identified through research.

Application Once an individual has committed to a vigorous long-term program, it is the responsibility of the exercise psychologist and fitness leader to help him maintain a lifelong

commitment to regular exercise. Knowledge of the determinants of exercise adherence and nonadherence should be used to anticipate potential drop-outs. Planned intervention strategies should be applied, when needed, to maintain motivation and commitment.

by researchers and theorists. This is an important part of the exercise psychology literature that must be addressed. Statistics are not available on the percentage of people who drop out of an exercise program and then get started again. Is it harder to resume an exercise program after once dropping out, or is it harder to start initially? Do people who resume their exercise programs after dropping out tend to be good adherers, or do they tend to drop out again? Are the determinants for exercise maintenance the same as those for exercise resumption, or is there a separate set of determinants? These questions and others need to be addressed by exercise psychologists.

THEORIES OF EXERCISE BEHAVIOR

Psychological models of human behavior have been applied to the exercise setting in an attempt to explain why people don't exercise, why they start to exercise, why they do or do not continue to exercise, and why they start exercising again if they stop. These models include (a) the theory of reasoned action, (b) the theory of planned behavior, (c) the transtheoretical model of stages of change, and (d) social cognitive theory. Each of these theories will now be briefly discussed.

Theory of Reasoned Action

Originated by Ajzen and Fishbein (1977), the *theory of reasoned action* proposes that the main precursor of a behavior such as exercise is the individual's *intention* to perform the behavior. The intention to perform the behavior is determined by the individual's *attitude* toward the behavior as well as *social norms* or social pressure to perform the behavior. Research has demonstrated that the theory of reasoned behavior is effective in predicting behavior when the individual has a great deal of personal control relative to the behavior (Yannis, 1994). Consequently, if an individual intends to maintain an exercise program, has social support to maintain it, and has personal control over her environment, then there is a good chance she will continue the program.

Figure 10.2

Schematic representation of the theory of planned behavior. Reprinted by permission from H. A. Hausenblas, A. V. Carron, and D. E. Mack, 1997, "Application of the theories of reasoned action and planned behavior to exercise behavior," *Journal of Sport & Exercise Psychology, 19*(1), 37.

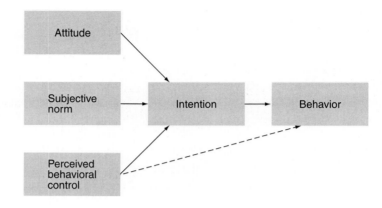

Theory of Planned Behavior

Originated by Ajzen (1985), the *theory of planned behavior* is an extension of the theory of reasoned action (Godin, 1994). The *intention* to perform a behavior is fundamental to the theory. Intention is determined by the individual's *attitude* toward the behavior and *social norms.* The difference between the two theories is the addition of *behavioral control* to the latter model. An individual will maintain or initiate an exercise program if his intention is firm and he feels in control. Intention is in turn a function of his attitude towards exercise and perceived social support. Research has demonstrated general support for the theory of planned behavior in predicting exercise behavior (Wankel & Mummery, 1993). It has been suggested, however, that expectation to exercise is a stronger predictor of exercise behavior than intention. These two terms are virtually identical, but it is believed that expectation to exercise takes into consideration noncognitive habits and perceived capabilities to a greater degree than intention does (Courneya & McAuley, 1993, 1994). The basic components and precursors to the theory of planned behavior are illustrated in figure 10.2. Strong support for the theory of planned behavior is provided through a meta-analysis reported by Hausenblas, Carron, and Mack (1997).

The Transtheoretical Model

The *transtheoretical model* was originally proposed as a stage theory of behavioral change by Prochaska and DiClemete (1982, 1983, 1986). Prochaska and Marcus (1994) provide an insightful explanation as to how the model is applied to exercise. According to the **transtheoretical model,** individuals pass through five dynamic stages in adopting healthy long-term exercise behavior. The stages are dynamic, because individuals may move in and out of the several stages before reaching the final stage, which is also dynamic. The five stages of change, illustrated in figure 10.3, include precontemplation, contemplation, preparation, action, and maintenance. Interventions called **processes of change** may be utilized to help exercisers move along the continuum from one stage to the next. It is important to know which stage an individual is in, because some

Figure 10.3

The transtheoretical model, showing stages of change and processes of change that interact to bring about improved exercise behavior.

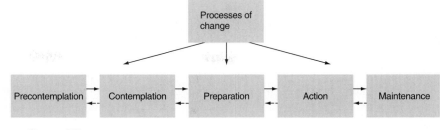

Stages of Change

interventions work better in one stage than in another. In applying the model, the exercise leader assesses the stage that the exerciser is in and then selectively applies a process of change intervention designed to help him move to the next level (Gorely & Gordon, 1995; Marcus & Simkin, 1994). Processes of change interact with the various stages of the transtheoretical model to bring about successful change in exercise behavior.

In the full model, in addition to processes of change, other factors interact with the stages of change to being about a change in behavior. These include self-efficacy, perception of gains and losses, and a set of psychological obstacles that may need to be addressed (e.g., personal or family conflicts). In general, the research has supported the transtheoretical model as a means to enhance exercise behavior (Armstrong, Sallis, Hovell & Hofstetter, 1993; Courneya, 1995; Marcus, Eaton, Rossi & Harlow, 1994).

Social Cognitive Theory

As proposed by Bandura (1986), *social cognitive theory* provides a viable way to explain exercise behavior. Individuals who are dissatisfied with their current exercise behavior, who exhibit high levels of **exercise self-efficacy,** and who set exercise goals are generally able to achieve their goals. Exercise self-efficacy is a powerful predictor of exercise behavior. Individuals who believe in themselves and believe that they can be successful at maintaining an exercise program generally are successful (DuCharme & Brawley, 1995; Poag & McAuley, 1992; Rudolph & McAuley, 1995).

While social cognitive theory has been presented here as a stand-alone theory of exercise behavior, tenets of the theory are best incorporated into other theories. For example, self-efficacy is included as an important component of the theory of planned behavior and the transtheoretical model. Current theory suggests that best results may be obtained by applying components of several theories into the same strategies for improving exercise behavior in sedentary individuals (Brawley, 1993; Dishman & Buckworth, 1996).

CONCEPT & APPLICATION 10.6

Concept The various theories of exercise behavior are useful in understanding human behavior and in designing interventions to help people adopt healthy exercise behaviors. *Application* Rather than pitting one theory against another, it is best to bring elements of different theories together to understand the psychology of exercise adoption and adherence.

For example, the transtheoretical model can be very helpful in understanding where people are relative to exercise behavior. This information can then be integrated with concepts of self-efficacy, intentions, attitudes, social norms, and personal control to design interventions that can help individuals adopt and maintain exercise programs.

FITNESS AS A MODERATOR OF LIFE STRESS

Given the positive relationship between exercise and improved mental health, it follows that physical fitness should serve as a buffer against life stress. This concept was introduced earlier in the chapter, when we discussed the important topic of *stress inoculation.* **Life stress** represents an accumulation of the daily hassles and challenges of living out our lives. Individuals who exercise regularly and maintain a high level of physical fitness should be less susceptible to the negative effects of life stress. Evidence for this hypothesis has been provided by Brown (1991) and by others. The investigation by Brown is of special interest, because objective measures of physical fitness and illness were assessed. Brown studied the relationship between level of physical fitness, as measured by the bicycle ergometer; life stress, as measured by the Life Experience Survey; and number of visits to the university health center. As illustrated in figure 10.4, the results of the investigation show an interactive relationship between life stress, physical fitness, and number of visits to the health center (illness). Being physically fit serves to inoculate the individual against illness during periods of high stress.Conversely, physically unfit individuals appear to be unprotected against high stress.

Tangentially related to the life stress issue is the observation that exercise and physical fitness is an effective treatment to reduce high blood pressure. Martin and Calfas (1989) provided a review of 17 uncontrolled or partially controlled studies and 13 controlled studies. The results of this review suggest that exercise is an effective nonpharmacologic treatment for hypertension. Chronic aerobic exercise produces a reduction in blood pressure that is independent of weight loss or diet.

Given the promising buffer effect that exercise has upon life stress, one wonders why more people do not take advantage of it. One possible explanation

Figure 10.4

Level of physical fitness
moderates the relationship
between life stress and
illness. Adapted with
permission from Staying fit
and staying well: Physical
fitness as a moderator of
life stress by J. D. Brown,
1991, *Journal of
Personality and Social
Psychology, 60,*
pp. 555–561. Copyright
1991 by the American
Psychological Association.

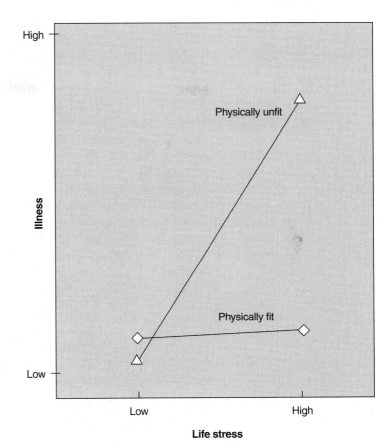

CONCEPT & APPLICATION 10.7

Concept Physical fitness is a buffer of life stress, reduces hypertension, and is associated with fewer visits to the doctor.

Application Time spent exercising is not wasted time. Because we live in a fast-paced stressful world, steps must be taken to buffer daily stress. Individuals must be encouraged to place daily vigorous exercise at the top of their priorities.

---

could be lack of knowledge about the beneficial stress inoculation effects of exercise. Another partial explanation might be the personalities of individuals who either choose or do not choose to exercise. Research suggests that individuals who regularly engage in exercise have distinctive personality characteristics. For example, Hartung and Farge (1977) reported that exercisers exhibit a profile of increased reserve, intelligence, seriousness, imagination,

Soccer provides exercise and psychological benefit to participants. Courtesy University of Missouri-Columbia Sports Information

forthrightness, and self-sufficiency when compared with nonexercisers. More recently, Schnurr, Vaillant, and Vaillant (1990) addressed the question of whether personality in young adulthood predicts exercise in later midlife. Male Caucasian Harvard graduates from the classes of 1942 to 1944 were traced to determine if personality characteristics measured in college were predictive of exercise habits later in life. As part of the Harvard longitudinal study begun in 1938, personality was assessed by two psychologists who used a review of 20 hours of interview transcripts. In college, hours and type of daily and weekly exercise were recorded. As part of the follow-up, subjects were asked about the amount and type of exercise they had engaged in since age 55. Results of the investigation showed that personality characteristics of vitality, integration, lack of anxiety, and lack of shyness during college were predictive of frequent exercise behavior later in life.

THE IMMUNE SYSTEM, CANCER, HIV, AND EXERCISE

In recent years research has linked two of the great plagues of our time (cancer and HIV) to exercise and its effect on the immune system. While exercise has generally been linked to benefits, in cases of excess it can have negative consequences. It is like a two-edged sword: it cuts both ways. If applied in moderation it can have beneficial effects, but if applied in excess it can have negative effects.

The Immune System and Cancer

Moderate exercise applied on a regular basis is associated with both psychological and biological benefits. Moderate exercise is linked to a lowered incidence of colon and breast cancer. Young women who regularly participate in physical exercise activities during their reproductive years have a reduced risk of breast cancer. Individuals who have cancer, but who exercise regularly, may benefit from improved psychological well-being, preservation of lean tissue, and enhanced immune systems (Bernstein, Anderson, Hanisch, Sullivan-Halley & Ross, 1994; Lee, 1995; Sternfeld, 1992). Benefits associated with exercise are linked to intensity and regularity. For someone to reap the biological and psychological benefits of exercise, it must be applied in moderation and on a regular basis. Whereas a moderate dose of endurance exercise has a potential beneficial effect upon the human immune response, more intense and more stressful exercise can have a persistent and adverse effect. It follows that strenuous exercise over a long period of time may compromise the effectiveness of the immune system to fight against cancer and other infections. Research shows that there is a dual response of the immune system to exercise. The integrity of the immune system is stimulated by moderate exercise but suppressed by intense exercise. It appears that there exists an optimal level of regular physical activity conducive to the resistance to illness. Apparently, you can have too much of a good thing (Mackinnon, 1994; Shephard, Rhind & Shek, 1995; Shephard & Shek, 1994).

CONCEPT & APPLICATION 10.8

Concept Immune function is stimulated by moderate exercise but suppressed by overly intense exercise. It appears that there exists an optimal level of regular physical activity conducive to the resistance to illness.

Application It is critical that coaches and exercise leaders recognize and understand the delicate balance between the beneficial effects of moderate exercise and the detrimental effects of overly intense exercise. When the integrity of the immune system is involved, the coach must be very sensitive to this balance. The most immediate concern is reduced immune system response and upper respiratory infection in the form of the cold virus and influenza. These illnesses weaken athletes and make them more susceptible to other diseases.

Exercise and the Human Immunodeficiency Virus

Magic Johnson's brief return to professional basketball and his participation in the 1992 summer Olympics in Barcelona, Spain, after contracting the **human immunodeficiency virus (HIV),** led to speculation as to the possible negative side effects of vigorous physical activity to his physical and psychological health. Since it is widely believed by the medical profession that the presence of the HIV ultimately leads to **acquired immune deficiency syndrome (AIDS),** there was cause for concern (Cinelli, Sankaran, McConatha & Carson, 1992). Evidence reported by Ironson, LaPerriere, Antoni, Klimas, Fletcher, and Schneiderman (1990) indicates that when asymptomatic gay males are informed of their HIV-positive status, they display a significant increase in anxiety and other distress scores. Furthermore, evidence has been accrued that links affective factors, such as depression and anxiety, with accelerated HIV infection (Ironson et al., 1990). Goodkin (1988) further suggests that increased anxiety and depression should be viewed as risk factors facilitating the development of AIDS. Because exercise has been positively linked with decreased anxiety and depression, it follows that chronic exercise should be effective in retarding the negative progression and effects of HIV. Three recent research reports support this position.

In a study reported by LaPerriere, Antoni, Schneiderman, Ironson, Klimas, Caralis, and Fletcher (1990), 50 gay males (ages 20 to 40) who had no symptoms of AIDS were randomly assigned to either an aerobic exercise training program or a control condition. None of the subjects knew whether they carried the HIV, but agreed to participate in the study to find out. Subjects in the experimental condition exercised on a bicycle ergometer three times per week for 45 minutes. Psychometric and blood immunologic measures were assessed after five weeks of training and constituted the prediagnosis test point. Seventy-two hours later, all subjects were informed whether they had tested HIV positive or negative. One week after being informed of their HIV test results, psychometric and blood immunologic measures were again assessed. The results of the investigation revealed that (a) subjects in the exercise condition showed significant improvement in cardiovascular fitness, (b) control group subjects who tested HIV positive suffered increased levels of anxiety and depression following the notification of the results of their blood test, and (c) HIV-positive controls but not HIV-positive exercisers displayed a significant decrease in blood natural killer lymphocytes. A decrease in natural killer cells is believed to result in a significant decrement in immune system resistance to infection.

A study by Rigsby, Dishman, Jackson, MaClean, and Raven (1992) addressed the concern that chronic aerobic exercise could lead to the suppression of the effectiveness of the immune system in individuals with an already compromised and weakened system. Noting from Simon's (1991) study that acute bouts of submaximal exercise are typically followed by transient increases in total leukocytes and total lymphocytes (including natural killer cells), Rigsby et al. (1992) tested the hypothesis that chronic aerobic exercise would have a beneficial effect on total leukocytes and total lymphocytes. Subjects were 37 males who had tested HIV positive and had been previously inactive. Subjects were assigned to either a 12-week exercise condition (bicycle ergometer) or a counseling control condition. Results revealed that exercisers improved their strength and endurance without suppressing an already compromised immune system (no change in total leukocytes and lymphocytes).

While the previous two investigations focused upon immune system response to aerobic exercise, a study by Lox, McAuley, and Tucker (1995) focused upon psychological response to aerobic exercise on the part of HIV-infected men. Thirty-three HIV-infected men were randomly assigned to an aerobic exercise treatment, a resistance weight-training treatment, or a stretching/flexibility control treatment for a period of 12 weeks. Results of the research indicated that aerobic exercise and weight training enhanced physical self-efficacy, positive and negative mood, and satisfaction with life. The control participants suffered declines in these three psychological measures. These results suggest that moderate exercise is an effective complementary therapy for treating psychological manifestations associated with HIV infection.

CONCEPT & APPLICATION 10.9

Concept The evidence suggests that asymptomatic HIV-positive individuals can enjoy the positive psychological and physiological benefits of chronic exercise without suppressing an already compromised immune system.

Application Under the supervision of a physician, asymptomatic HIV-positive individuals should be encouraged to engage in an aerobic exercise program designed to improve cardiovascular fitness and reduce the debilitating effects of anxiety and depression.

SOCIAL PHYSIQUE ANXIETY, EXERCISE ADDICTION, AND EATING DISORDERS

While social physique anxiety, exercise addiction, and eating disorders are really separate constructs, they have been linked together in the literature (Pasman & Thompson, 1988). This linkage has in some cases been unjustified, but in other cases it has been justified. Space does not allow an in-depth treatment of any of these topics, but in the paragraphs that follow I will introduce the concepts and show relationships where appropriate.

Social Physique Anxiety

People have perceptions about their physical physique. Some people like their physique, while others do not. For some people, a dissatisfaction about their physique may provide a motivation to adopt exercise as a means to improve it. Conversely, some people may avoid exercise because of the fear of being negatively evaluated relative to their physique. Still others have such distorted images of their bodies that they resort to bizarre eating habits in an attempt to make thin bodies even thinner.

Social physique anxiety is the anxiety that people experience when they perceive that other people evaluate their physique negatively. They may feel that others evaluate them as too thin, or too heavy, or too fat, and so on. From a health psychology perspective, the concern is that an individual who experiences social physique anxiety will be impeded relative to his exercise behaviors. Social physique anxiety is related to the concepts of body image and physical self-concept. Physical self-concept is a psychological construct measured by Fox and Corbin's (1989) Physical Self-Perception Profile (PSPP). The PSPP measures perceived body attractiveness, along with perceptions about physical competence, physical strength, and physical conditioning. The PSPP is the foundation of what has come to be referred to as the Fox (1990) Hierarchical Model of Physical Self-Concept. This model leads to the prediction that positive physical self-concept contributes to the development of global self-esteem. Individuals who enjoy a high level of positive physical self-concept are likely to enter into competitive situations and to feel good about exercising in the presence of other people. Conversely, individuals who suffer from low physical self-concept or who experience anxiety about their bodies are likely to avoid competitive situations or situations in which they are required to exercise in front of other people (Crawford & Eklund, 1994).

In an attempt to quantify the degree to which people experience social physique anxiety, Hart, Leary, and Rejeski (1989) developed the Social Physique Anxiety Scale (SPAS). The SPAS is a 12-item scale designed to assess the degree to which people become anxious when others observe or evaluate their physiques. Research with the SPAS has confirmed that women who score high on the SPAS may at times be reticent about starting an exercise program where other people will be present. It has also been demonstrated that women who score high on the SPAS adopt exercise programs for different reasons than women who score low on the SPAS. The higher social physique anxiety is, the more likely it is that women will choose to exercise for reasons associated with weight reduction, body tone, and improved physical attractiveness (Eklund & Crafword, 1994; Martin & Mack, 1996).

Exercise Addiction

Exercise addiction is generally defined as a psychophysiological dependence on a regular regimen of exercise. The normal benefits associated with regular exercise at a moderate intensity are lost for the exercise-addicted individual. Failure to exercise according to schedule results in a mood state disturbance in

CONCEPT & APPLICATION 10.10

Concept An individual's perception about her body and her physique can have either a positive or negative effect upon exercise behavior.

Application The Physical Self-Perception Profile (PSPP) and the Social Physique Anxiety Scale (SPAS) can be useful instruments for ascertaining people's perceptions about their bodies. The use of these inventories may provide important information to the coach or the fitness leader relative to the exercise behavior of some individuals. If an individual is avoiding exercise because of social physique anxiety, it may be possible to provide opportunities for exercise in less threatening surroundings.

the addicted individual. From an attributional perspective, the addicted exerciser is controlled by the activity, as opposed to the activity's being controlled by the exerciser. Compared to nonaddicted exercisers, addicted exercisers report being more restless and stressed out prior to an exercise bout. They also experience a higher degree of depression, anxiety, and general discomfort when they miss a scheduled workout. An important characteristic of the exercise addict is that he will generally insist on exercising in the face of physical pain or injury (Anshel, 1991). The **super-adherer** is generally believed to be addicted to exercise. The super-adherer is an exerciser who participates in and constantly trains for endurance events that require significant long-term effort and commitment. Often, these endurance events are "super-events" ranging from 50 to 100 miles at a time in length. The Running Addiction Scale (RAS) was developed by Chapman and Castro (1990) to measure exercise addiction. Another term used to describe the addicted exerciser is **obligatory runner.** Male runners are categorized as obligatory runners to a greater extent than female runners. Obligatory runners are highly motivated to exercise, and when they can't, they experience abnormal feelings of anxiety and psychological discontent (Conboy, 1994; Ogles, Masters & Richardson, 1995).

CONCEPT & APPLICATION 10.11

Concept Exercise addiction is associated with depression and anxiety in response to missing a regular exercise session. Additionally, individuals suffering from exercise addiction risk more serous injury or illness by refusing to take a day off in the face of sickness or an exercise-related injury.

Application From the perspective of attribution theory, it is not consistent with a wellness lifestyle to allow an exercise addiction to control a person's behavior. Steps should be taken to assist an individual who suffers from exercise addiction to take control of her own exercise behavior. Alternative forms of recreational activity should be used to replace addictive exercise behaviors when they become controlling.

Eating Disorders

A link between eating disorders and sport has been hypothesized. The fear is that a young athlete's desire to attain a "desirable" body weight or shape for a particular activity leads to eating behaviors that can be classified as pathogenic **eating disorders.** The worst eating disorders are anorexia nervosa and bulimia nervosa. **Anorexia nervosa** is a pathogenic eating disorder characterized by bizarre dieting behaviors and rapid weight loss. Anorexia nervosa is initially seen as self-control, but this is soon replaced by fear and anxiety that lost weight will be regained. It is often accompanied by intense ritualistic exercise behaviors designed to metabolize calories, but also to focus attention away from hunger pangs. **Bulimia nervosa** is also a pathogenic eating disorder. It starts out much as anorexia does, with the individual dieting in an effort to lose weight. At some point, however, the person's hunger drives her to engage in an eating binge. Guilt associated with the eating binge leads the person to purge the food she has eaten from her stomach (by vomiting). Initially the binge-purge cycle starts as sort of an experiment, but it soon escalates into a compulsion that in some cases cannot be controlled.

Anorexia nervosa and bulimia are effective in reducing body weight and making the individual seem disciplined, fashionably thin, and somehow liberated. But the euphoria over being thin and in control soon gives way to depression, hyperactivity, excessive exercise, insomnia, and bizarre eating patterns. What was initially a fairly innocent desire to lose weight may escalate into a behavior that could lead to serious illness or even death. Anorexia nervosa and bulimia are the most serious of the eating disorders engaged in by athletes, but not the only ones. Other eating disorders include use of diet pills, diuretics, fasting, fluid restriction, and use of laxatives. The link between eating disorders and athletics is especially strong with young women and activities such as gymnastics and dance. Due to Western society's emphasis on thinness in young women, the plague of pathogenic eating disorders is not restricted to athletes and performers (Biddle, 1993).

Since 1986, numerous studies have been reported that estimate percentages of female athletes who engage in some form of eating disorder. The percentages range a great deal from sample to sample and from sport to sport (Burckes-Miller & Black, 1988; Dummer, Rosen, Heusner, Roberts & Counsilman, 1987; Petrie, 1993a; Petrie & Stoever, 1993; Peirce, Daleng & McGowan, 1993; Rosen & Hough, 1988; Rosen, McKeag, Hough & Curley, 1986). All agree, however, that eating disorders are dangerous and must be seriously addressed by coaches and administrators. An example of the contrast between reported results can be readily observed in studies by Burckes-Miller and Black (1988) and by Petrie and Stoever (1993). Burckes-Miller and Black (1988), utilizing a large sample of female collegiate athletes from multiple sports, reported a bulimia nervosa rate of 39.2 percent. Petrie and Stoever (1993), utilizing a sample of female collegiate gymnasts, reported a bulimia nervosa rate of 4.1 percent. The large discrepancy between the results of these two investigations is attributed to measurement techniques and instruments used in the two studies. A careful reading of both articles leads to the conclusion that the Petrie and Stoever (1993) results are more accurate. The 4.1 percent incidence of bulimia nervosa in the sample of female collegiate gymnasts is roughly equivalent to that observed in the general population of collegiate females. Perhaps more troubling than the incidence of bulimia nervosa is the Petrie and Stoever observation that female collegiate gymnasts *regularly* engage in binge eating and resort to unhealthy behaviors such as excessive exercise, fasting, and strict dieting to control body weight. They made the following recommendations to professionals who work with female athletes:

1. Be aware that serous eating disturbances exist in the absence of diagnosed pathogenic eating disorders.

2. Conduct eating disorder screenings that allow for identification of dangerous eating behaviors as well as pathogenic eating disorders.

3. Develop intervention strategies that focus upon early education about, identification of, and treatment of unhealthy eating behaviors.

CONCEPT & APPLICATION 10.12

Concept The incidence of anorexia nervosa and bulimia nervosa among female athletes and females generally is of serious concern. Of even greater concern, however, is the very high rate of eating disturbances among female athletes that are not diagnosed as pathogenic. These tend to go untreated and unnoticed.

Application Eating disturbances of any kind should be of concern to athletes, coaches, and professionals associated with women's sports. Unhealthy behaviors such as fasting, dieting, and taking of weight-control drugs are particularly dangerous to young women engaging in

demanding training schedules. Athletes are under tremendous pressure to excel at their sports. When they come to believe that losing weight and becoming thin will help them perform better, they become particularly vulnerable to pathogenic eating disorders such as anorexia or bulimia. Extraordinary steps should be taken to educate female athletes about the danger of unhealthy eating behaviors. While we must be similarly concerned about eating disorders among boys and young men, they are far less prevalent in sport and in our society today.

In a very controversial article (Yates, 1987) and book (Yates, 1991), Yates hypothesized that obligatory male runners and anorexic females share common personality characteristics. This hypothesis that anorexics and obligatory runners share a core set of personality characteristics is called the **anorexia analogue hypothesis.** According to this hypothesis, obligatory runners use running to control their body weight. As they continue to run and diet to reduce body fat, they are following the anorexic format. The need to have absolute control over the body is similar to that found in the anorexic. Further, Yates argued, obligatory runners and anorexics have similar family backgrounds, socioeconomic status, personality characteristics, tolerance of pain, and quest for asceticism. Coen and Ogles (1993) examined the anorexia analogue hypothesis by contrasting personality characteristics of obligatory and nonobligatory runners. If obligatory runners are similar in personality characteristics to anorexic females, significant differences should emerge between the samples of obligatory and nonobligatory runners. Results provide partial support for the anorexia analogue hypothesis, in that obligatory runners were shown to differ from nonobligatory runners in terms of a number of psychological constructs, in the same way anorexic individual would. Obligatory runners exhibited higher levels of perfectionism and anxiety, but did not differ from nonobligatory runners in ego identity and anger.

The anorexia analogue hypothesis was also examined by Parker, Lambert, and Burlington (1994). They looked for evidence of psychopathology in samples of (a) eating-disturbed collegiate female runners, (b) normal college runners, (c) clinically diagnosed eating-disordered patients, and (d) nonathletic, non-eating-disordered college students. Results showed that only the clinically diagnosed eating-disordered patients exhibited psychopathogenic behaviors. Runners with eating-disturbed characteristics resembled the clinically diagnosed eating-disturbed patients in terms of eating behaviors, but not in terms of psychopathology. In conclusion, it would appear that obligatory runners and eating-disturbed females share a number of personality characteristics, but they do not seem to share the same psychological disturbances. Further research is required relative to the anorexia analogue hypothesis.

STALENESS, OVERTRAINING, AND BURNOUT IN ATHLETES

Much of the previous section on exercise psychology was devoted to the positive benefits associated with regular moderate exercise. It should be clear from this discussion that exercise in moderation yields powerful beneficial psychological and physiological effects. Near the end of that section, however, we touched briefly upon the negative effects of too much exercise, to the point of its becoming an obsession. Too much exercise can result in a reduction in the effectiveness of the immune system to fight disease and an increase in negative psychological mood. In a very practical way, exercise can be considered along a continuum from not enough exercise to too much exercise. Negative psychological and biological outcomes are associated with too little and too much exercise. Overtraining in athletes represents a paradox, because many of the benefits associated with exercise are reversed in the athlete who trains too much. For the athlete, the question of how much is too much is a complex one. Athletes are continually challenging the delicate balance between training and overtraining, since high levels of training are required for success in sport. Interestingly, Kuipers (1996) quantified the amount of training required for elite distance runners and stated that when total duration of training exceeds 15 hours per week, a performance decrement usually occurs. In sport and exercise, too much training leads to feelings of staleness, overtraining, and perhaps burnout. Burnout is the end product of too much training in the absence of intervention strategies to prevent it. Burnout usually means that the athlete withdraws from active participation in his sport for reasons of accumulated training stress. In the pages that follow I will (a) discuss the process that leads to burnout in sport, (b) discuss overtraining and mood disturbance, (c) introduce theoretical models of stress and burnout, (d) identify symptoms and interventions for burnout, and (e) make recommendations for athletes, coaches, and parents.

PROCESS LEADING TO BURNOUT

One important distinction between recreational activity and competitive activity is the imposed training that accompanies competition. Competition to excel is often so intense that athletes and coaches alike are continually looking for a physiological or psychological advantage. Often the competitive advantage is sought through increased training and practice. For long-distance runners, it means running more practice miles each day; for swimmers, it means swimming more laps each day; and so forth.

The net effect of the extra workouts is training stress. As explained by Silva (1990), **training stress** is a necessary by-product of the psychophysiological stress associated with training for competition in sport. The outcome of training stress may be positive or negative. The athlete's ability or inability to adapt to training stress determines whether the results will be negative or positive. As illustrated in figure 10.5, a positive adaptation to training stress results in **training gain.** Conversely, a negative adaptation to training stress results in a failure to make training gains.

Athletes typically respond to lack of training gain with increased training stimuli (e.g., they run more miles). If the athlete fails to make a positive adaptation to the increased training stimuli, it is likely that she will experience staleness. As explained by Silva (1990), **staleness** is the initial failure of the body to adapt to training stress. If the athlete fails to "train through" the staleness and make a positive adaptation to training stress, she will experience overtraining. Not to be confused with the physiological principle of training overload, **overtraining** is a psychophysiological malfunction: the demonstrated inability of the athlete to adjust to the demands of training stress.

If an athlete continues experiencing negative adaptation to training stress, lack of training gain, staleness, and overtraining, she will likely suffer burnout. As explained by Silva (1990), **burnout** is an exhaustive psychophysiological response to repeated unsuccessful efforts to meet the demands of training stress. Burnout is the third phase of what Silva (1990) has labeled the **training stress syndrome.** The three phases of the training stress syndrome are staleness, overtraining, and burnout. Once the athlete experiences burnout, withdrawal from the imposed stressful environment is nearly inevitable. As illustrated in figure 10.5, the final stage of the negative adaptation to training stress is burnout and withdrawal.

Figure 10.5

Negative and positive adaptation to training stress. Adapted with permission from An analysis of the training stress syndrome in competitive athletics by J. M. Silva, III, 1990, *Journal of Applied Sport Psychology, 2,* pp. 5–20.

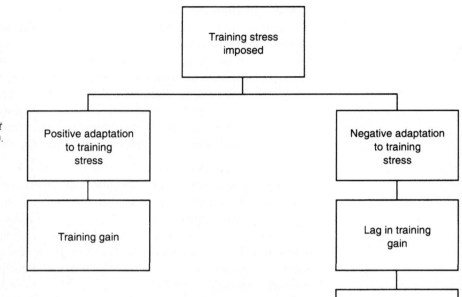
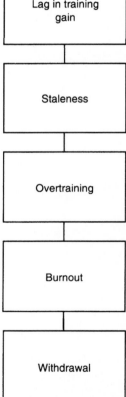

Is this athlete a candidate for burnout and withdrawal? Courtesy Kansas State University Sports Information

CONCEPT & APPLICATION 10.13

Concept How an athlete adapts to training stress will ultimately determine whether he will have a positive training experience or suffer staleness, overtraining, and burnout.

Application Athletes will make a positive adaptation to training stress if they are taught to recognize the signs of negative adaptation and are given the opportunity to cope. Relentless demands from coaches, parents, and teammates will interfere with the athlete's ability to cope.

OVERTRAINING AND MOOD DISTURBANCE

Perhaps the most critical aspect of Silva's concept of the training stress syndrome is overtraining because it is overtraining that leads to burnout. Coaches and athletes who engage in overtraining mistakenly confuse it with the beneficial effects of controlled training overload. Overtraining may be manifested in the form of mechanical overload (connective tissue, cartilage, and bone), metabolic overload (inadequate glycogen levels), and psychological overload (mood disturbance). Overtraining may be associated with fatigue during performance, decline in performance, mood disturbance, emotional instability, decreased motivation, and proneness to infection due to reduction in immune function (Kuiper, 1996). From a biological perspective, even acute bouts of overtraining can result in reduction in the immune system response (Fry, Grove, Morton, Zeroni, Gaudieri & Keast, 1994; Shephard & Shek, 1994). The failure of the immune system to combat infection and disease makes the athlete highly susceptible to the negative by-products associated with overtraining.

One of the indicators of overtraining is mood disturbance. Biopsies of exercised muscles demonstrate a clear connection between diminished muscle glycogen and increased mood disturbance (Puffer & McShane, 1992). Monitoring of mood disturbances through the use of the Profile of Mood States (POMS) is highly recommended as a means to recognize the onset of staleness and overtraining. For effective use of the POMS for monitoring psychological mood, a baseline measurement of mood must be determined. Berglung and Safstrom (1994) effectively used the POMS to monitor mood states of Swedish canoeists during a three-month period leading up to the Barcelona Olympics. They operationally defined mood disturbance as an increase in total mood to a level 50 percent above established baseline. When the criterion of 50 percent was passed, intervention was applied in the form of reduced or altered training. Short-term incidence of overtraining are typically referred to as *overreaching*. Mood disturbance has been repeatedly observed in swimmers and distance runners, but it also occurs with basketball players and other nonendurance sports (Raglin, Eksten & Garl, 1995; Raglin Koceja, Stager & Harms, 1996).

Mood disturbance is also related to personality of the athlete. Athletes who are high in the personality construct of hardiness are less likely to experience mood disturbance during training. Hardy individuals are able to alter their appraisal of stress, associated with overtraining, into a less stressful form (Goss, 1994). It is also interesting to note that the effects of mood disturbance on athletes tends to be long lasting. Kirkby (1996) observed that in some cases it takes several weeks for mood to return to pre-race levels. Given the important connection between overtraining and mood disturbance, it follows that (a) mood should be monitored, and (b) interventions should be applied in the form of reduced or altered training schedules when mood disturbance rises above a predetermined level (Hollander, Meyers & LeUnes, 1995).

CONCEPT & APPLICATION 10.14

Concept Many things, such as fatigue, performance decline, and proneness to infection, may signal overtraining in an athlete, but monitoring of mood states is one of the simplest and most effective ways to get an early warning of overtraining.

Application Mood states can be easily measured and monitored using the Profile of Mood States (POMS) or some variation of it. The important thing is to establish a baseline from which to work. The baseline represents the athlete's

normal healthy level of mood. It is from this baseline, which will differ for each athlete, that a determination of mood disturbance is made. A 50 percent increase in total mood is recommended as a criterion for concern. When using the POMS, total mood is determined by summing the five negative mood states and subtracting the score for vigor (see figure 2.5). Since this value may be less than zero, always add a constant of 100 to each total mood score.

MODELS OF BURNOUT

Silva's (1990) schematic of negative and positive adaptation to training stress illustrated the timeline and process by which burnout evolves and eventually results in withdrawal from sports participation. In a sense, Silva's schematic can be viewed as a model of burnout, but I prefer to view it as a defining process by which we can understand the relationship between staleness, overtraining, burnout, and finally withdrawal. In addition to Silva's schematic of burnout, several models of burnout have been proposed in the psychological and sport psychology literature. Two of these models will be discussed briefly in this section. A differentiation is made between withdrawal from sport and burnout. Burnout is just one of the reasons that athletes withdraw from sport. Research shows that the vast majority of athletes withdraw from sport for reasons associated with changing interests, time conflict, and lack of fun. The two models I will consider are Schmidt and Stein's' *investment model of burnout and dropout,* and Smith's *cognitive-affective model of stress and burnout.*

Schmidt and Stein's Investment Model of Burnout and Dropout

Based upon Rusbult (1980), Schmidt and Stein (1991) proposed an **investment model** of sports commitment that provides a clear prediction about conditions that promote continued participation, burnout, and withdrawal, respectively. As illustrated in figure 10.6, the Schmidt and Stein model is based upon five conditions. How the five conditions are perceived and interpreted by the athlete determines her commitment and possible withdrawal from sport. An athlete's involvement in sport is often based upon years and years of personal investment. Investments come in the form of time, friendship, emotional and physical energy, financial expense, and parental involvement. The athlete perceives that

Figure 10.6

Investment model showing two divergent types of commitment and withdrawal. From "Sport commitment: A model integrating enjoyment, dropout, and burnout" by G. W. Schmidt and G. L. Stein, 1991, *Journal of Sport & Exercise Psychology* (Vol. 13, No. 3), p. 260. Copyright 1991 by Human Kinetics Publishers, Inc. Adapted with permission.

Conditions	Commitment (enjoyment)	Commitment (burnout)	Withdrawal
1. **Rewards**	High (increasing)	Decreasing	Decreasing
2. **Costs (stress-induced)**	Low	Increasing	Increasing
3. **Satisfaction**	High	Decreasing	Decreasing
4. **Alternatives**	Low	Low	Increasing
5. **Investments**	High	High (increasing)	Decreasing

long-term investments will be lost if she withdraws from sport. As illustrated in figure 10.6, athletes remain committed to sports involvement for one of two reasons. The first reason is positive in nature and is based upon personal enjoyment. The individual who enjoys her commitment to sport experiences a high level of personal reward, satisfaction, and investment, while at the same time experiencing a low level of perceived (stress-induced) costs, and has few viable alternatives.

The second reason a person will stay involved in sport is unrelated to enjoyment. This person is a candidate for burnout because his continued involvement is motivated by a reluctance to give up years and years of personal investment and he sees few alternatives to continued involvement. Rewards and satisfaction associated with continued involvement gradually decrease, while stress-induced costs associated with commitment steadily increase.

According to investment theory, the only difference between the person who remains committed while experiencing burnout and the person who withdraws is the combination of alternatives and investments. The individual who perseveres in the face of burnout does so because of a perception that alternatives are unattractive (or nonexistent) and that personal investments are escalating. As long as the athlete perceives that investments are high and alternatives low, he will feel "trapped" and withdrawal will be difficult. The individual who finally does withdraw from active participation will do so because he comes to perceive that many other attractive alternatives exist, and that personal investment is decreasing.

Smith's Cognitive-Affective Model of Stress and Burnout

Smith's (1986) model of burnout is a four-stage model that parallels stages of the stress process first introduced in chapter 4 (see figure 4.4). The details of Smith's stress and burnout model are illustrated in figure 10.7. From the illustration it should be clear than an athlete's personality and level of motivation interact with all four stages. The situational, cognitive, physiologic, and behavioral components of the *general* stress process are paralleled by the situation-specific components of the burnout process.

In the first stage of the model, the athlete is confronted with objective demands that are beyond her ability to address. These demands are presented in the form of pressure to win, excessive practice and training time, and perhaps a

Figure 10.7

Smith's cognitive-affective model of stress and burnout. Adapted with permission from R. E. Smith, 1986, "Cognitive-affective mode of stress and burnout," *Journal of Sport Psychology, 8(1),* 40.

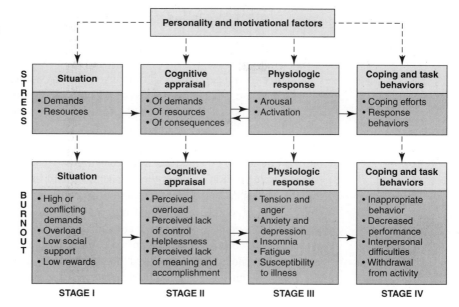

low return on her time investment (lack of playing time). In stage two a cognitive appraisal is made of the objective demands being placed on the athlete. The cognitive appraisal results in a threat to the athlete in the form of perceived overload, lack of control, feelings of helplessness, and lack of meaning. In stage three, perceived threat, as a consequence of cognitive appraisal, results in a physiologic response manifested in the form of anxiety/tension, depression, insomnia, fatigue, and/or susceptibility to illness. Finally, in stage four, the athlete responds with some sort of coping behavior or response, such as inappropriate behavior, decreased performance, interpersonal difficulties, and/or withdrawal from activity. Thus, burnout is viewed as a reponse to chronic stress. It is characterized by psychological, emotional, and perhaps physical withdrawal from a sport or activity the athlete formerly pursued and enjoyed.

CONCEPT & APPLICATION 10.15

Concept An athlete's perception of the conditions associated with sports training and involvement will determine the nature of her commitment and possible withdrawal.
Application For an athlete to enjoy her commitment to sport, she must perceive the rewards to be high and the stress-induced costs to be low. In addition, perceived satisfaction and investment must remain high, while attractive alternatives to continued involvement must be viewed as low. It is unrealistic to expect an athlete to remain happily committed to her sport activity if these conditions are not present.

SYMPTOMS OF AND INTERVENTIONS FOR BURNOUT

Researchers have addressed and identified physiological and psychological symptoms associated with burnout in athletes. As summarized in table 10.3, the athlete experiences a reversal of many of the physiological benefits associated with exercise, suffers from a loss of appetite and libido, gets more colds and respiratory infections, loses weight, loses sleep, becomes irritable or depressed, experiences feelings of exhaustion, suffers a loss of self-esteem, and experiences a negative change in interpersonal interactions.

Burnout can be identified through symptoms listed in table 10.3, and through the administration of either the Maslach Burnout Inventory (MBI) (Maslach & Jackson, 1986) or the Eades Athletic Burnout Inventory (EABI) (Eades, 1991). The MBI is composed of 22 self-report items, while the EABI is composed of 36. When symptoms of burnout are identified, steps must be taken to reverse debilitating effects as soon as possible. In the case of overtraining and sports burnout, Fender (1989) proposed three possible interventions, or steps for addressing burnout. The first and primary step in addressing burnout is self-awareness. The athlete must first recognize he is suffering from burnout and communicate his feelings to a sympathetic parent, coach, or sport psychologist. After he has taken the first step, the next is to take time off from the offending activity. If symptoms are identified early, taking a few days off from practice might be all that is necessary. If burnout has progressed to the point of withdrawal, however, total rest and relaxation might be necessary for the athlete's well-being. Finally, arousal control strategies (e.g., meditation, self-talk, and imagery) may be used successfully.

Recall that the three phases of negative stress syndrome are staleness, overtraining, and burnout. With this in mind, it follows that the best way to address the debilitating effects of burnout is to intervene while still in the staleness stage. The wise and experienced coach will recognize the signs of staleness and overtraining before they escalate to burnout. If each athlete is treated as a valued individual, little justification exists for a coach or leader to allow the negative stress syndrome to progress to the final stage of burnout and withdrawal. However, self-inflicted burnout and withdrawal are also possibilities.

CONCEPT & APPLICATION 10.16

Concept A completely linear relationship does not exist between increased training and enhanced strength, endurance, and performance. *Application* The mistaken belief that "more is better" when it comes to sports training may lead to staleness, overtraining, and burnout. Coaches and trainers must carefully monitor their training regimens to assure that their efforts actually result in increased performance and positive affect.

Table 10.3

Physiological and Psychological Symptoms of Burnout.

Physiological Symptoms
1. Increased resting and exercise heart rate
2. Icreased resting systolic blood pressure
3. Increased muscle soreness and chronic muscle fatigue
4. Increased presence of biochemical indicators of stress in the blood
5. Increased sleep loss
6. Increased colds and respiratory infections
7. Decreased body weight
8. Decreased maximal aerobic power
9. Decreased muscle glycogen
10. Decreased libido and appetite

Psychological Symptoms
1. Increased mood disturbances
2. Increased perception of physical, mental, and emotional exhaustion
3. Decreased self-esteem
4. Negative change in the quality of personal interaction with others (cynicism, lack of feeling, impersonal relating)
5. Negative cumulative reaction to chronic everyday stress as opposed to acute doses of stress

RECOMMENDATIONS FOR ATHLETES, COACHES, AND PARENTS

Few empirical studies of burnout have been conducted. An exception to this observation is a pair of studies reported by Gould, Udry, Tuffey, and Loehr (1996a); and Gould, Tuffey, Udry, and Loehr (1996b). These investigations involved the study of burnout in 30 junior tennis burnouts and 32 non-burnout comparison tennis players who were similar in age, playing experience, and sex. In the first study (1996a), the burned-out and non-burned-out junior tennis players were compared on a number of quantitative measures. In the second study (1996b), a qualitative analysis was conducted on 10 tennis players identified quantitatively in the first study as being most burned out. While a number of interesting results came out of these studies, two were of great importance. The first was that from a demographic, psychological, personal, and behavioral perspective, it was possible to differentiate between the two groups of athletes. The burned-out tennis players, in contrast to comparison players, exhibited higher burnout scores, were lower in motivation, were more withdrawn, were less likely to use coping strategies, and differed on a variety of perfectionism sub-scales (e.g., showed greater concern over mistakes). The second result of import was that through the qualitative analyses, recommendations were given to players, coaches, and parents as to how to avoid burnout in junior tennis. These recommendations are shown in tabular form in table 10.4.

Table 10.4

Recommendations (Advice) Given to Players, Coaches, and Parents on How to Avoid Burnout in Junior Tennis Players.

Gould et al., 1996b

Target Population	Recommendations
Player	1. Play for your own reasons. 2. Balance tennis with other things in your life. 3. If it is not fun then don't play. 4. Try to make practice and games fun. 5. Relax and take time off occasionally.
Coach	1. Cultivate personal involvement with player. 2. Establish two-way communication with athlete. 3. Solicit and utilize player input. 4. Work to understand player feelings and perspective.
Parent	1. Recognize the optimal amount of "pushing" needed. 2. Back off and lessen involvement. 3. Reduce importance of winning. 4. Show support and empathy for child's efforts. 5. Don't coach if not the coach, and separate roles if you are the coach. 6. Solicit child's input.

PSYCHOLOGY OF ATHLETIC INJURIES

Physical factors such as overtraining, equipment failure, and poor playing conditions are believed to be the major factors contributing to athletic injuries. Evidence is mounting, however, to suggest that psychological factors play an important role in the incidence, prevention, and rehabilitation of athletic injuries. Psychological factors associated with athletic injuries is the topic of this section of the psychobiology of sport and exercise chapter. Topics to be discussed include (a) psychological predictors of athletic injuries, (b) interventions to prevent injuries, (c) psychological trauma associated with injuries, and (d) rehabilitation of athletic injuries.

PSYCHOLOGICAL PREDICTORS OF ATHLETIC INJURY

A model for explaining the interactive relationship between athletic injury and such psychological factors as personality, life stress, coping resources, the stress response, and potential interventions was proposed by Andersen and Williams (1988). The Andersen and Williams model of stress and athletic injury is illustrated in figure 10.8. The key element of the model is the **stress response.** The stress response in this model is similar to the stress process illustrated in figure 4.4 of chapter 4. A potentially stressful athletic situation requires the athlete to complete a **cognitive appraisal** of the associated demands, resources, and consequences. If, in the athlete's judgment, the situational demands outstrip

Figure 10.8

A model of stress and athletic injury (Andersen & Williams, 1988). From "A model of stress and athletic injury: Prediction and prevention" by M. B. Andersen and J. M. Williams, 1988, *Journal of Sport & Exercise Psychology* (Vol. 10, No. 3), p. 297. Copyright 1988 by Human Kinetics Publishers, Inc. Adapted with permission.

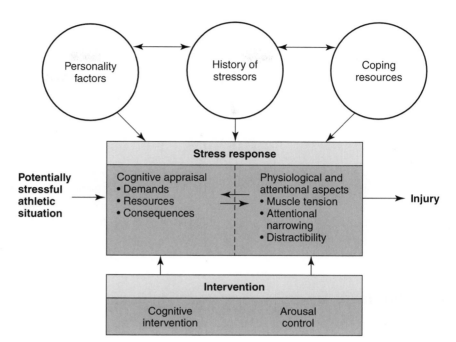

the personal resources needed to address the situation, the stress response will be significant. Conversely, if the athlete's perceived resources outweigh the demands, the stress response will be minimal. The elicitation of the stress response represents a perceived imbalance between the athlete's resources to cope with the demands of the situation and the actual demands. The elicitation of the stress response evokes selected physiological and attentional changes in the athlete. These changes include increased muscle tension, narrowing of the visual field, and increased distractibility. Each change is believed to enhance the chances of the athlete sustaining an athletic injury (Williams, Tonymon & Andersen, 1991). In addition to an imbalance between demands and resources, perceived consequences of the athletic situation can lead to the elicitation of the stress response. In essence, any cognitive appraisal that leads to the stress response puts the athlete at risk for injury. Factors that impact the stress response include personality of the athlete, history of stressors, coping resources, and potential interventions.

To reiterate, the key element of the model illustrated in figure 10.8 is the stress response. Whether or not psychological factors will contribute significantly to injury depends on the balance between an athlete's perceived ability to address a potentially threatening situation and the demands and consequences associated with the situation. If the situation results in a perceived imbalance (threat), the athlete will respond with increased muscle tension and inappropriately narrowed attention. It is the narrowed attention, attentional distractibility, and muscle tension that lead to a situation of increased vulnerability. As predicted by the model, athletes who score high on the ability to focus on a task experience fewer acute and chronic athletic injuries during the course of a season (Williams, Hogan & Andersen, 1993).

CONCEPT & APPLICATION 10.17

Concept   An athlete's perceived inability to respond to the demands of a potentially stressful athletic situation results in the stress response. The stress response in turn gives rise to increased muscle tension, narrowing of the visual field, and attentional distractibility.

Application   Once the athlete experiences the stress response, she is in a situation of heightened risk for injury. Every effort must be used to prevent this situation from developing in the first place.

As can be observed in figure 10.8, in addition to the key element of adjusting to the stress response, three other factors mediate the relationship between a potentially stressful athletic situation and an injury. These three factors include personality of the athlete, history of stressors, and coping resources available to the athlete. Each of these three factors will be briefly discussed.

Personality Factors
Personality factors that might have an effect upon how the athlete responds to a stressful athletic situation include hardiness, locus of control, sense of coherence, competitive trait anxiety, and intrinsic motivation. As can be observed in figure 10.8, personality factors affect the stress response directly, as well as indirectly, through history of stressors. They are not directly related to the incidence of athletic injuries, but are directly and indirectly related to how the athlete reacts to the stress response, which in turn directly predicts athletic injury (Hanson, McCullagh & Tonymon, 1992; Jackson, Jarrett, Barley, Kausch, Swanson & Powell, 1978; Diekhoff, 1984; Kelly, 1990; Lysens, Steverlynck, Vanden Auweele, Lefevre, Renson, Claessens & Ostyn, 1984).

History of Stressors
Factors incorporated under the category of history of stressors include stressful life events, daily hassles, and previous injuries. Taken together, these factors are believed to have an interactive effect upon the stress response leading to athletic injury.

Life Stress and Daily Hassles   As previously illustrated in figure 10.4, life stress is related to the incidence of illness. This relationship between stressful life events and increased illness is extended to the athletic domain. Life stress and daily hassles tend to undermine the ability of the athlete to effectively address the stress response and associated physiological and attentional consequences that may lead to injury vulnerability (Hanson et al., 1992). Positive life stress includes such events as studying for examinations, developing social relationships, and raising a family. Negative life stress includes such events as divorce, death in the family, and loss of job. The more life stress the athlete experiences, the greater is the incidence and severity of athletic injury. Moderating variables associated with this relationship include social support and playing status. The impact of life stress is moderated by an athlete's social support system and by whether or not he is a starter on his athletic team. Being a starter is more stressful than being a nonstarter and leads to increased incidence of athletic injury. Additionally, lack of social support leads to increased incidence of athletic injury. Social support is related to the notion of being part of a group of caring people, such as a family (Petrie, 1993b, 1993c).

Previous Injury How an athlete adjusts to a previous injury will determine its impact on the stress response to a potentially stressful athletic situation. Athletes who are worried about the recurrence of an injury, or about whether or not they have fully recovered from a previous injury, are vulnerable to further injury. This is the case because they will tend to be distracted and inappropriately focused during competition. As indicated in figure 10.8, negative appraisal may result if an athlete is psychologically unprepared to return to competition after sustaining an injury. Negative cognitive appraisal will almost certainly occur if an athlete is psychologically unprepared to return to competition. Intuitively, previous injury is an important factor to consider in the relationship between past history and the prediction of future injury or reinjury. Conversely, learning from the mistakes associated with past injuries can lower the probability of future injuries. In this regard, Rose and Jevne (1993) argue that there are *lessons* to be learned from past injuries, and that if these lessons are appropriately applied, they can result in a reduction in future injuries. Macchi and Crossman (1996) report that as a result of an injury sustained in ballet, many dancers learn to use correct technique, stretch more, and modify exercises that may lead to injury.

What if the injury an athlete sustains results in the end of her career. In this case we are not talking about the relationship between a previous injury and vulnerability for a future injury, but about the psychological well-being of the athlete. Some research has suggested that a career-ending injury results in decrement in self-esteem and life satisfaction. More recent research, however, has concluded that a decrease in life satisfaction results only if the individual suffering the career-ending injury had strong aspirations regarding a future career in professional sports (Kleiber & Brock, 1992).

Coping Resources

Coping resources available to the athlete include general coping behavior, social support, stress management techniques, and prescribed or self-prescribed medication. Collectively, these factors are believed to have an interactive effect on whether or not the athlete will experience the stress response.

Coping Behaviors Any behavior that assists an individual in dealing with a stressful situation is considered to be a **coping behavior.** The use of coping strategies or behaviors to address high-stress situations was discussed in detail in chapter 6. Coping behaviors are highly individualistic and varied in nature. In *Gone With the Wind,* for example, Scarlett O'Hara's strategy for coping with many stressful events was to say to herself, "I will think about it tomorrow." Well-developed general coping behaviors have been linked with the reduced incidence of athletic injuries in several research investigations. Hanson et al. (1992), for example, reported that coping resources are associated with reduced severity and frequency of track and field athlete injuries.

Social Support Social support is one of the important coping resources available to athletes to reduce the debilitating effect of the stress response (Petrie, 1993). Individuals and groups that provide social support for the athlete include parents, friends, coach, teammates, fraternity/sorority, clubs, and religious groups. In a study reported by Smith, Smoll, and Ptacek (1990), 20 different individuals or groups were identified that might provide social support to the athlete.

Stress Management Many athletes utilize stress management and cognitive intervention techniques as coping strategies for controlling the stress response. Often these same techniques are used by the athlete as cognitive intervention and arousal control strategies to buffer the effects of the stress response once it has developed. Research has demonstrated that effective reduction in the stress response is associated with a reduction in the number and severity of injuries sustained by athletes (Davis, 1991; Kerr & Goss, 1996).

Medication Drugs are used by athletes for various legitimate and illegitimate reasons, including performance enhancement, recreation, injury treatment, and pain management. Many drugs have the ability to influence the stress response, and thus the probability of injury. For example, animal and human research suggests that the side effects of anabolic steroids may include aggression, depression, anxiety, and social withdrawal. All these psychological effects have the potential to reduce the coping resources of the athlete (Gregg & Rejeski, 1990).

CONCEPT & APPLICATION 10.18

Concept Factors that determine whether or not the athlete will experience the stress response include the athlete's personality, history of stress, and coping resources.

Application From a psychological perspective, knowledge about these three factors may be useful in helping the athlete reduce the probability of injury. Understanding the person's personality and stress history will help the coach identify at-risk individuals. Assisting the athlete in developing coping skills and supportive social relationships will help her deal effectively with a potentially stressful environment.

An injured athlete
enjoys the
encouragement and
support of friends.
Courtesy Ball State
University Sports
Information

INTERVENTIONS

Two entire chapters in this book (chapters 5 and 6) have been dedicated to
arousal control techniques and cognitive-behavioral interventions that may be
utilized to enhance athletic performance as well as to inhibit the development of
the stress response. As illustrated in figure 10.8, these interventions play an
important role in determining whether or not a potentially stressful athletic
situation will lead to conditions conducive to athletic injury. These interventions
may include but are not restricted to cognitive restructuring, thought stopping,
confidence training, fostering team cohesion, relaxation skills, autogenic
training, meditation, hypnosis, imagery, attention control, and medication
modification.

PSYCHOLOGICAL ADJUSTMENT TO INJURY

There is a certain amount of physical pain associated with an athletic injury. In
addition, there is potential damage to muscle, bone, cartilage, and ligaments. All
of these require time to mend and heal. The damage to the athlete
psychologically is much more subtle. Yet in a sense, the psychological damage
may actually be more traumatic and long lasting than the physical damage. At
the time of a severe athletic injury, the athlete suffers significant mood
disturbance, with an increase in negative moods such as depression, anxiety, and
anger. At this time the athlete also suffers a decrement in positive moods such as
self-esteem and confidence. The mood disturbance may not return to pre-injury
levels until the athlete has been fully rehabilitated (Leddy, Lambert and Ogles,
1994; Quackenbush & Crossman, 1994; Smith, Stuart, Wiese-Bjornstal,
Milliner, O'Fallon & Crowson, 1993).

To further understand the psychological adjustments that an injured athlete goes through, models of psychological adjustment have been proposed. They are generally of two types: stage and cognitive appraisal models. Stage models conceptualize the psychological adjustments in terms of stages, or steps, that the athlete must pass through before full recovery can take place. Such stage models are patterned after models of grief. In this context, grief is defined as a response to a "loss" associated with an injury, as opposed to the loss of a loved one through death. As explained by Weiss and Troxel (1986) and Evans and Hardy (1995), the injured athlete goes through four stages that begin with stress associated with injury. These are (a) the stressor (injury); (b) cognitive appraisal of the situation, stressor, and response resources; (c) emotional response, and (d) consequences of stress. Cognitive appraisal models are similar to stage models, but reject the notion that the athlete passes sequentially through specific stages (Brewer, 1994). Based upon situational and personality factors, the athlete makes a cognitive appraisal of his ability to cope that gives rise to emotional and behavioral responses.

PSYCHOLOGICAL FACTORS INFLUENCING REHABILITATION

Following the incidence of serious injury (leading to being incapacitated three weeks or more), athletes experience significant disturbance of mood state. Mood disturbances occur within 24 hours following injury and dissipate as successful recovery progresses. The more serious the injury is, the more pronounced is the mood disturbance. It is believed that early detection and treatment of mood disturbance may facilitate the athlete's successful rehabilitation.

Research also suggests that athletes possess psychological profiles that will make them candidates for either hastened rehabilitation or slowed rehabilitation. Just as there are adherers and nonadherers to exercise programs, there are also adherers and nonadherers to injury rehabilitation programs. Early identification of likely nonadherers could lead to early psychological intervention, leading further to greater adherence to the prescribed rehabilitation program. Psychological variables of interest include goal orientation, intrinsic motivation, self-esteem, pain tolerance, and degree to which scheduling and environmental conditions are important. An athlete who presents an ego goal orientation, low intrinsic motivation, low self-esteem, and low pain tolerance, and who is

CONCEPT & APPLICATION 10.19

Concept Adherence to injury rehabilitation is related to selected psychological factors.
Application The early identification of athletes who are likely to experience adherence problems

should help the therapist in developing effective cognitive intervention strategies.

bothered by inflexible schedules and environmental conditions, is a candidate for slowed injury rehabilitation. Conversely, an athlete who presents a task goal orientation, high intrinsic motivation, high self-esteem, and high pain tolerance, and who is not bothered by schedules and the environment, is a candidate for hastened injury rehabilitation (Duda, Smart & Tappe, 1989; Green, 1992).

Psychological interventions that have proven to be effective include goal setting, use of imagery, counseling, and social support (Brewer, Jeffers, Petipas & Van Raalte, 1994). Goal setting allows the injured athlete to work towards predetermined markers indicative of rehabilitation adherence. An athlete recuperating from a knee injury, for example, would be able to set strength-gain goals that could hasten recovery. Imagery can be utilized by the athlete in visualizing goal achievement, or in carrying out specific instructions given by the trainer. The successful fulfillment of plans, instructions, and goals is visualized before these things are actually attempted. Counseling with members of the athletic training staff is also beneficial in helping the athlete maintain her rehabilitation schedule. Finally, attention given to the athlete by the athletic trainers and coach constitute social support, but of even greater importance is the support of family and close friends. Efforts to include family and friends in to the rehabilitation process can result in an effective intervention.

DRUG ABUSE BY ATHLETES

In writing this section on the use and abuse of drugs by athletes, I have relied upon four main sources: Anshel, 1993; Bahrke, 1993; NSCA, 1993 and Stone, 1993. These four references reflect the best scientific sources available that address both physical and psychological effects of drug abuse on athletes.

While of little scientific value, anecdotal evidence of drug abuse by high-profile athletes heightens our awareness of this problem. Ben Johnson, a Canadian world-record holder in the 100 meters, tested positive for anabolic steroids following his gold medal race in the 1988 Seoul Olympics. He set a new world record of 9.79, beating his old world record of 9.83 by .04 seconds. The International Olympic Committee (IOC) declared Johnson's race null and void, stripped him of his gold medal, and awarded it to Carl Lewis of the United States (Johnson & Moore, 1988). Lyle Alzado, a former National Football League (NFL) star, admitted to using anabolic steroids and human growth hormone for purposes of performance enhancement and blamed his drug abuse for a brain lymphoma (cancer) that a short time later would result in his death (Alzado, 1991). Alzado gave personal testimony to the incredible mood swings that he said made him mean, aggressive, and violent both on and off the field of play. In his dying words, he exclaimed, "It was addicting, mentally addicting. I just didn't feel strong unless I was taking them" (p. 24).

In previous sections of this chapter we have learned of athletes who succumb to eating disorders for purposes of performance enhancement. We have also learned of athletes who overtrain and experience burnout in an effort to perform at a level higher than that of their competitors. Similarly, in this section we learn

Speed skaters must be mentally and physically prepared for competition in order to avoid injury. Courtesy Corel Photo CD/Winter Sports

of athletes who turn to the use of drugs in an effort to gain an unfair advantage over their competitors. There are at least three problems associated with the use of drugs to enhance athletic performance (Anshel, 1993). The first one, which I have just mentioned, is the problem of ethics. Because drug use for purposes of performance enhancement is illegal, it is ethically wrong to take them in an effort to obtain an unfair advantage over the opposition. The second problem has to do with the potentially addictive properties of drugs. Once an athlete starts taking a drug for performance enhancement purposes, it may be difficult for her to stop taking them later on. Drugs may be physically and/or psychologically addictive. A third problem is related to the potentially lethal effects of drugs on the health and well-being of athletes. While it is often difficult to prove that the abuse of a drug led to the death or serious illness of an athlete, it is difficult to ignore the "gut-wrenching" testimonials of victims such as Lyle Alzado.

In this section I will (a) briefly address the hoped-for benefits and negative consequences of certain banned substances, (b) summarize a position statement of the NSCA, and (c) conclude with some suggestions for combating drug abuse.

PSYCHOPHYSIOLOGICAL EFFECTS OF CERTAIN BANNED SUBSTANCES

Each of the drugs or banned substances that I will mention in this brief review has both hoped-for benefit (the reason it is taken by the athlete) and a negative consequence. In some cases the negative consequences are well documented, but in other cases, due to limitations of research, they are not. I will first address the use and abuse of anabolic steroids because of their widespread use by athletes seeking greater size, aggressiveness, and strength.

Anabolic-Androgenic Steroids

Anabolic steroids are hormones that stimulate protein anabolism in the body. Athletes ingest anabolic steroids because they believe that they are responsible for alterations in body composition that result in greater size, strength, and power. What we call anabolic steroids are a group of synthetic derivatives of the male hormone testosterone that have been modified so that their presence in the bloodstream is prolonged. They have both an anabolic effect (increasing muscular strength and size) and an androgenic (masculinizing) effect on the user. Consequently, what we commonly refer to as anabolic steroids are really anabolic-androgenic steroids that are synthetically derived to increase muscle mass while at the same time minimizing the masculinizing, or androgenic, effect (Bahrke & Yesalis, 1993). While some researchers still maintain that the primary ergogenic benefits of anabolic steroids are derived from psychological effects, the physiological justification for application of anabolic steroids by athletes includes such results as increased body weight and mass, altered body composition, increased muscle size and strength, and increased blood volume and number of red blood cells (Stone, 1993). In addition to expected and desired physical changes, expected and desired behavioral changes include increased aggressiveness, competitiveness, training drive, and feelings of well-being.

If it can be assumed that all of the above reasons for taking anabolic hormones are true, one can readily see why they are banned! They could provide the user an illegal and unethical advantage over other athletes who do not use them. The prolonged use of large does of anabolic steroids is associated with a number of very disturbing side effects. Steroid use is psychologically addicting and may also be physically addicting. If as stated by Lyle Alzado, the athlete does not feel strong unless he is taking steroids, it is easy to see how he could become psychologically addicted to them. The appearance and progressive development of male secondary sex characters is a very obvious consequence of anabolic steroid use among young males and females. It has been suggested by many researchers that the abuse of anabolic steroids may lead to poor health. Organs that are particularly susceptible to negative consequences of anabolic steroid abuse are those, such as the kidneys and liver, that are responsible for the transport, metabolism, and detoxification of the drug. Since the liver serves a central role in the metabolism of drugs, it is not surprising that it is frequently damaged by their use and abuse. If a drug has a negative effect upon even one part of the body, the functional capacity of the entire body can suffer (Stone, 1993). If one of the hoped-for effects of anabolic steroid use is increased aggressiveness, competitiveness, and training drive, it is not surprising that a negative by-product of its abuse could be some sort of psychological aberration resulting in violent and antisocial behavior.

Stimulants

Stimulants, such as amphetamines and cocaine, increase the rate and work capacity of the central nervous system, respiratory system, and heart. The neural-stimulating and cardiac-stimulating effects of these drugs can provide a physiological advantage to the athlete by inhibiting mental and physical fatigue. The illegal and unethical use of stimulants may result in performance enhancement, but not without some danger to the athlete. These drugs are physically and/or psychologically addicting and their use may lead to serious health problems.

Depressants

Depressants, such as barbiturates, sedative-hypnotics, and alcohol, are designed to relive tension, depression, and anxiety in the athlete. Theoretically, this could help the fearful and anxious athlete by providing a steadying effect. These drugs, however, do not always have the desired effect on the athlete. Depressants may actually have the effect of reducing inhibition, reducing judgment, and heightening risk-taking behavior, which may in turn result in poor as opposed to superior performance. These drugs are also highly addictive, making it difficult to quit using them without severe withdrawal symptoms. As with all drugs, their abuse may lead to serious health consequences due to damage to organs responsible for metabolizing them.

Other Banned Drugs

Other drugs that have been banned by the International Olympic Committee (IOC) include diuretics, hallucinogens, and beta-adrenergic blockers. Diuretics are sometimes used by wrestlers, jockeys, and boxers to artificially induce an acute reduction in body weight through fluid elimination via the urine. Negative effects of diuretics may include nausea, heat stroke, blood clotting, reduced blood volume, and muscle cramps. The primary purpose of hallucinogens is to alter the perception of incoming stimuli. Because hallucinogens inhibit response and decision time as well as attentional focus, they tend to inhibit athletic performance instead of facilitating it. Beta-adrenergic blockers are used to steady and slow the heart rate, which may decrease anxiety/tension and indirectly enhance athletic performance.

POSITION STATEMENT OF NSCA

Athletes competing in the sport of weight lifting/power lifting have received more publicity for abusing drugs (particularly anabolic steroids) than any other group of athletes. In a sense this publicity has tarnished the reputation of this sport and profession. In an effort to protect the image of the sport, and the athletes who compete fairly in the sport, the National Strength and Conditioning Association (NSCA) published a position statement in opposition to the use of drugs in general and anabolic steroids in particular (NSCA, 1993). The position statement is based upon a comprehensive survey and analysis of the scientific literature dealing with the effects of anabolic steroids on athletic performance. In the paragraphs that follow I have paraphrased the ten statements that make up the NSCA Position Statement of 1993.

1. The use of anabolic-androgenic steroids (AAS) by athletes is illegal and punishable by law. Coaches or NSCA members who promote the use of AAS risk NSCA censure with potential legal penalties.

2. Strength and conditioning professionals must not condone the use of AAS. There is no compromise on this issue.

3. Competitive advantages may be derived from the use of AAS by users. These advantages may come in the form of increased lean body mass, decreased body fat, and increased strength and power, which may result in enhanced performance.

4. Those who use AAS face increased health risks, which can include liver disease, adverse effects on blood lipids, stroke and/or myocardial infarction, temporary infertility, and unwanted masculinization. Psychological aberrations are possible.

5. Both the risks and the benefits of AAS have been exaggerated by the lay press and general public, resulting in confusion and misinformation. The NSCA encourages full disclosure of known risks and benefits associated with AAS use.

6. Scientific investigations are encouraged that study the prevalence of AAS use in scholastic, collegiate, and professional athletes. Studies investigating the short- and long-term health risks associated with AAS use are also encouraged.

7. In order for drug testing to be a deterrent to AAS usage, it should be equally applied to all sports and levels of athletics.

8. A win-at-all-costs philosophy creates enormous pressure on athletes. Society in general and individuals that are supportive of athletics must work to change the philosophy that an athlete must win in order to be successful.

9. It is the aim of the NSCA to discourage AAS use and promote athletic performance that is based upon proper training methods and fair play.

10. The NSCA denounces the use of AAS for the purpose of performance enhancement.

COMBATING DRUG ABUSE IN SPORT

According to Anshel (1993), there are traditional as well as new approaches for combating drug use among athletes. Traditional approaches include deterrence, education, life skill strategies, alternative activities, and peer programs. New approaches for combating drug use among athletes are classified under the categories of cognitive and behavioral techniques. A careful reading of these two broad approaches (traditional and new) suggests that the real difference between them is that the new approaches are much more situation-specific. Focusing upon the new approaches, cognitive techniques utilize intellectual and psychological methods to influence behavior and attitude.Conversely, behavioral techniques shape the athlete's environment in ways that will elicit desirable responses and behaviors from the athlete.

Cognitive Techniques

Using cognitive techniques, the coach utilizes support groups among the players to encourage drug abstinence. The coach shows concern for athletes, sets limits on unacceptable behavior, develops team policy, and teaches athletes specific coping skills to deal with the pressure to excel. Coaches much be aware of each athlete's mental status, both in and out of the sport environment. Coaches can also help athletes by making them feel part of the team by seeking their input on important team decisions.

Behavioral Techniques

The vast majority of athletes take drugs for the purpose of performance enhancement. Therefore, the focus of behavioral techniques should be upon teaching athletes alternative ways to enhance performance that do not include the use of drugs. These alternative methods to increased performance are really traditional, since they include teaching motor skills and strategies that lead to increased performance. Coaches do not always spend much time in practice helping individual athletes improve their personal skills. They may instead run scrimmages in which individual skills are largely overlooked and assumed to already exist. Other behavioral techniques that are effective include peer involvement in drug education and drug prevention efforts. Young athletes are much more likely to take advice from an admired peer than from an adult. In fact, many athletes get involved in the use of drugs because they have listened to an admired peer who was not setting a good example. In setting up a drug-free environment, the coach may want to introduce mandatory drug testing, a clear course of action when drug abuse is detected, and interesting activities to engage athletes during free time. Athletes are much less likely to take drugs for purpose of performance enhancement if they fear detection through mandatory drug testing.

Better and more accurate research is needed relative to the use and abuse of drugs among scholastic, collegiate, and professional athletes. Underreporting is a serious limitation of research involving drug use among athletes. It is even more difficult to get accurate information from athletes about their coach's direct or indirect role in encouraging drug use for purposes of performance enhancement. Accurate data must be collected in a manner that would make it impossible to detect the name of the athlete reporting a result or the name of a coach associated with a particular athlete. This can only be accomplished if two conditions exist. First, data must be truly anonymous and untraceable, even in the face of a court subpoena. Second, the athletes filling out the questionnaires must believe that the data are truly anonymous and untraceable, even in the face of a court subpoena.

CONCEPT & APPLICATION 10.20

Concept Athletes are under tremendous pressure from coaches, parents, peers, and themselves to exhibit superior athletic performance. It does not seem to be enough to do your best any more; you must be better than everyone else. Since this is an unrealistic expectation, it is not too surprising that some athletes turn to "performance-enhancing" drugs.

Application It is the personal responsibility of all coaches and parents to make sure that no athlete they are associated with feels the pressure to excel to such a degree that she would resort to

"performance-enhancing" drugs to accomplish this. Coaches, teachers, and athletes must "buy into" the notion of task, or mastery, goal orientation, as opposed to ego orientation. Athletics should be about becoming the best that you can become, but not necessarily about being better than everyone else. Mandatory drug testing can serve as a deterrent to athletes prone to using drugs for purposes of performance enhancement, but it cannot address the deeper issue of why an athlete would resort to such illegal behavior in the first place.

SUMMARY   The chapter on the psychobiology of sport and exercise was divided up into four main areas, with subdivisions within each. The four main chapter headings included exercise psychology staleness, overtraining, and burnout; the psychology of athletic injuries; and drug abuse by athletes.

The broad area of exercise psychology was further subdivided into (a) general psychological benefits of exercise; (b) evidence of chronic benefits; (c) treating anxiety and depression; (d) theoretical explanations for positive relationships; (e) exercise adherence and determinants; (f) theories of exercise behavior; (g) fitness as a moderator of life stress; (h) the immune system, HIV, cancer, and exercise; and (i) social physique anxiety, exercise addiction, and eating disorders.

The psychological benefits of both chronic and acute exercise were considered. Numerous individual studies and three reviews were cited to substantiate the positive benefits of chronic exercise on mental health. Evidence suggests that the psychological benefits of a consistent and well-designed exercise program are as impressive as the physiological benefits. Several theoretical explanations for the positive relationship between exercise and improved mental health were considered. These explanations include the cognitive behavioral hypothesis, the social interaction hypothesis, and the distraction hypothesis. Physiological explanations include the cardiovascular fitness hypothesis, the amine hypothesis, and the endorphin hypothesis. Exercise adherence and exercise determinants were discussed within the framework of Sallis and Hovell's (1990) notion of the natural history of exercise. Theories of exercise behavior discussed included the theory of reasoned action, the theory of planned behavior, the transtheoretical model, and social cognitive theory. Fitness was discussed as a moderator of life stress. Exercise and fitness are viewed as buffers against life stress, or in terms of stress inoculation. Important connections between exercise and the immune system, the human immunodeficiency virus (HIV), and cancer were discussed. While too much exercise can compromise the responsiveness of the immune system, moderate exercise is viewed as an important moderator of HIV and cancer. Finally, the interactive relationships between exercise addiction, physique anxiety, and the incidence of eating disorders were explored.

The second main division of the chapter was on staleness, overtraining, and burnout in athletes. This section was further subdivided into discussions of (a) the process leading to burnout in sport, (b) overtraining and mood disturbance, (c) theoretical models of stress and burnout, (d) symptoms of and interventions for burnout, and (e) recommendations for athletes, coaches, and parents. The process leading to burnout in athletes was discussed using Silva's (1990) model of positive and negative adaptation to training stress. The three components of the training stress syndrome were identified as staleness, overtraining, and burnout. Schmidt and Stein's (1991) investment model of burnout was introduced. This model proposes two kinds of athletic commitment and withdrawal. The critical distinction between burnout and withdrawal lies in perceived alternatives and investments. In addition to Schmidt and Stein's investment model, Smith's cognitive-affective model of stress and burnout was introduced and discussed. Smith's (1986) model of burnout is a four-stage model that parallels stages of the stress process. The situational, cognitive, physiologic, and behavioral components of the general stress process are paralleled by the situation-specific components of the burnout process. Symptoms of burnout and suggestions for intervention were discussed, along with specific recommendation for athletes, coaches, and parents.

Topics discussed under the heading of the psychology of athletic injuries included (a) psychological predictors of athletic injuries, (b) interventions to prevent injuries, (c) psychological trauma associated with injuries, and (d) rehabilitation of athletic injuries. Physical factors such as overtraining, equipment failure, and poor playing conditions are believed to be the major factors contributing to athletic injuries. Evidence is mounting, however, to suggest that psychological factors play an important role in the incidence of sports-related injury. A model proposed by Andersen and Williams (1988) to explain the interactive relationship between athletic injury and such psychological factors as personality, life stress, coping resources, the stress process response, and potential interventions was introduced and discussed. Psychological factors influencing injury rehabilitation were also introduced. Just as psychological intervention may be used to reverse the debilitating effects of the stress response, intervention strategies are effective in enhancing injury recovery and rehabilitation. Research has linked rehabilitation and rehabilitation program adherence to treatment efficacy, social support, goal and task mastery, self-motivation, high pain tolerance, and the ability to be less bothered by scheduling and environmental conditions.

The final section of the chapter dealt with the important topic of drug abuse by athletes. Subsections of this topic included (a) psychophysiological effects of certain banned substances, (b) discussion of a position statement by the National Strength and Conditioning Association (NSCA), and (c) suggestions for combating drug abuse in sport. Drug abuse by athletes is associated with three main problems. First, the use of drugs by athletes for the purpose of performance enhancement is illegal, and therefore unethical. Second, the use of drugs for purposes of performance enhancement may be addictive. Once an athlete starts taking a drug it may be difficult for him to stop taking it. Third, the use of drugs may be detrimental to the health of the athlete, and in some cases, lethal. The section concludes with suggestions as to how the use of drugs by athletes seeking to improve performance can be discouraged.

REVIEW QUESTIONS

1. Differentiate between the terms *chronic exercise* and *acute exercise.*

2. What is a delayed anxiolytic response? Under what circumstance is it usually observed?

3. What is meant by *stress inoculation* relative to exercise? Relate some evidence for the effect.

4. What are some variables that have a mediating effect upon the relationship between exercise and psychological benefit? Explain.

5. Summarize the general psychological benefits of chronic and acute exercise.

6. Summarize the specific effects of chronic and acute exercise on depression and anxiety.

7. Differentiate between the terms *aerobic exercise* and *anaerobic exercise.*

8. What is the cause-and-effect relationship between exercise and positive mental health? Explain.

9. Identify, explain, and summarize three psychologically based theoretical explanations for the relationship between exercise and improved mental health.

10. Identify, explain, and summarize three physiologically based theoretical explanations for the relationship between exercise and improved mental health.

11. Diagram and explain Sallis and Hovell's (1990) natural history of exercise.

12. What are the characteristics of individuals likely to adopt a vigorous exercise lifestyle?

13. What are the primary determinants of adherence and nonadherence to a vigorous exercise program?

14. Identify, differentiate between, and explain four theories of exercise behavior.

15. Discuss the concept of fitness as a moderator of life stress.

16. What is the nature of the relationship between the immune system, cancer, and exercise?

17. Should an individual who has acquired the human immunodeficiency virus (HIV) engage in moderate physical exercise? Give reasons to justify your answer.

18. What is the nature of the relationship between social physique anxiety and exercise behavior?

19. Discuss the interactive relationship between the terms *exercise addiction, super-adherer,* and *obligatory runner.* Can we have too much of a good thing? Explain.

20. Provide a definitive explanation of the two major forms of pathogenic eating disorders.

21. Discuss the concept of unhealthy eating behavior as it relates to excessive exercise, fasting, and strict dieting.

22. What is the anorexia analogue hypotheses? Is there evidence to support this hypothesis? Explain.

23. Provide a detailed explanation of Silva's (1990) model for positive and negative adaptation to training stress.

24. Discuss the relationship between staleness, overtraining, and burnout. What is the training stress syndrome?

25. What is the relationship between overtraining and mood disturbance? Explain.

26. Identify, differentiate between, and thoroughly discuss the two models of burnout introduced in this chapter.

27. Identify symptoms of burnout and interventions that might be effective in treatment.

28. Discuss recommendations to athletes, coaches, and parents for avoiding staleness, overtraining, and burnout in athletes.

29. Provide a detailed explanation of Andersen and Williams' (1988) model of stress and athletic injury.

30. What are the possible steps for minimizing the occurrence and effect of the stress response relative to athletic injuries?

31. Identify and discuss the psychological factors that influence an athlete's injury rehabilitation.

32. Identify and discuss three general problems associated with the use of illegal drugs for the purpose of enhancing athletic performance.

33. Why do some athletes take anabolic steroids? What are the potential dangers associated with taking these drugs for the purpose of performance enhancement?

34. Why do some athletes take stimulants and depressants? What are the potential dangers associated with taking these drugs for the purpose of performance enhancement?

35. What are some of the other drugs that some athletes take? Why do they take these drugs? What are some of the potential dangers associated with their use?

36. Is there a clear cause-and-effect link between taking drugs such as anabolic steroids and improved athletic performance? Discuss this controversial issue. Refer to some of the references cited before completing this question.

37. Discuss measures that may be effective in combating drug abuse among athletes.

GLOSSARY

acquired immune deficiency syndrome (AIDS) Caused by the human immunodeficiency virus, the inability of the human immune system to combat disease.

acute exercise Short-duration, isolated bouts of exercise lasting approximately 30 minutes.

aerobic exercise Continuous and rhythmic exercise in which a sufficient supply of oxygen is available to the exerciser.

amine hypothesis Hypothesis that increased secretion of neurotransmitters associated with exercise is responsible for improved mental health.

anabolic steroids Hormones that stimulate protein anabolism in the body.

anaerobic exercise High-intensity and short-duration exercise requiring a period of recovery to replenish stored energy.

anorexia analogue hypothesis Hypothesis that anorexics and obligatory runners share a common core of personality characteristics.

anorexia nervosa Pathogenic eating disorder characterized by bizarre dieting behaviors and rapid weight loss.

bulimia nervosa Pathogenic eating disorder characterized by binge eating and vomiting to remain thin.

burnout Exhaustive psychophysiological response to repeated unsuccessful efforts to meet the demands of training stress.

cardiovascular fitness hypothesis Hypothesis that improved mental health associated with exercise is due to improved cardiovascular fitness.

chronic exercise A daily or regular exercise program across a long period of time.

cognitive appraisal Mental evaluation of a stressful situation.

cognitive behavioral hypothesis Hypothesis that exercise encourages and generates positive thoughts and feelings that serve to counteract negative mood states.

coping behavior Behavior that assists the athlete in dealing with a challenging or stressful situation.

delayed anxiolytic response Phenomenon that beneficial reduction in anxiety does not manifest itself until sometime following an acute bout of exercise.

distraction hypothesis Hypothesis that exercise affords the disturbed individual an opportunity to be distracted from worries and frustrations.

eating disorder Pathogenic condition in which an individual engages in unhealthy eating behaviors, such as anorexia nervosa or bulimia nervosa.

endorphin hypothesis Hypothesis that exercise is associated with brain production of chemicals that have a "morphine-like" effect on the exerciser.

exercise addiction Psychophysiological dependence on a regular regimen of exercise.

exercise adherence The process of adhering or complying to a prescribed exercise program.

exercise self-efficacy Confidence that one can initiate and/or maintain a personal exercise program.

human immunodeficiency virus (HIV) Communicable virus that leads to the weakening of the human immune system.

investment model Psychological model that predicts conditions that promote continued participation, burnout, or withdrawal from athletic participation.

life stress Positive and negative stress associated with living.

meta-analysis Statistical summary and comparison of independent samples.

obligatory runner A runner who is addicted to exercise (*See* exercise addiction).

overtraining Psychophysiological malfunction and demonstrated inability of the athlete to adjust to the demands of training stress.

processes of change Interventions used in the transtheoretical model to move from one stage of exercise to another.

social interaction hypothesis Hypothesis that improved mental health associated with exercise is due to social interaction with friends and colleagues who are also exercising.

social physique anxiety Anxiety that people experience when they perceive that other people evaluate their physique negatively.

staleness Initial failure of the body to adapt to training stress.

stress inoculation The ability of individuals to insulate, protect, or inoculate themselves against the stresses of life through regular exercise.

stress response Psychophysiological response associated with a perceived inability to respond to the demands of an athletic situation.

super-adherer Exerciser who participates in and constantly trains for endurance events that require significant long-term effort and commitment.

training gain Positive adaptation to training stress resulting in an improvement in performance.

training stress Necessary by-product of the psychophysiological stress associated with training for competition.

training stress syndrome Training syndrome that begins with staleness and overtraining, and culminates in burnout.

transtheoretical model A stage theory of behavioral change. When applied to exercise, the model proposes that individuals pass through five dynamic stages in adopting healthy long-term exercise behavior.

SUGGESTED READINGS

Andersen, M. B., & Williams, J. M. (1988). A model of stress and athletic injury: Prediction and prevention. *Journal of Sport & Exercise Psychology, 10,* 294–306.

Anshel, M. H. (1993b). Psychology of drug use. In R. N. Singer, M. Murphey, & L. K. Tennant (Eds.), *Handbook of research on sport psychology* (pp. 851–876). New York: Macmillan.

Bernstein, L., Henderson, B. E., Hanisch, R., Sullivan-Halley, J., & Ross, R. K.(1994). Physical exercise and reduced risk of breast cancer in young women. *Journal of the National Cancer Insitute, 86,* 1403–1408.

Brown, J. D. (1991). Staying fit and staying well: Physical fitness as a moderator of life stress. *Journal of Personality and Social Psychology, 60,* 555–561.

Carron, A. V., Hausenblas, H. A., & Mack, D. (1996). Social influence and exercise: A meta-analysis. *Journal of Sport & Exercise Psychology, 18,* 1–16.

Crews, D. J., & Landers, D. M. (1987). A meta-analytic review of aerobic fitness and reactivity to psychosocial stressors. *Medicine and Science in Sports and Exercise, 19,* 114–120.

Dishman, R. K. (1987). Exercise adherence and habitual physical activity. In W. P. Morgan & S. E. Goldston (Eds.), *Exercise and Mental Health* (pp. 57–83). Washington, DC: Hemisphere.

Dishman, R. K. (1994). The measurement conundrum in exercise adherence research. *Medicine & Science in Sports and Exercise, 26,* 1382–1390.

Dishman, R. K., & Buckworth, J. (1996). Increasing physical activity: A quantitative analysis synthesis. *Medicine and Science in Sports and Exercise, 28,* 706–719.

Gorely, T., & Gordon, S. (1995). An examination of the transtheoretical model and exercise behavior in older adults. *Journal of Sports & Exercise Psychology, 17,* 312–324.

Gould, D., Udry, E., Tuffey, S., & Loehr, J. (1996a). Burnout in competitive junior tennis players: I. A quantitative psychological assessment. *The Sport Psychologist, 10,* 322–340.

Hanson, S. J., McCullagh, P., & Tonymon, P. (1992). The relationship of personality characteristics, life stress, and coping resources to athletic injury. *Journal of Sport & Exercise Psychology, 14,* 262–272.

Kerr, G., & Goss, J. (1996). The effects of a stress management program on injuries and stress levels. *Journal of Applied Sport Psychology, 8,* 109–117.

Kuipers, H. (1996). How much is too much? Performance aspects of overtraining. *Research Quarterly for Exercise and Sports, 67,* Supplement to No. 3, 65–69.

LaFontaine, T. P., DiLorenzo, T. M., Frensch, P. A., Stucky-Ropp, R. C., Bargman, E. P., & McDonald, D. G. (1992). Aerobic exercise and mood: A brief review, 1985–1990. *Sports Medicine, 13,* 160–170.

Lee, I. (1995). Exercise and physical health. Cancer and immune function. *Research Quarterly for Exercise and Sport, 66,* 286–291.

Long, B. C., & Van Stavel, R. (1995). Effects of exercise training on anxiety: A meta-analysis. *Journal of Applied Sport Psychology, 7,* 167–189.

Lox, C. L., McAuley, E., & Tucker, R. S. (1995). Exercise as an intervention for enhancing subjective well-being in an HIV-1 population. *Journal of Sport & Exercise Psychology, 17,* 345–362.

Marcus, B. H., & Simkin, L. R. (1994). The transtheoretical model: Applications to exercise behavior. *Medicine and Exercise in Sports and Exercise, 26,* 1400–1404.

Morgan, W. P., & O'Connor, P. J. (1988). Exercise and mental health. In R. K. Dishman (Ed.), *Exercise adherence: Its impact on public health* (pp. 91–121). Champaign, IL: Human Kinetics.

North, T. C., McCullagh, P., & Tran, Z. V. (1990). Effect of exercise on depression. In K. B. Pandolf & J. O. Holloszy (Eds.), *Exercise and Sport Science Reviews, 18,* 379–415. Baltimore: Williams & Wilkins.

Pate, R. R., et al. (1995). Physical activity and public health. *Journal of the American Medical Association, 273,* 402–407.

Petrie, T. A., & Stoever, S. (1993). The incidence of bulimia nervosa and pathogenic weight control behaviors in female collegiate gymnasts. *Research Quarterly for Exercise and Sport, 64,* 238–241.

Petruzzello, S. J., Landers, D. M., Hatfield, B. D., Kubitz, K. A., & Salazar, W. (1991). A meta-analysis on the anxiety-reducing effects of acute and chronic exercise. *Sports Medicine, 11,* 143–182.

Rejeski, W. J., Brawley, L. R., & Schumaker, S. A. (1996). Physical activity and health-related quality of life. In J. O. Holloszy (Ed.), *Exercise and Sport Science Reviews, 24,* 71–108.

Rigsby, L. W., Dishman, R. K., Jackson, A. W., McClean, G. S., & Raven, P. B. (1992). Effects of exercise training on men seropositive for the human immunodeficiency virus-1. *Medicine and Science in Sports and Exercise, 24,* 6–12.

Sallis, J. F., & Hovell, M. F. (1990). Determinants of exercise behavior. In K. B. Pandolf, & J. O. Holloszy (Eds.), *Exercise and Sport Science Reviews, 18,* 307–330. Baltimore: Williams & Wilkins.

Schmidt, G. W., & Stein, G. L. (1991). Sport commitment: A model integrating enjoyment, dropout, and burnout. *Journal of Sport & Exercise Psychology, 13,* 254–265.

Silva, J. M., III (1990). An analysis of the training stress syndrome in competitive athletics. *Journal of Applied Sport Psychology, 2,* 5–20.

Stone, M. H. (1993). Literature review. Anabolic-androgenic steroid use by athletes. *National Strength and Conditioning Association Journal, 15,* 10–28.

Williams, J., Hogan, T., & Andersen, M. (1993). Positive states of mind and athletic injury risk. *Psychosomatic Medicine, 55,* 468–472.

Yannis, T. (1994). Planned behavior, attitude strength, role identity, and the prediction of exercise behavior. *The Sport Psychologist, 8,* 149–165.

Yates, A. (1987). Eating disorders and long-distance running: The ascetic condition. *Integrated Psychiatry, 5,* 201–204.

Yates, A. (1991). *Compulsive exercise and eating disorders: Toward an integrated theory of activity.* New York: Brunner/Mazel.

REFERENCES

A

Adams, R. M. (1995). Momentum in the performance of professional tournament pocket billiards players. *International Journal of Sport Psychology, 26,* 580–587.

Agnew, G. A., & Carron, A. V. (1994). Crowd effects and the home advantage. *International Journal of Sport Psychology, 25,* 53–62.

Aguglia, E., & Sapienza, S. (1984). Locus of control according to Rotter's S.R.I. in volleyball players. *International Journal of Sport Psychology, 15,* 250–258.

Ajzen, I. (1985). From intention to actions: A theory of planned behavior. In J. Kuhl & J. Beckman (Eds.), *Action-control: From cognition to behavior* (pp. 11–39). Heidelberg: Springer.

Ajzen, I. (1977). Attitude-behavior relations: A theoretical analysis and review of emperical research. *Psychological Bulletin, 84,* 888–918.

Alberti, R. E. (1977). Comments on differentiating assertion and aggression: Some behavioral guidelines. *Behavioral Therapy, 8,* 353–354.

Albrecht, R. R., & Feltz, D. L. (1987). Generality and specificity of attention related to competitive anxiety and sport performance. *Journal of Sport Psychology, 9,* 231–248.

Allport, G. W. (1937). *Personality—a psychological interpretation.* New York: Holt and Company.

Alzado, L. (July 8, 1991). I'm sick and I'm scared. *Sports Illustrated, 75,* 21–24, 27.

American Heart Association. (1992). *1993 heart and stroke facts statistics.* Dallas, TX: American Heart Association.

American Psychological Association. (1992). Ethical principles of psychologists and code of conduct. *American Psychologist, 47,* 1597–1611.

Ames, C. (1978). Children's achievement attributions and self-reinforcement: Effects of self-concept and competitive reward structures. *Journal of Educational Psychology, 70,* 345–355.

Andersen, M. B., & Williams, J. M. (1987). Gender role and sport competition anxiety: A re-examination. *Research Quarterly for Exercise and Sport, 58,* 52–56.

Andersen, M. B., & Williams, J. M. (1988). A model of stress and athletic injury: Prediction and prevention. *Journal of Sport and Exercise Psychology, 10*(3), 294–306.

Anderson, C. A., Deuser, W. E., & DeNeve, K. M. (1995). Hot temperatures, hostile affect, hostile cognition, and arousal: Tests of a general model of affective aggression. *Personality and Social Psychological Bulletin, 21,* 434–448.

Anshel, M. H. (1979). Effect of age, sex, and type of feedback on motor performance and locus of control. *Research Quarterly, 50,* 305–317.

Anshel, M. H. (1990). Commentary on the National Drugs in Sport Conference—1989. Treating the causes and symptoms. *Australian Journal of Science and Medicine in Sport, 22,* 49–56.

Anshel, M. H. (1991). A psycho-behavioral analysis of addicted versus non-addicted male and female exercisers. *Journal of Sport Behavior, 14*(2), 145–154.

Anshel, M. H. (1992). The case against the certification of sport psychologists: In search of the phantom expert. *The Sport Psychologist, 6,* 265–286.

Anshel, M. H. (1993a). Against the certification of sport psychology consultants: A response to Zaichkowsky and Perna. *The Sport Psychologist, 7,* 344–353.

Anshel, M. H. (1993b). Psychology of drug use. In R. N. Singer, M. Murphey, & L. K. Tennant (Eds.), *Handbook of research on sport psychology* (pp. 851–876). New York: Macmillan.

Anshel, M. H., & Wrisberg, C. A. (1988). The effect of arousal and focused attention on warm-up decrement. *Journal of Sport Behavior, 11,* 18–31.

Apter, M. J. (1982). *The experience of motivation: The theory of psychological reversals.* London: Academic Press.

Apter, M. J. (1984). Reversal theory and personality: A review. *Journal of Research in Personality, 18,* 265–288.

Arkes, H. R., & Garske, J. P. (1982). *Psychological theories of motivation* (2nd ed.). Monterey, CA: Brooks/Cole Publishing Company.

Armstrong, C. A., Sallis, J. F., Hovell, M. F., & Hofstetter, C. R. (1993). Stages of change, self-efficacy, and the adoption of vigorous exercise: A prospective analysis. *Journal of Sport & Exercise Psychology, 15,* 390–402.

Asken, M. J. (1991). The challenge of the physically challenged: Delivering sport psychology services to physically disabled athletes. *The Sport Psychologist, 5,* 370–381.

Associated Press. (1991, January 14). At least 40 die at South African soccer match. *Ball State Daily News,* 1.

Atkinson, J. W. (1964). *An introduction to motivation.* New York: D. Van Nostrand Company.

B

Bacon, S. J. (1974). Arousal and the range of cue utilization. *Journal of Experimental Psychology, 102,* 81–87.

Baer, L. (1980). Effect of a time-slowing suggestion on performance accuracy on a perceptual motor task. *Perceptual and Motor Skills, 51,* 167–176.

Bagnato, A. (1991, July 23). Dawson loses his cool; Dibble is at it again. *Muncie Evening Press,* 9, 10.

Bahrick, H. P., Fitts, P. M., & Rankin, R. E. (1952). Effect of incentives upon reactions to peripheral stimuli. *Journal of Experimental Psychology, 44,* 400–446.

Bahrke, M. W., & Morgan, W. P. (1978). Anxiety reduction following exercise and medication. *Cognitive Therapy and Research, 2,* 323–333.

Bahrke, M. S., & Yesalis, C. E. (1993). Psychological/behavioral effects of anabolic-androgenic steroids. In R. N. Singer, M. Murphey, & L. K. Tennant (Eds.), *Handbook of research on sport psychology* (pp. 877–887). New York: Macmillan.

Bakan, D. (1966). *The duality of human existence.* Chicago: Rand McNally.

Bakeman, R., & Helmreich, R. (1975). Cohesiveness and performance: Covariation and causality in an undersea environment. *Journal of Experimental Social Psychology, 11,* 478–489.

Ball, D. W. (1973). Ascription and position: Comparative analysis of stacking in professional football. *Canadian Review of Sociology and Anthropology, 10,* 97–113.

Bandura, A. (1973). *Aggression: A social learning analysis.* Englewood Cliffs, NJ: Prentice-Hall.

Bandura, A. (1977). Self-efficacy: Toward a unifying theory of behavioral change. *Psychological Review, 84,* 191–215.

Bandura, A. (1982). Self-efficacy mechanism in human agency. *American Psychologist, 37,* 122–147.

Bandura, A. (1986). *Social foundations of thought and action: A social cognitive theory.* Englewood Cliffs, NJ: Prentice-Hall.

Barber, T. X., Spanos, N. P., & Chaves, J. F. (1974). *Hypnosis, imagination, and human potentialities.* New York: Pergamon Press.

Bar-Eli, M., Hartman, I., Levy-Kolker, N. (1994). Using goal setting to improve physical performance of adolescents with behavior disorders: The effect of goal proximity. *Adapted Physical Activity Quarterly, 11,* 86–97.

Barnett, M. L., & Stanicek, J. A. (1979). Effects of goal-setting on achievement in archery. *Research Quarterly, 50,* 328–332.

Barnett, N. P., Smoll, F. L., & Smith, R. E. (1992). Effects of enhancing coach-athlete relationships on youth sport attrition. *The Sport Psychologist, 6,* 111–127.

Baron, R. A. (1971). Exposure to an aggressive model and apparent probability of retaliation from the victim as determinants of adult aggressive behavior. *Journal of Experimental Social Psychology, 7,* 343–355.

Baron, R. A. (1977). *Human aggression.* New York: Plenum Press.

Baron, R. A. (1989). *Psychology the essential science.* Boston, MA: Allyn and Bacon.

Barr, K., & Hall, C. (1992). The use of imagery by rowers. *International Journal of Sport Psychology, 23,* 243–261.

Baumeister, R. F., & Steinhilber, A. (1984). Paradoxical effects of supportive audiences on performance under pressure: The home field advantage in sports championships. *Journal of Personality and Psychology, 47,* 85–93.

Behling, O., & Schriesheim, C. (1976). *Organizational behavior: Theory, research, and application.* Boston: Allyn and Bacon.

Bell, G. J., & Howe, B. L. (1988). Mood state profiles and motivations of triathletes. *Journal of Sport Behavior, 11,* 66–77.

Bem, S. L. (1974). The measurement of psychological androgyny. *Journal of Consulting and Clinical Psychology, 42,* 155–162.

Bem, S. L. (1977). On the utility of alternative procedures for assessing psychological androgyny. *Journal of Consulting and Clinical Psychology, 45,* 196–205.

Benson, H., Beary, J. F., & Carol, M. P. (1974). The relaxation response. *Psychiatry, 37,* 37–46.

Bergandi, T. A., Shryock, M. G., & Titus, T. G. (1990). The basketball concentration survey:

Preliminary development and validation. *The Sport Psychologist, 4,* 119–129.

Berger, B. G., Friedmann, E., & Eaton, M. (1988). Comparison of jogging, the relaxation response, and group interaction for stress reduction. *Journal of Exercise Psychology, 10*(4), 431–447.

Berger, B. G., & Owen, D. R. (1988). Stress reduction and mood enhancement in four exercise modes: Swimming, body conditioning, hatha yoga, and fencing. *Research Quarterly of Exercise and Sport, 59*(2), 148–159.

Berger, B. G., Owen, D. R., & Frantisek, M. (1993). A brief review of literature and examination of acute mood benefits of exercise in Czechoslovakian and United States swimmers. *International Journal of Sport Psychology, 24,* 130–150.

Berglung, B., & Safstrom, H. (1994). Psychological monitoring and modulation of training load of world-class canoeists. *Medicine and Science in Sports and Medicine, 26,* 1036–1040.

Berkowitz, L. (1958). The expression and reduction of hostility. *Psychological Bulletin, 55,* 257–283.

Berkowitz, L. (1962). *Aggression: A social psychological analysis.* New York: McGraw-Hill.

Berkowitz, L. (1972). Sports, competition, and aggression. In I. D. Williams & L. M. Wankel (Eds.), *Proceedings of the Fourth Canadian Psychomotor Learning and Sport Psychology Symposium* (pp. 321–326). Waterloo, Ontario: University of Waterloo.

Berkowitz, L. (1993). *Aggression: Its causes, consequences, and control.* Philadelphia: Temple University Press.

Berkowitz, L., & Alioto, J. T. (1973). The meaning of an observed event as a determinant of its aggressive consequences. *Journal of Personality and Social Psychology, 28,* 206–217.

Berkowitz, L., & LePage, A. (1967). Weapons as aggression-eliciting stimuli. *Journal of Personality and Social Psychology, 7,* 202–207.

Bernstein, D. A., & Borkovec, T. D. (1973). *Progressive relaxation training.* Champaign, IL: Research Press.

Bernstein, L., Henderson, B. E., Hanisch, R., Sullivan-Halley, J., & Ross, R. K. (1994). Physical exercise and reduced risk of breast cancer in young women. *Journal of the National Cancer Institute, 86,* 1403–1408.

Betts, G. H. (1909). *The distribution and functions of mental imagery.* New York: Teachers College, Columbia University.

Beuter, A., & Duda, J. L. (1985). Analysis of the arousal/motor performance relationship in children using movement kinematics. *Journal of Sport Psychology, 7,* 229–243.

Biddle, S. J. H. (1993). Children, exercise, and mental health. *International Journal of Sport Psychology, 24,* 200–216.

Biddle, S. J. H. (1995). Exercise and psychosocial health. *Research Quarterly for Exercise and Sport, 66* (4), 292–297.

Biddle, S. J. H., & Hill, A. B. (1992). Relationships between attributions and emotions in a laboratory-based sporting contest. *Journal of Sports Sciences, 10,* 65–75.

Bird, A. M. (1977). Leadership and cohesion within successful and unsuccessful teams: Perceptions of coaches and players. In D. M. Landers & R. W. Christina (Eds.), *Psychology of motor behavior and sport* (Vol. 2). Champaign, IL: Human Kinetics Publishers.

Bird, A. M., & Horn, A. (1990). Cognitive anxiety and mental errors in sport. *Journal of Sport & Exercise Psychology, 12,* 211–216.

Bird, A. M., & Williams, J. M. (1980). A developmental-attributional analysis of sex-role stereotypes for sport performance. *Developmental Psychology, 16,* 319–322.

Bivens, S., & Leonard, W. M. (1994). Race, centrality, and educational attainment: An NFL perspective. *Journal of Sport Behavior, 17,* 24–42.

Black, S. J., & Weiss, M. R. (1992). The relationship among perceived coaching behaviors, perceptions of ability, and motivation in competitive age-group swimmers. *Journal of Sport & Exercise Psychology, 14,* 130–145.

Block, N. (Ed.). (1981). *Imagery.* Cambridge, MA: MIT Press.

Blumenstein, B., Bar-Eli, M., & Tenenbaum, G. (1995). The augmenting role of biofeedback: Effects of autogenic, imagery, and music training on physiological indices and athletic performance. *Journal of Sports Sciences, 13,* 343–354.

Botterill, C. (1996, October). *Cornerstones and challenges in performance enhancement: Looking at emotions in sport.* Paper presented at the meeting of the Association for the Advancement of Applied Sport Psychology, Williamsburg, VA.

Boutcher, S. H., & Rotella, R. J. (1987). A psychological skills education program for closed-skill performance enhancement. *The Sport Psychologist, 1,* 127–137.

Boutcher, S. H., & Trenske, M. (1990). The effects of sensory deprivation and music on perceived exertion and affect during exercise. *Journal of Sport & Exercise Psychology, 12,* 167–176.

Boutcher, S. H., & Zinsser, N. W. (1990). Cardiac deceleration of elite and beginning golfers during putting. *Journal of Sport & Exercise Psychology, 12,* 37–47.

Bowers, K. S. (1973). Situationalism in psychology: An analysis and a critique. *Psychological Review, 80,* 307–336.

Boyce, A. (1990). Effects of goal specificity and goal difficulty upon skill acquisition of a selected shooting task. *Perceptual and Motor Skills, 70,* 1031–1039.

Bradley, G. W. (1978). Self-serving biases in the attribution process: Reexamination of the fact or fiction question. *Journal of Personality and Social Psychology, 36,* 56–71.

Bramwell, S. T., Masuda, M., Wagner, N. N., & Holmes, T. H. (1975). Psychological factors in athletic injuries: Development and application of the Social and Athletic Readjustment Rating Scale (SARRS). *Journal of Human Stress, 1,* 6–20.

Brawley, L. R. (1984). Unintentional egocentric biases in attributions. *Journal of Sport Psychology, 6,* 264–278.

Brawley, L. R. (1993). The practicality of using social psychological theories for exercise and health research and intervention. *Journal of Applied Sport Psychology, 5,* 99–115.

Bray, S. R., & Carron, A. V. (1993). The home advantage in alpine skiing. *The Australian Journal of Science and Medicine in Sport, 25,* 76–81.

Bredemeier, B. J. (1978). The assessment of reactive and instrumental athletic aggression. *Proceedings of the International Symposium on Psychological Assessment.* Neyanya, Israel: Wingate Institute for Physical Education and Sport.

Bredemeier, B. J. (1983). Athletic aggression: A moral concern. In J. H. Goldstein (Ed.), *Sports Violence.* New York: Springer-Verlag.

Bredemeier, B. J. (1985). Moral reasoning and the perceived legitimacy of intentionally injurious sport acts. *Journal of Sport Psychology, 7,* 110–124.

Bredemeier, B. J. (1994). Children's moral reasoning and their assertive, aggressive, and submissive tendencies in sport and daily life. *Journal of Sport & Exercise Psychology, 16,* 1–14.

Bredemeier, B. J., & Shields, D. L. (1984). The utility of moral stage analysis in the investigation of athletic aggression. *Sociology of Sport Journal, 1,* 138–149.

Bredemeier, B. J., & Shields, D. L. (1986). Athletic aggression: An issue of contextual morality. *Sociology of Sport Journal, 3,* 15–28.

Bredemeier, B. J., Weiss, M. R., Shields, D. L., & Cooper, B. A. B. (1986). The relationship of sport involvement with children's moral reasoning and aggression tendencies. *Journal of Sport Psychology, 8,* 304–318.

Bredemeier, B. J., Weiss, M. R., Shields, D. L., & Cooper, B. A. B. (1987). The relationship between children's legitimacy judgements and their moral reasoning, aggression tendencies, and sport involvement. *Sociology of Sport Journal, 4,* 48–60.

Brewer, B. W. (1994). Review and critique of models of psychological adjustment to athletic injury. *Journal of Applied Sport Psychology, 6,* 87–100.

Brewer, B. W., Jeffers, K. E., Petipas, S. J., & Van Raalte, J. L. (1994). Perceptions of psychological interventions in the context of sport injury rehabilitation. *The Sport Psychologist, 8,* 176–188.

Broadbent, D. E. (1957). Mechanical model for human attention and immediate memory. *Psychological Review, 64,* 205–215.

Broadbent, D. E. (1958). *Perception and communication.* London: Pergamon Press.

Brodkin, P., & Weiss, M. R. (1990). Developmental differences in motivation for participating in competitive swimming. *Journal of Sport & Exercise Psychology, 12,* 248–263.

Broucek, M. W., Bartholomew, J. B., Landers, D. M., & Linder, D. E. (1993). The effects of relaxation with a warning cue on pain tolerance. *Journal of Sport Behavior, 16,* 239–254.

Brown, B. A. (1977). *Stress and the art of biofeedback.* New York: Harper & Row.

Brown, B. S., & Van Huss, W. D. (1973). Exercise and rat brain catecholamines. *Journal of Applied Physiology, 34,* 664–669.

Brown, D. R., Wang, Y., Ward, A., Ebbeling, C. B., Fortlage, L., Puleo, E., Benson, H., & Rippe, J. M. (1995). Chronic psychological effects of exercise and exercise plus cognitive strategies. *Medicine & Science in Sports & Exercise, 27,* 765–775.

Brown, J. D. (1991). Staying fit and staying well: Physical fitness as a moderator of life stress. *Journal of Personality and Social Psychology, 60*(4), 555–561.

Brown, J. D., & Lawton, M. (1986). Stress and well being in adolescence: The moderating role of physical exercise. *Journal of Human Stress, 12,* 125–131.

Brown, J. D., & Siegel, J. M. (1988). Exercise as a buffer of life stress. *Health Psychology, 7,* 341–353.

Brustad, R. J. (1996). Attraction to physical activity in urban school children: Parental socialization and gender influences. *Research Quarterly for Exercise and Sport, 67,* 316–323.

Buck, J. N. (1948, October). The H-T-P technique: A qualitative and quantitative scoring manual. *Journal of Clinical Psychology* (Monog. Suppl. No. 5).

Burckes-Miller, M., & Black, D. (1988). Male and female collegiate athletes: Prevalence of anorexia nervosa and bulimia nervosa. *Athletic Training, 23,* 137–140.

Burhans, R. S., Richman, C. L., & Bergley, D. B. (1988). Mental imagery training: Effects on running speed performance. *International Journal of Sport Psychology, 19,* 26–37.

Burke, K. L., & Houyseworth, S. (1995). Structural charting and perceptions of momentum in intercollegiate volleyball. *Journal of Sport Behavior, 18,* 167–182.

Bursill, A. F. (1958). The restriction of peripheral vision during exposure to hot and humid conditions. *Quarterly Journal of Experimental Psychology, 10,* 113–129.

Burton, D. (1988). Do anxious swimmers swim slower?: Reexamining the elusive anxiety-performance relationship. *Journal of Sport and Exercise Psychology, 10,* 45–61.

Burton, D. (1989a). The impact of goal specificity and task complexity on basketball skill development. *The Sport Psychologist, 3,* 34–47.

Burton, D. (1989b). Winning isn't everything: Examining the impact of performance goals on collegiate swimmer's cognitions and performance. *The Sport Psychologist, 3,* 105–132.

Burton, D. (1992). The Jekyll/Hyde nature of goals: Reconceptualizing goal setting in sport. In T. S. Horn (Ed.), *Advances in sport psychology* (pp. 267–297). Champaign, IL: Human Kinetics Publishers.

Burwitz, L., & Newell, K. M. (1972). The effects of the mere presence of coactors on learning a motor skill. *Journal of Motor Behavior, 4,* 99–102.

Buss, A. H. (1963). Physical aggression in relation to different frustrations. *Journal of Abnormal and Social Psychology, 67,* 1–7.

Buss, A. H. (1971). Aggression pays. In J. E. Singer (Ed.), *The control of aggression and violence: Cognitive and physiological factors.* New York: Academic Press.

Buss, A. H., & Durkee, A. (1957). An inventory for assessing different kinds of hostility. *Journal of Consulting Psychology, 21,* 343–348.

Buss, A. H., & Perry, M. (1992). The aggression questionnaire. *Journal of Personality and Social Psychology, 63,* 452–459.

C

Campbell, E., & Jones, G. (1994). Psychological well-being in wheelchair sport participants and nonparticipants. *Adapted Physical Activity Quarterly, 11,* 404–415.

Carlson, C. R., & Hoyle, R. H. (1993). Efficacy of abbreviated progressive muscle relaxation training: A quantitative review of behavioral medicine research. *Journal of Consulting and Clinical Psychology, 61,* 1059–1067.

Carron, A. V. (1975). Personality and athletics: A review. In B. S. Rushall (Ed.), *The status of psychomotor learning and sport psychology research.* Dartmouth, Nova Scotia: Sport Science Associates.

Carron, A. V. (1980). *Social psychology of sport.* Ithaca, NY: Mouvement Publications.

Carron, A. V. (1982). Cohesiveness in sport groups: Interpretations and considerations. *Journal of Sport Psychology, 4,* 123–138.

Carron, A. V., & Ball, J. R. (1977). An analysis of the cause-effect characteristics of cohesiveness and participation motivation in intercollegiate hockey. *International Review of Sport Sociology, 12,* 49–60.

Carron, A. V., & Bennett, B. B. (1977). Compatibility in the coach-athlete dyad. *Research Quarterly, 48,* 671–679.

Carron, A. V., Brawley, L. R., & Widmeyer, W. N. (1990). The impact of group size in an exercise setting. *Journal of Sport & Exercise Psychology, 12,* 376–387.

Carron, A. V., Hausenblas, H. A., & Mack, D. (1996). Social influence and exercise: A meta-analysis. *Journal of Sport & Exercise Psychology, 18,* 1–16.

Carron, A. V., Prapavessis, H., & Grove, J. R. (1994). Group effects and self-handicapping. *Journal of Sport & Exercise Psychology, 16,* 246–257.

Carron, A. V., & Spink, K. S. (1992). Internal consistency of the Group Environment Questionnaire modified for an exercise setting. *Perceptual and Motor Skills, 74,* 304–306.

Carron, A. V., Spink, K. S., & Prapavessis, H. (1997). Team building and cohesiveness in the sport and exercise setting: Use of interventions. *Journal of Applied Sport Psycholgoy, 9,* 61–72.

Carron, A. V., Widmeyer, W. N., & Brawley, L. R. (1985). The development of an instrument to assess cohesion in sport teams: The group environment questionnaire. *Journal of Sport Psychology, 7,* 244–266.

Cartwright, D. (1968). The nature of group cohesiveness. In D. Cartwright & A. Zander (eds.), *Group dynamics: Research and theory.* 3d ed. (pp. 91–109). New York: Harper & Row.

Caruso, C. M., Dzewaltowski, D. A., Gill, D. L., & McElroy, M. A. (1990). Psychological and physiological changes in competitive state anxiety during noncompetition and competitive success and failure. *Journal of Sport & Exercise Psychology, 12,* 6–20.

Case, B. (1987). Leadership behavior in sport: A field test of the situational leadership theory. *International Journal of Sport Psychology, 18,* 256–268.

Castiello, U., & Umilta, C. (1992). Orienting of attention in volleyball players. *International Journal of Sport Psychology, 23,* 301–310.

Cattell, R. B. (1965). *The scientific analysis of personality.* Baltimore: Penguin.

Cattell, R. B. (1973, July). Personality pinned down. *Psychology Today,* 40–46.

Cattell, R. B., Eber, H. W., & Tatsuoka, M. M. (1980). *Handbook for the Sixteen Personality Factor Questionnaire (16 PF).* Champaign, IL: Institute for Personality and Ability Testing.

Caudill, D., Weinberg, R., & Jackson, A. (1983). Psyching-up and track athletes: A preliminary investigation. *Journal of Sport Psychology, 5,* 231–235.

Chalip, L. (1980). Social learning theory and sport success: Evidence and implications. *Journal of Sport Behavior, 3,* 76–85.

Chapman, C. L., & Castro, J. M. (1990). Running addiction: Measurement and associated psychological characteristics. *The Journal of Sports Medicine and Physical Fitness, 30,* 283–290.

Chartrand, J. M., Jowdy, D. P., & Danish, S. J. (1992). The psychological skills inventory for sports: Psychometric characteristics and applied implications. *Journal of Sport and Exercise Psychology, 14,* 405–413.

Chass, M. (November 9, 1994). Teams look behind plate for managers. *Kansas City Star,* sec. D, 1, 4.

Chelladurai, P. (1978). *A multidimensional model of leadership.* Unpublished doctoral dissertation, University of Waterloo, Waterloo, Ontario.

Chelladurai, P. (1984). Discrepancy between preferences and perceptions of leadership behavior and satisfaction of athletes in varying sports. *Journal of Sport Psychology, 6,* 27–41.

Chelladurai, P., & Arnott, M. (1985). Decision styles in coaching: Preferences of basketball players. *Research Quarterly for Exercise and Sport, 56,* 15–24.

Chelladurai, P., & Carron, A. V. (1977). A reanalysis of formal structure in sport. *Canadian Journal of Applied Sport Sciences, 2,* 9–14.

Chelladurai, P., & Carron, A. V. (1978). *Leadership.* Canadian Association for Health, Physical Education and Recreation, Sociology of Sport Monograph Series.

Ottawa, Ontario: Canadian Association for Health, Physical Education and Recreation.

Chelladurai, P., Haggerty, T. R., & Baxter, P. R. (1989). Decision style choices of university basketball coaches and players. *Journal of Sport & Exercise Psychology, 11,* 201–215.

Chelladurai, P., Imamura, H., Yamaguchi, Y., Oinuma, Y., & Miyauchi, T. (1988). Sport leadership in a cross-national setting: The case of Japanese and Canadian university athletes. *Journal of Sport & Exercise Psychology, 10,* 374–389.

Chelladurai, P., & Saleh, S. D. (1978). Preferred leadership in sport. *Canadian Journal of Applied Sport Sciences, 3,* 85–97.

Cherry, E. C. (1953). Some experiments on the recognition of speech, with one and with two ears. *Journal of the Acoustical Society of America, 25,* 975–979.

Cinelli, B., Sankaran, G., McConatha, D., & Carson, L. (1992). Knowledge and attitudes of pre-service education majors about AIDS: Implications for curriculum development. *Health Education, 23,* 204–208.

Clark, L. V. (1960). Effect of mental practice on the development of a certain motor skill. *Research Quarterly, 31,* 560–569.

Clarke, J. C., & Jackson, J. A. (1983). *Hypnosis and behavior therapy: The treatment of anxiety and phobias.* New York: Springer Publishing Company.

Clifton, R. T., & Gill, D. L. (1994). Gender differences in self-confidence on a feminine-typed task. *Journal of Sport & Exercise Psychology, 16,* 150–162.

Clingman, J. M., & Hilliard, D. V. (1987). Some personality characteristics of the super-adherer: Following those who go beyond fitness. *Journal of Sport Behavior, 10,* 123–136.

Clingman, J. M., & Hilliard, D. V. (1990). Race walkers quicken their pace by tuning in, not stepping out. *The Sport Psychologist, 4,* 25–32.

Clingman, J. M., & Hilliard, D. V. (1994). Anxiety reduction in competitive running as a function of success. *Journal of Sport Behavior, 17,* 120–129.

Coen, S. P., & Ogles, B. M. (1993). Psychological characteristics of the obligatory runner: A critical examination of the anorexia analogue hypothesis. *Journal of Sport & Exercise Psychology, 15,* 338–354.

Cofer, C. N., & Johnson, W. R. (1960). Personality dynamics in relation to exercise and sports. In W. R. Johnson (Ed.), *Science and medicine of exercise and sport.* New York: Harper & Row.

Cohn, P. J. (1990). An exploratory study on sources of stress and athlete burnout in youth golf. *The Sport Psychologist, 4,* 95–106.

Cohn, P. J., Rotella, R. J., & Lloyd, J. W. (1990). Effects of a cognitive-behavioral intervention on the preshot routine and performance in golf. *The Sport Psychologist, 4,* 33–47.

Coleman, T. R. (1976). *A comparative study of certain behavioral, physiological, and phenomenological effects of hypnotic induction and two progressive relaxation procedures.* Ph.D. dissertation, Brigham Young University, Provo, UT.

Conboy, J. K. (1994). The effects of exercise withdrawal on mood states in runners. *Journal of Sport Behavior, 17,* 188–203.

Cooper, L. (1969). Athletics, activity, and personality: A review of the literature. *Research Quarterly, 40,* 17–22.

Corbin, C. B. (1967a). The effects of covert practice on the development of a complex motor skill. *Journal of General Psychology, 76,* 143–150.

Corbin, C. B. (1967b). Effects of mental practice on skill development after controlled practice. *Research Quarterly, 38,* 534–538.

Corbin, C. B. (1977). The reliability and internal consistency of the motivation rating scale and the general trait rating scale. *Medicine and Science in Sports, 9,* 208–211.

Corbin, C. B. (1981). Sex of subject, sex of opponent, and opponent ability as factors affecting self-confidence in a competitive situation. *Journal of Sport Psychology, 3,* 265–270.

Corbin, C. B., & Nix, C. (1979). Sex-typing of physical activities and success predictions of children before and after cross-sex competition. *Journal of Sport Psychology, 1,* 43–52.

Costa, A., Bonaccorsi, M., & Scrimali, T. (1984). Biofeedback and control of anxiety preceding athletic competition. *International Journal of Sport Psychology, 15,* 98–109.

Costill, D. L., Thomas, R., Robergs, R. A., Pascoe, D., Lambert, C., Barr, S., & Fink, W. J. (1991). Adaptations to swimming training: Influence of training volume. *Medicine and Science in Sports and Exercise, 23,* 371–377.

Courneya, K. S. (1995). Perceived severity of the consequences of physical inactivity across the stages of change in older adults. *Journal of Sport & Exercise Psychology, 17,* 447–457.

Courneya, K. S., & Carron, A. V. (1990). Batting first versus last: Implications for the home advantage. *Journal of Sport & Exercise Psychology, 12,* 312–316.

Courneya, K. S., & Carron, A. V. (1991). Effects of travel and length of home stand/road trip on the home advantage. *Journal of Sport & Exercise Psychology, 13,* 42–49.

Courneya, K. S., & Carron, A. V. (1992). The home advantage in sport competitions: A literature review. *Journal of Sport & Exercise Psychology, 14,* 13–27.

Courneya, K. S., & McAuley, E. (1993). Predicting physical activity from intention: Conceptual and methodological issues. *Journal of Sport & Exercise Psychology, 15,* 50–62.

Courneya, K. S., & McAuley, E. (1994). Factors affecting the intention-physical activity relationship: Intention versus expectation and scale correspondence. *Research Quarterly for Exercise and Sport, 65,* 280–285.

Cox, R. H. (1980). *Teaching volleyball.* Minneapolis: Burgess Publishing Company.

Cox, R. H. (1986). Relationship between skill performance in women's volleyball and competitive state anxiety. *International Journal of Sport Psychology, 17,* 183–190.

Cox, R. H. (1987a). *Relationship between psychological variables with player position and experience in women's volleyball.* Unpublished manuscript.

Cox, R. H. (1987b). An exploratory investigation of a signal discrimination problem in tennis. *Journal of Human Movement Studies, 13,* 197–210.

Cox, R. H. (1990). *Sport psychology: Concepts and applications.* 2d ed. Dubuque, IA: Wm. C. Brown Publishers.

Cox, R. H., & Davis, R. W. (1992, Spring). Psychological skills of elite wheelchair athletes. *Palaestra, 8,* 16–21.

Cox, R. H., Liu, Z. (1993) Psychological skills: A cross-cultural investigation. *International Journal of Sport Psychology, 24,* 326–34.

Cox, R. H., Russell, W. D., & Robb, M. (1998). Development of a CSAI-2 short form for assessing competitive state anxiety during and immediately prior to competition. *Journal of Sport Behavior, 21,* in press.

Cox, R. H., & Yoo, H. S. (1995). Playing position and psychological skill in American football. *Journal of Sport Behavior, 18,* 183–194.

Cox, T., & Kerr, J. H. (1989). Arousal effects during tournament play in squash. *Perceptual and Motor Skills, 69,* 1275–1280.

Craighead, D. J., Privette, F. V., & Byrkit, D. (1986). Personality characteristics of basketball players, starters, and nonstarters. *International Journal of Sport Psychology, 17,* 110–119.

Crandall, V. C. (1963). Achievement. In H. W. Stevenson (Ed.), *Child Psychology.* Chicago: University of Chicago Press.

Cratty, B. J. (1981). *Social psychology in athletics.* Englewood Cliffs, NJ: Prentice-Hall.

Cratty, B. J. (1983). *Psychology in contemporary sport: Guidelines for coaches and athletes.* Englewood Cliffs, NJ: Prentice-Hall.

Cratty, B. J., & Sage, J. N. (1964). The effects of primary and secondary group interaction upon improvement in a complex movement task. *Research Quarterly, 35,* 164–175.

Crawford, S., & Eklund, R. C. (1994). Social physique anxiety, reasons for exercise, and attitudes toward exercise settings. *Journal of Sport & Exercise Psychology, 16,* 70–82.

Crews, D. J. (1992). Psychological state and running economy. *Medicine and Science in Sports and Exercise, 24,* 475–482.

Crews, D. J., & Landers, D. M. (1987). A meta-analytic review of aerobic fitness and reactivity to psycho-social stressors. *Medicine and Science in Sports and Exercise, 19,* 114–120.

Crews, D. J., & Landers, D. M. (1993). Electroencephalographic measures of attentional patterns prior to the golf putt. *Medicine and Science in Sports and Exercise, 25,* 116–126.

Crocker, P. R. E. (1989). A follow-up of cognitive-affective stress management training. *Journal of Sport & Exercise Psychology, 11,* 236–242.

Crocker, P. R. E. (1992). Managing stress by competitive athletes: Ways of coping. *International Journal of Sport Psychology, 23,* 161–175.

Crocker, P. R. E., Alderman, R. B., & Smith, F. M. R. (1988). Cognitive-affective stress management training with high performance youth volleyball players: Effects on affect, cognition, and performance. *Journal of Sport & Exercise Psychology, 10,* 448–460.

Crocker, P. R. E., & Graham, T. R. (1995). Coping by competitive athletes with performance stress: Gender differences and relationships with affect. *The Sport Psychologist, 9,* 325–338.

Crossman, J., Jamieson, J., & Henderson, L. (1987). Responses of competitive athletes to lay-offs in training: Exercise addiction or psychological relief? *Journal of Sport Behavior, 10,* 28–38.

Cryan, P. O., & Alles, E. F. (1983). The relationship between stress and football injuries. *Journal of Sports Medicine and Physical Fitness, 23,* 52–58.

Csikszentmichalyi, M. (1975). Beyond boredom and anxiety. San Francisco, CA: Jossey-Bass.

Csikszentmichalyi, M. (1990). *Flow: The psychology of optimal experience.* New York: Harper and Row Publishers.

Cullen, J. B., & Cullen, F. T. (1975).The structure and contextual conditions of group norm violations: Some implications from the game of ice hockey. *International Review of Sport Sociology, 10,* 69–77.

D Dabbs, J. M., Jr., Johnson, J. E., & Leventhal, H. (1968). Palmar sweating: A quick and simple measure. *Journal of Experimental Psychology, 78,* 347–350.

Dahlstrom, W. G., & Walsh, G. W. (1960). *A Minnesota multiphasic personality handbook.* Minneapolis: University of Minnesota Press.

Dale, J., & Weinberg, R. (1990). Burnout in sport: A review and critique. *Journal of Applied Sport Psychology, 2,* 67–83.

Danielson, R. R. (1977). Leadership motivation and coaching classification as related to success in minor league hockey. In D. M. Landers & R. W. Christina (Eds.), *Psychology of motor behavior and sport, 1976* (Vol. 2). Champaign, IL: Human Kinetics Publishers.

Danish, S. J., Petitpas, A. J., & Hale, B. D. (1992). A developmental-educational model of sport psychology. *The Sport Psychologist, 6,* 403–415.

Danskin, D. G., & Crow, M. A. (1981). *Biofeedback: An introduction and guide.* Palo Alto, CA: Mayfield Publishing Company.

Davis, C., & Mogk, J. P. (1994). Some personality correlates of interest and excellence in sport. *International Journal of Sport Psychology, 25,* 131–143.

Davis, H. (1990). Cognitive style and nonsport imagery in elite hockey performance. *Perceptual and Motor Skills, 71,* 795–801.

Davis, H. (1991). Criterion validity of the athletic motivation inventory: Issues in professional sport. *Journal of Applied Sport Psychology, 3,* 176–182.

Davis, J. H. (1969). *Group performance.* Reading, MA: Addison-Wesley.

Davis, J. O. (1991). Sport injuries and stress management: An opportunity for research. *The Sport Psychologist, 5,* 175–182.

Davis, M., Eshelman, E. R., & McKay, M. (1988). *The relaxation & stress reduction workbook.* Oakland, CA: New Harbinger Publications, Inc.

Davis, M. H., & Harvey, J. C. (1992). Declines in major league batting performance as a function of game pressure: A drive theory analysis. *Journal of Applied Social Psychology, 22,* 714–735.

De Benedette, V. (1988). Spectator violence at sports events: What keeps enthusiastic fans in bounds? *The Physician and Sportsmedicine, 16,* 203–211.

DeCharms, R. C., & Carpenter, V. (1968). Measuring motivation in culturally disadvantaged school children. *Journal of Experimental Education, 37,* 31–41.

Deci, E. L. (1971). Effects of externally mediated rewards on intrinsic motivation. *Journal of Personality and Social Psychology, 18,* 105–115.

Deci, E. L. (1972). Intrinsic motivation, extrinsic reinforcement. *Journal of Personality and Social Psychology, 22,* 113–120.

Deci, E. L. (1975). *Intrinsic motivation.* New York: Plenum Press.

Deci, E. L. (1978). Intrinsic motivation: Theory and application. In D. M. Landers & R. W. Christina (Eds.), *Psychology of motor behavior and sport, 1977* (pp. 388–396). Champaign, IL: Human Kinetics Publishers.

Deci, E. L. (1980). *The psychology of self-determination.* Lexington, MA: Lexington Books.

Deci, E. L., Cascio, W. F., & Krusell, J. (1975). Cognitive evaluation theory and some comments on the Calder and Straw critique. *Journal of Personality and Social Psychology, 31,* 81–85.

Deci, E. L., & Ryan, R. M. (1985). *Intrinsic motivation and self-determination in human behavior.* New York: Plenum.

Dember, W. N. (1975). Motivation and the cognitive revolution. *American Psychologist, 29,* 161–168.

DePalma, D. M., & Nideffer, R. M. (1977). Relationships between the Test of Attentional and Interpersonal Style and psychiatric subclassification. *Journal of Personality and Assessment, 41,* 622–631.

Dewey, D., Brawley, L. R., & Allard, F. (1989). Do the TAIS attentional-style scales predict how visual information is processed? *Journal of Sport & Exercise Psychology, 11,* 171–186.

DeWitt, D. J. (1980). Cognitive and biofeedback training for stress reduction with university athletes. *Journal of Sport Psychology, 2,* 288–294.

DiCara, L. V. (1970). Learning in the autonomic nervous system. *Scientific American, 222,* 30–39.

Diekhoff, G. (1984). Running amok: Injuries in compulsive runners. *Journal of Sports Behavior, 7,* 120–124.

DiGuiseppe, R. A. (1973). Internal-external control of reinforcement and participation in team, individual, and intramural sports. *Perceptual and Motor Skills, 36,* 33–34.

Dishman, R. K. (1987). Exercise adherence and habitual physical activity. In W. P. Morgan & S. E. Goldston (Eds.), *Exercise and Mental Health* (pp. 57–83). Washington, DC: Hemisphere Publishing Corporation.

Dishman, R. K. (1991). Increasing and maintaining exercise and physical activity. *Behavioral Therapy, 22*(3), 345–378.

Dishman, R. K. (1994). The measurement conundrum in exercise adherence research. *Medicine & Science in Sports and Exercise, 26,* 1382–1390.

Dishman, R. K., & Buckworth, J. (1996). Increasing physical activity: A quantitative analysis synthesis. *Medicine and Science in Sports and Exercise, 28,* 706–719.

Dishman, R. K., & Gettman, L. R. (1980). Psychobiologic influences on exercise adherence. *Journal of Sport Psychology, 2,* 295–310.

Dishman, R. K., Sallis, J. F., & Orenstein, D. R. (1985). The determinants of physical activity and exercise. *Public Health Report, 100,* 158–172.

Dollard, J., Miller, N., Doob, I., Mourer, O. H., & Sears, R. R. (1939). *Frustration and aggression.* New Haven, CT: Yale University Press.

Donnelly, P. (1975). *An analysis of the relationship between organizational half-life and organizational effectiveness.* Paper completed for an advanced topics course, Department of Sport Studies, University of Massachusetts, Amherst.

Donnelly, P., Carron, A. V., & Chelladurai, P. (1978). *Group cohesion and sport.* Ottawa, Ontario: Canadian Association for Health, Physical Education and Recreation.

Draw, J., & Burton, D. (1994). Evaluation of a comprehensive psychological skills training program for collegiate tennis players. *The Sport Psychologist, 8,* 37–57.

DuCharme, K. A., & Brawley, L. R. (1995). Predicting the intentions and behavior of exercise initiatives using two forms of self-efficacy. *Journal of Behavioral Medicine, 18,* 479–497.

Duda, J. L. (1987). Toward a developmental theory of children's motivation in sport. *Journal of Sport Psychology, 9,* 130–145.

Duda, J. L. (1989). Relationship between task and ego orientation and the perceived purpose of sport among high school athletes. *Journal of Sport & Exercise Psychology, 11,* 318–335.

Duda, J. L., Olson, L. K., & Templin, T. J. (1991). The relationship of task and ego orientation to sportsmanship attitudes and the perceived legitimacy of injurious acts. *Research Quarterly for Exercise and Sport, 62,* 79–87.

Duda, J. L., Smart, A. E., & Tappe, M. K. (1989). Predictors of adherence in the rehabilitation of athletic injuries: An application of personal investment theory. *Journal of Sport and Exercise Psychology, 11*(4), 367–381.

Duda, J. L., & White, S. A. (1992). Goal orientations and beliefs about the causes of sport success among elite skiers. *The Sport Psychologist, 6,* 334–343.

Duffy, E. (1957). The psychological significance of the concept of arousal or activation. *Psychological Review, 64,* 265–275.

Duffy, E. (1962). *Activation and behavior.* New York: John Wiley and Sons.

Duke, M., Johnson, T. C., & Nowicki, S., Jr. (1977). Effects of sports fitness campus experience on locus of control orientation in children, ages 6 to 14. *Research Quarterly, 48*(2), 280–283.

Dummer, G. M., Rosen, L. W., Heusner, W. W., Roberts, P. J., & Counsilman, J. E. (1987). Pathogenic weight-control behaviors of young competitive swimmers. *The Physician and Sportsmedicine, 15,* 75–84.

Duncan, T., & McAuley, D. (1987). Efficacy expectations and perceptions of causality in motor performance. *Journal of Sport Psychology, 9,* 385–393.

Duquin, M. E. (1978). Attributions made by children in coeducational sport settings. In D. M. Landers & R. W. Christina (Eds.), *Psychology of motor behavior and sport,*

1977. Champaign, IL: Human Kinetics Publishers.

Durr, K. R. (1996). *Relationship between state anxiety and performance in high school divers.* Unpublished master's thesis, University of Missouri, Columbia.

Dweck, C. S. (1975). The role of expectations and attributions in the alleviation of learned helplessness. *Journal of Personality and Social Psychology, 31,* 674–685.

Dweck, C. S. (1980). Learned helplessness in sport. In C. H. Nadeau, W. R. Halliwell, K. M. Newell, & G. C. Roberts (Eds.), *Psychology of motor behavior and sport, 1979.* Champaign, IL: Human Kinetics Publishers.

Dweck, C. S., & Goetz, T. E. (1978). Attributions and learned helplessness. In J. H. Harvey, W. J. Ickes, & R. F. Kidd (Eds.), *New directions in attribution research* (Vol. 2). Hillsdale, NJ: Erlbaum.

Dweck, C. S., & Reppucci, N. (1973). Learned helplessness and reinforcement responsibility in children. *Journal of Personality and Social Psychology, 25,* 109–116.

E

Eades, A. (1991). *An investigation of burnout in intercollegiate athletes: The development of the Eades Athletic Burnout Inventory.* Paper presented at the North American Society for the Psychology of Sport and Physical Activity National Conference, Asilomar, CA.

Easterbrook, J. A. (1959). The effect of emotion on cue utilization and the organization of behavior. *Psychological Review, 66,* 183–201.

Ebbeck, V., & Becker, S. L. (1994). Psychosocial predictors of goal orientation in youth soccer. *Research Quarterly for Exercise and Sport, 65,* 355–371.

Edmonston, W. E., Jr. (1981). *Hypnosis and relaxation: Modern verification of an old equation.* New York: John Wiley and Sons.

Edwards, J. (1979). The home field advantage. In J. H. Goldstein (Ed.), *Sports, games, and play: Social and psychological viewpoints.* Hillsdale, NJ: Halstead Press.

Edwards, T., & Hardy, L. (1996). The interactive effects of intensity and direction of cognitive and somatic anxiety and self-confidence upon performance. *Journal of Sport & Exercise Psychology, 18,* 296–312.

Eklund, R. C., & Crawford, S. (1994). Active women, social physique anxiety, and exercise. *Journal of Sport & Exercise Psychology, 16,* 431–448.

Ellis, A. (1967). Rational-emotive psychotherapy. In D. S. Arbuckle (Ed.), *Counseling and psychotherapy: An overview* (pp. 78–99). New York: McGraw-Hill.

Ellis, H. C., Goggin, J. P., & Parenté, F. J. (1979). Human memory and learning: The processing of information. In M. E. Meyer (Ed.), *Foundations of contemporary psychology.* New York: Oxford University Press.

Emery, C. F., & Blumenthal, J. A. (1988). Effects of exercise training on psychological functioning in healthy Type A men. *Psychology and Health, 2,* 367–379.

Endler, N. S. (1978). The interaction model of anxiety: Some possible implications. In D. M. Landers & R. W. Christina (Eds.), *Psychology of motor behavior and sport— 1977* (pp. 332–351). Champaign, IL: Human Kinetics.

Engelhardt, G. M. (1995). Fighting behavior and winning national hockey league games: A paradox. *Perceptual and Motor Skills, 80,* 416–418.

Epstein, J. (1989). Family structures and student motivation: A developmental perspective. In C. Ames & R. Ames (Eds.), *Research on motivation in education* (Vol. 3, pp. 259–295). New York: Academic Press.

Epstein, M. L. (1980). The relationship of imagery and mental rehearsal to performance of a motor task. *Journal of Sport Psychology, 2,* 211–220.

Epstein, S., & Taylor, S. P. (1967). Instigation to aggression as a function of degree of defeat and perceived aggressive intent of opponent. *Journal of Personality, 35,* 265–270.

Essing, W. (1970). Team line-up and team achievement in European football. In G. S. Kenyon (Ed.), *Contemporary psychology of sport*. Chicago: The Athletic Institute.

Etnier, J. L., & Landers, D. M. (1996). The influence of procedural variables on the efficacy of mental practice. *The Sport Psychologist, 10,* 48–57.

Etzel, E. F. (1979). Validation of a conceptual model characterizing attention among international rifle shooters. *Journal of Sport Psychology, 1,* 281–290.

Fabianic, D. (1984). Minority managers in professional baseball. *Sociology of Sport Journal, 1,* 163–171.

Fallstrom, R. B. (Feb. 7, 1993). Antlers rack up reputation with opponents. *Columbia Daily Tribune* (MO), 5B.

Farrell, P. A., Gustafson, A. B., Garthwaite, T. L., Kalkhoff, R. K., Cowley, A. W., Jr., & Morgan, W. P. (1986). Influence of endogenous opiods on the response of selected hormones to exercise in man. *Journal of Applied Physiology, 61*(3), 1051–1057.

Fawcett, J., Mass, J. W., & Dekirmenjiar, H. (1972). Depression and MHPG excretion. *Archives of General Psychiatry, 26,* 246–251.

Fazey, J., & Hardy, L. (1988). *The inverted-U Hypothesis: A catastrophe for sport psychology?* British Association of Sports Sciences Monograph No. 1. Leeds: The National Coaching Foundation.

Feltz, D. L. (1988). Self-confidence and sports performance. *Exercise and Sport Sciences Reviews, 16,* 423–457.

Feltz, D. L., & Landers, D. M. (1983). The effects of mental practice on motor skill learning and performance: A meta-analysis. *Journal of Sport Psychology, 5,* 25–57.

Feltz, D. L., Lirgg, C. D., & Albrecht, R. (1992). Psychological implications of competitive running in elite young distance runners: A longitudinal analysis. *The Sport Psychologist, 6*(2), 128–138.

Feltz, D. L., & Mugno, D. A. (1983). A replication of the path analysis of the causal elements in Bandura's theory of self-efficacy and the influence of autonomic perception. *Journal of Sport Psychology, 5,* 263–277.

Fender, L. K. (1989). Athlete burnout: Potential for research and intervention strategies. *The Sport Psychologist, 3,* 63–71.

Fenz, W. D. (1975). Coping mechanisms and performance under stress. In D. M. Landers (Ed.), *Psychology of sport and motor behavior, 11,* (pp. 3–24). Penn State HPER Series, No. 10. University Park: Pennsylvania State University Press.

Fenz, W. D. (1988). Learning to anticipate stressful events. *Journal of Sport and Exercise Psychology, 10,* 223–228.

FEPSAC (1996a). Position statement of the European Federation of Sport Psychology (FEPSAC): I. Definition of sport psychology. *The Sport Psychologist, 10,* 221–223.

FEPSAC (1996b). Position statement of the European Federation of Sport Psychology (FEPSAC): II. Children in sport. *The Sport Psychologist, 10,* 224–226.

Feshbach, S. (1971). Dynamics and morality of violence and aggression: Some psychological considerations. *American Psychologist, 26,* 281–292.

Fiedler, F. E. (1967). *A theory of leadership effectiveness.* New York: McGraw-Hill.

Fiedler, F. E. (1971). *Leadership.* Morristown, NJ: General Learning Press.

Fiedler, F. E., & Chemers, M. M. (1974). *Leadership and effective management.* Glenview, IL: Scott, Foresman and Company.

Fiedler, F. E., Chemers, M. M., & Mahar, L. (1977). *Improving leadership effectiveness—the leader match concept.* New York: John Wiley and Sons.

Fimrite, R. (1985, November 4). K. C. had a blast. *Sports Illustrated,* 22–38.

Finn, J. A., & Straub, W. F. (1977). Locus of control among Dutch and American women softball players. *Research Quarterly, 48,* 56–60.

Fisher, A. C. (1976). *Psychology of sport.* Palo Alto, CA: Mayfield Publishing Company.

Fisher, A. C. (1986, April). *Imagery from a sport psychology perspective.* Paper presented at the meeting of the American Alliance for Health, Physical Education, Recreation and Dance, Cincinnati, Ohio.

Fisher, A. C., Domm, M. A., & Wuest, D. A. (1988). Adherence to sports-injury rehabilitation programs. *The Physician and Sports Medicine, 16*(7), 47–51.

Evans, L., & Hardy, L. (1995). Sport injury and grief responses: A review. *Journal of Sport & Exercise Psychology, 17,* 227–246.

Ewen, R. B. (1984). *An introduction to theories of personality.* 2d ed. New York: Academic Press.

Eysenck, H. J., & Eysenck, S. B. G. (1968). *Eysenck personality inventory manual.* London: University of London Press.

Fisher, A. C., Mancini, V. H., Hirsch, R. L., Proulx, T. J., & Staurowsky, E. J. (1982). Coach-athlete interactions and team climate. *Journal of Sport Psychology, 4,* 388–404.

Fisher, A. C., & Zwart, E. F. (1982). Psychological analysis of athletes' anxiety responses. *Journal of Sport Psychology, 4,* 139–158.

Fisher, R. J. (1982). *Social psychology of an applied approach.* New York: St. Martin's Press.

Fitts, P. M., & Posner, M. I. (1967). *Human performance.* Belmont, CA: Brooks/Cole.

Fodero, J. M. (1980). An analysis of achievement motivation and motivational tendencies among men and women collegiate gymnasts. *International Journal of Sport Psychology, 11,* 100–112.

Folkman, S., & Lazarus, R. S. (1985). If it changes it must be a process: Study of emotion and coping during three stages of a college examination. *Journal of Personality and Social Psychology, 48,* 150–170.

Fontaine, C. (1975). Causal attribution on simulated versus real situations: When are people logical, when are they not? *Journal of Personality and Social Psychology, 32,* 1021–1029.

Fortier, M. S., Vallerand, R. J., Briere, N. M., & Provencher, P. J. (1995). Competitive and recreational sport structures and gender: A test of their relationship with sport motivation. *International Journal of Sport Psychology, 26,* 24–39.

Fox, K. R. (1990). *The physical self-perception profile manual.* DeKalb, IL: Northern Illinois University, Office for Health Promotion.

Fox, K. R., & Corbin, C. B. (1989). The physical self-perception profile: Development and preliminary validation. *Journal of Sport & Exercise Psychology, 11,* 408–430.

Fox, K. R., Goudas, M., Biddle, S., Duda, J., & Armstrong, N. (1994). Children's task and ego goal profiles in sport. *British Journal of Educational Psychology, 64,* 253–261.

Frank, M. G., & Gilovich, T. (1988). The dark side of self and social perception: Black uniforms and aggression in professional sports. *Journal of Personality and Social Psychology, 54,* 74–85.

Franken, R. E., Hill, R., & Kierstead, J. (1994). Sport interest as predicted by the personality measures of competitiveness, mastery, instrumentality, expressivity, and sensation seeking. *Personality and Individual Differences, 17* (4)*,* 467–476.

Fredenburgh, F. A. (1971). *The psychology of personality and adjustment.* Menlo Park, CA: Benjamin-Cummings.

Frederick, C. M., & Ryan, R. M. (1995). Self-determination in sport: A review using cognitive evaluation theory. *International Journal of Sport Psychology, 26,* 5–23.

Freedson, P. S., Mihevic, P., Loucks, A., & Girandola, R. (1983). Physique, body composition, and psychological characteristics of competitive female bodybuilders. *The Physician and Sports Medicine, 11,* 85–90, 93.

Freischlag, J., & Schmedke, C. (1980). Violence in sports: Its causes and some solutions. In W. F. Straub (Ed.), *Sport psychology: An analysis of athlete behavior* 2d ed. Ithaca, NY: Mouvement Publications.

French, S. N. (1978). Electromyographic biofeedback for tension control during gross motor skill acquisition. *Perceptual and Motor Skills, 47,* 883–889.

Freud, S. (1933). *New introductory lectures on psychoanalysis.* New York: Norton.

Freud, S. (1950). Why war? In J. Strachey (Ed.), *Collected papers.* London: Hogarth.

Friedman, E., & Berger, B. G. (1991). Influences of gender, masculinity, and femininity on the effectiveness of three stress reduction techniques: Jogging, relaxation response, and group interaction. *Journal of Applied Sport Psychology, 3,* 61–86.

Frierman, S. H., Weinberg, R. S., & Jackson, A. (1990). The relationship between goal proximity and specificity in bowling: A field experiment. *The Sport Psychologist, 4,* 145–154.

Frieze, I. H. (1976). Causal attributions and information seeking to explain success and failure. *Journal of Research in Personality, 10,* 293–305.

Frieze, I. H., & Weiner, B. (1971). Cue utilization and attributional judgements for success and failure. *Journal of Personality, 39,* 591–605.

Fry, R. W., Grove, J. R., Morton, A. R., Zeroni, P. M., Gaudierei, S., & Keast, D. (1994). Psychological and immunological correlates of acute overtraining. *British Journal of Sports Medicine, 28,* 241–246.

Fung, L., & Fu, F. H. (1995). Psychological determinants between wheelchair sport finalists and non-finalists. *International Journal of Sport Psychology, 26,* 568–579.

Furst, D. M., & Tenenbaum, G. (1985). Influence of attentional focus on reaction time. *Psychological Reports, 56,* 299–302.

G

Gammon, C. (1985, June 10). A day of horror and shame. *Sports Illustrated, 62,* 20–35.

Garcia, A. W., & King, A. C. (1991). Predicting long-term adherence to aerobic exercise: A comparison of two models. *Journal of Sport and Exercise Psychology, 13*(4), 394–410.

Gardner, D. E., Shields, D. L. L., Bredemeier, B. J. L., & Bostrom, A. (1996). The relationship between perceived coaching behaviors and team cohesion among baseball and softball players. *The Sport Psychologist, 10,* 367–381.

Gardner, F. L. (1991). Professionalization of sport psychology: A reply to Silva. *The Sport Psychologist, 5,* 55–60.

Garland, D. J., & Barry, J. R. (1990). Personality and leader behaviors in collegiate football: A multidimensional approach to performance. *Journal of Research in Personality, 24,* 355–370.

Gauvin, L., & Rejeski, W. J. (1993). The exercise-induced feeling inventory: Development and initial validation. *Journal of Sport & Exercise Psychology, 15,* 403–423.

Gayton, W. F., Very, M., & Hearns, J. (1993). Psychological momentum in team sports. *Journal of Sport Behavior, 16,* 121–123.

Geen, R. G., & O'Neal, E. C. (1969). Activation of cue-elicited aggression by general arousal. *Journal of Personality and Social Psychology, 11,* 289–292.

George, T. R. (1994). Self-confidence and baseball performance: A causal examination of self-efficacy theory. *Journal of Sport & Exercise Psychology, 16,* 381–399.

George, T. R., & Feltz, D. L. (1995). Motivation in sport from a collective efficacy perspective. *International Journal of Sport Psychology, 26,* 98–116.

Geron, D., Furst, P., & Rotstein, P. (1986). Personality of athletes participating in various sports. *International Journal of Sport Psychology, 17,* 120–135.

Gilbert, B., & Twyman, L. (1983, January 31). Violence: Out of hand in the stands. *Sports Illustrated,* 62–68.

Gill, D. L. (1978). Cohesiveness and performance in sport groups. In R. S. Hutton (Ed.), *Exercise and Sport Science Reviews, 5,* 131–155.

Gill, D. L. (1980). Success-failure attributions in competitive groups: An exception to egocentrism. *Journal of Sport Psychology, 2,* 106–114.

Gill, D. L. (1988). Gender differences in competitive orientation and sport participation. *International Journal of Sport Psychology, 19,* 145–159.

Gill, D. L. (1993). Competitiveness and competitive orientation in sport. In R. N. Singer, M. Murphey, & L. K. Tennant (Eds.), *Handbook of research on sport psychology* (pp. 314–327). New York: Macmillan.

Gill, D. L., & Deeter, T. E. (1988). Development of the SOQ. *Research Quarterly for Exercise and Sport, 59,* 191–202.

Gill, D. L., Dzewaltowski, D. A. (1988). Competitive orientations among intercollegiate athletes: Is winning the only thing? *The Sport Psychologist, 2,* 212–221.

Gill, D. L., Dzewaltowski, D. A., & Deeter, T. E. (1988). The relationship of competitiveness and achievement orientation to participation in sport and nonsport activities. *Journal of Sport & Exercise Psychology, 10,* 139–150.

Gill, D. L., Gross, J. B., & Huddleston, S. (1983). Participation motivation in youth sports. *International Journal of Sport Psychology, 14,* 1–14.

Gill, D. L., Gross, J. B., Huddleston, S., & Shifflett, B. (1984). Sex differences in achievement cognitions and performance. *Research Quarterly for Exercise and Sport, 55,* 340–346.

Gill, D. L., Ruder, M. K., & Gross, J. B. (1982). Open-ended attributions in team competition. *Journal of Sport Psychology, 4,* 159–169.

Gill, D. L., & Strom, E. H. (1985). The effect of attentional focus on performance of an endurance task. *International Journal of Sport Psychology, 16,* 217–223.

Gillis, J. H. (1979). Effects of achieving tendency, gender, and outcome on causal attributions following motor performance. *Research Quarterly, 50,* 610–619.

Ginsburg, H., & Opper, S. (1969). *Piaget's theory of intellectual development.* Englewood Cliffs, NJ: Prentice-Hall.

Gladue, B. A. (1991). Qualitative and quantitative sex differences in self-reported aggressive behavior characteristics. *Psychological Reports, 68,* 675–684.

Glenn, S. D., & Horn, T. S. (1993). Psychological and personal predictors of leadership behavior in female soccer athletes. *Journal of Applied Sport Psychology, 5,* 17–34.

Godin, G. (1994). Theories of reasoned action and planned behavior: Usefulness for exercise promotion. *Medicine and Science in Sports and Exercise, 26,* 1391–1394.

Goldstein, J. H. (1983). *Sports violence.* New York: Springer-Verlag.

Goodkin, K. (1988). Psychiatric aspects of HIV infection. *Texas Medicine, 84,* 55–61.

Goranson, R. E. (1970). Media violence and aggressive behavior: A review of experimental research. In L. Berkowitz (Ed.), *Advances in experimental social psychology* (Vol. 5, pp. 1–31). New York: Academic Press.

Gordon, S. (1988). Decision styles and coaching effectiveness in university soccer. *Canadian Journal of Sport Sciences, 13,* 56–65.

Gorely, T., & Gordon, S. (1995). An examination of the transtheoretical model and exercise behavior in older adults. *Journal of Sports & Exercise Psychology, 17,* 312–324.

Gorton, B. E. (1949). The physiology of hypnosis. *Psychiatric Quarterly, 23,* 457–485.

Goss, J. D. (1994). Hardiness and mood disturbances in swimmers while overtraining. *Journal of Sport & Exercise Psychology, 16,* 135–149.

Goudas, M., Biddle, S., Fox, K., & Underwood, M. (1995). It ain't what you do, it's the way that you do it! Teaching style affects children's motivation in track and field lessons. *The Sport Psychologist, 9,* 254–264.

Gough, H. G. (1975). *Manual for the California psychological inventory.* Palo Alto, CA: Consulting Psychological Press.

Gould, D. (1983). Developing psychological skills in young athletes. In N. Wood (Ed.), *Coaching science update.* Ottawa, Ontario: Coaching Association of Canada.

Gould, D. (1986). Goal setting for peak performance. In J. M. Williams (Ed.), *Applied sport psychology: Personal growth to peak performance* (pp. 133–147). Palo Alto, CA: Mayfield Publishing Company.

Gould, D., Eklund, R. C., & Jackson, S. A. (1992a). 1988 U.S. Olympic wrestling excellence: I. Mental preparation, precompetitive cognition, and affect. *The Sport Psychologist, 6,* 358–382.

Gould, D., Eklund, R. C., & Jackson, S. A. (1992b). 1988 U.S. Olympic wrestling excellence: II. Thoughts and affect occuring during competition. *The Sport Psychologist, 6,* 383–402.

Gould, D., Eklund, R. C., & Jackson, S. A. (1993). Coping strategies used by U.S. Olympic wrestlers. *Research Quarterly for Exercise and Sport, 64,* 83–93.

Gould, D., Feltz, D., & Weiss, M. (1985). Motives for participation in competitive youth swimming. *International Journal of Sport Psychology, 16,* 126–140.

Gould, D., Finch, L. M., & Jackson, S. A. (1993). Coping strategies used by national champion figure skaters. *Research Quarterly for Exercise and Sport, 64,* 453–468.

Gould, D., Hodge, K., Peterson, K., & Giannini, J. (1989). An exploratory examination of strategies used by elite coaches to enhance self-efficacy in athletes. *Journal of Sport and Exercise Psychology, 11,* 128–140.

Gould, D., Horn, T., & Spreeman, J. (1983). Sources of stress in junior elite wrestlers. *Journal of Sport Psychology, 5,* 159–171.

Gould, D., Petlichkoff, L., Simons, J., & Vevera, M. (1987). Relationship between competitive state anxiety inventory-2 subscales scores and pistol shooting performance. *Journal of Sport Psychology, 9,* 33–42.

Gould, D., Petlichkoff, L., & Weinberg, R. S. (1984). Antecedents of, temporal changes in, and relationships between CSAI-2 subcomponents. *Journal of Sport Psychology, 6,* 289–304.

Gould, D., & Pick, S. (1995). Sport psychology: The Griffith era, 1920–1940. *The Sport Psychologist, 9,* 391–415.

Gould, D., Tammen, V., Murphy, S., & May, J. (1989). An examination of U.S. Olympic sport psychology consultants and services they provide. *The Sport Psychologist, 3,* 300–312.

Gould, D., Tuffy, S., Hardy, L., & Lochbaum, M. (1993). Multidimensional state anxiety and middle distance running performance: An exploratory examination of Hanin's (1980) zones of optimal functioning hypothesis. *Journal of Applied Sport Psychology, 5,* 85–95.

Gould, D., Tuffy, S., Udry, E., & Loehr, J. (1996b). Burnout in competitive junior tennis players: II. Qualitative analysis. *The Sport Psychologist, 10,* 341–366.

Gould, D., & Udry, E. (1994). Psychological skills for enhancing performance: Arousal regulation strategies. *Medicine and Science in Sports and Exercise, 26,* 478–485.

Gould, D., Udry, E., Tuffy, S., & Loehr, J. (1996a). Burnout in competitive junior tennis players: I. A quantitiative psychological assessment. *The Sport Psychologist, 10,* 322–340.

Gould, D., Weinberg, R., & Jackson, A. (1980). Mental preparation strategies, cognitions, and strength performance. *Journal of Sport Psychology, 2,* 329–339.

Gould, D., & Weiss, M. (1981). The effects of model similarity and model task on self-efficacy and muscular endurance. *Journal of Sport Psychology, 3,* 17–29.

Graen, G., & Cashman, J. F. (1975). A rolemaking model of leadership in formal organizations. In J. G. Hunt & L. L. Larson (Eds.), *Leadership frontiers.* Kent, OH: Kent State University Press.

Gray, S. W., & Fernandez, S. J. (1990). Effects of visuo-motor behavior rehearsal with videotaped modeling on basketball shooting performance. *Psychology: A Journal of Human Behavior, 26,* 41–47.

Green, L. B. (1992). The use of imagery in the rehabilitation of injured athletes. *The Sport Psychologist, 6,* 416–428.

Greenberg, J. S. (1990). *Comprehensive stress management.* 3d ed. Dubuque, IA: Wm. C. Brown Publishers.

Greene, D., & Lepper, M. R. (1974a). Effects of extrinsic rewards on children's subsequent intrinsic interest. *Child Development, 45,* 1141–1145.

Greene, D., & Lepper, M. R. (1974b, September). Intrinsic motivation: How to turn play into work. *Psychology Today,* 49–54.

Greenspan, M. J., & Feltz, D. L. (1989). Psychological interventions with athletes in competitive situations: A review. *The Sport Psychologist, 3,* 219–236.

Greenwell, J., & Dengerink, H. A. (1973). The role of perceived versus actual attack in human physical aggression. *Journal of Personality and Social Psychology, 26,* 66–71.

Greenwood, C. M., Dzewaltowski, D. A., & French, R. (1990). Self-efficacy and psychological well being of wheelchair tennis participants. *Adapted Physical Activity Quarterly, 7,* 12–21.

Greer, D. L. (1983). Spectator booing and the home advantage: A study of social influence in the basketball arena. *Social Psychology Quarterly, 46,* 252–261.

Gregg, E., & Rejeski, J. (1990). Social psychobiologic dysfunction associated with

anabolic steroid abuse: A review. *The Sport Psychologist, 4,* 275–284.

Grouios, G. (1992). Mental practice: A review. *Journal of Sport Behavior, 15,* 42–59.

Grove, J. R., Hanrahan, S., & McInman, A. (1991). Success/failure bias in attributions across involvement categories in sport. *Personality and Social Psychology Bulletin, 17,* 93–97.

Grove, J. R., Hanrahan, S. J., & Stewart, R. M. L. (1990). Attributions for rapid or slow recovery from sports injuries. *Canadian Journal of Sport Sciences, 15,* 107–114.

Grove, J. R., & Pargman, D. (1986). Attributions and performance during competition. *Journal of Sport Psychology, 8,* 129–134.

Grove, J. R., & Prapavessis, H. (1992). Preliminary evidence for the reliability and validity of an abbreviated profile of mood states. *International Journal of Sport Psychology, 23,* 93–109.

Grove, J. R., & Prapavessis, H. (1995). The effect of skill level and sport outcomes on dimensional aspects of causal attributions. *Australian Psychologist, 30,* 92–95.

Grusky, O. (1963). The effects of formal structure on managerial recruitment: A study of baseball organization. *Sociometry, 26,* 345–353.

Guyton, A. C. (1976). *Structure and function of the nervous system.* Philadelphia: W. B. Saunders Company.

H

Hackney, A. C., Pearman, S. N., III, & Nowacki, J. M. (1990). Physiological profiles of overtrained and stale athletes: A review. *Journal of Applied Sport Psychology, 2,* 21–33.

Halberstam, D. (1994). *October 1964.* New York: Villard Books.

Hale, B. D. (1982). The effects of internal and external imagery on muscular and ocular concomitants. *Journal of Sport Psychology, 4,* 379–387.

Hall, A., & Terry, P. C. (1995). Trends in mood profiles in the preparation phase and racing phase of the 1993 World Rowing Championships, Roundnice, the Czech Republic. *Journal of Sports Sciences, 13,* 56–57.

Hall, C. R., Mack, D., & Paivio, A. (1996). *Imagery use by athletes: Development of the Sport Imagery Questionnaire.* Manuscript submitted for publication.

Hall, C. R., & Martin, K. (in press). Measuring movement imagery abilities: A revision of the Movement Imagery Questionnaire. *Journal of Mental Imagery.*

Hall, C. R., & Pongrac, J. (1983). *Movement imagery questionnaire.* London, Ontario: University of Western Ontario.

Hall, C. R., Rodgers, W. M., & Barr, K. A. (1990). The use of imagery by athletes in selected sports. *The Sport Psychologist, 4,* 1–10.

Hall, E. G., & Erffmeyer, E. S. (1983). The effect of visuo-motor behavior rehearsal with videotaped modeling of free throw accuracy of intercollegiate female basketball players. *Journal of Sport Psychology, 5,* 343–346.

Hall, E. G., & Hardy, C. J. (1991). Ready, aim, fire . . . relaxation strategies for enhancing pistol marksmanship. *Perceptual and Motor Skills, 72,* 775–786.

Hall, H. K., & Byrne, A. T. J. (1988). Goal setting in sport: Clarifying recent anomalies. *Journal of Sport and Exercise Psychology, 10,* 184–198.

Hall, H. K., Weinberg, R. S., & Jackson, A. (1987). Effects of goal specificity, goal difficulty, and information feedback on endurance performance. *Journal of Sport Psychology, 9,* 43–54.

Hallander, D. B., Meyers, M.C., & LeUnes, A. (1995). Psychological factors associated with overtraining: Implications for youth sport coaches. *Journal of Sport Behavior, 18,* 3–20.

Halliwell, W. R. (1978). A reaction to Deci's paper on intrinsic motivation. In D. M. Landers & R. W. Christina (Eds.), *Psychology of motor behavior and sport, 1977.* Champaign, IL: Human Kinetics Publishers.

Halliwell, W. R. (1980). A reaction to Dweck's paper on learned helplessness in sport. In C. H. Nadeau, W. R. Halliwell, K. M. Newell, & G. C. Roberts (Eds.), *Psychology of motor behavior and sport, 1979.* Champaign, IL: Human Kinetics Publishers.

Halpin, A. W. (1966). *Theory and research in administration.* London: Macmillan.

Halpin, A. W., & Winer, B. J. (1957). A factorial study of the Leader Behavior Description Questionnaire. In R. M. Stogdill & A. E. Coons (Eds.), *Leader behavior: Its description and measurement.* Columbus: Ohio State University Press.

Halvari, H. (1989). The relations between competitive experiences in mid-childhood and achievement motives among male wrestlers. *Psychological Reports, 65,* 979–988.

Hanin, Y. L. (1980). A study of anxiety in sports. In W. F. Straub (Ed.), *Sport psychology: An analysis of athlete behavior* (pp. 236–249). New York: Mouvement Publications.

Hanin, Y. L. (1986). State-trait anxiety research on sports in the USSR. In C. D. Speilberger & R. Dias-Guerrero (Eds.), *Cross-cultural anxiety* (pp. 45–64). Washington, DC: Hemisphere.

Hanin, Y. L. (1989). Interpersonal and intragroup anxiety: Conceptual and methodological issues. In D. Hackfort & C. D. Spielberger (Eds.), *Anxiety in sports: An international perspective* (pp. 19–28). Washington, DC: Hemisphere Publishing Corporation.

Hanin, Y. L., & Syrja, P. (1995). Performance affect in junior ice hockey players: An application of the individual zones of optimal functioning model. *The Sport Psychologist, 9,* 169–187.

Hannaford, C. P., Harrell, E. H., & Cox, K. (1988). Psychophysiological effects of a running program on depression and anxiety in a psychiatric population. *The Psychological Record, 38,* 37–48.

Hanrahan, C., Tetreau, B., & Sarrizin, C. (1995). Use of imagery while performing dance movement. *International Journal of Sport Psychology, 26,* 413–430.

Hanrahan, S. J. (1995). Psychological skills training for competitive wheelchair and amputee athletes. *Australian Psychologist, 30,* 96–101.

Hanson, S. J., McCullagh, P., & Tonymon, P. (1992). The relationship of personality characteristics, life stress, and coping resources to athletic injury. *Journal of Sport and Exercise Psychology, 14*(3), 262–272.

Hanson, T. W., & Gould, D. (1988). Factors affecting the ability of coaches to estimate their athlete's trait and state anxiety levels. *The Sport Psychologist, 2,* 298–313.

Hardman, K. (1973). A dual approach to the study of personality and performance in sport. In H. T. A. Whiting, K. Hardman, L. B. Hendry, & M. G. Jones (Eds.), *Personality and performance in physical education and sport.* London: Kimpton.

Hardy, C. J., & Crace, R. K. (1991). The effects of task structure and teammate competence on social loafing. *Journal of Sport & Exercise Psychology, 13,* 372–381.

Hardy, C. J., & Riehl, R. E. (1988). An examination of the life stress-injury relationship among noncontact sports participants. *Behavioral Medicine, 14,* 113–118.

Hardy, C. J., Richman, J. M., & Rosenfeld, L. B. (1991). The role of social support in the life stress/injury relationship. *The Sport Psychologist, 5,* 128–139.

Hardy, L. (1990). A catastrophe model of performance in sport. In J. G. Jones & L. Hardy (Eds.), *Stress and performance in sport.* New York: John Wiley & Sons Ltd.

Hardy, L. (1996). Testing the predictions of the cusp catastrophe model of anxiety and performance. *The Sport Psychologist, 10,* 140–156.

Hardy, L., & Parfitt, G. (1991). A catastrophe model of anxiety and performance. *British Journal of Psychology, 82,* 163–178.

Hardy, L., Parfitt, G., & Pates, J. (1994). Performance catastrophes in sport: A test of the hysteresis hypothesis. *Journal of Sport Sciences, 12,* 327–334.

Harger, G. J., & Raglin, J. S. (1994). Correspondence between actual and recalled precompetition anxiety in collegiate track and field athletes. *Journal of Sport & Exercise Psychology, 16,* 206–211.

Harlow, R. G. (1951). Masculine inadequacy and compensatory development of physique. *Journal of Personality, 19,* 312–323.

Harrell, W. A. (1980). Aggression by high school basketball players: An observational study of the effects of opponents' aggression and frustration-inducing factors. *International Journal of Sport Psychology, 11,* 290–298.

Harris, D. V. (1980a). On the brink of catastrophe. In R. M. Suinn (Ed.), *Psychology in sports: Methods and applications* (pp. 112–118). Minneapolis: Burgess Publishing Company.

Harris, D. V. (1980b). Assessment of motivation in sport and physical education. In W. F. Straub (Ed.), *Sport psychology: An analysis of athlete behavior* (2d ed., pp. 126–135). Ithaca, NY: Mouvement Publications.

Harris, D. V., & Harris, B. L. (1984). *The athlete's guide to sports psychology: Mental skills for physical people.* New York: Leisure Press.

Harris, D. V., & Robinson, W. J. (1986). The effects of skill level on EMG activity during internal and external imagery. *Journal of Sport Psychology, 8,* 105–111.

Harrison, J., & MacKinnon, P. C. B. (1966). Physiological role of the adrenal medulla in the palmar anhidrotic response in stress. *Journal of Applied Physiology, 21,* 88–92.

Hart, E. A., Leary, M. R., & Rejeski, W. J. (1989). The measurement of social physique anxiety. *Journal of Sport & Exercise Psychology, 11,* 94–104.

Harte, J. L., & Eifert, G. H. (1995). The effects of running, environment, and attentional focus on athletes' catecholamine and cortisol levels and mood. *Psychophysiology, 32,* 49–54.

Harter, S. (1978). Effectance motivation reconsidered: Towards a developmental model. *Human Development, 21,* 34–64.

Harter, S. (1981). A model of intrinsic mastery motivation in children: Individual differences and developmental change. In A. Collins (Ed.), *Minnesota symposium on child psychology* (Vol. 14, pp. 215–255). Hillsdale, NJ: Erlbaum.

Harter, S. (1982). The perceived competence scale for children. *Child Development, 53,* 87–97.

Hartung, G. H., & Farge, E. J. (1977). Personality and physiological traits in middle-aged runners and joggers. *Journal of Gerontology, 32,* 541–548.

Hassmen, P., & Bomstrand, E. (1995). Mood state relationships and soccer team performance. *The Sport Psychologist, 9,* 297–308.

Hathaway, S. R., & McKinley, J. C. (1967). *Minnesota Multiphasic Personality Inventory manual.* New York: Psychological Corporation.

Hausenblas, H. A., & Carron, A. V. (1996). Group cohesion and self-handicapping in female and male athletes. *Journal of Sport & Exercise Psychology, 18,* 132–143.

Hausenblas, H. A., Carron, A. V., & Mack, D. E. (1997). Applicaiton of the theories of reasoned action and planned behavior to exercise behavior: A meta-analysis. *Journal of Sport & Exercise Psychology, 19,* 36–51.

Healey, T. R., & Landers, D. M. (1973). Effect of need achievement and task difficulty on competitive and noncompetitive motor performance. *Journal of Motor Behavior, 5,* 121–128.

Hecker, J. E., & Kaczor, L. M. (1988). Application of imagery theory to sport psychology: Some preliminary findings. *Journal of Sport & Exercise Psychology, 10,* 363–373.

Heider, F. (1944). Social perception and phenomenal causality. *Psychological Review, 51,* 358–374.

Heider, F. (1958). *The psychology of interpersonal relations.* New York: John Wiley and Sons.

Hellstedt, J. C. (1987). The coach/parent/athlete relationship. *The Sport Psychologist, 1,* 151–160.

Helmreich, R., & Spence, J. T. (1977). Sex roles and achievement. In R. W. Christina & D. M. Landers (Eds.), *Psychology of motor behavior and sport, 1976* (Vol. 2). Champaign, IL: Human Kinetics Publishers.

Hemphill, J. K., & Coons, A. E. (1957). Development of the leader behavior description questionnaire. In R. M. Stogdill & A. E. Coons (Eds.), *Leader behavior: Its description and measurement.* Columbus: Ohio State University Press.

Hendy, H. M., & Bower, B. J. (1993). Gender differences in attribution for triathlon performance. *Sex Roles, 29,* 527–542.

Henry, F. M. (1941). Personality differences in athletes, physical education, and aviation students. *Psychological Bulletin, 38,* 745.

Henschen, K. P., Horvat, M., & French, R. (1984). A visual comparison of psychological profiles between able-bodied and wheelchair athletes. *Adapted Physical Activity Quarterly, 1,* 118–124.

Henschen, K. P., Horvat, M., & Roswal, G. (1992). Psychological profiles of the United States Wheelchair basketball team. *International Journal of Sport Psychology, 23,* 128–137.

Hersey, P., & Blanchard, K. H. (1969). Life cycle theory of leadership. *Training and Developmental Journal, 23,* 26–34.

Hersey, P., & Blanchard, K. H. (1977). *Management of organizational behavior.* Englewood Cliffs, NJ: Prentice-Hall.

Hess, R. (1957). *Diencephalon-autonomic and extra-pyramidal functions.* New York: Grune and Stratton.

Heyman, S. R. (1987). Research and intervention in sport psychology: Issues encountered in working with an amateur boxer. *The Sport Psychologist, 1,* 208–223.

Hickman, J. L. (1979). How to elicit supernormal capabilities in athletes. In P. Klavora & J. V. Daniel (Eds.), *Coach, athlete, and the sport psychologist.* Champaign, IL: Human Kinetics Publishers.

Hill, K. L., & Borden, F. (1995). The effect of attentional cueing scripts on competitive bowling performance. *International Journal of Sport Psychology, 26,* 503–512.

Hin, P. (1992). Efficacy of Tai Chi, brisk walking, meditation and reading in reducing mental and emotional stress. *Journal of Psychosomatic Research, 36,* 361–370.

Hinkle, J. S. (1992). Aerobic running behavior and psychotherapeutics: Implications for sports counseling and psychology. *Journal of Sport Behavior, 15,* 263–277.

Hinkle, J. S. (1994). Integrating sport psychology and sports counseling: Developmental programming, education, and research. *Journal of Sport Behavior, 17,* 52–59.

Hinshaw, K. E. (1991). The effects of mental practice on motor skill performance: Critical evaluation and meta-analysis. *Imagination, Cognition, and Personality, 11,* 3–35.

Hird, J. S., Landers, D. M., Thomas, J. R., & Horan, J. J. (1991). Physical practice is superior to mental practice in enhancing cognitive and motor task performance. *Journal of Sport & Exercise Performance, 13,* 281–293.

Hobson, M. L., & Rejeski, W. J. (1993). Does the dose of acute exercise mediate psychophysiological responses to mental stress? *Journal of Sport & Exercise Psychology, 15,* 77–87.

Hole, J. W., Jr. (1981). *Human anatomy and physiology.* Dubuque, IA: Wm. C. Brown Publishers.

Hollander, E. P. (1971). *Principles and methods of social psychology.* 2d ed. New York: Oxford University Press.

Hollander, E. P. (1976). *Principles and methods of social psychology.* 3d ed. New York: Oxford University Press.

Hollandsworth, J. G. (1977). Differentiating assertion and aggression: Some behavioral guidelines. *Behavioral Therapy, 8,* 347–353.

Hollingsworth, B. (1975). Effects of performance goals and anxiety on learning a gross motor task. *Research Quarterly, 46,* 162–168.

Holloway, J. B., Beuter, A., & Duda, J. L. (1988). Self-efficacy and training for strength in adolescent girls. *Journal of Applied Social Psychology, 18,* 699–719.

Holsopple, J. Q., & Miale, F. R. (1954). *Sentence completion.* Springfield, IL: Charles C. Thomas.

Horn, T. S. (1984). Expectancy effects in the interscholastic athletic setting: Methodological considerations. *Journal of Sport Psychology, 6,* 60–76.

Horne, T., & Carron, A. V. (1985). Compatibility in coach-athlete relationships. *Journal of Sport Psychology, 7,* 137–149.

Horner, M. S. (1968). *Sex differences in achievement motivation and performance in competitive and noncompetitive situations.* Unpublished doctoral dissertation, University of Michigan, Ann Arbor.

Horner, M. S. (1972). Towards an understanding of achievement-related conflicts in women. *Journal of Social Issues, 28*(2), 157–175.

Horvat, M., Roswal, G., & Henshen, K. (1991). Psychological profiles of disabled athletes in competition. *Clinical Kinesiology, 45,* 14–18.

House, R. J. (1971). A path-goal theory of leader effectiveness. *Administrative Science Quarterly, 16,* 321–338.

House, R. J., & Mitchell, T. R. (1974, Autumn). Path-goal theory of leadership. *Journal of Contemporary Business, 5,* 81–97.

Hughes, S. (1990). Implementing psychological skills training in high school athletics. *Journal of Sport Behavior, 13,* 15–22.

Hull, C. L. (1933). *Hypnosis and suggestibility.* New York: Appleton.

Hull, C. L. (1943). *Principles of behavior.* New York: Appleton-Century-Crofts, Inc.

Hull, C. L. (1951). *Essentials of behavior.* New Haven, CT: Yale University Press.

Humphrey, J. H. (1986). *Profiles in stress.* New York: AMS Press, Inc.

Hunt, J. A., & Larson, L. L. (1974). *Contingency approaches to leadership.* Carbondale: Southern Illinois University Press.

Husak, W. S., & Hemenway, D. P. (1986). The influence of competition day practice on the activation and performance of collegiate swimmers. *Journal of Sport Behavior, 9,* 95–100.

Hutchinson, B. (1972). *Locus of control and participation in intercollegiate athletics.* Doctoral dissertation, Springfield College, Springfield, MA.

Hutchinson, T. P. (1981). A review of some unusual applications of signal detection theory. *Quality and Quantity, 15,* 71–98.

I

Ickes, W. J., & Layden, M. A. (1978). Attributional styles. In J. H. Harvey, W. J. Ickes, & R. F. Kidd (Eds.), *New directions in attribution research* (Vol. 2). Hillsdale, NJ: Erlbaum.

Ievleva, L., & Orlick, T. (1991). Mental links to enhanced healing: An exploratory study. *The Sport Psychologist, 5,* 25–40.

Ikai, M., & Steinhaus, A. H. (1961). Some factors modifying the expression of human strength. *Journal of Applied Physiology, 16,* 157–163.

Inciong, P. A. (1974). *Leadership styles and team success.* Unpublished doctoral dissertation, University of Utah, Salt Lake City.

Inlay, G. J., Carda, R. D., Stanbrough, M. E., Dreiling, A. M., & O'Connor, P. J. (1995). Anxiety and athletic performance: A test of Zone of Optimal Functioning theory. *International Journal of Sport Psychology, 26,* 295–306.

International Society of Sport Psychology (1992). Physical activity and psychological benefits: A position statement from the international society of sport psychology. *Journal of Applied Sport Psychology, 4,* 94–98.

Ironson, G., LaPerriere, A., Antoni, M., Klimas, N., Fletcher, M. A., & Schneiderman, N. (1990). Changes in immunologic and psychological measures as a function of anticipation and reaction to news of HIV-1 antibody status. *Psychosomatic Medicine, 52,* 247–270.

Irving, P. G., & Goldstein, S. R. (1990). Effect of home-field advantage on peak performance of baseball pitchers. *Journal of Sports Behavior, 13,* 23–28.

Isaac, A. (1992). Mental practice—does it work in the field? *The Sport Psychologist, 6,* 192–198.

Isaac, A., Marks, D. F., & Russell, D. G. (1986). An instrument for assessing imagery of movement: The vividness of movement imagery questionnaire (VMIQ). *Journal of Mental Imagery, 10,* 23–30.

Isaacs, P. (1982). *Hypnotic responsiveness and dimensions of thinking style and imagery.* Unpublished doctoral dissertation, University of Waterloo, Waterloo, Ontario.

Iso-Ahola, S. E. (1977a). Immediate attributional effects of success and failure in the field: Testing some laboratory hypotheses. *European Journal of Social Psychology, 7,* 275–296.

Iso-Ahola, S. E. (1977b). A test of the attributional theory of success and failure with Little League baseball players. In J. H. Salmela (Ed.), *Canadian Symposium for Psychomotor Learning and Sport Psychology, 1975.* Ithaca, NY: Mouvement Publications.

Iso-Ahola, S. E. (1978). Perceiving the causes of objective and subjective outcomes following motor performance. *Research Quarterly, 49*(1), 62–70.

Iso-Ahola, S. E. (1979). Sex-role stereotypes and causal attributions for success and failure in motor performance. *Research Quarterly, 50,* 630–640.

Iso-Ahola, S. E. (1995). Intrapersonal and interpersonal factors in athletic performance. *Scandinavian Journal of Medicine and Science in Sports, 5,* 191–199.

Ito, M. (1979). The differential effects of hypnosis and motivational suggestions on muscular strength. *Japanese Journal of Physical Education, 24,* 93–100.

J

Jackson, D. W., Jarrett, H., Barley, D., Kausch, J., Swanson, J. J., & Powell, J. W. (1978). Injury prediction in the young athlete. *American Journal of Sports Medicine, 6,* 6–14.

Jackson, S. A. (1992). Athletes in flow: A qualitative investigation of flow states in elite figure skaters. *Journal of Applied Sport Psychology, 4,* 161–180.

Jackson, S. A. (1995). Factors influencing the occurrence of flow state in elite athletes. *Journal of Applied Sport Psychology, 7,* 138–166.

Jackson, S. A. (1996). Toward a conceptual understanding of the flow experience in elite athletes. *Research Quarterly for Exercise and Sport, 67,* 76–90.

Jackson, S. A., & Marsh, H. W. (1996). Development and validation of a scale to measure optimal experience: The flow state scale. *Journal of Sport and Exercise Psychology, 18,* 17–35.

Jacobson, E. (1929). *Progressive relaxation.* 1st ed. Chicago: University of Chicago Press.

Jacobson, E. (1931). Electrical measurements of neuromuscular states during mental activities. *American Journal of Physiology, 96,* 115–121.

Jacobson, E. (1938). *Progressive relaxation.* 2d ed. Chicago: University of Chicago Press.

Jacobson, E. (1974). *Progressive relaxation.* reprint. Chicago: The University of Chicago Press.

Jambor, E. A., & Rudisill, M. E. (1992). The relationship between children's locus of control and sport choices. *Journal of Human Movement Studies, 22,* 35–48.

James, W. (1980). *The principles of psychology* (Vol. 1). New York: Henry Holt and Co.

Janssen, J. J., Sheikh, A. A. (1994). Enhancing athletic performance through imagery: An overview. In A. A. Sheikh, & E. R. Korn (Eds.), *Imagery in sports and physical performance*. Amityville, NY: Baywood.

Jefferies, S. C., & Esparza, R. (1992). Effects of imagery, relaxation, and self-talk on competitive interscholastic wrestling performance. *Research Quarterly for Exercise and Sport, 63* (Supplement), A-79.

Johnson, J. E., & Dabbs, J. M., Jr. (1967). Enumeration of active sweat glands: A sample physiological indicator of psychological changes. *Nursing Research, 16,* 273–276.

Johnson, W. O., & Moore, K. (Oct. 3, 1988). The loser. *Sports Illustrated, 69,* 20–27.

Johnson, W. R. (1961). Hypnosis and muscular performance. *Journal of Sports Medicine and Physical Fitness, 1,* 71–79.

Johnston, B., & McCabe, M. P. (1993). Cognitive strategies for coping with stress in a simulated golfing task. *International Journal of Sport Psychology, 24,* 30–48.

Jones, G. (1991). Recent developments and current issues in competitive state anxiety research. *The Psychologist: Bulletin of the British Psychological Society, 4,* 152–155.

Jones, G. (1995). More than just a game: Research developments and issues in competitive anxiety in sport. *British Journal of Psychology, 86,* 449–478.

Jones, G., & Hanton, S. (1996). Interpretation of competitive anxiety symptoms and goal attainment expectancies. *Journal of Sport & Exercise Psychology, 18,* 144–157.

Jones, G., Hanton, S., & Swain, A. (1994). Intensity and interpretation of anxiety symptoms in elite and non-elite sports performers. *Personality & Individual Differences, 17,* 657–663.

Jones, G., & Swain, A. (1992). Intensity and direction as dimensions of competitive state anxiety and relationships with competitiveness. *Perceptual and Motor Skills, 74,* 467–472.

Jones, G., & Swain, A. (1995). Predispositions to experience debilitative and facilitative anxiety in elite and nonelite performers. *The Sport Psychologist, 9,* 201–211.

Jones, J. G., & Cale, A. (1989). Precompetition temporal patterning of anxiety and self-confidence in males and females. *Journal of Sport Behavior, 12,* 183–195.

Jones, J. G., & Hardy, L. (1989). Stress and cognitive functioning in sport. *Journal of Sports Sciences, 7,* 41–63.

Jones, J. G., Swain, A., & Cale, A. (1991). Gender differences in precompetition temporal patterning and antecedents of anxiety and self-confidence. *Journal of Sport & Exercise Psychology, 13,* 1–15.

Jourden, F. J., Bandura, A., & Banfield, J. T. (1991). The impact of conceptions of ability on self-regulatory factors and motor skill acquisition. *Journal of Sport & Exercise Psychology, 13,* 213–226.

Jowdy, D. P., & Harris, D. V. (1990). Muscular responses during mental imagery as a function of motor skill level. *Journal of Sport & Exercise Psychology, 12,* 191–201.

K Kahn, R. I., & Katz, D. (1960). Leadership practices in relation to productivity and morale. In D. Cartwright & A. T. Zander (Eds.), *Group dynamics*. Evanston, IL: Row, Peterson and Company.

Kahneman, D. (1973). *Attention and effort*. Englewood Cliffs, NJ: Prentice-Hall.

Kane, J. E. (1970). Personality and physical abilities. In G. S. Kenyon (Ed.), *Contemporary psychology of sport: Second International Congress of Sports Psychology*. Chicago: The Athletic Institute.

Kane, J. E. (1976). Personality and performance in sport. In J. G. W. Williams & P. N. Sperryn (Eds.), *Sports medicine*. Baltimore: The Williams and Wilkins Company.

Kane, J. E. (1980). Personality research: The current controversy and implications for sport studies. In W. F. Straub (Ed.), *Sport Psychology: An analysis of athlete behavior* (2nd ed.). Ithaca, NY: Mouvement Publications.

Karteroliotis, C., & Gill, D. L. (1987). Temporal changes in psychological and physiological components of state anxiety. *Journal of Sport Psychology, 9,* 261–274.

Kaufmann, H. (1970). *Aggression and altruism*. New York: Holt, Rinehart and Winston.

Kavanagh, D., & Hausfeld, S. (1986). Physical performance and self-efficacy under happy and sad moods. *Journal of Sport Psychology, 8,* 112–123.

Kavussanu, M., & Roberts, G. C. (1996). Motivation in physical activity contexts: The relationship of perceived motivational climate to intrinsic motivation and self-efficacy. *Journal of Sport & Exercise Psychology, 18,* 264–280.

Kay, J. (1988, June 30). Trouble in river city: Players can't cite reason for Red's poor play. *Muncie Evening Press,* 15.

Keele, S. W. (1973). *Attention and human performance*. Pacific Palisades, CA: Goodyear Publishing Company.

Kelley, H. H. (1972). *Causal schemata and the attribution process.* Morristown, NJ: General Learning Press.

Kelley, H. H. (1973). The process of causal attribution. *American Psychologist, 28,* 107–128.

Kelly, J. K., Jr. (1990). Psychological risk factors and sport injuries. *The Journal of Sports Medicine and Physical Fitness, 30*(2), 202–221.

Keltikangas-Jarvinen, L., & Kelnonen, M. (1988). Aggression, self-confidence, and cardiovascular reactions in competitive performance in adolescent boys. *Aggressive Behavior, 14,* 245–254.

Kendall, G., Hrycaiko, D., Martin, G. L., & Kendall, T. (1990). The effects of an imagery rehearsal, relaxation, and self-talk package on basketball game performance. *Journal of Sport & Exercise Psychology, 12,* 157–166.

Kenow, L. J. (1992). Relationship between anxiety, self-confidence, and evaluation of coaching behaviors. *The Sport Psychologist, 6,* 344–357.

Kerr, G., & Goss, J. (1996). The effects of a stress management program on injuries and stress levels. *Journal of Applied Sport Psychology, 8,* 109–117.

Kerr, G., & Leith, L. (1993). Stress management and athletic performance. *The Sport Psychologist, 7,* 221–231.

Kerr, J. H. (1985). The experience of arousal: A new basis for studying arousal effects in sport. *Journal of Sports Sciences, 3,* 169–179.

Kerr, J. H. (1987). Structural phenomenology and performance. *Journal of Human Movement Studies, 13,* 211–229.

Kerr, J. H. (1989). Anxiety, arousal, and sport performance: An application of reversal theory. In D. Hackfort & C. D. Spielberger (Eds.), *Anxiety in sports: An international perspective* (137–151). Washington, DC: Hemisphere Publishing Corporation.

Kerr, J. H. (1993). An eclectic approach to psychological interventions in sport: Reversal theory. *The Sport Psychologist, 7,* 400–418.

Kerr, J. H., & Cox, T. (1988). Effects of telic dominance and metamotivational states on squash task performance. *Perceptual and Motor Skills, 67,* 171–174.

Kerr, J. H., & Svebac, S. (1989). Motivational aspects of preference for, and participation in 'risk' and 'safe' sports. *Personality and Individual Differences, 10,* 797–800.

Kihlstrom, J. F. (1985). Hypnosis. *Annual Review of Psychology, 36,* 385–418.

Kim, M. Y., & Sugiyama, Y. (1992). The relation of performance norms and cohesiveness for Japanese school athletic teams. *Perceptual and Motor Skills, 74,* 1096–1098.

Kimiecik, J. (1992). Predicting vigorous physical activity of corporate employees: Comparing the theories of reasoned action and planned behavior. *Journal of Sport and Exercise Psychology, 14,* 192–206.

Kimiecik, J. S., & Duda, J. L. (1985). Self-serving attributions among children in a competitive sport setting: Some theoretical and methodological considerations. *Journal of Sport Behavior, 8,* 78–91.

Kimiecik, J. C., Horn, T. S., & Shwin, C. S. (1996). Relationships among children's beliefs, perceptions of their parents' beliefs, and their moderate-to-vigorous physical activity. *Research Quarterly for Exercise and Sport, 67,* 324–336.

Kimiecik, J. C., & Stein, G. L. (1992). Examining flow experiences in sports contexts: Conceptual issues and methodological concerns. *Journal of Applied Sport Psychology, 4,* 144–160.

Kirkby, R. J. (1996). Ultraendurance: A case study. *International Journal of Sport Psychology, 27,* 109–116.

Kirkpatrick, C. (1987, February 2). Fight night. *Sports Illustrated, 66,* 59.

Kirschenbaum, D. S. (1992). Elements of effective weight control programs: Implications for exercise and sport psychology. *Journal of Applied Sport Psychology, 4,* 77–93.

Kirschenbaum, D. S., Wittrock, D. A., Smith, R. J., & Monson, W. (1984). Criticism inoculation training: Concept in search of a strategy. *Journal of Sport Psychology, 6,* 77–93.

Klavora, P. (1978). An attempt to derive inverted-U curves based on the relationship between anxiety and athletic performance. In D. M. Landers & R. W. Christina (Eds.), *Psychology of motor behavior and sport—1977,* (pp. 369–377). Champaign, IL: Human Kinetics Publishers.

Kleiber, D., & Brock, S. (1992). The effect of career-ending injuries on the subsequent well-being of elite college athletes. *Sociology of Sport Journal, 9,* 70–75.

Klint, K. A., & Weiss, M. R. (1986). Dropping in and dropping out: Participation motives of current and former youth gymnasts. *Canadian Journal of Applied Sport Sciences, 11*(2), 106–114.

Klint, K. A., & Weiss, M. R. (1987). Perceived competence and motives for participating in youth sports: A test of Harter's competence motivation theory. *Journal of Sport Psychology, 9,* 55, 65.

Knott, P. D., & Drost, B. A. (1972). Effects of varying intensity of attack and fear arousal on the intensity of counteraggression. *Journal of Personality, 4,* 27–37.

Kohl, R. M., Ellis, S. D., & Roenker, D. L. (1992). Alternating actual and imagery practice: Preliminary theoretical considerations. *Research Quarterly for Exercise and Sport, 63,* 162–170.

Kohl, R. M., Roenker, D. L., & Turner, P. E. (1985). Clarification of competent imagery as a prerequisite for effective skill imagery. *International Journal of Sport Psychology, 16,* 37–45.

Kolonay, B. J. (1977). *The effects of visuo-motor behavior rehearsal on athletic performance.* Unpublished master's thesis, Hunter College, New York.

Konttinen, N., & Lyytinen, H. (1992). Physiology of preparation: Brain slow waves, heart rate, and respiration preceding triggering in rifle shooting. *International Journal of Sport Psychology, 23,* 110–127.

Konttinen, N., & Lyytinen, H. (1993). Individual variability in brain slow wave profiles in skilled sharpshooters during the aiming period in rifle shooting. *Journal of Sport & Exercise Psychology, 15,* 275–289.

Konttinen, N., Lyytinen, H., & Konttinen, R. (1995). Brain slow potentials reflecting successful shooting performance. *Research Quarterly for Exercise and Sport, 66,* 64–72.

Kosslyn, S. M., Pinker, S., Smith, G. E., & Schwartz, S. P. (1981). On the demystification of mental imagery. In N. Block (Ed.), *Imagery.* Cambridge, MA: MIT Press.

Kraemer, R. R., Dzewaltowski, D. A., Blair, M. S., Rinehardt, K.F., & Castracane, V. D. (1990). Mood alteration from treadmill running and its relationship to beta-endorphine, corticotrophine, and growth hormone. *The Journal of Sports Medicine and Physical Fitness, 30*(3), 241–246.

Kramer, J. (1970). *Lombardi: Winning is the only thing.* New York: The World Publishing Company.

Krane, T. D., Marks, M. A., Zaccaro, S. J., & Blair, V. (1996). Self-efficacy, personal goals, and wrestlers' self-regulation. *Journal of Sport & Exercise Psychology, 18,* 36–48.

Krane, V. (1992). Conceptual and methodological considerations in sport anxiety research: From the inverted-U hypothesis to catatrophe theory. *Quest, 44,* 72–87.

Krane, V. (1994). The mental readiness form as a measure of competitive state anxiety. *The Sport Psychologist, 8,* 189–202.

Krane, V., Joyce, D., & Rafeld, J. (1994). Competitive anxiety, situation criticality, and softball performance. *The Sport Psychologist, 8,* 58–72.

Kroll, W. (1967). Sixteen personality factor profiles of collegiate wrestlers. *Research Quarterly, 38,* 49–57.

Kroll, W. (1970). Current strategies and problems in personality assessment of athletes. In L. E. Smith (Ed.), *Psychology of motor learning.* Chicago: The Athletic Institute.

Kroll, W., & Carlson, R. B. (1967). Discriminant function and hierarchical grouping analysis of karate participants' personality profiles. *Research Quarterly, 38,* 405–411.

Kroll, W., & Crenshaw, W. (1970). Multivariate personality profile analysis of four athletic groups. In G. S. Kenyon (Ed.), *Contemporary psychology of sport: Second International Congress of Sport Psychology* (pp. 97–106). Chicago: The Athletic Institute.

Kroll, W., & Lewis, G. (1970). America's first sport psychologist, *Quest, 13,* 1–4.

Kubitz, K. A., & Landers, D. M. (1993). The effects of aerobic training on cardiovascular responses to mental stress: An examination of underlying mechanisms. *Journal of Sport & Exercise Psychology, 15,* 326–337.

Kuipers, H. (1996). How much is too much? Performance aspects of overtraining. *Research Quarterly for Exercise and Sports, 67,* Supplement to No. 3, 65–69.

Kyllo, L. B., & Landers, D. M. (1995). Goal setting in sport and exercise: A research synthesis to resolve the controversy. *Journal of Sport & Exercise Psychology, 17,* 117–137.

L

Lacey, J., & Lacey, B. (1958). Verification and extension of the principle of autonomic response-stereotype. *American Journal of Psychology, 71,* 50–73.

LaFontaine, T. P., DiLorenzo, T. M., Frensch, P. A., Stucky-Ropp, R. C., Bargman, E. P., & McDonald, D. G. (1992). Aerobic exercise and mood: A brief review, 1985–1990. *Sports Medicine, 13*(3), 160–170.

Laird, D. A. (1923). Changes in motor control and individual variations under the influence of "razzing." *Journal of Experimental Psychology, 6,* 236–246.

Lan, L. Y., & Gill, D. L. (1984). The relationships among self-efficacy, stress responses, and a cognitive feedback manipulation. *Journal of Sport Psychology, 6,* 227–238.

Landers, D. M. (1988, April). *Cognitive states of elite performers: Psychological studies of attention.* Paper presented at the meeting of the American Alliance for Health, Physical Education, Recreation and Dance (Research Consortium Scholar Lecture), Kansas City, MO.

Landers, D. M. (1980). The arousal-performance relationship revisited. *Research Quarterly for Exercise and Sport, 51,* 77–90.

Landers, D. M. (1982). Arousal, attention, and skilled performance: Further considerations. *Quest, 33,* 271–283.

Landers, D. M. (1995). Sport psychology: The formative years, 1950–1980. *The Sport Psychologist, 9,* 406–417.

Landers, D. M., Boutcher, S. H., & Wang, M. Q. (1986). A psychobiological study of archery performance. *Research Quarterly for Exercise and Sport, 57,* 236–244.

Landers, D. M., & Courtet, P. A. (1979, June). *Peripheral narrowing among experienced and inexperienced rifle shooters under low and high stress conditions.* Paper presented at a meeting of the North American Society for Psychology of Sport and Physical Activity, Trois Rivieres, Quebec.

Landers, D. M., Furst, D. M., & Daniels, F. S. (1981, May–June). *Anxiety/attention and shooting ability: Testing the predictive validity of the test of Attentional and Interpersonal Style* (TAIS). Paper presented at a meeting of the North American Society for Psychology of Sport and Physical Activity, Monterey, CA.

Landers, D. M., Han, M., Salazar, W., Petruzzello, S. J., Kubitz, K. A., & Gannon, T. L. (1994). Effects of learning on electroencephalographic and electrocardiographic patterns in novice archers. *International Journal of Sport Psychology, 225,* 313–330.

Landers, D. M., Qi, W. M., & Courtet, P. (1985). Peripheral narrowing among experienced rifle shooters under low and high stress conditions. *Research Quarterly for Exercise and Sport, 56,* 122–130.

Lansing, R. W., Schwartz, E., & Lindsley, D. B. (1956). Reaction time and EEG activation. *American Psychologist, 11,* 433.

LaPerriere, A. R., Antonio, M. H., Schneiderman, N., Ironson, G., Klimas, N., Caralis, P., & Fletcher, M. A. (1990). Exercise intervention attenuates emotional distress and natural killer cell decrements following notification of positive serologic status for HIV-1. *Biofeedback and Self-Regulation, 15,* 229–242.

Layman, E. M. (1980). Meditation and sports performance. In W. F. Straub (Ed.), *Sport psychology: An analysis of athlete behavior.* 2d ed. Ithaca, NY: Mouvement Publications.

Lazarus, R. S., & Folkman, S. (1984). *Stress appraisal and coping.* New York: Springer.

Leddy, M. H., Lambert, M. J., & Ogles, B. M. (1994). Psychological consequences of athletic injury among high-level competitors. *Research Quarterly for Exercise and Sport, 65,* 347–354.

Lee, C. (1990). Psyching up for muscular endurance task: Effects of image content on performance and mood state. *Journal of Sport & Exercise Psychology, 12,* 66–73.

Lee, I. (1995). Exercise and physical health: Cancer and immune function. *Research Quarterly for Exercise and Sport, 66,* 286–291.

Lefavi, R. G., Reeve, T. G., & Newland, C. (1990). Relationship between anabolic steroid use and selected psychological parameters in male body builders. *Journal of Sport Behavior, 13*(3), 157–166.

Lefebvre, L. M. (1979). Achievement motivation and causal attribution in male and female athletes. *International Journal of Sport Psychology, 10,* 31–41.

Lefebvre, L. M., Leith, L. L., & Bredemeier, B. B. (1980). Modes for aggression assessment and control. *International Journal of Sport Psychology, 11,* 11–21.

Lefebvre, L. M., & Passer, M. W. (1974). The effects of game location and importance on aggression in team sport. *International Journal of Sport Psychology, 5*(2), 102–110.

Leirer, V. O., Yesavage, J. A., & Morrow, D. G. (1989). Marijuana, aging, and task difficulty effects on pilot performance. *Aviation, Space & Environmental Medicine, 60,* 1145–1152.

Leith, L. M. (1989a). Causal attribution and sport behavior: Implications for practitioners. *Journal of Sport Behavior, 12,* 213–225.

Leith, L. M. (1989b). The effect of various physical activities, outcome, and emotional arousal on subjective aggression scores. *International Journal of Sport Psychology, 20,* 57–66.

Leith, L. M. (1991). Do coaches encourage aggressive behavior in sport? *Canadian Journal of Sport Sciences, 16,* 85–86.

Leith, L. M., & Taylor, A. H. (1990). Psychological aspects of exercise: A decade literature review. *Journal of Sport Behavior, 13*(4), 219–239.

Lenk, H. (1969). Top performance despite internal conflict: An antithesis to a functional proposition. In J. W. Loy & G. S. Kenyon (Eds.), *Sport, culture, and society* (pp. 393–396). New York: Macmillan.

Lenney, E. (1977). Women's self-confidence in achievement situations. *Psychological Bulletin, 84,* 1–13.

Leonard, W. M. III (1989). The "home advantage": The case of the modern Olympics. *Journal of Sport Behavior, 12,* 227–241.

Lepper, M. R., & Greene, D. (1975). Turning play into work: Effects of adult surveillance and extrinsic rewards on children's intrinsic motivation. *Journal of Personality and Social Psychology, 31,* 479–486.

Lepper, M. R., & Greene, D. (1976). On understanding overjustification: A reply to Reiss and Sushinsky. *Journal of Personality and Social Psychology, 33,* 25–35.

Lepper, M. R., Greene, D., & Nisbett, R. E. (1973). Undermining children's intrinsic interest with extrinsic rewards: A test of the "overjustification" hypothesis. *Journal of Personality and Social Psychology, 28,* 129–137.

Lerner, B. S., & Locke, E. A. (1995). The effects of goal setting, self-efficacy, competition, and personal traits on the performance of an endurance task. *Journal of Sport & Exercise Psychology, 17,* 138–152.

Levenson, H. (1981). Differentiating among internality, powerful others, and chance. In H. M. Lefcourt (Ed.), *Research with the locus of control construct: Assessment methods* (Vol. 1, pp. 15–63). New York: Academic Press.

Levitt, E. E. (1980). *The psychology of anxiety.* Hillsdale, NJ: Erlbaum.

Li, F., & Harmer, P. (1996). Confirmatory factor analysis of the Group Environment Questionnaire with an intercollegiate sample. *Journal of Sport & Exercise Psychology, 18,* 49–63.

Linder, K. J., Johns, D. P., & Butcher, J. (1991). Factors in withdrawal from youth sport: A proposed model. *Journal of Sport Behavior, 14*(1), 3–17.

Lindsley, D. B., Schreiner, L. H., Knowles, W. B., & Magoun, H. W. (1950). Behavioral and EEG changes following chronic brain stem lesions in the cat. *Electroencephalography and Clinical Neurophysiology, 2,* 483–498.

Lirgg, C. D. (1991). Gender differences in self-confidence in physical activity: A meta-analysis of recent studies. *Journal of Sport & Exercise Psychology, 13,* 294–310.

Lirgg, C. D., & Feltz, D. L. (1989, March). Female self-confidence in sport: Myths, realities, and enhancement strategies. *Journal of Physical Education, Recreation, and Dance, 60,* 49–54.

Lirgg, C. D., & Feltz, D. L. (1991). Teacher versus peer models revisited: Effects on motor performance and self-efficacy. *Research Quarterly for Exercise and Sport, 62,* 217–224.

Lirgg, C. D., George, T. R., Chase, M. A., & Ferguson, R. H. (1996). Impact of conception of ability and sex-type of task on male and female self-efficacy. *Journal of Sport & Exercise Psychology, 18,* 426–434.

Llewellyn, J. H., & Blucker, J. A. (1982). *Psychology of coaching: Theory and application.* Minneapolis: Burgess Publishing Company.

Lochbaum, M. R., & Roberts, G. C. (1993). Goal orientations and perceptions of the sport experience. *Journal of Sport & Exercise Psychology, 15,* 160–171.

Locke, E. A. (1991). Problems with goal-setting research in sports—and their solution. *Journal of Sport & Exercise Psychology, 8,* 311–316.

Locke, E. A. (1994). Comments on Weinberg and Weigand. *Journal of Sport & Exercise Psychology, 16,* 212–215.

Locke, E. A., & Latham, G. P. (1985). The application of goal setting to sports. *Journal of Sports Psychology, 7,* 205–222.

Locke, E. A., & Latham, G. P. (1990). *A theory of goal setting and task performance.* Englewood Cliffs, NJ: Prentice-Hall.

Locke, E. A., Shaw, K. M., Saari, L. M., & Latham, G. P. (1981). Goal setting and task performance: 1969–1980. *Psychological Bulletin, 90,* 125–152.

Loehr, J., & Hahn, C. (1992). How to keep your mind on the game. *Tennis, 27,* 93.

Long, B. C., & Haney, C. J. (1988). Long-term follow-up of stressed working women: A comparison of aerobic exercise and progressive relaxation. *Journal of Sport and Exercise Psychology, 10*(4), 461–470.

Long, B. C., & Van Stavel, R. (1995). Effects of exercise training on anxiety: A meta-analysis. *Journal of Applied Sport Psychology, 7,* 167–189.

Long, B. S. (1980). Stress management for the athlete: A cognitive behavioral model. In C. H. Nadeau (Ed.), *Psychology of motor behavior and sport, 1979.* Champaign, IL: Human Kinetics Publishers.

Lorr, M., & McNair, D. M. (1988). *Manual for the Profile of Mood States—Bipolar Form.* San Diego: Educational and Industrial Testing Service.

Lott, A. J., & Lott, B. E. (1965). Group cohesiveness as interpersonal attraction. A review of relationships with antecedent and consequent variables. *Psychological Bulletin, 64,* 259–309.

Lowe, R. (1973). *Stress, arousal, and task performance of Little League baseball players.* Unpublished doctoral dissertation, University of Illinois, Urbana-Champaign.

Lox, C. L., McAuley, E., & Tucker, R. S. (1995). Exercise as an intervention for enhancing subjective well-being in an HIV-1 population. *Journal of Sport & Exercise Psychology, 17,* 345–362.

Loy, J. W. (1970). *Where the action is: A consideration of centrality in sport situations.* Paper presented at the meeting of the Second Canadian Psychomotor Learning and Sport Psychology Symposium, Windsor, Ontario.

Loy, J. W., & McElvogue, J. F. (1970). Racial segregation in American sport. *International Review of Sport Sociology, 5,* 5–24.

Loy, J. W., & Sage, J. N. (1970). The effects of formal structure on organizational leadership: An investigation of interscholastic baseball teams. In G. S. Kenyon (Ed.), *Contemporary psychology of sport.* Chicago: The Athletic Institute.

Luksa, F. (1980). *Time enough to win: Roger Staubach.* Waco, TX: Word.

Luxbacher, J. (1986). Violence in sport: An examination of the theories of aggression, and how the coach can influence the degree of violence in sport. *Coaching Review, 9,* 14–17.

Lykken, D. (1968). Neuropsychology and psychophysiology in personality research. In E. F. Borgatta & W. W. Lambert (Eds.), *Handbook of personality theory and research.* Chicago: Rand McNally.

Lysens, R., Steverlynck, A., van den Auweele, Y., Lefevre, J., Renson, L., Claessens, A., & Ostyn, M. (1984). The predictability of sports injuries. *Sports Medicine, 1,* 6–10.

M

Macchi, R., & Crossman, J. (1996). After the fall: Reflections of injured classical ballet dancers. *Journal of Sport Behavior, 19,* 222–234.

Mace, R. D., & Carroll, D. (1985). The control of anxiety in sport: Stress inoculation training prior to abseiling. *International Journal of Sport Psychology, 16,* 165–175.

Mace, R. D., & Carroll, D. (1989). The effect of stress inoculation training on self-reported stress, observer's rating of stress, heart rate, and gymnastic performance. *Journal of Sports Sciences, 7,* 257–266.

Mackinnon, L. T. (1994). Current challenges and future expectations in exercise imuunology: Back to the future. *Medicine and Science in Sports and Exercise, 26,* 191–194.

Madden, C. C., Kirby, R. J., & McDonald, D. (1989). Coping styles of competitive middle distance runners. *International Journal of Sport Psychology, 20,* 287–296.

Magill, R. A. (1985). *Motor learning: Concepts and applications.* Dubuque, IA: Wm. C. Brown Publishers.

Magni, G., Rupolo, G., Simini, G., DeLeo, D., & Rampazzo, M. (1985). Aspects of the psychology and personality of high altitude mountain climbers. *International Journal of Sport Psychology, 16,* 12–19.

Mahoney, M. J. (1989). Psychological predictors of elite and nonelite performance in Olympic weightlifting. *International Journal of Sport Psychology, 20,* 1–20.

Mahoney, M. J., & Avener, M. (1977). Psychology of the elite athlete: An exploratory study. *Cognitive Therapy and Research, 1,* 135–141.

Mahoney, M. J., Gabriel, T. J., & Perkins, T. S. (1987). Psychological skills and exceptional athletic performance. *The Sport Psychologist, 1,* 181–199.

Males, J. R., & Kerr, J. H. (1996). Stress, emotion, and performance in elite slalom canoeists. *The Sport Psychologist, 10,* 17–36.

Malmo, R. B. (1959). Activation: A neuropsychological dimension. *Psychological Review, 66,* 367–386.

Man, F., & Hondlik, J. (1984). Use of compulsory lessons of physical training for the stimulation of achievement motivation of pupils at an elementary school. *International Journal of Sport Psychology, 15,* 259–270.

Mann, L. (1974). On being a sore loser: How fans react to their team's failure. *Australian Journal of Psychology, 26,* 37–47.

Marcello, R. J., Danish, S. J., & Stolberg, A. L. (1989). An evaluation of strategies developed to prevent substance abuse among student athletes. *The Sport Psychologist, 3,* 196–211.

Marcus, B. H., Eaton, C. A., Rossi, J. S., & Harlow, L. L. (1994). Self-efficacy, decision making, and stages of change: An integrative model of physical exercise. *Journal of Applied Social Psychology, 24,* 489–508.

Marcus, B. H., & Simkin, L. R. (1994). The transtheoretical model: Applications to exercise behavior. *Medicine and Exercise in Sports and Exercise, 26,* 1400–1404.

Mark, N. M., Mutrie, N., Brooks, D. R., & Harris, D. V. (1984). Causal attributions of winners and losers in individual competitive sports: Toward a reformulation of the self-serving hypothesis. *Journal of Sport Psychology, 6,* 184–196.

Marks, D. F. (1973). Visual imagery differences in recall of pictures. *British Journal of Psychology, 64,* 17–24.

Marsh, H. W. (1994). Sport motivation orientations: Beware of jingle-jangle fallacies. *Journal of Sport & Exercise Psychology, 16,* 365–380.

Martens, R. (1971). Internal-external control and social reinforcement. *Research Quarterly, 42,* 307–313.

Martens, R. (1974). Arousal and motor performance. *Exercise and Sport Sciences Reviews, 2,* 155–188.

Martens, R. (1975). *Social psychology and physical activity.* New York: Harper & Row.

Martens, R. (1976). The paradigmatic crises in American sport personology. In A. C. Fisher (Ed.), *Psychology of sport.* Palo Alto, CA: Mayfield Publishing Company.

Martens, R. (1977). *Sport competition anxiety test.* Champaign, IL: Human Kinetics Publishers.

Martens, R. (1982). *Sport competition anxiety test.* Champaign, IL: Human Kinetics Publishers.

Martens, R. (1987). *Coaches guide to sport psychology.* Champaign, IL: Human Kinetics Publishers, Inc.

Martens, R. (1987). Science, knowledge, and sport psychology. *The Sport Psychologist, 1,* 29–55.

Martens, R., Burton, D., Vealey, R. S., Bump, L. A., & Smith, D. (1990). Development and validation of the competitive state anxiety inventory—2. In R. Martens, R. S. Vealey, & D. Burton (Eds.), *Competitive anxiety in sport* (pp. 117–190). Champaign, IL: Human Kinetics Books.

Martens, R., & Landers, D. M. (1969). Coaction effects on a muscular endurance task. *Research Quarterly, 40,* 733–737.

Martens, R., & Landers, D. M. (1970). Motor performance under stress: A test of the inverted-U hypothesis, *Journal of Personality and Social Research, 16,* 29–37.

Martens, R., & Landers, D. M. (1972). Evaluation potential as a determinant of coaction effects. *Journal of Experimental Social Psychology, 8,* 347–359.

Martens, R., & Peterson, J. A. (1971). Group cohesiveness as a determinant of success and member satisfaction in team performance. *International Review of Sport Sociology, 6,* 49–61.

Martens, R., Vealey, R. S., & Burton, D. (1990). *Competitive anxiety in sport.* Champaign, IL: Human Kinetics Books.

Martin, J. E., & Calfas, K. J. (1989). Is it possible to lower blood pressure with exercise? Efficacy and adherence issues. *Journal of Applied Sport Psychology, 1*(2), 109–131.

Martin, J. J., & Gill, D. L. (1991). The relationships among competitive orientation, sport-confidence, self-efficacy, anxiety, and performance. *Journal of Sport & Exercise Psychology, 13,* 149–159.

Martin, K. A., & Hall, C. R. (1995). Using mental imagery to enhance intrinsic motivation. *Journal of Sport & Exercise Psychology, 17,* 54–69.

Martin, K. A., & Mack, D. (1996). Relationship between physical self-presentation and sport competition trait anxiety: A preliminary study. *Journal of Sport & Exercise Psychology, 18,* 75–82.

Martin, L. A. (1976). Effects of competition upon the aggressive responses of college basketball players and wrestlers. *Research Quarterly, 47,* 388–393.

Maslach, C., & Jackson, S. (1986). *Maslach Burnout Inventory.* 2d ed. Palo Alto, CA: Consulting Psychologists Press.

Maslow, A. H. (1970). *Motivation and personality.* New York: Harper & Row.

Masters, K. S. (1992). Hypnotic susceptibililty, cognitive dissociation, and runner's high in a sample of marathon runners. *American Journal of Clinical Hypnosis, 34,* 193–201.

Masters, K. S., & Lambert, M. J. (1989). The relations between cognitive coping strategies, reasons for running, injury, and performance of marathon runners. *Journal of Sport & Exercise Psychology, 11,* 161–170.

Mastro, J. V., Canabal, M. Y., & French, R. (1988). Psychological mood profiles of sighted and unsighted beep baseball players. *Research Quarterly for Exercise and Sport, 59,* 262–264.

Mastro, J. V., Gench, B., & French, R. (1987). Psychological characteristics of elite visually impaired athletes: The iceberg profile. *Journal of Sport Behavior, 10,* 39–46.

May, J. R. (1986, Summer). Sport psychology: Should psychologists become involved? *The Clinical Psychologist, 39,* 77–81.

Maynard, I. W., & Cotton, P. C. J. (1993). An investigation of two stress-management techniques in a field setting. *The Sport Psychologist, 7,* 375–387.

Maynard, I. W., Hemmings, B., & Warwick-Evans, L. (1995). The effects of a somatic intervention strategy on competitive state anxiety and performance in semiprofessional soccer players. *The Sport Psychologist, 9,* 51–64.

Maynard, I. W., Smith, M. J., & Warwick-Evans, L. (1995). The effects of a cognitive intervention strategy on competitive state anxiety and performance in semiprofessional soccer players. *Journal of Sport & Exercise Psychology, 17,* 428–446.

McAuley, E. (1985). Modeling and self-efficacy: A test of Bandura's model. *Journal of Sport Psychology, 7,* 283–295.

McAuley, E. (1991). Efficacy, attributional, and affective responses to exercise participation. *Journal of Sport & Exercise Psychology, 13*(4), 382–393.

McAuley, E. (1992). The role of efficacy cognitions in the prediction of exercise behavior in middle-aged adults. *Journal of Behavioral Medicine, 15*(1), 65–88.

McAuley, E., & Courneya, K. S. (1992). Self-efficacy relationships with affective and exertion responses to exercise. *Journal of Applied Social Psychology, 22*(4), 312–326.

McAuley, E., & Courneya, K. S. (1994). The subjective exercise experiences scale (SEES): Development and preliminary validation. *Journal of Sport & Exercise Psychology, 16,* 163–177.

McAuley, E., Courneya, K. S., & Lettunich, J. (1991). Effects of acute and long-term exercise on self-efficacy responses in sedentary, middle-aged males and females. *The Gerontologist, 31*(4), 534–542.

McAuley, E., & Duncan, T. E. (1989). Causal attributions and affective reactions to disconfirming outcomes in motor performance. *Journal of Sport & Exercise Psychology, 11,* 187–200.

McAuley, E., Duncan, T. E., & Russell, D. W. (1992). Measuring causal attributions: The revised causal dimension scale (CDSII). *Personality and Social Psychology Bulletin, 18,* 566–573.

McAuley, E., & Gross, J. B. (1983). Perceptions of causality in sport: An application of the casual dimension scale. *Journal of Sport Psychology, 5,* 72–76.

McAuley, E., Poag, K., Gleason, A., & Wraith, S. (1990). Attrition from exercise programs: Attributional and affective perspectives. *Journal of Social Behavior and Personality, 5*(6), 591–602.

McAuley, E., Russell, D., & Gross, J. B. (1983). Affective consequences of winning and losing: An attributional analysis. *Journal of Sport Psychology, 5,* 278–287.

McAuley, E., & Tammen, V. V. (1989). The effects of subjective and objective competitive outcomes on intrinsic motivation. *Journal of Sport & Exercise Psychology, 11,* 84–93.

McCallum, J. (1987, June 8). The mystique goes on. *Sports Illustrated, 66,* 30–37.

McCallum, J. (1991, Nov. 11). For whom the Bulls toil. *Sports Illustrated, 75,* 106–118.

McCallum, J. (1994, March 28). Radical stupidity. *Sports Illustrated, 80,* 8.

McCarthy, J. F., & Kelly, B. R. (1978a). Aggression, performance variables, and anger self-report in ice hockey players. *Journal of Psychology, 99,* 97–101.

McCarthy, J. F., & Kelly, B. R. (1978b). Aggressive behavior and its effect on performance over time in ice hockey athletes: An archival study. *International Journal of Sport Psychology, 9,* 90–96.

McClelland, D. C., Atkinson, J. W., Clark, R. W., & Lowell, E. L. (1953). *The achievement motive.* New York: Appleton-Century-Crofts.

McCullagh, P. D., & Landers, D. M. (1976). Size of audience and social facilitation. *Perceptual and Motor Skills, 42,* 1067–1070.

McCutcheon, L. E. (1984). The home advantage in high school athletics. *Journal of Sport Behavior, 7,* 135–138.

McDonald, S. A., & Hardy, S. J. (1990). Affective response patterns of the injured athlete: An exploratory analysis. *The Sport Psychologist, 4,* 261–274.

McElroy, M. A., & Willis, J. D. (1979). Women and the achievement conflict in sport: A preliminary study. *Journal of Sport Psychology, 1,* 241–247.

McGhie, A., & Chapman, J. (1961). Disorders of attention and perception in early schizophrenia. *British Journal of Medical Psychology, 34,* 103–116.

McGill, J. C., Hall, J. R., Ratliff, W. R., & Moss, R. F. (1986). Personality characteristics of professional rodeo cowboys. *Journal of Sport Behavior, 9,* 143–151.

McGrath, J. E. (1970). A conceptual formulation for research on stress. In J. E. McGrath (Ed.), *Social and psychological factors in stress.* New York: Holt, Rinehart and Winston.

McGuire, E. J., Courneya, K. S., & Widmeyer, W. N. (1992). Aggression as a potential mediator of the home advantage in professional ice hockey. *Journal of Sport & Exercise Psychology, 14,* 148–158.

McInman, A. D., & Grove, J. R. (1991). Peak moments in sport: A literature review. *Quest, 43,* 333–351.

McNair, D. M., Lorr, M., & Droppleman, L. F. (1971). *Profile of Mood States manual.* San Diego, CA: Educational and Industrial Testing Service.

Mechikoff, R. A., & Kozar, B. (1983). *Sport psychology: The coaches' perspective.* Springfield, IL: Charles C. Thomas.

Mehrabian, A. (1968). Male and female scales of the tendency to achieve. *Educational and Psychological Measurement, 28,* 493–502.

Meichenbaum, D. (1977). *Cognitive behavior modification*. New York: Plenum Press.

Meichenbaum, D. (1985). *Stress inoculation training*. New York: Pergamon Press.

Metcalf, H. C., & Urwick, L. (Eds.). (1963). *Dynamic administration: The collected papers of Mary Parker Follett*, 277. London: Harper & Brothers.

Meyers, M. C., Sterling, J. C., & LeUnes, A. D. (1988). Psychological characterization of the collegiate Rodeo Athlete. *Journal of Sport Behavior, 11,* 59–65.

Meyers, M. C., Sterling, J. C., Treadwell, S., Bourgeois, A. E., & LeUnes, A. (1994). Psychological skills of world-ranked female tennis players. *Journal of Sport Behavior, 17,* 156–165.

Michaels, J. (1977). Classroom reward structures and academic performance. *Review of Educational Research, 47,* 87–99.

Mikalachki, A. (1969). *Group cohesion reconsidered*. London, Ontario: School of Business Administration, University of Western Ontario.

Miller, D. T., & Ross, M. (1975). Self-serving biases in the attribution of causality: Fiction or fact? *Psychological Bulletin, 82,* 213–225.

Miller, J. T., & McAuley, E. (1987). Effects of a goalsetting training program on basketball free-throw self-efficacy and performance. *The Sport Psychologist, 1,* 103–113.

Miller, N. E. (1941). The frustration-aggression hypothesis. *Psychological Review, 48,* 337–342.

Miller, T. W. (1982). Assertiveness training for coaches: The issue of healthy communication between coaches and players. *Journal of Sport Psychology, 4,* 107–114.

Milner, P. M. (1970). *Physiological psychology*. New York: Holt, Rinehart and Winston.

Mischel, W. (1986). *Introduction to personality*. New York: Holt, Rinehart and Winston.

Mizruchi, M. S. (1985). Local sports teams and celebration of community: A comparative analysis of the home advantage. *The Sociological Quarterly, 26,* 507–518.

Montagu, J. D., & Coles, E. M. (1966). Mechanism and measurement of the galvanic skin response. *Psychological Bulletin, 65,* 261–279.

Monte, C. F. (1977). *Beneath the mask: An introduction to theories of personality*. New York: Praeger.

Moore, J. C., & Brylinski, J. (1995). Facility familiarity and the home advantage. *Journal of Sport Behavior, 18,* 302–310.

Moran, A. (1993). Conceptual and methodological issues in the measurement of mental imagery skills in athletes. *Journal of Sport Behavior, 16,* 157–170.

Morgan, L. K., Griffin, J., & Heyward, V. H. (1996). Ethnicity, gender, and experience effects on attributional dimensions. *The Sport Psychologist, 10,* 4–16.

Morgan, W. P. (1969). Physical fitness and emotional health: A review. *American Corrective Therapy Journal, 23,* 124–127.

Morgan, W. P. (1972a). Hypnosis and muscular performance. In W. P. Morgan (Ed.), *Ergogenic aids in muscular performance* (pp. 193–233). New York: Academic Press.

Morgan, W. P. (1972b). Sport psychology. In R. N. Singer (Ed.), *The psychomotor domain: Movement behaviors*. Philadelphia: Lea and Febiger.

Morgan, W. P. (1974). Selected psychological considerations in sport. *Research Quarterly, 45,* 324–339.

Morgan, W. P. (1978, April). The mind of the marathoner. *Psychology Today,* 38–49.

Morgan, W. P. (1979a). Anxiety reduction following acute physical activity. *Psychiatric Annals, 9,* 141–147.

Morgan, W. P. (1979b). Prediction of performance in athletics. In P. Klavora & J. V. Daniel (Eds.), *Coach, athlete, and the sport psychologist* (pp. 172–186). Champaign, IL: Human Kinetics Publishers.

Morgan, W. P. (1980a). Sport personology: The credulous-skeptical argument in perspective. In W. F. Straub (Ed.), *Sport psychology: An analysis of athlete behavior*. (2d ed.) (pp. 330–339). Ithaca, NY: Mouvement Publications.

Morgan, W. P. (1980b). The trait psychology controversy. *Research Quarterly for Exercise and Sport, 51,* 50–76.

Morgan, W. P. (1981). Psychophysiology of self-awareness during vigorous physical activity. *Research Quarterly for Exercise and Sport, 52,* 385–427.

Morgan, W. P. (1985). Affective beneficence of vigorous physical activity. *Medicine and Science in Sports and Exercise, 17,* 94–100.

Morgan, W. P. (1994). 40 years of progress: Sport psychology in exercise and sports medicine. *40th Anniversary Lectures*. Indianapolis, IN: American College of Sports Medicine.

Morgan, W. P., & Brown, D. R. (1983). Hypnosis. In M. H. Williams (Ed.), *Ergogenic aids in sport* (pp. 223–252). Champaign, IL: Human Kinetics Publishers.

Morgan, W. P., Brown, D. R., Raglin, J. S., O'Connor, P. J., & Ellickson, K. A. (1987). Psychological monitoring of overtraining and staleness. *British Journal of Sports Medicine, 21*(3), 107–114.

Morgan, W. P., & Costill, D. L. (1972). Psychological characteristics of the marathon runner. *Journal of Sports Medicine and Physical Fitness, 12,* 42–46.

Morgan, W. P., & Johnson, R. W. (1977). Psychological characterizations of the elite wrestler: A mental health model. *Medicine and Science in Sports, 9*(1), 55–56.

Morgan, W. P., & Johnson, R. W. (1978). Psychological characteristics of successful and unsuccessful oarsmen. *International Journal of Sport Psychology, 11,* 38–49.

Morgan, W. P., & O'Connor, P. J. (1988). Exercise and mental health. In R. K. Dishman (Ed.), *Exercise adherence: Its impact on public health* (pp. 91–121). Champaign, IL: Human Kinetics Publishers.

Morgan, W. P., O'Connor, P. J., Ellickson, K. A., Bradley, P. W. (1988). Personality structure, mood states, and performance in elite male distance runners. *International Journal of Sport Psychology, 19,* 247–263.

Morgan, W. P., O'Connor, P. J., Sparling, P. B., & Pate, R. R. (1987). Psychological characterization of the elite female distance runner. *International Journal of Sports Medicine, 8,* 124–131.

Morgan, W. P., & Pollock, M. L. (1977). Psychologic characterization of the elite distance runner. *Annals of the New York Academy of Science, 301,* 382–403.

Moritz, S. E., Hall, C. R., Martin, K. A., & Vadocz, E. (1996). What are confident athletes imagining?: An examination of image content. *The Sport Psychologist, 10,* 171–179.

Morrow, G. R., & Labrum, A. H. (1978). The relationship between psychological and physiological measures of anxiety. *Psychological Medicine, 8,* 95–101.

Murgatroyd, S., Rushton, C., Apter, M. J., & Ray, C. (1978). The development of the telic dominance scale. *Journal of Personality Assessment, 12,* 519–528.

Murphy, A. (1987, March 30). A bloody mess. *Sports Illustrated, 66,* 24–31.

Murphy, S. M. (1994). Imagery interventions in sport. *Medicine and Science in Sports and Exercise, 26,* 486–494.

Murphy, S. M., Fleck, S. J., Dudley, G., & Callister, R. (1990). Psychological and performance concomitants of increased volume training in elite athletes. *Journal of Applied Sport Psychology, 2,* 34–50.

Murphy, S. M., Greenspan, M., Jowdy, D., & Tammen, V. (1989, October). *Development of a brief rating instrument of competitive anxiety: Comparisons with the CSAI-2.* Paper presented at the meeting of the Association for the Advancement of Applied Sport Psychology, Seattle, WA.

Murphy, S. M., & Jowdy, D. P. (1992). Imagery and mental practice. In T. S. Horn (Ed.), *Advances in sport psychology* (pp. 221–250). Champaign, IL: Human Kinetics Publishers.

Murphy, S. M., & Woolfolk, R. L. (1987). The effects of cognitive interventions on competitive anxiety and performance on a fine motor skill accuracy task. *International Journal of Sport Psychology, 18,* 152–166.

N Nagle, F. G., Morgan, W. P., Hellickson, R. V., Serfass, P. C., & Alexander, J. F. (1975). Spotting success traits in Olympic contenders. *Physician and Sports Medicine, 3*(12), 31–34.

Neff, C. (1990, January). Scorecard: They said it. *Sports Illustrated, 71*(27), 21–24.

Neiss, R. (1988). Reconceptualizing relaxation treatments: Psychobiological states in sports. *Clinical Psychology Reviews, 8,* 139–159.

Newcombe, P. A., & Boyle, G. J. (1995). High school students' sport personalities: Variations across participation level, gender, type of sport, and success. *International Journal of Sport Psychology, 26,* 277–294.

Nicholls, J. G. (1975). Causal attributions and other achievement-related cognitions: Effects of task outcome, attainment value, and sex. *Journal of Personality and Social Psychology, 31,* 379–389.

Nicholls, J. G. (1984). Conceptions of ability and achievement motivation. In R. Ames & C. Ames (Eds.), *Research on motivation in education: Student motivation* (Vol. I). New York: Academic Press.

Nicoloff, G., & Schwenk, T. L. (1995). Using exercise to ward off depression. *The Physician and Sportsmedicine, 23,* 44–56.

Nideffer, R. M. (1976a). *The inner athlete: Mind plus muscle for winning.* New York: Thomas Y. Crowell Company.

Nideffer, R. M. (1976b). Test of attentional and interpersonal style. *Journal of Personality and Social Psychology, 34,* 394–404.

Nideffer, R. M. (1978). *Attention control training.* New York: Wyden Books.

Nideffer, R. M. (1980a). Attentional focus—self-assessment. In R. M. Suinn (Ed.), *Psychology in sports: Methods and applications.* Minneapolis: Burgess Publishing Company.

Nideffer, R. M. (1980b). The relationship of attention and anxiety to performance. In W. F. Straub (Ed.), *Sport psychology: An analysis of athlete behavior.* 2d ed. Ithaca, NY: Mouvement Publications.

Nideffer, R. M. (1981). *The ethics and practice of applied sport psychology.* Ithaca, NY: Mouvement Publications.

Nideffer, R. M. (1985). *Athlete's guide to mental training.* Champaign, IL: Human Kinetics Publishers.

Nideffer, R. M. (1986). Concentration and attention control training. In J. M. Williams (Ed.), *Applied sport psychology* (pp. 257–269). Palo Alto, CA: Mayfield Publishing Company.

Nideffer, R. M. (1987). Issues in the use of psychological tests in applied settings. *The Sport Psychologist, 1,* 18–28.

Nideffer, R. M. (1989). Psychological aspects of sports injuries: Issues in prevention and treatment. *International Journal of Sport Psychology, 20,* 241–255.

Nideffer, R. M. (1990). Use of the Test of Attentional and Interpersonal Style (TAIS) in sport. *The Sport Psychologist, 4,* 285–300.

Nighswander, J. K., & Mayer, G. R. (1969). Catharsis: A means of reducing elementary school students' aggressive behaviors. *Personnel and Guidance Journal, 47,* 461–466.

Noel, R. C. (1980). The effect of visuo-motor behavior rehearsal on tennis performance. *Journal of Sport Psychology, 2,* 221–226.

Norman, D. A. (1968). Toward a theory of memory and attention. *Psychological Review, 75,* 522–536.

North, T. C., McCullagh, P., & Tran, Z. V. (1990). Effect of exercise on depression. In K. B. Pandolf & J. O. Holloszy (Eds.), *Exercise and sport science reviews, 18,* 379–415. Baltimore: William & Wilkins.

Noverr, D. A., & Ziewaez, L. E. (1981). Violence in American sports. In W. J. Baker & J. M. Carroll (Eds.), *Sports in modern America* (pp. 129–145). St. Louis: River City Publishers.

Nowlis, V. (1965). Research with the mood adjective checklist. In S. S. Tompkins & C. Izard (Eds.), *Affect, cognition, and personality.* New York: Springer Publishing Company.

NSCA (1993). Position statement: Anabolic-androgenic steroid use by athletes. *National Strength and Conditioning Association Journal, 15,* 9.

O

O'Connor, P. J., Bryant, C. X., Veltri, J. P., & Gebhardt, S. M. (1993). State anxiety and ambulatory blood pressure following resistance exercise in females. *Medicine and Science in Sports and Exercise, 25,* 516–521.

O'Connor, P. J., & Davis, J. C. (1992). Psychobiologic responses to exercise at different times of day. *Medicine and Science in Sports and Exercise, 24,* 714–719.

Ogilvie, B. C. (1968). Psychological consistencies within the personality of high-level competitors. *Journal of the American Medical Association, 205,* 780–786.

Ogilvie, B. C. (1976). Psychological consistencies within the personality of high-level competitors. In A. C. Fisher (Ed.), *Psychology of sport.* Palo Alto, CA: Mayfield Publishing Company.

Ogilvie, B. C. (1985). Sports psychologist and the disabled athlete. *Palaestra, 1,* 36–40, 43.

Ogilvie, B. C., Johnsgard, K., & Tutko, T. A. (1971). Personality: Effects of activity. In L. A. Larson (Ed.), *Encyclopedia of sport sciences and medicine.* New York: Macmillan.

Ogilvie, B. C., & Tutko, T. A. (1966). *Problem athletes and how to handle them.* London: Palham Books.

Ogles, B. M., Masters, K. S., & Richardson, S. A. (1995). Obligatory running and gender: An analysis of participative motives and training habits. *International Journal of Sport Psychology, 26,* 233–248.

Oglesby, C. (1980, May). Sport Psychology Academy. *Journal of Health, Physical Education, and Recreation, 51,* 42–43.

O'Halloran, A., & Gauvin, L. (1994). The role of preferred cognitive style in the effectiveness of imagery training. *International Journal of Sport Psychology, 25,* 19–31.

Onestak, D. M. (1991). The effects of progressive relaxation, mental practice, and hypnosis on athletic performance: A review. *Journal of Sport Behavior, 14,* 247–282.

Orlick, T. (1986). *Psyching for sport mental training for athletes.* Champaign, IL: Leisure Press.

Orlick, T., & Partington, J. (1987). The sport psychology consultant: Analysis of critical components as viewed by Canadian Olympic athletes. *The Sport Psychologist, 1,* 4–17.

Orne, M. T. (1959). The nature of hypnosis: Artifact and essence. *Journal of Abnormal and Social Psychology, 58,* 277–299.

Osborn, R. N., & Hunt, J. G. (1975). An adaptive-reactive theory of leadership: The role of macro variables in leadership research. In J. G. Hunt & L. L. Larson (Eds.), *Leadership frontiers,* Kent, OH: Kent State University Press.

Ostrow, A. C. (Ed.). (1996). *Directory of psychological tests in the sport and exercise sciences.* 2d ed. Morgantown, WV: Fitness Information Technology, Inc.

Oxendine, J. B. (1970). Emotional arousal and motor performance. *Quest, 13,* 23–30.

P

Paffenbarger, R. S. (1994). 40 years of progress: Physical activity, health and fitness. In *40th anniversary lectures* (pp. 93–109). Indianapolis, IN: American College of Sports Medicine.

Paivio, A. (1971). *Imagery and verbal processes.* New York: Holt, Rinehart and Winston.

Paivio, A. (1985). Cognitive and motivational functions of imagery in human performance. *Canadian Journal of Applied Sport Sciences, 10,* 225–285.

Palmer, S. L. (1992). A comparison of mental practice techniques as applied to the developing competitive figure skater. *The Sport Psychologist, 6,* 148–155.

Papaioannow, A. (1995). Different perceptual and motivational patterns when different goals are adopted. *Journal of Sport & Exercise Psychology, 17,* 18–34.

Parfitt, G., & Hardy, L. (1987). Further evidence for the differential effects of competitive anxiety upon a number of cognitive and motor subcomponents. *Journal of Sports Sciences, 5,* 62–63.

Parfitt, G., Hardy, L., & Pates, J. (1995). Somatic anxiety and physiological arousal: Their effects upon a high anaerobic, low memory demand task. *International Journal of Sport Psychology, 26,* 196–213.

Parker, R. M., Lambert, M. J., & Burlington, G. M. (1994). Psychological features of female runners presenting with pathological weight control behaviors. *Journal of Sport & Exercise Psychology, 16,* 119–134.

Partington, J. T., & Shangi, G. M. (1992). Developing an understanding of team psychology. *International Journal of Sport Psychology, 23,* 28–47.

Passer, M. W. (1981). Children in sport: Participation motives and psychological stress. *Quest, 33,* 231–244.

Pate, R. R., et al. (1995). Physical activity and public health. *Journal of the American Medical Association, 273,* 402–407.

Pedhazur, E. (1982). *Multiple regression in behavioral research.* New York: Holt, Rinehart & Winston.

Pemberton, C. L., & Petlichkoff, L. (1988, March). Sport psychology and the female Olympic athlete—an uncharted frontier. *Journal of Physical Education, Recreation and Dance, 59,* 55–58.

Peplau, L. A. (1976). Impact of fear of success and sex-role attitudes on women's competitive achievement. *Journal of Personality and Social Psychology, 34,* 561–568.

Peppler, M. (1977). *Inside volleyball for women.* Chicago: Contemporary Books.

Percival, L. (1971). The coach from the athlete's viewpoint. In J. W. Taylor (Ed.), *Proceedings for the First International Symposium on the Art and Science of Coaching* (Vol. 1). Willowdale, Ontario: Fitness Institute Productions.

Petitpas, A. J., Brewer, B. W., Rivera, P. M., & Van Raalte, J. L. (1994). Ethical beliefs and behaviors in applied sport psychology: The AAASP ethics survey. *Journal of Applied Sport Psychology, 6,* 135–151.

Petrie, T. A. (1993a). Disordered eating in female collegiate gymnasts: Prevalence and personality/attitudinal correlates. *Journal of Sport & Exercise Psychology, 15,* 424–436.

Petrie, T. A. (1993b). The moderating effects of social support and playing status on the life stress-injury relationship. *Journal of Applied Sport Psychology, 5,* 1–16.

Petrie, T. A. (1993c). Coping skills, competitive trait anxiety, and playing status: Moderating effects on the life stress-injury relationship. *Journal of Sport & Exercise Psychology, 15,* 261–274.

Petrie, T. A., & Stoever, S. (1993). The incidence of bulimia nervosa and pathogenic weight control behaviors in female collegiate gymnasts. *Research Quarterly for Exercise and Sport, 64,* 238–241.

Petrovsky, A. V. (1983). The new status of psychological theory concerning groups and collectives. *Soviet Psychology, 21,* 57–78.

Petruzzello, S. J., Landers, D. M., Hatfield, B. D., Kubitz, K. A., & Salazar, W. (1991). A meta-analysis on the anxiety reducing effects of acute and chronic exercise. *Sports Medicine, 11*(3), 143–182.

Petruzzello, S. J., Landers, D. M., & Salazar, W. (1991). Biofeedback and sport/exercise performance: Applications and limitations. *Behavior Therapy, 22,* 379–392.

Pie, J. S., Tenebaum, G., Bar-Eli, M., Eyal, N., Levy-Kolker, N., Sade, S., & Landers, D. M. (1996). Imagery orientation and vividness: Their effect on a motor skill performance. *Journal of Sport Behavior, 19,* 32–49.

Pierce, E. F., Daleng, M. L., & McGowan, R. W. (1993). Scores on exercise dependence among dancers. *Perceptual and Motor Skills, 76,* 531–535.

Pierce, E. F., & McGowan, R. W. (1992). Exercise dependence as a function of competitive orientation in runners. *Research Quarterly of Exercise and Sport, Supplement to 63*(1), Abstract A-81.

Poag, K., & McAuley, E. (1992). Goal setting, self-efficacy, and exercise behavior. *Journal of Sport & Exercise Psychology, 14,* 352–360.

Pollard, R. (1986). Home advantage in soccer: A retrospective analysis. *Journal of Sports Sciences, 4,* 237–248.

Populin, L., Rose, D. J., & Heath, K. (1990). The role of attention in one-handed catching. *Journal of Motor Behavior, 22,* 149–158.

Posner, M. I., & Boies, S. J. (1971). Components of attention. *Psychological Review, 78,* 391–408.

Powell, K. E. (1988). Habitual exercise and public health: An epidemiological view. In R. K. Dishman (Ed.), *Exercise adherence: Its impact on public health* (pp. 15–39). Champaign, IL: Human Kinetics Books.

Prapavessis, H., & Carron, A. V. (1988). Learned helplessness in sport. *The Sport Psychologist, 2,* 189–201.

Prapavessis, H., & Carron, A. V. (1996). The effects of group cohesion on competitive state anxiety. *Journal of Sport & Exercise Psychology, 18,* 64–74.

Prapavessis, H., & Grove, J. R. (1991). Precompetitive emotions and shooting performance: The mental health and zone of optimal function models. *The Sport Psychologist, 5,* 223–234.

Prapavessis, H., & Grove, R. (1994a). Personality variables as antecedents of precompetitive mood states. *International Journal of Sport Psychology, 25,* 81–99.

Prapavessis, H., & Grove, R. (1994b). Personality variables as antecedents of precompetitive mood state temporal patterning. *International Journal of Sport Psychology, 25,* 347–365.

Predebon, J., & Docker, S. B. (1992). Free throw shooting as a function of preshot routines. *Perceptual and Motor Skills, 75,* 167–171.

Pressman, M. D. (1980). Psychological techniques for the advancement of sports potential. In R. M. Suinn (Ed.), *Psychology in sports: Methods and applications.* Minneapolis: Burgess Publishing Company.

Prochaska, J. O., & DiClemente, C. C. (1982). Transtheoretical therapy: Towards a more integrative model of change. *Psychotherapy: Theory, Research, and Practice, 19,* 726–288.

Prochaska, J. O., & DiClemente, C. C. (1983). Stages and processes of self-change of smoking: Toward an integrative model of change. *Journal of Consulting and Clinical Psychology, 51,* 390–395.

Prochaska, J. O., & DiClemente, C. C. (1986). Toward a comprehensive model of change. In W. E. Miller & N. Heather (Eds.), *Treating addictive behaviors* (pp. 3–27). London: Plenum Press.

Prochaska, J. O., & Marcus, B. H. (1994). The transtheoretical model: The applications to exercise. In R. K. Dishman (Ed.), *Advances in exercise adherence* (pp. 161–180). Champaign, IL: Human Kinetics Books.

Puffer, J. C., & McShane, J. M. (1992). Depression and chronic fatigue in athletes. *Clinics in Sports Medicine, 11,* 327–338.

Pulos, L. (1979). Athletes and self-hypnosis. In P. Klavora & J. V. Daniel (Eds.), *Coach, athlete, and the sport psychologist.* Champaign, IL: Human Kinetics Publishers.

Q Quackenbush, N., Crossman, J. (1994). Injured athletes: A study of emotional responses. *Journal of Sport Behavior, 17,* 178–187.

R Raedeke, T. D., & Stein, G. L. (1994). Felt arousal, thoughts/feelings, and ski performance. *The Sport Psychologist, 8,* 360–375.

Raglin, J. S. (1992). Anxiety and sport performance. *Exercise and Sport Science Reviews, 20,* 243–273.

Raglin, J. S., Eksten, F., & Garl, T. (1995). Mood state responses to a pre-season conditioning program in male collegiate basketball players. *International Journal of Sport Psychology, 26,* 214–225.

Raglin, J. S., Koceja, D. M., Stager, J. M., & Harms, C. A. (1996). Mood, neuromuscular function, and performance during training in female swimmers. *Medicine and Science in Sports and Exercise, 28,* 372–375.

Raglin, J. S., & Morgan, W. P. (1988). Predicted and actual pre-competition anxiety in college swimmers. *Journal of Swimming Research, 4,* 5–8.

Raglin, J. S., & Morris, M. J. (1994). Precompetition anxiety in women volleyball players: A test of ZOF theory in a team sport. *British Journal of Sports Medicine, 28,* 47–51.

Raglin, J. S., Morgan, W. P., & Wise, K. J. (1990). Pre-competition anxiety and performance in female high school swimmers: A test of optimal function theory. *International Journal of Sports Medicine, 11,* 171–175.

Raglin, J. S., & Turner, P. E. (1993). Anxiety and performance in track and field athletes: A comparison of the inverted-U hypothesis with zone of optimal functioning theory. *Personality and Individual Differences, 14,* 163–171.

Raglin, J. S., Turner, P. E., & Eksten, F. (1993). State anxiety and blood pressure following 30 min. of leg ergometry or weight training. *Medicine and Science in Sport and Exercise, 25,* 1044–1048.

Raglin, J. S., Wise, K. J., & Morgan, W. P. (1990). Predicted and actual pre-competition anxiety in high school girl swimmers. *Journal of Swimming Research, 6,* 5–8.

Rainey, D. W., Amunategui, F., Agocs, H., & Larick, J. (1992). Sensation seeking and competitive trait anxiety among college rodeo athletes. *Journal of Sport Behavior, 15,* 307–317.

Ranson, S. W. (1939). Somnolence caused by hypothalamic lesions in the monkey. *Archives of Neurological Psychiatry, 41,* 1–23.

Raymond, C. (1990, June 27). Eighteen months after its formation, Psychological Society proves its worth to behavioral-science researchers. *The Chronicle of Higher Education, 36,* A5, A9.

Reddy, J. K., Bai, A. J. L., & Rao, V. R. (1976). The effects of the transcendental meditation program on athletic performance. In D. J. Orme-Johnson & I. Farrow (Eds.), *Scientific research on the transcendental meditation program* (Collected papers, Vol. 1). Weggis, Switzerland: MERU Press.

Reel, J. J., & Gill, D. L. (1996). Psychosocial factors related to eating disorders among high school and college female cheerleaders. *The Sport Psychologist, 10,* 195–206.

Reifman, A. S., Larrick, R. P., & Fein, S. (1991). Temper and temperature on the diamond: The heat aggression relationship in major league baseball. *Personality and Social Psychology Bulletin, 17,* 580–585.

Reilly, R. (April 22, 1996). Master strokes. *Sports Illustrated, 84,* 24–31.

Reis, J., & Bird, A. (1982). Cue processing as a function of breadth of attention. *Journal of Sport Psychology, 4,* 64–72.

Rejeski, W. J., & Brawley, L. R. (1983). Attribution theory in sport: Current status and new perspectives. *Journal of Sport Psychology, 5,* 77–99.

Rejeski, W. J., Brawley, L. R., & Schumaker, S. A. (1996). Physical activity and health-related quality of life. In J. O. Holloszy (Ed.), *Exercise and Sport Science Reviews, 24,* 71–108.

Renfrow, N. E., & Bolton, B. (1979). Personality characteristics associated with aerobic exercise in adult females. *Journal of Personality Assessment, 43,* 504–508.

Renger, R. (1993). A review of the Profile of Mood States (POMS) in the prediction of athletic success. *The Sport Psychologist, 5,* 78–84.

Richardson, A. (1969). *Mental imagery.* New York: Springer.

Richman, C. L., & Heather, R. (1986). The development of self-esteem through the martial arts. *International Journal of Sport Psychology, 17,* 234–239.

Riemer, B. (1975). Influence of causal beliefs on affect and expectancy. *Journal of Personality and Social Psychology, 31,* 1163–1167.

Riemer, H. A., & Chelladurai, P. (1995). Leadership and satisfaction in athletics. *Journal of Sport & Exercise Psychology, 17,* 276–293.

Rigsby, L. W., Dishman, R. K., Jackson, A. W., MaClean, G. S., & Raven, P. B. (1992). Effects of exercise training on men seropositive for human immunodeficiency virus-1. *Medicine and Science in Sports and Exercise, 24*(1), 6–12.

Roberts, G. C. (1972). Effect of achievement motivation and social environment on performance of a motor task. *Journal of Motor Behavior, 4,* 37–46.

Roberts, G. C. (1977). Win-loss causal attributions of Little League players. In J. Salmela (Ed.), *Canadian symposium for psychomotor learning and sport psychology, 1975* (pp. 315–322). Ithaca, NY: Mouvement Publications.

Roberts, G. C. (1980). Children in competition: A theoretical perspective and recommendation for practice. *Motor Skills: Theory into Practice, 4,* 37–50.

Roberts, G. C. (1982). Achievement motivation in sport. In R. Terjung (Ed.), *Exercise and sport science reviews* (Vol. 10). Philadelphia: Franklin Institute Press.

Roberts, G. C. (1993). Motivation in sport: Understanding and enhancing the motivation and achievement of children. In R. N. Singer, M. Murphey, & L. K. Tennant (Eds.), *Handbook of research on sport psychology* (pp. 405–420). New York: Macmillan.

Roberts, G. C., Kleiber, D. A., & Duda, J. L. (1981). An analysis of motivation in children's sport: The role of perceived competence in participation. *Journal of Sport Psychology, 3,* 206–216.

Roberts, G. C., & Pascuzzi, D. (1979). Causal attributions in sport: Some theoretical implications. *Journal of Sport Psychology, 1,* 203–211.

Roberts, G. C., & Treasure, D. C. (1995). Achievement goals, motivation climate and achievement strategies and behaviors in sport. *International Journal of Sport Psychology, 26,* 64–80.

Robinson, D. W. (1985). Stress seeking: Selected behavioral characteristics of elite rock climbers. *Journal of Sport Psychology, 7,* 400–404.

Rodgers, W., Hall, C., & Buckolz, E. (1991). The effect of an imagery training program on imagery ability, imagery use, and figure skating performance. *Journal of Applied Sport Psychology, 3,* 109–125.

Roeder, L. K., & Aufsesser, P. M. (1986, Winter). Selected attentional and interpersonal characteristics of wheelchair athletes. *Palaestra, 2,* 28–32, 43–44.

Rose, D. J., & Christina, R. W. (1990). Attention demands of precision pistol-shooting as a function of skill level. *Research Quarterly for Exercise and Sport, 61,* 111–113.

Rose, J., & Jevne, R. F. J. (1993). Psychosocial processes associated with athletic injuries. *The Sport Psychologist, 7,* 309–328.

Rosen, B. C., & D'Andrade, R. (1959). The psycho-social origins of achievement motivation. *Sociometry, 22,* 185–218.

Rosen, L. W., & Hough, D. O. (1988). Pathogenic weight-control behaviors of female college gymnasts. *The Physician and Sportsmedicine, 16,* 140–146.

Rosen, L. W., McKeag, D. B., Hough, D. D., & Curley, V. (1986). Pathogenic weight-control behavior in female athletes. *The Physician and Sportsmedicine, 14,* 79–86.

Ross, L. (1977). The intuitive psychologist and his shortcomings: Distortions in the attribution process. In L. Berkowitz (Ed.), *Advances in experimental social psychology* (Vol. 10, pp. 121–141). New York: Academic Press.

Ross, M. (1976). The self-perception of intrinsic motivation. In J. H. Harvey, W. J. Ickles, & R. F. Kidd (Eds.), *New directions in attribution research.* Hillsdale, NJ: Erlbaum.

Rotella, R. J., Gansneder, B., Ojala, D., & Billings, J. (1980). Cognitive and coping strategies of elite skiers: An exploratory study of young developing athletes. *Journal of Sport Psychology, 2,* 350–354.

Rotella, R. J., Malone, C., & Ojala, D. (1985). Facilitating athletic performance through the use of mastery and coping tapes. In L. K. Bunker, R. J. Rotella, & A. S. Reilly (Eds.), *Sport psychology.* University of Virginia: Authors.

Roth, D. L. (1989). Acute emotional and psychophysiological effects of aerobic exercise. *Psychophysiology, 26,* 593–602.

Roth, D. L., & Holmes, D. S. (1985). Influence of physical fitness in determining the impact of stressful events on physical and psychological health. *Psychosomatic Medicine, 47,* 164–173.

Rotter, J. B. (1966). Generalized expectancies for internal versus external control of reinforcement. *Psychological Monographs: General and Applied, 80*(1, Whole No. 609).

Rotter, J. B. (1971, June). External control and internal control. *Psychology Today, 5*(1), 37–42, 58–59.

Rowley, A. J., Landers, D. M., Kyllo, L. B., & Etnier, J. L. (1995). Does the iceberg profile discriminate between successful and less successful athletes? A meta-analysis. *Journal of Sport & Exercise Psychology, 17,* 185–199.

Royal, E. G., Whiteside, H., & McClelan, P. (1985). Attitude similarity and evaluation of an athletic coach. *International Journal of Sport Psychology, 16,* 307–311.

Ruder, M. K., & Gill, D. L. (1982). Immediate effects of win-loss on perceptions of cohesion in intramural and intercollegiate volleyball teams. *Journal of Sport Psychology, 4,* 227–234.

Rudisill, M. E. (1988). The influences of causal dimension orientations and perceived competence on adult's expectations, persistence, performance and the selection of causal dimensions. *International Journal of Sport Psychology, 19,* 184–198.

Rudisill, M. E. (1989a). Influence of perceived competence and causal dimension orientation on expectations, persistence and performance during perceived failure. *Research Quarterly for Exercise and Sport, 60,* 166–175.

Rudisill, M. E. (1989b). Putting attribution theory to work—improving persistence and performance. *Journal of Physical Education, Recreation and Dance, 60,* 43–46.

Rudolph, D. L., & McAuley, E. (1995). Self-efficacy and salivary cortisol responses to acute exercise in physically active and less active adults. *Journal of Sport & Exercise Psychology, 17,* 206–213.

Rudolph, D. L., & McAuley, E. (1996). Self-efficacy and perceptions of effort: A reciprocal relationship. *Journal of Sport & Exercise Psychology, 18,* 216–223.

Ruffer, W. A. (1975). Personality traits of athletes. *The Physical Educator, 32*(1), 105–109.

Ruffer, W. A. (1976a). Personality traits of athletes. *The Physical Educator, 33*(1), 50–55.

Ruffer, W. A. (1976b). Personality traits of athletes. *The Physical Educator, 33*(4), 211–214.

Rusbult, C. E. (1980). Commitment and satisfaction in romantic associations: A test of the investment model. *Journal of*

Experimental Social Psychology, 16, 172–186.

Rushall, B. S. (1970a). An evaluation of the relationship between personality and physical performance categories. In G. S. Kenyon (Ed.), *Contemporary psychology of sport: Second International Congress of Sports Psychology.* Chicago: The Athletic Institute.

Rushall, B. S. (1972). Three studies relating personality variables to football performance. *International Journal of Sport Psychology, 3,* 12–24.

Rushall, B. S. (1973). The status of personality research and application in sports and physical education. *Journal of Sports Medicine and Physical Fitness, 13,* 281–290.

Rushall, B. S., Hall, M., & Rushall, A. (1988). Effects of three types of thought content instructions on skiing performance. *The Sport Psychologist, 2,* 283–297.

Russell, D. (1982). The causal dimension scale: A measure of how individuals perceive causes. *Journal of Personality and Social Psychology, 42,* 1137–1145.

Russell, D., McAuley, E., & Tarico, V. (1987). Measuring causal attributions for success and failure: A comparison of methodologies for assessing causal dimensions. *Journal of Personality and Social Psychology, 52,* 1248–1257.

Russell, G. W. (1974). Machiavellianism, locus of control, aggression, performance and precautionary behavior in ice hockey. *Human Relations, 27,* 825–837.

Russell, G. W. (1981a). Conservatism, birth order, leadership, and the aggression of Canadian ice hockey players. *Perceptual and Motor Skills, 53,* 3–7.

Russell, G. W. (1981b). Spectator moods at an aggressive sporting event. *Journal of Sport Psychology, 3,* 217–227.

Russell, G. W. (1986). Does sports violence increase box office receipts? *International Journal of Sport Psychology, 17,* 173–183.

Russell, G. W. (1995). Personalities in the crowd: Those who would escalate a sports riot. *Aggressive Behavior, 21,* 91–100.

Russell, G. W., & Arms, R. L. (1995). False consensus effect, physical aggression, anger, and a willingness to escalate a disturbance. *Aggressive Behavior, 21,* 381–386.

Russell, G. W., & Drewery, B. P. (1976). Crowd size and competitive aspects of aggression in ice hockey: An archival study. *Human Relations, 29,* 723–735.

Russell, J. A., Weiss, A., & Mendelsohn, G. A. (1989). Affect grid: A single-item scale of pleasure and arousal. *Journal of Personality and Social Psychology, 57,* 493–502.

Russell, W. D. (1996a). The utility of family therapy in the field of sport psychology. *Family Therapy, 23,* 37–42.

Russell, W. D. (1996b). *Comparison of individuals' zone of optimal functioning across two different tasks: A laboratory examination of ZOF theory.* Unpublished doctoral dissertation, University of Missouri, Columbia.

Ryan, E. D. (1976). The questions we ask and the decisions we make. In A. C. Fisher (Ed.), *Psychology of sport.* Palo Alto, CA: Mayfield Publishing Company.

Ryan, E. D. (1980). Attribution, intrinsic motivation, and athletics: A replication and extension. In C. H. Nadeau (Ed.), *Psychology of motor behavior and sport, 1979.* Champaign, IL: Human Kinetics Publishers.

Ryan, E. D., & Lakie, W. L. (1965). Competitive and noncompetitive performance in relation to achievement motivation and manifest anxiety. *Journal of Personality and Social Psychology, 1,* 344–345.

Ryan, E. D., & Simons, J. (1981). Cognitive demand, imagery, and frequency of mental rehearsal as factors influencing acquisition of motor skills. *Journal of Sport Psychology, 1,* 35–45.

Ryan, F. (1981). *Sports and psychology.* Englewood Cliffs, NJ: Prentice-Hall.

Ryan, M. K., Williams, J. M., & Wimer, B. (1990). Athletic aggression: Perceived legitimacy and behavioral intentions in girls high school basketball. *Journal of Sport & Exercise Psychology, 12,* 48–55.

S   Sachs, M. L. (1982a). Exercise and running: Effects on anxiety, depression, and psychology. *Humanistic Education Development, 21,* 51–57.

Sachs, M. L. (1982b). Compliance and addiction to exercise. In R. C. Cantu (Ed.), *The exercising adult.* Boston, MA: The Collamore Press.

Sage, G. H. (1975). An occupational analysis of the college coach. In D. W. Ball & J. W. Loy (Eds.), *Sport and social order* (pp. 408–455). Reading, MA: Addison-Wesley.

Sage, G. H. (1984a). *Introduction to motor behavior: A neuropsychological approach.* 3d ed. Reading, MA: Addison-Wesley.

Salili, F., Maehr, M. L., & Gillmore, G. (1976). Achievement and morality: A cross-cultural analysis of causal attribution and evaluation. *Journal of Personality and Social Psychology, 33,* 327–337.

Sallis, J. F., Haskell, W. L., Fortmann, S. P., Vranizan, K. M., Taylor, C. B., & Solomon, D. S. (1986). Predictors of adoption and maintenance of physical activity in a community sample. *Preventive Medicine, 15,* 331–341.

Sallis, J. F., & Hovell, M. F. (1990). Determinants of exercise behavior. In K. B. Pandolf & J. O. Holloszy (Eds.), *Exercise and sport science reviews* (Vol. 18, pp. 307–330). Baltimore: Williams & Wilkins.

Salmela, J. H. (1992). *The world sport psychology sourcebook.* Champaign, IL: Human Kinetics.

Salmon, J., Hall, C. R., & Haslam, I. (1994). The use of imagery by soccer players. *Journal of Applied Sport Psychology, 6,* 116–133.

Sanguinetti, C., Lee, A. M., & Nelson, J. (1985). Reliability estimates and age and gender comparisons of expectations of success in sex-typed activities. *Journal of Sport Psychology, 7,* 379–388.

Sarason, I. G., & Smith, R. E. (1971). Personality. *Annual Review of Psychology, 22,* 393–446.

Sarason, S. B. (1954). *The clinical interaction with special reference to Rorschach.* New York: Harper.

Sarason, S. B., Hill, K. T., & Zimbardo, P. G. (1964). A longitudinal study of the relationship of test anxiety to performance on intelligence and achievement tests. *Monographs of the Society for Research in Child Development* (Serial No. 9829, Whole No. 7).

Schacham, S. (1983). A shortened version of the Profile of Mood States. *Journal of Personality Assessment, 47,* 305–306.

Schedlowski, M., & Tewes, U. (1992). Physiological arousal and perception of bodily state during parachute jumping. *Psychophysiology, 29,* 95–103

Scheer, J. K., & Ansorge, C. J. (1979). Influence due to expectations of judges: A function of internal-external locus of control. *Journal of Sport Psychology, 1,* 53–58.

Schmidt, G. W., & Stein, G. L. (1991). Sport commitment: A model integrating enjoyment, dropout, and burnout. *Journal of Sport and Exercise Psychology, 13*(3), 254–265.

Schmidt, R. A. (1988). *Motor control and learning.* 2d ed. Champaign, IL: Human Kinetics Publishers, Inc.

Schnurr, P. P., Vaillant, C. O., & Vaillant, G. E. (1990). Predicting exercise in later midlife from young adult personality characteristics. *International Journal of Aging and Human Development, 30,* 153–160.

Schomer, H. H. (1986). Mental strategies and the perception of effort of marathon runners. *International Journal of Sport Psychology, 18,* 133–151.

Schomer, H. H. (1987a). Mental strategy training programme for marathon runners. *International Journal of Sport Psychology, 18,* 133–151.

Schomer, H. H. (1987b). The relationship between cognitive strategies and perceived effort of marathon runners. *South African Journal for Research in Sport, Physical Education and Recreation, 10,* 37–64.

Schomer, H. H. (1990). A cognitive strategy training programme for marathon runners: Ten case studies. *South African Journal for Research in Sport, Physical Education and Recreation, 13,* 47–78.

Schultz, D. D. (1965). *Sensory restriction: Effects on behavior.* New York: Academic Press.

Schultz, J. H., & Luthe, W. (1959). *Autogenic training: A psychophysiological approach to psychotherapy.* New York: Grune and Stratton.

Schunk, D. H. (1995). Self-efficacy, motivation, and performance. *Journal of Applied Sport Psychology, 7,* 112–137.

Schurr, K. T., Ashley, M. A., & Joy, K. L. (1977). A multivariate analysis of male athlete characteristics: Sport type and success. *Multivariate Experimental Clinical Research, 3,* 53–68.

Schurr, K. T., Ruble, V. E., Nisbet, J., & Wallace, D. (1984). Myers-Briggs type inventory characteristics of more and less successful players on an American football team. *Journal of Sport Behavior, 7,* 47–57.

Schutz, W. C. (1966). *The interpersonal underworld.* Palo Alto, CA: Science and Behavior Books.

Schwartz, B., & Barsky, S. F. (1977). The home advantage. *Social Forces, 55,* 641–661.

Schwartz, G. E., Davidson, R. J., & Goleman, D. J. (1978). Patterning of cognitive and somatic processes in the self-regulation of anxiety: Effects of meditation vs. exercise. *Psychosomatic Medicine, 40,* 321–328.

Schwartz, M. S. (1987). *Biofeedback: A practitioner's guide.* New York: Guilford Press.

Scott, J. P. (1970). Sport and aggression. In G. S. Kenyon (Ed.), *Contemporary psychology of sport* (pp. 11–34). Chicago: The Athletic Institute.

Seabourne, T. G., Weinberg, R. S., & Jackson, A. (1982). *Effect of visuo-motor behavior rehearsal in enhancing karate performance.* Unpublished manuscript, North Texas State University, Denton, TX.

Seabourne, T. G., Weinberg, R. S., & Jackson, A. (1984). The effect of individualized practice and training of visuo-motor behavior rehearsal in enhancing karate performance. *Journal of Sport Behavior, 7,* 58–67.

Seabourne, T. G., Weinberg, R. S., Jackson, A., & Suinn, R. M. (1985). Effect of individualized, nonindividualized, and package intervention strategies on karate performance. *Journal of Sport Psychology, 7,* 40–50.

Seifriz, J. J., Duda, J. L., & Chi, L. (1992). The relationship of perceived motivational climate to intrinsic motivation and beliefs about success in basketball. *Journal of Sport & Exercise Psychology, 14,* 375–391.

Seligman, M. E. P. (1975). *Helplessness on depression, development, and death.* San Francisco: W. H. Freeman.

Selye, H. (1975). *Stress without distress.* New York: New American Library.

Selye, H. (1983). The stress concept: Past, present, and future. In C. L. Cooper (Ed.), *Stress research* (pp. 1–20). New York: John Wiley & Sons.

Sharp, M. W., & Reilley, R. R. (1975). The relationship of aerobic physical fitness to selected personality traits. *Journal of Clinical Psychology, 31,* 428–430.

Shaw, J. M., Dzewaltowski, D. A., & McElroy, M. (1992). Self-efficacy and causal attributions as mediators of perceptions of psychological momentum. *Journal of Sport & Exercise Psychology, 14,* 134–147.

Shay, K. A., & Roth, D. L. (1992). Association between aerobic fitness and visuospatial performance in healthy older adults. *Psychology of Aging, 7,* 15–24.

Sheehan, P. W. (1967). A shortened version of Betts' questionnaire upon mental imagery. *Journal of Clinical Psychology, 23,* 386–389.

Sheikh, A. A., & Korn, E. R. (1994). *Imagery in sports and physical performance.* Amityville, NY: Baywood.

Shelton, T. O., & Mahoney, M. J. (1978). The content and effect of "psyching-up" strategies in weight lifters. *Cognitive Therapy and Research, 2,* 275–284.

Shephard, R. J. (1990). *Fitness in special populations.* Champaign, IL: Human Kinetics Books.

Shephard, R. J., Rhind, S., & Shek, P. N. (1995). The impact of exercise on the immune system: NK cells, interleukins 1 and 2, and related responses. *Exercise and Sport Science Reviews, 23,* 215–241.

Shephard, R. J., & Shek, P. N. (1994). Potential impact of physical activity and sport on the immune system—a brief review. *British Journal of Sports Medicine, 28,* 247–255.

Sherwood, A., Light, K. C., & Blumenthal, J. A. (1989). Effects of aerobic exercise training on hemodynamic responses during psychological stress in normotensive and borderline hypertensive Type A men: A preliminary report. *Psychosomatic Medicine, 51,* 123–136.

Siedentop, D., & Ramey, G. (1977). Extrinsic rewards and intrinsic motivation. *Motor Skills: Theory into Practice, 2,* 49–62.

Silva, J. M., III. (1980a). Assertive and aggressive behavior in sport: A definitional clarification. In C. H. Nadeau (Ed.), *Psychology of motor behavior and sport, 1979* (pp. 199–208). Champaign, IL: Human Kinetics Publishers.

Silva, J. M., III. (1980b). Understanding aggressive behavior and its effects upon athletic performance. In W. F. Straub (Ed.), *Sport psychology: An analysis of athlete behavior* (2d ed.) (pp. 177–186). Ithaca, NY: Mouvement Publications.

Silva, J. M., III (1982). An evaluation of fear of success in female and male athletes and non-athletes. *Journal of Sport Psychology, 4*(1), 92–96.

Silva, J. M., III. (1984). Personality and sport performance: Controversy and challenge. In J. M. Silva, III & R. S. Weinberg (Eds.), *Psychological Foundations of Sport.* Champaign, Illinois: Human Kinetics Publishers.

Silva, J. M., III. (1989a). The evolution of AAASP and JASP. *Journal of Applied Sport Psychology, 1,* 1–3.

Silva, J. M., III. (1989b). Toward the professionalization of sport psychology. *The Sport Psychologist, 3,* 265–273.

Silva, J. M., III. (1990). An analysis of the training stress syndrome in competitive athletics. *Journal of Applied Sport Psychology, 2,* 5–20.

Silva, J. M., III. (1992). Psychological momentum and skill performance: A laboratory study. *Journal of Sport & Exercise Psychology, 14,* 119–133.

Silva, J. M., III, & Andrew, J. A. (1987). An analysis of game location and basketball performance in the Atlantic coast conference. *International Journal of Sport Psychology, 18,* 188–204.

Silva, J. M., III, Andrew, J. A., & Richey, S. (1983). *Game location and basketball performance variation.* Paper presented at the North American Society for the Psychology of Sport and Physical Activity Annual Convention, Michigan State University, East Lansing.

Silva, J. M., & Appelbaum, M. I. (1989). Association-dissociation patterns of United States Olympic marathon trial contestants. *Cognitive Therapy and Research, 13,* 185–192.

Silva, J. M., III, Hardy, C. J., & Grace, R. K. (1988). Analysis of psychological momentum in intercollegiate tennis. *Journal of Sport & Exercise Psychology, 10,* 346–354.

Silva, J. M., III, Shultz, B. B., Haslam, R. W., & Murray, D. (1981). A psychological assessment of elite wrestlers. *Research Quarterly for Exercise and Sport, 52,* 348–358.

Silva, J. M., III, Shultz, B. B., Haslam, R. W., Martin, T. P., & Murray, D. F. (1985). Discriminating characteristics of contestants at the United States Olympic wrestling trials. *International Journal of Sport Psychology, 16,* 79–102.

Silverman, J. (1964). The problem of attention in research and theory in schizophrenia. *Psychological Review, 71,* 352–379.

Simkin, L. R., & Gross, A. M. (1994). Assessment of coping with high-risk situations for exercise relapse among healthy women. *Health Psychology, 13,* 274–277.

Simon, H. B. (1991). Exercise and human immune function. In R. Ader, D. L. Felton, & N. Cohen (Eds.), *Psychoneuroimmunology* (2d ed.) (pp. 869–895). San Diego, CA: Academic Press.

Simon, J. A., & Martens, R. (1979). Children's anxiety in sport and nonsport evaluative activities. *Journal of Sport Psychology, 1,* 160–169.

Simons, A. D., Epstein, L. H., McGowan, C. R., Kupfer, D. J., & Robertson, R. J. (1985). Exercise as a treatment for depression: An update. *Clinical Psychology Review, 5,* 553–568.

Simons, C. W., & Birkimer, J. C. (1988). An exploration of factors predicting the effects of aerobic conditioning on mood state. *Journal of Psychosomatic Research, 32,* 63–75.

Singer, R. N. (1969). Personality differences between and within baseball and tennis players. *Research Quarterly, 40,* 582–587.

Singer, R. N. (1970). Effect of an audience on performance of a motor task. *Journal of Motor Behavior, 2,* 88–95.

Singer, R. N. (1975). *Myths and truths in sports psychology.* New York: Harper & Row.

Singer, R. N. (1984). What sport psychology can do for the athlete and coach. *International Journal of Sport Psychology, 15,* 52–61.

Singer, R. N. (1989). Applied sport psychology in the United States. *Journal of Applied Sport Psychology, 1,* 61–80.

Singer, R. N., & Cauraugh, J. H., Murphey, M., Chen, D., & Lidor, R. (1991). Attentional control, distractors, and motor performance. *Human Performance, 4,* 55–69.

Skinner, B. F. (1938). *The behavior of organisms: An experimental analysis.* New York: Appleton-Century-Crofts.

Skinner, B. F. (1953). *Science and human behavior.* New York: Macmillan.

Slater, M. R., & Sewell, D. F. (1994). An examination of the cohesion-performance relationship in university hockey teams. *Journal of Sports Sciences, 12,* 423–431.

Smith, A. L., Gill, D. L., Crews, D. J., Hopewell, R., & Morgan, D. W. (1995). Attentional strategy use by experienced distance runners: Physiological and psychological effects. *Research Quarterly of Exercise and Sport, 66,* 142–150.

Smith, A. M., Scott, S. G., O'Fallon, W. M., & Young, M. L. (1990). Emotional responses of athletes to injury. *Mayo Clinic Proceedings, 65,* 38–50.

Smith, A. M., Stuart, M. J., Wiese-Bjornstal, D. M., Milliner, E. K., O'Fallon, W. M., & Crowson, C. S. (1993). Competitive athletes: Preinjury and postinjury mood state and self-esteem. *Mayo Clinic Proceedings, 68,* 939–947.

Smith, B. D., & Vetter, H. J. (1991). *Theories of personality.* 2d ed. Englewood Cliffs, NJ: Prentice-Hall.

Smith, D. (1987). Conditions that facilitate the development of sport imagery training. *The Sport Psychologist, 1,* 237–247.

Smith, D. (1992). The coach as sport psychologist: An alternate view. *Journal of Applied Sport Psychology, 4,* 56–62.

Smith, G. (June 15, 1992). A few pieces of silver. *Sports Illustrated, 76,* 64–75.

Smith, M. D. (1980). Hockey violence: Interring some myths. In W. F. Straub (Ed.), *Sport psychology: An analysis of athlete behavior.* (2d ed.) Ithaca, NY: Mouvement Publications.

Smith, M., & Lee, C. (1992). Goal setting and performance in a novel coordination task: Mediating mechanisms. *Journal of Sport & Exercise Psychology, 14,* 169–176.

Smith, R. E. (1980). A cognitive-affective approach to stress management training for athletes. In C. H. Nadeau (Ed.), *Psychology of motor behavior and sport, 1979.* Champaign, IL: Human Kinetics Publishers.

Smith, R. E. (1986). Toward a cognitive-affective model of athletic burnout. *Journal of Sport Psychology, 8,* 36–50.

Smith, R. E., & Christensen, D. S. (1995). Psychological skills as predictors of performance and survival in professional baseball. *Journal of Sport & Exercise Psychology, 17,* 399–415.

Smith, R. E., Schultz, R. W., Smoll, F. L., & Ptacek, J. T. (1995). Development and validation of a multidimensional measure of sport specific psychological skills: The athletic coping skills inventory-28. *Journal of Sport & Exercise Psychology, 17,* 379–398.

Smith, R. E., & Smoll, F. L. (1990). Self-esteem and children's reactions to youth sport coaching behaviors: A field study of self-enhancement processes. *Developmental Psychology, 26,* 987–993.

Smith, R. E., Smoll, F. L., & Barnett, N. P. (1995). Reduction of children's sport performance anxiety through social support and stress-reduction training for coaches. *Journal of Applied Developmental Psychology, 16,* 125–142.

Smith, R. E., Smoll, F. L., & Curtis, B. (1979). Coach effectiveness training: A cognitive-behavioral approach to enhancing relationship skills in youth sport coaches. *Journal of Sport Psychology, 1,* 59–75.

Smith, R. E., Smoll, F. L., & Hunt, E. (1977). A system for the behavioral assessment of athletic coaches. *Research Quarterly, 48,* 401–407.

Smith, R. E., Smoll, F. L., & Ptacek, J. T. (1990). Conjunctive moderatory variables in vulnerability and resiliency research: Life stress, social support and coping skills, and adolescent sport injuries. *Journal of Personality and Social Psychology, 58*(2), 560–570.

Smith, R. E., Smoll, F. L., & Schutz, R. W. (1990). Measurement correlates of sport specific cognitive and somatic trait anxiety: The sport anxiety scale. *Anxiety Research, 2,* 263–280.

Smoll, F. L., & Smith, R. E. (1989). Leadership behaviors in sport: A theoretical model and research paradigm. *Journal of Applied Social Psychology, 19,* 1522–1551.

Smoll, F. L., Smith, R. E., Curtis, B., & Hunt, E. (1978). Toward a mediational model of coach-player relationships. *Research Quarterly, 49,* 528–541.

Snow, A., & LeUnes, A. (1994). Characteristics of sports research using profile of mood states. *Journal of Sports Behavior, 17,* 207–211.

Snyder, E. E., & Purdy, D. A. (1985). The home advantage in collegiate basketball. *Sociology of Sport Journal, 2,* 352–356.

Solomon, J., Hall, C., & Haslam, I. (1994). The use of imagery by soccer players. *Journal of Applied Sport Psychology, 6,* 116–133.

Sonstroem, R. J., & Bernardo, P. (1982). Intraindividual pregame state anxiety and basketball performance: A reexamination of the inverted-U curve. *Journal of Sport Psychology, 4,* 235–245.

Spence, J. T., & Helmreich, R. L. (1978). *Masculinity and femininity.* Austin: University of Texas Press.

Spence, J. T., Helmreich, R. L., & Stapp, J. (1975). Rating of self and peers on sex role attributes and their relationship to self-esteem and conceptions of masculinity and femininity. *Journal of Personality and Social Psychology, 32,* 29–39.

Spence, K. W. (1956). *Behavior theory and conditioning.* New Haven, CT: Yale University Press.

Sperling, G. (1960). The information available in brief visual presentations. *Psychological Monographs, 74*(11), 1–29.

Spielberger, C. D. (1971). Trait-state anxiety and motor behavior. *Journal of Motor Behavior, 3,* 265–279.

Spielberger, C. D. (1983). *Manual for the state-trait anxiety inventory* (Form Y). Palo Alto, CA: Consulting Psychologists Press.

Spielberger, C. D., Gorsuch, R. L., & Lushene, R. F. (1970). *Manual for the state-trait anxiety inventory.* Palo Alto, CA: Consulting Psychologists Press.

Spigolon, L., & Annalisa, D. (1985). Autogenic training in frogmen. *International Journal of Sport Psychology, 16,* 312–320.

Spink, K. S. (1978a). Correlation between two methods of assessing causal attribution. *Perceptual and Motor Skills, 46,* 1173–1174.

Spink, K. S. (1978b). Win-loss causal attributions of high school basketball players. *Canadian Journal of Applied Sport Sciences, 3,* 195–201.

Spink, K. S. (1992). Group cohesion and starting status in successful and less successful elite volleyball teams. *Journal of Sport Sciences, 10,* 379–388.

Spink, K. S. (1995). Cohesion and intention to participate of female sport team athletes. *Journal of Sport & Exercise Psychology, 17,* 416–427.

Spink, K. S., & Carron, A. U. (1992). Group cohesion and adherence in exercise classes. *Journal of Sport and Exercise Psychology, 14,* 78–86.

Spink, K. S., & Roberts, G. C. (1980). Ambiguity of outcome and causal attributions. *Journal of Sport Psychology, 2,* 237–244.

Stadulis, R. E., Eidson, T. A., & MacCracken, M. J. (1994). A children's form of the competitive state anxiety inventory (CSAI-2C). *Journal of Sport & Exercise Psychology, 16,* S109.

Staff. (1982, Fall). *Ethical standards for provision of services by NASPSPA members.* NASPSPA Newsletter, addendum.

Staff. (1992, September/October). AHA declares regular exercise to be a major factor in cardiovascular health. *President's Council on Physical Fitness and Sports Newsletter, 92*(5), 1, 5.

Steers, D. (1982, November). Trapped in Peru, U.S. women shouted down. *Volleyball Monthly,* 15–21.

Stein, G. L., Kimiecik, J. C., Daniels, J., & Jackson, S. A. (1995). Psychological antecedents of flow in recreational sport. *Personality and Social Psychology Bulletin, 21,* 125–135.

Stennet, R. C. (1957). The relationship of performance level to level of arousal. *Journal of Experimental Psychology, 54,* 54–61.

Stephens, D. E., Bredemeier, B. J. L. (1996). Moral atmosphere and judgments about aggression in girls' soccer: Relationships among moral and motivational variables. *Journal of Sport & Exercise Psychology, 18,* 158–173.

Sternfeld, B. (1992). Cancer and the protective effect of physical activity: The epidemiological evidence. *Medicine and Science in Sports and Exercise, 24,* 1195–1209.

Stogdill, R. M. (1948). Personal factors associated with leadership: Survey of literature. *Journal of Psychology, 25,* 35–71.

Stogdill, R. M. (1950). Leadership, membership, and organization. *Psychological Bulletin, 47,* 1–14.

Stone, M. H. (1993). Literature review: Anabolic-androgenic steroid use by athletes. *National Strength and Conditioning Association Journal, 15,* 10–28.

Straub, W. F. (1980). How to be an effective leader. In W. F. Straub (Ed.), *Sport psychology: An analysis of athlete behavior.* (2d ed.) Ithaca, NY: Mouvement Publications.

Straub, W. F. (1989). The effect of three different methods of mental training on dart throwing performance. *The Sport Psychologist, 3,* 133–141.

Suedfeld, P., & Bruno, T. (1990). Flotation REST and imagery in the improvement of athletic performance. *Journal of Sport & Exercise Psychology, 12,* 82–85.

Suinn, R. M. (1972). Removing emotional obstacles to learning and performance by visuo-motor behavior rehearsal. *Behavioral Therapy, 31,* 308–310.

Suinn, R. M. (1976, July). Body thinking: Psychology for Olympic champs. *Psychology Today, 10,* 38–43.

Suinn, R. M. (1980). Body thinking: Psychology for Olympic champs. In R. M. Suinn (Ed.), *Psychology in sports: Methods and applications.* Minneapolis: Burgess Publishing Company.

Suinn, R. M. (1983). *The seven steps to peak performance: Mental training manual for athletes.* Fort Collins, Colorado: Rocky Mountain Behavioral Sciences Institute.

Suinn, R. M. (1994). Visualization in sports. In A. A. Sheikh & E. R. Korn (Eds.), *Imagery in sports and physical performance* (pp. 23–42). Amityville, NY: Baywood.

Summers, J. J. (1991). Attentional style and basketball performance. *Journal of Sport & Exercise Psychology, 13,* 239–253.

Sutarman & Thompson, H. L. (1952). A new technique for enumerating active sweat glands in man. *Journal of Physiology, 117,* 51.

Svebac, S., & Kerr, J. H. (1989). The role of impulsivity in preference for sports. *Personality and Individual Differences, 10,* 51–58.

Swain, A., & Jones, G. (1992). Relationship between sport achievement orientation and competitive state anxiety. *The Sport Psychologist, 6,* 42–54.

T Tammen, V. V. (1996). Elite middle and long distance runners associative/dissociative coping. *Journal of Applied Sport Psychology, 8,* 1–8.

Tattersfield, C. R. (1971). *Competitive sport and personality development.* Unpublished doctoral dissertation, University of Durham, NC.

Taylor, J. (1991). Career direction, development, and opportunities in applied sport psychology. *The Sport Psychologist, 5,* 266–280.

Taylor, J. (1994). Examining the boundaries of sport science and psychology trained practitioners in applied sport psychology: Title usage and area of competence. *The Sport Psychologist, 6,* 185–195.

Taylor, J. (1995). A conceptual model for integrating athletes' needs and sport demands in the development of competitive mental preparation strategies. *The Sport Psychologist, 9,* 339–357.

Taylor, J., & Demick, A. (1994). A multidemensional model of momentum in sports. *Journal of Applied Sport Psychology, 6,* 51–70.

Taylor, J., Horevitz, R., & Balague, G. (1993). The use of hypnosis in applied sport psychology. *The Sport Psychologist, 7,* 58–78.

Taylor, T. (1992). Motivation for high school cross-country. *Scholastic Coach, 61,* 14–15.

Tenenbaum, G. (1984). A note on the measurement and relationships of physiological and psychological components of anxiety. *International Journal of Sport Psychology, 15,* 88–97.

Tenenbaum, G., & Furst, D. (1985). The relationship between sport achievement responsibility, attribution, and related situational variables, *International Journal of Sport Psychology, 16,* 254–296.

Tenenbaum, G., Pinchas, S., Elbaz, G., Bar-Eli, M., & Weinberg, R. (1991). Effect of goal proximity and goal specificity on muscular endurance performance: A replication and extension. *Journal of Sport & Exercise Psychology, 13,* 174–187.

Terry, P. C. (1993). Mood state profiles as indicators of performance among Olympic and World Championship athletes. In S. Serpa, J. Alves, V. Ferreira, & A. Paulo-Brito (Eds.), *Proceedings of the VIIIth ISSP World Congress of Sport Psychology* (pp. 963–967). Lisbon, Portugal: International Society of Sport Psychology.

Terry, P. C. (1995a). Discriminant capability of pre-performance mood state profiles during the 1993–94 World Cup Bobsleigh. *Journal of Sport Sciences, 13,* 77–78.

Terry, P. C. (1995b). The efficacy of mood state profiling with elite performers: A review and synthesis. *The Sport Psychologist, 9,* 309–324.

Terry, P. C., Keohane, L., & Lane, H. (1996). Development and validation of a shortened version of the profile of mood states suitable for use with young athletes. *Journal of Sports Sciences, 14,* 49.

Thayer, R. E. (1967). Measurement of activation through self report. *Psychological Reports, 20,* 663–678.

Theeboom, M., DeKnop, P., & Weiss, M. R. (1995). Motivational climate, psychological responses, and motor skill development in children's sport: A field based intervention study. *Journal of Sport & Exercise Psychology, 17,* 294–311.

Thirer, J., & Greer, D. L. (1981). Personality characteristics associated with beginning, intermediate, and competitive bodybuilders. *Journal of Sport Behavior, 4,* 3–11.

Thomas, P. R., Hardy, L., & Murphy, S. (1996). Development of a comprehensive test of psychological skills for practice and performance. *Journal of Applied Sport Psychology, 8,* Supplement, S119.

Thomas, P. R., & Over, R. (1994). Psychological and psychomotor skills associated with performance in golf. *The Sport Psychologist, 8,* 73–86.

Thune, A. R. (1949). Personality of weight lifters. *Research Quarterly, 20,* 296–306.

Titley, R. W. (1980). The loneliness of a long-distance kicker. In R. M. Suinn (Ed.), *Psychology in sports: Methods and applications.* Minneapolis: Burgess Publishing Company.

Tjeerdsma, L. (1992). Dealing with the psychological side of injury. *Scholastic Coach, 61*(7), 42–44.

Tompkins, S. S. (1947). *The Thematic Apperception Test: The theory and technique of interpretation.* New York: Grune and Stratton.

Treasure, D. C., Monson, J., & Lox, C. L. (1996). Relationship between self-efficacy, wrestling performance, and affect prior to competition. *The Sport Psychologist, 10,* 73–83.

Treasure, D. C., & Roberts, G. C. (1995). Application of achievement goal theory to physical education: Implications for enhancing motivation. *Quest, 47,* 475–489.

Treisman, A. M. (1965). Our limited attention. *The Advancement of Science, 22,* 600–611.

Tresemer, D. (1974, March). Fear of success: Popular but unproven. *Psychology Today, 7,* 82–85.

Tresemer, D. (1976). The cumulative record of research on "fear of success." *Sex Roles, 2,* 217–236.

Tricker, R., Cook, D. L., & McGuire, R. (1989). Issues related to drug abuse in college athletics: Athletes at risk. *The Sport Psychologist, 3,* 155–165.

Triplett, N. (1897). The dynamogenic factors in pacemaking and competition. *American Journal of Psychology, 9,* 507–553.

Tuckman, B. W. (1965). Developmental sequences in small groups. *Psychological Bulletin, 63,* 384–399.

Tuckman, B. W. (1972). *Conducting educational research.* New York: Harcourt Brace Jovanovich.

Turner, P. E., & Raglin, J. S. (1996). Variability in precompetition anxiety and performance in college track and field athletes. *Medicine and Science in Sports and Exercise, 28,* 378–385.

Tuson, K. M., Sinyor, D., & Pelletier, L. G. (1995). Acute exercise and positive affect: An investigation of psychological processes leading to affective change. *International Journal of Sport Psychology, 26,* 138–159.

Tutko, T. A., & Richards, J. W. (1971). *Psychology of coaching.* Boston: Allyn and Bacon.

Tutko, T. A., & Richards, J. W. (1972). *Coaches' practical guide to athletic motivation.* Boston: Allyn and Bacon.

U

Ulett, G. A., & Peterson, D. B. (1965). *Applied hypnosis and positive suggestion.* St. Louis: C. V. Mosby.

Ulrich, B. D. (1987). Perceptions of physical competence, motor competence, and participation in organized sport: Their interrelationships in young children. *Research Quarterly for Exercise and Sport, 58,* 57–67.

Ulrich, R. P. (1973). *The effect of hypnotic and non-hypnotic suggestions on archery performance.* Unpublished doctoral dissertation, University of Utah, Salt Lake City.

Ungerleider, S., Golding, J. M., Porter, K., & Foster, J. (1989). An exploratory examination of cognitive strategies used by master track and field athletes. *The Sport Psychologist, 3,* 245–253.

United States Olympic Committee (1983). U.S. Olympic Committee establishes guidelines for sport psychology services. *Journal of Sport Psychology, 5,* 4–7.

Ussher, M. H., & Hardy, L. (1986). The effects of competitive anxiety on a number of cognitive and motor subsystems. *Journal of Sports Sciences, 4,* 232–233.

V

Valle, V. A., & Frieze, I. H. (1976). The stability of causal attributions as a mediator in changing expectations for success. *Journal of Personality and Social Psychology, 33,* 579–587.

Vallerand, R. J. (1983). Attention and decision making: A test of the predictive validity of the Test of Attentional and Interpersonal Style (TAIS) in a sport setting. *Journal of Sport Psychology, 5,* 449–459.

Vallerand, R J., & Reid, G. (1984). On the causal effects of perceived competence on intrinsic motivation: A test of Cognitive Evaluation Theory. *Journal of Sport Psychology, 6,* 94–102.

Valzelli, L. (1981). *Psychobiology of aggression and violence.* New York: Raven Press.

Vandenberg, S., & Kruse, A. R. (1978). Mental rotations: A group of three-dimensional spatial visualization. *Perceptual and Motor Skills, 47,* 599–604.

Vanek, M., & Cratty, B. J. (1970). *Psychology and the superior athlete.* London: Macmillan.

Van Gyn, G. H., Wenger, H. A., & Gaul, C. A. (1990). Imagery as a method of enhancing transfer from training to performance. *Journal of Sport & Exercise Psychology, 12,* 366–375.

Van Raalte, J. L., Brewer, B. W., Lewis, B. P., Linder, D. E., Wildman, G., & Kozimor, J. (1995). Cork! The effects of positive and negative self-talk on dart throwing performance. *Journal of Sport Behavior, 18,* 51–57.

Van Raalte, J. L., Brewer, B. W., Rivera, P. M., & Petitpas, A. J. (1994). The relationship between observable self-talk and competitive junior tennis players' match performances. *Journal of Sport & Exercise Psychology, 16,* 400–415.

Van Schoyck, S. R., & Grasha, A. F. (1981). Attentional style variations and athletic ability: The advantages of the sports specific test. *Journal of Sport Psychology, 3,* 149–165.

Varca, P. E. (1980). An analysis of home and away game performance of male college basketball teams. *Journal of Sport Psychology, 2,* 245–257.

Vealey, R. S. (1986). Conceptualization of sport-confidence and competitive orientation: Preliminary investigation and instrument development. *Journal of Sport Psychology, 8,* 221–246.

Vealey, R. S. (1988a). Future directions in psychological skills training. *The Sport Psychologist, 2,* 318–336.

Vealey, R. S. (1988b). Sport-confidence and competitive orientation: An addendum on scoring procedures and gender differences. *Journal of Sport & Exercise Psychology, 10,* 471–478.

Vealey, R. S. (1989). Sport personology: A paradigmatic and methodological analysis. *Journal of Sport & Exercise Psychology, 11,* 216–235.

Vingerhoets, A. J. J. M., Croon, M., Jeninga, A. J., Menges, L. J. (1990). Personality and health habits. *Psychology and Health, 4,* 333–342.

Voelz, C. (1982). *Motivation in coaching a team sport.* Reston, VA: AAHPERD Publications.

Volkamer, N. (1972). Investigations into the aggressiveness in competitive social systems. *Sportwissenschaft, 1,* 33–64.

Vos Strache, C. (1979). Players' perceptions of leadership qualities for coaches. *Research Quarterly, 50,* 679–686.

Vroom, V. H., & Yetton, P. W. (1973). *Leadership and decision making.* Pittsburgh: University of Pittsburgh Press.

W

Wachtel, P. (1967). Conceptions of broad and narrow attention. *Psychological Bulletin, 68,* 417–429.

Walling, M. D., Duda, J. L., & Chi, L. (1993). The perceived motivational climate in sport questionnaire: Construct and predictive validity. *Journal of Sport & Exercise Psychology, 15,* 172–183.

Wankel, L. M. (1972). An examination of illegal aggression in intercollegiate hockey. In I. D. Williams & L. M. Wankel (Eds.), *Proceedings of the Fourth Canadian Psychomotor Learning and Sport Psychology Symposium* (pp. 531–542). Waterloo, Ontario: University of Waterloo.

Wankel, L. M. (1977). Audience size and trait anxiety effects upon state anxiety and motor performance. *Research Quarterly, 48,* 181–186.

Wankel, L. M., & Kreisel, S. J. P. (1985). Factors underlying enjoyment of youth sports: Sport and age group comparisons. *Journal of Sport Psychology, 7,* 51–64.

Wankel, L. M., & McEwan, R. (1976). The effect of privately and publicly set goals upon athletic performance. In K. F. Landry & W. A. R. Arban (Eds.), *Motor learning, sport psychology, pedagogy, and didactics of physical activity.* Miami: Symposia Specialists.

Wankel, L. M., & Mummery, W. K. (1993). Using national survey data incorporating the theory of planned behavior: Implications for social marketing strategies in physical activity. *Journal of Applied Sport Psychology, 5,* 158–177.

Wann, D. L., & Branscombe, N. R. (1990). Person perception when aggressive or nonaggressive sports are primed. *Aggressive Behavior, 16,* 27–32.

Watkins, B., Garcia, A. W., & Turek, E. (1994). The relationship between self-efficacy and sport performance: Evidence from a sample of youth baseball players. *Journal of Applied Sport Psychology, 6,* 21–31.

Watson, D., Clark, L. A., & Tellegen, A. (1988). Development and validation of brief measures of positive and negative affect: The PANAS scales. *Journal of Personality and Social Psychology, 54,* 1063–1070.

Watson, J. B. (1924). *Behaviorism.* Chicago: University of Chicago Press.

Watzlawick, P. (1978). *The language of change.* New York: Basic Books.

Weinberg, R. S. (1978). The effects of success and failure on the patterning of neuromuscular energy. *Journal of Motor Behavior, 10,* 53–61.

Weinberg, R. S. (1979). Intrinsic motivation in a competitive setting. *Medicine and Science in Sports, 11,* 146–149.

Weinberg, R. S. (1985). Relationship between self-efficacy and cognitive strategies in enhancing endurance performance. *International Journal of Sport Psychology. 17,* 135–155.

Weinberg, R. S. (1990). Anxiety and motor performance: Where to from here? *Anxiety Research, 2,* 227–242.

Weinberg, R. S. (1994). Goal setting and performance in sport and exercise settings: A synthesis and critique. *Medicine and Science in Sport and Exercise, 26,* 469–477.

Weinberg, R. S., Bruya, L. D., Garland, H., & Jackson, A. (1990). Effect of goal difficulty and positive reinforcement on endurance performance. *Journal of Sport & Exercise Psychology, 12,* 144–156.

Weinberg, R. S., Bruya, L. D., & Jackson, A. (1985).The effects of goal proximity and goal specificity on endurance performance. *Journal of Sport Psychology, 7,* 296–305.

Weinberg, R. S., Bruya, L. D., & Jackson, A. (1990). Goal setting and competition: A reaction to Hall and Byrne. *Journal of Sport & Exercise Psychology, 12,* 92–97.

Weinberg, R. S., Bruya, L., Jackson, A., & Garland, H. (1987). Goal difficulty and endurance performance: A challenge to the goal attainability assumption. *Journal of Sport Behavior, 10,* 82–92.

Weinberg, R. S., Bruya, L. D., Longino, J., & Jackson, A. (1988). Effect of goal proximity and specificity on endurance of primary grade children. *Journal of Sport & Exercise Psychology, 10,* 81–91.

Weinberg, R. S., Fowler, C., Jackson, A., Bagnall, J., & Bruya, L. (1991). Effect of goal difficulty on motor performance: A replication across tasks and subjects. *Journal of Sport & Exercise Psychology, 13,* 160–173.

Weinberg, R. S., Gould, D., & Jackson, A. (1980). Cognition and motor performance effect of psyching-up strategies on three motor tasks. *Cognitive Therapy and Research, 1980, 4,* 239–245.

Weinberg, R. S., & Hunt, U. V. (1976). The interrelationship between anxiety, motor performance, and electromyography. *Journal of Motor Behavior, 8,* 219–224.

Weinberg, R. S., & Jackson, A. (1979). Competition and extrinsic rewards: Effect on intrinsic motivation and attribution. *Research Quarterly, 50,* 494–502.

Weinberg, R. S., & Jackson, A. (1985). The effects of specific vs. nonspecific mental preparation strategies on strength and endurance performance. *International Journal of Sport Psychology, 8,* 175–180.

Weinberg, R. S., & Jackson, A. (1990). Building self-efficacy in tennis players: A coach's perspective. *Journal of Applied Sport Psychology, 2,* 164–174.

Weinberg, R. S., Jackson, A., & Kolodny, K. (1988). The relationship of massage and exercise to mood enhancement. *The Sport Psychologist, 2,* 202–211.

Weinberg, R. S., & Ragan, J. (1979). Effects of competition, success/failure, and sex on intrinsic motivation. *Research Quarterly, 50*(3), 503–510.

Weinberg, R. S., Seabourne, T. G., & Jackson, A. (1981). Effects of visuo-motor behavior rehearsal, relaxation, and imagery on karate performance. *Journal of Sport Psychology, 3,* 228–238.

Weinberg, R. S., Stitcher, T., & Richardson, P. (1994). Effects of a seasonal goal-setting program on lacrosse performance. *The Sport Psychologist, 8,* 166–175.

Weinberg, R. S., & Weigand, D. (1993). Goal setting in sport and exercise: A reaction to Locke. *Journal of Sport & Exercise Psychology, 15,* 88–96.

Weinberg, R. S., & Weigand, D. A. (1996). Let the discussions continue: A reaction to Locke's comments on Weinberg and Weigand. *Journal of Sport & Exercise Psychology, 18,* 89–93.

Weiner, B. (1972). *Theories of motivation: From mechanism to cognition.* Chicago: Rand McNally.

Weiner, B. (1979). A theory of motivation for some classroom experiences. *Journal of Educational Psychology, 71,* 3–25.

Weiner, B. (1981). The role of affect in sports psychology. In G. C. Roberts & D. M. Landers (Eds.), *Psychology of motor behavior and sport, 1980* (pp. 37–48). Champaign, IL: Human Kinetics Publishers.

Weiner, B. (1985). An attributional theory of achievement motivation and emotion. *Psychological Review, 92,* 548–573.

Weiner, B., Heckhausen, H., Meyer, U. U., & Cook, R. E. (1972). Causal ascriptions and achievement motivation: A conceptual analysis of effort and reanalysis of locus of control. *Journal of Personality and Social Psychology, 21,* 239–248.

Weiner, B., & Kukla, A. (1970). An attributional analysis of achievement motivation. *Journal of Personality and Social Psychology, 15,* 1–20.

Weiner, B., Russell, D., & Lerman, D. (1979). The cognition-emotion process in achievement-related contexts. *Journal of Personality and Social Psychology, 37,* 1211–1220.

Weiner, I. B. (1994). Rorschach assessment. In M. E. Maruish (Ed.), *The use of psychological testing for treatment planning and outcome assessment* (pp. 249–278). Hillsdale, NJ: Erlbaum.

Weiss, M. R., & Bredemeier, B. J. (1990). Moral development in sport. In K. B. Pandolf & J. O. Holloszy, (Eds.), *Exercise and sport science reviews, 18,* pp. 331–378. Baltimore: Williams & Wilkins.

Weiss, M. R., Bredemeier, B. J., & Shewchuk, R. M. (1985). An intrinsic/extrinsic motivation scale for the youth sport setting: A confirmatory factor analysis. *Journal of Sport Psychology, 7,* 75–91.

Weiss, M. R., & Friedrichs, W. D. (1986). The influence of leader behaviors, coach attributes, and institutional variables on performance and satisfaction of collegiate basketball teams. *Journal of Sport Psychology, 8,* 332–346.

Weiss, M. R., & Horn, T. S. (1990). The relationship between children's accuracy estimates of their physical competence and achievement-related characteristics. *Research Quarterly for Exercise and Sport, 61,* 250–258.

Weiss, M. R., McAuley, E., Ebbeck, V., & Wiese, D. M. (1990). *Journal of Sport & Exercise Psychology, 12,* 21–36.

Weiss, M. R., & Petlichkoff, L. M. (1989). Children's motivation for participation in and withdrawal from sport: Identifying the missing links. *Pediatric Exercise Science, 1,* 195–211.

Weiss, M. R., Wiese, D. M., & Klint, K. A. (1989). Head over heels with success: The relationship between self-efficacy and performance in competitive youth gymnastics. *Journal of Sport & Exercise Psychology, 11,* 444–451.

Weiss, M. R., & Troxel, R. K. (1986). Psychology of the injured athlete. *Athletic Training, 21,* 104–110.

Weitzenhoffer, A. M. (1963). *Hypnotism: An objective study in suggestibility.* New York: John Wiley and Sons.

Welford, A. T. (1962). Arousal, channel-capacity, and decision. *Nature, 194,* 365–366.

Welford, A. T. (1965). Stress and achievement. *Australian Journal of Psychology, 17,* 1–9.

Welford, A. T. (1973). Stress and performance. *Ergonomics, 16,* 567–580.

Weltman, G., & Egstrom, G. H. (1966). Perceptual narrowing in novice divers. *Human Factors, 8,* 499–505.

Weltman, G., Smith, J. E., & Egstrom, G. H. (1971). Perceptual narrowing during simulated pressure-chamber exposure. *Human Factors, 13,* 99–107.

Wenz, B. J., & Strong, D. J. (1980). An application of biofeedback and self-regulation procedures with superior athletes: The fine tuning effect. In R. M. Suinn (Ed.), *Psychology in sports: Methods and applications.* Minneapolis: Burgess Publishing Company.

Westre, K. R., & Weiss, M. R. (1991). The relationship between perceived coaching behaviors and group cohesion in high school football teams. *The Sport Psychologist, 5,* 41–54.

White, G. F. (1989). Media and violence: The case of professional football championship games. *Aggressive Behavior, 15,* 423–433.

White, R. (1959). Motivation reconsidered. The concept of competence. *Psychological Review, 66,* 297–323.

White, S. A., & Duda, J. L. (1993). Dimensions of goals and beliefs among adolescent athletes with physical disabilities. *Adapted Physical Activity Quarterly, 10,* 125–136.

White, S. A., & Duda, J. L. (1994). The relationship of gender, level of sport involvement, and participation motivation to task and ego orientation. *International Journal of Sport Psychology, 25,* 4–18.

Whiting, H. T. A., Hardman, K., Hendry, L. B., & Jones, M. G. (1973). *Personality and performance in physical education and sport.* London: Kimpton.

Whitmarsh, B. G., & Alderman, R. B. (1993). Role of psychological skills training in increasing pain tolerance. *The Sport Psychologist, 7,* 388–399.

Whitney, D. L., & Pratt, R. W. (1987). Paying attention: A study of attentional and interpersonal styles of hotel and restaurant administration students. *Hospitality and Education Research Journal, 11,* 43–58.

Widmeyer, W. N., Brawley, L. R., & Carron, A. V. (1985). *The measurement of cohesion in sport teams: The group environment questionnaire.* London, Ontario: Sports Dynamics.

Widmeyer, W. N., Brawley, L. R., & Carron, A. V. (1990). The effects of group size in sport. *Journal of Sport & Exercise Psychology, 12,* 177–190.

Widmeyer, W. N., & Williams, J. M. (1991). Predicting cohesion in coacting sport. *Small Group Research, 22,* 548–570.

Wiggins, D. K. (1984). The history of sport psychology in North America. In J. M. Silva & R. S. Weinberg (Eds.), *Psychological foundations of sport* (pp. 9–22). Champaign, IL: Human Kinetics Publishers.

Wilkes, R. L., & Summers, J. J. (1984). Cognitions, mediating variables, and strength performance. *Journal of Sport Psychology, 6,* 351–359.

Williams, J. M. (1980). Personality characteristics of the successful female athlete. In W. F. Straub (Ed.), *Sport psychology: An analysis of athlete behavior.* (2d ed.) (pp. 353–359). Ithaca, NY: Mouvement Publications.

Williams, J. M., & Hacker, C. M. (1982). Causal relationships among cohesion, satisfaction, and performance in women's intercollegiate field hockey teams. *Journal of Sport Psychology, 4,* 324–337.

Williams, J. M., Hogan, T., & Andersen, M. (1993). Positive states of mind and athletic injury risk. *Psychosomatic Medicine, 55,* 468–472.

Williams, J. M., & Straub, W. F. (1986). Sport psychology: Past, present, future. In J. M. Williams (Ed.), *Applied sport psychology* (pp. 1–13). Palo Alto, CA: Mayfield Publishing Company.

Williams, J. M., Tonymon, P., & Andersen, M. B. (1991). The effects of stressors and coping resources on anxiety and peripheral narrowing. *Journal of Applied Sport Psychology, 3*(2), 126–141.

Williams, J. M., Tonymon, P., & Wadsworth, W. A. (1986). Relationship of stress to injury in intercollegiate volleyball. *Journal of Human Stress, 12,* 38–43.

Williams, J. M., & Widmeyer, W. N. (1991). The cohesion-performance outcome relationship in a coacting sport. *Journal of Sport & Exercise Psychology, 13,* 364–371.

Williams, L. R. T. (1978). Transcendental meditation and mirror tracing. *Perceptual and Motor Skills, 46,* 371–378.

Williams, L. R. T., & Herbert, P. G. (1976). Transcendental meditation and fine perceptual motor skill. *Perceptual and Motor Skills, 43,* 303–309.

Williams, L. R. T., Lodge, B., & Reddish, P. S. (1977). Effects of transcendental meditation on rotary pursuit skill. *Research Quarterly, 48,* 196–201.

Williams, L. R. T., & Parkin, W. A. (1980). Personality profiles of three hockey groups. *International Journal of Sport Psychology, 11,* 113–120.

Williams, L. R. T., & Vickerman, B. L. (1976). Effects of transcendental meditation on fine motor skill. *Perceptual and Motor Skills, 43,* 607–613.

Williams, P. M., & Wassenaar, D. J. (1975). *Leadership.* San Jose, CA: Lansford.

Winter, B. (1982, May). Relax and win. *Sports and Athlete,* 72–78.

Winterbottom, M. R. (1953). *The relation of childhood training in independence to achievement motivation.* Unpublished doctoral dissertation, University of Michigan, Ann Arbor.

Wittig, A. F., Duncan, S. L., & Schurr, K. T. (1987). The relationship of gender, gender-role endorsement, and perceived physical self-efficacy to sport competition anxiety. *Journal of Sport Behavior, 11,* 192–199.

Wolpe, J. (1958). *Psychotherapy by reciprocal inhibition.* Stanford, CA: Stanford University Press.

Woodcock, A. J., & Corbin, C. C. (1992). The effect of verbal feedback on intrinsic motivation and perceived competence of cricketers. *Research Quarterly for Exercise and Sport* (abstract). Supplement to *63,* A-83.

Woodworth, R. S., & Schlosberg, H. (1954). *Experimental psychology.* Revised ed. New York: Holt, Rinehart and Winston.

Woolfolk, R. L., Murphy, S. M., Gottesfeld, D., & Aitken, D. (1985). Effects of mental rehearsal of task motor activity and mental depiction of task outcome on motor skill performance. *Journal of Sport Psychology, 7,* 191–197.

Wright, E. F., Voyer, D., Wright, R. D., & Roney, C. (1995). Supporting audiences and performance under pressure: The home-ice disadvantage in hockey championships. *Journal of Sport Behavior, 18,* 21–28.

Wrisberg, C. A. (1990). An interview with Pat Head Summitt. *The Sport Psychologist, 4,* 180–191.

Wrisberg, C. A., & Anshel, M. H. (1989). The effect of cognitive strategies on the free throw shooting performance of young athletes. *The Sport Psychologist, 3,* 95–104.

Wrisberg, C. A., & Pein, R. L. (1990). Past running experience as a mediator of the attentional focus of male and female recreational runners. *Perceptual and Motor Skills, 70,* 427–432.

Wrisberg, C. A., & Pein, R. L. (1992). The preshot interval and free throw shooting accuracy: An exploratory investigation. *The Sport Psychologist, 6,* 14–23.

Wrisberg, C. A., & Shea, C. H. (1978). Shifts in attention demands and motor program utilization during motor learning. *Journal of Motor Behavior, 10,* 149–158.

Wulf, S. (1987, November 2). World Series. *Sports Illustrated,* 28–41.

Y

Yanada, H., & Hirata, H. (1970). Personality traits of students who dropped out of athletic clubs. *Proceedings of the College of Physical Education,* (5), University of Tokyo.

Yannis, T. (1994). Planned behavior, attitude strength, role identity, and the prediction of exercise behavior. *The Sport Psychologist, 8,* 149–165.

Yates, A. (1987). Eating disorders and long distance running: The ascetic condition. *Integrated Psychiatry, 5,* 201–204.

Yates, A. (1991). *Compulsive exercise and eating disorders: Toward an integrated theory of activity.* New York: Brunner/Mazel.

Yeager, R. C. (1977, July). Savagery on the playing fields. *Readers Digest,* 23–24.

Yeager, R. C. (1979). *Seasons of shame: The new violence in sports.* New York: McGraw-Hill.

Yerkes, R. M., & Dodson, J. D. (1908). The relationship of strength of stimulus to rapidity of habit formation. *Journal of Comparative Neurology and Psychology, 18,* 459–482.

Z

Zaichkowsky, L. D, & Fuchs, C. (1988). Biofeedback applications in exercise and athletic performance. *Exercise and Sport Science Reviews, 16,* 381–421.

Zaichkowsky, L. D., & Sime, W. E. (1982). *Stress management for sport.* Reston, VA: AAHPERD Publications.

Zajonc, R. B. (1965). Social facilitation. *Science, 149,* 269–274.

Zeeman, E. C. (1976). Catastrophe theory. *Scientific American, 234,* 65–83.

Zervas, Y., & Kakkos, V. (1995). The effect of visuomotor behavior rehearsal on shooting performance of beginning archers. *International Journal of Sport Psychology, 26,* 337–347.

Zhang, L., Qi-Wei, M., Orlick, T., & Zitzelsberger, L. (1992). The effect of mental imagery training on performance enhancement with 7–10-year-old children. *The Sport Psychologist, 6,* 230–241.

Ziegler, S. G. (1980). An overview of anxiety management strategies in sport. In W. F. Straub (Ed.), *Sport psychology: An analysis of athlete behavior.* 2d ed. Ithaca, NY: Mouvement Publications.

Ziegler, S. G., Klinzing, J., & Williamson, K. (1982). The effects of two stress management training programs on cardiorespiratory efficiency. *Journal of Sport Psychology, 4,* 280–289.

Zientek, C. E. C., & Breakwell, G. M. (1991). Attributional schema of players before and after knowledge of game outcome. *Journal of Sport Behavior, 14,* 211–222.

Zimmerman, B. J., & Kitsantus, A. (1996). Self-regulated learning of a motoric skill: The role of goal setting and self-monitoring. *Journal of Applied Sport Psychology, 8,* 60–75.

Zuckerman, M., & Allison, S. N. (1976). An objective measure of fear of success: Construction and validation. *Journal of Personality Assessment, 40,* 422–430.

AUTHOR INDEX

Adams, R.M., 199
Agnew, G.A., 293
Agocs, H., 128
Aguglia, E., 219
Ahang, 179
Ajzen, I., 349, 350
Albrecht, R.R., 71
Alderman, R.B., 184, 185
Alexander, J.F., 35
Allport, G.W., 19, 23
Alzado, L., 379
Amunategui, F., 128
Andersen, M.B., 257, 372, 373, 374, 386
Anderson, C.A., 282
Andrew, J.A., 291
Annalisa, D., 144
Anshel, M.H., 9, 143, 181, 194, 359, 379, 380, 383
Ansorge, C.J., 218
Antonio, M., 356
Appelbaum, M.I., 76
Apter, M.J., 123, 124, 126
Arkes, H.R., 243
Arms, R.L., 284
Armstrong, C.A., 351
Armstrong, N., 252
Ashley, M.A., 30, 33
Asken, M.J., 45
Atkinson, J.W., 238, 239, 240, 241, 243, 267
Aufsesser, P.M., 45
Avener, M., 176

Bacon, S.J., 109
Baer, L., 156
Bahrick, H.P., 109
Bahrke, M.S., 345, 379, 381
Bai, A.J.L., 147
Bakeman, R., 302
Balague, G., 153
Bandura, A., 22, 23, 244, 267, 281, 344
Barber, T.X., 151, 152

Bar-Eli, M., 149, 178, 189
Bargman, E.P., 339, 343
Barley, D., 374
Barnett, N.P., 321
Baron, R.A., 57
Barr, K., 176
Barry, J.R., 36
Barsky, S.F., 293
Bartholomew, J.B., 143
Baumeister, R.F., 292
Beary, J.F., 140
Becker, S.L., 266
Behling, O., 308, 314, 328
Bell, G.J., 45
Bem, S.L., 255
Benson, H., 140, 144, 147, 150, 344
Bergandi, T.A., 71
Berger, B.G., 258, 337, 339
Berglund, B., 366
Berkowitz, L., 278, 280, 282
Bernardo, P., 106
Bernstein, D.A., 142, 355
Beuter, A., 108
Biddle, S.J.H., 220, 252, 339, 360
Billings, J., 177
Bird, A.M., 323
Bivens, S., 326
Black, D., 360
Black, S.J., 247
Blair, M.S., 346
Blair, V., 245
Blanchard, K.H., 314, 315
Block, N., 172
Blomstrand, E., 41
Blumenstein, B., 149
Blumenthal, J.A., 345
Boies, S.J., 86
Bonaccorsi, M., 149
Borden, F., 197, 198
Borkovec, T.D., 142
Bostrom, A., 318
Botterill, C., 178
Bourgeois, A.E., 41
Boutcher, S.H., 76, 149, 195, 200, 341

Bowers, K.S., 39
Boyer, B.J., 226
Boyle, G.J., 43
Bradley, G.W., 44, 76, 230
Brawley, L.R., 229, 298, 301, 340, 351
Breakwell, G.M., 228
Bredemeier, B.J., 280, 282, 284, 318
Brewer, B.W., 12, 168, 378, 379
Briere, N.M., 263
Broadbent, D.E., 64
Brock, S., 375
Brooks, D.R., 228
Broucek, M.W., 143
Brown, B.A., 147
Brown, B.S., 345
Brown, D.R., 150, 154, 156, 344
Brown, J.D., 352
Bruno, T., 181
Brustad, R.J., 340
Bryant, C.X., 339
Brylinski, J., 290
Buck, J.N., 26
Buckolz, E., 179
Buckworth, J., 351
Burckes-Miller, M., 360
Burke, K.L., 199
Burlington, G.M., 362
Bursill, A.F., 109
Burton, D., 97, 100, 108, 192
Buss, A.H., 284
Byrkit, D., 35

Cale, A., 98
Calfas, K.J., 352
Campbell, E., 340
Canabal, M.Y., 45
Caralis, P., 356
Carda, R.D., 118
Carlson, C.R., 142
Carlson, R.B., 35
Carol, M.P., 140
Carpenter, V., 217

Carroll, D., 184
Carron, A.V., 39, 231, 290, 293, 295, 298, 299, 301, 303, 304, 323, 325, 326, 348, 350
Carson, L., 356
Cartwright, D., 299
Case, B., 315, 316, 317
Cashman, J.F., 314
Castiello, U., 62
Castracane, V.D., 346
Castro, J.M., 359
Cattell, R.B., 23, 24, 27
Caudill, D., 157
Cauraugh, J.H., 70
Chapman, C.L., 359
Chapman, J., 63
Chartrand, J.M., 195
Chase, M.A., 254
Chass, M., 325
Chaves, J.F., 151
Chelladurai, P., 301, 314, 315, 317, 318, 325, 326, 328
Chemers, M.M., 313
Chen, D., 70
Chi, L., 252, 262
Christensen, D.S., 195
Christina, R.W., 69
Cinelli, B., 356
Claessens, A., 374
Clark, L.V., 173
Clarke, J.C., 150
Clifton, R.T., 253
Clingman, J.M., 33, 338
Coen, S.P., 362
Cofer, C.N., 25, 30
Cohn, P.J., 197
Coleman, T.R., 152
Coles, E.M., 91
Conboy, J.K., 359
Cooper, B.A.B., 30
Corbin, C.B., 28, 174, 254, 358
Corbin, C.C., 258
Costa, A., 149
Costill, D.L., 35
Cotton, P.C.J., 139
Counsilman, J.E., 360
Courneya, K.S., 290, 339, 350, 351
Courtet, P.A., 67, 109
Cowley, A.W.,Jr., 346
Cox, R.H., 34, 45, 71, 100, 103, 112, 115, 290, 302
Craighead, D.J., 35
Crandall, V.C., 238
Cratty, B.J., 143, 144, 308

Crawford, S., 358
Crenshaw, W., 33
Crews, D.J., 69, 77, 139, 340
Crocker, P.R.E., 170, 171, 185
Crossman, J., 375, 377
Crow, M.A., 147, 148
Crowson, C.S., 377
Csikszentmihalyi, M., 121, 122
Cullen, F.T., 286
Cullen, J.B., 286
Curley, V., 360
Curtis, B., 320, 321

Dabbs, J.M.,Jr., 91
Dahlstrom, W.G., 27
Daleng, M.L., 360
D'Andrade, R., 266
Daniels, F.S., 122
Danish, S.J., 171, 195
Danskin, D.G., 147, 148
Darst, 321
Davis, C., 35
Davis, H., 18, 28, 36, 376
Davis, J.C., 341
Davis, M., 143, 144, 145, 147
Davis, R.W., 45, 113
DeCharms, R.C., 217
Deci, E.L., 261, 268
Deeter, T.E., 252
Dekirmenjiar, H., 345
DeKnop, P., 252
DeLeo, D., 31
Demick, A., 199
DeNeve, K.M., 282
Deuser, W.E., 282
DiCara, L.V., 147
DiClemente, C.C., 350
Diekhoff, G., 374
DiLorenzo, T.M., 339, 343
Dimick, K., 239
Dishman, R.K., 336, 348, 351, 356
Docker, S.B., 197
Dodson, J.D., 105, 106, 128
Dollard, J., 22, 282
Donnelly, P., 301
Doob, I., 282
Draw, J., 192
Dreiling, A.M., 118
Drewery, B.P., 286
Droppleman, L.F., 41
Drost, B.A., 286
DuCharme, K.A., 351
Duda, J.L., 108, 229, 249, 250, 252, 262, 379

Duffy, E., 86, 90, 104
Duke, M., 218
Dummer, G.M., 360
Duncan, T.E., 209
Duquin, M.E., 222
Durr, K.R., 117, 118
Dweck, C.S., 223, 224, 230
Dzewaltowski, D.A., 45, 199, 346

Eades, A., 370
Easterbrook, J.A., 67, 108, 109
Eastman, 184
Eaton, C.A., 351
Ebbeck, V., 266
Ebbeling, C.B., 344
Eber, H.W., 23, 27
Edison, T.A., 103
Edmonston, W.E.,Jr., 151, 153
Edwards, J., 101
Egstrom, G.H., 109
Eifert, G.H., 78, 341
Eklund, R.C., 170, 358
Eksten, F., 339, 366
Ellickson, K.A., 44, 76
Ellis, A., 168
Ellis, S.D., 173
Emery, C.F., 345
Endler, N.S., 93, 97
Engelhardt, G.M., 286
Epstein, J., 265
Epstein, L.H., 344
Epstein, M.L., 177
Erickson, E., 21
Eshelman, E.R., 143
Esparza, R., 192
Etnier, J.L., 41, 173
Etzel, E.F., 71
Evans, L., 378
Eysenck, H., 23, 24
Eysenck, S.B.G., 24

Fabianic, D., 326
Fallstrom, R.B., 294
Farge, E.G., 353
Farrell, P.A., 346
Fawcett, J., 345
Fazey, J., 115, 116, 118
Fein, S., 285
Feltz, D.L., 71, 142, 173, 244, 245, 254
Fender, L.K., 370
Fenz, W.D., 98
Ferguson, R.H., 254

Fernadez, S.J., 182
Fiedler, F.E., 309, 311, 312, 313, 314, 328
Fimrite, R., 54
Finch, L.M., 170
Fishbein, 349
Fisher, A.C., 94, 97, 149, 172, 323
Fitts, P.M., 60, 72, 109
Fletcher, M.A., 356
Fodero, J.M., 241
Folkman, S., 170, 171
Fortier, M.S., 262
Fortlage, L., 344
Fortmann, S.P., 347
Fox, K.R., 252, 358
Franken, R.E., 34
Frantisek, M., 337
Fredenburgh, F.A., 26, 28
Frederick, C.M., 262
Freedson, P.S., 38
Fremouw, 184
French, R., 45
Frensch, P.A., 339, 343
Freud, S., 21, 23, 280
Friedmann, E., 258, 339
Friedrichs, W.D., 323
Frieze, I.H., 211, 222
Fromm, E., 21
Fry, R.W., 366
Fuchs, C., 149
Furst, D.M., 30

Gabriel, T.J., 195
Gannon, T.L., 69
Gansneder, B., 177
Garcia, A.W., 244
Gardner, D.E., 318
Gardner, F.L., 8
Garl, T., 366
Garland, D.J., 36
Garske, J.P., 243
Garthwaite, T.L., 346
Gaudieri, S., 366
Gauvin, L., 177, 179, 339
Gayton, W.F., 199
Gebhardt, S.M., 339
Gench, B., 45
George, T.R., 244, 245, 254
Geron, D., 30
Giannini, J., 266
Gill, D.L., 77, 97, 229, 244, 252, 253, 263
Gillmore, G., 216
Girandola, R., 38

Gladue, B.A., 284
Glenn, S.D., 314
Godin, G., 350
Goodkin, K., 356
Gordon, S., 351
Gorely, T., 351
Goss, J., 366, 376
Goudas, M., 252
Gould, D., 76, 97, 100, 106, 120, 141, 157, 168, 170, 244, 266, 371
Grace, R.K., 199
Graen, G., 314
Graham, T.R., 171
Grasha, A.F., 71
Gray, S.W., 182
Green, L.B., 379
Greenberg, J.S., 142, 143, 144, 145, 147
Greene, D., 260
Greenspan, M.J., 102
Greenwood, C.M., 45
Greer, D.L., 32, 293
Gregg, E., 376
Griffin, J., 216
Gross, A.M., 348
Gross, J.B., 219, 263
Grouios, G., 173, 174
Grove, J.R., 41, 119, 122, 224, 228, 231, 366
Grusky, O., 324, 325, 326
Gustafson, A.B., 346
Guyton, A.C., 87, 88

Hahn, C., 62
Halberstam, D., 313
Hale, B.D., 171, 176
Hall, A., 42
Hall, C.R., 176, 178, 179
Hall, E.G., 147, 182
Hall, J.R., 31
Hall, M., 198
Halpin, A.W., 310, 311
Hamilton, 184
Han, M., 69
Hanin, Y.L., 118, 120
Hanisch, R., 355
Hanrahan, C., 179
Hanrahan, S.J., 192, 228
Hanson, S.J., 374, 375
Hanson, T.W., 141
Hanton, S., 101, 102
Hardman, K., 25, 30
Hardy, C.J., 147, 182, 199

Hardy, L., 98, 101, 115, 116, 117, 118, 120, 195, 378
Harger, G.J., 118
Harlow, L.L., 351
Harlow, R.G., 32
Harmer, P., 299
Harms, C.A., 366
Harrell, W.A., 284, 285
Harris, B.L., 73, 95, 144
Harris, D.V., 73, 95, 144, 174, 176, 228, 256
Harrison, J., 91
Hart, E.A., 358
Harte, J.L., 78, 341
Harter, S., 245, 267
Hartman, I., 189
Hartung, G.H., 353
Harvey, J.C., 113
Haskell, W.L., 347
Haslam, R.W., 42
Hassmen, P., 41
Hatfield, 339, 342
Hathaway, S.R., 27
Hausenblas, H.A., 348, 350
Hausfeld, S., 244
Hearns, J., 199
Heath, K., 69
Hecker, J.E., 174
Heider, F., 208, 209, 210, 211, 216, 232
Hellickson, R.V., 35
Hellstedt, J.C., 160
Helmreich, R., 255, 302
Hemenway, D.P., 161
Hemmings, B., 139
Henderson, B.E., 355
Hendry, L.B., 25
Hendy, H.M., 226
Henry, F.M., 32
Henschen, K.P., 45
Herbert, P.G., 147
Hersey, P., 314, 315
Hess, R., 88
Heusner, W.W., 360
Heyman, S.R., 150
Heyward, V.H., 216
Hickman, J.L., 179
Hill, A.B., 220
Hill, K.L., 197, 198
Hill, R., 34
Hilliard, D.V., 33, 338
Hinkle, J.S., 4, 340
Hinshaw, K.E., 173
Hirata, H., 32
Hird, J.S., 173

Hirsch, R.L., 323
Hobson, M.L., 338
Hodge, K., 266
Hofstetter, C.R., 351
Hogan, T., 374
Hollander, E.P., 19, 20, 366
Holsopple, J.Q., 25
Horan, J.J., 173
Horevitz, R., 153
Horn, T.S., 97, 246, 314, 320, 340
Horne, T., 323
Horner, M.S., 242, 243
Horvat, M., 45
Hough, D.D., 360
House, R.J., 314
Houseworth, S., 199
Hovell, M.F., 346, 348, 351, 385
Howe, B.L., 45
Hoyle, R.H., 142
Hrycaiko, D., 181
Huddleston, S., 263
Hughes, S., 192
Hull, C.L., 22, 113, 239
Hunt, J.G., 314
Hunt, U.V., 90
Husak, W.S., 161
Hutchinson, T.P., 112

Inlay, G.J., 118
Ironson, G., 356
Isaac, A., 173
Iso-Ahola, S.E., 169, 222, 229
Ito, M., 156

Jackson, A.W., 76, 157, 160, 181,
    182, 266, 356
Jackson, D.W., 374
Jackson, J.A., 150
Jackson, S.A., 121, 122, 170, 370
Jacobson, E., 141, 142, 176
Jambor, E.A., 218
James, W., 54
Janssen, J.J., 174
Jarrett, H., 374
Jeffers, K.E., 379
Jefferies, S.C., 192
Jevne, R.F.J., 375
Johnsgard, K., 28
Johnson, J.E., 91
Johnson, R.W., 35, 42
Johnson, T.C., 218
Johnson, W.O., 379
Johnson, W.R., 25, 30, 156

Johnston, B., 171
Jones, G., 101, 102, 340
Jones, J.G., 98, 115
Jones, M.G., 25
Jowdy, D.P., 102, 172, 174, 195
Joy, K.L., 30, 33
Joyce, D., 117
Jung, C., 21

Kaczor, L.M., 174
Kahn, R.I., 310
Kahneman, D., 65
Kakkos, V., 182
Kalkhoff, R.K., 346
Kane, J.E., 31, 32
Karteroliotis, C., 97
Katz, D., 310
Kausch, J., 374
Kavanagh, D., 244
Kavussanu, M., 252
Kay, J., 296
Keast, D., 366
Keele, S.W., 55, 59, 60, 65
Kelly, J.K.,Jr., 374
Kendall, G., 181
Kendall, T., 181
Kenow, L.J., 319
Keohane, L., 41
Kerr, G., 184, 376
Kerr, J.H., 124, 125, 127, 128
Kierstead, J., 34
Kihlstrom, J.F., 151
Kim, M.Y., 303
Kimiecik, J.C., 122, 229, 340
Kirkby, R.J., 76, 366
Kitsantus, A., 190
Klavora, P., 106
Kleiber, D.A., 375
Klimas, N., 356
Klinzing, J., 184
Knott, P.D., 286
Knowles, W.B., 88
Koceja, D.M., 366
Kohl, R.M., 173
Kolonay, B.J., 182
Konttinen, N., 69, 177
Konttinen, R., 69, 177
Korn, E.R., 177
Kozimor, J., 168
Kraemer, R.R., 346
Kramer, J., 306
Krane, T.D., 245
Krane, V., 103, 116, 117
Kroll, W., 5, 33, 35

Kubitz, K.A., 69, 339, 340, 342
Kuipers, H., 362, 366
Kupfer, D.J., 344
Kyllo, L.B., 41, 188, 189

Lacey, B., 90
Lacey, J., 90
Lacy, 321
LaFontaine, T.P., 339, 343, 346
Lambert, M.J., 76, 362, 377
Lan, L.Y., 244
Landers, D.M., 5, 41, 67, 69, 70, 76,
    90, 97, 108, 109, 143,
    149, 173, 178, 188, 189,
    339, 340, 342
Lane, H., 41
Lansing, R.W., 108
LaPerriere, A.R., 356
Larick, J., 128
Larrick, R.P., 285
Latham, G.P., 186, 187, 188,
    189, 200
Layman, E.M., 144
Lazarus, R.S., 170, 171
Leary, M.R., 358
Leddy, M.H., 377
Lee, I., 355
Lefebvre, L.M., 286
Lefevre, J., 374
Leirer, V.O., 69
Leith, L.M., 184, 339
Lenney, E., 253
Leonard, W.M., 326
Leonard, W.M., III, 290
Lepper, M.R., 260
Lerman, D., 220
Lerner, B.S., 188
LeUnes, A., 41, 45, 366
Levenson, H., 218
Leventhal, H., 91
Levy-Kolker, N., 178, 189
Lewis, B.P., 168
Lewis, G., 5
Li, F., 299
Lidor, R., 70
Linder, D.E., 143, 168
Lindsley, D.B., 88, 108
Lirgg, C.D., 254
Lloyd, J.W., 197
Lochbaum, M.R., 120, 252
Locke, E.A., 186, 187, 188,
    189, 200
Lodge, B., 147
Loehr, J., 62, 371

Long, B.C., 339
Lorenz, K., 280
Lorr, M., 41
Loucks, A., 38
Lowe, R., 95
Lox, C.L., 245, 357
Loy, J.W., 325, 326
Luksa, F., 306
Luthe, W., 143
Lykken, D., 88, 90
Lyon, L., 28
Lysens, R., 374
Lyytinen, H., 69

Macchi, R., 375
MacCracken, M.J., 103
Mace, R.D., 184
Mack, D., 348, 350, 358
Mackinnon, L.T., 355
MacKinnon, P.C.B., 91
Maehr, M.L., 216
Magill, R.A., 76
Magni, G., 31
Magoun, H.W., 88
Mahar, L., 313
Mahoney, M.J., 157, 176, 195
Males, J.R., 128
Malmo, R.B., 86, 104
Malone, C., 144
Mancini, V.H., 323
Mann, L., 228
Marcus, B.H., 350, 351
Mark, N.M., 228
Marks, M.A., 245
Marsh, H.W., 122, 252
Martens, R., 6, 19, 23, 28, 91, 94,
        97, 98, 108, 120, 238
Martin, G.L., 181
Martin, J.E., 352
Martin, K.A., 178, 358
Martin, L.A., 286
Martin, T.P., 42
Maslach, C., 370
Maslow, A., 23, 239
Mass, J.W., 345
Masters, K.S., 76, 153, 359
Mastro, J.V., 45
Maynard, I.W., 139
McAuley, E., 209, 214, 215,
        219, 232, 339, 347,
        350, 351, 357
McCabe, M.P., 171
McCallum, J., 138, 313

McClean, G.S., 356
McClelland, D.C., 238, 239, 240,
        241, 243, 267
McConatha, D., 356
McCullagh, P.D., 339, 341, 374
McDonald, D.G., 339, 343
McElroy, M.A., 199, 242, 243
McElvogue, J.F., 326
McGhie, A., 63
McGill, J.C., 31
McGowan, C.R., 344
McGowan, R.W., 360
McGrath, J.E., 94
McInman, A., 122, 228
McKay, M., 143
McKeag, D.B., 360
McKinley, J.C., 27
McNair, D.M., 41
McShane, J.M., 366
Meichenbaum, D., 183
Mendelsohn, G.A., 103
Metcalf, H.C., 308
Meyers, 184
Meyers, M.C., 41, 45, 366
Miale, F.R., 25
Mihevic, P., 38
Miller, D.T., 228
Miller, N.E., 22, 282
Miller, T.W., 323
Milliner, E.K., 377
Milner, P.M., 88
Mischel, W., 22
Mitchell, T.R., 314
Mogk, J.P., 35
Monson, J., 245
Montagu, J.D., 91
Moore, J.C., 290
Moore, K., 379
Moran, A., 177
Morgan, L.K., 216
Morgan, W.P., 5, 29, 30, 31, 35, 37,
        38, 42, 43, 44, 76, 120,
        150, 154, 156, 345, 346
Morris, M.J., 120
Morrow, D.G., 69
Morton, A.R., **366**
Moss, R.F., 31
Mourer, O.H., 282
Mugno, D.A., 244
Mummery, W.K., 350
Murgatroyd, S., 126
Murphey, M., 70
Murphy, S.M., 102, 172, 174,
        181, 195

Murray, D.F., 42
Murray, H., 26
Mutrie, N., 228

Nagle, F.G., 35
Neff, C., 261
Neiss, R., 142
Newcombe, P.A., 43
Nicholls, J.G., 249, 251, 267
Nicoloff, G., 336
Nideffer, R.M., 70, 72, 73, 74, 76,
        142, 144, 145, 153
Nisbet, J., 34
Noel, R.C., 182
Norman, D.A., 64
North, T.C., 339, 341, 343, 344, 345
Nowicki, S.,Jr., 218

O'Connor, P.J., 44, 76, 118, 120,
        339, 341
O'Fallon, W.M., 377
Ogilvie, B.C., 5, 28, 30, 45
Ogles, B.M., 359, 362, 377
Oglesby, C., 6
O'Halloran, A., 177, 179
Ojala, D., 144, 177
Okwumabua, 184
Olson, L.K., 250
Onestak, D.M., 142, 151
Orlick, T., 4, 144, 179
Osborn, R.N., 314
Ostrow, A.C., 27, 95
Ostyn, M., 374
Over, R., 192
Owen, D.R., 337
Oxendine, J.B., 106, 158

Paffenbarger, R.S., 336, 337
Palmer, S.L., 173
Papaioannow, A., 252
Parfitt, G., 98, 117
Pargman, D., 224
Parker, R.M., 362
Parkin, W.A., 36
Partington, J.T., 4, 299
Pascuzzi, D., 212
Pasman, 357
Passer, M.W., 286
Pate, R.R., 44, 120, 336, 337
Pates, J., 98, 117
Pein, R.L., 78, 197

Pelletier, L.G., 337
Peplau, L.A., 243
Peppler, M.J., 226
Perkins, T.S., 195
Perry, M., 284
Peterson, D.B., 150, 154
Peterson, K., 266
Petipas, S.J., 379
Petitpas, A.J., 12, 168, 171
Petlichkoff, L.M., 100, 106
Petrie, T.A., 360, 361, 375, 376
Petrovsky, A.V., 299
Petruzzello, S.J., 69, 149, 339,
        342, 343
Piaget, J., 282
Pie, J.S., 178
Pierce, E.F., 360
Poag, K., 351
Pollock, M.L., 35, 76
Populin, L., 69
Posner, M.I., 60, 72, 86
Powell, J.W., 374
Prapavessis, H., 41, 119, 231,
        303, 304
Predebon, J., 197
Privette, F.V., 35
Prochaska, J.O., 350
Proulx, R.L., 323
Provencher, P.J., 263
Ptacek, J.T., 195, 376
Puffer, J.C., 366
Puleo, E., 344
Pulos, L., 154

Qi, W.M., 67, 109
Qi-Wei, 179
Quackenbush, N., 377

Raedeke, T.D., 103
Rafeld, J., 117
Raglin, J.S., 115, 118, 119, 120,
        339, 366
Rainey, D.W., 128
Ramey, G., 259
Rampazzo, M., 31
Rankin, R.E., 109
Ranson, S.W., 87
Rao, V.R., 147
Ratliff, W.R., 31
Raven, P.B., 356
Ray, C., 126
Raymond, C., 7

Reddish, P.S., 147
Reddy, J.K., 147
Reifman, A.S., 285
Reilly, R., 115
Rejeski, J., 376
Rejeski, W.J., 338, 339, 340, 358
Renger, R., 41
Renson, L., 374
Rhind, S., 355
Richards, J.W., 28
Richardson, P., 188
Richardson, S.A., 359
Riemer, H.A., 318
Rigsby, L.W., 356, 357
Rinehardt, K.F., 346
Rippe, J.M., 344
Rivera, P.M., 12, 168
Robb, M., 103
Roberts, G.C., 208, 212, 217, 222,
        229, 238, 252, 265
Roberts, P.J., 360
Robertson, R.J., 344
Robinson, D.W., 31
Robinson, W.J., 176
Rodgers, W., 179
Roeder, L.K., 45
Roenker, D.L., 173
Rogers, C., 23
Roney, C., 292
Rorschach, H., 26
Rose, D.J., 69
Rose, J., 375
Rosen, B.C., 266
Rosen, L.W., 360
Ross, M., 228
Ross, R.K., 355
Rossi, J.S., 351
Rotella, R.J., 144, 177, 195,
        197, 200
Roth, D.L., 340
Rotstein, P., 30
Rotter, J.B., 217, 218
Rowley, A.J., 41, 42
Ruble, V.E., 34
Rudisill, M.E., 218, 230
Rudolph, D.L., 347, 351
Ruffer, W.A., 18
Rupolo, G., 31
Rusbult, C.E., 367
Rushall, A., 198
Rushall, B.S., 28, 32, 35, 198
Rushton, C., 126
Russell, D., 209, 213, 214, 215, 219,
        220, 232
Russell, G.W., 4, 284, 286

Russell, J.A., 103
Russell, W.D., 103, 120
Ryan, E.D., 18, 26, 174, 263
Ryan, F., 222
Ryan, R.M., 261, 262, 268

Saari, L.M., 187
Sachs, M.L., 345
Sade, S., 178
Safstrom, H., 366
Sage, G.H., 88
Sage, J.N., 308, 309, 325, 326
Salazar, W., 69, 339, 342
Saleh, S.D., 315
Salili, F., 216
Sallis, J.F., 346, 347, 348, 351, 385
Salmela, J.H., 6
Sankaran, G., 356
Sapienza, S., 219
Sarason, I.G., 25, 242
Sarrazin, C., 179
Schacham, S., 41
Schedlowski, M., 98
Scheer, J.K., 218
Schleser, 184
Schlosberg, H., 90
Schmidt, G.W., 367, 386
Schmidt, R.A., 67, 76
Schneiderman, N., 356
Schnurr, P.P., 354
Schomer, H.H., 77
Schreiner, L.H., 88
Schriesheim, C., 308, 314, 328
Schultz, D.D., 90
Schultz, J.H., 143
Schumaker, S.A., 340
Schunk, D.H., 244
Schurr, K.T., 30, 31, 33, 34, 35
Schutz, R.W., 195
Schutz, W.C., 322
Schwartz, B., 293
Schwartz, E., 108
Schwartz, M.S., 148
Schwenk, T.L., 336
Scrimali, T., 149
Seabourne, T.G., 181, 182
Sears, R.R., 282
Seifriz, J.J., 252
Seligman, M.E.P., 223
Selye, H., 93, 94
Serfass, P.C., 35
Sewell, D.F., 302
Shangi, G.M., 299
Shaw, J.M., 199

Shaw, K.M., 187
Shay, K.A., 340
Shea, C.H., 66
Sheikh, A.A., 174, 177
Shek, P.N., 355, 366
Shelton, T.O., 157
Shephard, R.J., 45, 355, 366
Shields, D.L., 318
Shultz, B.B., 42
Shwin, C.S., 340
Shyrock, M.G., 71
Siedentop, D., 259
Silva, J.M.,III, 8, 11, 36, 42, 76,
    199, 291, 363, 366,
    367, 386
Silverman, J., 70
Sime, W.E., 136
Simini, G., 31
Simkin, L.R., 348, 351
Simon, H.B., 356
Simons, A.D., 344
Simons, J., 100, 108, 174
Singer, R.N., 5, 10, 33, 35, 70
Sinyor, D., 337
Skinner, B.F., 22, 55
Slater, M.R., 302
Slater-Hammel, Arthur, 5
Smart, A.E., 379
Smith, A.L., 77
Smith, A.M., 377
Smith, B.D., 23
Smith, D., 11, 125, 193
Smith, F.M.R., 185
Smith, M.D., 281
Smith, R.E., 185, 195, 242, 314,
    319, 320, 321, 368, 376
Smoll, F.L., 195, 314, 319, 320,
    321, 376
Snow, A., 41
Solomon, D.S., 347
Sonstroem, R.J., 106
Spanos, N.P., 151
Sparling, P.B., 44, 120
Spence, J.T., 255
Spence, K.W., 113, 239
Sperling, G., 56
Spielberger, C.D., 93, 94, 118, 120
Spigolon, L., 144
Spink, K.S., 217, 222, 229, 299, 303
Spreeman, J., 97
Stadulis, R.E., 103
Stager, J.M., 366
Stanbrough, M.E., 118
Staurowsky, E.J., 323
Steers, D., 293

Stein, G.L., 103, 122, 367, 386
Steinhiller, A., 292
Stephens, D.E., 282
Sterling, J.C., 41, 45
Sternfeld, B., 355
Steverlynck, A., 374
Stitcher, T., 188
Stoever, S., 360, 361
Stogdill, R.M., 308, 309
Stone, M.H., 379, 381, 382
Straub, W., 5, 6
Strong, D.J., 149
Stuart, M.J., 377
Stucky-Ropp, R.C., 339, 343
Suedfeld, P., 181
Sugiyama, Y., 303
Suinn, R.M., 181
Sullivan-Halley, J., 355
Summers, J.J., 157
Sutarman, 91
Svebac, S., 128
Swain, A., 98, 101
Swanson, J.J., 374
Sylva, J.M., 6
Syrja, P., 120

Tammen, V.V., 78, 102
Tappe, M.K., 379
Tarico, V., 215
Tatsuoka, M.M., 23
Tattersfield, C.R., 32
Taylor, A.H., 339
Taylor, C.B., 347
Taylor, J., 8, 10, 153, 155, 199
Taylor, T., 158
Templin, T.J., 250
Tenenbaum, G., 90, 97, 149, 178
Terry, P.C., 41, 42
Tetreau, B., 179
Tewes, U., 98
Theeboom, M., 252
Thirer, J., 32
Thomas, J.R., 173
Thomas, P.R., 192, 195
Thompson, 357
Thompson, H.L., 91
Thune, A.R., 32
Titus, T.G., 71
Tompkins, S.S., 25
Tonymon, P., 373, 374
Tran, Z.V., 339, 341
Treadwell, S., 41
Treasure, D.C., 245, 252, 265
Treisman, A.M., 64

Trenske, M., 341
Triplett, N., 5, 13
Troxel, R.K., 378
Tucker, R.S., 357
Tuckman, B.W., 94, 304
Tuffy, S., 120, 371
Turek, E., 244
Turner, P.E., 119, 120, 339
Tuson, K.M., 337
Tutko, T.A., 5, 28

Udry, E., 168, 371
Ulett, G.A., 150, 154
Ulrich, R.P., 156
Umilta, C., 62
Underwood, M., 252
Urwick, L., 308

Vaillant, C.O., 354
Vaillant, G.E., 354
Vallerand, R.J., 262
Vanden Auweele, Y., 374
Vanek, M., 143, 144
Van Huss, W.D., 345
Van Raalte, J.L., 12, 168, 379
Van Schoyck, S.R., 71
Van Stavel, R., 339
Varca, P.E., 291
Vealey, R.S., 39, 97, 192, 193,
    247, 267
Veltri, J.P., 339
Very, M., 199
Vetter, H.J., 23
Vevera, M., 100, 108
Vickerman, B.L., 147
Voelz, C., 158
Volkamer, N., 286
Voyer, D., 292
Vranizan, K.M., 347
Vroom, V.H., 314

Wachtel, P., 70
Wallace, D., 34
Walling, M.D., 262
Walsh, G.W., 27
Wang, M.Q., 76
Wang, Y., 344
Wankel, L.M., 263, 286, 350
Ward, A., 344
Warwick-Evans, L., 139
Watkins, B., 244
Weigand, D.A., 188

Weinberg, R.S., 76, 90, 115, 157, 160, 181, 182, 188, 244, 266
Weiner, B., 208, 209, 211, 212, 213, 219, 220, 222, 232
Weiner, I.B., 26
Weiss, M.R., 103, 244, 246, 247, 252, 323, 378
Weitzenhoffer, A.M., 156
Welford, A.T., 111, 112, 113
Weltman, G., 109
Wenz, B.J., 149
White, R., 245
White, S.A., 252
Whiting, H.T.A., 25
Whitmarsh, B.G., 184
Widmeyer, W.N., 298, 300, 301
Wiese-Bjornstal, D.M., 377
Wiggins, D.K., 5
Wildman, G., 168
Wilkes, R.L., 157

Williams, J.M., 5, 6, 38, 39, 257, 300, 301, 319, 372, 373, 374, 386
Williams, L.R.T., 36, 39, 147
Williamson, K., 184
Willis, J.D., 242, 243
Winterbottom, M.R., 266
Wise, K.J., 120
Wolpe, J., 181
Woodcock, A.J., 258
Woodworth, R.S., 90
Wright, E.F., 292
Wright, R.D., 292
Wrisberg, C.A., 66, 78, 143, 181, 197, 307
Wulf, S., 172

Yanada, H., 32
Yannis, T., 349

Yates, A., 361
Yerkes, R.M., 105, 106, 128
Yesalis, C.E., 381
Yesavage, J.A., 69
Yetton, P.W., 314
Yoo, H.S., 34

Zaccaro, S.J., 245
Zaichkowsky, L.D., 136, 149
Zajonc, R.B., 289, 327
Zalazar, S., 149
Zeroni, P.M., 366
Zervas, Y., 182
Ziegler, S.G., 74, 184, 185
Zientek, C.E.C., 228
Zimmerman, B.J., 190
Zinsser, N.W., 149
Zitzelsberger, 179
Zwart, E.F., 97

SUBJECT INDEX

ABC theory of personality, 168
Ability, attribution and, 209, 212
Able-bodied athletes, 45
Academic sport psychology, 6
Achievement motivation, 238–40.
    See also Motivation
    drive theory and, 238
    McClelland-Atkinson model of,
        238, 239–43
    performance and, 240–41
    in women, 242–43
Achievement situation, 238
Acquired immunodeficiency
        syndrome, 355–57
Activation-Deactivation
        Checklist, 96
Acute exercise, 337
    psychological benefits of,
        337–39
Addiction, exercise, 359
Additive principle, 259
Adherence
    to exercise program, 346–49
    to rehabilitation program,
        346–49
Aerobic exercise, 340
Affect, attribution and, 219–20
Aggression, 276–88
    vs. assertiveness, 279
    cathartic effect of, 278, 281,
        283–84
    definition of, 278
    examples of, 276–78
    by fans, 277–78, 284
        reduction of, 288
    frustration and, 282–83
    hostile, 278
    instinct theory and, 280–81
    instrumental, 279
    intent of, 279–80
    measurement of, 284
    moral reasoning theory and, 282
    performance and, 285
    reduction of, 287–88

social learning theory and,
        281–82
sport-specific factors in, 285–87
task vs. ego orientation and, 250
theories of, 280–83
AIDS, 355–57
American Association of Health,
        Physical Education, and
        Recreation (AAHPER), 6
American College of Sports
        Medicine (ACSM), 7
American Psychological
        Association (APA), 7
    ethical code of, 12–13
Amine hypothesis, 345
Anabolic-androgenic steroids,
        379, 381–82
Anaerobic exercise, 342
Androgyny, 255, 257
Anorexia analogue hypothesis,
        361–62
Anorexia nervosa, 360–62
Antidepressant effects, of exercise,
        341–44
Anxiety. *See also* Arousal
    assessment of, 141
    case study of, 91–93, 136
    cognitive state, achievement
        motivation and, 240
    control of. *See* Arousal
        adjustment strategies
    exercise and, 341–44
    gender role and, 257–58
    measurement of, 95–97
    multidimensional nature of,
        93, 97–103
    performance and, 98–128.
        See also Arousal,
        performance and
    prestart, 118
    relaxation techniques for,
        140–56. *See also*
        Relaxation response
    social physique, 357–58

somatic, 98–100
state, 93, 94
    cognitive, 98–100
    direction of, 101
    intensity of, 101–2
    precompetitive, 98, 118
stress and, 93–95
trait, 93
Anxiety-prone athlete, 157
Anxiety Rating Scale (ARS), 103
Anxiety/stress spiral, 140
Anxiolytic effects, of exercise,
        341–44
Applied sport psychology, 5, 6
Apter's reversal theory, 123–28
Arizona State University
        Observation Instrument,
        321–22
Arousal. *See also* Anxiety
    assessment of, 95–97
    attentional narrowing and,
        67–71, 73, 86, 108–10
    audience effect on, 289–90
    definition of, 86
    electrophysiological indicators
        of, 90–91
    neurophysiology of, 86–91
    optimal, 90, 118–21
    performance and, 67–69, 73,
        104–28
        catastrophe theory and,
            115–18
        cue utilization theory and,
            108–9
        drive theory and, 113–15,
            124–28
        individual variations in,
            137–39
        information processing
            theory and, 112–13
        inverted-U theory and,
            104–8
        reversal theory and,
            123–28

signal detection theory and,
110–12
zone of optimal functioning
and, 118–21
response criterion and, 111–12
Arousal adjustment, 376–77
Arousal adjustment strategies,
135–62
arousal energizing strategies,
157–61
bulletin boards, 159
coach-athlete-parent
interaction, 160
fan support, 160
goal setting, 158
pep talks, 159
precompetition workout,
160–61
publicity and new coverage,
160
self-activation, 160
gender and, 258
relaxation procedures, 140–56.
See also Relaxation
response
Arousal reaction, 88
Ascending reticular activating
system, 88
Assertiveness, 279
dysfunctional, 291
functional, 291
Assertiveness training, 323
Associaters, 76–79
Association for the Advancement of
Applied Sport Psychology
(AAASP), 6–7
certification process of, 8–9
ethical code of, 127
Athlete(s)
elite
disabled, psychological
profile of, 45–46
psychological profile of,
42–45
position of
leadership opportunity and,
324–26
personality and, 34–35
Athlete-coach compatibility,
322–23
Athlete-coach-parent interaction,
160
Athletic Coping Skills Inventory
(ACSI-28), 195

Athletic injuries, 372–79. *See also*
Injuries
Athletic Motivation Inventory
(AMI), 5, 28
Athletic performance.
See Performance
Attention, 53–79
amount of information and,
59–62
arousal and, 67–69, 73, 86.
See also Arousal
capacity model of, 65–66
definition of, 54
direction of, 70
distractibility and, 67
gating out and, 63
information processing and,
54–63
measurement of, 70–71
response delay and, 62–63
selective, 63–64
width of, 70
Attentional cueing, 198–99
Attentional focus, 67
flexible, 70–71, 73
internal vs. external, 72–73,
76–79
measurement of, 70–71
Attentional focus training, 72–76
Attentional narrowing, 67–71, 73,
108–10
Attentional refocusing, 76
Attentional strategies, associative
vs. dissociative, 76–79
Attentional style, 71
associative vs. dissociative,
76–79
exercise benefits and, 341
Attention and arousal set theory,
175–76
Attribution
ability and, 209, 212
affect and, 219–20
in competitive situations, 217–24
controllability and, 212
covariation principle and,
221–22
effort and, 209, 212
egocentrism in, 228–30
expectancy and, 222
gender and, 225–27
illogical model of, 228
learned helplessness and, 222–24
locus of causality and, 212

locus of control and, 211, 212,
217–22
logical, 221
logical model for, 228
luck and, 209, 210
measurement of, 212–15
open-ended, 212
outcome ambiguity and, 217
self-serving bias in, 228–30
sociocultural factors in, 216
stability of, 211, 222–24
task difficulty and, 209, 212
Attributional training, 230–32
Attribution research, bias in, 217
Attribution theory, 207–33
achievement motivation and, 209
definition of, 208
development of, 209–15
discounting in, 260
Heider's contribution to, 209–10
overjustification in, 260
Russell and McAuley's
contributions to, 212–15
Weiner's contribution to, 211–12
Audience effects, 288–94
crowd hostility and, 293–94
crowd size and, 293
home advantage and, 290–94
Autogenic training, 143–44
Autohypnosis, 153–55
Autonomic nervous system, 86–87
Autotelic experience, 121

Bandura's self-efficacy theory,
243–45, 344–45
Behavior
information processing model of,
55–56
stimulus-response model of, 55
Behavioral assessment
in anxiety measurement, 95–97
in attention measurement, 70
Behavioral techniques, for drug
abuse prevention, 384
Behavioral theories, 55–56
Behaviorism, 55
Bem Sex-Role Inventory, 255
Beta-adrenergic blockers, 382
Between-play routines, 197
Biochemical indicators,
of arousal, 90
Biofeedback, 147–49
Bit, 59

Blood pressure, arousal and, 91
Bracketed morality, 282
Brainwave training, 148
Bredemeier's theory of moral
reasoning and aggression,
282
Broadbent Model, 64
Bulimia nervosa, 360–62
Bulletin boards, 159
Burnout, 362–71
definition of, 363
identification of, 370
interventions for, 370
models of, 367–69
processes leading to, 363
symptoms of, 370

Canadian Society for Psychomotor
Learning and Sport
Psychology (CSPLSP), 6
Cancer, immune system and, 355
Capacity model, 65–66
Cardiovascular fitness hypothesis,
345
Case life cycle model, 315–17
Catastrophe theory, 115–18
Catharsis, 278, 281, 283–84
Cattell Sixteen Personality Factor
Questionnaire (16 PF),
27–28
Causal attribution, 207–33. *See also*
Attribution
Causal Dimension Scale,
213–15, 231
Causal Dimension Scale II,
215, 231
Centering, 73–75
Centrality, 325
Central nervous system, arousal
and, 87–88
Cerebral cortex, arousal and, 87
Certification, 7–9
Checklist, in personality
assessment, 25
Chelladurai's multidimensional
model of leadership,
317–18
Children
attributional training for, 230–32
exercise behavior in, 340
learned helplessness in, 222–24
locus of control in, 218
mastery environment for, 252

Chronic exercise, 337
psychological benefits of,
339–41
Chunking, 57
Clinical/counseling sport
psychologist, 8, 10
Closed-skill sports, 195
Coach(es). *See also* Leadership
assertiveness training for, 323
in self-confidence and
motivation development,
265–66
training of, 320–21
Coach-athlete compatibility,
322–23
Coach-athlete-parent interaction,
160
Coaching Behavior Assessment
System, 320–21
Coaching behaviors, assessment of,
320–22
Cognitive-affective model of stress
and burnout, 368–69
Cognitive appraisal, 372–73
in injuries, 378
Cognitive behavioral hypothesis,
344–45
Cognitive-behavioral interventions,
167–200
definition of, 168
goal setting, 186–91
imagery, 172–86
psychological skills training,
191–99
Stress Inoculation Training,
181, 183–84
Stress Management Training,
181, 185
Visual Motor Behavior
Rehearsal, 181–82
Cognitive Evaluation Theory, 261
Cognitive restructuring, 168
Cognitive Somatic Anxiety
Questionnaire, 96
Cognitive state anxiety, 98–100
achievement motivation and, 240
in catastrophe theory, 115–18
Cognitive techniques, for drug
abuse prevention, 384
Competence motivation, 245–47
Competition, definition of, 238
Competitive anxiety, 98–100
Competitive situations, attribution
in, 217–24

Competitive State Anxiety
Inventory, 96
Competitive State Anxiety
Inventory-2 (CSAI-2),
96, 97–98, 101–2
shortened version of, 102–3
Competitive State Anxiety
Inventory-2 for children
(CSAI-2C), 103
Competitive trait anxiety, gender
roles and, 257–58
Concentration. *See* Attention
Conflict theory, 21
Consideration, 310, 311
Contingent event, 124
reversal and, 124
Control
internal vs. external, attribution
and, 211
locus of, attribution and,
211, 217–22
Controllability, 212
Coping strategies, 170–200, 376
assessment of, 170
definition of, 170
drugs as, 376
effectiveness of, 170–71
emotion-focused, 170
imagery, 172–86
for injuries, 375–76
problem-focused, 170
social support as, 376
stress management as, 376
types of, 170–71
Covariation principle, 221–22
Credulous argument, 29
Cross-gender-typed, 257
Cross-lagged correlational
design, 302
Cueing, attentional, 198–99
Cue utilization theory, 67, 108–10
Cultural factors, in attribution, 216

Delayed anxiolytic response, 39
Depressants, 382
Depression, exercise and, 341–44
Descriptionists, 172
Direction
of anxiety, 101
of attention, 70
Disabled, exercise benefits for, 340
Disabled athletes, elite,
psychological profile of,
45–46

Discounting, 260
Dissociaters, 76–79
Distractibility, 67, 109
Distraction hypothesis, 345
Distress, 94
  behavioral responses to, 96
  coping strategies for, 170–71.
      See also Coping strategies
Diuretics, 382
Drive, 113
Drive theory, 113–15
  motivation and, 238
  reversal theory and, 124–28
  social facilitation and, 289
Dropouts, exercise, 348
  burnout and, 362–71. *See also*
      Burnout
  cognitive-affective model of,
      368–69
Drug abuse, 379–84
  anabolic-androgenic steroids in,
      379, 381–82
  beta-adrenergic blockers in, 382
  depressants in, 382
  detection of, 384
  diuretics in, 382
  hallucinogens in, 382
  National Strength and
      Conditioning Association
      position on, 382–83
  prevention of, 383–84
  reporting of, 384
  stimulants in, 382
Drugs, coping behavior and, 376
Drug testing, 384
Dysfunctional assertive
      behavior, 291

Eades Athletic Burnout
      Inventory, 370
Easterbrook's cue utilization theory,
      67, 108–10
Eating disorders, 360–62
Educational sport psychologist,
      8, 10
Effort, attribution and, 209, 212
Egocentrism, in attribution, 228–30
Ego-enhancing strategy, 228
Ego orientation, 249
Ego-oriented environment, 252
Ego-protecting strategy, 228
Elderly, exercise benefits for, 340
Electrocortical activity, arousal
      and, 90

Electroencephalogram (EEG),
      87, 90
  in biofeedback, 148–49
Electromyogram, 90
  in biofeedback, 148
Elite athletes
  disabled, psychological profile
      of, 45–46
  psychological profile of, 42–45
Endorphin hypothesis, 345
Ethics, in sport psychology, 10–13
Ethnic factors, in attribution, 216
European Federation of Sport
      Psychology (FEPSAC), 9
Eustress, 94
Exercise
  acute, 337
  aerobic, 340
  anaerobic, 342
  antidepressant effects of, 341–44
  anxiolytic effects of, 341–44
  cancer and, 355
  chronic, 337
  in eating disorders, 360–62
  HIV infection and, 354–57
  immune system and, 354–57
  natural history of, 346
  physical benefits of, 336, 354–57
  psychological benefits of,
      336–46
    in special populations, 340
    theoretical explanations for,
        344–46
  variables in, 341
  social physique anxiety and,
      357–58
  stress inoculation and, 340
Exercise addiction, 358–59
Exercise adherence, 346–49
  determinants of, 348
  exercise addiction and, 358–59
  self-efficacy and, 344–45, 347
Exercise behavior, theories of,
      349–51
Exercise dropouts, 348
  burnout and, 362–71. *See also*
      Burnout
  cognitive-affective model of,
      368–69
Exercise-Induced Feeling Inventory,
      339
Exercise program
  abandonment of, 348. *See also*
      Exercise dropouts
  adoption phase of, 347

  maintenance phase of, 348
  resumption of, 348–49
  super-adherence to, 359
Exercise psychology, 336–62
Exercise self-efficacy, 351,
      354–55, 357
Expectancy, attribution and, 222
External attentional focus, 73
  dissociative strategies and,
      76–79
External imagery, 176–77
External locus of control, attribution
      and, 211, 217–22
Extrinsic motivation, 241
  controlling aspect of, 261
  intrinsic motivation and,
      258–63

Factor analysis, 27
False consensus effect, 284
Fan support, 160
Fan violence, 277–78, 284
  reduction of, 288
Fazey and Hardy's catastrophe
      theory, 115–18
Fear of failure, 240, 257
Fear of success, 242–43, 253
Females. *See also* Gender roles
  achievement motivation in,
      242–43
  athletic vs. nonathletic,
      personality and, 37–39
  attribution by, 225–27
  fear of success in, 242–43
  self-confidence in, 253–54
Feminine attribute, 255
Fiedler's contingency theory,
      311–13
First-order traits, 27
Fitness. *See also* Exercise program
  as stress modulator,
      340, 352–54
Flow, 121–23
Fox Hierarchical Model of Physical
      Self-Concept, 358
Freud's psychodynamic theory, 21
Frustration, reversal and, 125
Frustration-aggression theory,
      282–83
Functional assertive behavior, 291
Fundamental Interpersonal
      Relations Orientation-
      Behavior Questionnaire,
      322

Galvanic skin response, arousal and, 91
Gating out, 63, 69, 109
Gender roles, 255–58. *See also* Females
    anxiety and, 257–58
    arousal adjustment strategies and, 258
    attribution and, 225–27
    self-confidence and, 253–54
Gender-typed, 257
Girls. See Females
Goal
    outcome, 190
    performance, 190
Goal orientation, 187, 251
    intrinsic motivation and, 262
Goal setting, 158, 186–91
    in rehabilitation, 379
Gravitational hypothesis, 31–32
Great man theory, 309
Griffith, Coleman Roberts, 5
Group cohesion, 295. *See also* Team cohesion
Group dynamics, 295–96
Group Environment Questionnaire, 298–99, 300

Hallucinogens, 382
Handicapped. See Disabled
Hanin's zone of optimal functioning, 118–21
Hardiness, 366
Harter's competence motivation theory, 245–47
Harter's Perceived Competence Scale for Children, 245
Heart rate, arousal and, 90
Heider, Fritz, 209
Henry, Franklin M., 5
Heterohypnosis, 153–54
Hierarchical Model of Physical Self-Concept, 358
Hierarchy of needs, 239
HIV infection, 355–57
Hollander's personality structure, 19–21
Home advantage, 288–89, 290–92
Hostile aggression, 278
Human growth hormone, 379
Human immunodeficiency virus infection, 355–57
Humanistic theory, 23
Hyperstress, 93

Hypnosis, 150–56
    autohypnosis, 153–55
    cognitive-behavioral theory of, 151–52
    definition of, 150–51
    effectiveness of, 156
    heterohypnosis, 153
    hypnotic trance theory of, 151
    improving effectiveness of, 155–56
    induction of, 152–53
    neutral, 153
    phases of, 152–53
    waking, 153
Hypnotic induction, 152
Hypnotic trance, 152
Hypostress, 93–94
Hypothalamus, arousal and, 87–88
Hysteresis, 117

Iceberg profile, 43–45
Illness, exercise and, 352–57
Illogical model, of attribution, 228
Imagery, 172–86
    attention and arousal set theory and, 175–76
    in cognitive-behavioral intervention programs, 181–85
    definition of, 172
    descriptionist theory of, 172
    effectiveness of, 177–79
    external (visual), 176–77
    internal (kinesthetic), 176–77
    measurement of, 177
    mental practice as, 172–74
    motivational function of, 178–79
    pictorial theory of, 172
    principles of, 180
    psychoneuromuscular theory of, 174–75
    in Stress Inoculation Training, 181, 183–84
    in Stress Management Training, 181, 185
    symbolic learning theory of, 175
    synonyms for, 172
    training in, 179–81
    in Visual Motor Behavior Rehearsal, 181–82
Immune system
    cancer and, 355
    exercise and, 352–57
    HIV infection and, 356–57

overtraining and, 366
    stress and, 354
Information
    amount of, 59–62
        response delay and, 62–63
    bits of, 59
    conveying of, 59–61
    measurement of, 58–63
    response to, 62–63
Information processing, 54–63
    chunking in, 57
    limited capacity for, 65–66, 86
    memory systems and, 56–58
    quantitative aspects of, 59–63
    sensory register in, 56, 58
    storage and retrieval in, 55–56
Information processing model, 55–56
Information processing overload, 54
Information processing theory, 112–13
Initiating structure, 310, 311
Injuries
    coping strategies for, 375–76
    predictors of, 372–79
    psychological adjustment to, 377–78
    psychology of, 372–79
    rehabilitation in, 378–79
    stress and, 372–75
Instinct theory, 280–81
Instrumental aggression, 279
Intensity, of anxiety, 101–2
Interactional model, of personality, 39–46
Interactive model, of psychological makeup, 169–70
Internal attentional focus, 73
    associative strategies and, 76–79
Internal-External Locus of Control Scale, 218
Internal imagery, 176–77
Internal locus of control, attribution and, 211, 217–22
International Journal of Sport Psychology, 6
International Society of Sport Psychology (ISSP), 5–6
Interpersonal factors, in psychological makeup, 169–70
Interventions, for arousal adjustment, 136. *See also* Arousal adjustment strategies

Interview, in personality assessment, 25
Intrapersonal factors, in psychological makeup, 169–70
Intrinsic motivation, 240
    development of, 263–67
    external rewards and, 258–63
Inverted-U theory, 104–8
    alternatives to, 115–28
    cue utilization theory and, 67, 108–10
    drive theory and, 113–15
    information processing theory and, 112–13
    signal detection theory and, 110–12
Investment model, 367–68

Journal of Applied Sport Psychology, 6–7
Journal of Interdisciplinary Research in Physical Education, 7
Journal of Sport Behavior, 7
Journals, 6–7

Kinesthetic imagery, 176

Lawther, John, 5
Leader, as facilitator, 314
Leader Behavior Description Questionnaire, 310, 315
Leadership, 306–26
    consideration in, 310, 311
    contingency approach to, 311
    initiating structure in, 310, 311
    relationship-motivated, 311
    situational favorableness and, 312–13
    subordinate maturity and, 315–17
    task-motivated, 311
Leadership Behavior Model, 319–22
Leadership behaviors, 308–9
    actual, 318
    preferred, 318
    prescribed, 318
    relationship-oriented, 311
    task-oriented, 311

Leadership opportunity, geographical location and, 324–26
Leadership styles, 311
Leadership theories, 307–22
    Chelladurai's multidimensional model, 317–18
    contingency, 311–22
    Fiedler's contingency theory, 311–13
    great man, 309
    Leadership Behavior Model, 319–22
    life cycle, 315–17
    path-goal, 314–15
    situation-specific, 314–22
    universal behavior, 310–11
    universal trait, 308, 309
Leadership traits, 308–9
    universal, 308
Learned helplessness, 222–24
Learning environment, 252
Least Preferred Co-Worker scale, 312
Levenson IPC scale, 218
Licensure, 7–9, 11
Life cycle theory, 315–17
Life development intervention, 171
Life stress. *See also* Stress
    exercise as moderator of, 352–54
    illness and, 352
    injury and, 372–75
Locus of causality, 212
Locus of control, attribution and, 211, 212, 217–22
Logical attribution, 221
Logical model, of attribution, 228
Long-term memory, 58
Luck, 209, 210

Mantra, 140, 144–45
Masculine attribute, 255
Maslach Burnout Inventory, 370
Maslow's hierarchy of needs, 239
Mastery environment, 252
    creation of, 265–66
Mastery orientation, 249
    intrinsic motivation and, 262
Matching hypothesis, 139
McClelland-Atkinson model, 238, 239–43
Media coverage, 160
Medicine and Science in Sports and Exercise, 7

Meditation, 144–47
Memory
    chunking and, 57
    long-term, 58
    sensory register and, 56, 58
    short-term, 56–58
    stages of, 58
    storage and retrieval of, 55–56
Mental devices
    in meditation, 144–45
    for relaxation, 140
Mental health model, 42–43
Mental practice, 172–74
Mental Readiness Form (MRF), 102–3
Meta-analysis, 41, 341
Metamotivational mode, 124–28
Minnesota Multiphasic Personality Inventory (MMPI), 27
Modeling, 22
Momentum, psychological, 199
Mood
    exercise and, 341–44
    monitoring of, 366
Mood disturbances. *See also* Anxiety; Depression
    injuries and, 377, 378
Mood states, 41–42
Morality, bracketed, 282
Moral reasoning theory, 282
Motivation
    achievement, 238–40
        drive theory and, 238
        McClelland-Atkinson model of, 238, 239–43
        performance and, 240–41
        in women, 242–43
    additive principle and, 259
    competence, 245–47
    ego orientation and, 249, 251–52
    extrinsic, 241
        controlling aspect of, 261
    goal orientation and, 251–52
    intrinsic, 240
        development of, 263–67
        external rewards and, 258–63
    multiplicative principle and, 260
    participation, 263–64
    relationship, 312
    task orientation and, 249, 251–52, 312
Motivational techniques, 137–39
Motive to achieve success, 240
Multidimensional anxiety theory, 97–103

Multidimensional leadership model, 317–18
Multiplicative principle, 260
Multivariate approach, 30
Muscle tension, 137
  arousal and, 90
Music, during exercise, 341

National Association for Sport and Physical Education (NASPE), 6, 7
National Strength and Conditioning Association (NSCA), 382–83
Negative stress syndrome, 362–71
Nervous system
  autonomic, 86–87
  sympathetic, 87
Neutral hypnosis, 153
News coverage, 160
Nicholls' developmentally based theory of perceived ability, 249–52
Noise, 110
Norman's Pertinence Model, 63
North American Society for the Psychology of Sport and Physical Activity (NASPSPA), 6
  ethical standards of, 12

Objective demand, 94
Obligatory runners, 359
  anorexics and, 361–62
Observation, in personality assessment, 25
Open-ended attribution, 212
Open-skill sports, 195
Optimal arousal, 90, 118–21
Optimal experience, 121–23
Optimal functioning, zone of, 118–21
Origin-pawn relationship, 217
Outcome goal, 190
Outcome goal orientation, 187
Overjustification, 260
Overreaching, 366
Overstress, 93
Overtraining
  burnout and, 362–71. *See also* Burnout
  definition of, 363
  mood disturbances and, 366

Palmar sweating, arousal and, 91
Parasympathetic nervous system, 87
Paratelic mode, 123–28
Parent, in self-confidence and motivation development, 266–67
Parent-athlete-coach interaction, 160
Participation motivation, 263–64
Participation Motivation Inventory, 263
Participatory modeling, 244
Path-goal theory, 314–15
Peak experience, 122
Pep talks, 137–39, 159
Perceived ability, 249–52
Perceived Motivational Climate on Sport Questionnaire, 252
Perceptions of Success Questionnaire, 252
Performance
  achievement motivation and, 240–41
  aggression and, 285
  arousal and, 67–69, 73, 104–28
  mood states and, 41–42
  personality and, 29, 30–39, 41–42
  psychological states and, 41–42
  state anxiety and, 98–128. *See also* Arousal, performance and
  team cohesion and, 301–2
Performance-enhancing drugs, 379–84
Performance goal, 190
Performance goal orientation, 187
Performance routines, 197
Personal Attributes Questionnaire, 255
Personality, 17–47
  in athletes vs. nonathletes, 30–31, 37–39
  athletic participation effects on, 31–32
  athletic performance and, 29, 30–39
  definition of, 19
  of exercisers vs. nonexercisers, 353–54
  of female athletes vs. nonathletes, 37–39
  injuries and, 374
  interactional model of, 39–46

measurement of, 24–28
  credulous vs. skeptical position in, 29
  multivariate approach in, 30
  predictive value of, 29
  projective procedures in, 24–27
  questionnaires in, 27–28
  rating scales in, 24
  mood states and, 41–42
  permeability and, 19–20
  psychologic core and, 19, 20
  role-related behaviors and, 19, 20
  situational factors and, 39–42
  skill level and, 35–36
  structure of, 19–21
  trait-state interactions and, 41–42
  type of sport and, 32–34
  typical responses and, 19, 20
Personality Factor Questionnaire (16 PF), 27–28
Personality theories, 21–24
  humanistic, 23
  psychodynamic, 21
  social learning, 22–23
  trait, 23–24
Personality traits
  of athletes vs. nonathletes, 30–31
  of exercisers vs. nonexercisers, 353–54
  first-order, 27
  second-order, 28
  source, 27
  surface, 28
Physically challenged persons. *See* Disabled
Physical self-concept, 358
Physical Self-Perception Profile, 358
Physiological indicators, in attention measurement, 70
Pictorialists, 172
Planned behavior theory, 350
Player position
  leadership opportunity and, 324–26
  personality and, 34–35
Positive and Negative Affect Schedule, 120
Poster-board displays, 159
Posthypnotic suggestion, 153
Postshot routines, 197
Practice, mental vs. physical, 172–73
Precompetition workout, 160–61

Precompetitive anxiety, 98, 118
Preshot routines, 197
Prestart anxiety. *See* Precompetitive
    anxiety
*Problem Athletes and How To
    Handle Them* (Ogilvie &
    Tutko), 5
Process goal orientation, 187, 190
Processing capacity, 65–66
Process of change, 350–51
Professional societies, 5–7
Profile of Mood States (POMS),
    41, 366
Progressive relaxation, 141–43
Projective procedures, 24–27
Propinquity, leadership opportunity
    and, 325–26
Psyching-up strategies, 157–61. *See
    also* Arousal adjustment
    strategies
Psychodynamic theory, 21
Psychological benefits, of exercise,
    336–46. *See also* Exercise
Psychological constructs, 239–40
Psychological core, 19, 20
Psychological makeup, interactive
    model of, 169–70
Psychological method, 193
Psychological momentum, 199
Psychological profile, of elite
    athletes, 42–45
    with disabilities, 45–46
Psychological skills, 193
    measurement of, 194–96
Psychological skills education,
    195–98
Psychological Skills Education
    Program (PSEP), 195–98
Psychological skills training,
    191–99
    attentional cueing in, 198–99
    definition of, 191
    guidelines for, 192–94
    psychological momentum
        in, 199
Psychological states, performance
    and, 41–42
Psychologic Skills Inventory for
    Sports (PSIS-5), 195
Psychoneuromuscular theory, of
    imagery, 174–75
Publicity, 160

Questionnaires, 27–28

Racial factors, in attribution, 216
Rating scales, 24
Reaction time probe technique, 66
Reasoned action theory, 349
Refocusing, 76
Rehabilitation, psychological
    factors in, 378–79
Relationship-motivated leaders, 311
Relaxation, progressive, 141–43
Relaxation response, 140
    autogenic training and, 143–44
    biofeedback in, 147–49
    in cognitive-behavioral
        intervention programs,
        181–85
    hypnosis and, 150–56
    meditation and, 144–47
    progressive relaxation and,
        141–43
    in Stress Inoculation Training,
        181, 183–84
    in Stress Management Training,
        181, 185
    in Visual Motor Behavior
        Rehearsal, 181–82
Research, personality. *See also*
    Personality theories
    credulous vs. skeptical approach
        to, 29
    gender issues in, 37–39
    trends in, 39
Research sport psychologist, 8, 10
Respiration rate, arousal and, 91
Response criterion, 111–12
Response delay, 62–63
Reticular formation, arousal
    and, 88
Retrieval, memory, 55
Reversal theory, 123–28
Role-related behaviors, 19, 20
Rorschach test, 26
Rotter Scale, 217–18
RT probe, 66
Runners, obligatory, 359
    anorexics and, 361–62
Running Addiction Scale, 359
Running Style Questionnaire
    (RSQ), 76–77

Satiation, reversal and, 125
Second-order traits, 28
Selective attention, 63–64
Self-activation, 160
Self-attention, 292

Self-confidence, 243
    development of, 263–67
    gender and, 253–54
Self-efficacy
    exercise, 351, 354–55, 357
    group, 303
Self-efficacy theory, 243–45, 254
Self-esteem, physical self-concept
    and, 358
Self-handicapping, 303–4
Self-reporting, in attention
    measurement, 70
Self-serving hypothesis, 228
Self-talk, 168
    in attentional cueing, 198–99
Sensoristasis, 90
Sensory register, 56, 58
Short-term memory, 56–58
Signal detection theory, 110–12
Signal plus noise, 110
Situational behaviors, 308
Situational traits, 308
Skeptical argument, 29
Skill, difficulty of, information bits
    and, 59–63
Skill level, personality and, 35–36
Skin temperature, in
    biofeedback, 148
Social cognitive theory, 351
Social cohesion, 297–98
Social comparison, 254
Social facilitation, 289–90
Social interaction hypothesis, 345
Social learning theory, 22–23,
    281–82
Social physique anxiety, 357–58
Social Physique Anxiety Scale, 358
Social psychology of sport, 275–328
Social reinforcement, 23
Sociocultural factors, in
    attribution, 216
Somatic state anxiety, 98–100
Source traits, 27
Spectator effects, 288–94
Spielberger's State Anxiety
    Inventory, 96, 97
Spielberger's Trait Anxiety
    Inventory, 96, 97
Sport(s)
    closed-skill, 195
    difficulty of, information bits
        and, 59–63
    gender-appropriate, self-
        confidence and, 253–54
    open-skill, 195

position in, personality traits
and, 34–35
type of, personality traits and,
32–34
Sport Anxiety Scale, 96
Sport Competition Anxiety Test, 96
Sport confidence, 247–48
Sport Grid, 103–4
Sport psychologist
certification of, 7–9, 11
clinical/counseling, 8, 10
educational, 8, 10
registry of, 8
research, 8, 10
training of, 8–9, 11
types of, 8, 10
Sport Psychologist, The, 6
Sport psychology
academic, 6
applied, 5, 6
clinical aspects of, 11
components of, 11
definition of, 4–5
ethics in, 10–13
history of, 5–7
professionalization of, 7–9
Sport Psychology Academy
(SPA), 6
Sport Psychology Registry, 8
Sports Orientation Questionnaire,
252
Sport-specific model of sport
confidence, 247–48
Stability dimension, of attribution,
211, 222–24
Stage model, of injury
adjustment, 378
Staleness, 363
State anxiety, 93, 94. *See also*
Arousal
cognitive, 98–100
achievement motivation
and, 240
in catastrophe theory, 115–18
direction of, 101–2
intensity of, 101–2
performance and, 98–128.
See also Arousal,
performance and
precompetitive, 98, 118
prestart, 118
somatic, 98–100
Steroids, anabolic-androgenic,
379, 381–82
Stimulants, 382
Stimulus-response model, 55

Stimulus-response theory, 22
Storage, memory, 55
Stress. *See also* Anxiety
burnout and, 368–69. *See also*
Burnout
cognitive-affective model of,
368–69
coping strategies for, 170–71,
375–76. *See also* Coping
strategies
definition of, 93
exercise as moderator of, 340,
352–54
illness and, 352–54
injuries and, 372–75
social support and, 376
training, 363
Stress inoculation, 340, 352–54
Stress Inoculation Training (SIT),
181, 183–84
Stress management, 136, 376–77.
See also Arousal
adjustment
Stress Management Training
(SMT), 181, 185
Stress process, 94
Stress response, 372
Structural rating scale, for
attribution, 212
Subjective Exercise Experience
Scale, 339
Substance abuse. *See* Drug abuse
Super-adherer, 33, 359
Surface traits, 28
Symbolic learning theory, 175
Sympathetic nervous system, 87

Tai Chi, 145
TARGET, 265
Task and Ego Orientation in Sports
Questionnaire, 252
Task cohesion, 297
Task dependence, leadership
opportunity and, 325–26
Task difficulty, attribution and,
209, 212
Task-motivated leaders, 311
Task orientation, 249
intrinsic motivation and, 262
Task-oriented environment, 252
creation of, 265–66
Teacher, in self-confidence and
motivation development,
265–66
Team building, 304–6

Team cohesion, 295–306
consequences of, 301–4
definition of, 295
determinants of, 299–301
development of, 304–6
group dynamics and, 295–96
homogeneity and, 303
measurement of, 296–99
performance and, 301–2
predictive value of, 303
self-efficacy and, 303
self-handicapping and, 303–4
stages of, 304
Team Psychology Questionnaire,
299–301
Team sports. *See also* Sport(s)
personality traits and, 33–34
position and, 34–35
Telic Dominance Scale
(TDS), 126
Telic mode, 123–28
Tension, 137
Test of Attentional and
Interpersonal Style
(TAIS), 70, 71
Test of Performance Strategies
(TOPS), 195
Thematic Apperception Test
(TAT), 26
Thought stopping, 73–75
Training, burnout and. *See* Burnout
Training gain, 363
Training stress, 363
Training stress syndrome, 363
Trait anxiety, 93
competitive, gender role and,
257–58
Trait-state interactions, 41–42
Trait theories, 23–24
of leadership, 309
Transcendental meditation,
144–47
Transtheoretical model, 350–51
Treisman's Attenuation Model, 64
Triplett, Norman, 5
Typical responses, 19, 20, 24

Understress, 93–94
United States Olympic Committee
(USOC), 8
Universal behavior theory of
leadership, 310–11
Universal traits, 308
Universal trait theory of leadership,
308, 309

Vealey's sport-specific model of
     sport confidence, 247–48
Violence. *See also* Aggression
   fan, 284
      reduction of, 288
Visual imagery, 176–77
Visual Motor Behavior Rehearsal
     (VMBR), 181–82

Waking hypnosis, 153
Wheelchair athletes
   elite, psychological profile of,
     45–46
   exercise benefits for, 340
Women. *See* Females
Workouts, precompetition, 160–61
World-class athletes. *See* Elite
     athletes

Yerkes-Dodson law, 106

Zajonc's Model, 289–90
Zone of optimal functioning,
     118–21